High Availability
IT Services

High Availability
IT Services

Terry Critchley

CRC Press
Taylor & Francis Group
Boca Raton   London   New York

CRC Press is an imprint of the
Taylor & Francis Group, an **informa** business
AN AUERBACH BOOK

CRC Press
Taylor & Francis Group
6000 Broken Sound Parkway NW, Suite 300
Boca Raton, FL 33487-2742

© 2015 by Taylor & Francis Group, LLC
CRC Press is an imprint of Taylor & Francis Group, an Informa business

No claim to original U.S. Government works

Printed on acid-free paper
Version Date: 20141020

International Standard Book Number-13: 978-1-4822-5590-4 (Hardback)

Visit the Taylor & Francis Web site at
http://www.taylorandfrancis.com

and the CRC Press Web site at
http://www.crcpress.com

To my wife, Chris; children, Philip and Helen; and the rest of my now extended family—Matt, Louise, and grandchildren, Ava, Lucy, and Ben

Contents

Foreword xxv

Preface xxvii

Acknowledgments xxxiii

Author xxxv

SECTION I AN AVAILABILITY PRIMER

1 **Preamble: A View from 30,000 Feet** 3

   Do You Know...? 3

   Availability in Perspective 4

      Murphy's Law of Availability 4

      Availability Drivers in Flux: What Percentage of Business Is Critical? 4

      Historical View of Availability: The First 7 × 24 Requirements? 6

      Historical Availability Scenarios 8

         Planar Technology 8

         Power-On Self-Test 9

         Other Diagnostics 9

         Component Repair 9

         In-Flight Diagnostics 10

   Summary 10

2 **Reliability and Availability** 13

   Introduction to Reliability, Availability, and Serviceability 13

      RAS Moves Beyond Hardware 14

      Availability: An Overview 15

      Some Definitions 15

      Quantitative Availability 16

      Availability: 7 R's (SNIA) 16

   Availability and Change 18

      Change All around Us 19

      Software: Effect of Change 20

      Operations: Effect of Change 20

      Monitoring and Change 20

Automation: The Solution? 22
    Data Center Automation 22
    Network Change/Configuration Automation 23
    Automation Vendors 23
Types of Availability 24
    Binary Availability 24
    Duke of York Availability 25
    Hierarchy of Failures 26
    Hierarchy Example 26
    State Parameters 27
Types of Nonavailability (Outages) 28
    Logical Outage Examples 29
    Summary 31
Planning for Availability and Recovery 31
    Why Bother? 31
    What Is a Business Continuity Plan? 31
    What Is a BIA? 32
    What Is DR? 33
Relationships: BC, BIA, and DR 33
    Recovery Logistics 33
    Business Continuity 34
Downtime: Who or What Is to Blame? 34
Elements of Failure: Interaction of the Wares 35
Summary 37
DR/BC Source Documents 37

3 Reliability: Background and Basics **39**
Introduction 39
    IT Structure—Schematic 40
    IT Structure—Hardware Overview 40
Service Level Agreements 42
    Service Level Agreements: The Dawn of Realism 42
    What Is an SLA? 43
    Why Is an SLA Important? 43
Service Life Cycle 43
Concept of User Service 45
Elements of Service Management 45
    Introduction 45
    Scope of Service Management 46
    User Support 46
    Operations Support 46
    Systems Management 47
    Service Management Hierarchy 47
    The Effective Service 48
    Services versus Systems 49
Availability Concepts 49

First Dip in the Water..49
Availability Parameters 50
Summary 52

4   What Is High Availability?...53
IDC and Availability 53
Availability Classification...54
Availability: Outage Analogy..56
A Recovery Analogy 56
Availability: Redundancy..57
Availability: Fault Tolerance 57
Sample List of Availability Requirements..57
System Architecture...57
Availability: Single Node 58
Dynamic Reconfiguration/Hot Repair of System Components......58
Disaster Backup and Recovery...58
System Administration Facilities 59
HA Costs Money, So Why Bother? 59
Cost Impact Analysis..59
HA: Cost versus Benefit..60
Penalty for Nonavailability 60
Organizations: Attitude toward HA 60
Aberdeen Group Study: February 2012 61
Outage Loss Factors (Percentage of Loss) 62
Software Failure Costs...62
Assessing the Cost of HA 64
Performance and Availability..64
HA Design: Top 10 Mistakes 65
The Development of HA...65
Servers 65
Systems and Subsystems Development 67
Production Clusters...67
Availability Architectures..69
RAS Features..69
Hot-Plug Hardware 69
Processors 69
Memory..70
Input/Output 71
Storage..71
Power/Cooling...71
Fault Tolerance 72
Outline of Server Domain Architecture..72
Introduction 72
Domain/LPAR Structure...73
Outline of Cluster Architecture 74

Cluster Configurations: Commercial Cluster...74
Cluster Components...74
Hardware...74
Software 75
Commercial LB 76
Commercial Performance 77
Commercial HA 77
HPC Clusters 77
Generic HPC Cluster 77
HPC Cluster: Oscar Configuration 78
HPC Cluster: Availability... 79
HPC Cluster: Applications 79
HA in Scientific Computing.. 80
Topics in HPC Reliability: Summary 80
Errors in Cluster HA Design 81
Outline of Grid Computing.. 82
Grid Availability 82
Commercial Grid Computing 83
Outline of RAID Architecture 83
Origins of RAID 83
RAID Architecture and Levels 84
Hardware... 84
Software 85
Hardware versus Software RAID 85
RAID Striping: Fundamental to RAID 85
RAID Configurations... 86
RAID Components.. 86
ECC 86
Parity.. 87
RAID Level 0 87
RAID Level 1 87
RAID Level 3 87
RAID Level 5 88
RAID Level 6 88
RAID Level 10 88
RAID 0 + 1 Schematic 89
RAID 10 Schematic 89
RAID Level 30... 89
RAID Level 50... 89
RAID Level 51 89
RAID Level 60... 90
RAID Level 100 90
Less Relevant RAIDs.. 90
RAID Level 2... 90
RAID Level 4... 90
RAID Level 7... 90
Standard RAID Storage Efficiency 91

SSDs and RAID..92
SSD Longevity 93
Hybrid RAID: SSD and HDD 93
SSD References..93
Post-RAID Environment..94
Big Data: The Issue...94
Data Loss Overview 95
Big Data Solutions? 95
Non-RAID RAID..96
Erasure Codes...97
RAID Successor Qualifications 97
EC Overview 98
EC Recovery Scope 99
Self-Healing Storage 100
Summary...101

SECTION II   AVAILABILITY THEORY AND PRACTICE

5   High Availability: Theory...105
Some Math 105
Guide to Reliability Graphs...105
Probability Density Function 105
Cumulative Distribution Function 107
Availability Probabilities 107
Lusser's Law...108
Availability Concepts...109
Hardware Reliability: The Bathtub Curve 109
Software Reliability: The Bathtub Curve 110
Simple Math of Availability 111
Availability 111
Nonavailability 112
Mean Time between Failures...112
Mean Time to Repair 112
Online Availability Tool 113
Availability Equation I: Time Factors in an Outage........................114
Availability Equation II 116
Effect of Redundant Blocks on Availability 117
Parallel (Redundant) Components 118
Two Parallel Blocks: Example...118
Combinations of Series and Parallel Blocks 119
Complex Systems..120
System Failure Combinations 120
Complex Systems Solution Methods.....................................121
Real-Life Example: Cisco Network Configuration 121
Configuration A 121
Configuration B 122
Summary of Block Considerations..123

Sample Availability Calculations versus Costs 124
Calculation 1: Server Is 99% Available..124
Calculation 2: Server Is 99.99% Available...124
Availability: MTBFs and Failure Rate 124
Availability Factors 125
Planned versus Unplanned Outages..125
Planned Downtime: Planned Downtime Breakdown 126
Unplanned Downtime 128
Security: The New Downtime 128
Disasters: Breakdown of Causes 128
Power: Downtime Causes...129
Power Issues Addenda..129
So What? 130
External Electromagnetic Radiation Addendum 131
Power: Recovery Timescales for Uninterruptible Power Supply 131
Causes of Data Loss...132
Pandemics? Disaster Waiting to Happen?...133
Disasters: Learning the Hard Way...133
Other Downtime Gotchas..133
Downtime Gotchas: Survey Paper 135
Downtime Reduction Initiatives..135
Low Impact Outages 135
Availability: A Lesson in Design 136
Availability: Humor in an Outage—Part I 137
Availability: Humor in an Outage—Part II..137
So What?..137
Application Nonavailability..137
Traditional Outage Reasons 138
Modern Outage Reasons 138
Summary..139

6   High Availability: Practice 141
Central Site...141
Service Domain Concept...141
Sample Domain Architecture 143
Planning for Availability—Starting Point..144
The HA Design Spectrum 145
Availability by Systems Design/Modification..145
Availability by Engineering Design..145
Self-Healing Hardware and Software 145
Self-Healing and Other Items..146
Availability by Application Design: Poor Application Design 147
Conventional Programs 147
Web Applications 147
Availability by Configuration 149

Hardware..149
Data 150
Networks..150
Operating System 150
Environment 150
Availability by Outside Consultancy...151
Availability by Vendor Support..151
Availability by Proactive Monitoring 151
Availability by Technical Support Excellence..152
Availability by Operations Excellence 152
First Class Runbook 153
Software Level Issues 153
System Time..154
Performance and Capacity..154
Data Center Efficiency..154
Availability by Retrospective Analysis..154
Availability by Application Monitoring..155
Availability by Automation 155
Availability by Reactive Recovery 156
Availability by Partnerships 157
Availability by Change Management 158
Availability by Performance/Capacity Management 158
Availability by Monitoring...159
Availability by Cleanliness...159
Availability by Anticipation 159
Predictive Maintenance 159
Availability by Teamwork 160
Availability by Organization 160
Availability by Eternal Vigilance...161
Availability by Location 162
A Word on Documentation 162
Network Reliability/Availability...163
Protocols and Redundancy 163
Network Types 164
Network Outages 164
Network Design for Availability 165
Network Security..166
File Transfer Reliability 167
Network DR..169
Software Reliability 169
Software Quality 169
Software: Output Verification...170
Example 1...171
Example 2...171
Example 3...171
Software Reliability: Problem Flow 171

Software Testing Steps...172
Software Documentation..173
Software Testing Model...173
Software Reliability—Models...175
The Software Scenario 175
SRE Models..175
Model Entities..176
SRE Models: Shape Characterization 177
SRE Models: Time-Based versus Defect-Based...178
Software Reliability Growth Model...178
Software Reliability Model: Defect Count...180
Software Reliability: IEEE Standard 1633–2008...181
Software Reliability: Hardening...182
Software Reliability: Installation...182
Software Reliability: Version Control 183
Software: Penetration Testing..183
Software: Fault Tolerance 184
Software Error Classification..185
Heisenbug...185
Bohrbug..185
Reliability Properties of Software...186
ACID Properties...186
Two-Phase Commit..186
Software Reliability: Current Status 187
Software Reliability: Assessment Questions...188
Software Universe and Summary..188
Subsystem Reliability...189
Hardware Outside the Server...189
Disk Subsystem Reliability 190
Disk Subsystem RAS..190
Tape Reliability/RAS..191
Availability: Other Peripherals...192
Attention to Detail...193
Liveware Reliability 193
Summary...194
Be Prepared for Big Brother!..195

7 High Availability: SLAs, Management, and Methods...197
Introduction 197
Preliminary Activities 198
Pre-Production Activities..198
BC Plan...199
BC: Best Practice..199
Management Disciplines...200

Service Level Agreements...201
    SLA Introduction 201
    SLA: Availability and QoS 201
    Elements of SLAs 201
    Types of SLAs... 203
    Potential Business Benefits of SLAs 203
    Potential IT Benefits of SLAs 204
    IT Service Delivery... 204
    SLA: Structure and Samples 205
  SLA: How Do We Quantify Availability?... 206
    SLA: Reporting of Availability 206
    Reneging on SLAs 207
HA Management: The Project 209
  Start-Up and Design Phase 209
    The Management Flow 210
    The Management Framework..210
    Project Definition Workshop..210
    Outline of the PDW...212
    PDW Method Overview 212
    Project Initiation Document...213
    PID Structure and Purpose 213
    Multistage PDW 215
  Delphi Techniques and Intensive Planning..215
    Delphi Technique...215
    Delphi: The Steps 216
    Intensive Planning 217
  FMEA Process 217
    FMEA: An Analogy 218
    FMEA: The Steps 218
    FMECA = FMEA + Criticality 219
    Risk Evaluation and Priority: Risk Evaluation Methods.........................219
  Component Failure Impact Analysis.. 220
    CFIA Development—A Walkthrough and Risk Analysis.......................... 220
    CFIA Table: Schematic...221
    Quantitative CFIA 222
    CFIA: Other Factors 222
Management of Operations Phase 223
  Failure Reporting and Corrective Action System 223
    Introduction 223
    FRACAS: Steps for Handling Failures 223
HA Operations: Supporting Disciplines 225
  War Room 225
    War Room Location 225
    Documentation 225
  Change/Configuration Management 226

Change Management and Control: Best Practice 226
Change Operations.. 227
Patch Management... 228
Performance Management 229
Introduction 229
Overview 229
Security Management 230
Security: Threats or Posturing? 230
Security: Best Practice 231
Problem Determination 231
Problems: Short Term 232
Problems: After the Event 232
Event Management 233
Fault Management...233
Faults and What to Do about Them 233
System Failure: The Response Stages 234
HA Plan B: What's That? 235
Plan B: Example I...235
Plan B: Example II 235
What? IT Problem Recovery without IT?..235
Faults and What Not to Do.. 236
Outages: Areas for Inaction 236
Problem Management.. 237
Managing Problems.. 237
Problems: Best Practice... 237
Help Desk Architecture and Implementation 238
Escalation Management.. 238
Resource Management 238
Service Monitors 239
Availability Measurement 239
Monitor Layers 240
System Resource Monitors..241
Synthetic Workload: Generic Requirements 241
Availability Monitors 242
General EUE Tools.. 243
Availability Benchmarks... 243
Availability: Related Monitors 244
Disaster Recovery 244
The Viewpoint Approach to Documentation 245
Summary...245

SECTION III VENDORS AND HIGH AVAILABILITY

8 **High Availability: Vendor Products** **249**
  IBM Availability and Reliability 250
    IBM Hardware 250
    Virtualization 251
      IBM PowerVM 251
      IBM Series x 251
    IBM Clusters 251
    z Series Parallel Sysplex 251
      Sysplex Structure and Purpose 252
      Parallel Sysplex Schematic 252
      IBM: High Availability Services 253
      IBM Future Series/System 253
  Oracle Sun HA 254
    Sun HA 254
      Hardware Range 254
      Super Cluster 255
      Oracle Sun M5-32 255
    Oracle HA Clusters 255
      Oracle RAC 12c 255
  Hewlett-Packard HA 256
    HP Hardware and Software 256
      Servers 256
      Software 256
      Services 256
    Servers: Integrity Servers 257
    HP NonStop Integrity Servers 258
      NonStop Architecture and Stack 258
      NonStop Stack Functions 259
  Stratus Fault Tolerance 260
    Automated Uptime Layer 260
    ActiveService Architecture 261
  Other Clusters 261
    Veritas Clusters (Symantec) 261
      Supported Platforms 261
      Databases, Applications, and Replicators 262
    Linux Clusters 262
      Overview 262
      Oracle Clusterware 263
      SUSE Linux Clustering 263

Red Hat Linux Clustering 263
Linux in the Clouds 263
Linux HPC HA 263
Linux-HA 263
Carrier Grade Linux 263
VMware Clusters 264
The Web and HA 264
Service Availability Software 264
Continuity Software 265
Continuity Software: Services 265
Summary 265

9 High Availability: Transaction Processing and Databases 267
Transaction Processing Systems 267
Some TP Systems: OLTP Availability Requirements 268
TP Systems with Databases 268
The X/Open Distributed Transaction Processing Model: XA and XA+ Concepts 269
CICS and RDBMS 270
Relational Database Systems 271
Some Database History 271
Early RDBMS 271
SQL Server and HA 272
Microsoft SQL Server 2014 Community Technology Preview 1 273
SQL Server HA Basics 273
SQL Server AlwaysOn Solutions 273
Failover Cluster Instances 273
Availability Groups 274
Database Mirroring 274
Log Shipping 274
References 274
Oracle Database and HA 275
Introduction 275
Oracle Databases 275
Oracle 11g (R2.1) HA 275
Oracle 12c 276
Oracle MAA 276
Oracle High Availability Playing Field 276
MySQL 277
MySQL: HA Features 278
MySQL: HA Services and Support 278
IBM DB2 Database and HA 278
DB2 for Windows, UNIX, and Linux 279
DB2 HA Feature 279
High Availability DR 279
DB2 Replication: SQL and Q Replication 280
DB2 for i 280
DB2 10 for z/OS 280

DB2 pureScale 280
InfoSphere Replication Server for z/OS 281
DB2 Cross Platform Development 281
IBM Informix Database and HA 281
Introduction (Informix 11.70) 281
Availability Features 282
Fault Tolerance 282
Informix MACH 11 Clusters 282
Connection Manager 283
Informix 12.1 283
Ingres Database and HA 284
Ingres RDBMS 284
Ingres High Availability Option 284
Sybase Database and HA 285
Sybase High Availability Option 285
Terminology 285
Use of SAP ASE 286
Vendor Availability 286
ASE Cluster Requirements 286
Business Continuity with SAP Sybase 287
NoSQL 287
NonStopSQL Database 288
Summary 289

SECTION IV   CLOUDS AND VIRTUALIZATION

10   High Availability: The Cloud and Virtualization 293
Introduction 293
What Is Cloud Computing? 294
Cloud Characteristics 294
Functions of the Cloud 294
Cloud Service Models 295
Cloud Deployment Models 296
Resource Management in the Cloud 297
SLAs and the Cloud 297
Cloud Availability and Security 298
Cloud Availability 298
Cloud Outages: A Review 298
Aberdeen: Cloud Storage Outages 299
Cloud Security 299
Virtualization 300
What Is Virtualization? 300
Full Virtualization 301
Paravirtualization 302
Security Risks in Virtual Environments 303
Vendors and Virtualization 303

IBM PowerVM 303
IBM z/VM 304
VMware VSphere, ESX, and ESXi 304
Microsoft Hyper-V 304
HP Integrity Virtual Machines 304
Linux KVM..304
Solaris Zones 304
Xen..305
Virtualization and HA..305
Virtualization Information Sources 306
Summary 306

11 Disaster Recovery Overview...307
DR Background...307
A DR Lesson from Space 307
Disasters Are Rare ... Aren't They? 308
Key Message: Be Prepared 308
DR Invocation Reasons: Forrester Survey 309
DR Testing: Kaseya Survey 310
DR: A Point to B Point..310
Backup/Restore..311
Overview 311
Backup Modes..311
Cold (Offline)...311
Warm (Online)..311
Hot (Online)...311
Backup Types 312
Full Backup...312
Incremental Backup..312
Multilevel Incremental Backup...312
Differential Backup...312
Synthetic Backup..312
Progressive Backup...312
Data Deduplication 313
Data Replication..314
Replication Agents..315
Asynchronous Replication...315
Synchronous Replication...316
Heterogeneous Replication..316
Other Types of Backup..316
DR Recovery Time Objective: WAN Optimization 317
Backup Product Assessments 318
Virtualization Review..318
Gartner Quadrant Analysis 318
Backup/Archive: Tape or Disk?...319
Bit Rot..319

Tape Costs..320
DR Concepts and Considerations 321
    The DR Scenario 321
        Who Is Involved?..321
    DR Objectives 322
    Recovery Factors 322
    Tiers of DR Availability 323
        DR and Data Tiering 323
        A Key Factor...324
The DR Planning Process 324
    DR: The Steps Involved 324
        In-House DR...324
    DR Requirements in Operations 327
        Hardware...327
        Software 327
        Applications...327
        Data 327
        DR Cost Considerations...328
        The Backup Site 328
        Third-Party DR (Outsourcing) 329
        DR and the Cloud 329
        HA/DR Options Described..329
        Disaster Recovery Templates 330
    Summary...330

SECTION V APPENDICES AND *HARD SUMS*

Appendix 1 ....**335**
    Reliability and Availability: Terminology...335
    Summary 371

Appendix 2 ....**373**
    Availability: MTBF/MTTF/MTTR Discussion 373
        Interpretation of MTTR..373
        Interpretation of MTTF 375
        Interpretation of MTBF..375
        MTTF and MTBF—The Difference 375
        MTTR: Ramp-Up Time 377
        Serial Blocks and Availability—NB..378
        Typical MTBF Figures 379
        Gathering MTTF/MTBF Figures 380
        Outage Records and MTTx Figures 380
    MTTF and MTTR Interpretation..381
        MTTF versus Lifetime 381
        Some MTxx Theory...381
        MTBF/MTTF Analogy..382
        Final Word on MTxx..382

Forrester/Zenoss MTxx Definitions 383
Summary 384

Appendix 3 ....**387**
Your HA/DR Route Map and Kitbag 387
Road to HA/DR 387
The Stages 387
A Short DR Case Study 391
HA and DR: Total Cost of Ownership 392
TCO Factors 392
Cloud TCO 393
TCO Summary 394
Risk Assessment and Management 394
Who Are the Risk Stakeholders? 395
Where Are the Risks? 395
How Is Risk Managed? 395
Availability: Project Risk Management 396
Availability: Deliverables Risk Management 400
Deliverables Risk Management Plan: Specific Risk Areas 402
The IT Role in All This 403
Summary 403

Appendix 4 ....**405**
Availability: Math and Other Topics 405
Lesson 1: Multiplication, Summation, and Integration Symbols 405
Mathematical Distributions 405
Lesson 2: General Theory of Reliability and Availability 406
Reliability Distributions 406
Lesson 3: Parallel Components (Blocks) 410
Availability: m-from-n Components 410
m-from-n Examples 410
m-from-n Theory 410
m-from-n Redundant Blocks 411
Active and Standby Redundancy 412
Introduction 412
Summary of Redundancy Systems 412
Types of Redundancy 413
Real m-from-n Example 414
Math of m-from-n Configurations 415
Standby Redundancy 415
An Example of These Equations 415
Online Tool for Parallel Components: Typical Calculation 416
NB: Realistic IT Redundancy 417
Overall Availability Graphs 418
Try This Availability Test 419

Lesson 4: Cluster Speedup Formulae 419
    Amdahl's Law 420
    Gunther's Law 421
    Gustafson's Law 423
    Amdahl versus Gunther 424
    Speedup: Sun-Ni Law 425
Lesson 5: Some RAID and EC Math 426
    RAID Configurations 426
    Erasure Codes 429
Lesson 6: Math of Monitoring 432
    Ping: Useful Aside 432
    Ping Sequence Sample 435
Lesson 7: Software Reliability/Availability 435
    Overview 435
    Software Reliability Theory 436
    The Failure/Defect Density Models 437
Lesson 8: Additional RAS Features 444
    Upmarket RAS Features 444
    Processor 444
    I/O Subsystem 445
    Memory Availability 445
    Fault Detection and Isolation 445
    Clocks and Service Processor 446
    Serviceability 446
    Predictive Failure Analysis 447
Lesson 9: Triple Modular Redundancy 447
Lesson 10: Cyber Crime, Security, and Availability 448
    The Issue 448
    The Solution 449
    Security Analytics 449
    Zero Trust Security Model 449
    Security Information Event Management 450
    Security Management Flow 450
    SIEM Best Practices 451
    Security: Denial of Service 452
    Security: Insider Threats 452
    Security: Mobile Devices (BYOD) 453
    BYOD Security Steps 454
    Security: WiFi in the Enterprise 455
    Security: The Database 455
    Distributed DoS 456
    Security: DNS Servers 456
    Cost of Cyber Crime 457
    Cost of Cyber Crime Prevention versus Risk 457
    Security Literature 458
Summary 458

Appendix 5 ....**461**
    Availability: Organizations and References 461
        Reliability/Availability Organizations 461
        Reliability Information Analysis Center 462
            Uptime Institute 462
            IEEE Reliability Society 462
            Storage Networking Industry Association 463
            Availability Digest 463
            Service Availability Forum 463
            Carnegie Mellon Software Engineering Institute............................ 464
            ROC Project—Software Resilience 465
            Business Continuity Today..465
            Disaster Recovery Institute 465
            Business Continuity Institute 466
            Information Availability Institute 466
            International Working Group on Cloud Computing Resiliency................. 466
            TMM*i* Foundation.. 466
            Center for Software Reliability 467
            CloudTweaks.. 467
        Security Organizations 467
            Security? I Can't Be Bothered.. 467
            Cloud Security Alliance...468
            CSO Online 468
            dark READING...469
            Cyber Security and Information Systems IAC 469
            Center for International Security and Cooperation 469
            Other Reliability/Security Resources... 469
        Books, Articles, and Websites 469
            Major Reliability/Availability Information Sources......................... 469
            Other Information Sources...470

Appendix 6 ....**479**
    Service Management: Where Next? 479
        Information Technology Infrastructure Library..479
        ITIL Availability Management 480
            Service Architectures 480
         Architectures 483
            Availability Architectures: HA Documentation............................... 483
            Clouds and Architectures 484

Appendix 7 ....**489**

Index **491**

Foreword

If you think high availability is expensive, try downtime.

With these words, Dr. Terry Critchley paints an exhaustive picture in his book *High Availability IT Services*, explaining how we can protect our critical applications effectively and economically from the plethora of faults that can take them down.

Terry's style is refreshingly informal and conversational. Even his most difficult topics are described in easily understandable terms with frequent vignettes relating his personal experiences that have spanned over four decades in the IT industry. However, he adds significant depth to each topic with frequent references to more detailed works, complete with URLs for easy access to these resources.

His book covers the entire gamut of high-availability topics, from hardware resilience to software reliability to service level agreements (SLAs) and even to the worst offender, the human fat finger. The book begins with a discussion of availability concepts and terms and looks at the cost of downtime. It stresses that change is the enemy of availability. The structure of a proper SLA is examined, and the basic requirements to achieve high availability are set forth. These requirements lead to discussions of high-availability architectures, including redundant server configurations, clusters, grid computing, and RAID disk arrays.

A simple look at the mathematics behind availability theory provides insight into how serial and parallel architectures affect reliability. This mathematical introduction is expanded in great detail in an appendix that can be referenced by the theorist who needs to calculate the potential availability of a proposed system.

The elimination of planned downtime is addressed along with the many causes of unplanned downtime. The role that networks play in service availability is discussed, and an extensive review of software reliability is accompanied by many references. The role of managing the high-availability project and its ensuing operation is covered in some detail. Offerings by many vendors of high-availability solutions are described.

The book continues with discussions of the availability considerations for OLTP (online transaction-processing) systems, virtualized systems, and clouds. A high-availability architecture is of little use if it cannot recover from an outage, so the book concludes with the disaster-recovery strategies that make high-availability work. The book's extensive 20-page Table of Contents makes it easy to find the coverage for any specific topic. At the expense of some redundancy, any chapter can be read independently of other chapters since each topic description is complete within itself. This makes the book an extremely valuable reference. Pull it off the shelf, browse the Table of Contents, locate the material you need, and become an instant expert.

As such, *High Availability IT Services* is an extremely valuable resource for IT professionals who need to become familiar with high-availability technology, for their management, for graduate programs in high-availability systems, and even for current high-availability practitioners like myself. The Glossary of Terms is unequalled in any comparable book.

Bill Highleyman
Availability Digest

Preface

Purpose of This Book*

What I have put in this book is from my own experience, from documented customer disasters and from the received wisdom of others. "There are people who know more about reliability, availability and availability management than I. For them, I have no message, but there are many people who know less, and less is not enough."† That's another reason for this book.

Not Another HA Book!

Yes, I'm afraid so. The difference is that this one is aimed at the availability of a *service* and not its components—hardware, software, and so on. A service is a set of business support processes run on an IT system. In a previous *life*, these processes may well have been manual. IT services comprise *people*, *products*, and *processes* in some sort of sequence. The acronym SOA, in the context of this book, could be interpreted as *service-oriented availability*. Keep this in mind throughout the book.

Very often this service component sequence is linear so that a fault in any of these components can result in a fault or outage of a service. Thus, a perfect system of *products* that are 100% operational does not necessarily mean the service is available to the user at the time he or she needs it. It may be that someone has run the wrong jobs, at the wrong time, or in the wrong order, rather like playing all the right notes of a piano concerto but in the wrong order. Everything is in working order but the service is not. These I call *logical outages*. They cause as much tribulation as the more familiar hardware failures.

Tell Me More

I developed this theme through a keen interest in availability and the legal possession of numerous articles on the subject, each with its own *take* on the topic. I felt the need for a single source of information about the principles, practices, and management of services in the pursuit of high

---

* This came from a saying by Sydney Smith, an eighteenth century UK wit and writer: "What you don't know would make a great book." Here is that book.
† I have paraphrased here a potent expression used in a religious context by Frank Sheed in his book *Theology and Sanity* (still available on Amazon, I think).

availability, backed up by references to more detailed expositions of the topics covered. In this respect, this document will hopefully act as a source book as well as a tutorial and guide on the reliability of products and the availability of services.

Another of my reasons for writing this book and other material was my delight in getting to understand a topic, whence I felt the urge to document it before I forgot it—a trait that helped me enormously when topics I'd forgotten came back to bite me. It reminds me of the expression of G. K. Chesterton's of someone *capering around a discovered truth*. I could well read this book myself in a year's time or two.

There are two basic ways of achieving a desired level of availability. One is to design availability *ab initio* (from the very start) into the system supporting critical services. The other is to retrofit availability onto an existing system—a much more expensive, difficult, and possibly risky option but one that may have to be taken.

The book is not a *how to* of high availability, and of the parent and sibling subjects business continuity (BC) and disaster recovery (DR), but an effort to educate the reader on the subject and the nuances of availability management. Availability, and its partner reliability, will be described fully in this book but perhaps *management* needs to be defined here. One definition is *the process of dealing with or controlling things or people*. The *thing* here is the availability of a system or systems providing a business function, for example, online orders or airline reservations. Availability in simple terms is the continued ability of the system or systems to perform their allotted function(s) at acceptable levels of accuracy, speed, and so on. These levels and their quantification are to be found in contracts called service level agreements (SLAs) drawn up between the business and the IT provider (which may be internal or external).

To use an analogy, this book attempts to describe ingredients, their interaction, and their associated recipes but draws the line at describing how to organize refreshments for a party, wedding reception, bar mitzvah, and so on. That type of work is the territory of the IT person, armed with a knowledge of *availability*, of his or her organization and its business requirements plus the various IT products employed in them.

The flip side of the availability coin is nonavailability and this can be assigned to any number of causes. These causes can be summarized here as due to the following: *hardware, software, firmware* and *embedded software, malware* (malicious attacks),* *liveware* (people—malicious or otherwise), *ambientware* (cooling, etc.), and *natureware* (natural phenomena). The percentage loss of availability due to hardware, software, and firmware is generally decreasing, whereas that due to malware and liveware is probably increasing, even if overall nonavailability is decreasing. Natureware is unpredictable but can be disastrous (Hurricane Sandy 2012 and, in H. G. Wells's words, *things to come*).

Thus it struck me while preparing this manuscript that hardware, firmware, and software may no longer be the prime whipping boys for system nonavailability (outages). Liveware and, more recently, malware are playing a part in downtime though not necessarily through physical outages. Any availability plan or exercise must therefore pay particular attention to *liveware* while not neglecting the other *wares*. Cyber-terrorism, beyond idiotic DDoS, may one day wander beyond government, military sites, and financial institutions to attack ordinary businesses, for whatever *cause* the malware originator is pursuing. We have been warned. See Appendix 5 for malware references, for natureware issues; see the Bible, Koran, Talmud, and other sacred texts.

---

* See Appendix 5 for malware references. Malware is mentioned over 60 times in this book.

In addition, there are often misplaced hopes and reliance on availability features of *vaporware*, unannounced vendor products that, we are assured, will deliver the promised silver bullet of 100% availability. Avoid!

The final subware in my classification is, for want of a better word, *ambientware* (sometimes called ecoware or the data center ecosystem), which is the environment the system lives in—heating, cooling, power, fire-retarders, and so on. The 'wares and some of their characteristics and interactions are shown in Figure 1.2 and Table 2.2.

Limitations of This Book

- The information in this book on vendors' approaches to high availability does not have consistent coverage since the same type of information on high availability has not been published by all vendors. I decided to publish *as is* rather than wait for an unknown time to get complete coverage from them.
- This book does not cover specific *how to* information for the numerous specific pieces of software such as TCP/IP, Active Directory, DNS, IMS, and Tuxedo. That would demonstrate ambition beyond my capabilities. It is more of an awareness of theory and fact and, hopefully, a valuable source book for pursuing topics of interest and importance further. In addition, this book does not lay claim to give definitive treatment to all availability features—see the references (URLs and other books) in the body of the book and in Appendix 6.
- I can't guarantee all the URLs cited will work forever. They worked for me at the time of writing and I checked some of them again before submitting the manuscript.

I have made liberal use of appendixes so that readers don't get mired with excessive detail when trying to negotiate a path through the principles in this book. If such detail is necessary for their further understanding, then they can dip into the appendix and return to the body of the book. Also, for similar reasons, I have made use of footnotes for additional information, references, and cautionary tales. They needn't be read at a first pass.

Structure of This Book

The book is divided into five sections (I–V), each of the first four sections containing several chapters and the final section, Section V, the appendixes. I have used US spellings except where proper names are involved. I have deliberately included a detailed table of contents so the reticent reader can pick his or her *itinerary* with which to traverse the book—the management, technical, or practice routes. There is quite a lot of math, mainly in the appendixes, but anyone who wishes to bypass it may do so without serious penalty in absorbing the essence of the subject. Just accept the conclusions reached, secure in the knowledge that someone, somewhere knows what it all means!

Section I: An availability primer and some reasons, mainly from surveys and enterprise experience, as to why anyone should bother about high availability:

- *Chapter 1:* A quiz, a history of the subject of availability, introduction to reliability and availability, general continuity planning elements and their relationships
- *Chapter 2:* An introduction to reliability and availability

- *Chapter 3:* The basics of availability SLAs, service management, and a first dip into availability concepts
- *Chapter 4:* A more detailed look at availability, redundancy, and fault tolerance, why HA, costs and reasons, and how high availability as a *subject* has developed. I then discuss availability architectures—RAS, clusters, grids, and RAID storage.

Section II: This section gives an outline of the theory of reliability and availability and the elements of actual practices in this HA area.

- *Chapter 5:* Some availability math, components as *blocks*, redundant blocks, series, parallel, and complex block diagrams with some real examples. The chapter concludes with a detailed look at failures (or outages)—planned and unplanned.
- *Chapter 6:* The practice of HA including seeking availability via a dozen different means, then onto network reliability and software reliability, including models, without which nothing works. I conclude with a look at reliability of other components of a system.
- *Chapter 7:* This takes us into the *management* areas of HA, including a deeper look at SLAs and the design and the operational phases of an HA setup plus some methods and techniques to help in these areas. There is a section on security management, now a key part of HA.

Section III: An examination of what the major hardware and software vendors have to offer in the HA world:

- *Chapter 8:* The chapter is devoted to major vendors of hardware, including fault tolerance and cluster offerings, including the emergent Linux clusters.
- *Chapter 9:* Again, a whole chapter is devoted to vendors and their products, this time in the areas of online transaction processing (OLTP) and relational databases (RDBMS), and how they blend together.

Section IV: A look at the ubiquitous world of clouds and virtualization and what availability considerations they present. There is also what I call a *route map* as a summary guide to what this is all about.

- *Chapter 10:* An overview of virtualization and cloud computing, cloud vendors, and *availability considerations* in these areas. It is not a tutorial on them.
- *Chapter 11:* This chapter covers the disaster recovery outline and stages in it, including when to test DR, when to invoke it, where to house the backup site (and where not to), and the usual roles and responsibilities issues. It is not a complete treatment and references are made to other literature.

Section V: This section lists appendixes, expanding on topics and subtopics raised in the book plus some simple math, which quantify some of the concepts covered. These appendixes are not vital to understanding the topic as a whole.

- *Appendix 1:* A large collection of the terminology on reliability, availability, and related subjects, which can serve as a refresher for someone who has forgotten the contents of the book.

- *Appendix 2:* An explanation of the time-related entities used in reliability and availability discussions—mean time to failure, mean time between failures, and mean time to repair. There exist a few clashes in how these concepts are defined, interpreted, and used.
- *Appendix 3:* This appendix examines the *route* to arrive at our main goals of a solid HA/DR system. It also deals with some peripheral but important issues such as risk assessment, risk management, costs of ownership, and plus a few other items. The chapter aims to assist and not prescribe solutions to the reader.
- *Appendix 4:* This appendix is the *meat* of the appendixes, where the math of reliability and availability are covered in some detail, together with items that I feel have some relevance to understanding the nuances of HA. The appendix is presented in 10 *lessons*, for want of a better word:
  - *Lesson 1:* Explanation of mathematical symbols used in the book
  - *Lesson 2:* A general theory of reliability and availability
  - *Lesson 3:* Theory of parallel components or blocks
  - *Lesson 4:* Cluster speedup formulae and types
  - *Lesson 5:* Some RAID math
  - *Lesson 6:* Simple math of monitoring
  - *Lesson 7:* Software reliability, models, and availability
  - *Lesson 8:* Additional RAS features developed over the years
  - *Lesson 9:* Triple modular redundancy arbitration
  - *Lesson 10:* Cybercrime, security, and availability
- *Appendix 5:* This appendix lists references to books, papers, and websites with information to supplement anything outlined in this book. I have tried to categorize them to make accessing a particular topic easier, with malware a prominent newcomer to availability references
- *Appendix 6:* This appendix discusses service management, which is where the subject of availability lives as one of the dozen or so elements in there. It has a brief outline of architectures for managing services.
- *Appendix 7:* I present a *pictorial* summary of the messages of the whole book.

Who Should Read This Book

Anyone whose company (and whose job) depends on *keeping the show on the road* and who cares about his or her company's well-being and prosperity. It is, however, open to anyone else who cares to read it.

It contains not only masses of information, but also a few laughs, many of them at my expense.

1. I believe all IT people involved in high availability and computer scientists and students could use the whole book, especially if management disciplines are their weak points.
2. Managers and team leaders would benefit from Chapters 1 through 3 and then Chapter 4 until they feel they are sinking, then stop, skim read Chapter 6, and devour Chapter 7. Back to skimming for Chapters 8, 9, and 10 then devour Chapter 11. Appendixes are optional.

There is a lot of information in this book. Not all of it is for remembering—some tables prove a point and can then be forgotten and referred to later if necessary.

Learning from This Book

I have found over the years in IT that there are various ways one might pick up and understand a subject. The methods I have found best for me are those where a subject is examined from different perspectives and at different levels of detail, which I refer to in the introduction to Section I. I have long realized that a single, long, detailed session of learning a subject does not work as well.

Accordingly, the reader may feel there is some repetition in the text but that is deliberate. In learning what I didn't already know to be able to write this book, I studied papers from many angles to try to master a particular topic before presenting it in the book.

The book is also a *portal* into many other areas related to high availability.

The Impetus for This Book

The world is full of tales of woe concerning organizations losing business, customers, and money through service outages, and lessons do not seem to have been learned. See the "Never Again" section of the Availability Digest at www.availabilitydigest.com.

In addition, a recent survey conducted by Continuity Software reveals that one-third of the organizations surveyed did not meet their service availability goals for mission-critical systems in 2012. It is discussed in Chapter 4 as well as at http://www.continuitysoftware.com/serv/2013-service-availability-benchmark-survey-cross-industry/.

About Me

I have been in and out of the IT arena since 1969, with 24 years in IBM, 3 years with Oracle, 6 years working for Sun Microsystems, and 1 year in a major UK bank. I have been involved with more areas of IT than you could shake a stick at: Y2K, IMS, CICS, storage, laser printing, OCR, OMR, UNIX, MVS, MUMPS, Pick, training, platform migrations, data center migration and customer planning, architecture, support, plus many other things.

In this book, I have made liberal use of diagrams and graphs as I believe the old adage that *a picture is worth a thousand words*. In addition, I have tried to lead people to solutions rather than push them with severe action checklists since I am unaware of readers' company business requirements, only where the pitfalls might lurk. I am also a minor authority on the Anglo-Zulu War of 1879, should any queries relating to that topic be raised by the contents of this book!

He that believeth in me and learneth from me, my learned colleagues, erudite correspondents, and other generous information sources shall not perish in the fires of eternal downtime but dwell in the Elysian fields* of (nearly) everlasting uptime.

T. A. Critchley

---

* From Greek mythology: the final resting places of the souls of the heroic and the virtuous.

Acknowledgments

In writing this book, I have tried to bridge the gap between literature written by experts for experts on the various aspects of reliability and availability, and mundane overviews, so that this knowledge is then accessible to nonexperts in digestible form. I could not have done this without the help of the experts acknowledged below, to whom I am very grateful.

Traditional acknowledgments written as prose bore me, I'm afraid, so I am reverting to a list format. I've named the people who have helped me in a variety of ways and also added minimalist details about them to indicate roughly where the evidence of their help resides in the book. Here we go, in no particular order:

- *Jeff Voas*, NIST; software reliability
- *Neha Miglani*, Assistant Professor, Computer Science, Kurukshetra University, India; software reliability models
- *Martin/Andrew (son) Shooman*, Verizon and EMC respectively; RAID details
- *Bill Highleyman*, editor of the *Availability Digest*; general support, encouragement, and review
- *Doug Hoffmann*, Quality Software; software testing and models
- *Seymour Morris*, Reliability Analytics; reliability advice and use of his online tools
- *Mike McCarthy*, Wilde Associates; reliability advice and guidance
- *Jim Metzler*, Webtorials; for permission to use their material
- *IDC*, permission to use a table they published some years ago, acknowledged in the text and deemed still valid
- *Doug Jensen*, Aberdeen Group; availability downtime, financial losses graph
- *Vendors of monitoring software*, many, especially SolarWinds, monitoring advice
- *Chris Barwise*, IBM Manchester; current IBM products
- *Mathew Heath*, IDC EMEA, HA classifications
- *Michael Lyu*, Chinese University of Hong Kong; software reliability and partial review
- *Bill Weinberg*, writer and Linux pundit; review of much of the material
- *Ed Gregory*, DePaul University, Chicago, IL; DR case study in Chapter 11
- *Professor James Plank*, University of Tennessee; erasure codes comments
- *Peter Judge*, technical author; general comments on the manuscript and its applicability
- *Others* who are acknowledged in the body of the book, many areas of assistance
- *Articles* by learned people—they filled lots of gaps in the book and my head ... and finally ...
- *Pacino's* and *Oca's crowd*, a Manchester pizza lunch group of *know-all* UK ex-IBMers, very little added to the sum total of information in this book, but fun to know and be with

Author

Dr. Terry Critchley is a retired IT consultant living near Manchester in the United Kingdom. He studied physics at the Manchester University (using some of Rutherford's original equipment!), gained an Honours degree in physics, and 5 years later with a PhD in nuclear physics. He then joined IBM as a Systems Engineer and spent 24 years there in a variety of accounts and specializations, later served in Oracle for 3 years. Terry joined his last company, Sun Microsystems, in 1996 and left there in 2001, after planning and running the Sun European Y2000 education, and then spent a year at a major UK bank.

In 1993, he initiated and coauthored a book on Open Systems for the British Computer Society (*Open Systems: The Reality*) and has recently written this book *IT Services High Availability*. He is also *mining* swathes of his old material for his next book, probably *Service Performance and Management*.

AN AVAILABILITY PRIMER

"Theirs not to reason why, theirs but to do and die ..."[*]

In the 1960s, I was teaching physics at a night class, subject refractive index μ. I was sailing along on the topic, throwing *sin i* and *sin r* about like confetti, when a student stopped me and asked *So what? Who cares?* but in more flowery language. I realized then that the student had taught me one of the most important things about teaching and writing—the *so what* test. I explained the importance of μ in optics and optical devices of many kinds—he was placated and peace was restored.

In this section, we cover some of the basic concepts of reliability and availability and, more importantly, the *why* of seeking high availability. Several concepts are mentioned briefly initially but are covered in more detail in Chapter 2 or through external sources referenced. This might be in a later section or an appendix, particularly the Terminology section.

I believe this is the best way to learn—looking at something from different perspectives over a period instead of wading through the same detail time after time. It is akin to learning the layout of a town by examining it from different viewpoints (car, walking, helicopter, map, talking to a resident) instead of tramping up and down the high street all day long. It works, believe me.

As a result, there is some repetition in this book, mainly deliberate, to introduce a topic, expand upon it, and, in the main, provide references for it. For any accidental repetition, my apologies.

---

[*] Alfred Lord Tennyson, *The Charge of the Light Brigade.*

Chapter 1

Preamble: A View from 30,000 Feet

Do You Know...?

1. The difference between resilience and reliability?
2. How to calculate the increase in reliability by adding a parallel component?
3. How to break up a server/network combination into physical domains for availability calculations?
4. What percentage of (recorded) outages are due to hardware failure?
5. What nonhardware factors cause outages? Can you name a dozen?
6. How a system can be *down* when all components are working?
7. The full breadth of what needs to be considered when designing and operating high availability services?
8. Enough about high availability to mentor someone in it? To tutor your boss?
9. What Lusser says about series components and reliability?
10. What Amdahl's/Gunther's/Gustafson's Laws all about?

If your answer to all the questions is *yes*, read no further and go out and play golf, go fishing, or drink beer (or all three). If any answers are *no*, please read on (see Figure 1.1).

This is our starting point in the discussion of availability, its theory, design, practice, and management, and I hope you and your organization will benefit from it. The management disciplines are the ones I found missing from most literature on high availability (HA) I've seen. Unmanaged technology can be like a loose cannon on a rolling ship—dangerous.

As well as learning from it, I hope you enjoy the book—I enjoyed writing it, unlike Hilaire Belloc did writing one of his books—*I am writing a book about the Crusades so dull that I can scarcely write it.* By *translating* erudite texts so that I could understand the topic enough to write about it has taught me a lot, for which I am grateful. I hope it helps you.

Figure 1.1 The curse of downtime! (From IBM Redbook: SG24-2085-00.)

Availability in Perspective

Availability seems an obvious entity to comprehend. In information technology (IT) terms, it is the presence of a working component or system, which is performing its job as specified. It has three connotations:

- Is it working or not?
- What percentage of time is it working according to specification?
- What is this specification that explains what *working* means?

We will see later that the last property above is the subject of an *agreement* between interested parties and is absolutely a key to the topic of HA.

Murphy's Law of Availability

This apparently immutable law, often called *The 4th Law of Thermodynamics*, states *If anything can go wrong, it will*. Hopefully, because the law is probabilistic, this book will help to minimize the impact of this law, certainly in the case of IT services and supporting systems. See Appendix 1 for the relationship between Murphy's and Sod's Laws.

Availability Drivers in Flux: What Percentage of Business Is Critical?

Until recently, the focus on HA was concerned with hardware and software and, unfortunately, still is in many organizations. There is a change in the need for HA, and the reasons for lack of it, as perceived by businesses and reported in a study by Forrester Consulting. It is dated February 2013 and titled "How Organizations Are Improving Business Resiliency with Continuous IT Availability."[*]

---

[*] http://www.emc.com/collateral/analyst-report/forrester-improve-bus-resiliency-continuous-it-avail-ar.pdf—
February 2013 study commissioned by EMC Corporation and conducted by Forrester Consulting.

Table 1.1   Top Risks to Business Services Availability

Driver of Increased Risk (to Availability)	Percentage of Responses
Increased reliance on technology	48
Business complexity of our organization	37
Frequency/intensity of natural disasters/weather	36
Increased reliance on third parties	33
Increased regulatory requirements	26
Increased threat of cyber attacks	25
Age of facility/data center infrastructure	16
Geographic distribution of our organization	15
Financial instability	14
Political and social instability	12
Power and fuel shortages/scarcity/outages	7
Increased frequency/risk of epidemics/pandemics	5
Other	5

The report indicates a shift in the types of risks, which businesses see as affecting the availability of their applications and services. These are outlined in Table 1.1, the result of surveying 246 global *business continuity (BC) decision makers*.

The outcome of these concerns is as follows:

■ Upgrading BC/disaster recovery (DR) is seen as a top IT priority (61% say *high/critical*).
■ Improving BC/DR drives the adoption of x86 virtualization (55% say *very important*).
■ Many organizations have already adopted active–active configurations (see Clusters in Chapter 4).
■ Continuous availability achieves both *operational* and *financial benefits*.
■ More organizations are ready for continuous availability.
■ About 82% lack confidence in their (current) DR solutions.
■ They believe that off-the-shelf continuous availability technology is mature.

The survey concludes saying:

Organizational demands for higher levels of availability will only increase. It's not a question of if but how IT operations will achieve these demands cost effectively. By combining HA/DR in a single approach organizations can achieve higher levels of availability, even continuous availability, without the huge capital expenditures and costly overhead of separate solutions and idle recovery data centers.

If things are changing, we need to try to understand and cater for emerging situations, which entails *knowledge and awareness*. I hope this book will help in achieving these goals. You may consider some aspects outlined trivial but even small insects can bite you and cause a lot of pain. There are lots of small *insects* in IT.

Another Forrester survey (2010) yielded the classifications of services supported by IT as approximately one-third each *mission critical*, *business critical*, and *noncritical*. This is a simple figure to bear in mind throughout this book when thinking *so what* as it tells us that two-thirds of a business activity is extremely important. Remember that *two-thirds*.

Historical View of Availability*: The First 7 × 24 Requirements?

System reliability has an interesting history with its genesis in the military. It is also notable that much of the theory of reliability was developed by and for the military and later, by the space programs. In fact, Lusser of Lusser's Law (see Chapter 5) worked with Werner Von Braun on the development of rocketry after the latter's sojourn with the German V1s and V2s in World War II.

If you look at the MIL handbooks produced by the US military, you will find the logic in the drive for component reliability. It is essentially the increasing reliance of military operations on electronics, and relying heavily on unreliable equipment in combat situations does not make sense. This focus on reliability of components was taken up by commercial manufacturers as a *survival* mechanism in a competitive world of selling goods. Service is also a key factor in winning business in this competitive world.

In the IT arena, reliability and availability go beyond simply using *quality* components because IT provides a service and the service needs to be reliable and hence available for use when needed. A service is composed of components that comprise working units, like disks that make up servers that combine to make systems and so on. Hence, we have a mill pond effect where this need for reliability spreads beyond the base components.

The following diagram shows, schematically not for the last time in this book, the viewpoints of server, system, and service (Figure 1.2). If you take this on board now, we are half way to our goal in this book.

As you move outward through the *onion rings* in the diagram, the theory of reliability and availability becomes more tenuous and difficult to predict exactly. However, one thing can be predicted and that is Murphy's Law—if a thing can go wrong, it will. The task of the availability person in IT is to predict how it might go wrong, what is the possibility of it going wrong and how do we design to avoid and when they happen, mitigate these failures.

In 1952, the US military was developing the SAGE system (semiautomatic ground environment) in the Cold War environment that pervaded East–West relations after World War II. It was essentially an early warning system (EWS) to monitor potential airborne attacks on the US mainland.[†] IBM, under Thomas J. Watson Jr., was bidding for the computer part of the SAGE business against Radio Corporation of America (RCA), Raytheon, Remington Rand, and Sylvania (where are they now?).

---

* The late Jim Gray (then at Digital Equipment Corporation [DEC]) and Daniel P. Siewiorek (Carnegie Mellon University): Draft IEEE paper c.1991.
  Also see *Why Do Computers Stop and What Can Be Done About It*? Tandem Technical Report 85.7 PN87614 (June 1985), also by Jim Gray.
† Probably the precursor to the proactive AWACS project.

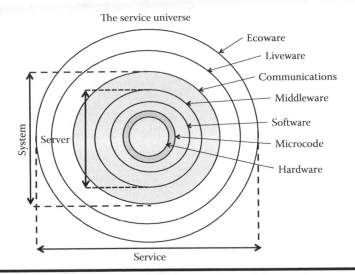

Figure 1.2 The service *universe*—Server, system, service.

In his book *Father, Son and Co.*, Watson says:

> ... the Air Force wanted the system to be absolutely reliable. In those days it was considered an accomplishment if someone could build a computer that would work a full eight-hour day without failing. But SAGE was supposed to operate flawlessly round the clock, year in and year out ... the storage circuitry we were using worked faster than the UNIVAC [*a competitor*], but it also 'forgot' bits of data more often." ... "The system even had the reliability that the Air Force wanted ... solved the problem by having the Q7s [*the new IBM computer*] work in tandem, taking turns. One machine would juggle the radar [*data*] while its twin was being serviced or standing by. By that method, the average SAGE center was able to stay on alert over 97% of the time."[*]

We *cognoscenti* recognize here (or will do shortly) the need for reliability in memory and for hardware redundancy via this rudimentary *cold standby* node cluster. Watson doesn't say anything about how the data were shared in those pre-SAN, pre-NAS, and pre-switch days, or how fast the switchover time was, but they blazed the system *availability* trail nevertheless.

Jim Gray had to say about the *old days*:

> Computers built in the late 1950s offered twelve-hour mean time to failure. A maintenance staff of a dozen full-time customer engineers could repair the machine in about eight hours. This failure-repair cycle provided 60% availability. The vacuum tube and relay components of these computers were the major source of failures: they had lifetimes of a few months. Therefore, the machines rarely operated for more than a day without interruption.
>
> Many fault detection and fault masking techniques used today were first used on these early computers. *Diagnostics* tested the machine. *Self-checking* computational

---

[*] Bantam Books (1990) ISBN 0-593-02093-4, probably available on Amazon and elsewhere.

techniques detected faults while the computation progressed. The program occasionally saved (*checkpointed*) its state on stable media.

After a failure, the program read the most recent checkpoint, and continued the computation from that point. This *checkpoint/restart* technique allowed long-running computations to be performed by machines that failed every few hours.

Things have certainly changed since then but my main thesis in this document is that *man cannot live by hardware alone*, a view supported by the Forrester survey outlined earlier. Logical errors and general *finger trouble* (by liveware) will sometimes outsmart any *NeverFallsOver* and *Semper Availabilis* vendors' hardware and software products.

The ham-fisted or underskilled operator can knock almost any system over. A new up-and-coming contender for *tripping up* systems is *malware* which is now increasingly recognized as a potential menace, not only to service availability, but to an organization's data, confidentiality, finances, and reputation.

Historical Availability Scenarios

Planar Technology

In the late 1950s, Fairchild and Texas Instruments (TI) went head to head in the race for smaller, more reliable electronic circuits. The requirements were driven partly by US military requirements, mainly the electronics in the Minuteman missile system. At that time, the move from glass tube circuits to transistors was underway but the problems of needing one transistor per function and the interconnection of many of them remained.

Fairchild was a *new boy* in this arena but was making progress with planar technology which enabled the connection of multiple circuits on a single substrate possible and avoided the problem of multiple interconnections via wires and solders in favor of metal strips on the insulating substrate. This was a massive leap in the technology—ICs or integrated circuits—and got round the reliability issue of earlier transistors. This was easily demonstrated by what was dubbed *the pencil tap test*, whereby a transistor could be made to malfunction in various ways simply by tapping it a few times with a pencil, not a desirable trait in military hardware delivered via a rocket or other *robust* means.

The names Robert Noyce and Jean Hoerni* are forever associated with this leap forward in transistor technology which was soon given further impetus by the avid interest of National Aeronautics and Space Administration (NASA) in fast, small, and *reliable* integrated circuitry. Interestingly, the intrinsic *reliability* of these new technologies was not the only issue. Their volume production was also of prime importance in the development and spread of computers and planar technology helped this in this goal.

It was IBM who, bidding to the military, asked Fairchild to produce suitable circuits for their purposes in this exercise. To the military, the initial cost of these *chips* (c. $100 each) was not an issue but for the volume sale of computers, it was. However, history shows us that such costs are now minimal (http://www.computerhistory.org/atchm/invention-of-the-planar-integrated-circuit-other-stories-from-the-fairchild-notebooks/).

An interesting article *Computer System Reliability and Nuclear War* can be found at the given link (http://www-ee.stanford.edu/~hellman/Breakthrough/book/chapters/borning.html), which illustrates beyond any argument the need for reliability, knowledge of reliability, and hence this book.

---

* Gordon Moore, of *Moore's Law*, was also part of the Fairchild setup in those days.

Power-On Self-Test

This series of diagnostic tests is run automatically by a device when the power is turned on. Today, it can apply to basic input/output systems (BIOS), storage area networks (SANs), mainframes, and many other devices and systems. Power-on self-test normally creates a log of errors for analysis and, in most cases, will not start any software until any problems are cleared. This is sometimes called built-in self-test (BIST).

Other Diagnostics

In my time at IBM, I saw many advances in the tools and techniques used by engineers for maintenance and diagnostic exercises. Originally, the engineers (called customer engineers or CEs then) used masses of A2 (42 cm × 60 cm) diagrams in oversized books, several of them kept in a hangar-sized metal bookcase in the machine room. They pored over these tomes while examining the innards of a machine with electrical probes, multimeters, and screwdrivers plus a few raised digits and swear words. The latter items will not be found in the terminology Appendix of this book but the reader will guess them anyway.

This could be a time-consuming exercise, as well as a strain on the engineer's back in lifting these books and make his eyes myopic trying to read incredibly complex diagrams. Taking a whole day to diagnose and fix a simple failure was not the norm but it was not unusual either. I can see those books now in my mind's eye and remain thankful that I did not have to use them in my work as a systems engineer.

These techniques did little to expose *soft* errors that might eventually become *hard* errors, possibly causing outages later. I remember meetings with customers where the IBM CE would summarize the latest hardware diagnostics and agree on a date and time for maintenance, or perhaps repair/replace activity, for components exhibiting higher than expected *soft* error rates, sometimes called *transient* errors.

In later years, these cumbersome diagnostic methods and books were replaced by maintenance devices (MDs), the equivalent of the clever diagnostic tools used in modern cars, but pre-Java. They shortened the diagnostic time and hence were a considerable boon to system availability and to the health of the engineer. Just to complete the picture, I was told by one engineer that there was an MD to diagnose a failing MD and so on! I should have guessed.

Component Repair

Repair could also be a time-consuming process that was eventually superseded by field replaceable units (FRUs), where failing items were replaced *in situ* (where possible) and the offending part taken away for repair, or to be scrapped. The part, if repairable, could then be used again on the same system or elsewhere.[*]

FRUs installed by the customer are called CRUs (customer-replaceable units), a fairly recent innovation. It is current modular system and component designs which make a replaceable units philosophy possible.

To be cost-effective, FRUs needed to be of a size that could be easily replaced and, if necessary, discarded if they could not be repaired after removal. This necessitates a granular approach to the system design but then more components making up a system means more things to go wrong.

---

[*] Contracts and consumer law permitting.

In-Flight Diagnostics

Later versions of the hardware and operating systems offered diagnostic recording and warning features that could be used either retrospectively (e.g., for identifying soft errors) or as an operational warning of potentially failing parts or components as work was in progress. A sophisticated level of self-test and diagnostics is implemented in hardware systems that offer fault tolerance (ft). These include Stratus and HP Nonstop, a system initially marketed by Tandem before their acquisition by HP (see Chapter 8).

Modern systems have these and other reliability, availability, and serviceability (RAS) features (see Chapter 2) which considerably enhance availability figures and are rarely unique to any one vendor. One characteristic of in-flight diagnostics is that the errors they detect can be either logged, flagged in real time to IT operations, or bypassed using fault-tolerant recovery techniques.

Summary

We have seen the early attempts to specify what causes our computers to fall over and to address the issues in various ways. The tackling of this problem is evolutionary and made very necessary by the consequences of failure to business and other systems. I can't think of any business today that isn't totally dependent on IT to run the whole operation or dependent on someone who is, for example, a third party.

Some enterprises only address the HA and DR aspects of running their IT when they get their fingers burned and for some, those burns are fatal. Funding HA IT is like paying for an insurance policy on your house—you hope you won't need it but when your house burns down you're glad you took the policy out. Your CFO may say *we've spent all this money on high availability and disaster recovery and I can't see any benefits.*

This issue reminds me of an appropriate story you might respond with:

> A man was walking round my home town of Warrington, UK, scattering a green powder. A second man saw this and asked the first man "Why are you scattering that powder?" to which the first man replied "To keep the elephants away." The second man looked puzzled and said "But there are no elephants in Warrington." "No" said the first man "this powder is very effective isn't it?"

Even if an enterprise decides to spend on these aspects of IT, they may either get it wrong or overspend with overkill *just to be on the safe side.* That's where knowing what you are doing comes in useful!

Many years ago, UK electricity boards built their networks using components, such as transformers, with large amounts of redundancy and capacity in them *just in case* and to save continually upgrading them as the load grew. Today, costs are such that networks are designed and provisioned using *power systems analysis tools* to design and install equipment with the ratings to do the job and have enough spare capacity to handle projected growth.

These power systems planning tools and the effort involved in using them are more than covered by cost savings from quality network design and component usage.

I know this because I spent several years of my IBM *life* working with and in public utilities— gas, water, and electricity.

Planning, quality design, implementation, and operations reap their own rewards and this applies in IT as well as in other service areas like utilities. The effects of such labors may not be obvious due to a form of IT hysteresis (see Appendix 1) but they are there nonetheless.

Remember: The three components of services—people, products, and processes—are like the three musketeers. All for one and one for all, in true *holistic* fashion. Together, they unite to provide a service to users/clients.

Chapter 2

Reliability and Availability

The two concepts reliability and availability are talked about, written about, equated with each other, and given star status but, in the main, remain somewhat one-dimensional concepts. In this chapter, and throughout this book, I hope to show that these concepts, particularly availability, have other dimensions and interpretations as well.

Introduction to Reliability, Availability, and Serviceability

Reliability represents the probability of components, parts, and systems to perform their required functions for a desired period of time, without failure, in specified environments with desired confidence. Reliability, in itself, does not account for any repair actions that may take place. Reliability accounts for the time it will take the component, part, or system to fail while it is operating. Reliability does not indicate how long it will take to get the unit under repair back into working condition and is often qualitative—*this car is much more reliable than my last one*. This assessment is usually based on how long it spent in the repair and servicing states.

Availability, to continue with the car analogy, is how long the car is in working order and how long you can travel before it fails, measured in operational and usage times, respectively (see Figure 2.2). These you will mentally note as the time between failures and how long it takes you to get the car back on the road.

> "Reliability, availability, and serviceability (RAS) is a computer hardware engineering term. The phrase was originally used by IBM as a term to describe the robustness of their mainframe computers. The concept is often known by the acronym RAS." See Wikipedia.

IBM did not *invent* RAS, but they put heavy emphasis on it in System/370 in 1970. They put robust features into succeeding mainframes to increase their ability to stay operational and then coined the acronym *RAS* for the outcome. RAS (reliability, availability, and serviceability) is evolving and the concept has been adopted by all hardware vendors and has now spread to the software domain.

Computers designed with higher levels of RAS have a multitude of features that protect data integrity and help them stay available for long periods of time without failure—this data integrity and uptime is a particular selling point for mainframes and fault-tolerant systems, despite their being more expensive.

In fact, reliability and availability characteristics could be developed for liveware.

Note: Reliability and availability do not have a one-to-one or a mathematical relationship that is universal (like Ohm's law, $V = IR$, or Einstein's $E = mc^2$). It is perfectly possible for component 1 to be less reliable than component 2 but deliver better availability. This scenario might occur when failures of 1 can be diagnosed and repaired much more quickly than those of 2 so that overall, the total outage time of 1 can be less than that of 2. Hence, the availability of 1, A%, is greater than that of 2, B%, even though reliability of 1, R_1, is lower than that of 2, R_2. Another way that less reliable components can "win" the availability contest is by using redundancy (duplicate components), like the original redundant arrays of independent disks (RAID) designs, but redundancy comes at a dollar cost.

See Availability Architectures in Chapter 4 for a discussion of RAS features.

Before we get into the body of this book, I'll outline some major areas that we will deal with in Chapters 6 and 7—a true view from 30,000 feet, part of the process of *learning via different viewpoints and angles.*

RAS Moves Beyond Hardware

An Intel document dated 2005 lists the following as factors that help RAS as well as pure hardware:

- *Highly reliable platforms:* Hardware, firmware, and software
- *Extensive hardware and software testing:* Vendor and user
- *Rigorous change management:* Supports my (and others') ideas that *volatility* can mean *outage*
- *Redundant architectures:* Used only where needed
- *Highly trained staff:* Liveware issues loom large in outages, as we will see
- *Well-established emergency procedures:* Runbooks, day-to-day and disaster recovery (DR)

We now need to add at least some mention of *security*, which can affect availability significantly these days, as do the other elements above; see http://www.intel.com/content/dam/www/public/us/en/documents/white-papers/reliability-availability-and-serviceability-for-the-always-on-enterprise-paper.pdf. This excellent paper contains a RAS table and a detailed glossary of RAS terms. Our RAS discussion in Chapter 3 of this book is generic and does not imply that all vendors have all the features mentioned in that chapter in their RAS environment.

Aside: I was reading an article about these things and its author, who is obviously knowledgeable, issued the *so what* comment about RAS features. In my mind, the *so what* is that the customer would like to know they are there, rather like knowing that there are safety features and procedures on aircraft without understanding them in detail. Basic RAS is the best platform to build on.

Availability: An Overview

Reliability is denoted mathematically as $R(t)$, a function of time described by a graph, which we will see shortly. At some time in the life of an item, its reliability may be assumed to be constant, to allow calculations to be made as we wallow at the bottom of the ubiquitous *bathtub* curve (see Chapter 5 under Availability Concepts).

Some Definitions

These definitions may seem superfluous but they often come in useful when we discuss with people about system availability—often boring but a good *anchor point* here to start a discussion of an important topic. Getting availability and reliability terms straight up front is akin to saying "according to Hoyle" when starting a game of cards. It prevents arguments. In the definitions that follow, an *item* may be a circuit board, a component thereof, a LAN, or even a whole server configuration and its associated network(s).

> *IEEE*[*]*: Reliability.* The ability of a system or component to perform its required functions under stated conditions for a specified period of time.
> *IEEE: Availability.* The degree to which a system or component is operational and accessible when required for use.
> *ITU-T*[†]*: Reliability.* The ability of an item to perform a required function under given conditions for a given time period.
> *ITU-T: Availability.* The ability of an item to be in a state to perform a required function at a given instant of time or at any instant of time within a given time interval, assuming that external resources, if required, are provided.
> *NIST FIPS: Availability.* This refers to "ensuring timely and reliable access to and use of information…" (44 U.S.C., Sec. 3542). A loss of availability is the disruption of access to or use of information or an information system.

Note: The definitions here point to *service* as the key entity in the definition of *availability*, the main thesis of this book.

> ***Shorter Oxford English Dictionary, 1988:*** *Reliability.* The quality of being reliable; reliableness.
> *Reliable.* That may be relied upon, in which reliance or confidence may be put, trustworthy, safe, and sure.
> These are all qualitative definitions. None of them, although comprehensible, implies any *quantitative properties* related to these two concepts.

---

[*] IEEE (Institute of Electrical and Electronics Engineers) 1990. *IEEE Standard Computer Dictionary: A Compilation of IEEE Standard Computer Glossaries.* New York, NY. http://en.wikipedia.org/wiki/Special:BookSources/1559370793.

[†] International Telecommunications Union, recommendations E800. https://www.itu.int/rec/dologin_pub.asp?lang=e&id=T-REC-E.800-198811-S!!PDF-E&type=items.

Quantitative Availability

Reliability of an *item* can be quantified by an equation (see Appendix 4) and is a function of MTBF,[*] whereas availability is not a fixed function of the *item* but varies depending on the reliability of the *item(s)* and the time taken to diagnose a problem and correct it. It is a function of MTBF and other parameters.

For the moment, let us take the number **A** representing availability as

$$\frac{\text{Time working}}{\text{Time working} + \text{Time not working}}$$

The plethora of definitions in the topic of reliability and availability can be confusing (as we will see) but the following diagram may ease the pain:

$$A = \frac{\text{\Large †††††}}{\text{\Large †††††} + \text{\Large ⚐⚐}} \tag{2.1}$$

A Primitive Availability Equation

> **Aside:** This visual representation reminds me of people of the Zulu and Navajo nations, where there is no written language—there may be others I don't know about. The Navajo language was used by the U.S. military intelligence in World War II for encoding messages in their Pacific operations, knowing the enemy couldn't possibly have had a hardcopy Navajo dictionary.

As we shall see, availability represents the probability that the system is capable of conducting its required function when it is called upon given that it has not failed or is undergoing a repair or an update action. Therefore, not only is availability a function of reliability, but it is also a function of the reparability, maintainability, or serviceability.

Figure 2.1 illustrates the factors that affect the definition of a system and its availability, that is, functioning according to its specification for a period of time. It should be noted here that there is a difference between the hours a system is actually working (switched on, lights flashing) and the hours it should be available to users, that is, fully supported, all relevant hardware and software initialized and all lights blazing.

Availability: 7 R's (SNIA)[†]

Mark Fleming (employed at IBM in 2008, the date of his presentation) lists 7 R's that impact availability:

Redundancy: To eliminate single points of failure (SPoFs).
Reputation: What is the track record of the key suppliers in your solution?

---

[*] Mean time between failures, covered in detail later along with its confusing companion, MTTF, mean time to failure. Don't worry, we'll get there by the end of Appendix 2.
[†] You can find the presentation on the SNIA website (www.snia.org).

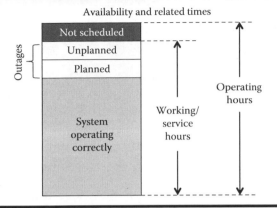

Figure 2.1 Visual availability: Definition of times.

Reliability: How dependable are the components and coding of the products?
Reparability: How quickly and easily can suppliers fix or replace failing parts?
Recoverability: Can your solution overcome a momentary failure without impacting the end users?
Responsiveness: A sense of urgency is essential in all aspects of high availability (HA).
Robustness: Can the solution survive a variety of forces working against it?

This same list can be found in Rick Schiesser's book *IT Systems Management* (2002)* so I am unsure of the true origin of the 7 R's discussion. It is the message that matters.

I put this in here because it is a useful memory jogger and even if you can't name all the components, at least you know you have seven to find!

With due respect to Mark Fleming, storage networking industry association (SNIA), and Rick Schiesser, I would add to and expand upon a few of their R's:

Resilience: Add as a measure of the ability and speed of recovery (*a la* the resilient boxer, who is able to get up and resume the fight where he left off after a knockdown).
Reputation: To Mark Fleming's words above in this category, I would add your own organization's reputation in avoiding commercial failures that impact existing customers and website failures that deter would-be customers.
Reparability: How soon can you complete problem determination (what and where) to decide which supplier or third party to ring if needed? In addition, for customer-replaceable field replaceable units (FRUs), what stock do you keep onsite? A few hours' driving to fetch an FRU will blow availability targets into the middle of the following week.
Return on investment (ROI): You will probably be asked to justify any extra expenditure or, put another way, say what will it cost the organization if we *don't* put this scheme in place and we get caught out?

On the last point, about ROI, 25 years ago, a senior information technology (IT) manager at a customer I looked after had a grand plan for a *new data center*. He was warned by an experienced external data center person that he should prepare a *cost case* when he presented his grand plan to the board as they would probably ask for such a thing. He didn't and they did!

---

* *IT Systems Management*, Prentice Hall PTR, ISBN 0-13-087678-X.

The situation then rebounded, however: he rang me and asked me to help prepare a cost case! Panic! I called around IBM data center personnel and, with their help, managed to put together a cost case involving productivity (IT staff/unit of power), software, and other savings associated with centralization and modernization.

I used the costs of the support staff per unit of power (the IBM RPP—relative processor power, then the 370/158)—IBM had 0.8 people/RPP, the customer at that time 1.8 per RPP. IBM was aiming for 0.2 people per RPP and I think we used the 0.8 figure as the benchmark for the customer's potential savings!

Someone in your organization will ask the very same question about *your* grand plans—HA, DR, or any other. You will need some sort of financial case involving total cost of ownership (TCO) (see Appendix 3) and benefits.

Availability and Change

Assume for the moment that we have a basic understanding of what availability means to an installation.

It seems unfair to some people that other organizations have better IT system availability than their organization has and they wonder why. Well, aside from breaking the *rules* that we will cover in this book, there is a factor that has occurred to me many times when reading about system *failures*. This is the fact that some organizations have rapidly changing operations and/ or business requirements, such as changing parameters related to time, disk space, and other entities when carrying out day-to-day work. They may also have system and application changes that might affect the potential availability of systems and data adversely. Then, there are software patches—system and application—including microcode and embedded code—across system(s) and networks.

Rapid change offers many opportunities for errors in implementing it and, in my view, can cause outages of the *liveware* kind. Note that there are permanent changes, such as patches and hardware additions, and transient ones, such as batch job parameters.

The *change* graph in Figure 2.2 assumes all other factors are equal (*ceteris paribus*) apart from the operations volatility factor. I think most people know what *data center volatility* is: changes to runtime parameters, job mixes, and scheduling changes to suit business circumstances. Change management is not the whole answer to this issue, although it will smooth the path.

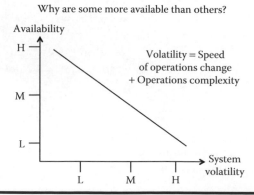

Figure 2.2 Availability and effects of change.

Human error can still occur in the best change management schemes.

> [O]ne of our engineers *accidentally changed a configuration* on our production SAN full of documents. His change immediately corrupted a terabyte of corporate data and started a series of events that led to a 72-hour restore. An entire company of thousands of workers sat idle while we watched stacks of tapes do their job.
>
> **Greg Shields**
> *ESJ Storage February 19, 2014*

Adding extra users to an existing system is also a change factor that can sometimes have unforeseen consequences. This is common occurrence, often done furtively, but rarely figures in change management discussions and activity.

Figure 2.2 shows schematically the relationship between the *velocity* of change and potential unavailability or instability. H, M, and L in the diagram are relative: they might be, for example, 99.99%, 99.5%, and 99%, respectively. They are there to illustrate my thesis that, other things being equal, volatility of systems, processes, and the work that runs on them can mean less availability in some circumstances.

One might add to the volatility axis a factor representing the ability to back out changes, which is a vital component of change management and hence availability.

In pseudo-mathematical expression, this might be written as follows:

$$\text{Nonavailability (system/data)} = f(V_{\text{OPS}}, V_{\text{CHNG}}) \qquad (2.1)$$

where V = volatility, and nonavailability might be a function of the two volatilities: operations and system changes.

Change All around Us

All change has the potential to cause failure or adverse results of some sort. The old data processing (DP) bureaus would qualify as volatile environments because of the often wild mixes of work they were asked to undertake by a bewildering array of customers. For example, the USAAF base at Burtonwood, near Manchester, and other local businesses used an IBM bureau facility for their changing payroll and we hope the airmen and their support staff got paid OK! I know about the volatility of the bureau, because I was there.

The old adage *if it ain't broke, don't fix it* was aimed at maintaining the *status quo* in the sure knowledge that change can often mean problems, some of which may be irreversible (the Humpty Dumpty syndrome). Unfortunately, *not fixing* is not always possible.

This *change can equal outage* concept was also supported in a webinar by *Continuity Software* on December 6, 2012, except the vertical axis in their graph was entitled Potential Downtime and Data Loss and the H, M, and L tags reversed. The conclusions are the same, however.

> ***Note:*** What I am saying here about change is also supported by an ORSYP survey (2012) on change and one by Forrester Consulting/Zenoss on IT Monitoring (August 2013), whose conclusions are outlined in the next section.

Software: Effect of Change

The volume of change to software for fault correction and maintenance can have a similar effect on reliability, just as other changes we have noted here. The need for strict change control here should be self-evident, as the JAFLOC syndrome (*it's just a few lines of code*) can cause havoc.

We are not just talking about application software here but any software supporting application. Major upgrades to the latter software would normally be subject to rigorous testing and verification but apparently minor changes, say, to a communications table, can be a source of outages. Incorrectly installed upgrades/patches can cause outages.

Cautionary Tale: I saw this happen in a major chemical company where a virtual telecommunications access (VTAM; an IBM telecommunications software application) table was altered by the company's communications staff without going through the change control procedures. The change clashed with other valid changes and brought the system down. IBM software customer engineers tried to locate the problem, believing it to be an IBM issue. Eventually, the internal communications staff owned up to the fact and the problem was solved quickly.

I know about this because I was the IBM systems engineer on that account but I was found *not guilty* of being an accessory in the crime.

Operations: Effect of Change

The study by ORSYP* on *pain* in IT operations produced several issues and suggestions that are germane to our discussion of availability, or the possible lack of availability. The survey questioned a sample base of worldwide organizations, ranging from major banks and financial institutions to retailers, and aimed at uncovering the factors that caused the most frustration for those organizations in managing their IT operations. To fully understand the methodology and riders, you should consult the ORSYP white paper.

The following statement from the white paper leads neatly into our thesis above about change and failure potential: "Among all the findings, it was clear that human factors and the dynamic nature of business operations will always represent potential problems for the management of IT operations."

This is precisely my argument in the Equation 2.1 in the previous section and is supported by Continuity Software in their webinar mentioned previously. One train of thought is to automate many repetitive tasks that often do not require the skills of a trained IT person and that often result in boredom. As we all know, boredom causes lack of interest and hence concentration and that is when the problems occur. A large proportion of downtime is due to liveware—bored staff are inattentive staff and as such are error prone. See Table 2.1 reproduced from the paper and condensed by the author into summary form.

Monitoring and Change

The Zenoss white paper referred to above, entitled *Amplifying the Signal in the Noise of IT Monitoring*, covers the challenges of IT monitoring, and hence control, of complex IT architectures.

---

* www.orsps.com, *Information Technology Operations Pains Report Management* 2012 (White Paper). Extracts here are reproduced with the kind permission of ORSYP.

Table 2.1   Operational *Pain* Factors and Possible Availability Impact

Reason for Operational "Pain"	Availability Impact
1. Lack of involvement of IT operations personnel in business projects	Possible poor design or architecture. *Shoddy* SLAs, suboptimal operations procedures, and documentation of them.
2. Cuts or freezes in IT budgets	Corner cutting on availability needs (redundancy, training, capacity, etc.).
3. Business constraints creating an ever-changing IT environment	Volatility, change = possible instability and human error.
4. Increased complexity of IT environment in management and administration	Volatility, change = possible instability and human error.
5. Security of IT systems, disaster recovery, data integrity, repetitive data processing	Inability to recover, logical outages (data loss, malware, other) if design is unsound.
6. Need to align IT with key business objectives, particularly SLAs	Differences between IT and business objectives, *malformed* or nonexistent SLAs, internecine friction.
7. Justification of IT investment (ROI) [*difficult*]	Possible *corner cutting* while expecting the best in availability and performance.
8. Skills balance and specialist and generalist synergy	Poor design, implementation, and operations [*finger pointing*].
9. Managing outages, procedures, recovery windows, unplanned outages	*Suboptimal* availability management and probably SLA compliance.
10. Mobility of workforce[a]	Management of availability and security can be compromised.

[a] This covers not just *users* but the possible need for itinerant (mobile) IT support and 7 × 24 if necessary.

The white paper includes the results of a Zenoss-commissioned Forrester Consulting study on IT service monitoring, which incorporates the response of "157 North American IT decision makers"* and was aimed at providing significant insight into why and how current monitoring solutions are failing to deliver expected productivity and efficiency benefits.

Their key findings are as follows:

- Complexity (i.e., IT complexity) continues to increase.
- Daily IT service issues are common.
- Existing monitoring tools are not effective.
- Monitoring provides benefits outside incident management.
- Unified monitoring is needed.

---

* http://blog.zenoss.com/2013/02/an-honest-discussion-about-why-repairing-it-services-takes-so-long/.

Although the survey was about *monitoring* issues, it uncovered some facts that in essence say that change can cause IT problems. The question and responses to one of the survey questions were as follows:

Question: What would you say are the three main causes of technology *performance* and *availability* issues in your environment today?

The five highest rated issues were as follows[*]:

■ Unplanned IT capacity or demand requirements
■ Inadequately tested changes in pre-production/test environments (which will of course will propagate into the production environment)
■ Configuration changes/drift in applications
■ Aging or poorly maintained technology infrastructure
■ Inadequately planned changes

If these results don't tell us that *change is a major factor* in causing problems that then become failures to meet expectations on availability and performance, I don't know what does (see http://www.zenoss.com/in/wp_signal_noise.html).

See Appendix 2 for *time* definitions (MTxx) in this paper, which you may find confusing at the present time.

To summarize, change *can* cause problems; as a matter o fact, uncontrolled, unmanaged, and unmonitored change *will* cause problems.

Automation: The Solution?

There is an illuminating article, "The Case for Automation," at http://www.kaseya.com/download/en-us/white_papers/Ziff.Automation.WP.pdf, profiling the use of internal and external staff in several availability-related areas of IT plus a list of candidate operations area for automation. It also highlights cost savings and productivity improvements, among other benefits of automating processes and actions.

In the absence of intelligent autonomic systems, these automation tools might be worth investigating. It should be remembered that *automation* and *autonomic* are not the same.

Automation is a step along the road to *intelligent operations, detection of errors,* and *corrective action,* which is basically what autonomic computing means, and today, there are a number of vendors offering automation solutions.

Data Center Automation

The case for automation of monitoring alerts and operational IT tasks often revolves around human factors—mistakes caused boredom and lack of concentration in people performing these often mundane tasks. The consequences of mistakes in tasks related to mission-critical systems can be severe. The question soon will be not *shall we automate* but *what shall we automate safely* in an attempt to mitigate the effects of change and human frailty in increasingly complex and volatile IT system environments. If a well-defined task is being carried out on a regular basis, then we have a candidate for automation.

---

[*] http://blog.zenoss.com/2013/02/an-honest-discussion-about-why-repairing-it-services-takes-so-long/.

Similarly, if staff turnover or reassignment is such that constant training and documentation updates are required, then automation may be a solution. There is of course the usual check and balance—what time and expense will it incur and will time and money savings accrue from that automation?

More importantly, will it reduce or eliminate failures and service level agreement (SLA) non-compliance, particularly those relating to critical business systems? Following are two case examples:

> ***Reference 1:*** A recent ORSYP paper (see Table 2.1) "IT Automation: How to Guide" is at http://info.orsyp.com/rs/orsypsoftwareinc/images/EN_eBook_IT_Automation_How_To_ Guide.pdf. This above paper looks useful and contains information about generic automation pitfalls, hints, and tips.
>
> ***Reference 2:*** The paper by Mike Resseler of Veeam is a useful guide to the why, wherefore, and how of data center automation (see http://go.veeam.com/go.veeam.com/go.veeam. com/go.veeam.com/wpg-backup-resseler-bringing-automation-to-datacenter.html; http:// resources.idgenterprise.com/original/AST-0109986_mike_resseler_bringing_automation_ to_the_datacenter.pdf).

Network Change/Configuration Automation

The network, because of its geography, is arguably the most difficult element of a service to monitor, control, modify, and repair. Manual procedures, prone as they are to error, may be difficult to police if errors are made in change and configuration. The effects of such errors may take some time, however, in becoming evident to a business service.

A white paper by Infoblox (www.infoblox.com) entitled "Is It Time to Automate Your Network Change and Configuration Processes?" contains a brief self-assessment of network control in these areas and suggestions for improvements via automation (see http://docs.media.bitpipe.com/io_11x/ io_113166/item_805232/Whitepaper_TimetoAutomateNetworkChangeConfigProcess.pdf).

Automation Vendors

There are several vendors who tout automation tools, including ORSYP, Veeam (see reference 2 above), and IBM. They also have useful general articles on their websites. In addition, another article, "IT Process Automation: Moving from Basics to Best Practices," written by Gartner Group for HP, identifies three elements that might *inhibit* the development of IT process automation solutions:

- Lack of IT organizational maturity* and appropriate skills
- Nonstandard IT infrastructure (software and hardware), which impede the achievement of IT process automation
- The costs of development, implementation, and administration

The Gartner/HP paper also lists the following as a sample vendor list for IT process automation: BMC Software, CA Technologies, Cisco, HP, iWave Software, Microsoft, NetIQ, Network Automate, UC4 Software, and VMware.

---

* Older readers will remember the *Nolan Curve* of IT maturity. Youngsters ask that old IT guy in the corner (the one with the gray beard) about it. You always wondered what he knew.
  See http://en.wikipedia.org/wiki/Stages_of_growth_model for a description of *Nolan*.

On this topic of *change*, a last quote:

> The more complex a system, the more potential failure points there will be, so it is clear that the most highly available systems must be those that are simplest and easiest to manage, and with the highest levels of inbuilt redundancy, failover options and backup.

(Computing/Double-Take article 2013)

> **Outcome:** *Change* is disruptive in varying degrees and can result in human error in IT situations. Process *automation* is a potential solution to human error caused by change. Also, remember that change management and all the other topics in this book are not simply the job of specialists—they should, given their importance, be in the *psyche* of everyone in IT at some appropriate level.

Types of Availability

Binary Availability

Availability is normally thought of as a "toggle" switch that can be turned on or off. We will see later that this is not strictly true, but let's pursue the *binary* case first. If you discuss *availability* with anyone, make sure you are playing the game Hoyle. There are shades of *off* and *on* that will become clear in due course.

Availability can be thought of in at least two forms:

1. The diagram below illustrates these *binary* states *available* or *down*. When the component/system at any point at time *t* is either up or down (operating or not operating), then its state of *availability A* is either 1 (up) or 0 (down), that is, availability $A(t) = 1$ or 0.

   In standard reliability terms and mathematically this is stated as

$$\text{State variable} = \begin{cases} 1 \text{ if the component is } \textit{functioning} \left(\text{to specification}\right) \text{ at time } t \\ \\ 0 \text{ if the component is in a } \textit{failed} \text{ state at time } t \end{cases}$$

2. The availability *A* is expressed as a percentage of the time it is available and working against the time (*T*) it is operational (*A*%). Operational time here is the period it is *meant* to be functioning. This is the time used to calculate availability, not elapsed or wall-clock time or the time it is *actually* operating to specification but not in use (see Figure 2.3).

> **Note:** Reliability is a *property* of a component, not a *state* like availability. Incidentally, a NASA publication describes a level of operation between 0 and 1 that it calls *limited operation* but doesn't give it a number, just that it is >0 and <1.

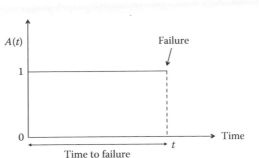

Figure 2.3   Availability state variable: Up or down.

Remember: This concept applies to a single item, not a collection of items such as a full-blown system where each component will have its own *state variable*. The state of the *assembly* of components will vary as we will see below.

Because we say "availability can be thought of in at least two forms," are there any others? Yes, the (grand old) Duke of York availability—my term for what is usually known as *degraded mode* (NASA's *limited operation*)—that assumes a system/service is operating but not as it is supposed to be according to the design or the SLA In place. This, incidentally, hammers home the importance of SLAs. No SLA means nobody cares how the service performs or how long it operates for. This is called anarchy.

Duke of York Availability

In the verse about our grand old duke marching his 10,000 men up and down a hill, there are the lines:

> When they were up they were up
> And when they were down they were down
> And when they were only half way up
> They were neither up nor down

The last line sounds better poetry than *they were neither state 1 nor state 0* and the diagram to the right of the verse represents *Duke of York* or *degraded* operations.

This situation can be applied to services that are neither up nor down but are forced by some component failure to operate in *degraded mode* in functionality, performance, or some other important agreed aspect of the service, probably via an SLA.

This mode of operation needs to be considered carefully in component failure impact analysis (CFIA) studies, particularly in relation to any SLAs in force for the service in question. Degraded service may also apply to DR plans, where a complete service cannot be supported by the DR configuration and some less critical services and applications may have to be *sacrificed* in the short term while total recovery of the primary site takes place. This is a business decision, based on a business impact analysis (BIA).

The concept of failed (state 0) components and operating (state 1) components becomes a little more complicated when there are several components operating together.

Consider the following failure hierarchy:

- Failure of *part* of a component: state 1 going to state 0
- Failure of a component: state 1 going to state 0
- Failure of part of a set of components (system): state?
- Failure within a system with software (service): state?

The answer to the third item in the bullet list above is it depends if the whole system (service) can still operate and deliver the *goods*, in which case it earns a 1. However, if it can still deliver but in a degraded mode that fails to meet its SLA, then the users would class it as state 0, even though to a hardware/software purist it is state >0 but <1.

It all depends on expectations and expectations are the province of SLAs.

Hierarchy of Failures

Figure 2.4 shows four purposes:

1. It demonstrates the hierarchy of elements in a service, each of which can have a state of 0 or 1 (down or up). The service illustrated comprises hardware, system software, and middleware tools and implies some other items. Each cascades down into component parts and the illustration shows the hardware parts explosion.
2. It can be a useful visual tool in performing CFIA, dealt with later in the book, along with the discussion of the failure mode and effects analysis (FMEA)/failure mode effects and criticality analysis (FMECA) methodology (see Chapter 7).
3. It is also amenable to fault tree analysis (FTA), which is, however, not covered in this book.
4. It can be used to analyze a system for SPoFs. A weak point in the chain may not appear to present a major problem but if the *business process* using that innocuous component depends 100% on it being available and accurate, it may comprise a major issue in the design of the overall system.

Hierarchy Example

Examples to illuminate the elements shown in Figure 2.4 are as follows:

- *Service:* Invoicing suite, stock control
- *System:* Hardware, software, environment—implied at level 2 in the diagram
- *Hardware (H/W):* Server, disk subsystem, and network
- *Software (S/W):* Operating system, middleware, *webware*, applications, and other elements
- *Assembly:* Motherboard or equivalent, memory card, and software program
- *Component:* CPU, memory chip, connections, and program module
- *Subcomponent:* Resistor, capacitor, clock, subroutine, scientific function (sin, cos, arctan, etc.), AND/OR gate, microcoded counter, timer, and so on

When subcomponent software from other sources is used, it is important to verify that the function it provides is what is needed (a type of SLA). In addition, the calling and results

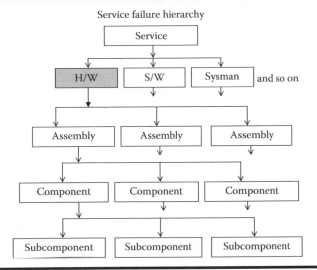

Figure 2.4   Service failure: Element hierarchy (tree).

delivery interfaces and formats application programming interfaces (APIs) need to be properly understood.

The software and *sysman* (systems management) and any other legs will have their own hierarchy, each with its own components, their equivalent of those of the hardware leg.

It is possible for a part of this hierarchy to fail but the whole service continues unaffected except, perhaps, for performance. For example, a failure in a memory component need not be fatal to the service if it can be *offlined* or the failure compensated for by a *mirrored* memory component.

Confusing, isn't it? The answer is that the SLA muddies the water as to whether the overall service is awarded 1 or 0 and whether quality of service (QoS) is included alongside availability requirements. QoS, for example, may include transaction response times, batch job turnaround times, and so on.

State Parameters

The diagram below shows a *service* delivered by identical configurations of, say, hardware and software. In situation A, there are two 0-state components but it is a working system. In situation B, there is only one 0-state component but the system will not work, that is, it is status 0. Obviously, this is due to the SPoF joining the two parallel sets of components.

$$\text{State}(A) = 1, \ \text{state}(B) = 0$$

The layout in the diagram is known as a *reliability block diagram (RBD)* (Figure 2.5).

This set of initials and method of display are often used in reliability studies, practical and theoretical, and are a fundamental part of designing systems for HA and rapid DR. See Appendix 1 for an outline description. The RBD diagrams are used to visualize systems for analysis purposes—availability, performance, functional *walkthroughs*, and so on. We will see more of them in this book.

It is easy to expand Figure 2.5 to a system configuration with many 0s but still merit an overall state 1 and a system with many 1's and a single 0 but an overall state 0. Again, the SLA has a part

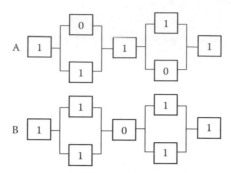

Figure 2.5 State parameter examples (0 or 1) for a service/system.

to play in the award of a 1 to the former system if the loss of one of the parallel components breaks an agreed SLA delivery parameter, for example, performance.

> *Note:* Figure 2.5 represents parallel and serial components and is not a *complex* configuration which will be dealt with briefly later.

> *Aside:* This reliability concept graph (Figure 2.3) can be applied to other situations where the horizontal axis, Time, takes on variations or other meanings, for example:
>
> ■ Calendar time (pure elapsed time)
> ■ Operational time (time the component is supposed to be working)
> ■ Number of kilometers covered by a vehicle before failure
> ■ Number of cycles for a periodically working component
> ■ Number of times a switch is operated, perhaps before failure
> ■ Number of rotations of a bearing, perhaps before failure

The term *availability* when applied to *hours of supported service* must not be confused with the definitions above. An application or service that is only offered for 100 hours per week has, on our definition (Figure 2.1), an availability of 100/168 or about 60%, which is patently not true. Within that 100 hours, the definitions above *do* apply, that is, *what percentage of that 100 hours is it available for work at a satisfactory level?*

In the rest of this book, I discuss mainly in terms of the second option, which is discussed in detail later and rediscussed, taken to pieces, and reassembled in Appendix 2.

Types of Nonavailability (Outages)

This discussion might seem a superfluous section, but wait. There are three basic classes of outage:

1. *Physical.* This class of outage refers to the scenario where something fails to operate. It might be hardware or software, directly or because of some external event like a flood. The failure may or may not impact the system or service that it supports. A hardware example of a

nonimpacting failure is the failure of one component of a parallel pair where the surviving component continues to function and support the system or service. A software example is an operating system or online transaction processing (OLTP) system that fails but is compensated for by the invocation of a *shadow* system, such as IBM's customer information control system (CICS) XRF (extended recovery facility).[*]

2. *Logical.* This class of outage refers to the scenario where nothing has failed but something prevents the system or service from operating properly or at all. Examples of this are extremely poor performance or some sort of *system limit* parameter that impacts the system or service, either totally or just partially.

   There might also conceivably be a combination of the scenarios 1 and 2. Examples of these might be where certain key parameters specifying system *resource limits* (or ceilings) are exceeded—*maxprocs, bufno, bufsize, maxusers,* and so on. If these parameters can be altered dynamically (without impacting system operation), then the service recovery can be swift: if not, then a reboot/re-IPL may be needed after altering the *offending* parameters. The latter case will involve a service outage.

3. *True outage.* This class of outage refers to the real time for which a service is unavailable and not the time that the supporting hardware and software is not available. The view that the operations staff have of an outage can differ significantly from that of the business's end user. For example, a hardware or software error that causes an outage might also have made erroneous changes to a database(s) that may then need to be recovered, perhaps from a log, so that proper business processing can resume. Such times, which are additional to physical outage times, are rarely, if ever, reflected in outage surveys. These times, which I term *ramp up* times, can be significantly larger than the nominal *fix* time. In such a situation, the true outage time for the *service* is

$$\text{True outage time} = \text{Detect time} + \text{Fix time} + \text{Ramp up time}$$

Outage causes repaired quickly does not necessarily mean low downtime:

> I'll never forget the longest day of my career. That day the sun rose, set, rose again, set again and finally rose a third time before I got to sleep. The reason: A major server crash—or, more specifically, *restoring all the data back to that server once its original problem was resolved.*

> **Greg Shields**
> *ESJ Storage February 19, 2014*

Logical Outage Examples

One example of a *logical outage* is illustrated by an IBM OLTP system—information management system (IMS). IMS was IBM's original DB/DC product before CICS became a *strategic* product.

---

[*] The extended recovery facility (XRF) enables an installation to run an alternate CICS system that monitors an active CICS region and takes over automatically or by operator control if the active system fails. It is just an example of software redundancy that is not unique to IBM.

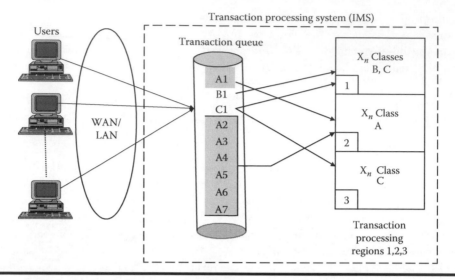

Figure 2.6   Logical outage example—*Vintage* IMS.

1. This is a real example I came across from this venerable IBM TP system IMS, 1980s vintage, and is illustrated in Figure 2.6. The various classes of IMS transaction, A, B, C, and so on, are routed (or directed) to regions assigned to process them. Here the regions are numbered 1, 2, and 3. From the schematic, it is evident that there is a glut of class A transactions and only one region available to service them, resulting in a queue of class A transactions waiting for region 2 to become free, and to be scheduled and executed.

   This imbalance might have happened over time as the pattern of work changed unpredictably and not necessarily through poor initial system setup, though that could be a cause. This could incidentally be avoided by knowledge of the workload characteristics in advance when assigning region-processing classes and changing the appropriate region class parameters to suit. This is called *planning*![*]

   If such changes are needed and can be done *in-flight*, then so much the better for availability and performance.

2. Another example of a logical (performance) outage I came across was using the record key *randomizing*[†] to populate a database. The key being hashed was only three characters long, which resulted in dozens of synonyms (*identical results*) for the record location and absurdly long times for the database software to follow these synonym chains to get the correct record. The same thing can happen in RDBMS scenarios where *hashing* is used to generate keys.

> ***Corollary:*** This is the origin of the SLA which, in general, specifies that the user wants a service to not only function, but to function within certain metrics involving parameters that he or she specifies and are important to the business.

---

[*] There is a useful expression that can be used to great effect in the right circumstances: *A lack of planning on your part does not constitute a crisis on mine.*

[†] Generating a location address for a record(s) from the record key using a randomizing algorithm that, if smart, will avoid synonyms, which are identical addresses for different keys.

Summary

The message in this chapter is that nonavailability is not a simple concept and a clear matter of *is it working or is it not*? Availability is really a matter of *is the service working as it should do to support me and if it isn't, it isn't available*. It may be that the system needs to *ramp up* or perform some extra work to get up to speed (see discussion of ramp up in Appendixes 1 and 2 for equivalent MTTV terminology used in reports by Forrester).

These metrics might include hours of service, performance characteristics, and other QoS entities. In the context of Figure 2.6, this performance metric was not explicitly specified but was raised to red alert when it happened.

Planning for Availability and Recovery

> *If you fail to plan, you plan to fail.*
>
> **Benjamin Franklin**
> *U.S. polymath and politician*

Why Bother?

Practically, all businesses rely to a great degree on information technology and most could not function at all without it. It is vitally important then that if IT support is not forthcoming (for whatever reason), the business can continue to function to a similar or lesser degree. That act of *carrying on* is known simply as *business continuity* (BC). Being unable to carry on has disastrous effects on some businesses in terms of financial losses, customer satisfaction, and other deleterious consequences. These issues are outlined elsewhere in this book, for example, Chapter 4, and in articles and papers on the Internet.

Although this book does not aim to cover aspects of total system recovery, it is instructive to look at the connection between planning for availability and subsequent recovery after major incidents that *take out* the normal IT operating environment. One aspect of availability planning and management is *what data and facilities do we put aside in our IT bank account for that rainy day*.

What Is a Business Continuity Plan?*

A business continuity plan (BCP) is a program of activity that develops, exercises, and maintains plans to enable an organization to

- Respond to a major disruption with minimum harm to life and resources.
- Recover, resume, and restore functions on a timescale that will ensure continuing viability of the organization involved.
- Provide crisis communications to all stakeholders (i.e., almost everyone connected in any way).

This includes an IT DR plan as a subset but also needs to cover temporary locations for displaced staff, emergency IT facilities (screens, desks, fax machines, etc.), communication with non-IT

---

* See *Disaster Recovery Journal* (http://www.drj.com/) for information and glossary.

facilities, third parties, and so on. It is no mean exercise. I have seen BC documentation and would not attempt to lift it for fear of lumbar damage. The plan usually takes input from mainly stakeholders and, among other things, the BIA (see below).

If you don't have a BCP, you emulate the man falling from a skyscraper who says halfway down *so far, so good*, and there are some wonderful tales of businesses *competing* for a Darwin award for BCP failures in the paper at http://www.webtorials.com/main/resource/papers/delphi/paper7/DR_Darwin_Awards.pdf.

One of these, a part of a BCP, is reproduced here, entitled "We Powered What?":

> One of the smaller telephone companies built a network operations center for their infrastructure transmission facilities. One day they discovered there was no backup power available at the site. Nothing had happened, they were planning ahead. The backup power was installed and demonstrated successfully.
>
> Eventually there was a power failure, but the equipment that was to be powered did not work. The electrical outputs were color coded to show where the backup power was connected. Unfortunately they got the color codes reversed. The only thing that worked after the power failure was the Christmas tree.

Test the system out and produce an RBD.

What Is a BIA?

A BIA assesses the consequences of disruption of a business function and process and gathers information needed to develop recovery strategies. Potential loss scenarios should be identified during the risk assessment (problem vs. probability of it occurring).

There are many possible disruption scenarios to consider, or even dream up, and assess their impact on the business—financial, image, share price, and so on. This exercise is ideal for a Delphi technique session (see Chapter 7).

The exercise should be carried out for each business unit* and documented. Examples of SBUs are invoicing, payroll, payments, and ledgers some more important than others and needing separate considerations in ensuring affordable availability.

Some terminology used in BIA relates to *tiers*, which are classifications of what downtime an application can tolerate without severe business impact. Typically, they might look as follows:

- *Tier 0:* One hour or less can be tolerated.
- *Tier 1:* Four hours downtime is tolerable.
- *Tier 2:* Extended downtime of a day or more is tolerable.
- *Tier 3:* Flexible but probably with a maximum, say, of *x* days.

Don't confuse these *tiers* with those describing the position of data as online, near-line, and so on, which is *data tiering* or *hierarchical data placement*.

This classification gives some discrete structure to the exercise, which would otherwise be difficult with an amorphous mass of services and applications. Which tier anything belongs to is a business decision, with the usual proviso *if you can't pay for it, you can't have it*.

---

* Often called SBUs or strategic business units.

What Is DR?

This book is not mainly about BC or DR but availability, or lack of it, although design for availability must take into account the requirements of both DR and some aspects of BC.

For example, it is pointless having a recovery time objective (RTO) that cannot be met because the dump/restore architecture and implementation mechanism are too slow to recover what is needed in this time.

BC/DR is the activity above and beyond the call of fault resolution and repair—it usually involves the total loss of the primary system, its applications, and user access. DR is not covered in detail here. It is a large topic in its own right and is very specific to the hardware and software involved as well as with the recovery requirements of the users defined in the SLA(s) negotiated with IT.

Figure 2.7 shows an early immersion reminder of the facets of DR, and all these will be reexamined in more detail in Chapter 11. This outline of DR includes some salutary examples and a methodology that is generally agreed by most other authors, particularly those who have been through it all. Remember that DR should be in the designers' minds when designing and planning for HA (see Figure 2.7).

There are murmurs about extending *cloud concepts* of software as a service (SaaS), platform as a service (PaaS), and the rest to other XaaS services like disaster recovery as a service (DRaaS) and high availability as a service (HAaaS). See Chapter 10 for an expansion of these ideas.

Relationships: BC, BIA, and DR*

Recovery Logistics

The word *recovery* has multiple meanings. Who is recovering what and for whom? This boils down to roles and responsibilities—IT and non-IT functions (Figure 2.8).

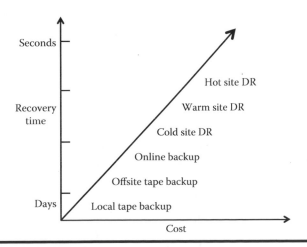

Figure 2.7   Preview: Disaster recovery in a nutshell.

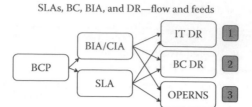

Figure 2.8   Major business/IT recovery requirements.

These recovery elements need to be understood and assigned to the appropriate personnel with a central point of control when the balloon goes up. In Figure 2.8, the highlighted numbers represent the following:

1. This is the recovery of IT-based hardware, software, applications, and communications. The phases of recovery will ideally follow a pattern dictated by the BIA.
2. There are numerous elements outside IT recovery that are necessary for the business to continue operating. For example, there is little point in recovering the IT infrastructure if the building housing the staff who use the IT services have no power or is inaccessible. There are logistics implications in BC. BC is *not* the same as DR since DR is a part of BC.
3. This is the area of running the business and supporting IT in the new environment. It is essentially a command and control activity for controlling people and processes in this *new world*. The overall control of the recovery process will look like a military operation with the exception that in a military situation, things may be *ad hoc* and planning must be done on the fly. In the case of BC/DR, the logistics and operational *modus operandi* should have been designed, documented, and rehearsed.

Business Continuity

The recovery of business premises and other non-IT sites does not concern us in this book but that is not to say it is not important if they form an integral part of mission-critical systems. If vital data entry, for example, is carried out from premises where power is lost for an extended period, then the functions of that site need to be *recovered* so that the business continues. Similarly, for floods and other catastrophic natural phenomena, it is pointless recovering IT when you have no user access to the services.

Organizations associated with *availability*, DR, and the like are referenced in Appendix 5. Their websites often contain valuable information on availability tools, techniques, and other organizations. For example, see the BCP and BIA references (http://www.csoonline.com/article/509539/how-to-perform-a-disaster-recovery-business-impact-analysis?page=1).

Downtime: Who or What Is to Blame?

I have no doubt that everyone has seen pie charts of what and who causes outages or downtime. They vary somewhat in the percentages displayed, depending on the survey date, but not in the factors that are responsible, except perhaps for cyber crime, unknown when some of the surveys were carried out. The broadest breakdowns cite people, processes, and products in roughly equal measure as responsible for outages.

The breakdown mentioned in the Preface to this book lists the following *culprits*:

- *Hardware:* Everyone knows what this is.
- *Software:* Covers nonembedded software of all kinds—application and system.
- *Ambientware:* The working environment of servers (ecosystem), disks, and so on.
- *Embedded software/microcode:* Built into hardware normally but *code* nonetheless.
- *Liveware* (or people)*:* People make mistakes and people in IT are no exception. They can err in minute-to-minute operations or in producing erroneous code or procedures that are used in production.
- *Malware:* Trojan horses, viruses, botnets, distributed denial of service (DDoS), and the whole gamut of *gremlins* that can cripple an IT system and/or its data.
- *Natureware:* Tornados, hurricanes, earthquakes, snow, floods, tsunami, terrorism, disaffected employees (yes), and so on.
- *Vaporware:* Has no impact on availability if you ignore it.

Each of these, apart from vaporware, has an effect on availability and should be the headings under which plans are made—plus estimating the probability of a particular occurrence multiplied by the business impact of that occurrence.

This will be covered a little later when I discuss the flow of activities in availability planning and, incidentally, in almost any IT project you undertake.

Elements of Failure: Interaction of the Wares

Table 2.2 summarizes the "'battleground" in the quest for high (or higher) availability of systems and services and my assessment of the maturity and solidity of the theory accompanying each availability area. It illustrates what is meant by failure rates and how mature the knowledge of the area is to allow prediction of these rates (see Table 2.2).

Faults in one *ware* area may propagate to other areas, as I have tried to emphasize in the following *impact* table. Sandys, Katrinas, tsunamis, and terrorist attacks or threats thereof often transcend our concerns about precise RAS features, so the perspective in Table 2.3 is a useful one

Table 2.2 Availability Theory: Its Maturity for the Various *Wares*

Ware	Inter-Failure Time (MTBF/MTTF) Meaning	Theory of Reliability: Maturity
Hardware (HW)	Well understood.	Established.
Software (SW)	Less precise than HW and mainly empirical.	Abundant but fluid and sometimes abstruse. There are numerous models and math distributions involved but none are universally applicable.
Ambientware (AW) (ecosystem)	Depends on simultaneous failures of equipment or crucial single one (power, air con, etc.).	Probably follows HW patterns and possibly NW.

(Continued)

Table 2.2 (Continued) Availability Theory: Its Maturity for the Various *Wares*

Ware	Inter-Failure Time (MTBF/MTTF) Meaning	Theory of Reliability: Maturity
Embedded SW or Microcode	Understood and probably long if testing is adequate. It usually is because of the nature of the code.	Probably follows the SW pattern, although microcode usually comprises less code. Embedded code can be millions of lines.
Malware (MW)	Variable MTBO (occurrences) decreasing and frequency depends on system vulnerability and benefit to miscreant of system *penetration*. On the increase in numbers and severity, especially high bandwidth DDoS.	Nonexistent as far as I know though it may be *according to Hoyle* possibility. Its frequency and damage potential is increasing year on year.
Natureware (NW)	Variable MTBO and nasty NW geographical areas should be avoided if possible or backup sites in a *friendly* NW environment.	Ways of predicting these phenomena developing—some are well known enough to avoid data centers in certain areas of the world.

Table 2.3 Scope and Interaction of Failures

Failure of can affect →

	HW	SW	AW	ESW	MW	LW	NW
HW		Y	Y	Y	D	Y	Y
SW	Y		Y	P	D	Y	Y
AW	Y	Y		N	D	Y	Y
ESW	Y	P	Y		D	P	Y
MW	P/D	P/D	Y	U		P	D
LW	A	A	U	N	D		Y
NW	N	N	N	N	N	N	

Legend:

Y = Can affect   A = Action needed   U = Uninvolved/unlikely
D = Doesn't matter   P = Possibly   N = No impact

HW = Hardware   SW = Software   AW = Environment/ecosystem
ESW = Embedded/microcode   MW= Malware   LW = Liveware
NW = Nature/Acts of God

to absorb and bear in mind when talking about *n* 9's availability. One Katrina at an unprepared site can blow a five 9's installation into the one 9 class for the next 10 years.

The decisions that have to be made are how much effort do we put in to prevention and how much into cure. In the case of widespread natural events, geographically separated sites may be the best DR solution.

I remember an organization using a supposedly sophisticated software package for selecting the best site for a data center based on road and rail access. It churned away for 10 minutes (using the Fibonacci series and Ohm's law for all I know) and then spurted out the ideal data center location—in the middle of the Bristol Channel! This is true.

Also, note that natural disasters vary and are often *native* to certain parts of the world and unknown in others. Tsunamis do not normally happen in the Sahara desert, nor do tornados in the United Kingdom.

Summary

In this chapter, I have presented an overview of availability, both as a concept and as a number and its related property, reliability. We've seen something of the environment of availability—its *history*, service delivery, elementary math, and the factors that influence the availability of systems and services and each other.

I have outlined the fact, still not recognized by some "informed" people, that there is more to availability than hardware—a whole host of things and subthings with subtle shades and nuances ready to trip up the unwary. I have also defined some terms related to availability to set the scene for later discussions.

> **Note:** A key understanding that should come out of this chapter is that there are different kinds of outages—*physical* and *logical* together with shades of degradation of service. The yardstick by which availability is measured is enshrined in the SLA, which can involve performance as well as availability.

I hope you got through this chapter unscathed and go on to enjoy the rest of the book. I feel it is more productive in HA design if one feels comfortable with the *subject* of availability than slavishly follow *prescriptive checklists*, although checklists do have their place in aiding, rather than leading, you. It is rather like wearing a well-made bespoke suit as opposed to one borrowed from a neighbor—you feel far more comfortable in the former outfit. Or, to take another analogy, would you like to have a major surgical operation when the *surgeon* involved needs to constantly read his or her checklist?

DR/BC Source Documents

Useful information on various aspects of DR and BC can be found at http://searchdisasterrecovery.techtarget.com/essentialguide/Essential-guide-to-business-continuity-and-disaster-recovery-plans?Offer=mn_eh121113DRCYUNSC_ww&asrc=EM_USC_25461043&uid=15414727&utm_medium=EM&utm_source=USC&utm_campaign=20131211_Our+top+DR%2FBC+content%3A+A+2014+planning+collection_. Also, see the Continuity Software's BC risk assessment at http://www.continuitysoftware.com/the-one-report-every-business-continuity-manager-is-asking-for/.

A lot of information is *nested* via references to other documents but it is a useful source of information to assist planning in these areas.

> **Note:** Access to *Search…* documents like the ones referenced in the above URL often requires registration, which is not an onerous task and, more often than not, is worth the effort.

Chapter 3

Reliability: Background and Basics

Introduction

The mainframe has long been the home of mission-critical applications in most organizations and still is in many instances.* Some twenty or so years ago, there was a move to nonproprietary systems, such as UNIX, Linux, and the proprietary Windows/NT. However, these systems did not traditionally have the maturity or stability of mainframe systems, especially as they tended to be combinations of client/server and distributed systems. The mainframe advantage in this arena was the fact that everything was on one system and each layer of software on it was aware of the others and the synergy, and *cooperation* between them was there.

In the IBM environment, for example, multiple virtual storage (MVS) understands the architecture and characteristics of Customer Information Control System (CICS), Information Management System (IMS), DL/I, DB2, and so on, and often vice versa. Gathering statistics across these software layers was relatively simple—MVS understood the concept of a CICS (online transaction processing [OLTP]) transaction or network traffic in a virtual telecommunications access method (VTAM) (teleprocessing communications) environment. Also, this *cooperation* made it easier to identify faults when the system failed. In UNIX, for example, the operating system only knew the software layers under it as processes with process numbers assigned and the *relationship* between them is much weaker than that of the software layers on mature legacy systems. Basically, UNIX had no idea what applications it was running.

It is this that made systems management of *open* systems more difficult than that of established mainframe platforms. Today, the software subsystems themselves (DBMS) and available monitors make the *open* world much more intelligent and manageable. For the mainframe (still with us) and the up-and-coming systems contenders—game on!

---

* I *cut my teeth* on mainframes at IBM, expensive monsters costing the earth, occupying half an acre and about as powerful as the PC I am producing this book on. One in my account had to enter the machine room using a big crane to lift it through an upper storey window.

The subject of availability is crucial for organizations dependent on mission-critical applications and services—loss of service more often than not means loss of revenue and/or customers. Quite simply, the *management* of availability is crucial to organizations moving to platforms other than the *tried and tested* legacy systems for mission- and business-critical work. *Having* is not a synonym of *managing*.

People soon recognized that availability was becoming important as more parts of an enterprise's business became increasingly reliant on what was then known as data processing (DP). Software came under scrutiny, particularly operating systems and communications software, the latter being charged with delivering packets of information without errors or at least being able to recover from transmission errors.

IT Structure—Schematic

Hardware and software are the basic building blocks that people think of when examining systems but there are other elements that need consideration.

Firmware or microcode when employed needed to be tested to destruction before being committed to production use as changing it was more difficult than changing pure software, especially if the function resided in hardware. The immediate physical environment surrounding the IT equipment also plays a major part in availability (Figure 3.1).

The architecture of *cloud* and *virtualization* environments is not shown here and is discussed in more detail in Chapter 10, but only in detail as far as the topic of *availability* is concerned.

However, it is now possible with current vendor hardware, software (operating systems and hypervisors), and services, along with third-party software, to achieve the manageability and availability of the managed mainframe of the *good old days*."

IT Structure—Hardware Overview

The IT landscape today (Figure 3.2) is very different from the one I grew up in.

The main differences are in *the web*, clouds, virtualization of entities like servers and storage, and a shift of emphasis from proprietary solutions to open systems, then to clouds. However, typical configurations like that in Figure 3.2 have a complexity and volatility which presents an

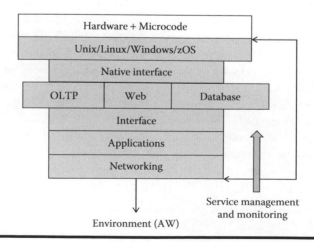

Figure 3.1 IT software layers today: Schematic.

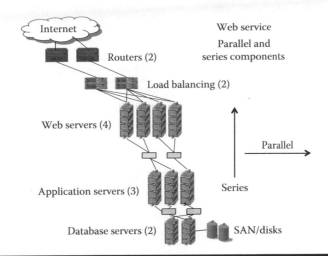

Figure 3.2   A web IT scenario today.

IT department with more availability and support considerations than previously. The management is more difficult without tools, skills, and techniques.

Although Figure 3.2 represents a web-based configuration, it could easily be modified to represent a *proprietary* or *non-web* environment.

One thing related to availability is illustrated in the diagram—that of calculating the operational availability of an end-to-end service taking into account the fact that some components work in parallel with each other, others in a serial or sequential fashion.

There are two sets of calculations that might be employed on such a configuration:

■ Vertical overall availability top to bottom (serial components)
■ Availability of one segment duplicated horizontally (redundant or parallel components), for example, the four web servers shown in Figure 3.2.

The math of this, while not too difficult, needs to be understood* when designing affordable high availability systems and services. Overconfiguration risks overspend, underconfiguration invites outages. I'll clarify what I mean by these last terms so that we have a level playing field for the rest of the book (assuming you are still with me so far).

Component: An item of IT equipment which, by itself, cannot be called a system and certainly not a service. Examples of components are a single disk, a network interface card, or a memory card. In software, it could be an application or piece of system software, such as middleware.
System: A set of hardware and software to do a particular job or jobs for end users and clients in and of an enterprise. Systems are made up of components.
Service: A set of whatever it takes to deliver an operational system to end users, including clients, in that enterprise. This will include a system, an application, development, support, and other elements. This is what the user deems *failed* when he or she cannot do their job via IT. The *system* or any *component* may or may not have failed. How this can be possible when no part of the system has failed has been mentioned already will be explored further as we progress.

---

* I'll bet you can't wait to get into Appendix 4, the Hard Sums in Appendix.

The title of this book contains the word *service* and this is the crux of most things in this book. Take a look at the quote from Michael Madden of CA Technologies given as follows:

> IT's role is shifting away from managing the infrastructure to providing high quality services based on Key Performance Indicators (KPIs), just as business units such as sales and manufacturing are judged. In addition, IT leaders will need to foster greater collaboration between technology teams managing data center resources to meet increasingly time-critical business demands.
>
> **Michael Madden**
> *General Manager, CA Mainframe Business Unit*[*]

His message echoes mine in this book: the quality of service is the key performance indicator (KPI) and not the status of the infrastructure or system, important though that is.

Note: A working infrastructure does not necessarily imply a working service.

Service Level Agreements

In legal terms, an agreement here is a contract (the United Kingdom) or tort (the United States) but applied to IT deliverables to a business via a service.

Service Level Agreements: The Dawn of Realism

If you want to buy a Ferrari or Maserati and walk into a car showroom dressed like detective Columbo, the salesman will immediately think *can this guy afford one*? The same sort of question is often asked when the business user states his business service requirements to the IT people as *responses of 0.02 second (or less) and 100% availability (or greater) until judgment day (and beyond if required)*. The IT department will dutifully go away and do their total cost of ownership (TCO) calculations for such a system/service and present it to business user management, to the nearest £10m ($15m), and ongoing, operational, and depreciation costs, in round millions.

The business people, having seen the estimate, will then retire crushed.[†] Over a coffee or a Jack Daniels and some financial reflection, they will modify their demands and settle for something the enterprise can afford and then the serious business of planning, designing, and delivering the service can begin. I know, because I saw a scenario similar to this played out at a well-known aerospace company in the United Kingdom where the users were setting impossible service level targets for IT.

When the dust settles, the parties involved will need to draw up an agreed set of deliverables, requirements, constraints, charges for a service, and penalties for nonfulfillment. This set is called a *service level agreement* or *SLA*. Notice the word *service* as opposed to *system*.

---

[*] Quoted with permission from Michael Madden, *Enterprise Executive November–December 2013: The Era of the Dynamic Data Center.* http://resources.idgenterprise.com/original/AST-0109764_build-the-future-the-era-of-the-dynamic-data-center.pdf.

[†] A wonderful expression for retreat, paraphrased here from the G.K. Chesterton Father Brown story called *The Queer Feet*.

What Is an SLA?

An SLA is a contract between a service provider, internal to a company or an outsourcing agency, and a customer that specifies, usually in measurable terms, what services the network service provider will furnish, when, and for how long, without interruption. Many Internet service providers provide their customers with an SLA. More recently, IT departments in major enterprises have adopted the idea of writing an SLA so that services for their customers (users in other departments within the enterprise) can be measured, justified, and perhaps compared with those of outsourcing network providers.

To be able to offer a quantifiable service or set of applications, the provider will need some IT disciplines to support and measure the components of the service. This set of disciplines is commonly known as system management. (Service management is a broader topic involving SLAs, operations, user liaison, and a host of other things.)

Why Is an SLA Important?

This basic *contract*, and it IS a contract, supplies a *raison d'être* for all the tools used and effort expended in IT for measuring everything that varies or moves. If the end users don't care about response times, availability, hours of service, and so on, SLAs don't matter. But users do care about these things, so they *do* matter, and the SLA is the *referee* between the two parties involved—IT and business.

I think that says all I wanted to say here about SLAs and their importance. SLAs are covered in more detail, with examples and references, in Appendix 4, along with supporting management disciplines and methodologies. In particular, see the section on user *viewpoints* in availability reporting (Figure 7.2).

They are key for end users, providing different perspectives on *IT life*.

Also covered in the same appendix are the benefits of SLAs to both *demander* and *provider*, an aspect often forgotten in some literature dealing with the topic.

Aside: SLAs are about targets or objectives. A question is appropriate here: *What is a problem?* An answer given by the *inventor* of IBM intensive planning meetings, after allowing his colleagues about an hour to think about it, was ... *something which stops you achieving an objective.* Illuminating, and difficult to argue with.

Corollary: A corollary of this is *if you don't have an objective, you can't have a problem.* SLAs are about objectives, their measurement, their management, and safe delivery. The UK elite forces motto can be paraphrased here in an SLA context as *Who cares, wins.*

Service Life Cycle

The concept of supplying a *service* as opposed to providing an application evolved from user insistence on receiving a complete service rather than *you can use this application when it's there. If it's not, that's tough, and don't expect any extras like speed either.* A service in the context of the end user is something that enables him or her to perform their job function, for example, using an application or suite of applications, commercial or scientific.

It is the availability of that service which is the key factor, not just the availability of its component parts (I hope this is now very clear to all).

The *life cycle* of a service and its components can be viewed as follows:

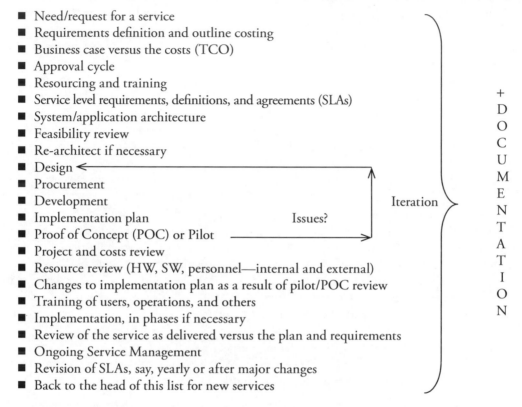

- Need/request for a service
- Requirements definition and outline costing
- Business case versus the costs (TCO)
- Approval cycle
- Resourcing and training
- Service level requirements, definitions, and agreements (SLAs)
- System/application architecture
- Feasibility review
- Re-architect if necessary
- Design
- Procurement
- Development
- Implementation plan
- Proof of Concept (POC) or Pilot
- Project and costs review
- Resource review (HW, SW, personnel—internal and external)
- Changes to implementation plan as a result of pilot/POC review
- Training of users, operations, and others
- Implementation, in phases if necessary
- Review of the service as delivered versus the plan and requirements
- Ongoing Service Management
- Revision of SLAs, say, yearly or after major changes
- Back to the head of this list for new services

In my experience, failed or *suboptimal* (a polite name I used with people meaning *lousy* or *screwed up*) projects are ones that have cut corners in the stages listed above. The avoidance of ATTAM projects (*All Things To All Men*) is also highly recommended.

Larger projects should be phased in design and implementation so that iterative amendments can be made before commitment to the final operational system. The key elements of project success I have found in my old acronym *FUMP* to be borne in mind in any development aimed at end users and the service factors they care about are as follows:

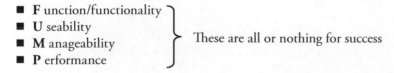

- **F** unction/functionality
- **U** seability
- **M** anageability
- **P** erformance

These are all or nothing for success

The **M** covers availability as well as other things and **P**, **U**, and **F** also impact availability, for example, if it can't be used properly, as per expectations and need, it isn't available.

The *service management* aspect is not to be treated in isolation as an add-on to the other steps—it must be borne in mind throughout the cycle. For example, if availability management is a user requirement, then availability issues must be addressed at the purchase, design, and implementation stages as well as in the production service. It is difficult and/or expensive to retrofit *availability* onto an existing system.

Concept of User Service

In the old *legacy* days, the computer center had little concept of serving the users and attending to their needs. They had a job to do and that was managing the complex monster called the IBM mainframe—users were just a blip on the horizon, a necessary evil. As the applications on offer moved out of the purely financial arena to areas like engineering, data warehouse, and online transactions, users were often charged for their use of the system.* Gradually, these users started asking what they were getting for their money and began to demand quantifiable *levels of service*, such as hours of service availability, uptime, response times, and so on. Eventually, this led IT and user to the concept of *service management*, a conscious effort by IT to offer a quantifiable service and not just CPU power and disk storage when they happened to be available. This concept of a service evolved into an agreement between users and IT as to what it should and should not include, together with costs, either internal (paper) money or real.

These *management* disciplines in IT are aimed at quantifying and improving the service offered to users in a variety of areas including the following:

- Application/service availability
- Application/service costs (real or internal *funny money*)†
- System availability
- Network availability
- More rapid recovery from failures
- Adequate response times
- Extended service hours when needed, for example, quarter/year end
- SLAs
- Service level reporting (SLR)
- Penalties for nonachievement of agreed service levels
- Regular review and renegotiation of the SLA(s)

Add to this list the two other vital … *ations*, *documentation* and *communications*. It helps to demonstrate due diligence when the fur starts to fly in difficult user–IT situations and possibly provide the means of getting out of them amicably.

Elements of Service Management

Introduction

What have these other service management bits and pieces got to do with me—I am Mr. Availability? The reason is that shortfalls in any of these design and support areas can impede availability activity, especially at *downtime*. Let us take an example.

---

* This was one reason engineers and scientists bought their own DEC systems. They eventually found that buying and running them more costly than they bargained for, however.

† Often, internal costs are disregarded by users but in one case I know, the user received, with his computer output, a slip showing what his job/transactions had cost the company in *real* money. It had a salutary effect on the numbers of badly thought out and unnecessary jobs submitted by users. *Funny money* is possibly a UK-only expression.

Imagine the user help desk is badly set up, and staff poorly trained, incompetently managed, and incented. It will be, in the vernacular, about as useful as a chocolate teapot or coffee pot. At crisis times, this is a focal point for communications between stakeholders and other parties, and poor performance of this function will impede fault detection, determination, and recovery, including disaster recovery (DR). The other parts of the support infrastructure also have a part to play in maintaining high availability. Someone of responsibility and stature should be in a position to take a *bird's-eye* view of things and ensure synergy of activity.

Scope of Service Management

Note: Why am I going on about this topic? The answer is that without proper service management disciplines, high availability is not really feasible because long detection, determination, and recovery times mean low availability.

The classification of service management topics is somewhat arbitrary but the following breakdown reflects the roles of the supporting personnel in an IT organization.

User Support

- User help desk (internal/external users, perhaps customers), including expedited communications channels for incident reporting and resolution
- User training in support methodology, roles and responsibilities (who rings who in support to report a fault?)
- Vendor hardware and software support—adequate coverage and hours of support
- RDBMS support (Oracle, SQL Server, etc.)—coverage and hours thereof
- Application support (SAP, Oracle Apps, others)
- Problem determination—procedures and communications
- Adherence to agreed SLAs
- Mobile/overnight/remote support when necessary

Case study: I witnessed a situation in a pharmaceutical company where the remote users were offline for over 24 hours, thinking the central server was *down*. Meanwhile, the server operations people thought the users had gone to sleep or resigned and left the company as the CPU and I/O utilizations were much lower than usual. The error? A new-fangled experimental LAN serving the users locally was out of action and was not *adopted* by any support group and so was not monitored and reported on.

Communication *faux pas* and a vital *unadopted* part of an important system.

Operations Support

- Batch operations
- Online operations
- Print management
- Recovery management
- Storage management
- Incident/problem management (part)

Systems Management

- Availability management, including cluster and subsystems—the subject of this document
- Application management
- Performance management ⎫ ⤶ Major availability siblings*
- Capacity management ⎭
- Storage management
- Network management
- Change management ⎫ ⤶ Important availability siblings
- Problem/incident management ⎭
- Audit/security management
- Software management
- Configuration/asset/facilities management
- Data management, including backup and recovery
- Print management, including recovery after failure
- Disaster recovery, the IT part of business continuity planning (BCP)

> *Note:* Almost every discipline listed above can have an impact on availability. For example, if printing is a key part of an application/service, for example, invoice production, then there must be availability, or *catch-up* capacity, built into the print management system. This may take the form of multiple printers or using a remote site printer as backup when a local printer fails. (There is a subtle difference between remote printing and network printing.†)

Service Management Hierarchy

Service management is illustrated as a hierarchy of interlinking disciplines as follows. Service management includes the discipline of availability management. To coin a phrase, *no discipline is an island* and these management disciplines interact and often interlock to support any respectable efforts at providing a five-star service to users. It should be noted that practically every discipline listed earlier with some partially shown in Figure 3.2 will require an *architectural* design, from trivial to major, to handle it.

Replacing the word *management* in the above context with the word *architecture* will give a new list of activities for an installation. Remember, *architecture* comes before *implementation*, *build*, and *usage*—just as it does when building a skyscraper.

Not simple is it? What the Figure 3.3 illustrates, in the fashion of an availability hierarchy, is that a mishap in one or more of the three disciplines above the *availability* element can have a negative impact on availability. Service management is the subject of a paper or a book in its own right and perhaps the best way to handle it is to do an Internet search for appropriate products, to develop and evolve the theme of service management.

For many installations, retrofitting availability management and architectural disciplines may be *mission impossible*, Tom Cruise or no Tom Cruise.

---

* Although most of the other disciplines do play a part.
† Network printing prints directly across network, remote printing needs a *catcher* system to receive the print job and then print it.

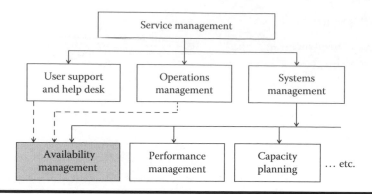

Figure 3.3 Availability management in service management context.

The Effective Service

Proposition: There is a subtle difference between *efficient* and *effective* (Figure 3.4).

One can be very efficient but doing the wrong thing very well. Effectiveness means achieving something useful as well as possible. There is a very potent expression I saw on a large sign outside an English church which read *It is all very well getting to the top of the ladder but not if it is propped against the wrong wall*, a wonderful expression that encapsulates brilliant but useless effort.

A service is a set of items that together enable an end user in a business to do his or her job effectively and productively. The end user expects the service provided

- To be there when he or she needs it.
- To deliver the correct results.
- To do this in an acceptable time.
- To do this over an extended period.

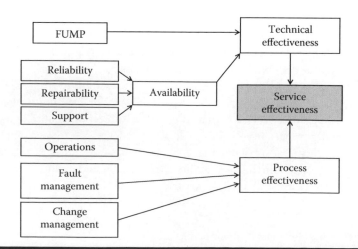

Figure 3.4 Elements comprising an effective service for users.

If it achieves these aims, it will be considered an effective service. The previous diagram will hopefully show the factors that synthesize to provide an effective service, meeting any SLAs attached to it.

Services versus Systems

A common mistake in talking about availability is not recognizing the difference between a system being unavailable and a service being unavailable. Books and papers, many well written by experts, pursue the silver bullet of perfect hardware and software and maintain that it represents *availability nirvana* if achieved. This is far from the truth for, as we shall see until we acknowledge it, that a 100% available system does not mean a 100% available service to an end user.

To set the record straight early on in this book, study the following diagram and accompanying description (Figure 3.5).

A system usually envisaged as the hardware and software and that is quite valid if that is all you care about in terms of availability. A service, however, comprises hardware, software, processes, and people plus an expectation of what that service should deliver. If it does not deliver that service at the level expected, it can be considered unavailable by some users. The business itself consists of services supporting other people and processes.

If the hardware or software becomes unavailable, it is very likely the service, or part of it, will be unavailable. However, we shall see that it is possible to have the hardware and software working fine but the service, or part of it, unavailable.

If services are unavailable due to circumstances that cannot be rectified in a time whereby business is not adversely affected, then business continuity plans need to be executed and this may involve plans for non-IT people and facilities as well as IT equivalents.

Availability Concepts

First Dip in the Water

There are a number of entities and related equations for most parts of reliability engineering. I will outline some of them here and they should become clear as we progress through the book. Most of these entities are described in the body of this book and encapsulated in the *Terminology* section in Appendix 1.

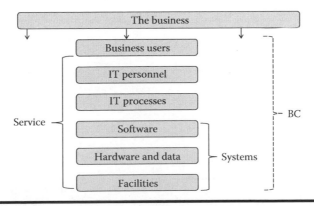

Figure 3.5 Business versus service versus system.

Availability Parameters

This section is therefore a *toe in the water* part of the promised repetition and immersion process of availability management. I hope the water isn't too cold. What follows is a short description of some of the key parameters that you will meet in reading or discussing high availability and sibling disciplines.

- *Availability calculations:* These are calculations carried out on connected components, each with its own reliability, to give an overall reliability/availability of the *system* of components. The components can be arranged in series, in parallel, or in a combination of both. Some combinations are known as complex configurations and are somewhat *complex* themselves to handle mathematically.

Reliability figures are not only applied to hardware but software as well though the predictability of the latter is not a clear-cut thing. One reason is there are many different prediction and estimation models and math functions within them. None are universally applicable in software reliability engineering (SRE).

- *A:* The availability of a component, often extended to a collection of components called a *system*. *A* is normally expressed as a ratio of times. However, for calculations, it is assumed to be the same as the steady-state reliability because it is the probability that the component is working at time t. It can be expressed as a decimal (<1) or a percentage (%). The *percentage* is the decimal value × 100. For reliability computations, the decimal value is used.
- *R:* The reliability of a component or unit. This is often expressed as a function of time, thus: $R(t)$. This suggests that it is impossible to do calculations using R because it keeps changing with time. There is a thing called the *steady-state* reliability which is the basis of *static* calculations. The steady-state value lies along the bottom of the hardware reliability versus time bathtub graph where the failure rate is in theory constant (Figure 3.6). The *burn-in* and *constant reliability* portions of the bathtub are shown in Figure 3.6. R_c is the constant value of R, valid for its useful life. Following that is the burnout phase (hardware only—software doesn't wear out).
- *R and A:* Basically, if the reliability of a component or combination is the decimal $0.x$, then the availability of that component/combination, on average, will be $x\%$.
- *Q or N:* These are used as the measure of nonavailability (unavailability) and is equal to $(1-R)$ because the sum of availability and nonavailability must equal 1. Q and N can be

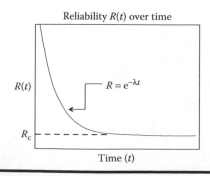

Figure 3.6   The steady-state value of reliability (*R*)—Exponential model.

expressed in the same terms as *A* above (decimal or as a percentage). This book uses *N* for nonavailability but you should remember *Q* is also used to denote the same thing.

■ *MTxx:* These express *mean* times for various activities in the active *life* of a component. xx stands for a number of things related to failures—time to get to a failure, time to repair a failure—which are explained as we progress and are beaten into shape in Appendix 2.

■ *Lambda:* The failure rate of a component (or system) which is the number of failures (outages) divided by the time the component is operating. It is usually expressed in failures per thousand hours, for example, a mean of two failures per 250,000 hours.

■ *Mu:* The repair rate of a component. It should be fairly obvious that the net failure rate over time is $(\lambda-\mu)$, an expression you might see many times in reliability calculations.

■ *RDB:* Reliability block diagram, a configuration diagram representing a system or part of a system and used in understanding points of failure in it. They are used for the purposes of calculations and visual *walkthroughs* of the design. It is the reliability equivalent of an electrical wiring diagram. It represents documentation that can be referred to in problem situations where the location and possible knock-on effects of a component failure need to be assessed. There are software tools available to aid in drawing up RBDs.

■ *RAS:* Reliability, availability, and serviceability. Three concepts, originally developed for hardware, to increase the reliability and operating time of hardware and latterly software. This is achieved by hardware and software design, recovery capability, and ease of maintenance as aids to availability.

■ *Distribution:* A mathematical *shape* describing the *adventures* of a component as it travels through time, usually depicting the probability of its *failure* or *survival* at any time *t*. These distributions have names, such as *Exponential* and *Weibull*, used when they are the best fit to the *life* pattern of a component. There are a score or more of them used in describing hardware and software reliability but we don't need to understand them all in their intricate detail.

■ *pdf, cdf:* Two distributions expressing reliability and probability of failure as a function of time. We will see these distributions later. The cdf $F(t)$ is derived from the pdf $f(t)$ and that's all we need to know at present.

■ *Management:* The understanding of the system and its design, proactive monitoring, control, and operation. This is achieved by *software tools, management techniques, knowledge,* and *common sense*, in reverse order. Knowledge and some management techniques will hopefully come out of this book. Software tools are an aid to management, not management itself and common sense is binary—you either have it or you don't.

■ *Infant mortality:* A phrase used to describe the early life or burn-in period of a component. It is used in describing the phases in the life of a component. The other phases are steady-state and burnout phases.

■ *Mean:* It is sometimes difficult to grasp a theory with numbers when the parameters involved vary with time or circumstance. In most reliability *theory, average* or *mean* values are used to make calculations. For example, we will use mean times between failures and *mean* times to repair them when dealing with quantitative availability.

See Appendix 1 under *Mean* for an explanation of both *arithmetic* and *geometric* mean values of quantities that are derived from a series of numbers. The mean of a set of numbers that are wildly different can be meaningless (no pun intended). For example, the mean value of the numbers 0.0013, 0.01, 0.2, 11.46, 102, 3012, 10,382 ... and so on will not tell us much about the entity being measured. Even with closer sets of numbers, don't place too much reliance on the mean as a universal truth, accurate to 3 places of decimals.

Summary

What we have seen here is a rapid run through the concepts of availability and reliability and why they are needed—basically to offer an effective service to end users who run the business pursued by the enterprise that IT serves.

Accordingly, we have examined services, a contract about service deliverables (SLA) and taken our first dip in the availability and reliability waters.

The parameters and concepts met in this *toe in the water* will be elaborated on throughout the book so that the reader emerges at the end of it wringing wet but very clean, armed with knowledge of the subject of availability.

Recommendation: Run through the *Availability concepts* section once more. It will be a useful exercise in the immersion process. Another recommendation, if you are getting lost in the book due to *jargon*, consult *Terminology* section in Appendix 1.

Chapter 4

What Is High Availability?

The phrase *high availability* (HA) begs the question of what is *normal or low availability*. For noncritical applications, an availability of 95% may be perfectly acceptable, for example, for an organization's internal staff holiday/vacation scheduling system, whereas 99.5% may be totally unacceptable for others, for example, airline reservations. According to internal data corporation (IDC), *a system is considered to be highly available if, when failure occurs, data are not lost and the system can recover in a reasonable amount of time*. What is *reasonable* will, of course, depend on the criticality of the application. What this definition does not cover is how often *failures* can be tolerated and in what, which raises the question *high availability of what?* The availability of the central processing unit (CPU), the storage subsystem, the whole system, the building containing the information technology (IT) equipment, the staff, and so on?

> *Note:* In general, availability should refer to the application or other *service* accessed by the end user in performing his critical work and this depends on the availability of the configuration of supporting *blocks*, such as local area networks (LANs), wide area networks (WANs), and routers as well as the computer system itself, with its layers of software (SW). The outage of a disk, tape, or other piece of hardware (HW) may cause an outage of one application or service but have no effect on the other.

IDC and Availability[*]

There are at least two ways of looking at HA: first, in terms of resilience of service blocks and second, in terms of numeric values.

The IDC *availability framework* describes five levels of service availability along with the **R**(eliability), **A**(vailability), and **S**(erviceability) definitions at each of these levels:

---

[*] *Source:* IDC January 1998. IDC have quite recently (8/12) agreed with these classifications.

Level 4: Services guaranteed. No outage or delay from any failure or service procedure.

R: Every component (hardware and software) has extremely high mean time between failure (MTBF).

A: Each component has a backup that can immediately replace it upon failure. Hardware is *fault tolerant*. Software can recover from many faults without causing failover.

S: Components should be replaced before they fail. Correct installation and configuration is required. Requires service contract to match guarantee (7 × 24).

Level 3: Services are guaranteed. Clients may experience a small delay during a failure or repair.

R: Every component (hardware and software) has high MTBF. Data services must survive server reboot.

A: Redundant, independent hardware with failover software.

S: Components can be replaced before they fail or immediately after failure. Correct installation and configuration is required. Requires service contract to match guarantee *(7 × 24 or 5 × 9 [9 am to 5 pm on weekdays]?).*

Level 2: Services are guaranteed to survive some failures transparently, other failures may cause service outages. Failures that cause service outage can be repaired quickly without outside intervention.

R: Every component (hardware and software) has industry standard MTBF. Data services may or may not survive server reboot.

A: Redundant, independent hardware with failover software.

S: Components can be replaced before they fail or immediately after failure. Correct installation and configuration is required. Requires service contract to match guarantee.

Level 1: Services are guaranteed to survive a small class of failures. Clients may experience a small delay during failures. Clients may experience a service outage during repair or failure.

R: Every component (hardware and software) has industry standard MTBF.

A: Partially redundant components. Some automated failure recovery.

S: Components replaced immediately after failure. Correct installation and configuration is required. Requires service contract to match guarantee (any level).

Level 0: Services are not guaranteed to survive failures or to be online serviceable.

R: Every component (hardware and software) has industry standard MTBF.

A: No redundant components necessary.

S: Service contract does not guarantee availability.

One crucial distinction between services is whether they are *managed* or *unmanaged*. This is made clear in the Availability Classification section discussed subsequently.

Note: Whichever way one looks at such definitions, there can be some leeway in what the customer considers to be critical, serious, a big nuisance, or just an annoyance. The main thing to remember is that their degrees of criticality, and each can be handled in a different way.

Availability Classification

The numeric availability figures and classifications discussed here are taken from Oslo University and were probably taken from those quoted by Jim Gray[*] and several other authors in many other

---

[*] "High Availability Computer Systems" *IEEE Computer* (September 1991).

publications. They represent a desired *nirvana* rather than an inalienable right. They have to be fought for and won.

The availability class can be derived quite neatly from the equation listed in the Gray* paper referenced above:

$$\text{Availability class} = \log_{10}\left[\frac{1}{1-A}\right]$$

(4.1)

Availability Class of Systems

Aside: In the draft paper which I planned to quote from, the equation is given as

$$\text{Availability class} = e^{\log_{10}[1/(1-A)]}$$

which is patently wrong. If you try the first equation with a few of the availability numbers in the table (Table 4.1) it is the correct one. An example is shown next. As of February 2013, the draft paper with this erroneous equation is still in existence on the Internet. Just a warning.

As a proving example, look at the 99% availability ($A = 0.99$) class in Table 4.1. According to Equation 4.1, the availability class is

$$\log_{10}\left(\frac{1}{1-0.99}\right) = \log_{10}100 = 2$$

(4.2)

Derivation of Availability Class

However, I suspect these figures apply to systems, or even just a central server and not a service level agreement (SLA)-driven service of the kind we have been discussing and I would hesitate to expect them to.

Table 4.1   Classes of System Availability (Gray)

System Class	Unavailability (min/yr)	Availability Class	Availability (%)
Unmanaged	50,000	1	90
Managed	5,000	2	99
Well managed	500	3	99.9
Fault tolerant	50	4	99.99
High availability	5	5	99.999
Very high availability	0.5	6	99.9999
Ultrahigh availability	0.05	7	99.99999

---

* Jim was posted "missing at sea" some years ago and declared "dead" a few years later. A sad loss to IT. Poor old James Martin (referenced in Appendix 5) was found dead at sea near his Caribbean holiday island in 2013, another sad departure. He had already given £100m to Oxford University. Who says there is no money in IT?

There is a dichotomy here. For example, 50 minutes outage per year (99.99% availability) might be composed of ten 5-minute outages, five 10-minute outages, two 25-minute outages, and so on. Looking at extremes, are a hundred 5-minute outages better or worse than a single 500-minute outage?

Availability: Outage Analogy

It depends on the ripple effect in getting the business functioning correctly again. If it takes 50 minutes to achieve this normal functionality each time, even though the system is *repaired*, then a single 500-minute outage is preferable.

A Recovery Analogy

To use an analogy, imagine a supermarket with one checkout for 10 items or less and another for an unlimited number of items, as illustrated in Figure 4.1. Imagine this scenario corresponds to a total outage of X units of time. In the case of checkout 1, there are four recoveries (goods check) and four system restarts (payment).

For checkout 2, there is one recovery and one system restart. It is clear that 40 items going through checkout 1 takes longer than 40 items going through checkout 2. The analogy is not exact but it should be clear that system restart, probably consisting of several common steps, can be longer for the multiple outage situation than the single outage one. The greater the number of outages, the greater the resulting overhead compared to the single outage case. It is also infuriating for the end user.

The difference in an IT situation will be more obvious if the time taken to restore the service to its *ramped up* status is relatively long.

In that case, we will have 10 ramp-up times in our *outage* against one, possibly a bit longer, in the case of a single, longer outage. The following two diagrams illustrate this theme.

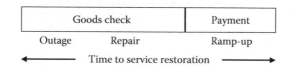

After the payment (scan goods, ramp-up), the service (serving the next customer) is restored.

Depending on the *ramp-up* time, my money is on the fewer, longer outages as the most desirable scenario.

An analogous discussion can be had about whether a mean response time of 2.4 s is better than a mean of 2.6 s. If the 2.4 s is made up of response times varying from 0.1 to 10 s and the other response times from within a much tighter margin, say 1.2–3.6 s, then the higher mean response time is probably preferable to users, mainly because it is more predictable and less stressful (due to fear of the unknown response time).

The topic of Performance Management is mentioned in Chapters 6 and 7 but not covered in any detail despite its importance. In detail, it is a separate exercise beyond the scope of this book.

However it is defined, *high availability* depends on your viewpoint but can be safely said to be availability beyond that offered by a normal system with little or no redundancy or credible recovery procedures (IDC level 0).

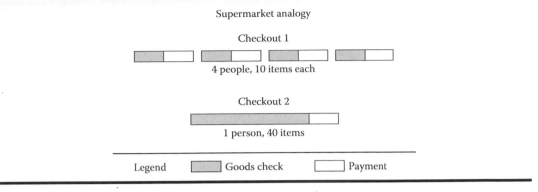

Figure 4.1 Outages pattern: Supermarket checkout analogy.

Availability: Redundancy

One way of increasing the availability of a system is by duplicating components in such a way that one component can take over operations if its partner fails. In such a situation, the extra component can either share the workload being supported or act as a backup should the other component fail. These modes of operation are called *active* and *standby* modes, respectively. The transfer of control from the failing unit to the partner unit is known as *failover* or, in some cases, it is called *switchover*. The difference between *active* and *standby* is that an active unit is ready to start operation, whereas a standby unit needs time to *get up to speed* or *energize* as some literature names the process.

> *Note:* The line between fault tolerance and redundancy is narrow—redundancy can imply some action needs to be taken to make use of the redundant component in recovery.
>   Fault tolerance is, in essence, *intelligent redundancy.*

Availability: Fault Tolerance

Bearing in mind that *availability* means the availability of an IT service and not any individual subsystem or component, we can see that if the elements are single points of failure (SPoFs), then the failure of one of them will bring the service down. Some systems have built in redundancy with transparent failover which represent special cases of redundancy.

A sample description of RAS (reliability, availability, and serviceability) fault tolerance and other redundancy features is given subsequently. It is a fictitious product but based on real life and illustrates the principles quite well.

Sample List of Availability Requirements[*]

System Architecture

The architecture and configuration will dictate to what extent can the system recover from a processing node failure:

---

* http://www.availabilitydigest.com/private/0206/benchmarking.pdf.

- RAS recovery (error correction code [ECC], parity)
- Single node
- Redundant Array of Inexpensive DRAM (RAID) disk arrays
- Cluster—cooperating systems
- Fault-tolerant duplication
- Active/active standby
- Remote data mirroring
- Demonstrated failover or recovery time

Availability: Single Node

Every critical component in the server should have a backup that is put into service automatically upon the failure of its mate (redundancy). These components include the following:

- Processors
- Memory
- Controllers
- Controller paths (fiber channel [FC], SCSI, NICs, etc.)
- Disks (RAID mirrors get a higher score than RAID 5)
- Networks
- Power supplies
- Fans and similar devices

A common argument against using redundancy willy-nilly is cost but this can often be mitigated by smart design.

Dynamic Reconfiguration/Hot Repair of System Components

Some components require power-down to repair but others can be repaired *in flight* in either working or quiescent mode.

- Failed components can be removed and replaced with operational components without taking down the system.
- All the components listed in Availability: Single Node section.

Note: Very often, a repair can be effected by use of field replaceable units (FRUs) that eliminate the need for lengthy diagnostics and repair in favor of immediately replacing a failing unit and repairing the failed unit later.

Disaster Backup and Recovery

In extreme cases, a situation can arise where fault recovery *in situ* is not possible, for example, flooding of a data center or massive power failure and the IT work of the enterprise cannot continue. The recovery of processing capability elsewhere is known as disaster recovery (DR). DR has several needs before it can be implemented, and among them are

- Availability of the backup site outside the *reach* of the outage cause
- Backup IT and other equipment capable of supporting the enterprise's workload or a critical subset of it at the very least
- Currency of backup data at, or available to, the backup site via
  - Backup tapes
  - Virtual tape
  - Asynchronous replication
  - Synchronous replication
  - Other means
- Demonstrated time to put the backup site into service (recovery time objectives [RTO]—see Terminology in Appendix 1)

System Administration Facilities

Since *finger trouble* is a frequent cause of outages, proper administration of high availability systems is a must.

- Monitoring of availability, performance, and other key parameters
- Fault reporting and recovery mechanisms
- Automatic recovery
- Self-healing

HA Costs Money, So Why Bother?

It seems quite obvious that HA is a necessary requirement for all applications. However, there is a cost involved, and should this cost outweigh the benefits, then the exercise may not be worthwhile.

Costs attributed to availability arise in almost all aspects of IT: hardware and software redundancy, duplicate databases, monitors, support, training, and several others. In addition to costs and financial benefits, companies can be hurt by loss of reputation with customers and with the market through visible and costly outages.

Note: High availability is therefore important to most enterprises for one reason or another.

Cost Impact Analysis

CIA is a very specific part of a business impact analysis (BIA) where an estimate of financial losses incurred as a result of failure of a certain duration. It is normally expressed in currency/hour for businesses with many transactions per hour with high cumulative value. Examples are a stock exchange or an airline reservation system. A company has to decide on whether to spend more on business continuity than it would save in losses for the sake of customer loyalty, brand image, and so on. The bottom line on HA is that it is up to the organization to decide the costs and benefits of purchasing hardware and software and designing the whole system for HA in its context. One man's *high availability* is another man's *low availability*.

HA: Cost versus Benefit

In normal life, for every benefit there is usually a cost (for someone, somewhere). This is illustrated in Figure 4.2, representing an IT scenario. The dotted line represents a nominal value of an organization's reputation and is the cost to it of losing that reputation in the worst-case scenario.

There is, however, a cutoff point where further spending outweighs the downside of outages though this is organization dependent.

An organization may attach a monetary value to its reputation that is greater than the loss attributable to outages. An IBM survey showed *organizations are investing more in IT due to concerns over reputational risk.* This is only one factor affecting a business due to IT service outages.

The old saying *if you think education is costly, try ignorance* could be rephrased *if you think high availability is expensive, try downtime.*

Penalty for Nonavailability

Organizations: Attitude toward HA

Research carried out by Vandon Bourne, commissioned and reported in a paper by SunGard Availability Services covered 450 IT directors in organizations with up to 1000 employees. The study tried to find what the attitude of these organizations was toward equating availability with their (business) performance.

In the survey, 66% of responders said that availability was important or crucial to the business and only 18% that it was *quite important* to business performance.

In answer to the question (paraphrased) *What are the consequences of not delivering an available IT capability?*, 58% thought they would lose business and 42% thought they would lose customers. A further 36% thought their job and the jobs or those reporting to them would be *on the line.* The overall percentages do not add up to 100% as people had the choice of selecting more than one *effect.*

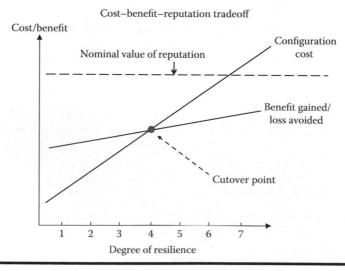

Figure 4.2   Availability: Cost versus benefit.

---

* http://www-935.ibm.com/services/us/gbs/bus/html/risk_study-2012-infographic.html. "How Security, Business Continuity and Technical Support Can Shape the Reputation and Value of Your Company."

So, customers think it is important for qualitative business reasons. What about quantitative reasons, like $$, ££, and €€ The Aberdeen Group study gives some answers to this question.

Aberdeen Group Study: February 2012

There is a cost implication for business if the critical IT systems that support the business are unavailable, for whatever reason.

The consequential loss will depend on many factors, including cash flow impact and the possible loss of customers or brand image. The estimates for loss of revenue in various industries were calculated by two studies of the cost of IT nonavailability in companies. This study was carried out as a refresh of a similar study carried out in 2010 involving 134 organizations. It was entitled

Datacenter Downtime[*]: How Much Does It Really Cost?

Aberdeen Group 2012

The results of both studies are shown in Figure 4.3—left hand bars are figures from 2010, right hand bars 2012. The yearly cost if downtime was calculated by combining the number of yearly events, the average length of a downtime event, and the average cost per hour of downtime as reported by survey respondents ($n = 134$).

Note: The *cost of downtime* increased by 65% over the period (less than two years) covered by this study. Extrapolate this if you dare.

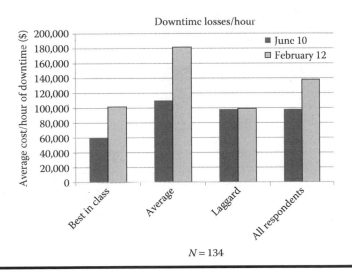

$N = 134$

Figure 4.3 Costs of outages from business interruptions. (Reproduced with permission from Aberdeen Group—Doug Jensen, February 2012. This study is no longer available on the Aberdeen website, please refer to http://v1.aberdeen.com/launch/report/perspective/8623-AI-downtime-disaster-recovery.asp).

[*] "Datacenter Downtime: How Much Does It Really Cost," Aberdeen Group, March 2012, Doug Jensen.

Outage Loss Factors (Percentage of Loss)*

What business and other losses accrue when IT systems or services fail? Again, there are factors that are specific to a company but others generally apply across the board.

If you still aren't convinced, I hope Table 4.2 finally answers the *why* of HA. There is, however, another *cost* question. As well as understanding what the cost of loss is, what does it cost to minimize this loss by increasing availability? An amusing story from the Internet is as follows:

> I am reminded of a (supposedly true) story about someone who took a new Rolls Royce across Europe. In the middle of nowhere the half-shaft broke and he called the factory. They sent an engineer with a replacement by helicopter. When he got back to UK he called the factory to enquire if there was any charge for the exceptional service in repairing the half-shaft and was told: 'Sir, Rolls Royce half-shafts do not break.†

Not, however, a defense for SLA noncompliance. There are costs attributable to software due to failures, known in software reliability engineering (SRE) as *poor quality*, and these are picked up by the vendor. This is dealt with briefly next.

Software Failure Costs

The chart and outline description discussed here is from the DACS magazine April 2010‡ showing the relative external costs of software failures among other costs outlined as follows:

Table 4.2 Outage Losses: Breakdown

Loss Item	Percentage
Business disruption	35.6
Lost revenue	23.4
End user productivity	19.0
IT productivity	8.4
Detection	4.4
Recovery	4.1
Ex-post activities	1.9
Equipments [*sic*] costs	1.8
Third parties	1.4

---

* "Why Every Practitioner Should Care About Network Change & Configuration Management"—Solarwinds, quoting "Gartner, Forrester and IT Analysis firms." See the website www.solarwinds.com.
† www.strobotics.com/reliability.htm.
‡ Design & Analysis Center For Software: Software Tech April 2010 Vol. 13 No. 1, after Webb and Patton.

- *Prevention costs:* Costs to prevent software and documentation errors including early proto-typing, requirements analysis, and training
- *Appraisal costs:* Costs of searching for errors during development such as design reviews, inspections (*walkthrough*), and black and glass [*white*] testing
- *Internal failure costs:* Costs of coping with errors discovered during development and testing

The potential costs of external failure in Figure 4.4 are as follows:

1. Cost to fix the defect
2. Customer cost to fix problems
3. Lost business for customer (customer's own *hit*—he won't be pleased about this.)
4. Lost customers (lost revenue)
5. Lost customer goodwill (reputation costs, bad publicity)

The thesis of the article is that the costs of developing good-quality software will offset the costs of poor quality, in other words, the return on investment (ROI) of *quality* (meaning *high reliability*) software is *positive*.

Remember: Software doesn't always fail like hardware does. It can be 100% available but it just doesn't do correctly what it is supposed to do. Failure costs may not be visible but they are very, very real. These are software *logical* failures.

See the article entitled "Software Project Failure Costs Billions ... Better Estimation & Planning Can Help" (http://www.galorath.com/wp/software-project-failure-costs-billions-better-estimation-planning-can-help.php).

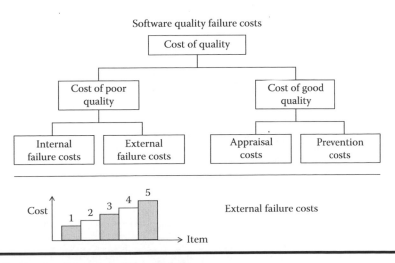

Figure 4.4   Costs of software quality and failure.

Assessing the Cost of HA

Total Cost of Ownership

There are complex models for total cost of ownership (TCO) but there are simpler models that might be useful in developing the cost case, if indeed one needs to be prepared. The main issue is covering all the areas involved in achieving the desired level of availability. One thing needs to be assessed before starting the exercise from either of the following:

- Is this a retrofit exercise on an existing system?
- Is this an *ab initio* exercise, that is, building from the very beginning?

The list of *costs* contained in Appendix 3 is mainly from the Gartner Group model, dating from 1987 and listed in Wikipedia. I have added some personal notes and observations contained in brackets after the Gartner items and others intermixed with Gartner bullet items and marked

- Like this (See Appendix 3 if TCO needs addressing now, otherwise read on.)

Performance and Availability

It may at first sight seem that performance has little to do with availability but it has. As I say *ad nauseam* throughout this book, outages are not always physical but can be logical and/or partial (Duke of York). A poorly performing system is often deemed *down* by users, the people whose opinions really matter in any judgement of the situation. If those *users* are potential customers and not internal staff, the effects can be drastic for business. The dramatic effect on business can be seen next from the results of a survey by Webtorials (http://resources.idgenterprise.com/original/AST-0067261_2012_Application_Service_Delivery_Handbook.pdf*).

The survey respondents were given a set of outcomes that could result from poor application performance. They were asked to indicate the type of impact that typically occurs if one or more of their company's business critical applications are performing badly, and they were allowed to indicate multiple impacts.

The impacts that were mentioned most often are shown in Table 4.3.

Table 4.3 Impact of Poor Application Performance

Impact	Percentage
The company loses revenue	62.0
IT teams are pulled together	59.8
Company loses customers	45.1
CIO gets pressure from his/her boss	45.1
Harder for IT to get funding	44.6
CIO gets other pressure	42.9

---

* "The 2012 Application & Service Delivery Handbook," quoted with the kind permission of Dr. Jim Metzler of Ashton Metzler consultants.

If a business critical application is performing poorly, it has a very significant business impact and it also has a very significant impact on the IT organization.

> *Note:* This is essentially a quality issue—ensuring the system is fit for purpose and getting it right first time. Poor quality means cost in correction and consequential loss.

HA Design: Top 10 Mistakes

The top 10 mistakes are as follows:

1. Underestimating the difficulty (*JAFLOC, skimpy plans*)
2. Not taking a phased approach (*big bang, burn your boats*)
3. Not planning for change (change *will* happen: fixes, requirements)
4. Over-engineering (redundant redundancy, so to speak)
5. Inadequate performance (*at switchover, normal or DR*)
6. Inadequate scalability (components should scale—hardware and software)
7. No standards or wrong standards (*replacements/add-ons' synergy*)
8. No integration (*software*)
9. Think of HA in isolation from management (*see title of this book*)
10. Not invented here (NIH) (RYO, DIY, software bias, nobody can teach us anything)

The full article by Jim Ewel can be found at www.embeddedintel.com/special_features.php? article = 90.

The Development of HA

We have looked at all the bad news so what has and is being done about it?* Having established in the foregoing sections that availability is important, it is instructive to see developments that have arrived to aid the cause of HA. Some time ago, Gartner developed a theme of development for HA (Figure 4.5). Reliability, and hence availability, was mistakenly thought of as the preserve of the hardware engineer but experience of outages not involving a single piece of hardware as the villain has changed all that.

The finger of suspicion can often be pointed at software, microcode, and plain and simple human error. The classical breakdown of outages is one-third each attributable to products, processes, and *people*.

Servers

Figure 4.5 positions the development of central computers from monolithic uniprocessors to symmetric multiprocessors (SMPs), massively parallel processors (MPPs), and cluster configurations against the criteria of scalability and availability. MPP systems are normally used for high

---

* Mark Twain. "Everyone is talking about the weather but nobody is doing anything about it."

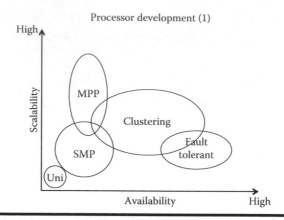

Figure 4.5   Development of high availability.

performance computing/computation (HPC) applications in a *shared nothing* approach with message passing between the nodes as their communication method.

The cluster technology shown in Figure 4.5 has also been adapted to HPC with large numbers of nodes that would be impractical for commercial applications.

One difference between SMPs and clusters/MPPs is that in the first configuration, the CPUs in an SMP share the operating system (OS), whereas the CPUs in others have one OS per *node*.

More recently, clustering has moved forward from simply duplicating nodes for failover toward databases, middleware, and applications. For example, there are HA implementations of Oracle, Sybase, Informix, NFS, Tuxedo, and SAP.

Figure 4.6 illustrates scalability* advances on a single node:

■ Tightly coupled SMPs
■ MPPs
■ Clustered processors (nodes)

The search for scalable architectures brings with it the need to maintain overall reliability because in general, more components equal higher probability of failure (Figure 4.6).

There have also been numerous developments in availability features in IT equipment other than servers. One of the earliest of these was RAID, originally standing for redundant arrays of inexpensive disks but now called redundant arrays of independent disks. These were the brainchild of David Andrew Patterson, an American computer pioneer and academic who has held the position of professor of computer science at the University of California, Berkeley, California, since 1977. It made little sense to have a perfect 100% available server when the disks were prone to falling over every few days, thereby disrupting the services supported.

Patterson is also noted for his pioneering contributions to reduced instruction set computing (RISC) processor design, having coined the term RISC (although IBM might dispute this), and by leading the BerkeleyRISC project. He and his colleagues are also known not only for their initial

---

* A characteristic of a system, model, or function that describes its capability to cope and perform under an increased or expanding workload. It is also taken to mean that a system can scale in capacity by adding processors, preferably linearly, that is, if the number of processors increases by X%, the "power" of the system to do work increases by the same or similar amount.

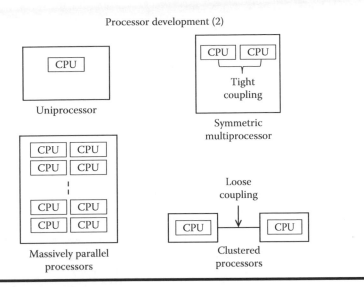

Figure 4.6 **Schematic of multiple processor configurations.**

publication, but for subsequent research on RAID disks. RAID is now being implemented using solid-state drives (SSDs) even on existing RAID controllers.[*] It is still alive and evolving, but only just according to some pundits. Others will recommend it without hesitation.

Systems and Subsystems Development

The history of computer multiprocessors and clusters is best captured by a footnote in Greg Pfister's *In Search of Clusters*: "Virtually every press release from DEC mentioning clusters says 'DEC, who invented clusters …'." This is not strictly true. IBM did not invent them either.

Customers invented clusters, as soon as they could not fit all their work on one computer, or needed a backup. The date of the first is unknown, but it would be surprising if it was not in the 1960s, or even late 1950s.[†] Remember, clusters are partly a result of the failure of computer power advances to keep abreast of demand and partly due to the demand for higher availability.

Figure 4.7 illustrates the development of processors over the years in the pursuit of HA and scalability.

The figure reads from bottom left (a single processor) to top right (self-healing systems) and shows the developments that helped to increase performance and availability of computer systems over the past 40 years or so.

Production Clusters

Practical, commercial *production* clusters were probably first introduced by digital equipment corporation (DEC)—the VAX cluster in 1984, although it is said that the first commercial clustering product was ARCnet, developed by Datapoint in 1977 but it was not a great success. It was

---

[*] See, for example, http://www.kingston.com/us/community/articletype/articleview/articleid/204/accelerating-system-performance-with-ssd-raid-arrays.aspx.

[†] See Wikipedia http://en.wikipedia.org/wiki/History_of_computer_clusters.

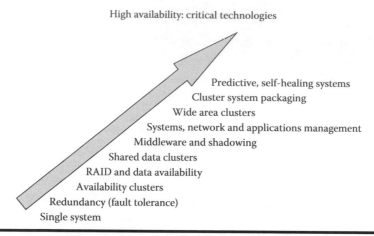

High availability: critical technologies

Predictive, self-healing systems
Cluster system packaging
Wide area clusters
Systems, network and applications management
Middleware and shadowing
Shared data clusters
RAID and data availability
Availability clusters
Redundancy (fault tolerance)
Single system

Figure 4.7   High availability technologies. (Data from Gartner Inc.).

whispered by competitors that DEC had to cluster to achieve higher performance than a uniprocessor as the year on year power increases of their systems did not match power demand from users.

Early DEC clusters were asymmetric with a master controlling all other nodes in the cluster. If the master went down, so did the cluster but this was solved over the years by a controlled handover to a *second in command* node. IBM was forced to introduce SMP systems (3081D in 1981) as the yearly increase in single processor power was, believe it or not, only 18%, whereas demand for power (and disk storage) was growing by 40%. Necessity is the mother of . . . guess what.

One article cited IBM's HASP (Houston Automatic Spooling) as an early example of parallel computing but it was not. It was a master–slave relationship where jobs were handled in their entirety by HASP and the processing done by an attached computer, essentially serial processing. It was definitely not a cluster. Neither was an ASP (attached support processor), an earlier IBM product offering similar functions.*

Aside: As an aside, when IBM put two 360/65 systems together in a hybrid cluster/SMP, the increase in throughput of both systems compared to a single one was 10% and that was after a great deal of effort, tuning and swearing. Hardly worth the extra cost of a 360/65 system, very expensive in those days. This desired *speedup* is the subject of *Amdahl's Law*, along with other *Laws*, outlined in Appendix 4, the *hard sums* appendix.†

Incidentally, see Wikipedia on *Hypervisors* for the IBM 360/65s foray into virtual machine territory when hosting a normal system and an emulation of an older machine to maintain backward compatibility on new machines.

As the central system gained in reliability (hence availability) and resilience, the next component in the service chain was the disk subsystem, which needed to improve its availability characteristics to match the mainframe. Individual disks were manufactured with better availability but

---

* The successors to these were JES2 and JES3 (Job Entry Subsystems 2 and 3).
† The term used by a senior mathematician at a big company when asked about his job.

a major advance was the introduction of RAID technology. It was the antithesis of SLEDs (single large expensive disks).

As we shall see later, RAID is coming up against its limitations when used in environments with huge amounts of data, commonly called *big data*. One limitation pointed out by gurus is the *recovery time* for ever-larger volumes of data on ever-larger disk units. The resilience of the individual *bits* that comprise data is not increasing as fast as the disks are getting bigger, so each disk is likely to fail sooner the bigger it gets.

> ***Note:*** The solutions involve techniques that have been around for some time in telecommunications but not applied to disks until RAID start to creak.

Availability Architectures

Architecture is the key element in building lasting systems with scalability, hence the title of this major section.

*RAS Features**

Hot-Plug Hardware

Hot-plug devices have special connectors that supply electrical power to the board or module before the data pins make contact. Boards and devices that have hot-plug connectors can be inserted or removed while the system is running. The devices have control circuits to ensure they have a common reference and power control during the insertion process. The interfaces are not powered on until the board is inserted and the system controller (SC) instructs them to. The CPU and memory boards used in many systems are hot-plug devices. The process of adding them is usually called *dynamic reconfiguration* and often involves software recognition of the fact that it has happened. (See Terminology in Appendix 1 for *availability* and *reliability* terms.)

Processors

RAS features today go beyond simple hardware chips and can involve duplication of hardware and software. In this and succeeding sections (to Fault Tolerance), RAS features in various parts of a system are outlined.

- Processor instruction error detection (e.g., residue checking of results) and instruction retry, including alternative processor recovery
- Processors running in lock-step to perform master-checker or voting schemes
- Machine check architecture to report errors to the OS, usually via interrupt handlers
- Hot plug (see Hot-Plug Hardware section)
- ECC

---

* These are mainly hardware RAS features. Other documents include items such as dual NICs, redundant components, and software failover under "RAS."

Memory

Memory availability is important in trying to preserve data, particularly OLTP data, across memory failures. Several techniques can be employed.

Hot Plug: See Hot-Plug Hardware section.

ECC: Parity or ECC protection of memory components (cache and system memory), as well as memory bus, bad cache line disabling, memoryscrubbing, memory sparing, bad page offlining (*blacklisting*), redundant bit steering (RBS), memory mirroring, and chipkill memory. Random access memory (RAM) with *ECC* can detect and correct errors. As with parity RAM, additional information needs to be stored and more processing needs to be done, making ECC RAM more expensive and a little slower than nonparity and logic parity RAM.

This type of ECC memory is especially useful for any application where uptime is a concern: failing bits in a memory word are detected and corrected on the fly with no impact to the application. The occurrence of the error is typically logged by the OS for analysis by a technical resource. In the case where the error is persistent, server downtime can be scheduled to replace the failing memory unit.

This mechanism of detection and correction is known as *extended error correction* (*EEC*) (not *ECC*).

Memory scrubbing: A technique where all the memory is periodically addressed and any address with an ECC error is rewritten with the faulty data corrected.

Memory mirroring: Memory mirroring is roughly equivalent to RAID-1 mirroring in disk arrays, in that memory is divided in two parts and one part is mirrored to the other half simultaneously. If a read from one of the memory parts returns incorrect data due to an uncorrectable memory error, the system retrieves the data from the mirror. Because all mirroring activities are handled by the hardware, memory mirroring is OS independent in most implementations.

Memory sparing: Sparing provides a degree of redundancy in the memory subsystem, but not to the extent of mirroring. In contrast to mirroring, sparing leaves more memory for the OS. In sparing mode, the trigger for failover is a preset threshold of correctable errors being exceeded.

Chipkill memory: Chipkill memory technology, an advanced form of error checking and correction. Chipkill protects the memory in the system from any single memory chip failure. It also protects against multi-bit errors on a single memory chip:

> IBM engineers have solved this problem for Netfinity servers by placing a RAID processor chip directly on the memory DIMM. The RAID chip calculates an ECC checksum for the contents of the entire set of chips for each memory access and stores the result in extra memory space on the protected DIMM. Thus, when a memory chip on the DIMM fails, the RAID result can be used to "back up" the lost data, allowing the Netfinity server to continue functioning. This RAID technology is similar to the RAID technology used to protect the contents of an array of disk drives. We call this memory technology Chip-kill DRAM.[*]

Chipkill is an IBM term. Hewlett–Packard (HP) uses the term *Chipspare* and Intel *SDDC* (single device data correction) for the same feature.

---

[*] IBM paper "IBM Chipkill Memory"; http://www.ece.umd.edu/courses/enee759h.S2003/references/chipkill_white_paper.pdf.

RBS provides the equivalent of a hot-spare drive in a RAID array. It is based on the memory controller, and it senses when a chip on a DIMM* has failed and when to route the data around the failed chip.

Bad page offlining: A common class of memory errors is a single *stuck bit* in DIMM. The bit stays stuck in a specific state and cannot be rewritten anymore. Other bits in the same DIMM or on the same channel are not affected. With ECC DIMMs, this error can be corrected. Taking things *offline* is sometimes known as *blacklisting* but normally applied to nodes in a cluster or processors in an MPP,

Lockstep memory: In this mode, two memory channels (memory parts) operate as one and are accessed simultaneously but different contents are written to each. Cache data are split across both memory channels so that different parts of the same cache are stored in multiple places.†

Pellston technology: Now known as *Intel Cache Safe* technology. This technology disables cache that is giving too many ECC errors. It checks whether a cache line is bad or not by an ECC algorithm on the 32 ECC bits which protect the Level 3 (L3) cache lines, thus acting on ECC errors rather than simply reporting them.‡

Input/Output

Highly available central servers and memory are of little value in normal data processing if the input/output subsystems (I/O) are prone to regular failures. These I/O systems include telecommunications as well as disk channels etc.

- Cyclic redundancy check (CRC), which are checksums for data transmission/retry and data storage, for example, PCIe advanced error reporting, redundant I/O paths.
- Longitudinal redundancy check (LRC) for confirming data in network transmissions, comparing sent and received LRCs.

Storage

Moving down the chain of data takes us to the storage media, usually disks, used for long term retention and access of data. These too have something to offer in the RAS stakes.

- Native storage device RAS
- Hardware RAID configurations, both standard and proprietary
- Checksums on both data and metadata, and background scrubbing
- Dual controllers and connections

Power/Cooling

In line with the saying that a chain is as strong as its weakest link, we come to the power that drives all our IT equipment. It isn't rocket science to work out that if the power fails, everything else does too.

---

* Dual Inline Memory Module.
† See www.lenovo.com/thinkserver—This is an excellent paper and recommended.
‡ Memory has joined the "tiering" movement with, initially, a single cache level, for example the original IBM Risc System/6000 (1990). Later, second and third level caches were added, mimicking the external data tiering we see today. Cache handling algorithms are key to performance and bigger, faster cache is not always the winner.

- Over-designing the system for the specified operating ranges of clock frequency, temperature, voltage, vibration
- Temperature sensors to alter the operating frequency when temperature goes out of specification
- Surge protector, uninterruptible power supply (UPS), auxiliary/dual power (internal generator or utility supplier)—see Terminology in Appendix 1.

Eaton have produced a paper entitled "10 Ways to Increase Power System Availability in Data Centers," and this can be found at http://powerquality.eaton.com/About-Us/news-events/whitepapers/whitepaper.asp?doc_id = 12316&paperID = 1.

Fault Tolerance

Fault-tolerant designs extended the idea by making RAS the defining feature of their computers for applications like stock market exchanges or air traffic control, where system crashes would be catastrophic. Fault-tolerant computers (e.g., Tandem Computers via HP's Nonstop and Stratus Technologies), which tend to have duplicate components running in lock-step for reliability, have become less popular, due to their high cost. HA systems, using techniques like computer clusters, are often used as cheaper alternatives. For further details of fault-tolerant systems, over and above RAS features, see Chapter 8.

Today, RAS is relevant to software as well and can be applied to networks, application programs, OSs, personal computers, servers, and supercomputers. Software reliability is important as well as hardware reliability because without software, hardware is *down*.

There are several other ways of increasing the availability of systems by engineering, rigorous operations, and so on but two major architectures stand out in this area—*Clusters* and *RAID*. Like all things connected with achieving high (or higher) availability, cost effectiveness springs to mind as a key consideration. All sorts of add-ons may attract a designer as his *hot buttons* but they rarely cost *buttons*. With that rider, let us have a look at these major architectures.

> *Note:* Fault tolerance can also be applied to software but is a little trickier than redundant hardware because a redundant software module, a copy of a failing one, will probably fail itself! This is dealt with later in the book (see Chapter 6 under Software Reliability).

Outline of Server Domain Architecture

Introduction

IBM introduced the concept of splitting the resources of a server, including peripherals, between workloads and called it partitioning. The separate sets of isolated resources—CPUs, memory, and disks—were called *logical partitions* or LPARs. In the mainframe environment, LPARs are, in practice, equivalent to separate mainframes. These were also evident in the Cray 6400, which became the Sun Microsystems E10000, and other large systems and are common place today in virtualized environments.

The OS in each LPAR is IPLed (*booted up*) separately, has its own copy of its OS, has its own operator console (if needed), and so forth. If the system in one LPAR crashes, there is no effect on the other LPARs (isolation). The concept of LPARs developed so that they could be reconfigured to exchange resource between LPARs to balance workloads, for example. This concept is today in general use and the separate sets of server resources are often called *domains*.

Domains and LPARs can be static, where a system needs to be taken down to alter the configuration of resources and dynamic, where this can be done *on the fly*. The control of these LPARs/domains is done by a piece of software sometimes called a service processor.

Domain/LPAR Structure

Figure 4.8 shows an example of a server and its resources shared out into LPARs or domains which can then be allocated to different workloads.

A typical workload split might be as follows:

- Domain/partition 1 (P1)—production
- Domain/partition 2 P2)—development and testing
- Domain/partition 3 (P3)—office software

Previously, these environments would have occupied separate systems.

Each domain uses a separate boot disk with its own instance of the OS, as well as I/O interfaces to network and disk resources. CPU/memory boards and I/O boards can be separately added and removed from running domains using dynamic reconfiguration provided they are not also assigned to other domains.

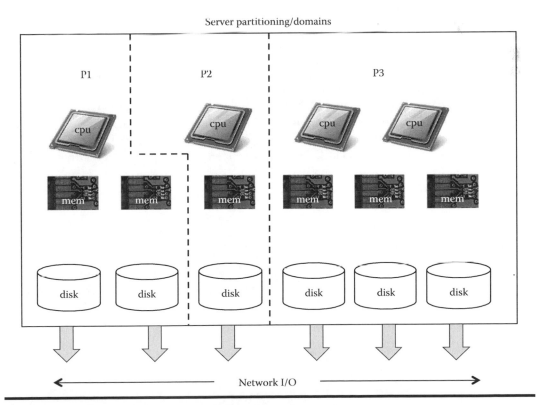

Figure 4.8 Server partitioning/domaining schematic.

Security between domains is maintained through various security methods. Data from one domain is isolated from other domains at the hardware level. This separation is enforced by the SC, ensuring one domain cannot access data packets from another domain. In practice, the partitions are almost the same as separate servers in terms of isolation but can communicate with each other if necessary.

These *isolation* features of domains have the availability *plus* that domains cannot interfere with each other, especially if they *crash* for whatever reason. In a single node, a system crash brings down everything with it—OS, middleware applications—the whole lot.

The next section deals with the features, including availability, of combinations of servers or nodes—clusters. This has developed into today's virtualization of various IT resources.

Outline of Cluster Architecture

There are two basic reasons for clustering, that is, linking multiple systems for various reasons. We will examine the use of such configurations in the quest for higher availability than that offered by a single system and outline the others. Clusters as we saw earlier developed as a *need* that was the mother of the cluster invention. DEC brought the cluster into supported production use and was soon followed by other vendors. History lesson complete, we will now look at clusters and their various manifestations.

Clusters can be implemented in a variety of ways to cater for different requirements that are as follows:

- Load balancing (LB)
- Performance
- HA
- Parallel processing, mainly scientific HPC

HA clusters provide continuous availability of services by eliminating SPoFs and by failing over services from one cluster node to another in case a node becomes inoperative. Typically, services in a HA cluster read and write data (via read-write mounted file systems). Therefore, a HA cluster must maintain data integrity as one cluster node takes over control of a service from another cluster node. This is done with volume and lock managers which are integral parts of clustering software.

Node failures in a HA cluster are not visible from clients outside the cluster. HA clusters are sometimes referred to as failover clusters and are available on a number of popular OSs. Clusters today are, in essence, business as usual.

Cluster Configurations: Commercial Cluster

A basic two-system (2-node) commercial (HA, LB) cluster might look as shown in Figure 4.9.

See Terminology in Appendix 1, for four other cluster topologies that are described and illustrated there.

Cluster Components

Hardware

The basic high availability block in a cluster is the duplication of hardware components which are outlined below.

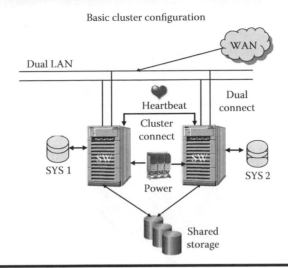

Figure 4.9 Basic two-node cluster configuration.

- A network, here shown as a WAN, connecting users to the *system*
- A duplicated LAN connecting the two processing systems (switches are not shown explicitly in the diagram)
- Dual connections LAN-to-processors
- Two processors, each with its own *system* disks, but sharing *data disks*, which themselves may be RAID-configured
- A power switch connecting power to both systems (processor and disk) that can be used to isolate a failing processor (*fencing*)
- Dual connections (FC or SCSI) to shared disks or SAN (storage area network)

Software

1. Cluster software including a *heartbeat* for processors to monitor each other's *health*, namely, *are you still there Charlie?* Cluster software can be given the life and death decisions over which applications survive when, for example, two working systems are reduced to one by the failure of one or the other. There are also pieces of software to handle any contention issues that will arise when two or more system nodes try to access the same resources. A cluster manager keeps track of cluster quorum by monitoring the count of cluster nodes (Figure 4.10).

2. If more than half the nodes are active, the cluster has quorum. If half the nodes (or fewer) are active, the cluster does not have quorum, and all cluster activity is stopped. Cluster quorum prevents the occurrence of a *split-brain* condition—a situation where two instances of the same cluster are running. A split-brain condition would permit each cluster instance to access cluster resources, for example, data, without knowledge of the other cluster instance, resulting in corrupted cluster integrity.

3. Quorum is determined by communication of messages among cluster nodes via Ethernet. Optionally, quorum can be determined by a combination of communicating messages via Ethernet and through a quorum disk. For quorum via Ethernet, quorum consists of 50% of the node votes plus 1.

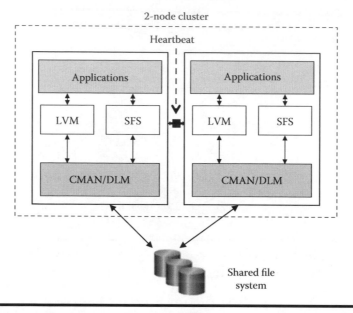

Figure 4.10 Cluster management software configuration. CMAN, cluster manager; DLM, distributed lock manager; LVM, logical volume manager.

4. Lock management is a common cluster-infrastructure service that provides a mechanism for other cluster infrastructure components to synchronize their access to shared resources. A distributed lock manager does what it says on the tin where locking software runs in each cluster node: lock management is distributed across all nodes in the cluster.
5. The usual OS, middleware, and applications software.

Commercial LB

LB is a method of distributing workloads across multiple computers or a computer cluster, network links, CPUs, disk drives, or other resources (Figure 4.11). LB optimizes resource use and

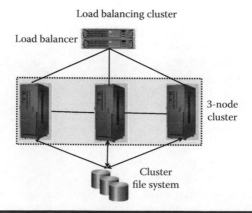

Figure 4.11 Load balancing cluster: Schematic.

throughput, minimizes response time, and avoids overload on any target system that it/they serve. Using multiple components with LB instead of a single component may increase the balancer's reliability through redundancy.

LB is usually provided by dedicated software or hardware, such as a multilayer switch or a Domain Name System server process, often alongside the systems it is balancing across, for example, the Resonate product.

A cluster of nodes can be used with a load balancer to direct work to the appropriate node for that type of work or simply balance incoming work across the nodes (round robin is one way, lowest utilization next). It is assumed that each node has access to a shared file system (SFS). SFSs are often specific to the cluster vendor. The cluster might typically consist of web or commercial application servers or a database cluster.

Obviously, LB is superfluous if the second/third nodes are simply there as standby and will accept no work.

Commercial Performance

Scalability is achieved simply by adding nodes to the cluster and updating the tables that the cluster manager holds and maintains. See *Amdahl's Law* and modifications thereof in Appendix 4 (Gustafson's and Gunther's Laws).

Commercial HA

HA can be achieved by using one or more nodes as standby for others to take over in the event of failure. This assumes that all other SPoFs have been eliminated. There is a white paper from Continuity Software outlining the *Top Ten Cluster/High Availability Risks*[*] from a technical viewpoint. It highlights *ten of the top high availability risks identified in leading data centers worldwide*, specifying the problem, the reason, the impact, and the resolution.

HPC Clusters

Generic HPC Cluster

An HPC cluster looks different in that they usually make use of cheaper components but large numbers of them often PCs or workstations.

An example of such a beast is shown in Figure 4.12.

Communication between nodes in such a cluster is achieved by using a Message Passing Interface (MPI), which is very fast if it is to create the illusion of a large computer made up of many small ones. MPI is a standardized and portable message-passing system designed by a group of researchers from academia and industry to function on a wide variety of parallel computers.

The standard defines the syntax and semantics of a core of library routines useful to a wide range of users writing portable message-passing programs in http://en.wikipedia.org/wiki/Fortran_77 or the C programming language. Several well-tested and efficient implementations of MPI include some that are free and in the public domain.

---

[*] http://continuitysoftware.com/wp-content/uploads/2013/06/Top10-Cluster-HA-risks.pdf.

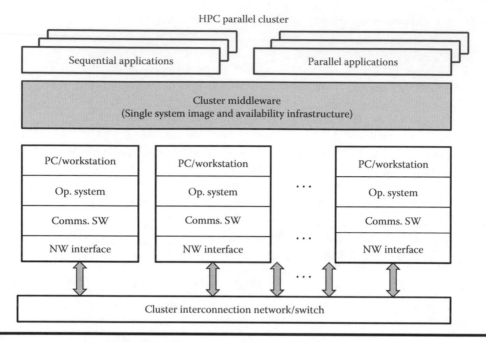

Figure 4.12 Generic HPC cluster.

HPC Cluster: Oscar Configuration

Open Source Cluster Application Resources is an initiative to develop scientific HPC without paying *mega bucks* for the privilege. Its philosophy is similar to that of RAID, using arrays of less expensive servers to perform the scientific calculations. OSCAR allows users to install a Beowulf-type HPC cluster. Beowulf clusters are scalable performance clusters based on commodity hardware, on a private system network, with an open source software (Linux) infrastructure. The OSCAR project aims to support as many different Linux distributions as possible. Some Linux distributions mentioned on the OSCAR website are OpenSUSE, Red Hat Enterprise Linux, and Ubuntu.

HA computing has long been played a critical role in industry mission-critical applications. On the other hand, HPC has equally been a significant enabler to the R&D community for their scientific discoveries. With the combination of HA and HPC, together will clearly lead to even more benefits to both industry, academic and research fields of endeavor.

HA-OSCAR (high availability open source cluster application resources) is an open source project that aims to provide a combined power of HA and performance computing solution. The goal is to enhance a Beowulf (an earlier HPC cluster system) system for mission-critical grade applications. To achieve HA, component redundancy is adopted in HA-OSCAR cluster to eliminate this SPoF. HA-OSCAR incorporates a self-healing mechanism, failure detection and recovery, automatic failover, and fail-back.

Figure 4.13 illustrates the concept of clusters of essential commodity, cost-effective systems for scientific computing.

This initiative is an offshoot of OCG (the Open Cluster Group). It is an informal group of people dedicated to making cluster-computing practical for HPC.*

---

* http://www.openclustergroup.org/.

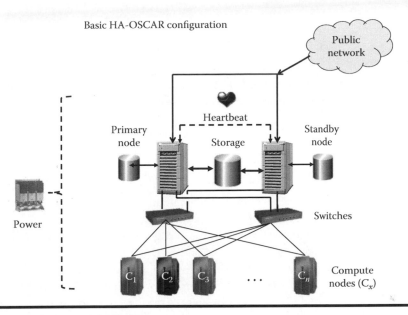

Figure 4.13 HA-Oscar configuration.

HPC Cluster: Availability

HPC work often requires HA especially when running very long jobs (days, weeks, or even months in duration) where failure means starting all over again.

For example, weather forecasting can be more accurate if more granularity is introduced into the layers of the atmosphere, yielding more data from more simultaneous equations to be solved.

HPC Cluster: Applications*

One category of applications where cluster computing is rapidly becoming the architecture of choice is Grand Challenge Applications (GCA). GCAs are defined as fundamental problems in science and engineering with broad economic and scientific impact whose solution can be advanced by applying High Performance Computing and Communications (HPCC) technologies. The high scale of complexity in GCAs demands enormous amounts of resource, such as processing time, memory, and communication bandwidth. A common characteristic of GCAs is that they involve simulations that are computationally intensive. Examples of GCAs are applied fluid dynamics, environmental modeling, ecosystem simulation, biomedical imaging, biomechanics, molecular biology, molecular design, cognition, and computational sciences.

Obviously, *availability* is a key issue in very long-running simulations in applications like those mentioned in the paragraph above.

---

* http://www.cloudbus.org/papers/ic_cluster.pdf (*with some corrections to the English*).

HA in Scientific Computing

Engelmann and Scott of Oak Ridge National Laboratory discuss the combinations of active and supporting systems for scientific high-end computing (HEC) but the concepts apply to clusters of two or more nodes in the commercial world. A summary of these modes of failover operations follows and is of great interest to us in a commercial IT environment:

Active/cold standby: Cold standby comprises two nodes or systems, one active and the other waiting in the wings. When the primary (active) system fails, the standby node is initialized and replaces the failed node. Although there is hardware redundancy here, there is no software redundancy to keep the two nodes in synchronization so the *state* information from the failing node is lost.

Active/warm standby: This provides some software redundancy as well as the hardware redundancy, and state information is communicated to the standby node on a regular basis, a form of lockstep. The information lost between the two systems will be that which changed after the last information exchange between the nodes.

Active/hot standby: This is similar to warm standby except that state information is transmitted to the standby system each time it changes (using something akin to two-phase commit— 2PC) so the standby node is in a position to take over the work of the failed primary node immediately upon its demise.

Topics in HPC Reliability: Summary

The topics relevant to HPC reliability can be summarized in the *Topics of Interest* in an HPC symposium held in San Francisco in 2005[*]:

- Error detection, mitigation, and recovery
- Error rates and types
- Characterization of errors (radiation-induced, hard, intermittent, etc.)
- Detection mechanisms
- Monitoring tools and techniques
- Error detection latencies
- Performance impacts/overheads
- Techniques for error recovery
- Reliability design
- Caches/memory architecture
- Interconnect architecture
- Fault prediction
- Fault modeling
- Self-healing/autonomics for error handling in cluster/grid environments
- Hardware redundancy techniques to decrease error rate

Two reasons for considering HA in HPC are as follows:

- Compute jobs today can be very long and failures expensive, as we have alluded to already.
- Commodity (*cheap*) components are employed for economy reasons.

---

[*] 1st Workshop on High Performance Computing Reliability Issues.

As a taster, the sessions included one topic called "High Performance Computing Reliability Issues." How appropriate!

Errors in Cluster HA Design

Continuity Software has produced several papers on service availability and, in particular, an e-book on the *Top Ten Cluster/High Availability Risks* (http://continuitysoftware.com/wp-content/uploads/2013/06/Top10-Cluster-HA-risks.pdf):

> This eBook highlights ten of the top high availability risks identified by Availability Guard/Cluster in leading datacenters worldwide, including information about risk cause, potential impact, and suggested resolution.

I have reproduced the 10 issues with the kind permission of Continuity Software as follows:

1. Incomplete storage access by cluster nodes
2. SAN fabric with a SPoF
3. Business concentration risk in the private cloud
4. Erroneous cluster configuration
5. No database file redundancy
6. Reused hardware
7. Network configuration with a SPoF
8. Geo-cluster with erroneous replication configuration
9. Inconsistent I/O settings
10. Host configuration differences between cluster nodes

The list therefore is not simply academic but based on *real data center experiences*. Some of the issues will probably have been caused by the errors and omissions we have been discussing about in this book.

On a more general HA front, Continuity Software[*] has produced a paper with the detailed, graphical results on an availability survey, which is entitled "2013 Enterprise Service Availability Benchmark Survey" (see http://continuitysoftware.com/wp-content/uploads/2013/05/IT-Service-Availability-Survey-Enterprise-2013.pdf).

The introduction to this paper is as follows:

> This benchmark survey presents service availability metrics and related corporate practices that allow IT executives to compare their organization's performance and practices to their peers.
>
> The results presented here are based on responses from 147 professionals from a wide range of industries and geographies collected through an online survey.

One telling fact uncovered in this survey is quoted verbatim below:

> However, 32% of the organizations surveyed did not meet their service availability goals for mission-critical systems in 2012.

---

[*] Results from Continuity Software.

The best outage statistics were achieved by the telecommunications industry, followed by high-tech industries. The worst figures were from Healthcare, followed by financial services and public sector bodies.

Continuity Software also offers a *Service Availability Assessment* that might tie in with Chapter 11.

Outline of Grid Computing*

Grid computing is often likened to *pay as you go* to emulate a utility charging mechanism where one only pays for what one consumes in terms of electricity, gas, and so on. It has taken on a wider meaning in the sense that often it can use the power of many distributed systems or workstations in a *grid* to support a workload. For example, workstations and desktop systems have been found to have average CPU utilizations of 5% or less, offering scope for using the *spare* capacity in some way, provided the hardware and, more importantly, software technology is available.

Grid Availability

To ensure the availability of the workload in the absence of every participating node having HA characteristics, certain parts of the grid environment need to have HA properties, for example:

- Workload management and the ability to run parallel copies of applications in case of failure in one of the nodes
- Grid directory
- Security services
- Data storage with redundancy, RAID
- Grid software clustering
- Load-balanced network
- HA routing protocols
- Redundant firewalls
- Parallel processing
- Backup and recovery
- Alerts and monitoring to signal a failure

Not all workloads are suited to this grid *sharing* mode of operation. Those that are should be able to continue working if one of the nodes in the grid configuration is unavailable and be capable of parallelism.

Figure 4.14 shows the nominal CPU capacity of the grid systems (black fill rectangle) and the portion used, leaving spare capacity to be *soaked up* by the distributed grid workload. Studies on workstations suggest that their CPU utilization is often quite low and there is nearly always spare capacity to be had from them. There are other ideas about what *grid computing* is but because it was a fairly fluid concept when someone suggested distributed computing rather like the electricity grids we are familiar with and is therefore open to interpretation. The main point regarding availability is that such a computing system needs software resilience as well as hardware resilience which means parallel execution of code and, where necessary, dual copies of code kept in the same *state*.

---

* For a readable introduction to grid computing see IBM Redbook; http://www.redbooks.ibm.com/redbooks/pdfs/sg246895.pdf.

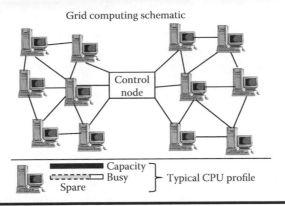

Figure 4.14   Grid computing schematic.

Commercial Grid Computing

For a commercial slant on grid computing, see http://domino.watson.ibm.com/library/cyberdig. nsf/papers/6D8B284209BCD48B85256CB600731D4C/$File/RC22702.pdf.

This reference states in its Abstract … *provides an overview of commercial applications of grid computing* … but majors on performance and response times with little emphasis on reliability and availability.

There is a report to be found at http://www.insight-corp.com/reports/grid06.asp and it states

> Grid computing has moved out of the laboratory and into a wide variety of commercial applications. No longer the exclusive tool of researchers seeking to harness enough compute power for massive computational challenges such as weather modeling or weapons test simulations, today grids are being deployed in more traditional commercial computing applications.

The reference (http://www.insight-corp.com/reports/grid06.asp) also has a pertinent section called the Commercial Acceptance of Grid Computing.

Unfortunately, if you want to follow the reference and obtain the main report, it will set you back just under $3000. This book is a far better bargain. Although grid computing could be used commercially, it finds its *metier* in HPC.

There is another reference which, although 10 or more years old, outlines much of the ground that needs to be covered to use grid technology in a commercial environment (see http://ubiquity. acm.org/article.cfm?id = 782793).

Outline of RAID Architecture*

Origins of RAID

In 1988, David A. Patterson, Garth Gibson, and Randy H. Katz at the University of California Berkeley, published a paper entitled "A Case for Redundant Arrays of

---

* See http://en.wikipedia.org/wiki/Standard_RAID_levels. For other "redundancy and duplication features," see the RAID sections of this book.

Inexpensive Disks (RAID)." This paper described various types of disk arrays, referred to by the acronym RAID. The basic idea of RAID was to combine multiple small, inexpensive disk drives into an array of disk drives which yields performance exceeding that of a Single Large Expensive Drive (SLED). This array of drives appears to the computer as a single logical storage unit or drive.

The Mean Time between Failure (MTBF) of the array will be equal to the MTBF of an individual drive, divided by the number of drives in the array. Because of this, the MTBF of an array of drives would be too low for many applications. However, disk arrays can be made fault-tolerant by redundantly storing information in various ways.

Five types of array architectures, RAID 1 through RAID 5, were defined by the Berkeley paper, each providing disk fault-tolerance and each offering different trade-offs in features and performance. In addition to these five redundant array architectures, it has become popular to refer to a non-redundant array of disk drives as a RAID 0 array.[*]

RAID is an example of *fault tolerance* achieved via *redundancy* of resources, in this case, disks and parity, although we should note the difference between automatic fault tolerance and that gained by doing some work after a failure. Patterson and his colleagues reasoned that cheaper, less reliable disks could be used if they could build in some redundancy so that in the event of a disk failure, data could either be kept safe or reconstructed from the data and control features on the remaining disks.

An example similar to this concept is that of *byte parity* where a byte can be reconstructed from the parity bit when a data bit is lost for whatever reason. Whichever RAID level is used, it should be remembered that a single disk controller supporting RAID configurations is a SPoF and should therefore be duplicated for HA.

RAID Architecture and Levels[†]

First of all, we need to look at *who* performs the work to construct RAID disks. Basically, RAID can be implemented either in the storage controller or in the software.

The implementation of RAID involves hardware, software, and some esoteric algorithms, which can be sleep-inducing unless you are a mathematician. Figure 4.15 shows the bare outline of the components of most RAID disk configurations.

One of the main considerations about RAID is the time taken to recover and format in the original RAID format after a failure.

Ever larger disks and amounts of data increase recovery times, which equal longer outages and hence longer mean time to repair (MTTR), which in RAID can mean a full recovery. The march of ever larger, mission-critical databases puts a strain on the recovery times for standard RAID systems such that alternatives are being looked at. If recovery times increase too much, there is the possibility of disk failure during recovery where recovery time approaches MTBF and the company will go out of business!

Hardware

RAID controllers use proprietary data layouts, so it is not usually possible to span controllers from different manufacturers. Most hardware implementations provide a read-write cache, which, depending on the I/O workload, improves performance.

---

[*] IBM Redbook SG24-2085-00, as good a "history" of RAID as any I have found.
[†] Superb discussion and animation of RAID levels at http://www.acnc.com/raid.

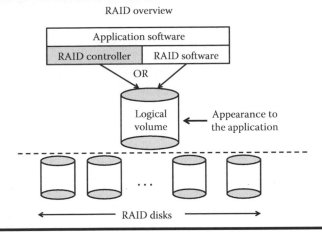

Figure 4.15   RAID schematic.

In most systems, the write cache is non-volatile (i.e. battery protected), so pending writes are not lost in the event of a power failure.

Software

RAID implementations are now provided by many OSs. Software RAID can be implemented as

- A layer that abstracts multiple devices, thereby providing a single virtual device, often called a *logical volume*, which the application programmer imagines he is accessing.
- A more generic logical volume manager (provided with most server-class OSs).
- A component of the file system.

Hardware versus Software RAID

Hardware implementations provide guaranteed performance, add no computational overhead to the host computer, and can support many OSs: the controller simply presents the RAID as another logical drive.

There are several RAID configurations that one can choose, but only a subset satisfy most commercial requirements. These requirements vary from pure availability to performance and some need a combination of both. Cost is often a consideration plus performance in recovering data in outage and DR scenarios. This is a classic case of *one size does not fit all*. For a detailed comparison table of *hardware* versus *software* RAID, see www.cyberciti.biz/tips/raid-hardware-vs-raid-software.html.

RAID Striping: Fundamental to RAID

RAID striping is a way of concatenating multiple drives into what appears to the server and applications as a single logical unit or volume. With striping, the drive's storage sectors are partitioned into *strips*, which can vary in size from 512 bytes to several megabytes, depending on the implementation. The operating environment and application requirements will dictate the optimum stripe size.

When writing a file, segment 1 is written to volume 1, segment 2 to volume 2, and so on until the last volume is reached. RAID then starts writing again onto volume 1 and so on. With striping, the I/O load is more balanced than that of multiple drives without striping. Large records and large blocks can be accessed more efficiently using striping because data access occurs in parallel across multiple drives. Such access is transparent to the program and the user because the configuration is viewed as a logical volume.

RAID Configurations

RAID levels can be Level 0, 1, 2, 3, 4, 5, 6, 7, 10, 0 + 1, 1 + 0, 30, 50, and 60, plus some proprietary levels.[*]

The more popular levels are discussed and illustrated next and the others noted in passing. It is not my intention to repeat long descriptions and diagrams of RAID configurations but to give the best reference sites I have come across for outlining these RAID configurations or levels—see Reference Sites for RAID in Appendix 5.

RAID Components

RAID configurations or levels (of which there are many) are, in the main, composed of relatively few elements—stripes, mirrors, ECC, and parity codes. These are illustrated in Figure 4.16.

ECC

ECC stands variously for error correction code, error correcting code, and a few other terms but they all mean the same. It is a code manipulation to enable detection and correction of single-bit errors and detection of double-bit errors. It is based on a technique known as *Hamming code* (after its *inventor*).[†] Reed Solomon coding is used in RAID 6.

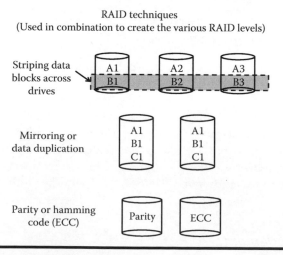

Figure 4.16 **Elements used in building RAID levels.**

---

[*] There are murmurings about the "death of RAID." See sections Post-RAID Environment and Erasure Codes.
[†] For the actual Hamming code calculation, see; http://users.cs.fiu.edu/~downeyt/cop3402/hamming.html.

The hamming code technique was developed in the 1950s for large arrays of dynamic RAM (DRAM) and extended more recently to disks and RAID. It is still used in memory architectures as we have seen earlier.

Parity

Parity is the result of adding an extra bit to a bit string to allow checking (not correction) of errone-ously changed bits. The normal convention is that a parity value of 1 indicates that there is an *odd* number of ones in the data, and a parity value of 0 indicates that there is an *even* number of ones. If the number of bits changed is even, the check bit will be valid and the error will not be detected.

Moreover, parity does not indicate which bit contained the error, even when it can detect it. A parity example is shown as follows:

1 1 0 0 1 0 0 1 (even) Parity bit = 0
1 1 0 1 1 0 0 1 (odd) Parity bit = 1

However, if the first and second 1s in the second line are dropped for 0s, the parity bit will still be *correct* even though there is an error in the byte because the number of 1s is still odd. Single-bit error correction and double-bit error detection are the RAS goals at this level.

RAID Level 0

This level was not covered in the Patterson et al. research (1987) and paper (1988) but is normally included as a *bona fide* RAID level. RAID 0 offers nonredundant arrays but *no data protection* via parity or ECC hamming codes. It comprises *striping* of data blocks across disks.

RAID 0 does not offer any data protection and is only classed as a RAID level to avoid causing offence, although it does perform well.

RAID Level 1

RAID 1 comprises *mirroring* (or duplication) of data blocks across disks, offering a *second bite at the cherry* if one set of blocks fails.

This obviously needs twice the capacity that the data would normally need. Data are not striped. Read performance is increased over a single data copy because either copy can be accessed but write performance is the same.

Another type of RAID one uses disk *duplexing* that involves a second disk controller, thus eliminating the SPoF of a single controller for a RAID array.

RAID 1–3 as it is sometimes known is a RAID 1 configuration with double mirroring, that is, three sets of the data—one original, two copies. This is shown in Figure 4.17.

The configuration shown will obviously offer higher availability but at a cost in storage effi-ciency (here it is 33% of nonduplicate data).

RAID Level 3

RAID 3 operates by dividing blocks of data into stripes that are written across disks or a disk array. Parity is generated and written on separate disks. Data are checked on reads via the parity information generated on writing.

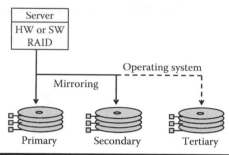

Figure 4.17   RAID 1 with double mirror.

RAID 3 double parity is RAID 3 with a second byte-level parity disk and is marginally slower than standard RAID 3. It can, however, provide failure protection for two disks against the one for standard RAID 3.

RAID Level 5

RAID 5 operates in a similar fashion to RAID 3 but distributes the parity information across the same disks as the data and is the most common RAID implementation. It provides more *usable storage* (storage efficiency 67%–94%) than RAID 1 (50%) or RAID 10 (50%). When the array disks are of differing size, the RAID 5 usable size is $(N-1) \times S_{min}$, where S_{min} is the size of the array's smallest disk and N is the number of disks in the array.

RAID 5 uses disks more efficiently than other RAID implementations by overlapping read and write operations.

RAID Level 6

RAID 6 operates in a similar fashion to RAID 5 but has two sets of distributed parity information that gives better data recovery after failure. It can, however, recover from two disk failures as opposed to the one covered by RAID 5. For disks of different sizes, the RAID 6 usable size is $(N-2) \times S_{min}$. The *parity* data in RAID 6 is often tagged P and Q. P is standard parity, Q is Reed Solomon coding.

Some RAID configurations are combinations of the standard RAID configurations and are known as *nested* RAID. Some of these are discussed in the subsequent sections.

RAID Level 10

RAID 10 is a hybrid of RAID 0 and RAID 1 and exists in three forms: RAIDs 10, 0 + 1, and 1 + 0.

- RAID 0 + 1 is where data are striped across multiple disks and then these striped disk sets are mirrored (Figure 4.18).
- RAID 1 + 0 is where data are mirrored and the mirrors are striped.
- RAID 10 is a Linux inspired level but equivalent to 1 + 0 and recognized as a bona fide RAID level (see Wikipedia for hybrid and nested RAID discussions).

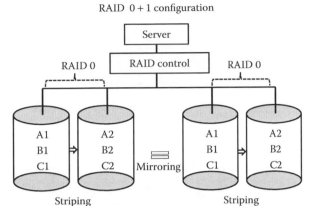

Figure 4.18   RAID 0 + 1 configuration.

RAID 10 needs a minimum of four disks and is called a *stripe of mirrors*. It has excellent redundancy (as blocks are mirrored) and excellent performance (as blocks are striped and retrieval can be achieved using multiple heads).

RAID 0 + 1 Schematic

These nested levels can be extended, for example, to RAID 100, which is RAID 1 plus RAID 0 plus RAID 0.

RAID 10 Schematic

This is a combined mirror/striping configuration as shown in Figure 4.19.

RAID Level 30

This is a combination of RAID levels 3 and 0 and combines high data transfer rates with high data reliability.

RAID Level 50

RAID 50 or RAID 5 + 0 consists of RAID 5, data and distributed parity, mirrored as per RAID 0. It is more fault tolerant than RAID 5 but has twice the parity overhead.

RAID Level 51

RAID 51 (or RAID 5 + 1) consists of two RAID%s that are mirrors of each other. In general, each RAID 5 configuration resides on a separate controller otherwise the availability would be compromised by a SPoF.

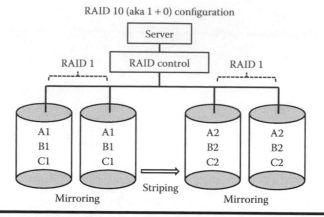

Figure 4.19   RAID 10 configuration.

RAID Level 60

RAID 60 is similar to a RAID 50 array. A RAID 60 array—also referred to as *dual drive failure protection*—is built from at least eight disk drives configured as two or more RAID 6 arrays and stripes stored data and two sets of parity data across all disk drives in both RAID 6 arrays.

RAID Level 100

RAID 100 (often called RAID 10 + 0) is a combination of RAIDS 1 + 0 + 0.

Less Relevant RAIDs

RAID Level 2

This level works at the bit level and comprises striping of data across disks and writing a set of hamming codes, giving the equivalent of ECC, which is common in memory, data paths, and disk controllers. It is thus superfluous in environments where ECC is in-built and is not widely used. In addition, it involved an overhead in having to read and decode the ECC each time data were read from a disk, attracting a relatively high space overhead of 3 parity bits for each 4 data bits.

RAID Level 4

This is similar to RAID 3 where striped data are in blocks and not RAID 3 bytes to improve random access performance. Data protection is via a dedicated parity disk or HDD, although this can create a bottleneck. It is similar to RAID 5 but that uses distributed parity. If all N drives are the same size, the storage efficiency is $[(N-1)/N] \times 100\%$.

RAID Level 7

This level of RAID was developed by Storage Computer Corporation, now defunct, and required a specialized proprietary controller and backup power to maintain cache data. It is an enhanced version of RAIDs 3 and 4 and uses parity as the recovery mechanism. The real-time OS handles the caching and parity calculations, and hence, the need for backup power for the hardware involved.

In management, SNMP (simple network management protocol) agents allowed remote monitoring and management of RAID 7 arrays while the ability to declare multiple attached disk drives as hot standby devices.

I think this is enough of RAID discussions so I'll leave it to the references I have given in Appendix 5 to take it further. One question about RAID is the efficiency with which it utilizes storage—nominal versus usable and we deal with this next.

Standard RAID Storage Efficiency

The effective storage capacity of RAID arrays depends on the consumption of space by the RAID level overheads—mirrors, parity, ECC. Table 4.4 outlines this efficiency (% *useful data storage*) for eight standard RAID levels. Nonstandard and proprietary RAID level configuration efficiencies will, of course, vary.

Table 4.4　RAID Characteristics Comparison (Partial)

RAID Level	Minimum Drives (n)	Data Protection	Storage Utilization	Array Failure Rate
0	2	None	100%	$1 - (1 - r)^n$
1	2	1 drive $n - 1$	50% $1/n$	r^n
1E	3	1 drive	50%	–
2	3	1 (maybe)	71%–82% $1 - 1/n[\log_2(n-1)]$	Variable
3	3	1	$1 - (1/n)$	$1 - (1 - r)^{(n-2)/2}$
4	3	1	$1 - (1/n)$	$1 - (1 - r)^{(n-2)/2}$
5	3	1 drive	67%–94% $1 - (1/n)$	$1 - (1 - r)^{(n-2)/2}$
5EE	4	1 drive	50%–88%	–
6	4	2 drives	50%–88% $1 - (2/n)$	$1 - (1 - r)^{(n-3)/2}$
10	4	1/subarray	50% $2/n$	–
50	6	1/subarray	67%–94%	–
60	8	2/subarray	50%–88%	–

n, the number of drives in the configuration; *r*, the drive failure rate.

> *Note:* There is a set of math associated with storage utilization percentage in various RAID configurations and this is outlined in Appendix 4.

A tool that allows one to calculate the storage efficiency of RAID levels 1, 2, 3, 4, 5, and 6 for various numbers of disks available in an array can be seen at http://www.ecs.umass.edu/ece/koren/architecture/Raid/raidiator.html.

RAID levels are now many and varied and the choice of which to use depends on the service requirements and the company's bank balance.

> *Note:* It should be remembered that not all the available disk space is used as a matter of course, RAID or otherwise. Some installations keep some storage available as contingency. Thus a nominal efficiency of 50% might only turn out to be 40% to preserve some additional space as contingency. Efficiency used in talking about disks has different meanings and you should be aware of who is talking about what.

For a comparison of RAID configurations with different characteristics listed, including simple mathematical expressions for read and write performance, see Wikipedia entry (https://en.wikipedia.org/wiki/RAID#Comparison).

For some calculations on the *reliability* of various RAID configurations, see the Dell paper (also referenced in Appendix 5) (http://www.dell.com/downloads/global/power/ps2q08-20080190-Long.pdf).

Table 4.4 gives an outline of some of the key features of RAID levels:

> Appendix 4 contains a discussion of some of the math associated with RAID operation, with kind the permission of Professor Marty Shooman.

Some additional RAID information and more detailed math can also be found in Appendix 4, Lesson 5.

SSDs and RAID*

Solid-state storage (SSS) is a type of computer storage media that is made from silicon microchips, rather like main memory. SSS stores data electronically instead of storing magnetically, as spinning hard disk drives (HDDs) and magnetic oxide tapes do. SSS is not new and is often used as a *cache* (staging post) between servers and processors and standard HDD. It is important that the solid-state medium used is *nonvolatile* to emulate that of HDDs.

In fact, IBM had a big job persuading customers to stick with IBM HDDs when it was patently obvious that SSDs were perfect for paging, needing about 10–50 MB instead of a full 100 MB drive, and other temporary activities which stored and retrieved data. It would also have been much faster than HDDs. The era I am talking about was the 1980s. It is now possible to implement RAID on

---

* See http://searchsolidstatestorage.techtarget.com/definition/Solid-State-Disk-SSD-RAID and, for detailed performance, http://www.tomshardware.co.uk/ssd-raid-iops,review-32151.html.

SSDs and take advantage of the data security of redundancy along with the increased performance SSD enjoys over normal disks. SSD RAID can be a strategy for improving performance that involves dividing and storing the same data on multiple SSDs instead of HDDs. SSDs can be used in RAID configurations, reaping the same benefits, and have some advantages over HDDs.

First, the sustainable I/O rate can be up to 100 times (a figure quoted by Samsung), but in practice about 10, that of an HDD and its power consumption can be much less. Second, the environmental costs of using SSDs can be much less than that of HDDs. However, there are some disadvantages to SSD RAID.

SSD Longevity

SSD stands for solid-state drive or device and not solid-state disks as is sometimes said and written.

Their life expectancy (as I write) is not as good as that of HDDs and the cost per megabyte is higher than HDDs. This has an effect on MTBF and accounting depreciation (amortization)—one technical, one financial. In addition, employing SSD for the more esoteric RAID configurations where usable capacity (storage efficiency) is half or less than half the configured capacity can be very expensive.

However, ideal SSD RAID performance requires the optimum combination of *cache*, microprocessor, software, and hardware *resources*. When all these factors work together in optimal fashion, an SSD RAID can significantly outperform an HDD RAID of comparable storage capacity. However, failure to properly dovetail the underlying technologies can result in performance that does not exceed, and may actually fall behind, mechanical HDDs.

It is a matter of *you pay your money and you take your choice* or, better still, take advice from your vendor or services provider, especially for *hybrid RAID* outlined subsequently.

> *Note:* There is nowadays talk of *flash-based* storage that is directly attached to the processor and uses direct memory access (DMA) to interface with it.

This is not covered in this book but I thought I would tell the reader anyway.

Hybrid RAID: SSD and HDD

It is possible to *mix and match* SSD and HDD in RAID configurations as long as the supporting software or controllers are up to the task. Hybrid RAID is a redundant storage solution that combines high capacity, low-cost SATA, or higher-performance SAS HDDs with low latency, high Input/Output (Operations) per second (IOPs) SSDs, and an SSD-aware RAID adapter card. In hybrid RAID, read operations are done from the faster SSD and write operations happen on both SSD and HDD for redundancy purposes.

The job involved here is deciding where to put what data—application data and redundancy data—and having controllers that can optimize the use of SSDs as well as HDD.[*] SSD can be used as a high-speed cache as well as a data storage device in its own right.

SSD References

RAID, SSD, HDD, and flash memory, coupled with post-RAID technologies, are evolving subjects that are far too volatile to commit to paper here. They can be found in the usual places in

---

[*] See http://searchsolidstatestorage.techtarget.com/tip/RAID-with-SSD-A-primer.

the Internet, many involving the name of Professor Jim Plank. However, there is what looks like a *living* set of SSD documents to be found at http://www.storagesearch.com/enterprise-ssd-ha.html.

Post-RAID Environment

Big Data: The Issue

One of the issues facing RAID technology today is the growth in stored data and the problems in recovering that data in the event of a disaster or massive data loss for some other reason. This is the world of *big data* that carries not only the burden of physical *real estate* but brings problems of data organization and *time for data recovery* (RTO) after failure.

Papers today quote disk storage as growing at 40% per annum compound as if it is a startling figure, newly discovered. From my earliest days in storage, this figure was being used and even formed the basis of sales forecasts for disk storage.

However, a paper by Aberdeen Group "Big Data Trends" (February 2013) indicates that not only is the amount of data growing, but growing at an increasing rate, that is, it is accelerating, from 29% compound per annum in December 2009 to 56% in December 2012. At $r\%$ growth (expressed as a fraction 0.r), the amount of data needing to be stored after n years would be

$$C_n = C_0(1+r)^n$$

(4.3)

Compound Growth of Data

At 56%, $C_n = C_0 \times (1.56)^n$ where C_0 is the amount of data today, which is sixfold increase in four years. Add to this a Forrester Report[*], produced in conjunction with IBM, which claims that 90% of all computer data were gathered in the past two years. Big data indeed, and what will the next two to five years yield?

My memory tells me that in about 1980, only about 3% of data were computer accessible, that is, online or on magnetic storage. It isn't clear what that percentage is today but it is large I am sure.

Hadoop is a clustering process for handling *big data* and structured or free from data. An ebook on it can be obtained from various sources via a web search using *hadoop illuminated, ebook* as search terms. This ebook defines big data as *very large, loosely structured data set that defies traditional storage*. According to this source, big data arise from multiple sources, some unheard of years ago, such as

- Web data
- Photographs, music, and videos
- Social media data (Facebook, Twitter, and LinkedIn)
- Click stream data (When users navigate a website, the clicks are logged for further analysis that is important for online advertising and e-commerce.)
- Sensor data (from numerous sources including road traffic analysis, petroleum production, and weather forecasting)

Examples of big data given in the Hadoop ebook are as follows:

- Facebook has 40 PB of data and captures 100 TB/day.
- Yahoo has 60 PB of data.
- Twitter handles 8 TB/day.

---

[*] Survey results from Forrester Research.

- eBay has 40 PB of data and handles 50 TB/day.
- US Library of Congress has 235 TB of stored data.
- Boeing collects 640 TB per flight.
- Wal-Mart has 2.5 PB of stored data.

Add to this the normal business data—databases, emails, documents, and so on—and that archived for various reasons and you have the picture of a world drowning in data when it wants information. Information in my book is data, trimmed and cooked, ready to eat and easily digested.

> **Note:** One question some people are asking is *Do we need it all in raw form*? To which I answer *I don't know: it's an organization's business requirements issue.* Maybe they do, maybe they don't.

Data Loss Overview

A major problem in availability is actual loss of data for one reason or another. The damage caused by such losses depends on the size of the organization according to surveys. The breakdown of causes of data loss, like service and system outage figures, depends on the survey in question but the main causes appear to be

- Drive failure, which may include bit-flip or bit-rot and possibly firmware failure, perhaps in rarely accessed code
- Drive read instability, often from a *dying* drive
- Software issues
- User error, for example, erroneous disk recovery in RAID
- Other causes, heat, cold, moisture, and so on

Given that data loss is a distinct possibility, it is important to anticipate, design, and plan for detection and retrieval of it.

The article below and the reference (http://www.deepspar.com/wp-data-loss.html) have a detailed discussion on data loss and recovery (with some selling).

A form of data loss is *compromised data* which is data that has been stolen or data that has been tampered with. This form is a *security issue* and can be equated to a service outage, especially if the service is suspended for investigation and/or repair or perhaps to prevent further breaches. Data loss that can be recovered and put back into service is one thing, and data loss as in *stolen* by an outside agency can have much more wide-reaching effects on a business.

Big Data: Solutions?

There are new techniques available which might resolve some of these deficiencies. In 2012 alone, 4 terabyte (TB) disks were announced and 6 TB disks promised, with pundits talking about 60 TB disks *on the horizon*.

The base from which data it is growing is already large today as we have seen above from ordinary alphanumeric data in the 1970s to the enormous amounts of data stored for analytic purposes and unstructured data for video, image, audio, business intelligence, and other forms, plus regulatory requirements for long-term storage.

In the 1970s, the upper limit of bit density for disks was thought to be about 2 Mb/in^2 but now it is being talked about in terms of 20 Gb/in^2 and even higher. Unless the *bit rot* and *bit failure* rates decrease in line with the growth in areal density and drive capacity, the mean time to failure (MTTF) of drives will decrease, that is, be less reliable. Improvements *today* are sought in the areas of materials science, magneto-optical recording heads, and ECC (in the broadest sense).

Incidentally, *future* technologies and efforts for the dense storage of data, far beyond post-RAID, include the following:

■ Biological materials
■ Holographic systems
■ Microelectromechanical devices

Two papers[*] discuss the *end of RAID* suggesting its days may be numbered (September 2009).

Estimates have been made of the total time taken to read and reconstruct HDDs of various sizes. The 2009 1500 GB drive weighs in at 22 hours. For drives in 2013, storage papers talk about *days* as the read/reconstruct times, calling to mind a variation on the hoary old benchmark expression *you don't need a watch to time the recovery, you need a calendar*.

The practical applications of these techniques are emerging at the time of writing this book. However, just because a new technology is a *world beater* doesn't mean it will take over RAID territory in double-quick time. The arbiters of such a transition will be the customers and the vendors. If the cost of switching to a new technology is large, the vendors will hedge their bets as will the customers. In short, RAID is unlikely to *shuffle off this mortal coil* quickly because of three laws of IT:

■ Law of people and financial inertia
■ Laws of economics
■ Law of *if it ain't broke, don't fix it* (until it breaks, then you have to fix it)

Of the technologies hinted at earlier, and there are four main subspecies of the main contender, erasure codes (ECs), which are outlined in the next sections.

Non-RAID RAID

This hybrid technology covers variations on RAID and some claim they are not RAID, others claim they are. Whatever it is called, it looks like RAID and is a mutation of it, attempting to remedy drawbacks in classical RAID, particularly in recovery.

There are a number of proprietary (nonstandard) RAID configurations mainly limited to the relevant vendor, for example, RAID 4. Some of these may be appropriate for special purposes but if an organization is *standards-based* then these options may not be appealing. Some of the nonstandard RAID configurations are as follows:

■ Double parity RAID (RAID DP, NetApps, and others)
■ RAID 7 (Storage Computer Corporation, now defunct)
■ RAID 1.5 (HighPoint: Striping and mirroring with integrated *hot* spare plus the usual parity data)

---

[*] http://www.enterprisestorageforum.com/technology/features/article.php/3839636/RAIDs-Days-May-Be-Numbered.htm also use "3847396" in above URL for the second paper.

- RAID 5E, 5EE, RAID 6E, 50EE
- Intel Rapid Storage Technology (RAID 1 + 0 with extensions)
- Linux MD RAID 10 (variable RAID levels)
- RAID-Z (see https://blogs.oracle.com/bonwick/entry/raid_z)
- RAID-K (Double parity RAID 4)
- UnRAID (Embedded NAS, Lime Technology)
- X-RAID (Netgear technology, "X" for eXpandable)
- Vendor variations on RAID (HP, IBM and others—RAID-X [a variation of RAID 10], IBM EVENODD, RAID-DP, RAID-TM, etc.)
- Others, such as Data Robotics *BeyondRAID*, a sort of RAID *hypervisor* adding transparency to the underlying RAID structure.

There may be newer RAIDs but that is probably like rearranging the deck chairs on the Titanic or ordering more ice for your drink.

See some of the RAID extensions listed earlier at www.tomshardware.co.uk and http://cdn.ttgtmedia.com/searchStorageUK/downloads/1210_ST_eG_RAID.pdf.

For other reference sites for RAID, see Appendix 5 under the RAID heading.

Erasure Codes

EC and its various implementations (information dispersal [IDA], forward error correction [FEC], and so on) are mooted as the main contenders for the *Storage Availability* title. Incidentally, the word *erasure* is synonymous with *failure*. The qualities that this successor will need to possess at the very least are remedies for the approaching *limits* of RAID capability.[*]

RAID Successor Qualifications

Most papers in the *Death of RAID* camp cite the following qualities needed by a worthy successor to RAID:

- Handling and protecting *big* data
- Ability to handle simultaneous failures (>2 at least)
- Recovery times to match RTOs and be less liable to failure during recovery (MTTDL [mean time to data loss] >> MTTR)
- Large-scale cost-effectiveness
- Does not necessarily insist on data being local (IDA)

*EC*s are a general name that encompasses[†] Reed-Solomon coding, FEC, and IDA.[‡]

The main thrust in looking for RAID replacements is the handling of large amounts of data and their recovery after noncorrectable failure. RAID 5 (single parity) can handle one failure, RAID 6 (double parity, P and Q) handles two failures. The search is on for a method of storage that can handle k failures where $k > 2$.

---

[*] Other suggestions are Object Storage and declustered RAID (Garth Gibson of Panasas and an original "RAID" man alongside Patterson et al.). See also http://citeseerx.ist.psu.edu/viewdoc/summary?doi=10.1.1.49.7954.

[†] James Plank, University of Tennessee (Private communication 2013).

[‡] Information here is mainly from a Cleversafe Inc. paper 2011, www.cleversafe.com.

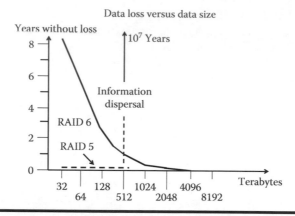

Figure 4.20 Information dispersal versus RAID 5 and RAID 6. (Data from Cleversafe Inc.)

Figure 4.20 illustrates the decreasing time that can elapse before failure for different amounts of data. Given that bit failure rates are improving, the sheer size of disk nodes means that any one disk becomes more and more likely to fail as they grow.

One major concept in all this is *MTTDL*, which is usually expressed as an equation involving our old friends MTTF and MTTR as well as factors specific to EC. This quantity is of importance for overall reliability needs and should be maximized so that failures are less likely to occur in recoveries taking significant time—failure within a recovery.

We will leave this particular topic of RAID successors here for the moment but just be aware of the term *erasure codes* and the fact that there are different implementations of the concept. An outline of EC is given next.

EC Overview

The *nomenclature* in the EC literature varies in specifying numbers of disks for data and those used for recovery coding. We use the Jim Plank conventions here where n is the total number of disks in an EC situation, k is for data, and m is for *coding* (the EC equivalent of pure parity in RAID 5 and 6).

Briefly, the nomenclature used in erasure coding and retrofitted to RAID is as follows (Figure 4.21):

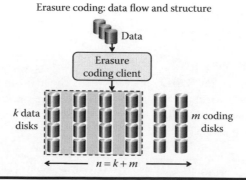

Figure 4.21 Erasure coding data flow and disk configuration.

- *m* is the number of coding disks (sometimes referred to as fragments).
- *n* is the total number of disks.
- *k* is the number of disks dedicated to data.
- $n = m + k$.
- *r* is called the encoding rate and is equal to *m/n*.

The way the data and recovery code information is stored can take at least two forms given as follows:

1. A *horizontal* code separates the data and codes onto separate sets of disks, as illustrated in Figure 4.21.
2. A *vertical* code mixes data and codes on the same disks.

The RAID 5 and 6 equivalents of this configuration have one and two sets of parity data for recovery, which would logically sit where the *m coding disks* are in Figure 4.21. EC uses a mathematical function to describe a set of numbers or codes so they can be recovered if one is lost.

For the record, these mathematical functions are referred to as *polynomial interpolation* or *oversampling*.

Applying this nomenclature to RAID configurations, the following are true:

- For RAID 1, $m = 1$, $n = 2$.
- For RAID 5, $m = 4$, $n = 5$.
- For RAID 6, $m = (n - 2)$.
- For replication with two copies, $m = 1$, $n = 3$, $r = 1/3$.

EC Recovery Scope

In Figure 4.21, it is possible to recover (tolerate) up to *m* failures with *m* disks encoded supporting *k* disks of data.

Another way of saying this is that $(n-k)$ failures can be handled because $n = k + m$. A typical set of numbers might be 16 devices, 10 for data, and 6 for coding.

> ***Endnote:*** In the EC documentation, there is quite a bit of theoretical work on probability of *failures during recovery*. It doesn't bear thinking about, given the need to understand EC writing data before recovery is considered.

> ***Bottom Line:*** The way the recovery *coding* disks are written is where the different names for EC coding arise.

Some of the theory behind RAID, EC, and its siblings can be found in Appendix 4, Lesson 5. Also, see the Plank/Huang presentations entitled "Tutorial: Erasure Coding for Storage Applications" given at the *Usenix* Storage conference in February 2013 (http://web.eecs.utk.edu/~plank/plank/papers/FAST-2013-Tutorial.html).

My *mentor* in tackling the subject of EC has been Jim Plank (University of Tennessee) and a list of papers he and others have written can be seen at http://web.eecs.utk.edu/~plank/plank/papers/.

And finally, a paper called "Erasure Coding vs. Replication: A Quantitative Comparison" by Hakim Weatherspoon and John D. Kubiatowicz (Computer Science Division, University of California, Berkeley, CA) states the position of EC in the abstract to their paper:

Abstract. Peer-to-peer systems are positioned to take advantage of gains in network bandwidth, storage capacity, and computational resources to provide long-term durable storage infrastructures. In this paper, we quantitatively compare building a distributed storage infrastructure that is self-repairing and resilient to faults using either a replicated system or an erasure-resilient system. We show that systems employing erasure codes have mean time to failures many orders of magnitude higher than replicated systems with similar storage and bandwidth requirements. More importantly, erasure-resilient systems use an order of magnitude less bandwidth and storage to provide similar system durability as replicated systems.

They aim to demonstrate the availability and bandwidth gains by using EC against replication methods. A little more detail from this paper can be found in Appendix 4, Lesson 5 under the heading Some RAID and Erasure Code Math (https://oceanstore.cs.berkeley.edu/publications/papers/pdf/erasure_iptps.pdf).

They will keep you busy for some time to come, especially the math in the last paper cited.

Self-Healing Storage

In the June 2009 Storage magazine, an article by Marc Staimer defined this topic thus:

"Self-healing is [most] accurately defined as transparently restoring both data and storage from failure." That might seem like splitting hairs, but it's not. It's the difference between treating the symptoms and fixing the cause.

The author identified three categories of storage self-healing given as follows:

- End-to-end error detection and correction
- *Heal-in-place* systems attempt to repair a failed disk before initiating a RAID rebuild
- *Fail-in-place* systems would not require failed hard drives to be replaced during the warranty life of the configuration

Vendors offering products in the last two areas, heal-in-place and fail-in-place, are discussed next.

Heal-In-Place

There are developing methods for storage healing (recovering) from data errors without stopping the disks and rebuilding. These are often known as *heal-in-place* techniques.

- DataDirect Networks S2A *Series* employs embedded parity calculations and parallelization of reads and writes.
- NEC D-Series *SANs* offers dual parity RAID 6 and disk rebuilds in some cases. It also separates out unresponsive drives from RAID groups, which continue to operate, and put

the drives *under supervision*. If data are recovered, they are put back in the RAID group avoiding, according to NEC, 30%–50% of RAID rebuilds which would otherwise be required.

■ *Panasas Inc. ActiveStor* employs ActiveScan that monitors data objects, RAID parity, and underlying disk devices to catch errors before they occur (*presumably transient errors*). If such errors are found, ActiveScan can copy the data from the problem disk, avoiding reconstruction in most cases like this.

Fail-In-Place

A variation of heal-in-place provides sufficient built-in redundancy to cater for failures without *fixing* anything or recovering via data reloads.

■ *Atrato Inc. Velocity 1000* is a unit containing sealed subunits of disk drives, each of which holds a set of four mini-units inside.
  – Subunits and mini-units are referred to as SAIDs (self-managing array of identical disks). The sealed *boxes* contain enough hard drives to offer parity protection in virtual RAID groups and automatically *swap in* spares if one hard drive should fail. It is claimed that the V1000 can go for three to five years without hardware maintenance or replacements.
■ *Xiotech Corp. Emprise 5000/7000* builds storage systems from units called intelligent storage elements (ISE), which are based on a technology acquired from Seagate. It is claimed that ISEs reduce the two main causes of disk failure—heat and vibration—giving more than 100 times the reliability of a normal disk drive in a standard bay.
■ The V1000 can perform diagnostics and error correction on bad drive sectors and *write* around then if necessary. Xiotech claims that the product will need zero servicing in five years of normal operation.

This kind of storage *self-healing* technology (which IBM calls *self-managing*) is a branch of the *autonomic computing* subject (see http://searchstorage.techtarget.com/tip/Self-healing-systems-and-RAID-technology).

Summary

RAID as proposed in 1988 has done sterling work for online information systems and other vital applications in reducing the impact of disk failures on the service being performed. However, the increasing amount of data generated by video, audio, business analytics, and other growth is finding the RAID configurations used today struggling to cope with some time requirements, such as RTOs.

The areas giving problems are the size of disk units themselves, the bit error rates that make a larger disk more liable to failure than a smaller one and the recovery times for large volumes of data after a failure. *Proprietary RAID* variations, particularly of RAID 6, offer a temporary solution to the problems but are prone to the same errors outlined here. Currently, there are efforts at extending the life of RAID using triple parity and other technology *gizmos*.

The use of extensions to parity and ECC, often known as *erasure codes* (EC), is in the picture as longer-term solutions to the RAID ailments. Although the theory of these codes is much older than RAID, the implementations and practice are embryo. Current EC implementers include Cleversafe, EMC, Amplidata, and Nippon Electric Corporation (NEC).

One major factor that recovery must cater for is the sheer volume of data being stored today, commonly known as *big data*. One important factor concerns the way data is stored and how fast it can be restored when lost or compromised in some way, which has implications for normal recovery and DR (see Chapter 11).

For example, key online data supporting important business transactions will need rapid recovery so as not to impact the company's business. Old Laurel and Hardy videos, vitally important though these are, can await storage and recovery by some more leisurely method. It all hinges on costs and the need to put the service show back on the road.

AVAILABILITY THEORY AND PRACTICE

"The complexity of a system is proportional to the square of its components."*

In this section, we cover new things and things we have seen before as part of the immersion process. As I intimated previously, I am not trying to teach the reader the breaststroke or the crawl or any other swimming stroke. What I am attempting to do is make the reader comfortable in the water and make his or her own mind up as to how to progress.

I had to swallow a lot of IT water and nearly drowned in theory to be able to do this but I hope the result is worthwhile.

Topics covered and uncovered include simple reliability mathematics leading to the use of reliability block diagrams (RBDs), the causes of outages both planned and unplanned plus a couple of laughs at my expense. Another topic unveiled is the numerous areas in IT which can help or hinder high availability and, to some extent, disaster recovery. Part of this is semi-technical but a major element in this whole arena is influencing the IT availability and recovery *mindset* of *what happens if* . . . .

This section finishes by considering the reliability of networks, software, and other entities supporting the main parts of IT systems, for example, disks and tapes. I believe this last section to be unique in books dealing with high availability but these elements are no less important in some environments than the central processors.

---

* Fink's Fifth Law.

Chapter 5

High Availability: Theory

Some Math

There are some mathematical issues that can be skipped in understanding the basics of availability and some that cannot. We will deal with the latter in the next few sections.

Guide to Reliability Graphs

Probability Density Function

Two graphs are fundamental to reliability (and hence availability) studies. The first, the probability density function (pdf), represents the probability of an event happening as a function of some related quantity. To understand this generic definition, here are some examples:

- A graph of the probability of a car breaking down as a function of distance traveled
- A graph of the probability of the failure of a component as a function of time

The last situation is illustrated in Figure 5.1.

The graph shows the probability of failure, $f(t)$, as a function of time. The interpretation of this is that the probability of failure between times:

$$t \text{ and } (t + \delta t)$$

where δt is a small number and is represented by the area under the probability curve between those two points. At some point on the horizontal time axis, there will be a point that represents the highest tendency to fail, t_H, and the mean time between failures (MTBF), t_M.

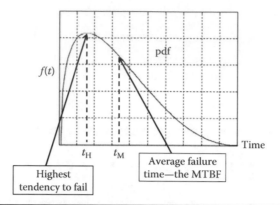

Figure 5.1   A sample probability distribution function.

This is the point where the areas under the curve before and after that point are equal, namely, t_M, so that

$$\text{Left area} \int_{0}^{t_M} f(t)dt = \text{Right area} \int_{t_M}^{\infty} f(t)dt \tag{5.1}$$

MTBF Time on pdf f(t) *curve*

The total area under the curve represents 1, that is, certainty of failure between time = 0 and time = infinity, and thus,

$$\text{Left area} \int_{0}^{t_M} f(t)dt + \text{Right area} \int_{t_M}^{\infty} f(t)dt = \int_{0}^{\infty} f(t)dt = 1 \tag{5.2}$$

Total Area Under $f(t)$ *—Failure Is Certain*

Figure 5.2 shows the development of the cumulative distribution function (cdf) curve from the pdf curve, which is a plot of the area under $f(t)$ between 0 and a where a goes in small increments from 0 to infinity.

At first glance, it is sometimes difficult to work out what the $f(t)$ curve means when the $F(t)$ curve tells us the failure probabilities. If you imagine that $f(t)$ represents a number of men and the time axis of their height, it is unlikely we would ask how many men are exactly 1.8323199044 m tall. More likely, we would ask a question like *how many men are there whose heights lie between 1.84 and 1.86 m?*

Similarly, in the case of the pdf, we might ask what the probability is of the component being modeled failing between time 1.84 and 1.86 years, say. Just as the probability of a man being between 1 m and 10 m tall is almost certainly 1 (unless you live in a strange country), the probability of component failure between time 0 and infinity is also 1, that is, absolutely certain at some time.

The cdf curve is drawn calculating the probability of failure between times 0 and $(0 + \Delta t)$, 0 and $(0 + 2\Delta t)$, $(0 + 3\Delta t)$, and so on, each number giving a point on the $F(t)$ curve.

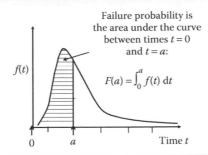

Figure 5.2   Failure probability between two times.

This is essentially an *integration* rather than a *summation* as Δt approaches 0. There are a number of graphical functions used in reliability engineering—some continuous, others discrete. The ones often used are Weibull, exponential, and Poisson (see Terminology in Appendix 1).

Cumulative Distribution Function

The curve generated as described above looks as shown in Figure 5.3. Imagine moving along the time axis and each point calculating the area under the curve and plotting it against time. At time *t*, this will give the probability of failing at or before time *t*. If we plot values of this area against time, then we derive what is known as a cdf, a sample of cdf is shown in Figure 5.3.

As time goes toward infinity, the probability of failure goes toward 1, or certain failure as it must fail at some time in this period! The graphs shown in Figures 5.1 through 5.3 are generic and the actual shape of the pdf depends on the *failure* model in question. There are a number of mathematical distributions used in reliability engineering, as we have seen, and they vary in selection depending on whether hardware or software reliability is being pursued.

Some of these distributions are outlined in Appendix 4 in the context of hardware and software reliability and availability and briefly covered in the Appendix 1 Terminology section.

Availability Probabilities

Application availability depends on the availability of other elements in a system, for example, network, server, operating system, and so on, which support the application. Concentrating solely on the availability of any one block will not produce optimum availability of the application for the

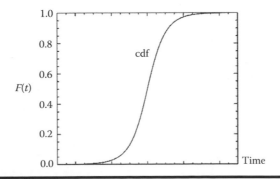

Figure 5.3   Cumulative distribution function.

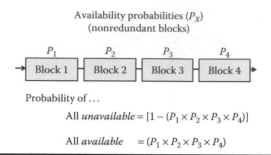

Figure 5.4 Series of system of *components* or *blocks*.

end user. In Figure 5.4, a *linear* or nonredundant configuration of elements supporting the user application is shown. In vendor engineering publications, these elements are referred to as *blocks*, although other publications may refer to them as *components*. It is evident that if any block in the configuration fails, the user loses the use of the application. The application is as available as the weakest link in the chain, or so it would appear.

Figure 5.4 is a schematic showing a linear chain of blocks, henceforth known as *nonredundant blocks* or blocks in *series*. It is easy to see that the failure of any block in the chain will cause a failure of the service to the end user. There are, of course, other blocks in the chain, such as operating system, middleware, and so on (not shown here) but the principle is the same. A single component whose failure causes overall failure of a system or service is called a single point of failure (SPoF).

Equations 5.1 and 5.2 demonstrate that a series of blocks is weaker than its weakest component simply because of the multiplication of several factors, all of which are <1.

Lusser's Law

Lusser's Law is a prediction of reliability named after Robert Lusser.[*] It states that the reliability of a *series* system (of our *blocks*) is equal to the product of the reliability of its component subsystems, if their failure modes are known to be statistically independent. This is what we see in Figure 5.4. The law can be stated as follows:[†]

$$P_{n-\text{components}} = \prod_{i=1}^{n} P_i \quad \text{which is } P_1 \times P_2 \times \ldots \times P_n \tag{5.3}$$

Lusser's Law for Serial (Series) Components

> ***Note:*** This lays to rest the theory that a chain is as strong as its weakest link, the thinking at the time. Lusser's Law deals with the reality of this situation.

Later in section Effect of Redundant Blocks on Availability, we will discuss using *components in parallel* and how to make the assessment of availability more IT-specific and not just deal with anonymous blocks or components which might represent anything in a reliability context—valves, pipes, and so on.

---

[*] He worked on Wernher von Braun's US rocketry program post-WWII.
[†] See Appendix 4 for an explanation of ∏.

Part of availability management is to examine the service failure points in the configuration between application and user, assess their impact on service availability, and subsequently devise proactive monitoring and reactive recovery procedures for all services or applications. The word *management* is significant here and does not mean the same as *monitoring*.

Monitoring is a passive activity, whereas management is an active, preemptive process, which seeks to avoid problems in the first instance rather than cure them, possibly multiple times. If proactive processes fail, there must be adequate reactive processes and procedures in place to minimize problem determination and recovery time.

Availability Concepts

To understand the idea of availability and attempt to quantify and optimize it, it is necessary to be aware of some of the terms involved. Most of the terms will be explained briefly in context in this book but for a fuller treatment, see Appendix 1.

Hardware Reliability: The Bathtub Curve

Over 50 years ago, a group called AGREE (Advisory Group for Reliability of Electronic Equipment) found that hardware failure rates took the shape of the *bathtub* illustrated in Figure 5.5 and likened it to the death rate of people with the horizontal axis representing a person's age and the vertical axis the death rate. The relatively high death rate in early life was known as the *infant mortality* phase, burn-in, and the right hand rise is *old age* or, in equipment terms, burnout.

In general, when parts are first manufactured, they experience a relatively high failure rate. After an initial period of *early life* failures, there is an extended period of time where parts will fail at a fairly steady, but slower, rate, $R(t) =$ constant. Then, as components begin to wear out, there is a period of time where component failures occur at an increasing rate.

Vendors often use a variety of techniques during the manufacturing process to identify early life parts failures before servers are shipped to clients. Corrective action can then be taken. Accelerated life testing often speeds up this *discovery* process.

Incidentally, the fault occurrences predicted by the Weibull distributions (Appendix 4) of failure rate differ in shape depending on the parameters used in drawing the curves.

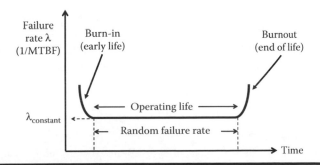

Figure 5.5   Hardware reliability *bathtub* curve.

Table 5.1   Hardware Bathtub Failure Modes

Early Life	Operating/Useful Life	Wearout Phase
Manufacturing	Random chance failures	Mechanical
Shipping		Batteries
Storage		Capacitors
Installation		Solid state
Deployment		
Environment		

Scott Speaks of Vicor points out[*] that combining several Weibull curves with different distribution parameters yields a curve very close to the *bathtub* curve we have just discussed.

In *hardware failure mechanisms*, there are numerous ways in which hardware can fail—soft fail or hard fail. Table 5.1 shows some of these but not all variations of each. For example, mechanical failure can be caused by stress, heat, fatigue, and torque. The failures are presented under the three areas shown in the bathtub curve.

$$\text{Early life}: \text{Reliability} = f(t);\ \text{Useful life} = \text{constant } R_0;\ \text{Wearout} = \text{erratic } F(t)$$

Software Reliability[†]: The Bathtub Curve

Software does not have the same reliability characteristics as hardware, which is illustrated in Figure 5.5. Software does not *age* like hardware and errors are often phased out over the life of a product. The possible issue then becomes *is the new release of that particular software as reliable as the old one?* The software reliability curve in Figure 5.6 is reproduced from a paper by Jiantao Pan of Carnegie Mellon University.[‡]

Jiantao points out a major difference between the hardware and software curves in that the software failure rate does not increase at the end of life stage as the hardware does.

He also informs us

> that in the last phase, software does not have an increasing failure rate as hardware does. In this phase, software is approaching obsolescence: there are (*sic*) no motivation for any upgrades of changes to the software.

The discontinuities shown in Figure 5.6 may occur when software is upgraded, either by fixes or replaced with a new version. The shape of the software bathtubs varies depending on your information source but essentially shows the error rate in the software as delivered. The software *as delivered* can go through phases of error detection and correction and many papers make reference to these two activities.

---

[*] "Reliability and MTBF Overview."

[†] For an introduction, see https://journal.thecsiac.com/issue/3/39 an article by John Musa. This will ease the pain of tackling other, more esoteric papers.

[‡] http://www-2.cs.cmu.edu/~koopman/des_s99/sw_reliability/.

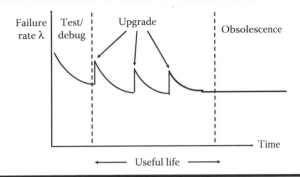

Figure 5.6   Software reliability *bathtub* curve.

Other curves (see the Rayleigh curve in Appendix 4) show the error rates at various stages of software development—unit test, system test, and so on.

Simple Math of Availability[*]

Availability: This is often applied to IT blocks (components) in a system, such as CPU, disk, and so on. Availability uses the language of probabilities, which assigns numeric values to the possibility of events occurring or not occurring. Probabilities are always less than or equal to 1—the closer the probability is to 1, the more likely it is to occur. If, for example, the weather forecast states that there is a 70% chance of rain tomorrow it means the probability of rain is 0.7. Conversely, the probability there will not be rain is 0.3 because the total probability of there being rain or no rain is 1, that is, 100% certain.

Expressing this mathematically, if the probability of event A *occurring* is, say, P_A, then the probability of event A *not occurring* is $(1-P_A)$. Probabilities are in the range 0–1, 0 meaning never and 1 meaning certainty.

If we use the notation P_A as the probability of a block being available (i.e., working)

$$P_N = (1 - P_A) \text{ and } P_N + P_A = 1$$

Relationship of Availability to Nonavailability

(5.4)

Availability

Availability (A) is the percentage of time in any time interval that a particular block, for example, disk, is operating normally. This can be expressed as

$$A(\%) = P_A \times 100\%$$

For example, if a block has a probability of being available of 0.92, then its availability is

$$A(\%) = \text{Probability } 0.92 \times 100 = 92\%$$

---

[*] For a bit more detail on this, see Appendix 4.

Nonavailability

Nonavailability (N) is the percentage of time in any time interval that a particular block, for example, disk, is not operational due to component failure. This can be expressed as

$$N(\%) = P_N \times 100 = (1 - P_A) \times 100\%$$

For the availability example mentioned earlier, its nonavailability is

$$N(\%) = (1 - 0.92) \times 100 = 8\%$$

Nonavailability can also be called *downtime*, although the implication that something is broken is not necessarily true. It means that the application or service is not available as the user wants it (logical outage), as we shall see.

However, there is a dilemma here. A disk may be working well for application A but may be unavailable for application B, for example, due to surface faults on a track. The question arises *is the disk unavailable?* It obviously depends on your viewpoint—an engineer or user of application B would say it is not operational, and an unaffected user (application A) may disagree because he is working normally.

In availability, there may be differing viewpoints about what is actually available. It is easy to see that the following is also true:

$$N + A = 100\%$$

The probability, P, that the block is available can be worked out from a given availability figure:

$$P(A) = \frac{A}{100} \quad (\leq 1)$$

By *block*, we mean a recognizable (or orderable) unit of hardware or software, for example, a disk array, network component, or version of Windows. The availability of, for example, a disk will be a function of the availability of the components of which it is made, each of which will have its own Weibull (or other) distribution *failure* curve, or in some cases, other distributions. Failure of a single component may or may not cause the disk to be unavailable, depending on how it is configured.

> *Note:* Some availability concepts need to be introduced at this point and they involve *mean* values of quantities (see Terminology in Appendix 1).

Mean Time between Failures

MTBF of a block or component—start of failure 1 to start of failure 2. We will expand on this definition a little later and in Appendix 2 as it is open to various interpretations and a few misinterpretations.

Mean Time to Repair

Mean time to repair (MTTR) the component applies to each block in the configuration supporting an application or service. The MTBF for an assembly of components will obviously be a function of the individual MTBFs and the way in which the blocks are configured. *Time to repair* covers

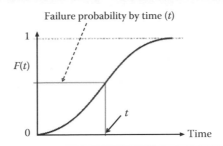

Figure 5.7   Failure probability distribution—Weibull cdf.

many things beside simply fixing something (see Figure 5.9 for a detailed breakdown of this time element.)

In addition to this, it is known that the MTBF is exactly what it says—it is a *mean* or *average*. For a random distribution of failure times, the curve (Figure 5.7) shows the distribution of failure intervals for any particular block in the service configuration.

Weibull is a common distribution applied to reliability studies and hence availability and failure rates/probabilities. See Figure 5.7 and refer to Appendix 4, where the significance of the parameters and other data about the Weibull and other distributions are explained. We have seen this curve earlier in Figure 5.3 but here it is again as part of the immersion process.

The graph shown in Figure 5.7 is known as the cdf and shows the probability of failure of a component as a function of time in operation. Eventually, failure is a certainty and its probability is therefore 1. As time progresses, the probability of failure gets closer and closer to 1, that is, a certainty.

There are other distributions possible—exponential, binomial, gamma, and so on, but some of them are, as we shall see, variations or subsets of the Weibull distribution.

The cdf is a derivative (integral) of the pdf when it is continuous and a summation when the distribution is discrete. Whatever the distribution, there will be a distribution of failure times about the mean, however, that is calculated.

This topic is expanded in Appendix 4 where a list of reliability mathematical distributions can be found. It is sometimes difficult to work out any sensible information when dealing with distribution curves but help is at hand for some of the calculations.

Online Availability Tool

See Appendix 4 for details of an online tool for assessing the availability of, say, *m* units out of a complement of *n* parallel * redundant) units from data supplied by you. It saves massive effort in doing calculations for the availability of parallel components in systems, using the formulae given in that Appendix. It is many times easier than wading through the parallel blocks formulae (also in Appendix 4), which may be intellectually satisfying but hard to use. The online tool is from Reliability Analytics Corporation, courtesy Seymour Morris (www.reliabilityanalytics.com) and there are various combinations of reliability configurations that can be modeled on input provided by the user.

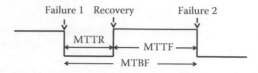

Figure 5.8   Schematic for availability equation.

Availability Equation I: Time Factors in an Outage

The availability (*A*) of a system block is usually expressed in terms of MTTF and MTTR in Figure 5.8 (we will see this figure and its derivatives in Appendix 2) plus the supporting equation:

$$A(\%) = \frac{MTTF}{(MTTF + MTTR)} = \frac{MTTF}{MTBF} \times 100\%$$

(5.5)

Simple Availability Equation (%)

MTTF plus MTTR is the total time the block is observed and MTTF is the time it is operational during that period, hence the equation above.

> ***MTPD:*** There is another key parameter in recovery times and that is the mean time for problem determination (MTPD) on top of the actual repair time (MTTR) when the problem is finally identified. Very few *availability* articles mention this important part of recovery. The quoted text below is an exception (http://www.computerworld.com/s/article/105781/MTBF).

> MTTF and MTBF are sometimes used interchangeably, but they are in fact different. MTTF refers to the average (the mean, in arithmetic terms) time until a component fails, can't be repaired and must therefore be replaced, or until the operation of a product, processor design is disrupted. MTBF is properly used only for components that can be repaired and returned to service. This introduces a couple of related abbreviations occasionally encountered: MTTR (mean time to repair) and, less common, MTTD (mean time to diagnose). With those notions in mind, we could say that MTBF = MTTF + MTTD + MTTR.
>
> **Russ Kay**
> *October 31, 2005*

There is a detailed discussion of MTxx parameters in Appendix 2. It's very simple when you know how they and availability are defined. Here Kay uses MTTD, whereas I have used MTPD but they are essentially the same thing. Another document* states, in adding a factor to MTTR (mean time to repair or recover):

MTTD is classified as Mean Time To Detection.

I dispute this as meaning detection (*Houston, we have problem*!) as it doesn't tell us what the problem is—that is the role of problem determination and thence to the repair/recovery phase.

---

* http://www.ece.cmu.edu/~koopman/des_s99/traditional_reliability/presentation.pdf.

It may be implied but it is not obvious. Yet another document[*] supports the separation of determination and repair:

> Mean Time To Restoration: Mean Time To Recovery: MTTR
> *Symbol:* MTTR (abbreviation)
> *Definition:* The expectation of the time to restoration of the component

> ***Note:*** The use of "Mean Time To Repair" is deprecated as it gives the wrong impression of the steps within the diagnose/recover arena.

MTTR is a factor expressing the mean active corrective maintenance time required to restore an item to an expected performance level. This includes for example troubleshooting, dismantling, replacement, restoration, and functional testing, but shall not include waiting times for resources.

Thus, from the end user's point of view, Equation 5.5 above should really be written differently, taking into account problem notification and determination.

> ***Note:*** The reason for this split is to emphasize the importance of problem determination, which can in some cases be much more than the MTTR. If you don't know what the problem is, you can't fix it.

In Figure 5.9, t_1 is the MTPD, t_2 is the response time of the agent, and t_3 is the actual repair time. The *real* MTTR, therefore, is:

$$MTTR = (t_1 + t_2 + t_3 + t_1 + t_2) \tag{5.6}$$

Components of Real Time to Recover

where Δt_1 and Δt_2 are the times to detect a failure has occurred and the time taken to restore the service to normal operation, respectively.

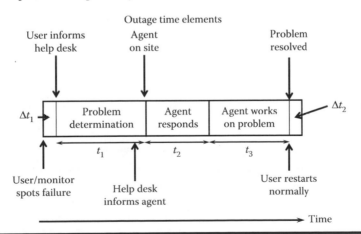

Figure 5.9   Time elements in an outage.

---

[*] http://www.epsma.org/*pdf*/MTBF%20Report_24%20June%202005.pdf.

Note: These times may not be insignificant, especially Δt_2, since there may be a time lapse between the actual fixing of the root problem and the resumption of normal service (ramp up time). The service level agreement (SLA) should be clear on this point to avoid fisticuffs and penalties on IT for nonachievement. We shall see examples of this later.

It is evident that minimizing these times is the core of availability management. In addition, it is important, therefore, to state exactly what is meant by *availability* and from which viewpoint. This sequence of events is shown in Figure 5.9, covering the following:

- Discovery
- Location
- Diagnosis
- Get parts (and possibly staff) (These may include travel.)
- *Cure* and ramp-up

The differentiation between these various factors is important in attempting to *minimize* them because each requires different actions to reduce the time to complete them. You can't do this unless you recognize them as entities. Ramp-up or full-service restoration needs consideration at the design stage. A fix of 5 minutes, ramp-up time 120 minutes is a *lower outage* than a 20-minute fix, ramp-up time 30 minutes. Think about it.

Availability Equation II

The previous availability equation can now be rewritten as

$$A(\%) = \frac{\text{MTTF}}{\text{MTTF} + [t_1 + (t_2 + t_3)]} = \frac{\text{MTTF}}{\text{MTTF} + (\text{MTPD} + \text{MTTR})} \times 100\% \quad (5.7)$$

Availability as a Percentage—Rewritten

where the problem determination, recognition, and service resumption factors are recognized and catered for in design, calculations, and service levels.

The user may be aware of the failure immediately, whereas the help desk and the relevant agent does not know about it until sometime later. The *agent* is whichever body is deemed responsible for correcting the failure and could be a software vendor, a hardware supplier, or the organization's own IT staff.

It is evident from either distribution curves for MTTR/MTTF that the *mean* time between failures/*mean* time to repair is indeed an average and the intervals between failures can vary from short to very long. For example, if the MTTR is X hours and an SLA has been agreed for X hours to bring the system back, there will still be instances where the recovery time is greater than X hours and instances where it is less. People involved in the drawing up and delivery of SLAs should be aware of this fact.

The distribution for MTPD is not immediately obvious but will definitely depend on the completeness of the problem determination procedures, documentation, and the skills of the staff and supporting organizations in the installation.

Note: Availability is sometimes expressed as *time available/elapsed time.* This can be misleading if the elapsed time contains a period when nonavailability is acceptable, for example, a 2-week shutdown of a manufacturing plant or weekends where the system is not used or needed. In these cases, the availability should be realistically expressed as

$$A(\%) = \frac{\text{Time actually operating to spec}}{\text{Time supposed to be operating to spec}} \qquad (5.8)$$

Availability Times Explained

where *time supposed to be working* is the time the system is *expected* to be delivering a service, as opposed to wall-clock time. This was outlined diagrammatically in Figure 1.3.

Also, the military have an acronym MLDT which is *mean logistical delay (time)*, that is essentially the time taken to retrieve the appropriate part or person to resolve the fault. IT may not include this in the repair time but should recognize it may exist. Most organizations would insist on such items being located on-site to avoid MLDT delays.

Initially, one may attempt to ascertain MTBFs for all the blocks providing service to the end user and calculate the failure rate for the whole system. Although this is feasible for hardware blocks, it is difficult for software blocks. Unless the MTTFs for each block in the service *configuration* are known, the overall service availability could not be calculated. See Appendix 4 for a more detailed explanation of standard reliability theory (if you are interested).

Probability of application being available is simply the availability as A% converted to a probability for all *n* blocks in a series configuration, that is:

$$P(\text{total}) = P_1 \times P_2 \times P_3 \times \ldots P_n = \frac{A_1 \times A_2 \times A_3 \times \ldots A_n}{100^n}$$

The availability probabilities for parallel (redundant) configurations of components or blocks, for example, ISDN backup lines, are discussed next.

Effect of Redundant Blocks on Availability

The discussion so far has dealt with linear chains of blocks (blocks in *series*, to use an electrical analogy), where the whole chain is weaker than its weakest link—*Lusser's Law.*

To carry this analogy further, it is possible to use blocks in parallel to increase the availability of the chain, assuming that one block can take over from a failed block, and also assuming that the blocks fail independently. Figure 5.10 illustrates this for the two blocks.

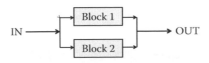

Figure 5.10   Parallel or redundant blocks.

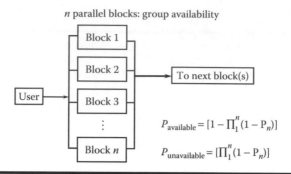

n parallel blocks: group availability

Block 1

Block 2 → To next block(s)

User → Block 3

Block n

$P_{\text{available}} = [1 - \prod_1^n (1 - P_n)]$

$P_{\text{unavailable}} = [\prod_1^n (1 - P_n)]$

Figure 5.11   Group availability of *n* parallel blocks (π means *the product of*; Σ means *the sum of*).

These *blocks* might be network interface cards (NICs), disks, servers, or other parts of a working system. The general case for *n* parallel blocks is shown in Figure 5.11, together with the equations for availability and nonavailability probabilities.

Parallel (Redundant) Components

Figure 5.11 illustrates the components configured in parallel as opposed to in series as we have seen already.

The math of these configurations is similar to Lusser's math except we deal with *unreliability* instead of *reliability* entities in the math.

The basic premise in these calculations is that if the probability of being available is *P*, then the probability of not being available is *N* where *N* = (1–*P*) and *P* = (1–*N*) because the total availability of being *available* or *not available* is 1. In reality, a system will consist of several sets of redundant components, for example, disks, servers, network card, lines, and so on. These will feed into each other, possibly mixed with single components.

Figure 5.11 shows the general case of *n* blocks in a parallel configuration. This might represent one set of components for a subsystem such as a RAID configuration or set of NICs. Such a configuration can be difficult to handle mathematically so a *reduction* technique is usually employed. This is dealt with later when discussing domains and examples of parallel components.

Two Parallel Blocks: Example

Picture two components in parallel, one with availability probability P_a and the other P_b. The probability of both blocks being *unavailable*, that is, the chain is broken, is

$$(1 - P_a)(1 - P_b)$$

Nonavailability of Dissimilar Parallel Components

(5.9)

This assumes the blocks have different availability characteristics, P_a and P_b. If they were the same, say $P_a = P_b = P$, then the probability that both are not available is given by the following relationship:

$$\text{Nonavailability} \quad N = (1 - P)^2$$

(5.10)

Nonavailability of Similar Parallel Components

which is essentially a variation of Lusser's Law using the nonavailability probabilities as multipliers instead of availability probabilities. The probability that n redundant blocks are unavailable is $(1-P)^n$ and the probability that they are all available is given by the relationship $[1-(1-P)^n]$, the general case of Equation 5.10.

As an example, consider two parallel blocks, each with an availability of 99.5%. The probability that both are unavailable is

$$N = (1 - 0.995) \times (1 - 0.995) = 0.000025$$

Hence, its availability (compared with the availability of a single nonredundant case of 99.5%) is

$$A(\%) = (1 - N) \times 100 = (1 - 0.000025) \times 100\% = 99.9975\%$$

The knowledge of each value of P and some mathematical skills would be needed to solve the problem of service availability for a combination of serial and parallel service blocks, which is often the case in real life.

Combinations of Series and Parallel Blocks

In Figure 5.12 and the logic and simple math discussed in this section, it is often the case that any set of components composing a system will comprise a combination of series and parallel items and we need a way of calculating their net or overall availability. Figure 5.12 demonstrates the *reduction* technique referred to earlier.

In Figure 5.12, we need to reduce the availability of the two parallel components to one and then treat the whole set as a series of blocks. The availability of block S_1 is A_1, say, 0.97, that of S_2 is A_1, say, 0.98, and that of the combined parallel blocks A_{P12}. Assume $A_{P1} = A_{P2} = 0.95$, then the math goes as given in the equations next.

If N_{P12} is the nonavailability of the two parallel blocks, then

$$N_{P12} = (1 - A_{P1}) \times (1 - A_{P2})$$

$$\text{i.e., } N_{P12} = (1 - 0.95) \times (1 - 0.95) = 0.0025$$

$$A_{P12} = (1 - N_{P12}) = 0.9975$$

$$A_{tot} = 0.97 \times 0.9975 \times 0.98 = 0.948 \text{ or } 94.8\% \text{ available}$$

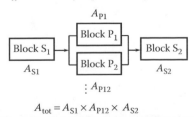

Series (S) and parallel (P) blocks
A_X = Probability of path X being available

$A_{tot} = A_{S1} \times A_{P12} \times A_{S2}$

Figure 5.12   Combination of serial and parallel components.

Note that we can express these figures as a decimal or as a percentage. Reliability is often quoted as a decimal, for example, 0.9987, and availability as a percentage, which is the decimal multiplied by 100.

> **Design Note:** In the design of a system with redundant components, there are logistic considerations. Are the parts always on site? If not, how long will it take to get them? Are we using redundancy to sidestep the intrinsic unreliability of the parts we are using? ... and so on.

There is another configuration that can complicate matters and that is the one where blocks have multiple connections to other blocks. These are normally called *complex system*s and these are outlined in the next section.

Complex Systems[*]

There are connections of components that are neither series nor parallel but what are called *complex*. A schematic example follows but the essence of these types of reliability block diagrams (RBDs) is that they can be treated in different ways. The system in Figure 5.13 cannot be broken down into a group of series and parallel systems. This is primarily due to the fact that component 3 has two paths leading away from it, whereas 2 and 4 have only one.

A schematic diagram outlining this typical complex study is shown in Figure 5.14 using real IT system components to illustrate it (note the cross links that make the configuration more complex).

A working example video of the analysis of a complex system using Reliasoft's BlockSim software can be found at https://www.youtube.com/watch?v=8PgWszSvF3U. There are numerous Blocksim examples on YouTube – parallel, k-from-n etc. – which can be found by simple searches on *reliasoft* and *blocksim*.

The video study gives typical MTTFs for the components of the system to be used in the development of a solution.

A very good Dell paper covers similar ground to this topic at http://www.dell.com/content/topics/global.aspx/power/en/ps3q02_shetty?c=us.

System Failure Combinations

The combinations of component failures that will cause the system to be unavailable are shown in the video that takes the viewer through the procedure of working on this problem using the BlockSim tool (referenced above).

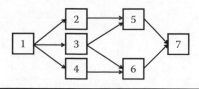

Figure 5.13   RBD schematic of a complex system.

---

[*] http://reliawiki.com/index.php/RBDs_and_Analytical_System_Reliability#Reliability_of_Nonidentical_k-out-of-n_Independent_Components.

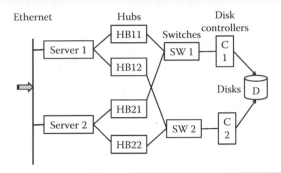

Figure 5.14 Complex cluster RBD example. (Data from ReliaSoft.)

For the record, there are 10 combinations of component failures that will make the illustrated combination unavailable.

The math of this involves equations covering these *failing* combinations and is not recommended bedtime reading, but it is a useful CFIA (component failure impact analysis) exercise using a suitable software tool.

Complex Systems Solution Methods

Several methods exist for obtaining the reliability of a complex system including the following:

- The decomposition method
- The event space method
- The path-tracing method

The methods, in essence, remove components one by one and perform the calculations on the resulting configurations. This is quite a laborious task for configurations with many components and links between them.

An erudite discussion of these methods can be found at http://reliawiki.com/index.php/RBDs_and_Analytical_System_Reliability.

Real-Life Example: Cisco Network Configuration

See Figure 5.15, which is a Cisco schematic of a network configuration. It can be analyzed by working out the reliabilities of the individual components for configuration **A**, assuming they are all the same, say, *P*, which will yield the equation.

Configuration A

The equation for the reliability of the configuration **A** is

$$P^3 \times [1 - (1 - P)^2] \times P^3 = 0.999855 \quad \text{(Lusser + Parallel equation)}$$

which would need to be solved in some way.

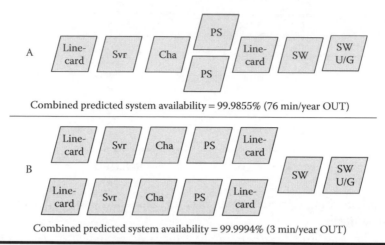

Cisco availability example: redundancy

A

Combined predicted system availability = 99.9855% (76 min/year OUT)

B

Combined predicted system availability = 99.9994% (3 min/year OUT)

Figure 5.15   Cisco parallel components example.

Configuration B

Similarly, the equation for configuration **B**, the second configuration, would be

$$[1-(1-P)^2]^5 \times P \times P = 0.999994 \quad \text{(Lusser + Parallel equation)}$$

Relate these equations to the A and B sections of Figure 5.15.

> *Note:* These calculations make assumptions about the configuration of the components. To illustrate this, look at Figure 5.16 where a configuration of components shown before is connected in *two different ways*.

It might at first sight seem that because the layout of the components is the same, the overall reliability of the chain will be the same but this is not quite the case.

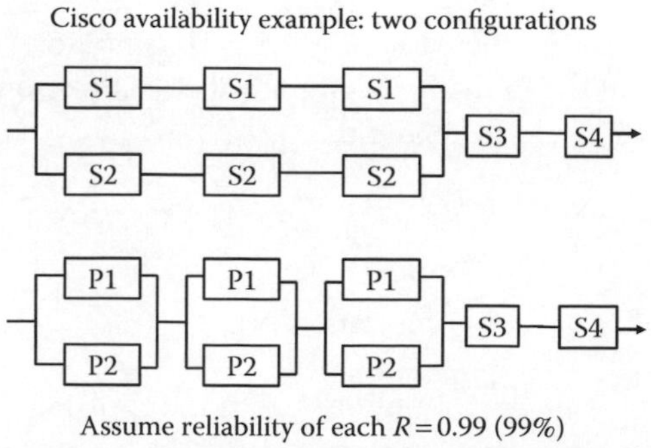

Cisco availability example: two configurations

Assume reliability of each $R = 0.99$ (99%)

Figure 5.16   Reliability of different configurations—Same components.

1. In the first configuration (A), the reliability of the series components, because all reliability numbers are $P = 0.99$, is

$$3 \times \text{serial } S1 := P^3 = 0.99^3 = 0.970 = P_{\text{top}} = P_t$$

$$3 \times \text{serial } S2 := P^3 = 0.99^3 = 0.970 = P_{\text{bottom}} = P_b$$

Combining these parallel, reduced sets of serial components yields what appears to be two parallel components of availability 0.970. Using the usual formula gives

$$P_{t+b} = [1 - (1 - P_t)(1 - P_b)] = [1 - (0.03)^2] = 0.9991 = 99.91\%$$

This now reduces the problem to three serial components: $P_t + {}_b$, S_3, and S_4, which is a simple three-parameter multiplication, answer 0.979, to save you from any trouble.

2. In the second case (B), we need to solve the problem for three sets of two components in parallel, each of $R = 0.99$. We know from the above formula what the net reliability of two parallel components is, that is,

$$P_{12} = [1 - (1 - P_1)(1 - P_2)] = [1 - (0.01)^2] = 0.9999 = 99.99\%$$

We now have the following series of five components to solve P_{12}, P_{12}, P_{12}, S_3, and S_4:

$$0.9999, 0.9999, 0.9999, 0.99, \text{ and } 0.99$$

$$= 0.9999 \times 0.9999 \times 0.9999 \times 0.99 \times 0.99$$

$$= 0.98 = 98\% \text{ (actually } 97.981)$$

See the Cisco paper related to this exercise showing typical MTBF values for their equipment (http://www.webtorials.com/main/resource/papers/cisco/paper139/Redundant-Supervisors.pdf).

Summary of Block Considerations

This section aims to clarify and underline the simple theory above that deals with series and parallel blocks (reliability terminology) or components (IT terminology).

Formulae were discussed and are outlined further in the famous Appendix 4, along with a URL from Reliability Analytics[*] which reduces the labor involved in performing parallel block/component calculations to a minimum.

■ *Series blocks:* In discussing this, we outlined Lussers' Law for the overall reliability of a series on n blocks, that is, the availability probability is the product of the individual reliabilities *not* the reliability of the weakest block. This *chain* is not as strong as its weakest link—it is weaker if all the other components have a reliability of less than 1.
■ *Parallel blocks:* Parallel blocks were discussed in terms of the following:
    – The reliability of n blocks in parallel
    – The reliability afforded by m blocks out of n originally available

---

[*] Courtesy of Seymour Morris, Reliability Analytics.

Sample Availability Calculations versus Costs

The two calculations, based on the theory of series and parallel blocks outlined previously, show the effect on making one block in a chain much more available.

P_n is the probability of each of 4 blocks being available, $n = 1, 2, 3,$ and 4. Let us imagine that in real life the blocks are as follows:

1. A workstation—reliability $P_1 = 0.99$
2. A LAN—reliability $P_2 = 0.97$
3. A server—reliability $P_3 = 0.99$
4. A disk array—reliability $P_4 = 0.98$

The purpose of the calculation is to show that *upping* the availability/reliability of one part of the configuration, possibly at great cost, can yield little overall benefit and that concentrating effort elsewhere might be a more productive exercise at a lesser cost.

Calculation 1: Server Is 99% Available

$$P_1 \times P_2 \times P_3 \times P_4 = 0.99 \times 0.97 \times 0.99 \times 0.98 = 0.93$$

The combined availability probability is 0.93 or 93%.

Calculation 2: Server Is 99.99% Available

Imagine we improve the availability of the server by whatever means available to yield $A = 99.99\%$ availability. The new overall probability of the chain of blocks being available is now 0.94,

$$P_1 \times P_2 \times P_3 \times P_4 = 0.99 \times 0.97 \times 0.9999 \times 0.98 = 0.94 \text{ or } 94\%$$

94% availability, up from 93%, not a vast increase considering the probable cost of increasing the availability of the server from 0.99 to 0.9999. This is one reason why highly available servers or fault tolerant are not necessarily the sole element in an HA (high availability) solution.

Lusser strikes again!

Availability: MTBFs and Failure Rate

> *Aside:* It is easy to get confused about failure rates, MTBFs, and lifetimes. The MTBF of a rechargeable battery might be a few weeks but with recharging, it can function again and have a lifetime of several recharges. A rechargeable battery is a *repairable* component, a non-rechargeable one isn't. There are other ways of looking at MTBFs, by relating them to failure rates, λ, which is used in reliability theory and is illustrated in Figure 5.17 and summarized in Equation 5.11.

It is often convenient to work in terms of failure rate, λ, so please make a mental note of it here as we deal with it later in the Hard Sums in Appendix 4.

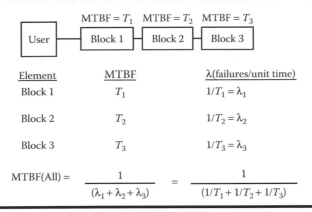

Figure 5.17 MTBFs and failure rate.

In summary, the relationship between MTBF and failure rate in a system of n components is

$$MTBF_{SYS} = \frac{1}{\sum_{i=1}^{n} \lambda_i}$$

(5.11)

Relationship of MTBF to Failure Rate

The relationship between MTBF and λ for *one* item or component is $MTBF = 1/\lambda$. Equation 5.11 assumes an exponential relationship between t and failure probabilities.

Availability Factors

Planned versus Unplanned Outages

The availability of a system, and hence the services which run on it, can be impacted by planned outages as well as the unexpected. A study[*] of the frequency of planned and unplanned downtime showed the following results:

■ Unplanned downtime (13%)
■ Planned downtime (87%)

IBM gives their breakdown of these figures in manual SG24-6547 (Table 5.2).

Figures such as these can vary of course, depending on the mix of vendor hardware, software, in-house developed code, and so on. As the system availability features of hardware improve with facilities such as hot-swap, redundant components, and so on, planned downtime is reducing with each generation of hardware. This often applies to software.

---

[*] By Strategic Research. The 87% figure is endorsed by IBM in Redbook SG24-6547 *IBM System Storage Business Continuity: Part 1 Planning Guide.*

Table 5.2 Components of Planned and Unplanned Outages (IBM)

Type	Planned (%)	Unplanned (%)
Software	13	30
Hardware	8	15
Application	8	27
Network	10	n/a
Operations	52	25
Other	9	3

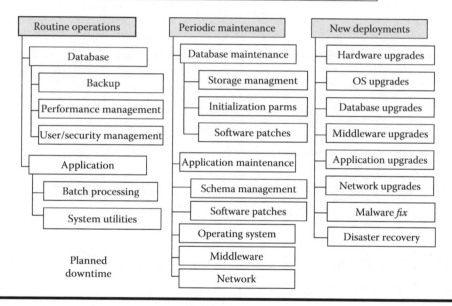

Figure 5.18 Planned downtime factors—87% of total.

There are many reasons for planned and unplanned downtime; both sets are illustrated in Figures 5.18 and 5.19.

Whatever set of figures you take for the spread of outages across causes, you will still have to look across the whole spectrum of possibilities in HA design and failure mitigation.

Planned Downtime: Planned Downtime Breakdown

As we have just seen, this is the main cause of nonavailability of services and sometimes, when improperly carried out, causes unplanned downtime.

Figure 5.18 lists many causes of outages that are planned for various reasons. It is not an exhaustive list and may be expanded taking account of customer circumstances and IT environment.

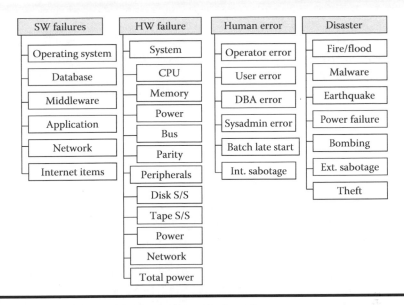

Figure 5.19 Unplanned downtime factors—13% of total.

The planned outages are change-based in the main, except perhaps for recovery of RAID failures. Although it would seem at first glance that these changes are necessary and the time taken irreducible, this is probably not so. The software aspects of these outages can be reduced by planning them as if building a hardware configuration.

I have seen too many problems caused by systems programmers *tweaking* things with the best intentions but sometimes causing systems grief.

Note: Change management as well as planning is key to reducing the number of times these things happen.

Remember that we are looking at the availability of a service not just its components so in all the hardware and software elements listed in Figures 5.18 and 5.19 may be embedded *liveware* issues that are to blame. It is perfectly feasible for *everything* to be operational but the service might not be. An example is the running of the wrong job, a sequence of jobs in the wrong order or at the wrong time and so tunnel vision in looking for physical outage *gotchas* is not the right way of looking at things.

Some of the unplanned downtime issues mentioned earlier may only affect one application, which may or may not be mission critical. It is important to develop procedures for the detection, determination, and correction of errors on a business priority basis. As a matter of interest, and complementing the previous table (Table 5.2) showing planned and unplanned downtime, Table 5.3 illustrates the breakdown of planned downtime.

Table 5.3 Planned Downtime Outage Components

HW Upgrade	SW Upgrade	Backup	Reconfigurations	Maintenance
28%	29%	13%	13%	17%

For many people, achieving HA means concentrating on minimizing hardware failures via redundancy, hot-swap disks, and so on. In real life, many outages are caused by factors other than hardware. It is appropriate at this stage to differentiate between a system failure (or outage) and the nonavailability of an application/service to the end user.

Unplanned Downtime

These are the circumstances that catch enterprises on the hop, so to speak.

They could be unforeseen or unforeseeable or expected because of cost-cutting or incompetent design.

The probability of occurrence is dictated by how many possible entities can cause an outage of a system and what mitigation has been built into the design and operation of the system. Redundancy is an obvious solution but location of a data center is also important in areas of extreme weather conditions.

We have made the point several times that human *finger trouble* is also a likely candidate for bringing a system down or rendering it not really fit for purpose. In short, many planned and unplanned outages are not necessarily inevitable. In any case, planned or unplanned, there are numerous outage possibilities, and I hear you say *how can we possibly cater for them all?* It's the same problem as eating a mammoth—you eat it one bite at a time.

Unplanned outages are the failures that hit the headlines, particularly in banks, where their effects ripple outward to humanity very quickly. One bank in the United Kingdom has been especially vulnerable to unplanned outages and this has been attributed to underinvestment in robust IT. On a personal note, some two decades ago I read some figures about percentages of turnover invested in IT by banks and other organizations.

This bank was notable by its very low% investment compared to the other banks, approximately one half the others. The chickens came home to roost very recently.

Security: The New Downtime

Unauthorized intrusion into IT systems is now a fact of life and a growing threat in terms of both volume and severity—the more recent surveys attest to this. From being a nuisance to individuals on PCs it has become a serious contender for knocking out a business or part thereof. The effects of these intrusions, often caused by malicious software (malware), can vary but can cause a service interruption or outage and are therefore of interest to us as ultraorthodox *availabilians*.

The immediate result of intrusions is not necessarily outage time but may eventually cause a cessation of a service due to actual outages, security exposures or reactive mitigation, and recovery actions. For example, if a malicious agent has stolen the details of 100,000 credit card customers, the service may have to be suspended pending investigation and recovery. We (at least in the United Kingdom) are familiar with situations where people have their valid credit cards failing to operate, often in embarrassing circumstances, due to some internal IT error.

More details on this topic can be found in Appendix 4, Lesson 10, and suffice it to say at this point that the situation is *here*, it is *now*, and it is potentially *lethal* to services.

Disasters: Breakdown of Causes*

These percentages, shown in Table 5.4, are of course country/location and, it seems, vendor dependent. In the surveys, it is also difficult to differentiate between, for example, power outages caused by weather and those intrinsic to the power supply components themselves.

---

* http://www.thegeeksclub.com/computer-disaster-recovery-planning-tips-resources-sb/.

Table 5.4   Disaster Causes Breakdown

Cause	Percentage (%)
Tornado/miscellaneous	12
Fire/explosion	7
Bomb	5
Earthquake	5
Hardware	24
Power	16
Hurricane	16
Flood	15

For example, if the IT power fails because of a flood, the IT department isn't going to build levees but might get a secondary power supply for the IT systems via a different transformer or route.

Again, were some hardware failures might be caused by power transients or surges—who knows? See Table 5.4 for the list of disasters that causes breakdown.

The figures quoted by IBM[*] are very roughly the same and, given the rider above, even major variations can probably be explained by the interpretation of *causes* which may in fact be the cause of a cause. For example, a flood may be registered as the cause of an outage but the final cause might have been a flooded transformer site, that is, a power outage.

Power: Downtime Causes[†]

Obviously, the precautions and design factors considered must take account of things that vary by geography, the possible impact of them on IT service plus the probability that it might happen (Table 5.5).

For example, there aren't many major earthquakes in the United Kingdom and those that do occur are only powerful enough to make a person spill his or her tea, although that can be very distressing to the British. Floods, however, are a different matter these days.

Power Issues Addenda

There are some additional facts on power which may be of interest:

1. The Power Systems Group at Manchester University (UK) has carried out work on power outage avoidance employing GPS technology. The following is an extract from the URL (http://www.eee.manchester.ac.uk/our-research/research-impact/gps-protects-power-networks-against-failure/):

   > Our pioneering global positioning system (GPS) based method for preventing electricity blackouts has been included in international grid management standards and also features in technical guidelines on best practice. National Grid expects to save £0.5 million each year as it implements the

---

[*] "Virtualizing disaster recovery using cloud computing"—January 2012.

[†] *Source:* APC (Schneider) Corporation. http://www.apcmedia.com/salestools/vavr-5wklpk/vavr-5wklpk_r1_en.pdf.

Table 5.5   Breakdown of Power Outage Causes

Cause	Total Percentage
Other circuit breakers	40
PDU and circuit breakers	30
UPS failure	20[a]
Balance of system	10

Note: PDU, power distribution unit; UPS, uninterruptible power supply.

[a] Strange isn't it? An UPS is accounting for 20% of the power-related interruptions! An UPS is often more than a roomful of batteries, as can be seen in Appendix 1 under the **UPS** entry and in the discussion below. Murphy's Law again.

system across the UK ... Researchers, led by Professor Peter Crossley, have developed algorithms, prototype devices, concepts and operating strategies to enhance the reliability of protection systems used in electrical transmission networks. Their work focused on network synchronisation using time signals from global positioning system (GPS) satellites.

2. Schneider-APC (American Power Corporation) lists the following as potential power issues[*]:
   a. Transients
   b. Interruptions
   c. Sag/undervoltage and swell/overvoltage
   d. Waveform distortion
   e. Voltage and frequency fluctuations

The likelihood of occurrence of these issues and how they affect *different countries* will depend on the nature and stability of the electricity supply.

So What?

Here are some real-life situations which can affect the quality of power supplies:

1. A famous US *brownout* occurred about 30 years ago when the singer Tiny Tim (6 feet 6 inches tall singer and ukulele player) got married in a televised ceremony during the night when power suppliers did not expect large demands on power.
2. Undervoltage, for example, can cause the picture on a TV to *roll* around in a vertical direction and do strange things to IT equipment and hence the service it supports.
3. When I worked with a UK electricity board, I was informed that the supply engineers would scan the newspapers and TV magazines to see what imminent TV programs might attract large audiences and hence consume more power. This was especially necessary in the United Kingdom because in such circumstances, large quantities of tea would be brewed and consumed during the program and at program intervals.

[*] Voltage issues will vary by country. For example, the United Kingdom tends not to suffer from *brownouts*.

Your IT site could be on the wrong end of one of these outages or brownouts so it pays to consider the options available.

For reference, see the Uptime Institute site for the paper "Fault Tolerant Power Compliance Specification" (_http://uptimeinstitute.com/images/stories/Mission_Critical_Product_Certification/Industry_Specifications/ftpc_specifications_v2.pdf).

External Electromagnetic Radiation Addendum

Some years ago, a new IT installation on the English south coast was frequently experiencing *glitches*, such as dropped parity, in their computers. This remained a mystery until someone did a test for external electromagnetic radiation hitting the site. Such radiation was found to be coming from a Government site close by—radar I think. They apparently solved the problem by *papering* the walls with thin chicken wire mesh to absorb the radiation. Rumor also had it that they used the silver wrapping from their bars of chocolate to paper the walls as an extra radiation *reflector*, but no one starved as a result.

New data center sites would benefit from such a study, which can often be carried out by electrical engineering departments on Universities. One of my own accounts carried out this exercise and was found to be *clean*. In the scale of the costs of the new data center and such errors, the fee for this service was trivial but the potential benefits enormous.

Note: A *system failure* is the failure of a server system either in whole or in a block of the system which renders it unusable. The *nonavailability of an application or service* to an end user can be caused by many factors other than hardware or system software failure, for example, an overrun of overnight batch work that precludes the use of an online application until it is complete. If this pushes availability of the online application back from the expected 8 am start to 10 am, that is, two hours of *downtime*, and bang goes your 99.999% availability for several years!!

Think about that one. It could trip you up over time as batch work grows (plug for Capacity Planning/Management).

Another example of application nonavailability is *data loss or inadvertent corruption*, covered in the next section.

The data volumes and percentages represent ever increasing importance over the years due to the critical nature of many of the applications it supports. Data loss and recovery is discussed in a little more detail in the section on RAID Configurations in Chapter 4, where the rapidly increasing volumes of data, both structured and unstructured, disk capacity areal bit density compete against a more slowly improving bit *survival* rate.

This dichotomy demands innovative solutions if the reliability and availability of data is to be maintained or increased over the next *data hungry* years.

Power: Recovery Timescales for Uninterruptible Power Supply

There is an illuminating article "15 Seconds versus 15 Minutes" on perceptions and misconceptions about power backup at http://www.edsenerji.com.tr/userfiles/files/WP%20107%2015%20Seconds%20vs%2015%20Minutes.pdf.

Two interesting snippets from this article are given below:

A. The paradigm of requiring 15 minutes or more of battery backup for mission critical UPS system reliability is an antiquated and flawed perception. When properly integrated and maintained, standby generators can and will reliably support the critical load in 10 seconds or less. This challenges the idea lead-acid batteries and extended backup time are necessary. The growing intolerance to a "graceful shutdown" also renders 15 minutes of backup moot. The UPS system can be designed with much higher reliability and predictability by using more reliable backup energy methods and applying proper design techniques. This paper discusses the issue and methods of implementing a short ride-through system with higher reliability and predictability than with traditional methods. ...

B. Some engineers and power system designers feel there is a significant difference between typical applications of 25 to 30 seconds of reserve time as with a flywheel UPS system, and 15 minutes as in a conventional static UPS and battery system. There is a reliability difference, but the actual advantage may surprise many.

See Appendix 1 (Terminology) for a diagram illustrating the use of redundancy in power supply, covering some of the devices mentioned in the reference above.

Causes of Data Loss

There are other surveys where the results differ because of interpretation of errors and their causes and the country or countries of survey. Refer to the survey in the URL under Table 5.6 for the whys and wherefore of these figures of *perceived* and *actual*. One thing to note is that current surveys will list *security* issues as a separate item because lumping it in with the most convenient existing *outage* category blurs the focus on it and it is wise to keep it as a separate entity.

According to the National Archives & Records Administration,[*] 93% of companies who lost their data for 10 days or more went bankrupt within a year of the loss and 3% of companies which run into some computer disasters never reopen.

One survey, referenced in the footnote, yielded the following results (Table 5.6):

Table 5.6 Breakdown of Data Loss Causes

Issue	Perceived (%)	Actual (%)
Hardware error	78	56
Human error	11	26
Software error	7	9
Virus	2	4
Natural disaster	1–2	1–2

Source: KrollOnTrack (http://www.zdnet.com/blog/storage/how-data-gets-lost/167).

---

[*] The National Archives and Records Administration (NARA) is the US nation's record keeper, to be found at http://www.archives.gov/.

Something to think about here. What we have outlined here are major outages with dire consequences. There are other circumstances that we will examine in the subsequent sections.

Pandemics? Disaster Waiting to Happen?

There are no figures I am aware of for outages caused in pandemic situations but fairly recent scares on bird flu and other *nasties* means that a pandemic or epidemic is not impossible. It would be wise to imagine such an occurrence and work out what additional steps need to be taken over and above those for other major disasters.

It differs from other disasters in that it only affects *liveware*. This is part of business continuity plan (BCP) but will involve IT staff.

Disasters: Learning the Hard Way

Here are some examples of lessons learned at *metropolitan* levels after disaster struck—sometimes unexpectedly, as is their way.

1. The Bishopsgate bombing of April 24, 1993, occurred when the Provisional Irish Republican Army (IRA) detonated a truck bomb on Bishopsgate, a major thoroughfare in London's financial district, the City of London. As a result of the bombing, the *ring of steel* was introduced to protect the City, and many firms introduced disaster recovery plans in case of further attacks ... The attack also prompted British and American financial companies to prepare disaster recovery plans in case of future terrorist attacks. DEC lost a data center in this atrocity but IBM loaned them office space to reinstall and recover their facilities. Who said chivalry was dead?
2. The World Trade Center 1993 bombings in February 1993 caused bankruptcy in 40% of affected companies within two years of the attack (International Data Corporation [IDC] and quoted in Wikipedia). For nearly all organizations concerned in such *disasters*, it was a lesson learned.
3. Hurricane Sandy, Katrina, and so on. These are the current *attention grabbers* as people realize that some places are safer than others in which to store your *IT crown jewels*.

Other Downtime Gotchas*

These are some of the things that *go bump in the night* and cause palpitations. They are not listed in order of impact on services. That's your job.

■ Planned maintenance overrunning into *production* time.
■ Distributed Denial of Service and transaction overload. This is a fairly common issue with popular public websites and often causes a *shutdown*. Lotteries with a huge rollover *payload* often suffer from fatal overload in the hours before the draw.
■ Other overruns impacting a subsequent service, for example, online day starting significantly after the expected time.
■ File, log, DBMS, and so on overflow.
■ Unacceptable performance or usability, often causing users to consider the service *down*.

---

* Gotchas are things that jump out and bite you unexpectedly (an IBM term?).

- Data corruption/data loss* from external or internal *agents*.
- Poorly tested new configurations (clusters).
- Cluster failover failures (a double whammy) due to incorrect configurations and other support reasons. One estimate puts unplanned outages in failover situations at 5%–10% of failures.
- Poorly tested applications (Logical errors can occur. Wrong results in any program equals logical downtime requiring recovery.).
- Rogue processes (runaway tasks, CPU *hogs*, memory leakage, memory stealers, etc.) having a dramatic effect on performance.
- Other hardware failures (adapters, cables, overheating, damp, etc.).
- System *limit* parameters (*maxprocs* exceeded, *maxmem* exceeded, etc.) causing *non-usability* problems for service users, despite there being no *real* outage. These we have classified as *logical outages*.
- In the era of *data tiering*, it is important that the lower tiers of the storage hierarchy are as *availability conscious* as the highly visible online tiers.
- Failed communications with another system which does not have the availability characteristics of the primary system (*fault propagation*) and cannot supply the latter with the information it needs, as illustrated in Figure 5.20.

This might be a domain name server (DNS) subsystem, part of the main systems, or another machine altogether which fails to respond to the primary system because of its own outage. If the traffic is one way, primary to secondary, it may be of little or no consequence but if the primary system requires a reply and/or data in response to proceed, it may render that application(s) on the primary system effectively unavailable.

This type of situation was also a distinct possibility in the Y2000 saga—compliant system to/from noncompliant system data transfer. This is the problem I surmised was caused at the London Stock Exchange on March 1, 2000, by the two DEC systems out of sync because one recognized February 29th, the other didn't, resulting in jobs running in the wrong order.

- Growth in required capacity of networks, processor, and disk *creeping up* on an installation, leading to logical *performance* outages or slowdowns. It goes without saying that monitoring is the key here.

Communication with another system

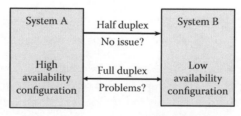

Is critical system A dependent on instant
and accurate replies from system B ?

Figure 5.20 System dependence on other systems' availability.

---

* Did you know that if you put a magnetic tape on an operating washing machine, it can wipe bits off the data? I know, because I did it—once.

- Inadequate data protection planning. In a 2009 survey by ExaGrid/CIO Pulse, 97% of IT professionals felt their data are vulnerable to a data protection or a data incident.
- Growth in data volumes leading to increased backup (and hence recovery) times. These may eat into the online day, an outage by any other name and impact recovery time objectives (RTOs) in an SLA.
- Transcription or transposition errors in producing *operational* documentation from hand-written or retyped data and instructions which may result in *finger trouble* issues.
- Contamination of vital system components (*dirty* machine room/operations bridge).
- Devising and implementing solutions to which there is no problem, that is, fixing things when they aren't broken.
- Missing personnel whose skills are vital to some recovery situations—do you have backup skills in other words.
- There must be others for the reader to fill in, writing on one side of the paper only ... a gloomy picture but forewarned is forearmed.

Downtime Gotchas: Survey Paper

There is a good white paper from FORTRUST called "Evaluating Data Center and Colocation High-Availability Service Delivery" which contains a Data Center Evaluation Checklist for *evaluating data centers and colocation service providers* which is essentially a data center health check that looks useful as a thought provoker and discoverer of *gotchas* specific to your facility, in-house, cloud, or otherwise. It covers aspects of the data center design and operation under the following headings (http://www.fortrustdatacenter.com/wp-content/uploads/2013/09/FORTRUST_ White-Paper_Evaluating-Data-Center-and-Colocation-High-Availability-Service-Delivery.pdf):

- Location and risk mitigation
- Business stability and compliance
- Data center IT equipment
- Access and connectivity
- Physical security
- Operational process and service assurance controls, maintenance and lifecycle strategies
- Critical Systems Infrastructure Management and Capacity Planning

Downtime Reduction Initiatives

It is possible to reduce downtime in an existing installation by taking hopefully nondisruptive actions on the system. IDC has reported on the *positive impact* on downtime of implementing certain initiatives in operations scenarios and these are summarized in Table 5.7.

Low Impact Outages

It is possible for a system to fail and an application can continue to be used, for example: a client/server application designed so that data entry can continue on the client in the event of server system failure:

- A standby system takes over
- A message queuing application where the *sender* retains the messages until the failed *receiver* is active again

Table 5.7   Reducing Downtime via Specific Initiatives

Initiative Taken	Reduction (%)
Management tools	65
Upgrade servers, storage, networking	50
Failover clustering for internally faced applications	43
Standardization on single desktop operating system	30
Comprehensive PC security	28
Thin clients/blades	25
Deploying multiple antivirus, anti-spam solutions	15
Using industry best practices (ITIL CobiT)	13
Server virtualization	10

Source: IDC's Business Value Research, 2009. With permission from IDC.

Notes: Percentages *do not* add up to 100%. Effects were measured independent (*sic*) of each other.

It is also possible for an application to be effectively *unavailable* even though it is operational on an active system. This is the case where response time is so poor that the users cease to use the system and fall back to other methods of doing their work. Another example of effective nonavailability (very topical) is a badly designed website front end that users find difficult or impossible to use. Every part of the system is functioning correctly but the *application* is essentially unavailable—a virtual outage I suppose.

It should be clear now that availability is a complex area which needs much consideration when designing architectures for the creation and management of mission-critical systems, including websites. Throw the old idea of what an *outage* is out of the window.

Availability: A Lesson in Design

Just after my *1287 period*, I was involved with the use an IBM mark reader (cutely named a 3881 OMR) used in a UK Examination Board. It was employed for marking multiple choice questions from school examinations after a successful experience using an IBM bureau 1287 OCR (optical character recognition). Part of the system design was the use of a mechanical numbering unit on the reader and these printed numbers formed a vital part of the whole marking system and subsequent results processing.

On discussing this project with an engineer, he pointed out that the numbering unit on the mark reader was added as a design afterthought and was the least reliable part of the whole system. We quickly changed the flow of the marking system before we were confronted with irate parents complaining about botched exam results for their Cyrus II or Peggy Sue.

Don't base your design of service *processes*, even non-IT ones, on a SPoF, especially one which is unreliable and cannot be duplicated for redundancy. We got away with this one by what was essentially a *walkthrough* of the system with an expert in CIFA, a topic discussed next.

This particular SPoF would have not only affected the components below it in the hierarchy but could have effectively destroyed the usefulness of all those components above it as well as the validity of the whole work flow.

Availability: Humor in an Outage—Part I

In the early 1970s, I was heavily involved in OCR for IBM, a niche skill. One customer, a public utility, installed an IBM 1287 OCR machine and *driver* computer (IBM 360/22), which I oversaw and provided a bespoke course on programming and running the system. The system was running smoothly until, one day, I received an urgent call from the operations manager at the utility.

"We have a problem with the 1287 …" Without hesitating, I launched into my vast repertoire of possible causes: "Was it an 0C4 data check?," "A CCW chain overrun?," "Buffer overflow," "documents too small?" …

"No" came the reply "None of those. It just caught fire!"… and it had! This nearly spelled the end of my OCR career.

Problem determination: Assuming nothing and listening to the symptoms.

Availability: Humor in an Outage—Part II

The same customer as above but at installation time. When any 1287 OCR was installed, it was routinely broken into two large pieces and wheeled into place on low *bogeys*. In taking one piece to the machine room, the removal men got the part-1287 up to a speed such that it was difficult to stop. It crashed through the machine room doors, leaving one of them flat on the floor and seriously altering the orientation of the other.

A senior customer IT person arrived, surveyed the damage, and proceeded to go somewhat berserk. Instead of being worried about the doors, he was pointing excitedly at the 2311 disks whose software would drive the whole system.

Problem determination: One front panel was red, the other was blue, and he was not pleased.
Problem resolution: I drove back to the IBM office in Manchester with the red panel, exchanged it
   for a blue one from the IBM internal system, then drove back to the customer and *installed* it.
MTTR: About 3 to 4 hours—2 minutes to fix, the rest of the time travel (logistics time).

No SLA (for color scheme in this case), delivery of wrong part.

So What?

> You need to look at all these factors and weigh them up in the context of their possible impact on your organization. Nobody said it was easy, except perhaps a few well-meaning but glib papers and webinars. Mammoths take time to eat.

Aside from software tools, monitors, and stop watches, there are ways of understanding, enhancing, and improving availability. Some of these are outlined in Chapter 7, which covers nontechnical management disciplines and techniques. They are the keys to control and management of systems and services.

Application Nonavailability

The outage study below differs from many we have seen quoted in concentrating on the nonavailability of applications to the end user. This includes factors such as late start due to overrun of overnight housekeeping, backups, and so on, as well as hardware failures. Let us remind ourselves here about outages and their classification.

I have seen about 10 or 12 *outage* studies over the past 10 years and they are as follows:

1. All different
2. All the same
3. Show change with age

> **Question:** How can this be? Well, the percentages attributed to various causes are different, which accounts for (1). The surveys all show a wide range of factors responsible for outages, accounting for (2). Item (3) shows that *cyber* threats are coming to the fore—they did not exist in older studies or were unrecognized as such.

Traditional Outage Reasons

A service can be totally out of action (*state* = 0) or fully operational (*state* = 1). It can also be in a *Duke of York* mode (*state* = *unknown*) where the service survives but in a reduced or degraded mode, which may or may not be SLA compliant.

The first, study illustrated below,[*] is from a mature mainframe environment and was put together by a particularly meticulous IBM systems engineer (Figure 5.21). It probably reflects the mature environments we come across today, except there are no *malware* figures there. Note that it, and studies like it, assumes that the outages recorded are total, that is, *state* = 0.

The studies I have seen date from about 1987 and show increasing levels of detail. I don't think the actual numbers matter too much—just the fact that there are many areas of possible outages to examine and cater for in design and recovery.

Modern Outage Reasons

Figure 5.22 is from the report "2013 Enterprise Service Availability and Business Continuity Benchmark Survey" by *Continuity Software*[†].

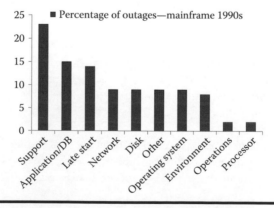

Figure 5.21   Outage causes 1: IBM mainframe study 1990s.

---

[*] Study was a Private Communication from Richard Mahony (IBM).
[†] Results from Continuity Software.

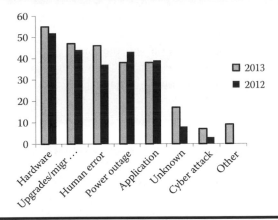

Figure 5.22 Outage causes 2: Analysis 2012–2013.

While these and similar charts show variations in the contributions made by different factors to nonavailability, they do illustrate the following points forcefully:

■ Hardware is only part of the availability equation and this is supported by other studies I alluded to above. The contribution of each cause of the nonavailability depends on the maturity of the hardware and software components of the system.
■ *Finger trouble* (*human error* in Figure 5.22) is a prime suspect and persists across the studies and the years.
■ Given the hardware RAS features of current servers, it is probably safe to assume that the IBM chart (Figure 5.22) will probably be more applicable to data center installations than other *vintage* charts, provided good service management disciplines are in place (see Chapter 7). However, the *cyber* attack aspect is absent or unrecognized in this study.
■ Only shown in Figure 5.22 is the increasing *outage* or sabotage threat from *malware* in all its manifestations, more than doubling in the interval 2012–2013.

Note: However, the *usual suspects* are involved at 1% level or another.

Summary

This chapter is somewhat of a gallop through the subject of availability and, in true immersion fashion, many of the topics covered will be dealt with again later. The key entities introduced are as follows:

■ The *probability density function* that can take the form of one of a number of mathematical distributions (see Terminology in Appendix 1)
■ The *cumulative distribution function* that is derived from the pdf and is a key quantity in reliability engineering.
■ The concepts of availability and availability probabilities and the law relating the overall availability of a *series* of components (Lusser's Law).
■ Graphs showing the reliability of *hardware* and *software* components as a function of time, the so-called *bathtub curves*.

- Some simple math of reliability and availability and two forms of the *equation* for *availability—raw* and, hopefully, more *elegant.*
- The handling of reliability and availability of components in *parallel* (or *redundant* configurations) and the simple math thereof. We have also seen combinations of parallel and series components with several examples, numeric and real-life cases (Cisco).
- Factors affecting availability and the topic of *outages* of systems, both *planned* and *unplanned.* Numerous types of outage have been discussed together with some discussions and references related to many of them.
- Some humorous but instructive anecdotes relating to outages and the *conclusions* and *lessons* that can be drawn from them.
- *Causes* of *outages* from two eras of computing, 20 years apart, demonstrating the relentless march of cybercrime in IT.
- *Lessons* that we can all learn and steps we should recognize can avoid or minimize outages or shorten their duration. These include knowledge of your business and IT, shared experience, and rigid management disciplines applied at all stages of inception through to operations, review, and revision.

Chapter 6

High Availability: Practice

Central Site

This chapter examines the practice of availability in its many guises in an objective fashion. The way vendors implement these practices is covered in Chapter 8.

Service Domain Concept[*]

In order to impose some structure on the blocks in the service configuration, it is convenient to split the configuration into *domains* of blocks with similar characteristics, for example, local server, local area network (LAN), wide area network (WAN), and remote server. In this section, we depart from the generic concept of *blocks* in a chain between service and service requestor. These domains can then be treated in the same mathematical way as the blocks were in the previous discussions. A schematic of a domain structure is illustrated in Figure 6.1.

Once the domains have an aggregate availability calculated, the math can be applied to a smaller number of items, three in the case discussed here, and their combined availability probabilities. This method has the advantage that specialists in various areas can concentrate on their area of expertise for calculating aggregate domain availability, for example, the network. It is important to include the *connection* between domains in the availability calculation.

It is using a diagram like that in Figure 6.1 or Figure 6.2 which will enable an IT department to develop the CFIA (component failure impact analysis) table in Chapter 7. In addition, a diagram like this (Figure 6.1 or Figure 6.2) will allow the calculation of reliability and availability percentages using the reduction technique we saw for handling parallel (redundant) components

---

[*] A February 2010 NIST publication *Guide for Applying the Risk Management Framework to Federal Information Systems* uses a similar system breakdown concept, albeit with a different name. See http://csrc.nist.gov/publications/nistpubs/800-37-rev1/sp800-37-rev1-final.pdf. They are called *subsystems* which is a subdivision of an IT system. To set the record straight, and to dispel any thoughts of plagiarism, my idea of these *domains* was developed c.1998/99 when at Sun Microsystems and incorporated in the HA paper of that time, which forms the basis of this book.

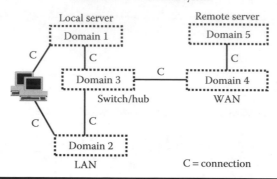

Figure 6.1   Schematic showing domains.

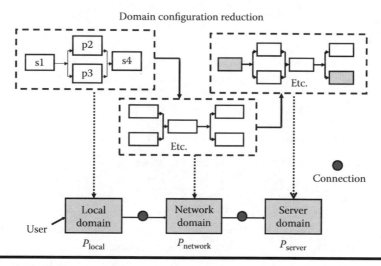

Figure 6.2   Domain block *reduction*.

in a system. Thus, the detailed set of parallel and series components in the hypothetical system is reduced to series of three equivalent blocks in the subsequent paragraph.

This concept of *domain reduction* is similar in principle to the reduction technique used in electrical engineering where a relatively complex network is reduced to a single *feed* to a newly designed addition to the network. This concept was dealt with earlier in the section on series and parallel components (section Availability Concepts in Chapter 5) and their mathematical treatment.

In the configuration shown in Figure 6.2, the overall probability of the whole end-to-end system being available is, according to Lusser,

$$P_{SYS} = P_{local} \times P_{network} \times P_{server}$$

(6.1)

Overall availability of domains

… and don't forget the connections and their reliability in the calculation. If they are relatively complex network components, refer to Chris Oggerino's *Network Availability* book referenced in Appendix 5.

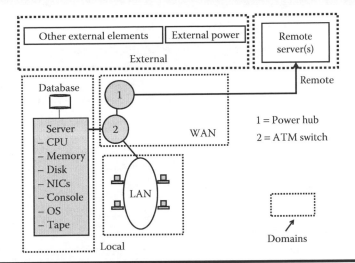

Figure 6.3 Domains in distributed systems.

Examples of real-life domains are shown in Figure 6.3. It isn't difficult to see that we couldn't have these reduced elements in parallel; hence, Lusser has to be applied to them. Breaking a system architecture up like this makes visualization simpler and will also help in CFIAs and walkthroughs in the design and review stages of a high availability and disaster recovery (HA/DR) project.

Sample Domain Architecture

Figure 6.3 represents a system with a local server, LAN, and switches plus a remote server to which this system connects on a real-time basis.

Hint: It implies that HA of the application system is not the only availability consideration in this arena. It is possible to *dilute* a highly available configuration to cater for a less critical application, which in essence means reuse of an existing configuration or architecture. Saves time, effort, and money, two of which are not renewable resources.

Note: A good backup/restore procedure is part of designing a HA solution but not if the hardware performing the backup/restore tasks is more liable to failure than the system it supports.

If a local service depends on external blocks or systems, then the service level requirements of that service will need to be reflected in the supporting services (see Figure 6.3). For example, if local service 1 depends on external service 2, then external service 2 must have availability and recovery characteristics equivalent to that of the local service or have any shortfall recognized in the service level agreement (SLA).

Planning for Availability—Starting Point*

There are about twenty or so main areas I will consider in the design and management of availability and its sibling discipline, recovery. *You are having us on* I hear you say. Not so, look at these areas, refer to the myriad survey items I have outlined and then set to work. An hour before I typed these words, I read a news flash on my internet service provider (ISP)'s system about my own bank's new IT system crashing through the floor.

Why? I don't know, I haven't read about it in detail yet but my money (if I have any left) is on *change management* as the bank has just split into two semiautonomous parts and I am not too sure how well that transition was managed. The 23 items (areas) are listed as follows:

1. System design/modification for availability
2. Engineering design (reliability, resilience, fault tolerance)
3. Application design and testing
4. Configuration (redundancy, uninterruptible power supply [UPS], redundant arrays of independent disks [RAID])
5. Outside consultancy (consultancies)
6. Vendor support
7. Proactive monitoring of components for performance and availability
8. Technical support excellence—both internal and external
9. Operations excellence
10. Retrospective monitoring/analysis and reactive problem determination
11. Application monitoring
12. Operations task automation
13. Reactive recovery (operations)
14. Using partnerships where feasible (learning from others)
15. Using change management
16. Using performance and capacity management techniques and tools
17. Using availability monitoring for early diagnosis, SLAs, and reporting
18. Operating theatre *cleanliness* of bridge/machine room
19. Anticipation of availability *gotchas* specific to the service or application
20. First-class teamwork and cooperation
21. Organizational relevance, appropriateness, and skills evolution
22. Security vigilance, the up-and-coming threat to service, and system availability
23. By choice of location

Most of these items are in the realm of internal IT responsibility but some rely on outside help. Item 2 is in the hands of the company evaluator/purchaser of vendor IT equipment (hardware and software) for mission-critical applications and services.

---

* I have just found (January 11, 2014) a 2003 paper by Oracle which promotes a similar theme to what follows here: http://docs.oracle.com/cd/B12037_01/server.101/b10726/operbp.htm#1008007. To avoid charges of plagiarism, I should point out that the origins of my *availability* list given in this section were laid down in the late 1990s in a paper I wrote when at Sun Microsystems.

The HA Design Spectrum

Most of the documentation on HA/DR I have come across majors on hardware, mainly redundant or fault tolerant, and, to some extent, software. My thesis is that the spectrum of activity needed to design, implement, and maintain a HA business IT system and recover from failures small and large (DR) is much, much greater. In section Planning for Availability—Starting Point, I have listed 23 areas (1 to 23) which can have an impact on the availability of business services that are IT-based. I am sure it will be evident that these areas can have a significant impact on the availability and nonavailability of any service or system.

> **Remember:** Focusing on availability and focusing on avoidance of nonavailability are not the same thing, if you think about it.

Availability by Systems Design/Modification

Highly available systems need to be designed or existing systems modified to meet the needs of crucial applications. The design stage with the tools and techniques which can help in this area are covered in Chapter 7. The design stage can be aided by judicious use of reliability block diagrams (RBDs) and some of the techniques and methods outlined in Chapter 7. Where feasible, relevant calculations should be employed and documented.

Availability by Engineering Design

This area lies directly with the hardware and software engineering functions within the hardware vendor organization but will cover things like error correction code (ECC), RAID, hot-swap devices, automatic software recovery (shadow), and so on (essentially RAS [reliability, availability and serviceability]). Nowadays, these features are offered by most hardware vendors who want to stay in business.

You can't really influence or use these features—it's just nice to know they are there. Software *engineering* is the responsibility of the vendors of commercial off the shelf (COTS) and middleware; the responsibility for in-house software reliability lies with the organization itself.

Self-Healing Hardware and Software

A useful (but marketing) article by IBM gives us the following information about self-healing, generally talked about as part of *autonomic computing*. In a nutshell, self-healing hardware applied to *chips* often means that built in conducting material is built in and used to *seal* gaps in broken circuitry (Figure 6.4).

> Autonomic computing will help customers reduce the cost and complexity of their e-business infrastructures, and overcome the challenges of systems management using systems that self-optimize, self-configure, self-heal and self-protect. System z plays a major role in the IBM autonomic computing initiative, since self-management capabilities available for System z will function as a model for other IBM servers. z/OS provides ... functions to address the goals of the IBM autonomic computing initiative.

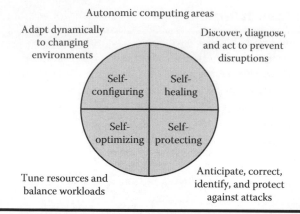

Figure 6.4 Autonomic computing areas (the goal).

Self-Healing and Other Items

In an article* from nearly 20 years ago, Jim Gray stated *Administration and maintenance people are doing a better job than we have reason to expect .... The only hope is to simplify and reduce human intervention in these aspects of the system.* Was he an autonomic computing sage?

Although a level of operations automation is available today, full autonomic computing is still a goal with the following requirements, among others:

- Detection of various faults and even automatic switching to backups where available (Chipkill memory, ECC cache, central processor, service processor, system bus, Multipath I/O, etc.)
- Plug and play and hot-swap I/O
- Capacity upgrade on demand
- Intrusion detection services
- System automation providing policy-based self-healing of applications, system and sysplex resources
- Security features such as LDAP, Kerberos, secure sockets layer (SSL), digital certificates, and encryption

In a *self-healing software system*,† the system monitors itself for anomalous behavior (after the *norm* has been established). When such behavior is detected, the system enters a self-diagnosis mode that aims to identify the fault and extract as much information as possible as to its cause, symptoms, and impact on the system (not the service, which it does not understand). Once these are identified, the system tries to adapt itself by generating candidate *fixes*, which are tested (assessed) to find the best candidate state.

The nearest we get to autonomic computing today is automation of various functions and some human intervention in others.

---

* "Why Do Computers Stops and What Can Be Done About It?" TANDEM Technical Report 85. June 7, 1984 PN87614 (Jim Gray).
† A.D. Keromytis, http://www.cs.columbia.edu/~angelos/Papers/2007/self-heal.pdf.

Availability by Application Design: Poor Application Design

It is possible to increase the availability of systems by judicious application design. Two examples are shown in Figure 6.5—using message queuing and implementing local spooling (and possibly error checking) in a client/server environment. Although the server part of the application is not available, recovery can be effected faster when it does become available—no reentry of transaction data and so on. The poor application design into two things: conventional programs and web applications.

Conventional Programs

For internally developed systems, the design and coding obviously have a bearing on the correct functionality and availability of the applications supporting business services based on IT systems. This is in the province of software availability and QoS (quality of service) covered in this chapter under section Software Reliability.

In general, experienced users will try to avoid poorly designed systems, which are sometimes developed without their input in terms of functions and usability. I have seen such user revert to manual methods where possible to avoid trying to use the unusable.

Web Applications

An illuminating article[*] lists 10 faults designed *to drive away your readers* from a customer-facing website (August 2012) given as follows:

1. Use impossible navigation on your site (see Figure 6.6).
2. Put up more advertisements than content.
3. Do not maintain your site (refer clients to other, non-existent, sites).
4. Require (*ask for*) too much information.
5. Be too cutting edge (require clients to be rocket scientists or Philadelphia lawyers).
6. Crash your customers' browsers.
7. Use sound on a business site (except as a valid, requested webinar, for example).
8. Put up too many images.

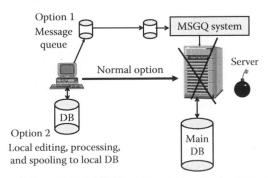

Application availability design schematic: options

Figure 6.5 Availability by design—two sample options.

---

[*] http://webdesign.about.com/od/webdesignbasics/tp/aa122101a.htm.

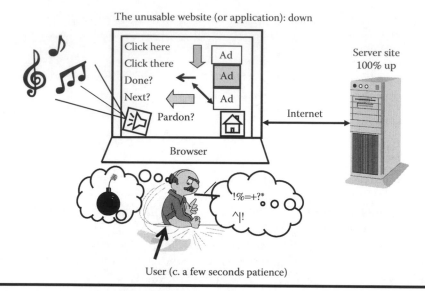

Figure 6.6   Nonavailability: the unusable website or application.

9. Embed too many tables.
10. Pay no attention to your readers' (*needs/feedback*).

These *failures* can cause a *logical outage* or, at the least, a partial outage by sending some or all potential customers (or internal staff) away from your site. One such site, guaranteed to lose a company business, and possibly the designer his job, is illustrated in Figure 6.5 in all its over-the-top glory.

I am a recognized authority on unusable and irritating websites which are, for all intents and purposes, *down* because they are not delivering the service they were designed for and possibly divert me to other sites to transact my business.

This *poor design* thesis is supported by the 2012 report "How to Stop Webpage Speed from Killing Your Marketing" by Limelight Networks, Inc., which indicates that when website page loading is slow, 62% of mobile device users abandon their session and nearly one-third of those never return. This is not good for business. What does that suggest to us?

Later Research: The seven-second *patience limit* in Figure 6.6 may be too optimistic. In 2009, a study by Forrester Research[*] found that online shoppers expected pages to load in two seconds or fewer—and at three seconds, a large share abandons the site. Only three years earlier, a similar Forrester study found that the average expectations for page load times were four seconds or fewer. See the *New York Times* article in the given URL (http://www.nytimes.com/2012/03/01/technology/impatient-web-users-flee-slow-loading-sites.html?pagewanted=all&_r=1&) where it talks about 250 milliseconds being the *patience limit*.

Monitoring performance and user experience at the sharp end of things should be mandatory for *designers* and *operators* of websites. Marketing people too have a major part to play in this as well, although you may have to advise them because they are unlikely to have read this book.

---

[*] Survey results from Forrester Research.

Availability by Configuration

Hardware

Some of the ways that the availability of vendor servers, associated hardware, and databases can be improved include the following:

- Hardware redundancy, for example, RAID, memory mirroring
- Putting CPUs on different boards wherever possible
- Putting memory on different boards wherever possible
- Putting I/O cards on different system boards wherever possible
- Connecting redundant resources to different power supplies
- Hot-swap/plug facilities for cards and peripherals
- Redundant operating system (OS) boot disks
- Duplicate consoles
- Failover software (OS, middleware, applications)
- Clustering*
- Employing fault-tolerant hardware and associated software
- Use of monitoring software independent of the system being monitored
- Other redundant *ecosystem* devices (fans, sprinklers, etc.)

The availability from basic hardware RAS to full fault-tolerant features comes at a cost as shown schematically in Figure 6.7. It may be that the level of availability aimed for in an enterprise depends on the final total cost of ownership (TCO). This diagram does not emphasize the other factors, both physical and logical, which can affect the users' view of the *usable* availability of a service that is governed by an SLA.

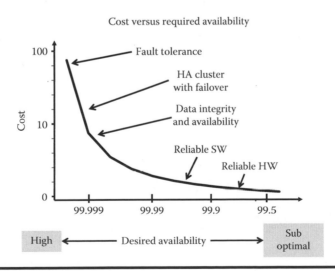

Figure 6.7   Costs of reliable/available configurations.

---

* There are various forms of clustering used here: active/cold, active/warm, active/hot, and active/active/standby as we discussed in Chapter 4.

Data

High availability of a service usually means high availability of the associated data. Some of the tools and techniques for achieving this are listed below.

- Using RAID techniques, weighing safety against recovery times, and operational update times (this affects response times of transactions)
- Disk mirroring—local or remote (geographic)
- Table layout, for example, partitioning, as in Oracle
- Duplicated logs and recovery files on separate drives
- Backup/archive software, part of DR
- Database *image* copy software (local, remote)
- Redundant backup hardware
- Worst-case scenario—key it in again from the beginning!

Networks

Networks, too are a vital link in the availability chain.

- Redundancy
- Integrated services digital network (ISDN) backup
- Alternate/virtual routing

Operating System

It goes without saying that if the operating system (OS) goes down, everything else underneath it goes down too. The availability of the OS is thus vital.

- Recovery features (shadow OS, online transaction processing [OLTP])
- Fast reboot after failure
- Automatic restart
- Journal file system
- Live OS maintenance facilities
- Logging, backup, recovery utilities
- Post-dump analysis

Environment

In recent years, the environment, particularly the weather, has been instrumental in causing severe outages of IT data centers. We can't do much about the weather except to be prepared for it and, when it does its worst, be able to recover from the outage(s) caused by it.

- UPS (sometimes a mass of batteries)
- Separate electricity supply from utility or own generators
- Over-configured cooling, fire sprinklers, Halon gas, etc.
- Machine environment cleanliness

As outlined before, it is not good economics to configure a system and network for availability where the costs of doing so outweigh the benefits. In most situations, HA solutions will be designed and managed on a financial *need* basis, taking account of the criticality of the applications to the business and the consequences of their failing.

Figure 6.7 (based on an IBM Redbook diagram) shows the cost effects of opting for configurations yielding higher and higher availability, but not to scale, just indicative of possible steep increases in cost for little availability return. It is opportune at this stage to emphasize that spending vast amounts of money on hardware and software HA will be to no avail if the service provided is unavailable or not performing according to requirements for other reasons.

By all means focus on the hardware/software area, but not at the expense of other areas as outlined *ad nauseam* in this book.

Availability by Outside Consultancy

Several vendors and IT consultancies offer specialist services related to achieving HA. These can cover availability assessments of current systems, availability design/modifications for new/current systems, remote proactive monitoring, creation of operational procedures for backup and recovery, and so on.

Your vendors would be a good start for HA assistance but others specialize in this kind of work as well.

Availability by Vendor Support

To ensure rapid response by vendors to outages caused by their products, it will be necessary to have suitable service contracts with those. This includes software and other vendors—not just hardware vendors. The chain of availability is only as strong, at theoretical best, as its weakest link. It is pointless having a 24 × 7 support contract for the hardware but only 8 × 5 on the database which supports the application. In addition, most IT vendors offer a remote monitoring and diagnostic service for proactive observation of system hardware and, in some cases, software. Ask your vendor(s) about these facilities and make sure you understand the difference between bronze, silver, gold, and platinum.

Availability by Proactive Monitoring

Given that suitable tools are available, it is often possible to predict where failures might occur if corrective action is not taken in time. Failures include hardware, database overflow, and other *full* conditions, which might lead to application nonavailability, plus the question of physical and logical security.

There are a number of other tools that can help with proactive monitoring of overutilized resources such as the network. Bottlenecks should be anticipated before they disrupt (change management) or degrade the service (capacity planning).

Remember, poor performance can often be construed by users as an outage of their system. A form of performance degradation is the presence of *rogue* or *runaway* tasks that may hog CPU and I/O resources. It is desirable to have a process for detecting and *killing* such tasks where necessary.

The key disciplines of *change, capacity*, and *performance management* are key ingredients in baking a successful *availability* cake, along with other aspects of service management.

Availability by Technical Support Excellence

To ensure maximum availability, it is key that staff supporting the Data Center Systems are adequately trained and work hand in hand with the incumbent vendor(s). Many outages can be attributed to *finger trouble* by technical support staff as well as operators—the ever-present *liveware* threat.

A paper by IDC* says that "to maximize the benefits of systems and technology ... an organization's workforce must be high performing and well skilled." This phrase applies in this section, the next, and, to a lesser extent, elsewhere. A study quoted in the paper indicates that these two main factors contributing to the success of the IT technology function are team skills (61%) and support of the technology vendor (19%). The figures quoted above are for IT managers' perceptions by looking at the key IT operating metrics:

- Data and backup recovery
- Endpoint/perimeter security
- HA
- Archiving and retrieval
- Client (*user*) management

The paper is well worth some study, especially as it points out that skills lag the use and need for various technologies in a form of *hysteresis*. An example today would be the recognition of security and performance as key to maintaining proper service availability but with a possible skills lag.

The items following are further examples of areas where support and operational errors can occur and often have far reaching implications for availability. There are doubtless many others.

> **Summary of availability by technical support excellence:** The major ongoing task here is *education* and maintaining currency of skills. It involves the organizational structure of IT and, believe it or not, some parts of the business. As availability targets are raised, the list of items that need consideration grows beyond just obvious hardware and software reliability. Remember, a little knowledge is dangerous.

Availability by Operations Excellence

Many outages of application nonavailability can be attributed to poor operations and technical actions. Vendors and their installations can quote several instances of *failure* caused by inadequately trained administration personnel.

One such instance is the recovery from failure of mirrored disks where the good mirror in brought into synchronization with the corrupt mirror instead of vice versa. Another example is switching a machine off to recover from a *stalled* situation. A further example is entering the wrong

---

* "Information Security and Availability: The Impact of Training on IT Organizational Performance," http://eval.symantec.com/downloads/edu/Impact_of_Training_on_Organizational_Performance.pdf., which was sponsored by Symantec.

time/date at some point causing havoc with the execution of *cron* jobs or applications, which rely heavily on accurate times/dates for their correct functioning.

These incidents were all too common in many modern environments and are still occurring today in all probability in IT organizations called *laggards* by some Gartner reports on various topics. See notes in the section Availability by Technical Support Excellence.

First Class Runbook[*]

Information and technical procedures in the Runbook should provide in support of the following areas:

- *System configuration information:* Build and configuration information about the installation is documented with mechanisms for update.
- *Routine housekeeping:* Recommended actions to be performed on a regular basis.
- *Platform tools:* Guidelines and procedures showing how to use the toolsets which vendors supply.
- *Startup/shutdown:* Technical procedures for starting up and shutting down hardware and software.
- *General administration:* Technical procedures to ensure that the platform is running in an optimum state such as checking logs.
- *Maintenance:* Technical procedures that upgrade or otherwise change the configuration of the platform such as adding new components and upgrading a running in Cluster environment.
- *Troubleshooting:* Information to help identify faults and ensure rapid escalation into the vendor(s).
- *Backup procedures:* These should be at least semiautomated but knowledge of them is needed if they don't run according to plan.
- *Recovery:* Recovery procedures to be run following a variety of fault scenarios.
- *Documentation library:* Electronic and web-based set of internal and vendor product and procedure manuals.

A Runbook should not attempt to replicate the information gained through training courses, but assumes an appropriate level of skill of operations and administration staff. It is not simply a prescriptive set of instructions—it should be a *living document*, updated regularly and containing received wisdom from ongoing operations.

Software Level Issues

I have observed that often, when pieces of software interact with each other, for example, that driving communications hardware, OS, and middleware, there are sometimes *glitches* in this interface. What happens then is they cease to communicate or cooperate causing an embarrassing *wait* between them but no tangible evidence of an outage. The key to this is to make sure interfacing software is at the level specified in the release documentation.

For example, if SW A only works with SW B at levels (0) and (–1) and you expect it to work with SW B at level (–2) or lower (earlier version), you may cause trouble. This happened several years ago with a pair of IBM communications controllers (3705s) where contact was lost because

---

[*] See Appendix 1 for a Runbook (operations manual) overview.

each controller was waiting for the other to reply in some way (*ack* [acknowledgement] or *nak* [negative acknowledgement] or similar). There was no indication of an outage except an embarrassing *nothingness*, followed by similar.

System Time

Some errors that result in nonavailability of applications are independent of hardware failures. An example is the incorrect setting of system clocks by administrators. This can result in *cron*-related jobs being run at the wrong time or even wrong day. Some installations keep their system clocks synchronized to a reliable external clock, such as the Rugby (UK) clock. There will be others which provide this facility.

Some installations reduce *finger trouble* issues by using software to automate times and other things, such as job scheduling and backup of databases. Previously, this was thought to lead on to the nirvana of the unattended or *dark* machine room, which is illustrated technically in Figure 6.8.

Performance and Capacity

Rigorous *performance* and *capacity* management are essential if the system appears to the end user to have stalled because of very poor response times. To him or her, the application is in essence unavailable. These disciplines are not covered in any detail in this book because they are somewhat detailed and I believe that a little knowledge is more dangerous than none. I therefore recommend the use of other resources for these tasks.

Data Center Efficiency*

It goes without saying that in data centers, *running a tight ship* should be the watchword to provide against outages.

> Automation is typically the next step in the data center journey. Introducing higher levels of automation enables greater levels of flexibility and helps support even higher levels of availability. Greater reliance on automation tools and technologies offloads manually intensive tasks for system administrators, reduces error rates and ensures the performance of applications against their SLAs. (from the referenced IBM report)

The major ongoing task here, as before, is *education* and maintaining *currency* of skills.

Availability by Retrospective Analysis

This is essentially the data analysis part of root cause analysis (RCA—see Appendix 1) should it be required. When errors occur, it is sometimes possible to interrogate log files post-event (performance, change, OS, etc.) to ascertain what the cause of an outage was and any attendant circumstances that might be included in the RCA and operations documentation. Manual operations logs (handwritten or perhaps PC-based) can also offer clues to outages if they are kept as working documents.

---

* IBM report called "Data Center Operational Efficiency Best Practices," http://docs.media.bitpipe.com/io_10x/io_105085/item_542158/Data_Center_Study.pdf.

Dark machine room

Figure 6.8   The unattended (*dark*) machine room.

Digital Equipment Corporation (DEC) used to supply a leather-bound operations log book in the heady days of good business. These may or may not avoid a similar outage occurring again as can *déjà vu* from observant technical support.

Exactly what can be done further here depends on what the relevant vendor and associated third parties can offer in the areas of monitoring. There is a philosophy of mine, which says *capture everything that changes or moves and worry about whether it is of any use later.* If you haven't got it you can't do anything with it and you can always delete it when it is past its *sell by* or *useful date.*

Availability by Application Monitoring

In recent years, COTS software, particularly Enterprise Resource Planning (ERP), has been subject to monitoring. This is often provided by the COTS vendor but often by vendors of systems management software, such as BMC and Tivoli. In fact, some ERP packages provide HA functions for their software in conjunction with operating on, and cooperating with, hardware clusters and other HA facilities.

The development of problem determination, backout and recovery procedures, and training are vital to increasing application availability by reducing downtime. These procedures will obviously depend on the application(s) in question.

Availability by Automation

We have alluded to this earlier but the idea of automating activities is receiving acclaim for various reasons, including productivity, speed, and the elimination of many (not all) user errors. Keep an eye open for this topic which is gaining ground and whose nirvana, full autonomic computing, is illustrated in Figure 6.4. Torches with long-life batteries or *fully* automated procedures are needed to function in this environment.

Remember that automation has degrees of sophistication and effectiveness and is not yet fully autonomic computing.

There is still the need for

- Understanding of your IT operations and areas *ripe* for automation. You might choose to run a Delphi session on the subject supported by a BIA (business impact analysis)
- Correct choice of tools

- Effective use of automation the tool(s)
- Ongoing operations skills to reduce *finger trouble*
- Other items specified in various places in this book

You will find an increasing number of articles about this topic and often accompanied by product descriptions.

There are numerous existing articles on automating backup and even DR, for example, at the given URL (http://www.itbusinessedge.com/blogs/infrastructure/time-to-automate-your-disaster-recovery-program.html). For others, search on *backup automation, disaster recovery*. See section Automation: The Solution? in Chapter 2.

Availability by Reactive Recovery

This is the normal operational actions for a problem—detect, locate, identify, and fix. Recovery from failure is a key element in availability management. Recovery after a problem occurs is reactive but proactive monitoring can prevent problems from occurring in many instances. This latter might be called *virtual recovery*, whereas reactive recovery is very real. An example of proactive recovery would be the servicing or replacement of parts which show soft errors above a recommended threshold.

A second example might be a tuning exercise undertaken when a service's response time is increasing and might eventually break some clause in an SLA.

When proactive actions do not avoid problems, then thorough, documented recovery procedures (often known as *Runbooks*) need to be in place.

The following example illustrates the scope of problem determination and recovery. Procedures such as that listed in the example need to be *living* procedures, modified in light of experience of availability issues.

Example 1: Operations Procedures—Recovery

Application: Online orders
System element: Opsys1 operating system
Proactive monitoring information: Opsys1 console
Problem determination: PROB09
Auto-recovery facilities: Automatic reboot
Availability architecture: Shadow OS
Business impact: Delayed or lost orders
Impact (H/M/L): H
Recovery procedures: REC07 if auto reboot fails
Estimated recovery time: 10 mins
Recovery contacts: Service desk × 3456, technical support × 4567
MTBF this type: 1500 hours
Last occurrence: 13:45, December 5, 2013

There are tools, usually tied to vendor products, for automating some aspects of Runbook development. Ideal Runbooks are online and maintained religiously. Procedures such as the example given above will need to be developed for the other *elements* in the service chain between user and the servers and within the servers.

It is obvious that online operations procedures are more effective and maintained *but* don't put them on the system(s) you are monitoring, for obvious reasons. Use a separate PC and duplicate it (see Availability Monitoring section). This should be repeated for other parts of the chain of hardware and software from end user to the applications.

Another perspective on recovery is to classify problem determination by domains, which were discussed in section Service Domain Concept. For example, consider the following as usable domains:

- Remote server domain recovery
- LAN domain recovery
- WAN domain recovery
- External domain recovery, for example, external power supply
- Server recovery
- Data recovery
- Application recovery
- Recovery of other vital components and/or peripherals

Recovery Times: The time to recover (MTTR) will be between two values:

$$T_{\text{MAX}} \text{ and } \sum T_i$$

where:

T_{MAX} is the longest component recovery time for completely overlapped recovery

ΣT_i is the total of the individual recovery times (T_i) for totally nonoverlapped recovery—end-to-end recovery

It is important that the service agreements for each block in the service configuration match the availability requirements. For example, it is not feasible to have a 7 × 24-hour service agreement for relational database management system (RDBMS) databases and only a 5 × 8-hour agreement for the vendor's hardware or other components of the service configuration. This covers things like asynchronous transfer mode (ATM) switches, software, and application cover.

Availability by Partnerships

It is usually the case where systems experience faults or crash that there will be more than one vendor who may need to help in problem determination and resolution. If these vendors do not cooperate, there is often *finger pointing* or *not our product* activity. Cooperating vendors can aid in designing HA systems and reduce problem determination and recovery time in an installation. They should also be on hand to expedite recovery from failures involving their products.

It may also be beneficial to consult other organizations on IT matters like HA/DR where there is a common interest (and no business competition).

There is synergy and cross fertilization of ideas in this sort of cooperation, but your company may have to initiate it.

*Availability by Change Management**

Bank loses data. This was all over the UK newspapers, radio and television in June 2012 when a major bank had an outage, blocking updates, transfers and withdrawals from the bank. It transpired that there had been a *scheduling software upgrade* which resulted in the non-availability issue. The outage, which had wide-ranging effects, lasted several days and, although the bank said it would underwrite any consequential loss, it was a case of "egg all over their faces."

> … and lo and behold, there was another outage at the same bank in early March 2013, this time attributed to *hardware*. Although the fix apparently took effect after 3 hours, there were ripple effects on other institutions connected with the bank as well as the bank itself.

Of course, the hardware was probably fine in the first instance but this was a typical *logical outage* which hardware at 99.999 availability would not have solved—only cost the customer a lot of money. As it transpired, the *caper* costs the bank a direct £125m and an unknown amount in customer defections.

Change management is mentioned elsewhere in this document but suffice it to say here that one of the prime considerations in changes is that they should be capable of being *backed out* if they fail. This doesn't mean that any outages caused by the original change will not be serious. *Risk-laden* changes ought to be pre-tested if possible.[†]

It transpired that a piece of scheduling software was involved but it isn't known who *goofed*— the software or operations liveware.

Availability by Performance/Capacity Management

We have seen that performance issues can masquerade as outages when user work is seriously interrupted or degraded by poor responses. These topics are covered in Chapter 7 but suffice it to say what the fundamental differences between them are discussed subsequently.

Performance *management* is a proactive *operational* exercise, mainly concerned with the *here and now* of resource consumption, response, and turnaround times and the provision of data for capacity management. On the other hand, performance *monitoring* is more of a passive exercise, whereas capacity *management* (or planning) is the prediction of, and planning for increased resource utilization in systems with a view to proactive solutions. It is *tactical* and, in some cases, *strategic*.

Capacity management has two major legs (or arms):

■ The use of performance data and its intelligent extrapolation based on business volumes and their resource requirements.
■ The estimation of resource requirements for new business applications and services, often using operational data from similar workloads already running. It is important to understand the difference between a *business transaction* and the subsequent multiple *system* transactions when assessing resource requirements.

---

[*] Excellent document and checklist set on Change Management at http://www.cisco.com/warp/public/126/chmgmt.pdf.
[†] Amazon website's "caper" in October 2012.

The two disciplines, performance and capacity, should not be confused in their objectives, methodology, conclusions, or output. One is tactical and operational, the other planning and strategic.

Availability by Monitoring

It is now fairly common to have a pseudo-client accessing services, such as websites and business applications. The *client* acts as a real user submitting transactions or reading data from a live system. It is plain to see that if this *client* is to monitor availability as well as other items, it must survive outages of the system being monitored. Common sense dictates that this *client* be duplicated. For example, one at the center and one in an end user location or locations. A complete center outage can be compensated for by the continuing activity of a remote *client*. This could not happen if component and redundant component are side by side in a flooded room.

An adjunct to monitoring availability will be tools for measuring KPIs (key performance indicators), for example, for performance and capacity management. They will assist in situations where the users consider a system *down* based on its performance characteristics (see Chapter 7).

Availability by Cleanliness

The machine room should resemble a hospital operating theater (the better ones anyway) in its cleanliness. Coffee, hamburgers, and sundry other comestibles have no place in a machine room for fear of contamination. I have seen a console keyboard ruined when coffee was spilt on it and the miscreant tried to dry it with a hair dryer the keyboard just buckled and died. The system it was controlling wasn't pleased and the end users didn't think much of it either. There was no duplicate console facility.

Anything exposed that carries data, such as a tape reel, should not be handled with dirty hands. Another possible *gotcha* can be introduced by extraneous electronic equipment in the machine room because it can be picked up by the circuitry in the systems, possibly causing bits to drop off at random.

Availability by Anticipation

One of the benefits of experience is that a person can judge where problems might arise and concentrate more effort in those areas. Such experience ought, where feasible, to be enshrined in operational Runbooks so that less experienced personnel can learn. For example, if operations staff have found by experience that when item 1 happens, items 6 and 7 are likely culprits and should be checked out first, it provides valuable insight into problems and should be recorded in operations Runbooks. This allows other, less experienced operators to minimize problem determination time and hence recovery time.

In the future, this might be done by software that is capable of learning and making judgments. In the meantime though, it is a human's task to learn from experience and pass this learning on.

Predictive Maintenance

Predictive maintenance, as the name implies, is the maintenance or replacement of parts of systems (generic) based on certain criteria that might indicate imminent or near-future failure. The technique is very often applied to mechanical systems such as oil rigs and large machines but is a little harder to fit into an IT environment. It is still worth investigating for applicability to your IT environment, an example being the detection, logging, and analysis of *soft* errors in system parts. An IBM Redbook gives an overview of the topic in the first chapter of http://www.redbooks.ibm .com/redpapers/pdfs/redp5035.pdf.

There is also an Aberdeen Report "Asset Management: Using Analytics to Drive Predictive Maintenance" which, although mainly applicable to manufacturing, has uses in *telecoms and IT management*, according to the report Abstract (http://aberdeen.com/Aberdeen-Library/8380/ AI-predictive-asset-analytics.aspx.aspx).

> It should now be glaringly obvious that there are many bases to be covered in the search for HA and I have outlined quite a few here. You may think of others. If you do, elaborate on them and tell others (not your competitors though).

Availability by Teamwork

Marty Brounstein in *Managing Teams for Dummies* lists 10 qualities necessary for effective team-work and the headings of team member qualities are reproduced here.

1. Demonstrating (*personal*) reliability
2. Communicating constructively (this includes documentation in my opinion)
3. Listening actively (remembering he or she has two ears and only one mouth)
4. Functioning as an active participant (*no passengers or deadweights*)
5. Sharing openly and willingly (information, knowledge, experience) (*no bragging though*)
6. Cooperating and pitching in to help (nothing to contribute here—fetch the coffee)
7. Exhibiting flexibility (change is inevitable—swim with it, not against)
8. Showing team commitment (no *sickies* to watch a ball game)
9. Working as a problem solver (especially useful in Delphi exercises)
10. Treating others in a respectful and supportive manner (*giving strokes*)

In my usual style, I would add another quality to an excellent list—*good timekeeping* and a quotation to support item 3 in the list given above:

> I like to listen. I have learned a great deal from listening carefully. Most people never listen. Ernest Hemingway

However you define *good* teamwork, a good team will design, implement, operate, and maintain a better HA/DR system than a *so-so* or downright *poor* team. Also, a team is probably only as good as its worst player.

Availability by Organization

HA and DR are (or should be) becoming more important in business IT, which means that IT is evolving. It stands to reason that if business IT and its requirement are evolving, then the organization of people using and supporting business IT should evolve in line with the much-vaunted principle of *aligning IT with the business*. What does this mean in practical terms?

- Appropriate parts of the business community should be HA-aware, meaning they understand the principles of HA/DR, what it means to the company's business and what their role in it is. Each business unit, however that is defined, should have an HA/DR-aware person, not necessarily full time, plus a deputy or substitute
- IT skills should be regularly reviewed in light of the evolution of IT requirements and the evolving nature of any threats to the stability of that IT, be it malware, performance, functionality, or anything else that might breach SLA requirements and specifications.

Availability by Eternal Vigilance

This is a key factor in keeping the show *on the road* and relates to the *security aspects of systems and services*. A compromised system may be 100% available but unable to perform its allotted functions because of lost functionality or data caused by *malware* attack. This item never appears on outage surveys over about 10–15 years old as the problem was virtually unknown, particularly in large organizations.

Today, it is not unknown. It may now be *known but it is not fully understood*. Moreover, even where it is understood, there is often little proactive activity in the monitoring, detection, and mitigation of such attacks. Such activity is encompassed in SIEM (Security Information [and] Event Management—Gartner 2005), outlined in Chapter 7 and other papers referred to in this book.

Analysis of security event logs helps security analysts detect and investigate advanced threats often missed by simple tools or manual methods. Good security analysis provides converged network security monitoring and centralized security information and event management. Threats are not necessarily what the EMC reference below calls *smash and grab* but often involve illicit seeding of malware entities on a system to facilitate malicious and potentially damaging access to systems and data.

There is also a *liveware aspect* to this area because software tools cannot really monitor people and they are potential *criminals*. Methods and processes need to be adopted and revised so that the opportunity for system damage by people—both internal and external—is reduced to a minimum. Even then, that minimum should be worked on in light of experience in one's own organization and in others, although companies are often loath to admit that their defenses have been breached.

Physical security beyond simple lock-and-key mechanisms is in use or available today to counter some liveware threats; some of them are listed as follows:

- RFID badges for unattended access
- Security personnel and normal identity badges*
- Face and iris recognition techniques
- Video/CCTV surveillance at entry points and round location/campus perimeters
- Fingerprint scanning
- Body heat detectors

Often, data theft is not just a case of stealing data by network or other nonphysical intrusion but by walking away with smaller systems completely, as happened more than once at one of the companies I worked for in the past. It was rumored that these systems were *stolen to order* as the stolen

---

* The late Edwin Nixon, when CEO of IBM UK visited the IBM Warwick site. As he signed in, the guard noticed his badge was out of date and refused him entry. He was about to explode when he realized that the guard was correct in what he did and commended him for his vigilance.

items were not just random pieces of IT equipment but complete systems. A solution here might be position sensing devices used to track stolen cars (*trackers*).

Availability by Location

It goes without saying that the location of data centers—primary and disaster—needs careful consideration, especially in areas prone to extreme weather conditions, earthquakes, *sink holes*, or other disruptive influences. For example, it is not recommended that you place your data center in the middle of the Bristol Channel as a location *finder* did in England based on information fed into a program.

You also need to consider the supply and possible resupply in emergency of

- People
- Power, water (controlled), other *eco* supplies
- Accommodation
- Documentation (copies of *current* documents)
- Communications—electronic and transport
- Medical support
- Other things connected with your IT and business and essential to its continued operation day to day

There are a number of articles on the web dealing with location selection but don't forget to think about your own particular business and needs. No *blind following* of checklists.

Final Words: If you understand these areas of availability, do something about them. If you don't, take advice and then do something about them. Don't pay a third-party lots of money for a report that sits on a shelf gathering dust. See references http://uk.emc.com/collateral/software/solution-overview/h11031-transforming-traditional-security-strategies-so.pdf; http://reports.informationweek.com/abstract/21/11076/Security/How-Attackers-Target-and-Exploit-Critical-Business-Applications.html?cid=SBX_iwk_fture_Analytics_default_newsletters&itc=SBX_iwk_fture_Analytics_default_newsletters.

A Word on Documentation

This is the bane of the life of everyone connected with IT and is worth a word. Documentation is really a history lesson which can not only teach us things but get us out of a tight spot. It is needed in program development, design, implementation, operations, and other areas. Some may be temporary, some permanent but all should be kept. Documentation should be accurate, accessible, useful, and concise and should be used *to avoid repeating the mistakes of history*.

I was heavily involved in the Y2000 *caper* when at Sun Microsystems and at the end of the day I wondered, like everyone else, what the fuss was all about. Planes did not fall from the sky, global positioning satellite (GPS) kept on working, and a 1001 other disasters failed to materialize. The main reason for the disquiet was that it was not easy to find out where the two digit dates were in the IT universe and so we speculated what might happen if the two digit feature was everywhere. Why? Because we weren't sure. Why weren't we sure? Because in many cases the relevant documentation either didn't tell us or didn't exist.

Simple but true. Documentation matters. Period.

Network Reliability/Availability*

During the World War II, broken lines of communication were bypassed by using carrier pigeons or dispatch riders on motor bikes to ferry messages between groups of military people. Before the advent of the telegraph (*singing wires*) in the United States, Wells Fargo and the Pony Express carried out the task of delivering mainly urgent communications across large distances. These backup processes are not really feasible in today's globalized environment, suffering as they did from very high latency, absence of redundancy, and the danger of being attacked by arrows and rifles.

Today's networks differ from those used as recently as 20 years ago in their sophistication and the arrival of embedded and microcoded software, operating in areas where *dumb* hardware used to sit. This brings benefits but has the downside that there is more to go wrong in data and protocol paths through the network.

Protocols and Redundancy

Network availability is somewhat different from hardware and software because it involves both hardware, software, microcode, or embedded software and the design of alternate (redundant) paths for traffic denied access to the regular path. These paths need not necessarily be the same type as the failing path, for example, an organization might use virtual private network (VPN) backup to stand in for a failed non-VPN circuit.

Of course, hardware redundancy can still be employed in dual network interface cards (NICs), switches, and so on. A prime example of redundancy in networks is the use of *timer* servers other than the primary server or perhaps secondary *DNS* servers.

Protocols also have a part to play in data shipping. For example, UDP sends data in very large *chunks*, initially without too much regard to whether it reached its destination intact. TCP on the other hand, politely asks the recipient whether he received a block of data intact and, if not, resends it.

The result is that UDP is faster but TCP is more caring about data in its charge. One thing to watch out for is the emulation of one network protocol by another. It is likely that the resulting performance might be dire and, although staying *available*, may blow an system network architecture (SLA) out of the water. I have seen it in the 1970s with DEC emulation of system network architecture (SNA) protocols.

Many protocols employ ECC and LRC (longitudinal redundancy checking) to ensure the integrity of transmitted data.† Protocol communication across heterogeneous systems may need consideration for performance issues.

---

* See http://www.ciscopress.com/articles/article.asp?p=361409 and the book referenced therein, plus the *Chris Oggerino* book referenced in Appendix 5.
† Some telecommunications protocol redundancy methods have been *lifted* to use in disk data transfer implementations, theory, and other literature.

Network Types

Circuit switch (connection oriented) and *packet switch* (connectionless) networks are what we normally come across in IT communications. Circuits are essentially paths between communicating entities and is assigned to that *conversation* for its duration. Packet switching involves breaking up a message into components and routing it by different paths or *hops* to its destination, where it is reconstituted. The header information for the latter contains, among other things, the destination for the message.

The technologies used for these transmissions might be *frame relay* (FR) or ATM. Packet switch technology and TCP/IP protocol is used for Internet traffic where security is important in such an *open* environment. There is a trade-off in networks of security versus performance, depending on the protocol adopted and whether acceleration techniques are employed.

Network Outages

It is difficult to pinpoint a single point of failure (SPoF) in a network as there are normally alternative paths/routes available for the traffic to traverse. In a reasonably well-designed network, it is unlikely that there would be a SPoF component causing an outage. A logical outage due to overload is more feasible however. Network outage causes include the following:

- Complete or partial failure of (multiple) hardware and software components
- Power outages supporting network components
- Microcode/embedded software failure in components
- Unavoidable scheduled maintenance
- Configuration errors by operations (liveware)
- Acts of nature, floods, earthquakes, and so on
- Misplaced digging equipment and the like[*]

A University of Michigan study of an IP service provider found the following breakdown of outages:

- 23% router failure, including hardware/software faults and Distributed Denial of Service (DDoS)
- 32% link failures, including fiber cuts and network congestion (*performance*)
- 36% for router maintenance, including software/hardware upgrades
- 9% for miscellaneous reasons

Another study indicated that *router software* failures caused 25% of all the router outages, with the *router control-plane* the biggest culprit within that percentage.

> ***Note:*** We should remember that MTTR includes reestablishment of the fully operational system or *ramp-up* time. Actual repair time in these situations may be low but any reconfiguration required will take time and can introduce human errors into the actual recovery of components—the *double whammy* of the recovery procedure.

---

[*] I have seen a photograph of a cable passing through the middle of a sewer pipe in a UK water board as the constructor could not be bothered to go round it.

Network Design for Availability

A network has two possibly conflicting demands on its design: costs and HA. The availability and performance characteristics will be embedded in an SLA and the balancing act is to meet them with a network implementation that doesn't *break the bank* and which can be monitored and managed. Some key elements and considerations of a highly available network are as follows:

- SLA requirements covering security, response, and recovery times
- SPoF elimination
- Reliable and maintainable hardware and software (high MTTF and low MTTR, ramp-up)
- Redundancy versus costs incurred by the users
- Redundant components (twin NICs, routers, etc.), for example, router clustering* for WANs
- Nonstop routing around failed links
- Rapid failure detection mechanisms (monitors)
- Rapid intrusion detection mechanisms (monitors)
- Rapid replacement/fix operations but this will of course depend on the network design and the location of the components
- Ensuring bandwidth requirements are met via modeling or other calculations on traffic peaks, peak-to-average, seasonal variations, and other key figures
- Operations, support, recovery procedures, and operator training
- Documentation—design and operations (Runbooks)

An initial network design should have a RBD drawn up and any SPoFs identified and supplied with redundant partners—active or passive.

Redundancy configurations in networks may be

- One for N (1:N) where there is one standby component for every N active component
- One for one (1:1) where there is a standby component for every active component
- One plus one (1 + 1) which is similar to 1:1 but here the traffic is transmitted simultaneously on both active and standby components (active/active in our terms)

It will only be possible to make reliability calculations if there is real data available for the chosen components, that is, MTBF/MTTF figures. MTTR (repair) times may also be available from the vendor which can put the design on a *quantitative* basis. Obviously, which option is chosen will be dictated to a large extent by costs (TCO).

For hints and tips on HA network design considerations, see the presentation at http://ws.edu .isoc.org/data/2006/976764518448225b69b1c0/redundant.ppt.

There is an apt quotation in the presentation above which says

> In the Internet era, reliability is becoming something you have to build, not something you can buy. That is hard work, and it requires intelligence, skills and budget. Reliability is not part of the basic package. Joel Snyder—*Network World Test Alliance October 1, 2000*

---

* http://www.fatpipeinc.com/router_clustering.php.

Endnote: A new US FCC body—Public Safety and Homeland Security Bureau (PSHSB). Within PSHSB, there is a system (US only I think) for reporting major network outages. See the presentation "Resilient Network Design Concepts" if interested, otherwise go to Network Security source (http://transition.fcc.gov/pshs/services/cip/nors/nors.html).

The Cisco website documentation also provides some good general network reliability material.

This HA documentation also includes a presentation on network HA (http://www.cisco.com/en/US/prod/collateral/iosswrel/ps6537/ps6550/prod_presentation0900aecd8031069b.pdf) plus "Cisco IOS Management for High Availability Networking: Best Practices White Paper" (http://www.cisco.com/c/en/us/support/docs/availability/high-availability/25562-ios-management.html#t3).

The first presentation mentioned above includes some suggestions for improving hardware and software availability in networks, summarized in Table 6.1. Cisco documentation is very often generic enough to help in designing networks for HA and, incidentally, for implementing change management.

The presentation also outlines what it calls a *HA tool kit* that lists the entities that offer resilience at the following levels (foil 237 in the presentation above):

- Application level
- Protocol level
- Transport/link level
- Device level

Network Security

Basic network hardware is not so complex as to be riddled with poor reliability and, to a lesser extent, the software. What can cause a network to be unavailable are security issues like DDoS, data stealing, and all the other nasty things that malcontents might try to do to and via a network. Conventional wisdom in this area suggests the following:

Table 6.1 Improving Network Availability—Cisco

Improving Hardware Availability	*Improving Software Availability*
Load sharing redundant components	Improved software quality
Active/standby redundancy—processors, power, fans, line cards	Process independence—restart and protected memory
Active/standby fault detection	Routing processor switchover
Cards with high MTBF (100K hours)	Nonstop forwarding (NSF)
Separate control and forwarding plane	Line card switchover
Low node rebuild time	Faster reboot (*our ramp-up time!*)
Nondisruptive (*hitless*) upgrades	Routing convergence enhancements
Robust component hot-swap	Uplink fast/backbone fast/HSRP (hot standby router protocol)

- *Protect* the network by correct design and configuration.
- *Monitor* the network for normal problems and to *detect* large increases in traffic that can't be explained in terms of business growth, year/month end/special offer processing and the like.
- *React* to warnings from monitoring, especially those suggesting malware is at work.
- *Refine* the network design and monitoring method where necessary.

The same wisdom suggests tackling:

- Defense in depth—firewalls, anti-malware software, segmented networks, role-based access, and other controlling mechanisms
- Use of cryptography employing strong modern algorithms (AES, superseding DES)
- Rigorous access, authentication, and authorization mechanisms (AAA)*
- Separation of duties to avoid staff fraud and *mutiny* (*but not spying on friends*)
- Endpoint security—vital in days of wireless access and access by BYOD (bring your own device and plug it into our network)
- Try to secure web-based data and information, perhaps by implementing *atomic* services in a service-oriented architecture, which is essentially a form of *security hardening* as discussed elsewhere under software reliability

Make no mistake, someone, somewhere wants your data and he or she may be cleverer and more network *savvy* than you—unless you do something about it.

It boils down to being alert and following up with *search and destroy*. Security, as I never tire of saying, is the up and coming threat to the HA of services and of the data they rely on (see http://www.csoonline.com/article/print/342820 and references therein).

File Transfer Reliability

Despite being a world of websites, OLTP, clouds, and other clever things, file transfers still figure in most business organizations. In terms of the reliability of transmission and speed (a possible logical constraint), there are a number of software packages that offer nearly lossless transmission and transfer speed enhancements. I have deliberately not used the term *availability* in the context of file transfer because that is essentially a function of the network itself. When sending files (data, media, Word, Excel, etc.) over a network, it is nice to know after the transmission that

1. It got there in one piece and as transmitted, so to speak.
2. It got there in time for some important subsequent processing where delays might have a deleterious effect.
3. It only went to, and can be accessed by, the person(s) it was meant for.

What needs to be done to achieve this? Well, an Axway paper about secure file transfer lists 10 of the reasons that file transfer protocol (FTP), part of the TCP/IP family, may not be appropriate for reliable file transfer:

---

* Access to data is a fairly simple concept, authentication means *prove you are who you say you are* and authorization means *we know who you are now but there are certain things you can't do and places you can't go.*

- It has no encryption capabilities (*open to wire-tapping*).
- It does not protect usernames and passwords (*ditto*).
- It does not have integrity checking (*over and above LRC*).
- It has no checkpoint-restart feature (failure/total resend takes time).
- It does not offer nonrepudiation (*proof that files have been sent*).
- It cannot compress data (*possible speed/performance issue*).
- It cannot *push* or *pull* files unless the client is available (*uncertain wait times can result—SLA issue?*).
- It does not provide visibility (*via a suitable monitor facility*).
- It can be hard to manage.
- It is not really free (security features need bolting on for full function).

The reasons behind these drawbacks are explained in the actual paper at http://resources.idgenterprise.com/original/AST0087939_axway_whitepaper_mft_survival_guide_en_0.pdf.

In addition, an Attachmate white paper on its FileXpress product lists typical requirements under "Essential Elements of Secure File Transfer" as follows:

- *Encrypt* files for transfer to ensure that only *intended* recipients have access to data in those files.
- *Authenticate* the identity of partners in the transfer as *bona fide* recipients. This might entail using digital certificates using SSL protocol. This may be in addition to the standard *user name* and *password* mechanism.
- Ensure the *integrity* of files transferred by using a secure file transfer solution rather than straight FTP.
- *Audit* and *report* on the transfer process. File transfer can take place at any time and present high volumes, and reporting on this transfer, perhaps on an exception basis, is desirable. Typical information in this process might include success/failure, who or what was authenticated as a recipient and other management data for capacity planning and SLA reporting.
- Use *suitable products*, of which FileXpress is just one, makes it possible to
  - Make files available to partners and customers across z/OS, Windows, Linux, and UNIX.
  - Allow partners and customers to upload files to the organization's servers—a dangerous activity without rigid security.
  - Support a host of FTPs required externally by authorized parties, for example, HTTPS, FTP, FTPS, SFTP, and PGP protocols.
  - Delegate administration tasks to partners and help desk personnel who have the appropriate authorization.

Osterman Research also published a survey on file transfer in December 2013. It is called "The Need for Enterprise-Grade File Transfer" and was sponsored by Attachmate. One theme is that *email continues to be the primary platform that individuals use to send electronic content*, used in 99% of the organizations surveyed, while two-thirds use *vanilla* FTP and only about one-quarter use enterprise-grade file transfer.

The survey lists trends in file transfer which can necessitate *industrial strength* file transfer methods, including the need for better data security, organizations becoming more globally distributed, and remote working (BYOD) becoming more common. The report also outlines other issues affecting standard file transfer methods such as email and FTP and mentions the lack of security and cost implications of file transfer via data burned onto CDs or DVDs (see www.ostermanresearch.com and reports within this URL).

End Note: If *file transfer* is used in an organization and it is connected with *important business* functions, then such file transfer needs attention at the HA design stage just like any other aspect of a service needing HA. A business impact analysis (BIA) should qualify this when carried out.

Network DR

It is somewhat difficult to see a whole network becoming unusable at one time and having to failover to a secondary or backup network of similar capacity—that would be expensive. Normally, network component redundancy will take care of outages by switching routes in some way. The DR issue for networks is *how do we build them so that when the primary server site is out for the count our users can still access the secondary (DR) site*. Not a simple task.

It is more than likely that a *DR* plan for the network will have to be drawn up between the IT department and network supplier(s) with the objectives that

1. It will transport the surviving users to the DR site (IP switching).
2. The RBD and other *homework* (RCA, walkthrough) on the backup transport has been done.
3. It will support the DR traffic, whose resource requirements will lie between *full production* traffic to that of a *skeleton* service for the mission-critical services (bandwidth, latency, etc.).
4. It won't cost the earth in over-engineered networks because item 3 was not carried out properly.

Articles about this topic abound on the Internet but most of them seem to be *selling* something rather than *educating*. Some flipchart markers and large pieces of paper are needed here to understand the company's network in *normal mode, modest recovery mode* (main site still active), and *full DR mode*. I think perspiration and inspiration are called for. Incidentally, there is a *checklist* about network DR in the given URL (http://searchstorage.techtarget.com/tip/Network-disaster-recovery-checklist).

Software Reliability*

Software reliability is defined as the probability of failure-free software operation for a specified period of time in a given environment. This is a similar definition to that for hardware reliability but that is where the similarity ends.

Software Quality

Software quality is a subject in its own right. Common causes of poor software quality (=reliability) are found in noncompliance with good architectural and coding practices. Suffice it to say that the

---

* See http://www.sans.org/reading_room/whitepapers/basics/bugs-biting_1135 and http://www.cs.colostate.edu/pubserv/pubs/Li-malaiya-p-li95.pdf.

quality of application software is a function of many other factors too, some of them human and therefore prone to incipient errors and subsequent failures:

- Design faults
- Poor or no reviews or walkthroughs
- Lack of standards—coding, interfaces, application programming interfaces (APIs), and so on
- Poor change management, especially if specifications change
- Development errors
- Software complexity and size
- User requirements not properly captured and/or not understood
- Misunderstanding of correctly specified requirements
- Suboptimal (*synonym for poor*) testing at various test stages
- Poor project management in some or all stages (*lack of granularity in timelines**)
- Technology or domain new to developers or programmers
- Poor coordination and synergy within a programming team
- The quality or incorrect use of third-party components, such as external libraries and functions, can have an adverse effect on software reliability for the following reasons:
  - The external software is inherently unreliable or experimental.
  - The usage of this software is incorrect in some way which is not readily apparent in testing.
  - Its interface with the *calling* program is not clear or consistent. This *calling* is important in high performance computing (HPC) where numerous libraries exist to aid scientific computations of all kinds.
  - The programmer does not know what he or she is doing.

Software errors do not necessarily cause obvious outages or crashes. They can be insidious and may simply produce erroneous output directly or be transmitted to other systems and applications. We are talking here about both commercial and scientific applications.

There is a subtle difference between the *reliability* of a piece of software and its *fault content*. One would expect a *high reliability* piece of software to have a *low-fault* content. However, a piece of software can contain multiple faults but they may be hidden in code paths (or subroutines or modules) that are only rarely executed. An example might be code which is only executed in a leap year on February 29th but is riddled with faults. Until that fateful day, it might be considered a model of reliability, and then on February 29th, the wheels fall off the IT service wagon. Here, the software may be 100% reliable, except for once every four years.

Software: Output Verification

Errors in output can be classed as *logical* whereas a crash of the software we can consider a *physical* outage, rather like a hardware failure in that it is very visible. Errors of the former type may not be

---

* This is vital in assessing progress and avoiding the *we are 90% finished boss* syndrome when nobody has any idea where the project item or phase is up to. I know, I've been there.

obvious until their inaccuracy results in tangible consequences, such as paying an invoice twice, invoicing a customer for the incorrect amount, or a returning space shuttle landing in Timbuktu instead of Florida. The physical errors become immediately apparent, but the logical ones may take some time to detect and can result in financial loss and an organization's credibility before they are.

The validity of any output should be verified by people versed in the application(s) domain.

Example 1

There was a case in space exploration* where some key measurements were quoted in metric (*cgs*) and others in imperial (*fps*). I think the errors were spotted before the flight. The program concerned may not have noticed because it was dealing simply with numbers and perhaps did not understand *units*. In this case, interfacing routines were written by different subcontractors who made different assumptions about units of measurements. The interface between the modules only passed values, which were presumably *unitless*, so the computations were correct for the units assumed.

Example 2

In my early IT days, I was given the task of writing a program in the new-fangled language RPG (report program generator), ideal for producing tables and various analyses from raw data. My job was to produce a table of students in various pass grades A, B, C, and so on from examination marking data. I did this with ease and sat back smugly, waiting for applause.

A person from the examination board studied the results carefully and informed me that according to my figures, more people achieved grade A than had entered the exam!

Example 3

I was writing a program in IBM Assembler which necessitated the clearing of a data field after processing on a particular record had finished and using it again for the next record. The length of the field was contained in a 4-byte field at the start of it and this was used to step through the data field *zeroizing* it until the end of the field was reached and that was it.

Unfortunately, I made an error in this *stepping* operation and carried on past the field end, obliterating everything in my path until I reached my own blanking instruction when the system choked and died in an act of *hara kiri*. A subsequent core dump showed the memory full of "00 .. 00 ..." up until the *suicidal* instruction, the memory of which I retain to this day.

> ***Note:*** Programs/services producing erroneous output are *down* as far as the service user is concerned.

Software Reliability: Problem Flow

Appendix 5 cites a paper by Wohlin, Host, Runeson, and Wesslen called "Software Reliability," which describes the relationships between software errors, faults, and failures, whose definitions can be found in Appendix 1 under Terminology.

---

* USA I'm afraid.

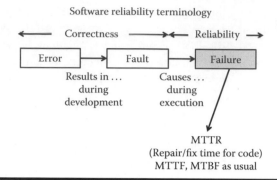

Figure 6.9 Software reliability terms—error, fault, failure.

They produce a diagram, adapted for Figure 6.9, which uses the terms *correctness* and *reliability* as entities in the software quality field. In addition, they use the following phrases to spell out what a failure is:

> Failure is a dynamic description of a deviation from the expectation. In other words, a failure is a departure from the requirements of the externally visible results of program execution. Thus, the program has to be executed for a failure to occur. A fault is the source of a failure, statically residing in the program, which under certain conditions results in a failure. The term *defect* is often used as a synonym to fault. The fault in the software is caused by an error, where an error is a human action.

The general term for describing good software is *quality* which also trades under the name *reliability* but is harder to pin down numerically like hardware reliability.

Software Testing Steps

The breakdown of time and effort in end-to-end software development is known, but the breakdown within those elements is less well defined and, moreover, documented. A paper sponsored by IBM and titled "E-Guide: Software Quality and Testing Best Practices" breaks the testing process into elements and assigns them to Gartner-like quadrants, called Agile testing quadrants in this document.

Examples of testing types are as follows:

- Unit tests
- Component tests
- Functional tests
- Prototypes
- Simulations
- Exploratory tests
- Usability tests
- User acceptance tests (UATs)
- Alpha/beta tests
- Performance and load tests
- Security tests (pentests and others)
- (Personally, I would add test plan and test results documentation)

Software Documentation

A critical factor here, reinforced by my experience in Y2000 "caper" is that many unknowns in that area were caused by *lack of documentation* for much of the software involved—microcode, embedded, and normal. I have alluded to this earlier but let us review it here.

As it turned out, most Y2000 date/time formats were valid and, in reality, the only possible candidates for the rollover issue were older legacy programs written in the *save all the memory you can* days of coding. Documentation therefore of what has been tested and what hasn't is key to subsequent problem determination and repair. Faster diagnosis and repairs equals higher availability.

Such documentation should contain the test plan and the test results as observed so that questions like *How is the date formatted?* can be answered without massive effort.

I came across a very good example of *retrospective use documentation* in installing a system for a pharmaceutical application concerned with the *safety of medicines*. This system was to capture medical test data from a variety of dissimilar systems and then consolidate it. The output of this system was a very deep printout and an accompanying file. I asked what this detailed mass of documentation was for and was told it was to refer back to if the medicine in question had any unpredicted side effects after reaching the market, to check if that angle had been covered in the tests. The whole point for the pharmaceutical company was to show it had exercised due diligence in its testing of emerging medications and would be less liable to litigation for serious side effects.

Remember, *all steps* in the design, coding, and testing phases of software development can either introduce errors or fail to spot them where they exist and are thus key to HA software. Documentation is a key factor here. See *Software Quality and Testing Best Practices* at http://docs.media.bitpipe.com/io_11x/io_112849/item_810616/IBM_sSoftwareQ_IO%23112849_Eguide_112613_LI%23810616.pdf.

Software Testing Model

The following rationale for the test-execution model was developed by Doug Hoffman[*] and wording (not the content) modified by myself to fit the style of this book. Doug has given permission to use this section and some references and terms of use of his material are given at the end.

Doug Hoffman is President of Software Quality Methods, LLC. and has written papers and presented talks on a variety of subjects relating to software quality assurance.

> The model describes the domains of influences on behavior of the Software Under Test (SUT)[†] and domains of potential outcomes. Most developers and test designers primarily focus on the inputs and results—the test exercise and the expected behaviors. They often take the data sets into consideration since the existence or non-existence of referenced data has dramatic effect on SUT behavior. Consider adding a new customer to a database and the behavior with and without a current customer with the same name.
>
> Other significant influences on SUT behavior are the internal program state, for example, is the right screen being displayed and external environmental factors: are network services available, what OS is the program running in, how much memory is

---

[*] With permission from Doug Hoffman.
[†] Not to be confused with *system* under test, a term used in benchmarking, for example, TPC benchmarks and normally refers to a server and relevant peripheral devices as the *SUT*.

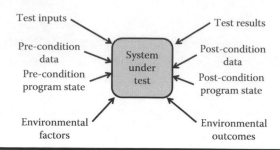

Figure 6.10 Hoffman's test-execution model. (From Doug Hoffman. Copyright 2000–2008, SQM, LLC. http://2009.stpcon.com/pdf/Hoffman_Extended_Model_for_Test_Execution.pdf. With permission.)

available, how much network bandwidth is available and so on. The expected behavior of the SUT can be significantly different given the state of the program and the environment.

The model also shows the domains that may be affected when bugs are present. Expected results are nominal behaviors. However, bugs may manifest anywhere in the system. Other data may be modified, perhaps change permissions for one user and the permissions for some other users are also changed, the internal or external program state may be changed for example or the wrong window is displayed, and the environment may be affected. An example might be Microsoft Word leaving some temporary files around the file system or 100% CPU utilization for 10 seconds when doing simple arithmetic.

What this means for reliability is that there are an infinite number of ways the SUT behavior can be influenced, all of which cannot be considered in programming or testing. Undiscovered faults may exist, just waiting for the right combination of circumstances. When we encounter a failure that cannot be reproduced it is likely due to one or more unnoticed influences.

In terms of outcomes, there are an infinite number of ways failures can occur and go unnoticed in spite of comprehensive design reviews, code reviews, and testing. Unexpected data may be modified, added, or deleted in the data the SUT references or elsewhere in the system. Internal program states may be wrong but go undetected, for example, printer dot density changes that aren't reset. Environmental effects may be transient or persistent. Transient effects occur during execution, for example, CPU utilization or file access, where persistent effects leave traces that might be discovered later such as temporary files not removed or a reset system variable.

Doug Hoffman grants permission to use the diagram (Figure 6.10) or other of his material in accordance with Creative Commons Attribution-Noncommercial 3.0 Unported License, which means it can be used as you like as long as you attribute where you got it (see http://creativecommons.org/licenses/by-nc/3.0/). Doug's other papers and slide sets are available at http://www.softwarequality-methods.com/html/papers.html.

You will find the following quote among Doug's writing:

It seems a shame to make the same old mistakes when there are still plenty of new ones to discover.

This is the philosophy guiding this book in looking beyond just hardware and software, virtual or otherwise, cloud or no cloud, in pinning down HA of services.

Software Reliability—Models

Software reliability is more difficult to define and quantify than hardware reliability. Nevertheless efforts have been made to put the topic on an objective basis via a series of models.

> The work on software reliability models, part of what is known as SRE (Software Reliability Engineering) started in the early 70's, the first model being presented in 1972. Various models proposed in the literature tend to give quite different predictions for the same set of failure data. It should be noted that this kind of behavior is not unique to software reliability modeling but is typical of models that are used to project values in time and not merely represent current values.
>
> Furthermore, a particular model may give reasonable predictions on one set of failure data and unreasonable predictions on another. Consequently, potential users may be confused and adrift with little guidance as to which models may be best for their applications. Models have been developed to measure, estimate and predict the reliability of computer software. Software reliability has received much attention because reliability has always had obvious effects on highly visible aspects of software development, testing prior to delivery and maintenance.[*]

The Software Scenario

Michael Lyu in his paper "SRE: A Roadmap"[†] outlines the lifecycle of faults or defects in software products and they can be summarized as follows:

- *Fault prevention:* To avoid, by construction, fault occurrences.
- *Fault detection:* Whose existence is via verification (*walkthrough?*) and validation (testing).
- *Fault removal:* Correction that leads to the concept of mean time to repair (MTTR) often quoted in software reliability engineering (SRE) literature. Obviously, MTTR for software can be more *fluid* than that for hardware because an apparent simple error may have far-reaching effects elsewhere.
- *Fault tolerance:* To provide, by redundancy, a service complying with the (program) specification in spite of faults having occurred or occurring.
- *Fault/failure forecasting:* To estimate, by evaluation, the presence of faults, and the occurrences and consequences of failure. This has been the main focus of *SRE modeling*.

SRE Models

A software model is an expression, usually mathematical, derived using real failure data, calibrated against it and, when it is satisfactory, used to predict the reliability of similar software. It is *not* the same as a software development process model because SRE models are concerned with errors in the development stages and not the stages themselves (specification, design, implementation,

---

[*] "A Detailed Study of NHPP Software Reliability Models"—Lai, Garg http://ojs.academypublisher.com/index .php/jsw/article/download/jsw070612961306/4896 (Note: This link does not function as at April 7, 2014, but is listed in a Google search.)

[†] http://dl.acm.org/citation.cfm?id=1254716.

verification, and maintenance). The SRE models are often given slightly different names depending on who wrote the article/book you are reading.

This field of software engineering is closely packed with mathematical models and distributions to predict software reliability characteristics. *Gompertz, Rayleigh, Gumbel, Gamma-Lomax, Goel-Okumoto, Hossian-Dahiya, Yamada (exponential and Rayleigh distribution forms, of course), Weibull,* and *LogNormal* are not names of theories, models, and distributions that immediately spring to mind when thinking or learning about SRE.

The basic idea emanating from early model work is to invoke past software failure data and use it to predict future behavior using a model of some sort. The models now number over 200 types and the situation being modeled will essentially dictate which model is most appropriate—there is no *one size fits all* model available at present. Most software reliability models have the following characteristics:

- Assumptions
- Factors taken into account
- The software environment they operate in (real time, applications, etc.)
- A mathematical function that relates the reliability with these factors and can be used in prediction of the number of faults in a unit time or the numbers of faults (density) encountered or the time between faults

There are some tools available on the Internet which allow a user to fit his or her data to various mathematical distributions to find a *best fit*, although this seems to me like reading various weather forecasts until you get one you like.

Most models vary in their assumptions about parameters, for example, the decay rate of failure intensity. Basili et al. suggest that the failure rate or intensity *falls* with increasing module size irrespective of any *fix* activity, although it sounds counter-intuitive.

The flow of activity to develop a model is

- Have an initial model in mind, for example, exponential or other mathematical function.
- Measure the parameters you wish to model on running software and plot them against time.
- Try to fit the results to the model and modify it if necessary.
- Use the model to predict software failures in a real situation if it passes the test.
- If it works, frame it and hang it on the wall: if it doesn't, try again (or rename it).

Attempts have been made to compare the ability of some of these models in predicting reliability but this has proven difficult, mainly in trying to compare apples with oranges when all the entities, assumption, parameters, and software environments involved are different.

Model Entities

There are a number of models going back over 30 years which, from my short investigation of them, show widely differing results in predicting software errors. The various models attempt, as we have just seen, to quantify entities like the following:

- Number of residual faults (in the software)—*defect density* or defects per lines of code (LOC) or failures/unit time
- Defect or failure rate per unit time is called *failure intensity*, symbol λ

- Number of faults detected up to a certain time t (cumulative), symbol μ
- Time between failures of the software—*MTTF*. There is also the software equivalent of the hardware *MTTR* but this is not as easy to predict as many hardware repairs or replacements often are.
- Assigning a *reliability figure* to the software, often synonymous with quality

The parameters from these models can be used, by the appropriate people, to estimate the future reliability of software and to assess when it can be released for general usage or to put a mission into space.

SRE Models: Shape Characterization

Models usually produce graphs of various entities against time and they assume various shapes, even within models, depending on the parameters chosen and assumptions.

> *Aside:* There are variations in model *names* reflecting combinations of ways of looking at the problem and the laying out of these names would at least double the depth of Table 6.2. I have seen them laid out in a thesis where the same model but with a different *announcement* date is treated as another model. Thus, the pseudomodel Smith Jones (1983) and Smith Jones (1991) are listed as different models, although they are essentially the same. Some model names and their characteristic defect-time shapes are shown in Table 6.2 and expanded upon in Appendix 4.

The model *types* in Table 6.2 take their names from the shape of a software *defects versus time* plot, a favorite SRE graph. The base shapes are *concave* and *S-shaped* and an example of the latter is shown in Figure 6.11.

The *concave* curve essentially looks like the top right hand part of this *S*-curve and drawing it would insult your intelligence. The number of defects plotted is usually the total found by time t, not those found at a particular time t or time interval. The numbers of errors per unit time or per 1000 LOC and their distance apart in time are the primary characteristics of SRE models.

Table 6.2 Selected Reliability Models

Model	Type/Shape
Musa–Okumoto	Concave
Inflection *S*-shaped	*S*-shaped
Goel–Okumoto	Concave
Delayed *S*-shape	*S*-shaped
Logistic growth	*S*-shaped
Yamada exponential	Concave
Gompertz	*S*-shaped
Generalized Goel	Concave

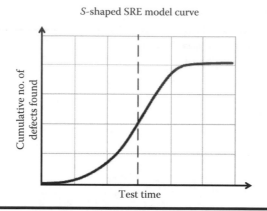

S-shaped SRE model curve

Figure 6.11   Software reliability *S*-shaped defect curve.

The use of various models in the field of software reliability is an attempt to predict the reliability of a piece of software via a model, usually in the form of an equation describing a graph or curve, calibrated with real data. Some of the math describing these model shapes can be found in Appendix 4.

> ***Note:*** In science, a model or theory that explains current behavior and correctly predicts behavior or results that are subsequently verified is considered *the truth*. When it fails to predict observed behavior correctly, then it is either modified or consigned to the scrap heap.

SRE Models: Time-Based versus Defect-Based

There is no shortage of models in the SRE arena whose aim is to predict *failure* or *defect* rates in developing or developed software. The use of defect data is considered in two basic ways as we will see in the next section—time between failures and number of failures or defects in a piece of software.

Many papers on SRE are 1990s-vintage but sometimes a later review of some models appear from various sources—universities and conferences being major *contributors*. Most of these papers explain their SRE models and quote several tables of real-life software development data used to *calibrate* or *justify* the model(s) under discussion.

Software Reliability Growth Model*

Software reliability growth model (SRGM) is one of the most well-known theoretical time-based models for estimating and predicting software reliability in development and maintenance. Software reliability is defined as the probability that the software will work without failure for a specified period of time. In SRGM, software reliability growth is defined by the mathematical relationship between the time span of program testing and the cumulative number of detected faults.

SRGM is a mathematical model that tells us how the reliability of a piece of software improves as faults are detected and repaired. One benefit of this foresight is it can be used to predict when a

---

* http://pdf.aminer.org/000/364/870/software_reliability_growth_model_from_testing_to_operation.pdf. Michael Lyu (editor) book, free online version; http://www.cse.cuhk.edu.hk/~lyu/book/reliability/.

particular level of reliability might be achieved. Various SRGMs have been developed over the past 30 or more years and can provide information on improving software reliability.

A good SRGM can furnish metrics like time period, number of remaining faults, MTBF, and MTTF. MTTR is not really calculable as it is a human activity often of unknown duration. Apart from this, there are several parallels in SRE with hardware engineering. In SRGM, the Weibull distribution figures prominently in various software studies, including survival analysis (operating time without failure). There are several SRGMs as we mentioned earlier in this section and some of the conventional ones are as follows:

- Goel–Okumoto model
- Gompertz model
- Logistic growth model
- Yamada delayed *S*-shaped model
- Yamada Weibull-type testing-effort function model
- Several others (there are at least 15 variations according to one SRE article)

Characteristics of the SRGMs depend on the model and any riders associated with it but common ones are as follows:

- They assume the reliability of the software growth after a fault has been detected and fixed.
- They can be used by a *test* panel to decide whether to stop or continue testing some software.
- They can be divided in *concave* or *S-shaped* versions by the shape of the predicted *reliability* versus *time* graph and described by relevant equations.

Assumptions of the SRGMs are illustrated in Table 6.3.*

The Tandem report goes on to say the following about SRGM assumptions:

Table 6.3 SRGM Assumptions and Their Assessment

Assumption	Reality
Defects are repaired immediately they are discovered.	Normally they are not.
Defect repair is perfect.	Defect repair introduces new ones.
No new code is introduced during QA test.	New code is frequently introduced, both defect repair and new features.
Defects are only reported by the product testing group.	They are reported by lots of groups.
Each unit of time (calendar, execution, no. of test cases) is equivalent.	Not true for calendar time or test cases.
Tests represent operational profiles.	Profiles are difficult to define.
Failures are independent.	A reasonable assumption overall.

---

* Summarized from the Tandem SRGM Report.

It is difficult to determine how the violation of the model assumptions will affect the models. For instance, introducing new functionality may make the curve less concave, but test reruns could make it more concave. Removing defects discovered by other groups comes closer to satisfying the model assumptions but makes the model less useful because we are not including all the data (which may also make the results less statistically valid).... Given the uncertainties about the effects of violating model assumption, the best strategy is to try the models to see what works best for a particular style of software development and test.

Parameters of SRGM are discussed here. Like other models, there is a method of calibration with real data observed in the past and many papers exhibit models and compare them by quoting metrics observed in real life and those predicted by the models. There is often significant disagreement. The SRGM type of model works on the following basis[*]:

- Collect and study software failure data
- Choose appropriate SRGMs for the software system (in question)
- Identify model's characteristics that describe model performance
- Compute quantitative measures and use SRGMs to make management decisions
- Obtain estimated parameters of the SRGMs using maximum likelihood estimates (MLE) or least squares estimate (LSE) based on collected data over a period of time (*I would call this exercise calibration*)
- Obtain the fitted model by substituting the estimated parameters in the selected SRGMs
- Use appropriate calculations and adopt some criteria to assess the predictability of model performance

SRGMs were used by Tandem Computers (now part of Hewlett Packard) in their software development, and their paper on "Software Reliability Growth Models" is an excellent introduction to them (http://www.hpl.hp.com/techreports/tandem/TR-96.1.pdf).

A more recent paper "On the Choice of an Appropriate Software Reliability Growth Model" by Neha Miglani[†] of Kurukshetra University, India, proposes a technique for the selection of an appropriate reliability model for an ongoing software development project and validates it on sets of test data.

Software Reliability Model: Defect Count

Defect density (sometimes called *error density*) is a measure of the total of confirmed defects divided by the size of the software entity being measured. *Defect or failure intensity* is the measure of defects per unit time at some time during program execution. There are definitions of *faults*, *errors*, and so on, as we have seen, but in software modeling, most people settle for the word *bug*, which is understood by all.

Defects can cover a mass of *sins* or *bugs* the origins of which are listed in Table 6.4. Logic (liveware) errors are prominent in this table at 37% of the total.

---

[*] "Software Reliability," a presentation by Nikta Naseri and Javier Vazquez—http://users.encs.concordia.ca/~dssouli/INSE%206250%20folder/Survey%20papers%2012%20folder/S_Reliability.pptx (quoted earlier).

[†] See *International Journal of Computer Applications* (0975-8887) Vol. 87 - No. 9, February 2014; http://www.ijcaonline.org/archives/volume87/number9/15237-3772.

Table 6.4 Software Defect Distribution by Type

Defect Type	Percentage of Faults
Logic (*human error*)	37
Inter-process communication (IPC)	13
Hardware interface	2
Functional description	2
Data handling	6
Data definition	4
Computation	2
User interface	2
Nonreproducible	2
Test hardware	6
Software interface	6
Requirements	2
Not a defect	6
Module/interface implementation	4
Module design	6

Programs are usually composed of modules which, in turn, are composed of instructions. Size is an important parameter and is often expressed as LOC or KiloLOC (KLOC). Defects per KLOC is a metric sometimes used in SRE modeling.

Note: A more detailed discussion on the *defect density model* can be found in Appendix 4.

Software Reliability: IEEE Standard 1633–2008*

The methods for assessing and predicting the reliability of software, based on a lifecycle approach to SRE, are prescribed in this recommended practice. It provides information necessary for the application of software reliability measurement to a project, lays a foundation for building consistent methods, and establishes the basic principle for collecting the data needed to assess and predict the reliability of software. The recommended practice prescribes how any user can participate in software reliability assessments and predictions. The standard is outlined and *onward* references are supplied in the given URL (http://standards.ieee.org/develop/project/1633.html).

---

* Not to be confused with Resolution 1633 (2008) from the Council of Europe which concerns the consequences of the war between Georgia and Russia.

Software Reliability: Hardening

Some software, while being secure in itself, may use and be reliant on other software that does not have the same security characteristics. System hardening is a process undertaken to eliminate as many security and contamination risks as possible. This is typically done by removing all non-essential, unnecessary user privileges and dormant utilities from the computer. Although these programs may offer useful features to the user, if they provide *back-door* access to the system, they must be removed during system hardening. *Hardening* software requires known security *vulnerabilities* to be eliminated or their effects mitigated.

Vulnerability is any weakness or flaw in the software design, implementation or administration and configuration of a system, which provides a mechanism for a threat to exploit the weakness of a system or process.

> All security standards and Corporate Governance Compliance Policies such as PCI DSS, GCSx CoCo, SOX (Sarbanes Oxley), NERC CIP, HIPAA, HITECH, ISO27000 and FISMA require Windows and UNIX servers, workstations, firewalls, routers and switches to be secure and configured properly in order to protect and secure confidential data.[*]

For hardening, most systems require adjustment of OS security settings in order to become PCI compliant. Basically, this means reviewing vendor *default* software system security level settings, object security, device and services security, password policy settings, time synchronization, and others.

This software *hardening* process applies to OSs, web services, firewalls, and other software and will probably require help from the vendor of the software to assess the vulnerability of the whole system. Workstations are not excluded from this process as they often contain valuable data and need to be protected. A forum on the Internet suggests the following hardening steps:

- Remove unnecessary software from key systems.
- Disable or remove unnecessary usernames and passwords.
- Disable or remove unnecessary services.
- Implement auditing of accounts and privileges.
- Implement the *principle of least privilege* (for users and other resources).
- Immediately remove the user accounts of people who leave the company.
- Remove dormant or unused accounts—part of the audit follow-up.
- Perform vulnerability tests on the system and its software.

Software Reliability: Installation

How can a software installation cause outage problems—physical or logical? Easy for liveware. We have already seen how an erroneous installation of VTAM tables caused severe problems. Two other tales involve an aerospace company who decided to install IBM's security product RACF (resource access control facility) and a chemical company installing HSM (data tiering).

---

[*] http://www.newnettechnologies.com/server-hardening.html and also the NIST paper: http://csrc.nist.gov/groups/STM/cmvp/documents/fips140-3/physec/papers/physecpaper01.pdf.

Aerospace company tale: The company installed the RACF modules and then started the system up—or tried to. It wouldn't let anyone do anything at all. They tried to uninstall RACF but it wouldn't let them do that either—*just doing its job*. It took them several hours of trial and error to get the miscreant out of the system. This was possibly a case of misinterpretation of parameter settings but the reasons behind the issue were never found.

Chemical company tale: The company installed the HSM (hierarchical storage manager) modules with the intention of tiering their data. It did not do quite what they expected so, because they were within the trial period, decided to uninstall it. This seemed to work but for weeks subsequently, *ghost* HSM messages kept appearing, issuing warnings or instructing them to take certain actions, threatening dire consequences if disobeyed.

They reinstalled HSM then immediately uninstalled it successfully which laid the *ghost* of HSM to rest (and lost IBM all that lovely revenue).

These are obviously examples (true) of liveware installation *gotchas* which can result in all manner of problems affecting availability targets. There will be others.

Software Reliability: Version Control

Version control (also known as a *revision control*) is a repository of files, often the source code of software, with monitored and controlled access. Every change made to the source is tracked, along with who made the change, reasons for the change, and references to problems fixed, or enhancements introduced, by the change.

This is an area akin to a minefield in a foreign country if it isn't treated as a discipline. This control applies to internal software and third-party software. The point does not need laboring here because the practice of *free for all* updates and revisions of software is known by everyone to be dangerous. The control of software change is an integral part of the change control discipline, and there are a number of vendors offering such control software. Don't neglect it.

The Cisco paper "Configuration Management: Best Practices White paper" contains a section on software version control and a number of other *change control* practices which you may find generically useful (see http://www.cisco.com/c/en/us/support/docs/availability/high-availability/15111-configmgmt.html).

Software: Penetration Testing

Penetration testing services, occasionally called *pentests* or *pen tests*, are methods of evaluating computer and network security by simulating an attack on a computer system or network purporting to come from external and internal threats. These penetration testing services can be extremely helpful in terms of strengthening a company's security knowledge.

These are often carried out for an enterprise by third parties, partly because of niche skills involved and also the implied impartiality of the testing. Penetration tests can be performed in three basic ways:

- *White box testing*, where the tester knows details of the system under test (SUT) as if he were an *insider* in the enterprise.
- *Black box testing*, where the tester does not have such knowledge. This mode of testing probably mirrors the attack by someone unfamiliar with the system, either internal or external, but attempting to break into it for one purpose or another.
- *Gray box testing*, where the tester has limited knowledge of the system.

These types of testing are also applied to software quality testing. A good introduction to the subject overall is at http://www.softwaretestinghelp.com/penetration-testing-guide/ and http://www.lo0 .ro/2011/07/08/top-10-web-application-penetration-testing-tools-actually-11/.

The choice of *pentest* partner depends on how paranoid the CEO/CIO are about the system, but there is a paper on choosing such a partner at http://reports.informationweek.com/abstract/21/11475/Security/Strategy:-Choosing,-Managing-and-Evaluating-A-Penetration-Testing-Service.html.

The banking site I was working with a few years ago outsourced all their penetration testing to maintain neutrality in the objectives and results of the tests. It made sense in their case because the outsourced third party was far more knowledgeable than the bank about the subject.

However, this is what Dave Shackleford[*] had to say about *external* testers in an article recommending *internal* pen test teams except where regulations forbid it:

> Many organizations have a legal or compliance requirement to have an external party perform at least one penetration test per calendar year. In addition to this, it's a good idea to have external firms perform some tests that require extensive knowledge on platforms that your team may not know well or tests your team is not capable of performing for some other reasons.
>
> It's also a very good idea to rotate through several pen testing firms for a variety of reasons. First, you can ensure the firm you are using does not become too comfortable with your environment and its details: performing regular testing could lead to a scenario where the testing firm becomes complacent and misses potential vulnerabilities. Second, you can get a different perspective from a variety of pen testers, each of whom brings his or her own skills and approach to the table. In general, the more eyes you can get on your environment, the more potential security issues you can find.

For further information on this topic, see Wikipedia[†] or the "corsaire" site.[‡]

Software: Fault Tolerance

Software fault tolerance (ft) is based mainly on concepts developed for hardware ft, that is, redundancy. Such redundancy can work for faults which are not design errors, whereby a fault is replicated in several places. For example, N-version software redundancy mimics hardware ft redundancy where applicable. Metrics and tools in this area of software development are few but there are some techniques to aid software ft:

■ *N-version software:* In this technique, modules are made up with several different implementations, each performing the same task but in a different way. In this manner, a faulty block does not propagate the same error in its alternatives. Each version submits its answer to an *arbiter or decider* and, if the results agree, returns them to their planned destination. This technique (and that of recovery blocks discussed next) depends on accurate specifications to ensure a software ft working model.

---

[*] From the article "Testing from Within" by Dave Shackleford in *Information Security Essential Guide* February 2013.

[†] http://en.wikipedia.org/wiki/Penetration_test.

[‡] http://www.penetration-testing.com/home.html.

- *Recovery blocks:* These blocks are developed by Randell (http://www.cs.ncl.ac.uk/publications/ inproceedings/papers/341.pdf), which operate via an adjudicator (referee) to confirm or otherwise the results of different implementations of the same algorithm. When this concept is used, a software system is constructed of recoverable ft blocks. In the case where the adjudicator decides that a primary software unit has failed, *he* tries to *roll back* the system state and tries the secondary alternative. If the adjudicator does not accept the results of all the alternative units, then *he* declares a *program exception* and invokes the OS exception handler. The main problem with this technique is having the ability to *roll back* the actions of the failing unit, which means building the system in the manner of a transaction system (OLTP).

- *Self-checking software:* This advance on ft, used for extremely reliable and safety-critical systems, includes extra checks, such as amount check pointing and rollback recovery methods. Despite not being a rigorous method, it is apparently very effective, which is good news if you are flying to Mars in 2025. The next step is to develop ultra-ft software.

It is currently difficult to quantify the improvement in software reliability attributable to these techniques. In addition, software ft is not as mature and reliable as hardware ft but has to be better than nothing in getting round human design faults which, like the poor and taxes, will always be with us.[*]

Software Error Classification

Heisenbug

In software development, *Heisenbug* is a classification of an unusual software bug that disappears or alters its behavior when an attempt to isolate it is made. Due to the unpredictable nature of a *Heisenbug*, when trying to recreate the bug or using a debugger, the error may change or even vanish on a retry.

The name *Heisenbug* is derived from *Heisenberg's uncertainty principle* which states, "it is fundamentally impossible to predict the position and momentum of a particle at the same time." One common example of a *Heisenbug* is a bug that appears when the program is compiled with an optimizing compiler, but does not appear when the same program is compiled without optimization.

Bohrbug

In computer programming, the *Bohrbug* is a classification of an unusual software bug that always produces a failure on retrying the operation which caused the failure. The *Bohrbug* was named after the Bohr atom because the bug represents a solid and easily detectable bug that can be isolated by standard debugging techniques.

A mature piece of software in the operational phase, released after its development and testing stage, is more likely to experience failures caused by *Heisenbugs* than *Bohrbugs*. Most recent studies on failure data have reported that a large proportion of software failures are transient in nature, caused by phenomena such as overloads or timing and exception errors.

The study of failure data from Tandem's fault-tolerant computer system supports this in that 70% of the failures noted were *transient* or *soft* failures, caused by faults like timing problems or memory leakage.

---

[*] http://www.ece.cmu.edu/~koopman/des_s99/sw_fault_tolerance/.

Reliability Properties of Software[*]

ACID Properties

In nonsimple software interactions, particularly those involving middleware, there can be synchronization issues in data updates. One way of ensuring consistency is via the properties in the acronym ACID (*atomicity, consistency, isolation,* and *durability*). These are the mainstays of OLTP and databases, particularly in a distributed environment.

- *Atomicity:* All changes to data are performed as if they are a single operation. That is, *all the* changes are performed, or *none* of them are. For example, in an application that transfers funds from one account to another, the atomicity property ensures that, if a debit is made successfully from one account, the corresponding credit is made to the other account. Doing one without the other is not allowed.
- *Consistency:* Data are in a consistent state when a transaction starts and when it ends. For example, in an application that transfers funds from one account to another, the consistency property ensures that the total value of funds in both the accounts is the same at the start and end of each transaction.
- *Isolation:* The intermediate state of a transaction is invisible to other transactions. As a result, transactions that run concurrently appear to be serialized. This property is sometimes called *Independence.*

     For example, in an application that transfers funds from one account to another, the isolation property ensures that another transaction sees the transferred funds in one account or the other, but not in both, nor in neither.
- *Durability:* After a transaction successfully completes, changes to data persist and are not undone, even in the event of a system failure. For example, in an application that transfers funds from one account to another, the durability property ensures that the changes made to each account will not be reversed.

Two-Phase Commit

Another property of software which ensures consistency of results is *two-phase commit* (2PC), where database updates and transaction completions in related units of work are completed and abide by the ACID properties discussed earlier.

This type of discipline is key to consistent data and transaction integrity and has an implication for availability when one partner in the 2PC exchange fails and the whole task is not completed.

It comprises, in simple terms, the communication exchanges involving updates/changes:

- Commit-request phase (*are you ready Bill?*)
- Ack(nowlegment) (yes I am ready Charlie)
- Commit phase (Charlie: *then let's go Bill*)
- Commit the change(s)

Figure 6.12 illustrates schematically systems involved in updates and employing the two-phase commit protocol method to ensure the consistency of updates of databases on the two systems. In this case, the players are one *coordinator* (2PC requestor) and one *cohort* (partner in the 2PC).

---

[*] Mainly concerned with transaction processing and related database access.

Example of two-phase commit protocol

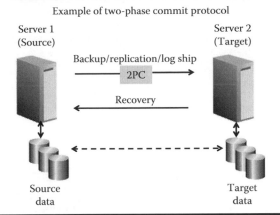

Figure 6.12   Sample two-phase commit (2PC).

There might be more than one cohort in the exercise. Both/all keep logs to restore the *status quo* if commit agreement is not reached and the transaction may have to be rerun.

> ***Summary:*** A 2PC commit operation is, by definition, an all-or-nothing affair. If a series of operations bound together as a transaction cannot be completed, the rollback must restore the system (or cooperating systems) to the pre-transaction state.

Software Reliability: Current Status[*]

Software reliability is still an active field of research with the literature full of models, their benefits, and their critics. However, what is generally recognized is that if we do come up with a correct model for software reliability, it could have the following uses:

1. Helping a software development team to know when to stop testing and debugging a software and release it. This is called *target reliability* and could guarantee a customer a certain minimum period of fault-free running of the software. We have alluded to this before.
2. A software company would be interested in knowing whether the reliability of newer versions of software the company has been releasing is increasing (or not).
3. The company might also like to correlate a software reliability metric of their software with features in their development environment. For example, one question worth answering would be to determine whether the usage of certain open source C++ libraries as opposed to a competing in-house library increases the reliability of the software. Such questions and their answers could lead to formulating software development best practices aimed at increasing software reliability (quality).

---

[*] http://ge.geglobalresearch.com/blog/software-reliability-a-stochastic-process-based-perspective/ (June 2011).

Software Reliability: Assessment Questions*

These are some useful questions to ask about your planned software where multiple *yes* answers could spell trouble (for internal or third-party applications):

- Is the software delivered late?
- Are software releases made too frequently?
- Are software versions different at each site or for each customer?
- Is there a reliance on over-staffing to make a release date?
- Are low-level faults (those related to coding and design) found during system testing?
- Do corrective actions result in disabling of functions that previously worked?
- Are corrective actions repeated more than once for the same fault?
- Is software delivered with faults that were removed in previous versions?
- Is there a slow response time to correct faults?
- Is fault information scattered and incomplete?
- Does software management use little or no method for verifying and scheduling software releases?
- Are there few or no procedures in place for developing and testing software?
- Does management have difficulty determining where to start improving the reliability of software?
- Is there a high turnover rate of software professionals, and is there a high percentage of short-term contract software professionals?
- Is there growing discontent among the software staff?
- Are field support personnel making software changes in field?
- Are software engineers doing on-site field support?
- How easy or difficult is the installation?
- Has the software been fully tested in an operational environment?
- Is there a reference installation you can contact with installation and operational queries?
- Are there alternatives if the software doesn't live up to expectations?
- Is the negotiated vendor support contract in line with your availability SLAs? For example, is your availability target 6d × 24h but your support contract 5d × 8h?

Outcome: Significant numbers of *yes* responses spell trouble for the software in question and will require an overhaul of your program development or a change of third-party software supplier.

Software Universe and Summary

Figure 6.13 summarizes most of the areas we have looked at in software availability and quality. This figure is the software equivalent of the service *onion* of Chapter 1 and shows the main areas of the software *universe*—application, development, and production environments.

---

* "Tactical Software Reliability," http://ismi.sematech.org/docubase/document/2967agen.pdf.

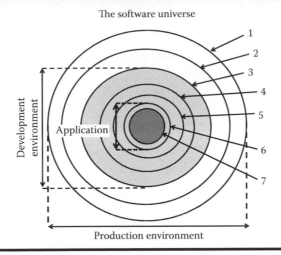

Figure 6.13 **The software *universe* onion.**

The legend to this diagram, all of which items we have covered previously, is as follows:

1. Other software environments to which this one interacts with, for example, an application on another system. For commercial software, this area would include the vendor; for internal software, the developer
2. Hardening the environment in which the software lives and ensuring the security of it and the data it uses
3. Software testing/piloting commercial software
4. Coding standards, reuse, documentation, and other related administrations
5. *Harness* software, for example, middleware, OS, and so on
6. Subroutines and *imported* functions, particularly in the scientific environment
7. The core software and application

We have alluded many times to the fact that HA encompasses more than just hardware and software. Even within the software environment, there are microenvironments all of which might have an impact on the availability and quality of any software employed in providing a service to users. The figure is not totally encompassing but does indicate there is more to the software aspect of HA than meets the eye. Remember, even "working" software that delivers incorrect results can be considered unavailable.

The final HA aspect we consider is the subsystems without which the server and associated software will not function. It is of little use having a 100% available server and software if the peripherals on which it relies for data access and transmission are unreliable.

Subsystem Reliability

Hardware Outside the Server

The title *subsystem* covers other devices that attach to, or feed servers and provide a complementary service of some sort. Each of these will have its reliability characteristics and will vary by vendor and type of device. The trend for decades has been to offload function from server to subsystem resulting in greater intelligence in many subsystems. However, they only need *careful* attention if their operation is a key to business operations.

Supporting subsystems might include the following:

- Disks (storage subsystems)
- Tapes
- Printers
- Unit record (card readers/punches, paper tape, and the like)
- MICR and OCR/OMR (magnetic ink/optical character/optical mark readers)
- Communications subsystems and adapters
- Other devices and subsystems (telephone systems, sensors, etc.)

All these systems, with the exception of disks and tapes, usually rely on *very cold* standby redundancy and backup devices to provide *RAS*, although there are exceptions I'm sure. *Clever* firmware will play a part in some of these areas. We will concentrate mainly on disks and tapes in this discussion because they are used in normal processing and backup/restore situations … but don't forget the possible importance of other devices to the availability of a service.

Disk Subsystem Reliability

Modern disk subsystems are composed of more than just disks and a simple controller as they were when I started in IT. They contain power and cooling, CPUs, host and device adapters, switches, some microcode, and a hardware management console (HMC). Many have built-in RAS and processors, sometimes more than one, to perform their functions. For all I know, the latest examples of storage technology may have coffee-making facilities as well as super HA.

Disk Subsystem RAS

The amount and sophistication of RAS and redundancy features varies from vendor to vendor and no attempt is made here to cover these differences. Instead a list of feasible options is presented, many of which might be implemented by the various vendors.

Availability features might include the following:

- A firmware hypervisor if appropriate.
- Management console (HMC) for control of the various parts of the subsystem which controls all storage configurations and service actions.
- Dual HMC in case of failure or an alternative subsystem *aware* device.
- Dual pathing for various connections—internal and external.
- Fault tolerance.
- Remote support and/or *call home* support for error resolution.
- Dual power supplies, battery backup, and cooling devices* … plus environmental monitoring and reporting (*ecosystem/ambientware*)
- The inherent RAS features of the CPU(s) which control the subsystem
- Resource de-allocation on excessive error count (threshold exceeded)

---

* An amusing variation I saw on the word *fan* was *air movement device*!

- Subsystem internal CPU failover and failback (if more than one CPU or, as sometimes called, central electronic complex—CEC)
- Dual copies of data during write—one in cache, the other in nonvolatile storage (NVS) until completion
- Alternate pathing, controlled by the host OS, on failure of a data path
- Redundancy checks (metadata) on data passing to and from the subsystem
- Ability to withstand power variations for a time (typically tens of milliseconds) via a power line *disturbance* feature
- Other control mechanisms may be employed, such as emergency power off for safety reasons
- The usual disk/SSD features—RAID, predictive failure analysis, etc.

In the case of most subsystems/peripheral devices, there is little in the way of design that isn't already in them, except for perhaps redundancy where costs are not prohibitive and the benefits tangible (*what does it mean to our business?*).

Tape Reliability/RAS

Tape devices are rarely, if ever, used as online real-time data vehicles supporting OLTP, web servers, and so on. Where *RAS* features are needed are in consistent recording accuracy and nondegrading tape media for storage and retrieval. Storage and accurate retrieval of data may be necessary for legal and DR reasons so *longevity* is a requisite for such data media. Speed, of course, is also a necessary feature of modern tapes for dump and restore purposes, particularly for DR. The KPI of RTO and RPO will rely on performance aspects of recovery devices.

The *availability* of tapes and the applications they serve can depend on any or all the following features:

- Vendor support and skills, plus *your* operations skills
- Advanced media and recording mechanism (durability)
- Low power dissipation with sleep-mode support (sleeps when unloaded and idle for a certain time)
- Built-in temperature sensor
- Automatic in-drive media quality management function with alerts
- Drive load/thread reliability (hardened loader)
- On-site hot spares kit
- Ask for MC[S]BF (mean cycles[swaps] between failures), MTBF, MTTR, or any other *measure between failures* the vendor has

Typical figures are

MC[S]BF: 2,000,000 h; MTBF: 250,000–500,000 h
MTTR: (3 min hot-swap, 20–30 min non-hot-swap)

- Highly integrated ASIC modules and electronics packaging
- Graceful dynamic braking on power loss (avoids media damage)
- Flangeless rollers to eliminate tape edge contact
- Robotic libraries

- Thermal monitoring, fan monitoring, and control:
  - Monitor and report any changes in reliability
  - Pro-active error analysis and alerting systems
- Implements a highly efficient service strategy, such as
  - Concurrent firmware/embedded software update capability
  - Single field replaceable unit (FRU) drive replacement strategy
  - Hot plug, quick disconnect drive replacement
  - Persistent drive attributes through a service action
  - Pay attention to media considerations
  - Cycle tapes to spread the wear and keep a record (see point 3 in Notes)

Notes:

1. If you buy a tape subsystem, make sure you test the *restore*. A Gartner study showed that 34% of purchasers never tested the restore capability of tape subsystems they had installed.
2. Make sure you understand and have tested the tape load/unload *characteristics* if you are using tape for DR (necessary for meeting RTO and RPO). This of course will normally depend not just on raw speed but on backup mechanism—full dump, incremental and the restore mechanism—image copy, reload from transaction a log, and so on
3. Tapes that are stored for a long time can suffer *bit rot* and conventional wisdom suggests that a simple test is performed on them every so often to check that all is OK with the data on them.

The guide referenced below suggests that the lifetime of magnetic tapes before significant degradation sets in is between 10 and 20 years.

For details of caring lovingly for tapes, see *Ampex Guide to the Care and Handling of Magnetic Tape*—it may save your business from oblivion if you use tape backup for DR purposes and want to make sure you can retrieve the data again (http://www.clir.org/pubs/reports/pub54/care_and_handling.html).

Availability: Other Peripherals

The importance of availability of peripherals like printers, OMR, card readers, and so on depends on their status in supporting a business service. If, for example, a printer is only used for producing some statistics at the end of each week or month, then redundant printers may not be necessary. However, if output is vital to a service and must be available when desired, a second or third printer may be needed to back up the primary one.[*]

---

[*] Make sure the configuration is suitable for backup/recovery purposes. I once made a configuration error when installing dual printers in a public utility. They worked fine except for the fact that initially they printed successive print lines on alternate printers!

Attention to Detail

In addition, it is important to assess the need for reliability of a *peripheral on a peripheral* if it is a key part of a service workflow. An example is the page numbering unit on the 3881 OMR I alluded to earlier (see Availability: A Lesson in Design). In the normal scheme of things, one would not attach much importance to it in an HA environment as it was at the bottom of the failure hierarchy but it was the crux of the exam system workflow and therefore vital. It wasn't logistically possible to have a redundant numbering unit as *backup* on the OMR, so the workflow had to be redesigned—not the hardware or the software. Another factor here is the reliance of a critical system or service on another system to accept and return data (distributed processing).

That other system should also be highly available for obvious reasons. This type of *gotcha* should be picked up in a walkthrough exercise involving the appropriate people.

In this case, it was spotted by an engineer who was *au fait* with the OMR—he was one of the *appropriate* people.

Liveware Reliability

A NASA publication (weighing in at 700+ pages) suggests some reliability actions for *liveware* or people. Given the impact on availability of *finger trouble* this seems a reasonable idea. Their suggestions cover the following:

- Design for immunity to human error, that is, make it difficult to louse things up without trying very hard.
- Design an easy and friendly human interface, not one that requires a PhD in human factors to use. Intuitive is the word that springs to mind.
- Try to minimize the likelihood of human error, possibly by simplicity where possible and feasible.
- Develop design and operational checklists. Make their use mandatory *unless the operators can name all the US states from memory*.
- Develop rigorous design, operations (Runbooks), and procedures manuals.
  - Use FMEA and other management disciplines to generate RDBs.
  - Write manuals for operations and maintenance people.
  - Make warnings, cautions, and suggestions clear and unambiguous.
  - Revise this documentation when the system is revised.

(*I would add to this:*)

- Ensure the correct level and currency of training is in place. *Remember, a fool with a tool is still a fool* (as I keep saying).
- Revise the problem determination and *fix* procedures to reflect new issues that have been resolved and reflect this in any training.

Hopefully, these actions will minimize or eliminate *I didn't realize that pressing that button would ....*, *I naturally assumed that ....*, *where is Jim? He is the only one who knows anything about this*, and so on *ad disastrum*. The watchword here should be *Assume nothing*. In addition, I believe there is little room for artistic creativity in designing and operating HA systems, except perhaps for the human interface.

Summary

There are a number of areas to be considered in enhancing the availability of systems and these have been covered in generic fashion in this section. Remembering the fact that much downtime is caused by factors other than hardware, it is key to have covered all the *availability by . . .* sections in order to achieve HA.

The service chain in IT is only as robust as its Lusser-calculated link availability, which is less than the weakest link.

Note: Figure 6.14 illustrates a schematic HA system containing many of the topics we have discussed in this section.

The journey from users desk through the system and back is long and fraught with *gotchas* which IT must anticipate and mitigate or avoid completely.

Many of the *availability* aspects outlined earlier are aimed at avoiding the possible effects of finger trouble either in operations or *ad hoc* changes forced by poor design. The essence of this is getting it right first time with a *quality* solution. Quality is, if you remember, creating something *fit for purpose*. In addition, the velocity of change is a potential factor in causing outages. If it cannot be avoided, it should be controlled and, if feasible, automated.

I hope it will be pinned on the wall of any *availability* guru's office and a copy hand-painted on the side of his or her coffee cup.

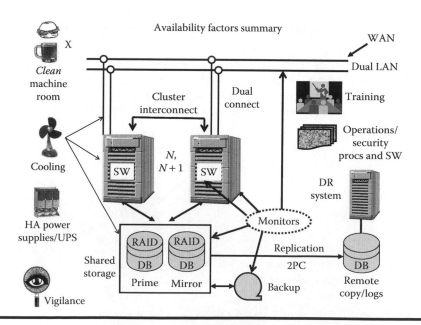

Figure 6.14   Summary of availability factors: Schematic.

Be Prepared for Big Brother!

The other issue looming over HA is security and the detection and neutralization of attacks from botnets, DDoS, and so on and the subsequent building up security against them.

These types of attacks are maturing and becoming immune to attempts to block them, rather like bacteria and their nemesis antibiotics. It is unlikely that an SLA will have specific anti-attack requirements but that doesn't mean they should not be anticipated. They can impact any agreed availability targets like any other outage type.

Not only are these threats not going to go away, they are going to increase in intensity and sophistication over the years. Appoint a *security* person and have him/her keep in touch with the security websites and organizations listed in Appendix 5.

Note: Murphy's Law is especially virulent in this sector of risk.

Chapter 7

High Availability: SLAs, Management, and Methods

Introduction

This chapter suggests the areas where installations might improve the level of service of an e-commerce initiative. All the activities in this document have a bearing on business continuity (BC) in terms of system availability and disciplines aimed at meeting service levels and most of them can be used in projects other than those related to HA.

What follows are areas where activity needs to be focused and are basic to IT whatever the underlying technology. They do not age, only increase in importance as *clouds* and *virtualization* descend on IT systems.

Some installations I came across used to try to buy their way to success by buying expensive software to do the management tasks involved in all IT design, implement and operate projects. For *XYZ Management*, they would purchase *The Ultimate XYZ Management Package*, light the blue touch paper and stand back. This would be repeated for managing ABC, DEF, and so on.

This sounds fine and might be if:

- It has a pedigree but doesn't break the bank.
- You know how to use it.
- You understand the subject it addresses.

Regarding the above list, there is a saying "A fool with a tool is still a fool" and unless the third, and most important, point above is fulfilled, the chances of success are greatly reduced. If this point *is* fulfilled, you can almost certainly *manage XYZ* and the rest using a school exercise book as your tool project documentation better than you could mishandling a software package.* In this section, we will examine some of the tools and techniques that might add value to availability projects.

---

* c. 1985. A customer I dealt with had a performance person in IT. His office wall was covered with multicolored charts of *anything* versus *everything* plotted on them. One day I plucked up courage and asked him what they all meant (the *so what* test). He wasn't really sure, although we both agreed they were very pretty and covered the ugly wall nicely. This is a true story—only the name of the man has been left out.

> *Note:* They are neither compulsory nor strictly sequential in their employment but they are extremely useful in imposing a degree of discipline and structure to activities where failure is not an option.

The following management disciplines and techniques are of prime importance in maintaining high availability (HA) in the various incarnations we have discussed:

- Preliminary activities
- Pre-production
- Business continuity plan (BCP)
- Management disciplines (methods and techniques)
- Service level agreements (SLAs)
- Project definition workshop (PDW)
- Delphi technique and intensive planning
- Failure mode effects (and criticality) analysis (FMEA/FMECA)
- Component failure impact analysis (CFIA)
- Walkthroughs
- War room
- Change management
- Problem and fault management
- Risk management
- Security management
- Resource management
- Performance
- Capacity
- Network
- Data and storage
- Software
- Assets
- Other items listed in context later

These disciplines are outlined in this chapter and covered in more detail in Appendix 3 under HA/DR Route Map. This is in line with my philosophy of not impeding the flow of the book with excessive detail in the body.

Preliminary Activities

Pre-Production Activities

There are several pre-production activities needed to ensure a successful implementation of applications and supporting hardware software in a HA production environment. Some of these activities are business as usual, whereas others are aimed at risk reduction in the project. Among these activities are

- Identification of a business sponsor
- Environmental planning (heat, power, space)
- A full definition of the project to include objectives, deliverables, and overall timescales for delivery. This is a precursor to actual project management, task assignment, and so on.
- External hardware, software, and project management services
- Internal skills development
- Service management architecture design (help desk, operations, systems, and network management)
- Develop SLA with business people representing the *end users.*
- *Addressing mission-critical issues*—what this book is about
- Plans for
  - Development
  - Testing and quality of service (QoS)
  - Coordination of third parties involved in the project
  - Adequate notification of the need for temporary extended hours of service, including support coverage
  - Adequate user notification by IT of planned outages
  - Current system workload and capacity
  - Growth forecasts for the applications

... and, the usual plea, *documentation.*

Documentation is a two-edged sword—it can get you into jail in the wrong circumstances but get you out of jail in IT disasters by demonstrating *your* due diligence.

BC Plan

Recent surveys on business reliance on technology indicate that system outages can cost some businesses hundreds of thousands of pounds per hour. In addition, other studies indicated that companies unable to recover their operations within two weeks are typically out of business within six months. According to a recent UK study, the three most commonly identified consequences of a computer disaster are as follows:

- Loss of business/customers/reputation
- Loss of credibility/goodwill (*share price*)
- Cash flow problems

It is in the interest of most businesses to have an availability and disaster recovery (DR) strategy to allow recovery from complete failure of systems supporting their business operations. This recovery strategy is outside the normal recovery plans invoked when a piece of hardware or a database is lost but the installation as a whole is still operational.

BC is outside the scope of this book but is outlined here as a crucial part of *availability* of systems and services. We have seen how BCP, DR, and business impact analysis (BIA) are related and that IT DR is a subset of BC.

BC: Best Practice

A disaster is something which prevents critical parts of the business being carried on as usual and requires some level of reproduction of normal facilities to carry on essential parts of a business.

There are various checklists, advice, and warnings about this topic but the main actions in my view are as follows:

1. Get the company to take it seriously (senior sponsor).
2. Appoint people and pin responsibility on them (accountability).
3. Get on do something about it.

> *Note:* Some considerations are outlined below and what I hope are *useful references* can be found in Appendix 5, but it is mainly *your* common sense and knowledge of the business that are required.

- Appoint a BC coordinator and a responsible senior executive as sponsor—a sponsor is an *owner* and *gauleiter* or *fixer*.
- Establish a *virtual team*—a full-time team would be a waste of resources in what will hopefully be a very rare occurrence—along with roles and responsibilities. Business people should be involved and the vendors used by the business might well form part of this team for short lead time supply of goods and services.
- Train the virtual team and, if necessary, develop training for them.
- Establish conditions that might cause disruption which needs to invoke *disaster* activity and assess their likelihood, perhaps as a% chance. For example, a tsunami is practically 0% likely in England but has a much higher likelihood in the Far East. A continuity plan will depend on exactly which type of disaster hits the organization and the requirements for mitigation will vary accordingly.
- Establish what physical parts of the business could be affected—people, locations, IT, other technology, data, supplies and stocks. and anything else on which the business depends.
- Establish which parts of the business are crucial to survival and prioritize them via a BIA and all that entails.
- Create plans for the *recovery* of those strategic business functions according to the disaster being considered.
- Walk through those plans, rather like walking through an application program or a RBD for an HA system. An external *devil's advocate* is a good idea.
- Based on these plans, outline an emergency *SLA* as to what level of service the business units can expect in a disaster scenario.
- Develop a staff BC awareness plan and make them aware of their role in recovery plans. It seems sensible to appoint BC representatives in the business units.
- Document the plan and circulate, in summarized and tailored form where necessary. The HR manager is not interested in the domain name service (DNS) recovery plan.
- Review and update the plan regularly.
- Physical security of IT sites is also a prime consideration.

Management Disciplines

What have all these other disciplines got to do with availability and its management I hear you say? To quote Frank Sheed in *Theology and Sanity*, he relates an incident where a driver is heading straight for an oak tree when his passenger warns him of the imminent danger. The driver replies

It's no good telling me—I'm not a botanist!. I trust you see his point and mine. The first thing we need before we actually start work is an SLA, even a draft one, to get a feel for the size of the HA/DR task.

Service Level Agreements

SLA Introduction

In the days before *IT*, computing was done in the data processing department by gurus with little or no contact with the business users. The primary use of the systems was in accounting and very often, the DP manager reported to the finance director. As more applications were put on the system, it often became necessary to give priority to certain applications at peak times and this was done without reference to the users.

As charge back became more prevalent, users began to ask what they were getting for their money and would make certain demands about the service they wanted to receive. This developed into the idea of agreements about levels of service which became known as SLAs.

An SLA is a document drawn up between the organization's IT service providers and representatives of the business users. The agreement covers the levels of service needed by the users. Often, there will be SLAs for individual applications whose requirements differ from other applications, for example, order entry may demand a higher level of service than the HR application. We will now examine the reasons why SLAs are a good thing for IT accounts.

SLA: Availability and QoS

Depending on how an SLA is phrased, it is possible for its terms to be met but the QoS delivered not what was expected. For example, a service might comfortably meet its target for availability but with poor or erratic response times, giving an uneven and substandard QoS. Performance and the response time variations might be caused by unexpected increases in the numbers of users or unforeseen peak loads which were not reflected in the drawing up of the SLA then in force.

If these increases are deemed to be permanent, the existing SLA should either be ignored or renegotiated by both sides. I have seen *undeclared* extra users affect a system's performance adversely.

There can be many elements of *service* in a SLA but three are important in designing and maintaining HA—availability (obviously!), performance (logical outages), and in modern times, security. This is illustrated in Figure 7.1 as an *aide memoire*.

Elements of SLAs

The following are things to consider and, where appropriate, include in an SLA. They are in no particular order and not necessarily complete:

- Background and brief description of the application and its importance, that is, why it needs the requested level of service
- Parties to the agreement—IT and user
- Roles and responsibilities
- Current system workload and capacity

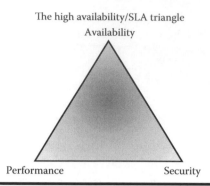

Figure 7.1   **Major elements of an SLA.**

■ Growth forecasts for the application
■ Workload pattern forecasts, for example, changes in transaction mixes towards the heavier transactions over time or at period-ends
■ Measurement methods for SLA reporting—hours of service, uptime, response times, and so on. This can get quite involved with 90th percentile numbers, what they mean and so on. If you not sure about this topic, take advice.
■ *Response times* and deadlines, for example, for batch reports
■ Business *security* requirements
■ Recovery times and status of recovered data (RTO)
■ Charging mechanism, for example, by transaction, by CPU second, by disk occupancy, lines printed
■ Service level metrics, that is, what is to be measured and why?
■ Service level reporting, e.g., *availability*—for IT and for users
■ Ongoing communications between users and IT on SLA achievements and changes
■ User compensation for nonachievement of targets by IT
■ User and IT staff training
■ User responsibilities, for example, not deleting the database and then demanding immediate recovery, notifying IT of unusual working, for example, weekends or evenings
■ Any exclusions, for example, acts of God, floods unless these are covered by a DR plan
■ Another exclusion might say *response times cannot be guaranteed during quarter, half-year and year-end processing when these workloads are superimposed on the normal workload.*
■ The term of the agreement, for example, 9 months when the SLA will be either revised or renegotiated. SLAs have a *sell by date*, especially in a volatile business environment.

The following are expansions of some SLA specifics:

1. *Hours of service* for the application access. This can range from 9 to 5 days a week to 24 h × 365 days. The hours of service put constraints on certain activities such as backup, scheduling maintenance and the duration of housekeeping activities. It is necessary for the nonprime shift activities (usually overnight batch work and housekeeping) to complete before the start of the prime shift user activity.
2. The actual availability of the system during those hours of service. If it is 100%, then availability equals hours of service divided by hours of service.

3. *Response times* for application transactions or elapsed time for batch and reporting applications. Interactive transaction usually have a response time requirement phrased something like *the application will, at peak times, deliver 90% of the transactions within 2 seconds*. This is called a 90th percentile.
4. *Security requirements* implies setting up the system to block unauthorized access to the system, the application, and the associated data. It often means that attempts at unauthorized access should be logged and kept for audit and other reporting.
5. *Advance notification* of users of planned downtime, for example, hardware or software upgrades, new installations, and so on, and immediate notification of unplanned downtime

> ***Note:*** Poor *system performance* can often present a logical outage, especially in Internet applications, such as on-line finance. Studies have shown that a users *patience span* in browsing websites is about *7 seconds*, which, in terms of the general public means he or she will not use the system if the response time is longer than this or is very erratic. The service is then effectively unavailable for its purpose.

Types of SLAs

An SLA is usually related to a business function and it's specific requirements for service. A single SLA does not normally cover a whole business since this might prove expensive and, in the case of minor functions, unnecessary.

Examples of SLA types are shown below:

1. 7 × 24 production systems. Planned downtime notification is needed.
2. Systems that are normally available for extended working hours, say, 6 am to 9 pm. Planned downtime notification is needed.
3. Systems that are available during normal working hours but can be taken down after hours without official notice.
4. Systems that can be taken down during working hours with one or two hours notice.
5. Systems that can be taken down with little or no notice.
6. Systems that can be taken down immediately if the resource they use is needed for the more important system. An example is a power outage where minimal power is available and what there is devoted to the most important systems.

> ***Note:*** Notifications here should form part of the *change management* procedures.

Potential Business Benefits of SLAs

Some of the potential benefits of an SLA can be classified under *business benefits* and *IT benefits*.

■ Stable production environment
■ Consistent response times
■ User effectiveness and satisfaction

- Resilience, especially for mission-critical work
- Improved QoS
- Competitive edge

Some of the reasons for using SLAs* are as follows:

1. Define performance levels required (58%)
2. Measure service level provided (52%)
3. Measure customer satisfaction (35%)
4. Set and manage/customer/user expectations (34%)
5. Expand services (30%)

Potential IT Benefits of SLAs

Some of the IT benefits of SLAs are as follows:

- Skills development
- Increased productivity
- Helps IT to be viewed as a benefit not just an overhead

IT Service Delivery

Once an SLA is drawn up, the IT department then has to devise ways of meeting these requirements and determine the cost of doing so. In fact, an SLA is the main driver in what processes, procedures, and products are used in obtaining information which shows whether the SLA is being met. In addition, an SLA gives the IT department something to aim at rather than trying to achieve the mythical subsecond response times with 100% availability.

Of course, every user will ask for these service characteristics but cost is the great leveler. If the cost of a desired service level is too great for the users, then a less stringent SLA must be worked out with them.

To meet nontrivial SLA needs, a service management infrastructure has to be set up or, if one exists, be adapted to cover the new SLA. It is often convenient to modify an existing SLA for a similar business service rather than negotiate from *scratch*.

The service management infrastructure would typically cover the following, with assistance from vendors and other outside agencies where necessary:

- Service level objectives from the SLA
- Help desk
- Operations
- Applications/middleware
- Operating system
- Hardware
- Network

---

* *Source:* Lucent Technologies (acquired by Alcatel in 2006).

The last four items in this list represent the scope of systems management, although the management of applications is becoming feasible with the advent of application knowledge modules (KMs).

One way of classifying service management is to break the service delivery infrastructure into the following disciplines:

■ User support
■ Operations and support
■ Systems management

We have seen these expanded in Chapter 3 under section Elements of Service Management.

SLA: Structure and Samples

1. The following text is extracted from a vendor SLA and shows the elements covered by the agreement. These elements do not include availability or response times but the structure is informative.
   a. Title page
   b. SLA commitments, one signature from each side
   c. Technical support SLA signature list
   d. Purpose, goals, and scope
   e. Responsibilities and guidelines
   f. Technical support services
   g. Desktop services
   h. Server administration services
   i. Network access services
   j. Other technical support services
   k. SLA clarifications for users (*what are their responsibilities?*)
   l. SLA clarifications for vendors (*what are their responsibilities?*)
2. The following is the outline of a sample *security* policy covering security policy and regulations for a fictional company. The structure could be used in an SLA in the security section.
   a. Introduction
   b. Security guidelines
   c. Security policy and standards
   d. Data owners
   e. Data custodian
   f. Data users
   g. Security administrator
   h. Data classification
   i. Access controls
   j. User identification
   k. Password management
   l. Data access controls
   m. Business resumption planning
   n. Security self-assessment
   o. Enforcement and legal responsibilities
   The purpose of showing these differing SLA structures is to highlight the fact that each SLA depends very much on what the user needs and is asking for—the two are not necessarily the same!

3. An SLA agreement from Martin County, Florida, is reproduced below:
   Service Level
   a. The Martin County physical computer network must be operational 7 days a week, 24 hours a day.
   b. The network can never be brought down *intentionally* Monday to Friday, am to 5 pm (*no planned outages in daytime*).
   c. Any intentional downtime (installations), maintenance and repair) must be announced to users at least 24 hours prior to the outage.
   d. Any unplanned network outage occurring Monday through Friday between 8 am and 5 pm will be corrected within 4 hours of its being reported.
   e. Any unplanned outage occurring any other time will be corrected by midnight the following regularly scheduled work day.
   f. Excluding planned network outages, the network must be available 99.9% in any 28-day period.

It is the SLA that dictates the requirements and deliverables for service management. It is hoped that what has gone before on SLAs will be sufficient for you to face the users and talk sensibly about wants, needs and the realities of IT life.

SLA: How Do We Quantify Availability?

This begs the question again of *availability of what and to whom?* Some elements of an application system or other service might be as follows:

- Users' screens/PCs—local and remote from the IT system
- LAN connecting around a site
- WAN connecting across sites and to the central IT system(s)
- Internet for appropriate applications
- Server, central, remote, or both
- Operating system(s), depending on the mix of vendor hardware/software
- Middleware (OLTP, web applications, web supporting applications)
- Database (traditional hierarchical, network, object, chained file, and relational)
- Application (in-house or COTs)
- Disks, directly or network attached
- Other peripherals, tapes, OCR, MICR
- Other parts of a system supporting the user service

At the end of the day, it is the availability of whatever is specified in the SLA between IT and the business. Some people might concentrate on the availability of the server, others the ability of users to access their application(s).

SLA: Reporting of Availability

Different people will have different *viewpoints* of what is *available* and what is *not available* or *down*. The operations manager may have several disks and tapes out of action but the end user may not even notice if there is, for example, disk mirroring in place. This concept of *views* also applies to entities such as mean time between failures (MTBF) which is dealt with later. The question is *availability* or *failure* of what?

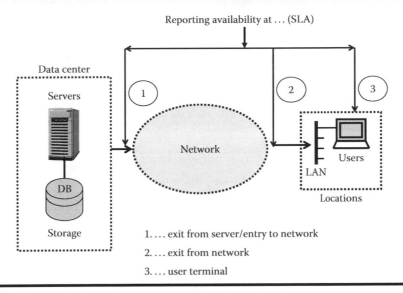

Reporting availability at … (SLA)

1. … exit from server/entry to network
2. … exit from network
3. … user terminal

Figure 7.2 SLA reporting: Availability—viewpoints.

In Figure 7.2, we see three different parts of a *system* where availability has a meaning, depending on where you *sit*. At point 1, the center operations people might say *the system is up*, even if the network is down. If the network is up and the service is operating up to point 2 (the network exit), the center and network operations people say the whole system is up, even if some outage, such as power, might mean that the end user is still seeing no service, that is, for him/her, the system is down.

It is likely that different groups within IT will have different responsibilities and SLAs. For example, a center SLA will be concerned with the service in all its aspects to point 1, the network peoples' SLA from point 1 to point 2 and a location personnel SLA covering point 2 to point 3. It would be difficult for people at the center to cover the area from 2 to 3.

In practice, I have seen responsibility and an SLA for operations staff which covers the service from the server through point 1 to point 2 and *location* personnel responsible downstream from point 2 to point 3. Table 7.1, in the SLA report for the service or system, might look as follows with *agreed* (with the users) points of recording:

There are of course many other aspects of service level reporting than just availability of a service. It is the unambiguous clarification of this question which will decide on what being *available* means. The availability of whatever is agreed upon may be measured manually or by software though the latter will cease to function if the server on which it resides goes down server on which it resides goes down.

Reneging on SLAs

> *Note:* The user reactions to poor service follow a gradual pattern of simple moaning over their morning coffee to the *you wouldn't like me when I'm angry* scenario. Remember, the days of *you'll have what you're given* attitude, common in the bad old days, has given way to a more cooperative working relationship between the business and the IT department. In fact, it is now a major task for a CIO or senior IT person to demonstrate that IT adds value to the business and is not just an unavoidable cost.

Table 7.1   Sample SLA Availability Table

Service Point	Availability (%)
Server exit, to Point 1 as seen by ops	99.7
Network, Point 1 to Point 2	99.9
Service, at Point 2	99.6[a]
Service, Point 2 to Point 3	99.9
Service, at Point 3 as seen by users	99.5[a]

[a] We see here a prime example of Lusser's Law of reliability multiplication here in this simple model of a service (see Chapter 5).

The following paragraphs are from a book on *High Availability* by Floyd Piedad and Michael Hawkins,[*] quoted here with permission.

> *User unhappiness* is the first and least severe stage. Users simply express unhappiness with poor system availability. The IT organization may either recognize a problem or deny it, citing their host or network availability statistics as proof. Those who deny the problem's existence bring their organization to the next stage of user alienation.
>
> *User distrust* is characterized by user disbelief in much of what the IT organization says. Users may begin to view IT's action plans as insufficient, or view the IT organization as incapable of implementing its plans. They gradually lose interest in helping IT with end user surveys and consultations. IT organizations that can deliver on promises and provide better availability *from the user's point of view* can prevent users from moving to the next stage of user alienation.
>
> *User opposition* is the third stage of alienation. Here, users do not merely ignore IT plans—they begin to actively oppose them, suggesting alternatives that may not align with IT's overall plans. Users start to take matters into their own hands, researching alternatives that might help solve their problems. The challenge for the IT organization is to convince users that the IT plan is superior. The best way to meet this challenge is to conduct a pilot test of the user's suggested alternative, then evaluate the results hand-in-hand with users. In contrast, we have seen some IT organizations react arrogantly, telling users to *do what you want, but don't come crying to us for help*. These organizations find themselves facing the final stage of user alienation.
>
> *User outsourcing* is the final stage of user alienation. Users convince management that the best solution lies outside the IT organization. Outsourcing can take the form of hiring an outside consultant to design their system, going directly to an outside system supplier, or even setting up their own IT organization. At this stage, users have completely broken off from the IT organization, and reduced—if not totally eliminated—the need to fund it.

---

[*] *High Availability*—F. Piedad and M. Hawkins (Prentice Hall PTR), ISBN 0-13-096288-0. This book is very useful for topics about the management aspects of HA, among other things.

> *Aside:* Incidentally, I maintain that DEC (Digital Equipment Corporation) gained footholds in IBM *camps* in the 70s and 80s due to the situation in the last paragraph.

They did not go for IBM's *jugular* and try to replace the mainframe but concentrated on users, especially scientific ones, and their immediate requirements. These could often be satisfied by a DEC system and a DEC partner application. DEC spotted the value of applications running on their machinery long before other vendors did and, in the 1970s and 1980s, had the then largest catalogue of applications in the industry.

For more detailed examples of SLAs, see the very good papers in the two references below:

1. *Cisco (Network):* http://www.cisco.com/en/US/tech/tk869/tk769/technologies_white_paper09186a008011e783.shtml#step4]
2. *RL Consulting:* http://www.itsm.info/Sample%20SLA%20Templates.pdf

SLAs in a managed *cloud environment* are a different proposition because IT will need to negotiate with the cloud provider on behalf of the users in his own organization and the question of *who reports what to whom* decided between all interested parties.

HA Management: The Project*

In another IBM paper (other than the one referenced below), Joseph Gulla writes:

> Have you ever noticed there are two basic kinds of IT projects? The *first* is a project in name only. It has executive interest but not true support. It has a team, but its members have other jobs as well. The project has a goal but it might not be firm or it changes in an unmanaged way. Let's call them "self-styled projects."
>
> The **second** category is the formal project with funding, executive support, dedicated resources, deadlines and serious consequences for failure. These are the "real projects."

Start-Up and Design Phase

There is a diagram I used to illustrate the *cost of correcting errors* in software development and other projects. It was a curve that showed rapidly increasing costs involved in correcting problems as the project proceeded. The curve was used to demonstrate that *well begun is half done* and getting the project out of a hole after much digging became a massive task.

That is why the start-up and design phase is singled out here for attention. Most of what follows can be used in other projects apart from HA. I have found that using the time notation (P-w), where P is production day and w the number of weeks before P that a particular activity should start, is a useful header to documented project activity. It focuses the mind quite effectively. Thus, P-12 is an activity due 12 weeks (3 months) before production date. This is a documentation

---

* See *Seven Reasons Why Projects Fail* (Joseph Gulla, ex-IBM, now Alazar Press). See http://www.ibmsystemsmag.com/mainframe/tipstechniques/applicationdevelopment/project_pitfalls/.

method I find very useful, particularly with fellow IT people who have an aversion to calendars and clocks.

The Management Flow

Figure 7.2 shows the activity flow from concept, through design and on to implementation and operation. It is roughly chronological and suggests tools and techniques which might be employed in this sequence of activities.

A more detailed sequence is shown in Appendix 3 headed Your HA/DR Route Map and Kitbag and the Appendix also covers cost of ownership (TCO) and risk assessment and management at both project and *deliverables* level.

> *Design/Startup:* As said, the use of these tools is not prescriptive or mandatory but knowledge of the tools and techniques can generate synergy of thinking among participants of Delphi, PDWs, and so on. The process should start with the need which is normally a business request for a new or modified service. The next step would normally be a PDW to give the project an initial *shape* and scope. This will require someone skilled as a facilitator to oversee this activity, though he or she need not be a project manager.
>
> *Operations/management:* The next phase after implementation of the service is the day to day running of the service which is just as important as the design stage since it here that SLAs are achieved or not. There are a number of areas involved here and the basic ones are shown in Figure 7.3. Operation and management are not passive activities but an active discipline which not only records but acts on service events.

The Management Framework

Figure 7.4 illustrates the management framework.

Project Definition Workshop

A short conversation from Lewis Carroll's *Alice in Wonderland* will outline the need for, and indicate the direction of, a PDW:

Alice: "Would you tell me, please, which way I ought to go from here?"
Cheshire Cat: "That depends a good deal on where you want to get to," Alice: "I don't much care where—"
Cheshire Cat: "Then it doesn't matter which way you go,"
Alice: "—so long as I get SOMEWHERE,"
Cheshire Cat: "Oh, you're sure to do that, if you only walk long enough."*

This conversation illustrates to a *T* my take on PDWs, a simple principle which you can expand to implement in several ways. The bare bones of the process are as follows:

---

* I have lived in Cheshire (UK) all my life and very close to Lewis Carroll's original home at Daresbury. However, I still have no idea what a Cheshire Cat is or how if differs from other cats.

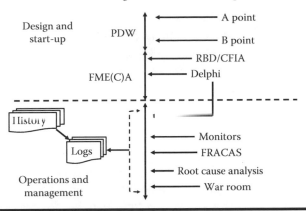

Figure 7.3   **Design and operation: Flow of activity.**

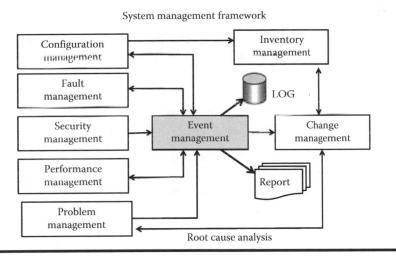

Figure 7.4   **The HA management framework.**

- Define the *A Point*, which is where you are now.
- Define the *B Point* which is where you want to get to.
- Develop and refine the activities needed for the transition state A to state B.
- Classify them under disciplines—operations, development, systems management, security, and so on.
- Develop an action plan against these items and assign to people.
- Document in a project initiation document (PID; see section Project Initiation Document) and get on with it.
- Seek a peer review by someone not involved directly.

The beauty of the PDW is that it works!

Outline of the PDW

Today, a PDW is a common vehicle for setting up projects and was common fare in IBM in the 1970s and 1980s and still exists today but under a different name. It is *not* a project management and control technique but a way of defining a project as unambiguously as possible. It does not replace project management tools and technologies and is usually independent of them, although such tools can be used in carrying out the actions and work items coming out of the PDW.

The purpose of the PDW is to allow an organization to reach a common understanding of the business requirements and operational parameters for the delivery of an identified project, in this case an HA design and implementation. This information will allow the development of a solution to meet the users' requirements and to manage the integration of the proposed project approach into the users' business with maximum chance of success and minimum disruption.

A PDW can be used at several stages of the project. Outputs from the workshop enable the top-level deliverables, project acceptance and signoff criteria to be agreed. The key skills and resources are identified and the project pricing expectations are set.

To aid the PDW process, a *project brief* should be prepared, which will describe the requirements and environment for the project and will normally include the following inputs:

- Background—where it came from and who it is for and the sponsor
- Outline business case and drivers—cost and business impact of downtime
- Project definition, explaining what the project needs to achieve and including
  - Project goals
  - Project scope—setting boundaries to change and technology
  - Outline project deliverables or desired outcomes
  - Critical success factors (CSFs)—not cost, as that is a constraint not a CSF
  - Exclusions, constraints, assumptions and interfaces
- Success and acceptance criteria—IT and user
- Risks involved—these are to be addressed in the PDW
- Project organization (overall responsibilities only)—detailed roles and responsibilities come out of the PDW actions

Output: The output of a PDW will be a draft *PID*, covering many of the same topics, but eventually in more detail and with more certainty.

PDW Method Overview

The normal way of running a PDW is via a facilitator, internal or external. That person will direct operations but an overview will be presented here. It is assumed that the A point and B point are defined in some way or other, perhaps via a Delphi session.

It is then necessary for the team and facilitator to extract all the actions needed for the journey A to B. A typical rough output of such a session is a series of activities across a number of charts or black/whiteboards. It is then necessary to decide what area each activity comes under (operations, security, application development, database, OLTP, etc.) and a manager assigned to that area, in Figure 7.5 they are the responsibilities of Jim, Fred,..., and Sue.

The progress in these areas should be subject to frequent meetings, both within the discipline and cross-discipline and hence be subject to the organization's *change management* methodology. All this is driven by, and feeds into, the *PID*. The PID is the project startup *blueprint*. You can see this graphically in Figure 7.5.

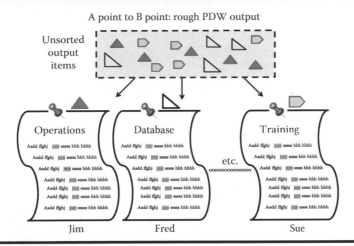

Figure 7.5 PDW: Session(s) output categorized and assigned.

Project Initiation Document

PID is a core document for the project and its format and content is pretty consistent across vendors, consultants, and the like. I have worked on several of these documents in a big UK bank, not all initiated by me, but maintained, updated, and used as input to various reviews. The documents were a very useful inheritance for me at contract start and for people who took over from me at contract end. We'll examine a typical structure and content headings and discuss its creation, maintenance, and use.

Of course, if your organization has its own mandatory document standards, it shouldn't be difficult to fit a PID around the appropriate ones.

There are two basic ways of developing a HA solution:

1. *Ab initio*, that is from nothing through to a working solution
2. A *delta* increment across the whole of an existing configuration

The output of the PDW will obviously be different in both cases. In my view, the second scenario will be the messiest to handle, partly because nearly everything done will be a change. A third possible route is specific *delta* work on a few components of an existing system that are proving the most vulnerable to outages. The route chosen will depend on users requirements, costs, and available skills.

PID Structure and Purpose

Purpose

The PID is the document that will answer the questions why, what, when, and who, which covers management information and approval, what it entails, progress via milestones and who is doing what to ensure that progress. Whatever project management method is used, it can fit in with a PID, even if it mandates its own documentation. PIDs are recognized by PRINCE2 (projects in a controlled environment) and so cooperation is not a big issue. A major thing to remember is that the PID should be a *living* document nurtured by progress and any changes rendered necessary by circumstances.

The working flipcharts and notes generated at the PDW plus the events and documentation leading up to the PDW, including previous attempts or experience from similar projects are the inputs.

Structure

PRINCE documentation suggests the following table of contents for a PID but *they are not carved in stone* and I have seen variations used to cater for an organization's own needs,* often using their own documentation standards:

- Purpose of the document—what is this project all about? Relate to business
- Background to the need for it
- Project definition—I would hammer the *A point to B point* and *viewpoints* way of looking at things
- Method of approach, probably devised and communicated by the facilitator
- Business case, including losses if we don't do it
- Project organization
- Communications plan
- Project quality plan
- Initial project plan
- Project controls
- Initial risk and issues log—these pages will get *red hot* I can assure you. The document should chart actions and progress against these issues and risks.
- Financial management—this could be a totally different document. This log needs frequent review and follow-up.
- Contingency plans
- Project filing structure, that is, where can I find things out regarding this project.

PID Notes

Some key features of a Project Initiation Document (PID) are as follows.

1. The beginning of the document can contain the usual features of your organization—who has copies, contact names, revisions and dates, and so on.
2. A PID need not be a single monolithic document but an outline and holding document which points to other, separately maintained documents.
3. The document will obviously state what is in the project plan but equally important is an understanding of what is *not* in the plan, in other words, exclusions. This has been found necessary to avoid situations where certain things have been assumed as implicit in the plan when they have not been requested or designed explicitly.
4. The reader will be aware by now of my discomfort at following prescriptive activities blindly. The key here is to use common sense, decide on who the document is written for, and ask yourself if everyone involved disappeared, would the PID be enough for a new team to take up the reins and drive on?

---

* See Appendix 3 for an expansion of these topics *a la* PRINCE2 and my comments and additions.

There are several sample PIDs to be found on the Internet. Searching on *pid, sample document* will yield a number of PIDs from various sources.

Multistage PDW

Where a project is large or requires phasing, it is convenient to have several A points and B points, where the B point of phase 1 is the A point of phase 2 and so on. Each one then requires a mini-PDW, handled exactly the same as before while ensuring *continuity* from one phase to succeeding phases. It may be advisable to have a multistage PID unless you wish to produce a single PID, resembling *War and Peace* in size and scope.

Delphi Techniques and Intensive Planning

> *Note:* These topics cover activities where raw brain power, prejudices, and pet ideas are subjugated to the pursuit of solutions to defined objectives by a superior being called a facilitator.

In HA and DR planning and implementation, it is not acceptable to take the opinions of *n* people, add them together and divide by *n* to get a mean solution. It should be more like a decision made by an informed jury so that the end result is sound and you don't find the wrong man guilty.

Delphi Technique[*]

One process used to *facilitate* the meeting is called the *Delphi Technique*. Its name comes from the all-knowing Oracle at Delphi and the actual method was developed during the cold war to forecast the impact of technology on warfare.

This technique was further refined and developed by the RAND Corporation for the US Department of Defense in the 1950s. Although originally intended for use as a psychological weapon during the cold war, it has since been adapted for use in business and other areas of endeavor. Before going into the technique itself, a little tale about the surprising outcome of a Delphi-like session involving an IBM facilitator and senior executives from a large chemical company.

> The facilitator asked them to work alone and produce a list of the six most pressing issues in the business then present them briefly to the rest of the executives.
>
> The outcome was an eye opener. They disagreed totally on what the major issues were and expressed surprise at some of the issues raised by their peers in their own sector of the business. "I didn't know that stock levels were a serious issue" said the Finance Director, "I could have helped you there". The same scenario was repeated among them for other important issues, each new to someone in the team. Even though their expectation was one of immediate consensus on what the issues were, they found the exercise very useful in bringing these thoughts to the surface.

That is one of the beneficial effects of Delphi.

---

[*] For the knowledge geek, http://is.njit.edu/pubs/delphibook/delphibook.pdf is a 618 page document on Delphi and, for all I know, the Freudian and Jungian implications of the method.

Although the executives were unaware of the technique, they were actually partaking in a diluted, short-term version of it.

> ***Note:*** In general, the Delphi method is useful in answering one, specific, single-dimension question. There is less support in the field for its use to determine complex forecasts involving multiple factors. Such complex model building is more appropriate for other, more esoteric models, perhaps with Delphi results serving as inputs. This makes it useful for single IT issues in the right circumstances and with today's communication methods and networks the traditional snail-mail and days/weeks timeframes can be short-circuited.

This is what I have called the *turbo-Delphi technique*, an exercise tailored to fit the necessary decision timescale for an IT issue. Look at the simplified flowchart of the technique below with the steps explained (Figure 7.6).

Delphi: The Steps

The essence of the technique is as follows (refer to Figure 7.6):

1. A *facilitator* is chosen, probably for the whole project or subproject. It should be someone familiar with the project and having some leadership and analysis skills. If this is part of a major project, it should already have a *sponsor*.
   He or she should initiate any documentation on the *project*.
2. A *panel of experts* is chosen. This is more than likely the IT team involved in the availability work together with a business contact. An *expert* can be defined as *an individual with relevant knowledge and experience of a particular topic*.
3. Define the *problem* that needs to be understood and input given on.
4. Set out the *questions* that require input from the experts. The answers should be correlated for commonality of views. A second set of questions based on the input should then be issued. In a *turbo* version of Delphi, the whole thing might be done in conference mode around a table with *think* breaks to gain independent input from the team. Collect the results.

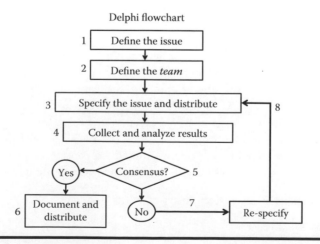

Figure 7.6   Delphi technique flowchart.

5. *Analyze* the input and findings and put an *action* plan together for the issue in question. If the facilitator finds broad agreement, the *solution* is documented and distributed. If not, the variations of opinion are documented and distributed and a second round of opinions is sought and the analysis repeated.

6. When some form of consensus is reached, *initiate* the project.

There are other design and evaluation methods, one of which is discussed below. They sometimes overlap and it is up to the account which elements of which method it uses. The *common sense* method should be applied here.

Intensive Planning

This is really what I feel is an extension of the Delphi technique with more and discipline. It appears to have originated with IBM. It is not well documented anymore but I will add the comments made on it by an ex-IBM friend who suffered the process. I have modified his specific objectives to suit our purposes:

> ... the original sessions were 2 weeks and started at 8:29 and other –:x9s times during the day which was an excellent idea. Late arrivals were excluded from that session. Each session posed a question and couldn't end until there was unanimous agreement. One of the main things was to agree on the real issues ... not necessarily the obvious ones (I seem to remember it was called the Kluge although I can't find any reference to that term elsewhere).
>
> My main memory is that it was a very wearing 2-week experience.

I think you will recognize the similarity with the Delphi technique exercise but with *heavy weights* being lifted.

FMEA Process*

Failure mode and effects analysis (FMEA) is a methodology designed to identify potential failure modes for a product or process, to assess the risk associated with those failure modes, to rank the issues in terms of importance, and to identify and carry out corrective actions to address the most serious concerns. The FMEA dates back to 1949 and was used initially by the US Military.

Failure mode and effects and criticality analysis (FMECA) is essentially FMEA with a criticality analysis, outlined briefly below. This is optional as it was aimed at areas involving possible loss of life or equipment.

> ***Note:*** None of the management/design methods and techniques outlined in this book is mandatory. If you already have your own methods, approved by the organization, then use them. You will, however, probably find some useful add-ons in these discussions.

---

* A very good exposition of FMEA (64 pages and readable) can be found at the International Marine Contractors Association (IMCA) website: http://www.imca-int.com/media/73361/imcam166.pdf.

FMEA: An Analogy

In the 1850s–1860s during the westward migrations of people in the American West, there was person called a *wagon master* who was responsible for the safety of people migrating from the East to California and states in between. He was effectively the precursor of the captains of ships and aircraft today. His job was to *anticipate* hurdles on the journey and *circumvent* them in some way.

There would be rivers to cross, mountains to negotiate, supplies to be gathered en route, and hostile personnel to be avoided—by scout reconnaissance—or repulsed. There would be options open to him: move up/down river for a crossing, climb/circumvent the mountain, seek out water and game, and avoid or fight hostile elements. After a few trips, the wagon master would have some mental documentation to help in overcoming new hurdles which might arise.

> ***Note:*** Sound familiar? This was the FMEA and CFIA of the Wild West.

FMEA: The Steps

Slight differences are found between the various FMEA/FMECA standards. An FMECA analysis procedure typically consists of the following logical steps (*my comments thus*):

- Assemble your (virtual) team and estimate a timescale.
- Define the system components (usual user involvement as in any service).
- Define ground rules and assumptions in order to help drive the design.
- Construct system block diagrams (and try to reduce them for availability calculations if necessary).
- (Perform any *useful* calculations with what you have learned from this book and elsewhere).
- Identify failure modes (piece, part level or functional) (*CFIA*).
- Analyze failure effects/causes (ditto and lessons from previous designs).
- Feed results back into design process.
- Classify the failure effects by severity (see Table 7.2).
- Perform criticality calculations (*for DR decision purposes*).
- Rank failure mode criticality if this entity is employed (FMECA).
- Determine critical items including SPoFs.
- Feed *this needs attention* results back into design process.
- Identify the means of failure detection, isolation and compensation (*Monitoring*).
- Perform maintainability analysis (what is the expected MTTR and what stock is necessary).
- Document the analysis, summarize uncorrectable design areas, and identify special controls necessary to reduce failure risk (mitigation).
- Make recommendations (*to stakeholders*) and develop SLA(s).
- Follow up on corrective action in design and implementation/effectiveness.

We are in effect performing a *walkthrough* with a FMEA exercise. It is probably at this stage that the criteria for the declaration of DR are established and the ground laid for a DR plan if one does not already exist.

Table 7.2 CFIA Activity Table Schematic

Failure Point	Impact	Recovery Action	Notes/Owner
Data center firewall	All remote services would stop	Switch IP address to *warm* standby within 4 hours (SLA)	Migrate to BT firewall Svc?/Alan V. Proc. 23
Application 1 DB	Data is RAID so loss can be catered for	None needed initially	Harry S. to schedule recovery Proc 26
Image scanner	Other scanners will take over	Recover failing component and re-instate. Check RCA/document	Remaining scanners must support peak load/Joe S. Proc 33
Fax server	Other fax servers would continue but impact felt at peak period	Recover server using Runbook section 3.1	Install another fax server as warm standby?/Dave D. Proc 43B
System console	Temporary *blip*	Configure multiple console support	Done already?/Alan V. If not done Proc 7
Loss of data center	Total loss of service	Invoke DR and reroute traffic to London DR site	Team/review DR plan afterwards Procs DR1–16

 Etc.

FMECA* = FMEA + Criticality

FMECA is a *extra* on FMEA where the *C* stands for criticality which adds an evaluation of how critical a failure is in terms of immediate effect and consequences. The criticality factor was aimed mainly at projects where severe damage of loss of life might occur and an attempt has been made to quantify this factor. This may not be useful to IT services but it is covered here for completeness.

Risk Evaluation and Priority: Risk Evaluation Methods

A typical failure modes and effects analysis incorporates some method to evaluate the risk associated with potential problems identified through analysis. One of the most common methods, risk priority numbers, is discussed next.

In order to use these numbers to assess risk, the analysis must

- Rate the severity of each effect of a failure.
- Rate the likelihood of occurrence for each cause of failure.

---

* FMECA, used in military, aerospace, and so on. Its value in IT projects is debatable as representing possible overkill.

- Rate the likelihood of prior detection of cause of failure (i.e., the likelihood of detecting the problem before it reaches the end user or customer).
- Calculate the RPN by taking the product of the three rating

$$RPN = \text{severity} \times \text{occurrence} \times \text{detection}$$

Each of these ratings can be given a number between 1 and 10 so the maximum value of RPN is 1000 (10 × 10 × 10) and the minimum is 1. This RPN can then be used to compare issues/faults within the analysis to prioritize problems for corrective action (repair). There are some people who doubt the validity and usefulness of the RPN but it has some standing and support in the world of reliability standards.

As I said earlier, these techniques are for you to choose the best fit to your organization and *modus operandum*. However, the next topic is I feel, a *must have*.

Component Failure Impact Analysis

CFIA[*] is a proactive method to determine the potential impact on service delivery in the event that a particular component (or configuration item) should fail. It can be used in the *design* and *operational* phases of development and implementation. In the operational phase, failure to deliver to expectations (SLAs) can be looked at from different angles for causes:

- Incorrect design ? Back to the drawing board.
- Incorrect *build*? Rework?
- Incorrect installation? Reinstall?
- Incorrect operation? Review procedures and implement.
- Incorrectly maintained?—Ditto.
- *Bad* external influences (malware, malice) or *hostile* environment? Review and improve if possible.
- Deliberate damage or interference? Interview personnel.

CFIA is a useful tool as it can create a visual tabular view of services and their required component items and, if used, a searchable information base for analyzing future problems.

The CFIA as part of the availability management process will involve technical specialists who understand the way that the infrastructure is arranged and organized. A basic CFIA will target a specific section of the infrastructure: just looking at simple binary choices (e.g., if we lose component x, will a service degrade or simply stop working)?

CFIA Development—A Walkthrough and Risk Analysis

A risk analysis identifies important functions and assets that are critical to a firm's operations, then subsequently establishes the probability of a disruption to those functions and assets. Once the risk is established, objectives and strategies to eliminate avoidable risks and minimize impacts of

---

[*] Definition from http://itsm.certification.info/cfia.html.

unavoidable risks can be set. A list of critical business functions and assets should first be compiled and prioritized. Following this, determine the probability of specific threats to business functions and assets. For example, a certain type of failure may occur once in 10 years—what is the impact when it does happen?

From a risk analysis, a set of objectives and strategies to prevent, mitigate, and recover from disruptive threats should be developed. Structured walkthroughs are familiar things in program development. It is possible, even desirable to perform a similar exercise on a system/service to develop the CFIA list discussed earlier, otherwise there is a lot of guesswork involved.

How do we do this? It is a question of getting a group of peers together to *walk through* the delivery process of a service[*] through a system, usually via a facilitator and a blackboard to plot the flow of work. At each stage of this journey, the things to be done and the questions to be asked are as follows[†]:

- Determine the function of the system/service components.
- Create functional and reliability block diagrams (RBDs).
- Document the above and the objectives/requirements of the system/service.
- What happens if this component fails (failure effect)?
- Can we prevent the failure upfront—buy the best, keep it cooler?
- How easy and practical is it to fix without undue business impact? To hand or will someone have to mail it to us?
- Can we cover for the failure in some way if it is permanent (redundancy, hot plug, alternate route, etc.) but not a DR situation?
- What other functions or services are affected if it fails?
- What is the total business impact of each failure identified? FMEA suggests ranking the failures for criticality but, as I implied above, this is optional.
- Rank the exposed failures in terms of impact and recovery effort/time and weigh against available resources.
- Which failures constitute DR invocation situations? If this cannot be decided here, suggest some criteria for making the decision when a major failure occurs.
- Develop follow-up and corrective actions ... we are going to document all this aren't we!!
- ... and so on. A *business person* and an appropriate *technical expert* should help.

The analysis should be used to create a CFIA table, a schematic of which is shown below. In real life, it will be much more detailed and organization-specific.

CFIA Table: Schematic

The exercise could be carried out on an existing system or on the design and architecture of a proposed system. Table 7.2 is extracted from a real-life impact/SPoF analysis of a single service of a large bank. It ran to five pages and involved several stakeholders in a review of the outcome. Knowledge of the application is vital to assessing the impact of any failure. *Proc* in the table below refers to *procedures* to be followed.

---

[*] Obviously, this exercise is applied to services critical to the business—high *S* value.
[†] Some of these are FMEA recommendations.

222 ■ High Availability IT Services

> **Note:** Such a table should generate documents that highlight SPoFs, recovery options, and their recovery times and what action is recommended to reduce similar incidents.

More advanced CFIAs can be expanded to include a number of variables, such as likelihood of failure, recovery time, and cost of failure. Remember, the seriousness (S) of an outage situation is

$$S = (business)impact \times probability\ (likelihood)\ of\ occurrence$$

Some installations may make an assessment of the probability of any particular failure based on either experience or vendor data.

Have you ever wondered whether the operator or other vital support *personnel are SPoFs*? If one of your DBAs is on vacation/strike and the only other one has just walked under the number 12 bus, what do you do? Have a backup support agreement with a consultancy or vendor on a *pay if we use you* basis? (See Appendix 3.) If you think this is far-fetched, look at the following true incident of a personnel SPoF:

> Then a serious disruption occurred. On a Saturday, with all 750 Anytown branches open in 17 states, most storage area network (SAN) connectivity was lost, forcing branches to conduct limited business offline for six hours. "Essentially, one of the existing solutions blew up," says Jim. "Joe [Bloggs] was away celebrating a wedding anniversary and Harry [Lime] was on vacation." [*Bank incident 2011: From a Banking IT magazine with names changed to protect the guilty*]

Quantitative CFIA

My experience of CFIA in IBM was quantitative as well as qualitative where the configuration was communicated to IBM Customer Engineering for analysis. They had figures of estimates for the reliability of various IBM components that were used to provide an estimate of the reliability of a configuration as specified. Such output was obviously vendor specific but could be done for other vendors, given that the reliability figures for the components of the system were available. However, not all vendors publish such figures, even if they are known.

CFIA: Other Factors

It may escape notice but there may be other services which depend on the service in question when carrying out a CFIA, for example:

- Were there files and other data sets being created which are used elsewhere and left open after the failure?
- Is there a *job* waiting for output from the failing system and what is the impact if it cannot run on time?
- Is there a mechanism for informing all *stakeholders* of the failure?

> **Note:** In essence, I am asking if there might be *knock-on* effects on other services and systems from the failure of the service we are dealing with. No application is an island.

Management of Operations Phase

Technology without management and control can do more harm than good in many situations. A service is only as good as the worst aspect of its design and implementation and its continued QoS is a function of its operation and maintenance. That is the reason for including this section of the book.

Failure Reporting and Corrective Action System

Again, this, like FMEA, is an outline of a tried and tested methodology for post-operational monitoring and control of a system. It is not mandatory but you may find it useful, failure reporting and corrective action system (FRACAS). The US Military Guide MIL-STD-2155(AS) says of the relationship between FMECA and FRACAS. I have made the leap of faith that when they say FMECA I can substitute FMEA:

> FME(C)A's primary purpose is to influence the system and component design to either eliminate or minimize the occurrences of a hardware failure or the consequences of a failure. The FRACAS represents the *real world* experience of actual failures and their consequences. An FME(C)A benefits the FRACAS by providing a source of comprehensive failure effect and failure severity information for the assessment of actual hardware failure occurrences. Actual failure experience reported and analyzed in FRACAS provides a means of verifying the completeness and accuracy of the FME(C)A.

> **Note:** Basically, they are saying that FMECA and FRACAS go together like ham and eggs, which is why they are included in this book as optional management methods and techniques.

Introduction

FRACAS is an example of closed loop failure reporting fixing system inasmuch as it goes round its loop of activity in *learning and review* mode. "The essence of a closed loop FRACAS is that failures and faults of both hardware and software are formally reported, analysis is performed to the extent that the failure cause is understood and positive corrective actions are identified, implemented and verified to prevent further recurrence of the failure" (MIL-STD-2155[A] July 24, 1985).

We now realize that there are other types of failure other than hardware and software but the FRACAS principle still holds.

FRACAS: Steps for Handling Failures

The step names in the FRACAS process will change, depending on whether you are building an aircraft or running an IT installation or huge data center. The description below applies to Figure 7.7 and is IT oriented. The IT system as designed (by FMEA) is installed and RBD diagrams are available.

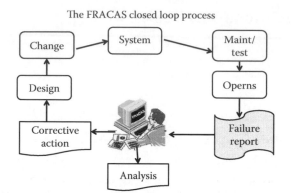

The FRACAS closed loop process

Figure 7.7   The FRACAS closed loop failure process.

1. Maintenance or tests may uncover potential failures which are reported.
2. The occurrence of real errors is also reported to the FRACAS system.
3. The failure(s) is analyzed and resolved.
4. The resolution is incorporated into the new design which is implemented using change control.
5. The whole cycle repeats.

The analysis might also be repeated periodically to categorize and perhaps *pigeonhole* errors for subsequent occurrences and speed resolution.

Typical *failure modes* might include the following:

■ Untimely operation (job2 runs before job1, result chaos)
■ Failure to operate when required, the normal definition of failure
■ Loss of any output
■ Erroneous output/results
■ Invalid output

Sometimes it is instructive to construct a table of three columns headed thus[*]:

Device/component	Failure mode	Failure effect

The *failure effects*, decided at the outset, might look as follows:

■ System failure
■ Degraded operation (Duke of York)
■ System status failure (not quite right)
■ No immediate effect

Although the documentation makes FRACAS (and FMEA) look frighteningly serious and prescriptive, you must remember that developments were often military or space ventures with serious

---

[*] This would complement the assessment table in the CFIA described previously.

consequences for failure, hence the apparent *belt, braces and spare pair of backup braces* approach. Use it as you think fit for your organization.

HA Operations: Supporting Disciplines

War Room

I came across this concept in my early days in IBM. The *war room* was a room dedicated to problem and issue management in its broadest sense, mainly for extensive problems. It contained charts, listings, and so on concerning the current issue(s) being handled. It also contained operations manuals, the history of resolved issues and related CFIA and root cause analysis (RCA) documents in case they might throw light on current problems being experienced.

War Room Location

Today, if all necessary data is online and accessible, the war room can be a virtual room, convened wherever needed, as long as the necessary information is available. In true HA fashion, it may be wise to have two rooms, similarly equipped and with key information duplicated. One might indeed be a movable vehicle if there is a possibility of the original room being unavailable because of a disaster affecting the location. This could possibly be called *peripatetic* operation after the walking Greek philosopher.

A gathering of the *war cabinet* would be called by a designated *problem manager*, attendees being decided on when the rough area of concern could be ascertained—hardware, software, network, and so on. IBM had a system called RETAIN which was a world-wide system of symptoms and solutions.

An engineer in Tokyo experiencing a problem could dial into this systems and, with appropriate keywords, initiate a search for problems matching his own. Where there was a *hit* on the particular symptoms, there might be one or more solutions posted that could solve or help to solve his current problem. Typical attendees would be the application owner, operations manager or deputy, and so on.

Once the *size and shape* of the problem is determined, the issue would be assigned an *owner* who would pursue the issue using any resources he or she needed to bottom it. This owner would need temporary empowerment to pursue his or her mission, from the service sponsor.

Documentation

Documentation—quality and pictorial systems visibility—is a key to the success of the war room and should contain information pertaining to any SLAs in force relating to the issue(s) in progress. They are enterprise specific but should contain at least the following:

- Location and backup location
- Scope of the war room activity—which services are covered
- Communication channels for all stakeholders—*very important*
- Facilitator name and contact details plus stand-in
- Service representatives and contact details plus stand-in
- BIAs and SLAs for the services covered
- Roles and responsibilities of participants by service (not necessarily specific names)

- The process which should be followed upon major issue or DR invocation
- Access to previous problems, preferably on a dedicated *server*, for example, a simple search facility* on a PC (with a standby of course)
- Visual equipment for viewing all aspects of the issue in hand, even to the extent of walls full of handwritten flipcharts
- Anything else that would help the situation

War room staff are sometimes called a *Failure Review Board* (q.v.).

> *Note:* The war room is for all intents and purposes a command and control center (CCC) for IT problems. One major benefit of the technique is it minimizes the *headless chicken syndrome*.

Change/Configuration Management

We have seen early in this book that *change* and operational *volatility* can have an adverse effect on availability or, at least, predispose systems to fail.

Change management and configuration management are very close together in terms of what they seek to achieve. Change management seeks to make changes to resources in a system in a controlled and consistent manner while understanding the impact on other parts of the system.

Change Management and Control: Best Practice

The basic elements of this key discipline are as follows:

- Identify a change management team (virtual, containing relevant skills) plus a change controller.
- Devise documentation and meetings plans (what, where, and when).
- Request for a change (initiation) from the business, IT, user, or problem resolution.
- Change impact analysis—will a change to system software X related to application A have an adverse effect on application B?†
- Authorization for the change from an appropriate authority.
- Publish the impending change—to IT staff concerned and any users who might be affected. You don't need to tell everyone about every minor change though (Figure 7.8).
- Scheduling and tracking the change(s) as a mini-project.
- Change installation, coordination, and verification.
- Backout procedures for the change where the change causes other problems. This ability is vital to an installation making changes.
- If the change does not have the desired results, then a RCA should be carried out to avoid repetition in the future.
- Change review, document, and publish the results.

---

* A customer of mine used a simple PC search tool to access previous or similar problem situations along with suggested lines of progressing and possible solutions. It worked beautifully and eliminated the need for and expense of commercial *tools*.
† I've seen it happen when the A to B connection wasn't raised in a customer—result was a big problem.

Schematic flow of change management

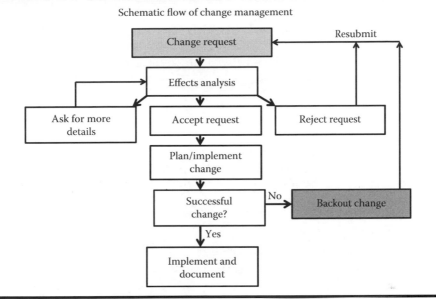

Figure 7.8 Change control schematic flow.

- Areas where change management is required include:
  - Operating environment patch management
  - Application patch/upgrade management
  - Concurrent upgrade of hardware or software
  - Installation of new hardware or software
  - Changing system or application parameters, for example, tuning the operating system or reorganizing an application database
  - Other changes which might impact business services' availability or correct functioning. A service which doesn't deliver what it is supposed to deliver can be considered *unavailable* without necessarily involving outages of hardware or software
- As ever, update and maintain the change documentation. You never know when you might need it.

The shaded box *backout change* is a vital step in the change management process. If this cannot be done, or is very slow to complete, the service will remain in limbo until the *status quo* is restored. This will result in extra time added to any subsequent *ramp-up* time. In the case of a UK bank in 2013, the delay in complete restoration of all services ran into days and very large amounts of money in compensation.

Backout and subsequent ramp-up time after a failed change are critical factors in service uptime.

Change Operations

This is the job of the change team using the established, agreed, and understood procedure for changes:

- The request for a change to be made is generated.
- A change impact analysis is performed, especially clashes with other changes.
- The change is authorized by IT and management of the requestor.

- The change is scheduled and tracked.
- The change is performed and verified.
- The change is backed out if unsuccessful.
- The requestor(s) are informed who provide change feedback.
- The change is reviewed and documented.

Patch Management

A major factor in the volatility of a service is the application of patches to the various layers of software, including the operating system. This is a change management issue as assumes greater importance the more patches that need to be applied. There are at least three philosophies pertaining to patch management:

- Put them all on a.s.a.p.
- Only put on the patches that our system needs.
- Don't bother with any of them—not recommended.

The decision which route to take may be different for different types of patch. Hot fixes are usually offered to fix a specific problem which your organization may or may not have. Other are a series of patches—rollups and service packs.

There are several papers on the topic which might be useful in deciding the patch philosophy your organization should adopt in the HA environment. The second reference (from Cisco) contains other references, including the NIST documentation on patch management. Two general references are listed below:

1. http://docs.media.bitpipe.com/io_11x/io_113690/item_831844/patch-management-ebook%5B2%5D.pdf.
2. http://blogs.cisco.com/security/patch-management-overview-challenges-and-recommendations/.

The NIST reference, NIST: Special Publication 800-40 Revision 3, Guide to Enterprise Patch Management Technologies, can be found at http://nvlpubs.nist.gov/nistpubs/SpecialPublications/NIST.SP.800-40r3.pdf (478 KB PDF).

This reference, Six Steps for Security Patch Management Best Practices, can be found at http://searchsecurity.techtarget.com/Six-steps-for-security-patch-management-best-practices.

This is not such a big task as it may appear here. Myself and the customer did it without expensive software tools: just common sense and the commitment of management to the process. Looking at the myriad of statistics about what factors contribute to downtime, whichever set you study, the *human factor* looms large.

> ***Note:*** The output of change management can be of vital importance in RCA inasmuch as it may give a clue to the possible cause from the sequence of events preceding the *outage*.

There is a quote saying "There are people who make things happen, people who watch things happen and people who say 'what happened?'" Which category are you?

Performance Management

Introduction

This, along with change management, represents a key factor in maintaining availability and complying with performance clauses in any SLAs.

Performance management is covered briefly here as a *pointer* to texts which show the *how and why* of the discipline.

One issue with performance management is *do we monitor and optimize the performance of every service and application we have?* The answer is probably *No*, unless you have resources and money to burn. That leaves the same decision to be made that applied to DR and normal recovery—what are the most important services and what performance characteristics do they require?

In addition, the monitoring aspect will need some consideration. Do we monitor, report, and analyze everything or do we work on an *exception reporting basis*? If yes, then you will need an acceptable baseline and threshold for the things you don't report on, which might include

- Maximum CPU load
- Maximum disk utilization
- Maximum network traffic
- Maximum memory utilization and so on

If one or more of these limits is breached, alerts and appropriate action should follow.

Overview

Usually, the most important services are online and it is on these services that monitoring, analyzing, and reporting is aimed. What is of interest for critical online services, aside from availability, is total response time as seen by the service user. This is the sum of the times spent in the various journey components. These times are made up of the actual time to service the request for that resource plus the time waiting to be served by that resource.

A schematic service flow is shown in Figure 7.9.

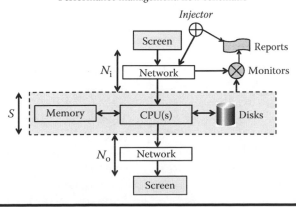

Performance management: flow schematic

Figure 7.9   Performance factors schematic.

Monitors need to be available to measure the utilization of those service resources and the total response time in that resource. In the diagram, an *injector* and monitor systems are shown. The injector system is a user emulator injecting or ping transactions into the system to check for availability and performance. Suitable monitors are used to measure (or allow calculation of) traffic, response times, and utilizations. For a transaction

N_i = network time for input traffic, N_o = network time for output traffic, S = time in system

Transaction response time at screen = $N_i + S + N_o$ = time seen by user

The *report* represents analysis of captured data, reporting, and notification of off-baseline numbers. This of course is a simple case that assumes screen painting time is zero and the system does not interact with other systems or agents.

There are some useful general sections in the following references which will help in setting up a performance management process with suitable products for any particular organization:

1. End to End Performance Management on IBMi (http://www.redbooks.ibm.com/redbooks/pdfs/sg247808.pdf).
2. Capacity and Performance Management: Best Practices White paper (Cisco) (http://www.cisco.com/c/en/us/support/docs/availability/high-availability/20769-performwp.html).

More information specific to a vendor's own environment can be found by searching on *<vendor name>, performance management*, for example, *windows, performance management*.

Security Management

Security: Threats or Posturing?

A quote from Eugene Kaspersky, chief executive of security firm Kaspersky Lab, at Infosecurity Europe 2013 in London:

> Every company is a victim of cyber attacks, whether they know it or not. For this reason, companies should be doing everything they can do to keep their data safe and to avoid being a stepping stone for attackers to go after higher level organizations.
>
> Enterprises have a critical role to play in stopping attackers from going up or down the supply chain,... Even consumers had a duty to protect their computers and digital worlds.
>
> Governments too, have a critical role to play, especially in making critical IT systems more robust by moving them on to more secure operating systems (OS), networks and applications.
>
> At present, all these elements are insecure, making it extremely difficult to defend critical infrastructures from attack. It is easier and cheaper for enemies to develop cyber weapons than it is to develop traditional weapons, and this could usher in an era of cyber weapons and cyber wars.

Today, the security threat to HA is REAL and increasing in volume and severity.

Security: Best Practice

The following points are made to provide a context for developing a security mechanism for your organization and they represent a consensus of security experts.

- Appoint an IT security manager with adequate authority in the organization
- Develop a security policy in line with the importance of the data to the business and assign ownership
- Understand any regulatory or legal security aspects which apply to your industry
- Perform risk analysis on key business areas
- Develop security mechanisms for
  - Physical and electronic components, for example, locks, card access, and shielding from radiation.
  - Authentication mechanisms.
  - Access control mechanisms, including physical access.
  - Communication security mechanisms.
- Ensure that security is not compromised when falling back to operating at a DR site.
- Use standard security features and not proprietary unless necessary.
- Evaluate security methods and software, especially those with good audit trails.
- Make security an integral part of any project and the PDW.
- Take system and data security seriously.
- Develop a security information event management system (SIEM). See Lesson 10 in Appendix 4 for SIEM and other *cyber security* topics.

Also, refer to the *Security* references in Appendix 5 for more detailed information on security threats and fighting them over and above that in Appendix 4 (http://www.availabilitydigest.com/public_articles/0807//mobile_threats.pdf).

> **Reminder:** Security does not appear as an outage cause in surveys and studies over a few years old but today, security incidents, particularly distributed denial of service, are becoming more prevalent. That is why I have placed much emphasis on security in this book.

There is a substantial report by Verizon titled "2014 Data Breach Investigations Report" that claims to give *fresh insight into cyber espionage and denial-of-service attacks ... identifies nine attack patterns, grouped by industry, making it easier to indentify the types of threats you can encounter.* See http://www.verizonenterprise.com/DBIR/2014/ (Download request page).

> **Note:** Cultivate paranoia as your watchword and guide to security and HA. This and eternal vigilance is the price you pay for HA services.

Problem Determination

In the expanded formula for availability we have seen, there is a factor MTPD, mean time to problem determination. MTTR is the actual repair time once we have located and determined the nature of the fault.

$$\text{Availability}(A) = \frac{\text{MTTF}}{\text{MTTF} + \text{MTTR} + \text{MTPD}}$$

What does this entail for the team tasked with this? Obviously maximizing the top line and minimizing the bottom line. Both are within the sphere of influence of the designer and the system operators.

Problems: Short Term

There are a number of things which must be done as soon as possible after a failure (or outage) to detect and cure the cause and, in addition, record enough information to do a Root Cause Analysis (RCA) subsequently. The latter activity is important in avoiding a repetition of that failure.

- Recognize that a fault has occurred and start brief online documentation.
- Don't panic (HCS).* Panic is the preserve of nonplanners.
- Inform those affected by the fault and those responsible for *repair*.
- Assess its severity and impact on other components or linked systems which may be affected but not the root cause. For example, have they lost synchronicity, *forgotten* the time of day, have outdated key tables, and so on?
- Identify and contact *fixers*.
- *Fixers* identify its *location* (disk, router, PDU, and so on).
- *Fixers* identify the cause.
- If serious or intractable enough, convene the *War Room*.
- Identify the *immediate* impact (invoicing *out*, Memphis location *out*, and customer website *down*), using a documented CFIA—see how useful they are?
- Devise a solution, based on previous experience if appropriate.
- Implement the solution.
- Ramp up the system to normal operation.
- Inform those affected.
- Have a Plan B.

Problems: After the Event

When the dust dies down, there are further activities to be carried out to bottom the real cause of the outage and ensure no repeat performance of it.

- Perform RCA (if not done in the *immediate* steps above).
- Document the issue and its resolution.
- If possible, fix it in such a way that an identical failure does not occur.
- Update operations, problem *logs*, and any user documentation/procedures.
- Amend any *short-term* activities found wanting and document for implementation.
- Action to replace any components which, although operational again, may be showing signs of wear and tear, for example, through more frequent transient or intermittent errors.

---

* Headless chicken syndrome (HCS). UK readers will remember Corporal Jones shouting *don't panic* while running round in manic circles.

Event Management*

To effectively manage a total system, including servers, network, storage, applications, and so on, it is essential to have almost total knowledge of what happening across the system, or at least those systems supporting critical business applications. The generic way of alerting staff to actual or impending problems is by using some means of generating *events* which are communicated to support staff.

The events can be simple information messages or something more serious. The latter are called *alerts*. Alerts can often be tailored to specific site needs—a serious alert for one site may not be so for another.

Alerts come in two basic flavors—a *hard* problem that needs to be rectified and warnings that need to be acted upon. A disk failure is an example of a hard alert. A threshold exceeded is an example of a *warning* of a potential problem alert. Thresholds can be things like CPU utilization, database space short, memory shortage, and so on.

There are vendor tools for generating *alerts* for the following:

- Hardware
- Software
- Databases
- Commercial applications (ERP, CRM)
- Breaches of security (SIEM), from remote device and BYOD to servers
- Environmental factors like voltage and temperature (data center infrastructure management or DCIM)

> *Note:* These are often called *knowledge modules*. In today's environment, *security event monitoring* (SIEM) has become very important, indeed, mandatory in my view.

The judicious selection and implementation of these can aid maintaining HA in conjunction with trained people and rigorous service management processes and techniques.

Fault Management

Faults and What to Do about Them

> *Note:* Normally, a system is not available when it is supposed to be due to a fault or faults. These can be *physical* (failing disk, memory card, network component outage, CPU failure, operating system or application crash, and so on) or *logical* (wrong job is run, time of day entered is wrong, incorrect data is produced, and many others).

What can we do about faults? The obvious solution is to fix them but another method is to build fault tolerance into the system design, both hardware and, in some cases, software. Before we look at fault tolerance, let us see what should happen in a normal fault situation.[†]

---

* Terminology in these areas varies—words may be the same but interpretation different. Don't get hung up on it, just define them as you see fit and map to any documents that use other terms.

† Siewiorek, D.P., Swarz, R.S., *Reliable Computer Systems—Design and Evaluation*, 2nd Edition, 1992, Digital Press and other documents.

System Failure: The Response Stages

Once a fault has occurred in a system, the system may go through as many as eight distinct stages to respond to the occurrence of a failure [siewiorek92]. While a system may not need, or be able to use all 8, any reliable design will use several, coordinated techniques. The stages are fault confinement, fault detection, diagnosis, reconfiguration, recovery, restart, repair, and reintegration. Each stage is discussed briefly below:

Fault containment: The purpose of this stage is to limit the spread of the effects of a fault from one area of the system into another area. This is typically achieved by making liberal use of fault detection (early and often), as will multiple request/confirmation protocols and performing consistency checks between modules.

Fault detection: This is the stage in which the system recognizes that something unexpected has occurred. Detection strategies are broken into two major categories, online detection and offline detection. A system supporting online detection is capable of performing useful work while detection is in progress. Offline detection strategies (like a single user diagnostic mode) prevent the device from providing any service during detection.

Diagnosis: If the detection phase does not provide enough information as to the nature and location of the fault, the diagnosis mechanisms must determine the information. Once the nature and location of the fault have been determined, the system can begin to recover.

Reconfiguration: Once a faulty component has been identified, a reliable system can reconfigure itself to isolate the component from the rest of the system. This might be accomplished by having the component replaced, by marking it offline and using a redundant system.

Alternately, the system could switch it off and continue operation with a degraded capability. This is known as *graceful degradation*, although users call it something different.

Recovery: In this stage, the system attempts to eliminate the effects of the fault. A few basic approaches for use in this stage are fault masking, retry, and rollback.

Restart: Once the system eliminates the effects of the fault, it will attempt to restart itself and resume normal operation. If the system was completely successful in detecting and containing the fault before any damage was done, it will be able to continue without loss of any process state. The time taken to restart will depend on whether it is a *warm* or *cold* start.

Repair: During this stage, any components identified as faulty are replaced. As with detection, this can be either offline or online.

Reintegration: The reintegration phase involves placing the replaced component back in service within the system. If the system had continued operation in a degraded mode, it must be reconfigured to use the component again and upgrade its delivered service.

In my experience, when an interruption occurs, several other things need to take place:

■ Gather data about the fault and its duration (from monitoring tools and previous experience).
■ Assess the business impact (do we need to invoke DR)?
■ Perform RCA (later), based on history and data from the current situation. This may also involve some kind of configuration database where the age and history of components is recorded.
■ Document the fault, its resolution, and update operations procedures to try to avoid a repeat of the incident.

HA Plan B: What's That?

I often think when in almost any situation where some sort of IT automation is used *what would they do if that IT item failed?* An example is the payment of a restaurant bill by credit card where they use a wireless credit card device for payments—in fact, I have asked the question in restaurants and been met with blank stares. They do not have a Plan B, a fallback method. This is not however, the opportunity for a free lunch as some restaurants *do* have a fallback plan of a card number *pressing* machine, hardcopy documents, and demanding old-fashioned signatures instead of security codes.

Plan B: Example I

Another example is a supermarket local server failure affecting the checkout tills. When this has happened, at least in the United Kingdom, the buyer and vendor look at the shopping trolley and agree an estimate of what it should cost and settle for that. This is the supermarket's Plan B. Plan B, however simple, will prevent the staff and management running around like headless chickens instead of making the best of the situation. Document it and distribute it—the *Panic Manual*—to all who *need to know.*

Plan B: Example II

Some years ago, I attended a talk by a meteorology expert on the use of the then biggest IBM system, a System 360/195, in improving weather forecasting. He explained the way it could solve more equations in a shorter time to refine short-term forecasts. Previously, short-term forecasts were less accurate because of the time taken by slower systems. At the end of the illuminating talk, a member of the audience asked what they did if the 360/195 *crashed.* His immediate answer was *We have a piece of wet seaweed on the wall and that does the same job.* I know this is a true story because I was there.

What? IT Problem Recovery without IT?

Plan B is an action sequence to be taken when the system is down, the problem is difficult to diagnose/trace and DR is not necessary. It is a plan for carrying on the business as possible without the IT support that has just gone to sleep and is difficult to wake up. There may be a manual method, supported by any functioning IT, to carry on the business in such a way that the IT system can be updated when it returns to state 1.

Plan B may involve entering data into a PC for later transmission to the main IT system or simply writing in a school exercise book. There may be many other ways of developing a Plan B and implementing it but it will pay dividends to have one. Think of it as the business equivalent of CFIA. This could be an ideal scenario to design via the turbo-Delphi technique.

A crucial part of Plan B has to be communication with all affected by the failure and the prospect of no early return to normality. This *population* will include one's own end users and external users, which in essence means customers and prospective customers accessing a failed website. Internal and external communications between IT departments and with vendors where necessary need to be planned and documented.

> ***Note:*** Make sure the involved vendors are aware of the *game plan* too, since they aren't mind readers or users of your systems.

Faults and What Not to Do

This section may be skipped by readers with no interest in negative actions but you will miss some salutary lessons by doing so.

Outages: Areas for Inaction

The tribal wisdom of the Dakota Indians, passed from generation to generation, warns:

> *When you find that you are riding a dead horse, best strategy is to dismount.*

However, in some IT installations, this advice is translated into more advanced recovery tactics and ensuing strategies, such as the following:

- Switching the system *off* and then *on* again (tell your boss this is the *global master reset* technique in case he asks. It is used by TV repair men to fool the customer that he knows what he is doing)
- Kicking the system components harder, perhaps changing your boots first
- Changing the system operators
- Hiring outside contractors to operate the system
- Appointing an IT committee to study the system and report back in six month's time
- Arranging pleasant visits to other countries to see how other enterprises handle *dead* systems—countries with warm climates are preferred
- Lowering the SLA standards so that dead systems can be accepted as *operational* within its terms and rewriting the incriminating aspects of the SLA
- Reclassifying the system as *availability impaired* instead of *dead**
- Doing a productivity study to see if fewer users would improve the availability of the *availability impaired* system
- Clustering several dead systems together to increase the availability and speed (Amdahl's, Gunther's, and Gustafson's Laws)
- Seeking additional funding and/or training to improve the dead system's performance and resilience via redundancy and cluster upgrades
- Declaring that because the *dead* system does not have to be operated and maintained, it is less costly, carries lower overheads, and therefore contributes substantially more to the enterprise's bottom line than working systems.
- Initiating the search for the guilty, punishment of the innocent, and promotion of nonparticipants: standard *failed project* practice in many installations.

Note: If you don't understand this theory, or you think it is untrue, you probably haven't been in IT long enough.

---

* If you need to be *au fait* with this language, study *The Official Politically Correct Dictionary and Handbook* (HarperCollins), ISBN 0 586 21726 6. It could save your job or get you promoted.

Problem Management

This is an expansion of a FRACAS activity. Problems and faults are not necessarily identical—a fault is normally a visible failing somewhere in the system, a problem may be something less tangible but may lead to a fault if it isn't resolved or bypassed in some way. Either way they are items to chase, monitor progress on, and resolve. This is therefore not fault management—the fault is an abstraction to this discipline and just a *thing* to be progressed. However, roll it into fault management if you wish.

There needs to be a procedure in place to handle loss of service from various causes, for example, network, disk, or server failure. This is linked together by the help desk and may or may not involve software tools. The *war room* idea is often implemented, where relevant persons meet to discuss problems and their resolution on a regular basis with all relevant information to hand. The frequency of these meetings depends on the criticality of the problems.

Some vendors have relationships with other, noncompeting vendors allowing them to offer a *one stop* reporting point. In such a relationship, the first vendor in the group called by the customer assumes responsibility for resolving the issue with the other vendors.

Managing Problems

Problem management is essentially a methodology, usually implemented via software tools, for the tracking and resolution of problems affecting service to the users. It feeds off the activities of those engaged in the determination of the cause and the resolution thereof (fault management). It should develop a *modus operandi* from the list above. Documentation, the bane of everyone's life, is necessary for situations where the relevant team might not be available and stand-ins perform the function.

Problem management is often called *trouble ticketing* if you have come across the term. It sometimes pays to study and try to relate terms which seem different but mean roughly the same thing.

Problems: Best Practice

It is imperative that an enterprise works with the appropriate vendors to set up problem determination procedures, some pointers below:

- Devise a problem determination process from user seeing the problem to service resumption, including escalation procedures and when they should be invoked (help desk).
- Set up the problem determination communications process—who rings who and when.
- Set up problem determination procedures, with software tools, for resolving the cause—consider the section War Room.
- Set up a system for recording problem status, both internally and when the problem is with the vendor(s).
- Set up RCA for problems and revise operations procedures to avoid repetition where possible.
- Avoid *finger pointing*.
- Work with vendors in setting up any problem determination procedures as they know their products.

Note: Hopefully, these steps can be melded into the FRACAS flow of activity for operational systems and be the basis for fault management. In essence, this is setting up the system for handling problems and fault management is *cracking* the problem/fault within this framework.

Help Desk Architecture and Implementation

The help desk is the focal point for communication of problems which arise. Experience by industry analysts suggest that in about three quarters of performance and availability issues (74% according to ATERNITY) are discovered by IT only when the users call the help desk. Its mission, setup, and communications *modus operandi* are therefore very important, as are the skills of the personnel manning it.

The problems reported by various parties are often placed in categories, for example:

Priority 1: Threat to business, for example, loss of customer or revenue
Priority 2: Threat to a part of the business
Priority 3: Inconvenience
Priority 4: Minor issue

Other methods are to use a *color coding* system, such as red, amber, and green with perhaps a flashing light for emergencies. In any case, the severity has to be decided in advance where possible, usually on a business case. For example, the HR vacation system failing is not as serious as the billing or an online sales system failing.

Escalation Management

As well as assigning ratings to service interruptions, it is necessary (in the impact analysis) to determine how long the problem can remain unresolved before it is escalated, internally and externally. Most organizations have some process of escalation process defined, probably from year 2000 efforts in many cases. The process should start in the CCC.

As with availability management and DR, an impact analysis needs to be carried out on what degree of protection is needed for each business system supported by IT. One of the key issues in problem management is the clear definition of roles and responsibilities, for example between operations and technical support.

Resource Management

A detailed discussion of the management of resources needed to support HA systems and services is beyond the scope of this book. These resources and their management are nonetheless very important.

They include the management (not just measurement) of the following:

■ Performance
■ Capacity

- Network
- Data and storage
- Software
- Assets
- Configuration
- User chargeback
- Other items needing control by the enterprise, especially those which can impact HA, DR, and SLA

The last listed item is there because of my fear of relying solely on generic checklists which may not reflect the actual requirements of your organization. That is your job.

It is difficult to see how HA can be achieved and SLAs terms met without reasonable understanding and control of these resources. It is almost certain that existing procedures cover many of these areas but may need revision in the light of other requirements thrown up by the HA/DR project.

Service Monitors

This section covers the *why*, *how*, and often the *who* and *what* of monitoring a service. It should be evident that *if you can't measure it, you can't manage it* and at least three things will happen as a consequence:

- You will blow your SLA(s) out of the water.
- You will lose control of what is going on in the systems that are providing user services that pay your salary.
- You will be *flying blind*—not recommended.

Availability Measurement

This is essentially the measurement of time that a system or component is operating as specified, as we have seen. If the system is operating in *degraded mode* and the SLA specifies performance criteria as well as uptime, then other factors may need to be measured and correlated.

This topic goes under several names, all meaning roughly the same thing, that is, what *availability* and *response time* does the end user (the business person) observe in his or her work? One major reason for measuring these parameters is for reporting on SLA that might well specify limits for them.

Common names and current acronyms are as follows:

- Synthetic monitoring
- End user experience (EUE)
- Real user monitoring (RUM)
- End user monitoring (EUM)
- End user view

and combinations of these words making other acronyms!

Monitor Layers

There is a hierarchy of entities that can be monitored and might be called a monitoring stack. However, for our purposes, the main entity which is of interest is the end user and his or her service. The layers might be represented as follows:

- End user layer monitoring (ping)
- Synthetic transaction monitoring (response times)
- Application monitoring and, in parallel, operating system and middleware monitoring
- Cloud monitoring/virtual server monitoring
- *Traditional* server (CPU, memory) and web server monitoring
- Network monitoring (response times, traffic, utilization, intrusion events, etc.)
- Database monitoring (performance, utilization, capacity, etc.)

Synthetic monitoring is *synthetic* in the sense that it does not represent measurements taken from real users in operation but by some entity pretending to be a user. This entity is normally a computer of some sort—a PC, a server—driving scripts or transactions into a server that may be a web server or a standard server hosting BICARSA* and other important enterprise applications. This *entity* might take the form of a web browser emulation program/script or a transaction generator for say, a CICS or Tuxedo OLTP system.

It is the end user equivalent of the remote terminal emulator (RTE) in system performance benchmarking where a system *injects* transactions into a remote or local server to assess its performance characteristics, for example the venerable TPC-A and TPC-B transactions and the hardy annual TPC-C. You may also come across the terms *injector* or *injection* in the EUE arena.

The scripts for such monitoring can be

- Best guess at user interactions with the server(s), mainly for critical applications, generated using vendor EUM tools.
- Derived from detailed monitoring of user interactions with the server, taking account of the various navigational paths taken by typical users.
- Simple *pinging* applications that essentially tell us whether the server is there or not and how long it takes for the ping to traverse the network.

In most cases, the synthetic view of availability and performance may fit what the real user experiences but, in general, will not be clever enough to detect that the data returned is not quite right. An example might be where a data set or database used by the application in question is incorrect for some reason, a fact which might only be evident to a user when viewing the results of transaction and based on his or her experience—*that doesn't look quite right*. We will now take a brief look at monitors, both generic (a model) and those supplied by hardware and software vendors.

Note: The inclusion of vendors' products, services and documentation in this book does not constitute an endorsement of those products nor a recommendation to use them, neither does it imply there are not others that offer similar facilities.

---

* Billing, inventory control, accounts receivable, and sales analysis, a term used when the finance director/CFO was in charge of IT and IT spend.

System Resource Monitors

Synthetic Workload: Generic Requirements

In the *old days*, metric gurus measured everything tangible—CPU utilization, memory utilization, I/O queuing, I/O times, and so on—and be able to declare that everything was fine, or not, as the case might have been. This will not necessarily be the users' view in today's environments that are much more complex than they were in the old mainframe days. Units like *pages accessed, pages transmitted,* and *average page size* will be involved in Internet considerations.

It is a matter of tools understanding and catering for a multiplicity of software environments and services. Figure 7.10 illustrates a schematic monitor of an application system. In theory, one would like to pretend to be a user and experience what the user sees at various times in the operating cycle of a system, that is, the period over which it is meant to offer an available service.

One thing you should note. The view the user has of work and data *entering* his or her environment, together with its speed of access, is not the same as the server operator sees *leaving* his or her system environment.

Figures 7.10 and 7.11 illustrate the principle of this *pseudo-user* or observer, plus the flow of two modes of *injection* into operational servers.[*] The *observer* injects pseudo or real transactions into the system and measures the resulting response times and ongoing availability of the target system(s).

There are local and remote observers to allow for a broken network suggesting to the remote observer that the system or server component is down, when in reality it is not.

This mode of operation is often called *synthetic* transactions and the exercise *EUE* because in this environment, communication with a system can be via web browser emulation or scripts that generate transactions for the server—in web or non-web mode.

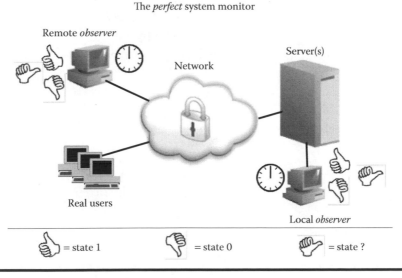

The *perfect* system monitor

Remote *observer*

Network

Server(s)

Real users

Local *observer*

= state 1   = state 0   = state ?

Figure 7.10   Monitor: Observer of system behavior.

---

[*] Compuware calls them *robot* workstations that execute synthetic, scripted transactions. These agents *simulate user activity so issues are discovered and fixed before they degrade your end-user experience*: Compuware dynaTrace.

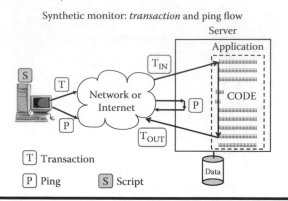

Figure 7.11 Synthetic user of a system—flow schematic.

Results can be observed live (real time) or in post-operation processing, and constitute part of the SLA report. However, without proper monitoring *all-seeing* tools, knowledge of what is happening end-to-end is limited to what various log files and intelligent network devices can tell the operations people. Compuware, for example, claims to sidestep these blind-spots to monitor, among other things, activity on web clients and servers, Java/.NET servers, messaging and database systems, services, and transaction gateways.

Availability measurements are valid even if there are no real users accessing the system. However, response times of synthetic transactions will vary depending on the number of active users and their resource consumption—storage, network, CPU, and so on.

This is simple queuing theory, an example of which is given in Lesson 6 of Appendix 4, which illustrates both *injection* cases—a *real* transaction generated and sent to the server (or a set of web requests) and a simple *ping* mechanism with response parameters being analyzed. The next figure shows the flow of pings and real transactions across a network (or they could be local) with a schematic indication of what happens to them when they arrive at the server.

The ping has a very short way to travel, the transaction has a longer journey though some middleware, and application code.

Availability Monitors

The following list represents a subset of vendors whose names came up in an Internet search for *availability monitors* and does not constitute an evaluation or an endorsement of any products, neither does it imply there are not other products offering similar functions.

- BMC—EUE Monitoring
- CA—Customer Experience Manager
- HP—Real User Monitor
- IBM—ITCAM for Transactions

Some of them have useful diagrams illustrating specific modes of operation to aid understanding of their operation. The tools often include *network* and *performance* monitoring facilities that can be useful in availability design and SLA fulfilment.

General EUE Tools

The URL below lists a staggering number of *End User Experience Monitoring Tools* (40+) and appears to be updated from time to time, especially with user comments, which are often useful in evaluations of any of the products mentioned. See http://www.real-user-monitoring.com/the-complete-list-of-end-user-experience-monitoring-tools/.

My own thoughts are to keep the *monitor* software isolated from the systems being monitored so that, for example, it or any of its agents don't die if the system being monitored goes down. Even so, it may be necessary to add redundancy to the monitoring *server* as well.

> **Note:** Some of the *ping* tools mentioned below include other features such as packet loss, round trip time, and hops in the trace route. Another list of monitoring tools and their websites can be found in Appendix 5.

Availability Benchmarks

Not many people know this,[*] but there are *benchmarks* for measuring various aspects of availability,[†] including this paper by Continuity Software and one supervised by David Patterson.[‡] These papers discuss the relevant metrics (or measurable parameters) that would characterize such benchmarks, with emphasis on RAID 5 and the recoverability aspects of any failures.

The Abstract of the Patterson/Brown paper is given below:

> Benchmarks have historically played a key role in guiding the progress of computer science systems research and development, but have traditionally neglected the areas of availability, maintainability, and evolutionary growth, areas that have recently become critically important in high-end system design. As a first step in addressing this deficiency, we introduce a general methodology for benchmarking the availability of computer systems. Our methodology uses fault injection to provoke situations where availability may be compromised, leverages existing performance benchmarks for workload generation and data collection, and can produce results in both detail-rich graphical presentations or in distilled numerical summaries. We apply the methodology to measure the availability of the software RAID systems shipped with Linux, Solaris 7 Server, and Windows 2000 Server, and find that the methodology is powerful enough not only to quantify the impact of various failure conditions on the availability of these systems, but also to unearth their design philosophies with respect to transient errors and recovery policy.

There are noises from certain quarters about including some availability aspects to standard benchmarks like Standard Performance Evaluation Corporation (SPEC) and Transaction Processing Council (TPC), but I'm not aware of anything concrete emerging so far. This could not sensibly involve waiting for the MTBF time to see when the component/system failed and

---

[*] See http://en.wikipedia.org/wiki/Non-standard_RAID_levels.

[†] http://www.continuitysoftware.com/sites/default/files/Service-Availability-Survey.pdf.

[‡] http://www.cs.rutgers.edu/~rmartin/teaching/spring03/cs553/readings/brown01.pdf.

would need artificial outages (fault injection in the text quoted above) to be simulated and recovery performed. RAID apart, I'm not sure how this would work for other components.

Availability: Related Monitors

There are dozens of vendors offering scores of monitoring tools, from the *big players* like IBM, HP, BMC, CA, and others to niche players, some of whom have very sophisticated tools on offer. The only issue with niche players, especially small ones, is that they may go to the big IT grave-yard in the sky.* However, if you architect an availability solution such that they can be replaced by another vendor product, then it might not be a big problem. Several vendors have *catholic* products which offer APIs for the inclusion of other products in the monitoring arena, with facilities to inter-face with them.

The main areas of monitoring which can impact availability and SLAs are as follows:

- Network availability and performance
- Server performance and memory capacity
- Disk performance and storage capacity
- Configuration, fault, problem, and other day-to-day areas of IT administrative activity
- Security—soup to nuts, speaking in the vernacular, meaning from remote, and nomadic access devices to the central server(s)
- Ambientware (or ecosystem) conditions—Emerson and Schneider/APC (American Power Corporation) are examples

Note: Security incidents are a growing threat to data, system and service availability and should comprise a large part of availability planning, design and operation. For a compre-hensive list (A to Z) of potential threats see http://www.sophos.com/en-us/threat-center/threat-analyses/threatsaurus/a-to-z-of-threats.aspx.

Disaster Recovery

This important topic is not covered in any detail here. See Chapter 11 in this book for DR coverage but it is judicious to round off the availability topics with some pointers and key references to the subject of DR. The first thing to note is that DR is a personal thing, designed for the organization and based on its requirements, finances, skills, and business impact caused by any failure neces-sitating invocation of DR.

Specific activities in the DR area include the following:

- Appointing a DR manager and DR *virtual team*, perhaps *au fait* with the Delphi technique as a tool
- Assessing types of disaster and possibility of occurrence
- Performing impact analysis of the effect on business of a disaster—which business functions need the most *first aid* and on what timescale

---

* I've seen several such vendors *disappear* in my time in IT and, sadly, some of them had products that beat the pants off the *big boys* at the time.

- Defining minimum processing for business areas when normal operations are not available (what do we need to run to keep various business functions *alive*)
- Assessing DR alternatives and selecting a strategy
- Looking at total remote replication of a primary site with frequent or real time copies of primary data to that site
- Selecting appropriate tools, for example, remote data replication products
- Developing the plan
- Testing and implementing the plan
- Monitoring and maintaining the plan, basing it on experience in testing
- Testing the plan at appropriate intervals—all checklists I have seen ask how often this is done and the answers are sometimes *not very often at all* or *never*

See Chapter 11 for an outline of DR and some references to the topic. DR or BC is also covered at length in several articles on various websites, particularly vendor sites.

Nearly all the availability, recovery, normal, and disaster will depend for their success on the quality of documentation as well as personnel skills. People forget, documents do not.

The Viewpoint Approach to Documentation

This is a topic dear to my heart. It recognizes that there are a number of ways of expressing things and presenting them to different types and levels of people inside and outside an organization. I have seen supposed IT architecture diagrams that look like NASA wiring diagrams for the Saturn rocket and presented to a business person. At the other extreme is the sketch on a cigarette packet detailing the whole system and shown to the operations manager. This, as the saying goes, is *not* a good thing.

It is a good thing to angle descriptions and diagrams to the intended recipient and not assume that one size fits all:

- *Do not* show the chief financial officer a diagram containing server and network components plus the relevant software, including release and patch levels.
- *Do not* show the chief operations manager a diagram containing invoice flows, expected return on investment, and Sarbanes–Oxley compliance status.
- *Do not* show anybody the network diagrams except people interested in networks.
- I have seen the above *Do nots* actually *done* to the detriment of the person and the project.

I think you get the drift—if you want to communicate effectively with someone, speak his or her language.

Summary

This section of the book has been concerned with manageability aspects of HA—design and implementation. The disciplines are not mandatory but if you haven't got any or the existing ones are weak, use them or, if you prefer, mix and match to get a comfortable fit for your organization.

Security awareness, detection, and action are now a mandatory part of designing and achieving HA services and the point has been made forcefully in this chapter. There are other aspects of HA that are mainly connected with potential *logical outages* so don't forget these. Living on a diet of hardware and software reliability only is bad for the health of your services. Think outside this system box.

We know by now that liveware is a source of outages and, with the best will in the world, will continue to be so. Education is one obvious help in reducing the incident of *finger trouble* but a tried and tested discipline to follow can have significant benefits. I have been amazed at the outcome of Delphi, PDWs, or equivalents where it contained ideas and solutions we didn't realize we the participant had in us. Trust me—they work.

Remember also, I have great faith in your common sense. You must have some to read this book and have got this far.

> *Note:* Remember that in general, poor management = poor outcome = failure, no matter how detailed your knowledge of reliability and availability is.

VENDORS AND HIGH AVAILABILITY

"Caveat Emptor"*

This section looks at availability products, features, and techniques offered by IT vendors in the areas of servers, software, services, and, in some cases, literature (collateral). In particular, database and systems management tools are covered in varying degrees of detail. It should be borne in mind that the vendor information may age and detailed plans should not be drawn up on the basis of information in this book.

The fact that a product gains mention in this book does not constitute an endorsement of that product nor a recommendation that it be used. It does not moreover imply that there are not other products which cater for the same areas of activity in high availability.

Although this section covers major players, other companies and organizations do make an appearance in references in this book, mainly in Appendix 5.

---

* Latin for *Let the buyer beware*. It is also the basis of the shout *cavey!* used in English public schools to warn miscreants of the imminent arrival of authority.

Chapter 8

High Availability: Vendor Products

Note 1: Any mention of commercial products or reference to commercial organizations is for information only; it does not imply recommendation or endorsement by me nor does it imply that the products mentioned are necessarily the best available for the purpose.

Note 2: The information presented in this and the next chapter is in the main about current, evolving products. If you are planning any serious work on these products, please refer to the relevant current documentation from the vendors and other accredited sources. The same caveat applies to cited URLs throughout this book. They have an annoying habit of committing *hara kiri* without warning or redirection.

In this chapter, we will cover some of the offerings from various vendors where they have an impact on *availability*. These will be mainly hardware discussions with some nondatabase software aspects thrown in where appropriate.

No attempt is made to compare and contrast the offerings of the various vendors. That is often done by analyst/survey organizations like Gartner, Forrester, Aberdeen, and some others. I find them more objective than vendors' own reports and competitive comparisons and therefore I am happy to quote those relevant to our themes.

In addition, I can only discuss information made available by the vendors and, if the coverage seems light in some cases, it is because the required information is not available on the Internet.

IBM Availability and Reliability

IBM is generally credited with introducing the concepts of reliability, availability, and serviceability (RAS) in its mainframes. The concepts and advanced implementations of them have been introduced into other IBM and non-IBM systems, such that today RAS is a common currency on most server hardware.

Note that all RAS implementations are not necessarily the same in functionality, even if they share the same RAS name. In addition, not all generic RAS features mentioned in this book are available on all platforms which claim RAS as part of their offerings.

> To avoid repetition, I have only listed the full (or nearly full) set of IBM RAS features instead of spelling them out each time for every vendor with the same, a subset or a superset of these features. If individual RAS items are important to you, consult the relevant vendor and/or his website.

IBM Hardware

The current IBM hardware revolves around the following:

- System z, the mainframe environment, OS z/OS
- System x, the Intel-based environment, OS Windows, and Linux
- System p, the AIX (UNIX) environment, formerly Risc System/6000
- System i, the previous AS/400 environment, now OS IBM i
- Virtualized environments involving these architectures
- Linux on System z
- Parallel Sysplex

Some references are provided as follows:

Series z RAS: SG24-7833-01
Series x RAS: REDP-4864-00, http://www.redbooks.ibm.com/redpapers/pdfs/redp4864.pdf
The RAS presented in the above reference is not as comprehensive as that given for power architecture, but significant nonetheless.
Power7 RAS: http://www-03.ibm.com/systems/es/resources/Key_Aspects_of_Power_System_Reliability_Availability_and_Serviceability.pdf.
Series i RAS: See power RAS above, bearing in mind not all features are available on the various levels of IBM i operating system nor the various models of power architecture available.

> **Note:** These features are not necessarily available on all power-based platforms nor supported by all valid power operating systems (AIX, IBM i, Linux varieties—Red Hat, SUSE). See the reference above or www.ibm.com/power.

First seen in 1997, IBM developed a hardware design methodology called *first failure data capture* (*FFDC*) in all IBM Power System servers. This methodology uses hardware-based fault detectors to perform extensive checks on internal system components. Each detector is a diagnostic probe capable of reporting fault details to a dedicated service processor in the machine.

The overriding *mission* is to identify *which component* caused a fault—*on the first occurrence of the fault*—and to prevent any reoccurrence of the error.

The next section shows the emergence of a new power implementation of the venerable AS/400, facilitated by the abstraction layers built into it from the beginning (1988). These were the remnants of IBM's Future Systems project.

Virtualization

IBM PowerVM

IBM PowerVM is a combination of hardware and software that enables the virtualization platform for AIX (System p), Linux, and IBM i (System i—old AS/400) environments for IBM Power Systems. See sg24-7940, http://www.redbooks.ibm.com/redbooks/pdfs/sg247940.pdf.

IBM Series x

These are the X86 servers that can be virtualized in various modes employing VMWare vSphere, Microsoft Hyper-V, Oracle VM, and Citrix XenServer. See REDP-4480-00, http://www.redbooks.ibm.com/redpapers/pdfs/redp4480.pdf.

IBM Clusters

IBM is able to cluster IBM i, IBM p, and IBM x systems in the normal manner of clustering.

The detailed features may vary across platforms and the references given below should be consulted as a starting point:

IBM i: (formerly AS/400), http://pic.dhe.ibm.com/infocenter/iseries/v7r1m0/index.jsp?topic=%2Frzaue%2Frzaigconcepts.htm.

IBM p: Power HA (formerly HACMP—high availability clustered multiprocessing), http://public.dhe.ibm.com/common/ssi/ecm/en/pod03013usen/POD03013USEN.PDF.

IBM x: (X86 based), http://public.dhe.ibm.com/common/ssi/ecm/en/cld00221usen/CLD00221USEN.PDF.

z Series Parallel Sysplex

In a nutshell, the IBM Parallel Sysplex is the mainframe z Series equivalent of Windows, *UNIX*, or Linux clustering.

> **Aside:** I first learned about Sysplex when attending an IBM Consultants Class in 1986 near Brussels, Belgium. Hal Lorin, a colorful author, teacher, and IBM researcher,* told the class about this architecture without actually calling it a *sysplex*. The actual system was not announced until a few years later and it then dawned on me what Hal had been talking about. Its main features were designed to give workload balancing, scalability, single system image, and HA.

---

* Hal has now apparently forsaken IT completely and writes novels and poetry.

Sysplex Structure and Purpose

The IBM Parallel Sysplex is a technology aimed at highly reliable, redundant, and robust configurations to achieve *near-continuous availability* (IBM words). It is a z Series entity and comprises one or more z/OS and/or OS/390 operating systems images linked by a coupling facility (CF). These images can be combined to form clusters of 2–32 images, offering maximum availability.

Characteristics of the Parallel Sysplex include the following:

- There are no SPoFs (single points of failure).
- Automatic, dynamic workload balancing across systems
- Parallel Sysplex technology can be configured up to 32 z/OS systems.
- These systems behave like a single, logical computing facility.
- Parallel Sysplex remains virtually transparent to users, networks, applications, and even operations.
- Concurrent planned maintenance of hardware and software components, allowing additional images to be added without disruption to workloads
- Networking technologies to provide multinode persistent session, virtual IP addressing, and other features to deliver fault-tolerant network connections
- Coexistence of different releases of z/OS and OS/390 to facilitate rolling maintenance
- Applications can be *data sharing enabled* and cloned across images to allow the following:
  - Workload balancing
  - No loss of application availability in the event of an outage
- Many automated operational and recovery processes reducing the need for human intervention.

Parallel Sysplex Schematic

Figure 8.1 shows an outline of a parallel sysplex with two integrated coupling facilities and one as a Sysplex LPAR (logical partition). The disk subsystems (not shown) are shared between the Sysplex images.

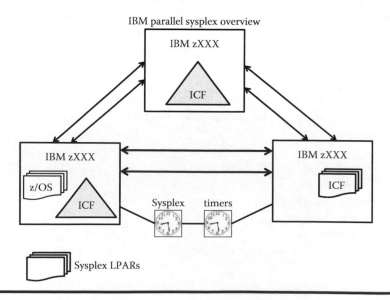

Figure 8.1 A sysplex (very) schematic.

The sysplex timer is to synchronize system clocks across the sysplex images and to coordinate recovery from time-stamped logs (see Wikipedia entry for IBM Parallel Sysplex).

IBM: High Availability Services

High Availability (HA) does not always come in *ready-to-use* hardware and software packages but often requires human intervention to maximize their effectiveness. This is the role of the HA services which IBM and other vendors offer.

- Availability assessment
- HA planning
- HA process design (http://www-935.ibm.com/services/uk/en/it-services/high-availability-services.html)
- Business continuity and resilience services (http://www-935.ibm.com/services/uk/en/it-services/business-continuity-and-resiliency.html?lnk = mseIS-bcar-uken)
- IBM HA center of competence (http://www-03.ibm.com/systems/services/labservices/solutions/hacoc.html)

The services offered by IBM and other vendors will vary so use the appropriate websites for current details. If there isn't an offering that suits your requirements, ask the vendor to tailor one for you.

You do it for a suit, why not do it for your HA and disaster recovery (DR) needs?

IBM Future Series/System

This is neither a pre-announcement nor a prediction but just a little true story[*] to tell your children or grandchildren and to round off this discussion about IBM hardware:

> Long, long ago (I will plump for 1975–1976) and far, far away (I would try Poughkeepsie) there was much talk and wild rumor about a revolutionary new system coming out from IBM which would knock the pants off the competition and indeed IBM's own then current range (System/370). It would have a huge address space, brand new hardware and software and a host of other wonderful things, including an exciting range of panel colors and pastel shades for lady CIOs and CFOs—the usual ones were red, blue, yellow, and pearl. It got customers asking IBMers, including me, what this was all about and should they delay IT purchases until nirvana arrived?
>
> This of course put the wind up IBM and for that and other reasons they eventually shelved the project. One *other* reason was that moving to the new system would entail a migration on a scale akin to that in migrating from, say DEC to IBM or vice versa and the customers would not like that at all. IBM didn't *un-announce* FS since in theory it didn't exist but let it ride away into the sunset (Who was that masked man?).
>
> Knowing that people had suspected this new product, IBM reiterated, without acknowledging that FS ever existed, that it was in the game of evolution and not revolution in developing the product line and verily this prophecy came to pass. You can still run programs written for System 360 in, say, 1965 on today's servers and the FS *revolution* is but a distant memory.

---

[*] It was true from where I was sitting at the time. I had not signed a Letter 112, a famous piece of admin in IBM which customers had to sign if they were to be given access to information about future products. This would have been on a *need to know* basis or an *if you don't tell me what's coming, I'll stop buying your kit* basis. Needless to say, IBM didn't think much of the last sentence.

(*) The FS concept in essence was a newly architected way of computing with three isolating interface layers to shield the programmer/user from lower level changes in hardware and software. One key factor was developing the idea of a single level storage view of data storage from the programmer/user perspective so that memory, disks, and tape became unknown to these people. This would lead on to systems managed storage (SMS) to make life easier for users. The architecture was in flux over the years of the early 1970s—announcement timescale and estimated costs began to escalate. In the mid-1970s, the project was eventually abandoned.

To prove that it is an ill wind that blows nobody any good, IBM salvaged some of the FS concepts, like 64-bit addressing and some hardware abstraction, and embedded them in the System/38 and its follow-on product, the AS/400 (announced in 1988), now living happily as System i or IBM i.

FS, of course, would have had 100% availability until the end of time, just like most *vaporware* . . . and everyone would live happily ever after . . . and that is the end of the story. Time for bed children.

Some years after this, Sun Microsystems joined the popular *nirvana tomorrow* movement with its Genesys program in the late 1990s. I saw it arrive and be touted everywhere but I didn't see it go—another mysterious *masked man*.

Future Systems/Series is discussed at length in a rather large book at 800+ pages, entitled *IBMs 360 and Early 370 Systems* by Pugh, Johnson, and Palmer, from IBM Research. It is a fascinating look at IBM in the 1960s/1970s and gives an insight into management thought processes as well as technical information (MIT Press, ISBN 0-262-16123-0, 1991).

Oracle Sun HA

Oracle and Sun tied the marriage knot in 2008 and appeared to have settled happily into their new relationship, although they had always had close ties. There followed the inevitable rationalization of personnel and products and things seem to be moving smoothly. Oracle of course are the suppliers of Oracle database, MySQL, applications, and middleware as well as services related to these.

The HA properties of Oracle and MySQL are covered in Chapter 9. Sun within Oracle are the suppliers of mainly scalable processor architecture (SPARC)-based hardware and some software for running their systems, including Solaris, the son of SunOS.

Sun HA

Hardware Range

Oracle Sun supplies a range of servers based on SPARC and ×86 architectures, plus some telecommunications servers (Netra):

- Servers T4-1B, T4-1, T4-2 and T4-4 T5-1B, T5-2, T5-4, T5-8
- Server M5-32
- Fujitsu M10-1, M10-4, M10-4S
- ×86 based (Intel) servers

As stated in Oracle's comparison of RAS between SPARC and IBM Power systems, RAS can vary with model and release configuration and the same applies to any RAS considerations here.

A paragraph in an Oracle publication states

> Delivering RAS capabilities means much more than just having reliable components. It includes a combination of hardware and software features combined with advanced, integrated management and monitoring. Together these capabilities enable the SPARC T5 servers to deliver mission-critical uptime and reliability.

For reference see http://www.oracle.com/us/products/servers/overview/index.html.

RAS is covered in the following publication of the Oracle website and includes RAS features of the Oracle Solaris operating system, such as the fault management architecture (FMA) and other features:

http://www.oracle.com/technetwork/server-storage/sun-sparc-enterprise/documentation/o13-027-t5-ras-1924294.pdf?ssSourceSiteId = ocomen.

The paper cited above also covers other features aimed at HA and virtualization or the **T5** models:

- Oracle VM Server for SPARC
- Oracle Solaris Cluster (see reference below)
- Integrated systems monitoring
- Oracle Supercluster T5-8
- Other features

Super Cluster

Super cluster can be seen at http://www.oracle.com/technetwork/server-storage/sun-sparc-enterprise/documentation/supercluster-t5-ras-1963195.pdf?ssSourceSiteId = ocomen.

Oracle Sun M5-32

This is relatively a recent addition to the SPARC stable and its documentation shows many of the SPARC/Solaris RAS features (http://www.oracle.com/us/products/servers-storage/servers/sparc/oracle-sparc/m5-32/sparc-m5-32-ds-1922642.pdf).

Oracle HA Clusters

Oracle offers a cluster called real application cluster (RAC), said to be the culmination of the development of the HA stack.

Oracle RAC 12c

Oracle RAC provides a very high database availability by removing the single database server as an SPoF. In a clustered server environment, the database itself is shared across a pool of servers, which means that if any server in the server pool fails, the database continues to run on surviving servers. Oracle RAC is a key component of Oracle's maximum availability architecture (MAA—see reference below), a set of best practice blueprints that addresses the common causes of unforeseen and planned downtime. It complements the HA features native to the Oracle database itself.

Oracle RAC not only enables continued processing database workloads in the event of a server failure, it also helps to further reduce the cost of downtime by reducing the amount of time databases are taken offline for planned maintenance operations. Using complementary solutions, such as the new *application continuity* feature available with Oracle Database 12*c* (see reference below). Oracle RAC provides even better user experience by enabling the replay of failed transactions in a nondisruptive manner, effectively masking any database outage from the end user.

References are provided as follows:

*Oracle 12*c: http://www.oracle.com/technetwork/database/availability/maximum-availability-wp-12c-1896116.pdf?ssSourceSiteId = ocomen.
RAC: http://www.oracle.com/technetwork/products/clustering/rac-wp-12c-1896129.pdf.
MAA: http://docs.oracle.com/cd/B28359_01/server.111/b28281/architectures.htm.

Hewlett-Packard HA

HP Hardware and Software

HP offer a range of hardware, software and services which can be configured to suit the various levels of high availability which might be required.

Servers

The HP server range contains architectures from vendors they have acquired over the years. Compaq (DEC) and Tandem, which gives them some flexibility in high availability system design but has the possible attendant issues of support for those architectures if used in combination.

- Integrity: Superdome2, server blades, rack servers
- Integrity: NonStop servers
- ProLiant servers
- AlphaServers

Each of these platforms has RAS features in various degrees and can be clustered to various degrees and node-count. See the website information on individual models for clarification of these details.

Software

To support the architectures listed above, appropriate software is required. HP supplies this as follows.

- HP-UX, OpenVMS, Linux, Windows
- Various middleware, database, and transaction software, including for a time a version of IBM's CICS OLTP

These operating systems have RAS features to some extent, some totally in software, others cooperating with hardware RAS.

Services

To complete the picture, HP offer high availability services to meld the hardware and software above into a cohesive system.

- Business critical services (various)
- UNIX operating system services (various)
- Open VMS operating system services (various)

Hewlett-Packard of course offers a range of other products—PCs, printers, software, and services. HP and Dell used to lead the field in PC sales but Lenovo came up on the rails and overtook them both in 2012.

Servers: Integrity Servers

The main enterprise servers are contained in the integrity family comprising

- Enterprise servers with symmetric multiprocessing (SMP) architecture, blade systems, and Superdome 2.
- NonStop fault-tolerant servers with massively parallel processor (MPP) architecture using inbuilt triple modular redundancy (TMR—see Lesson 9 in Appendix 4). The nonStop servers were descendants of the Tandem fault-tolerant systems which emerged from the HP takeover of Tandem.

The HP *standard integrity servers* have the processor and other hardware RAS features[*] expected of today's servers (error correction code [ECC], parity protection, memory scrubbing, etc.) plus features HP call *differentiators* in their literature (Figure 8.2), which are listed as follows:

- Double chip memory sparing, claimed to be 17 times better than single chip sparing, is reflected in the annual field replaceable unit [FRU] repair rates.
- Dynamic processor resiliency (DPR), a set of error monitors which flags when a processor has experienced a certain number of correctable errors over a specific time. DPR then deallocates the suspect CPUs before the errors become hard and *topple* the operating system.
- Enhanced machine check architecture (MCA) recovery, a technology composed of processor, firmware, and operating system features. This combination caters for uncorrectable errors that cannot be hardware-recovered by passing it on to the operating system.

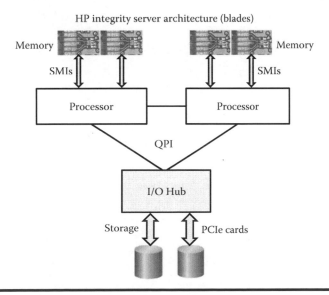

Figure 8.2   HP i2 and rx2800 platform RAS.

---

[*] Remember that the "RAS" of a system is composed of the RAS of the chips and so on, which make up the components (*processor, storage or I/O, etc.*) plus RAS features added when the components are "architected" into a system, for example, on interconnections.

■ Processor hardened latches to minimize the bit-switch errors caused by *particle strikes*. The newer processor include new circuit topologies that reduce the susceptibility of core latches and registers to these strikes, reducing latch soft errors by a factor of about 100, registers by about 80.
■ Intel cache safe technology (Pellston) determines whether multibit errors are transient (soft) or persistent (hard). If persistent, the bad cache location is removed from use.
■ Passive backplane contains little or no circuitry. Instead, the supporting circuitry is either contained on a separate plug-in blade (making it easier to swap out) or on a separate piece of circuitry that sits behind the passive backplane, handling the supporting functions.
■ Quick path interconnect (QPI) and scalable memory interconnect (SMI) error recovery features or point-to-point self-healing. These data *lanes* ship data back and forth between memory and processor and processor and I/O as shown in Figure 7.1.

In addition to these features, the Integrity Superdome has other HA features:

■ Electrically isolated partitions (*hard* partitions) which can be hot-swap modified to mask failures
■ Fault-tolerant fabric with redundant links and guaranteed delivery of transport layer packets. *Strong* cyclic redundancy checks (CRCs) are used to guarantee data integrity.
■ Crossbar (XBAR) fault resilience via hot-swap replaceable units (XFMs) and fault-tolerant communication paths
■ An analysis engine comprise management processors charged with monitoring fundamental hardware health—voltage, fans, power, and temperature which alert OS and hence administrator of errors requiring external attention
■ Redundant hot-swap clock tree
■ Extra, advanced I/O RAS features
■ Enclosures enhancing serviceability of major components and FRUs

For reference see http://www8.hp.com/us/en/products/integrity-servers/product-detail.html?oid=431 1905#!tab=features.

HP NonStop Integrity Servers

The NonStop servers do not simply rely on hardware but as with advanced RAS, other complementary and synergistic features to increase overall availability. Examples of this are NonStop J-series operating system and the NonStop SQL RDBMS.

As we have stated, the NonStop systems use triple modular redundancy (TMR) to verify the correctness of various processor operations (see Appendix 4, Lesson 9 for TMR).

NonStop Architecture and Stack

HP describe the architecture of their fault-tolerant system (although they don't use the words *fault-tolerant* much) as a *fully virtualized integrated stack* which is shown in Figure 8.3.* NonStop is not just a hardware architecture but has supporting software. It is an MPP

---

* The information about HP supplied in this book may be dated, although the bulk of my information comes from the paper referenced which is dated 2012–2013. There are, however, several papers about NonStop still on the web despite their being 11 or 12 years old. You should check before assuming that information in them is still current.

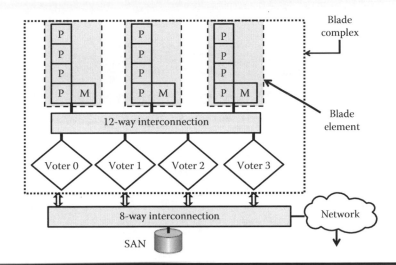

Figure 8.3   HP NonStop system architecture.

architecture and operates via a message passing protocol because MPPs within a node need to communicate. In the NonStop architecture, workloads are divided among many independent processors on the MPP to limit the sphere of influence of failures of hardware or system and application software.

The parallel architecture is assisted by the ServerNet interconnect technology to give near-zero latency to intercomponent transfers (processor to processor, processor to I/O, etc.).

NonStop Stack Functions

The components of this architecture are listed below with a minimalist description—the detail is in the paper referenced at the end of this section.

Hardware: Models NS2200, NS2100, and BladesystemNB54000c servers can be clustered.

Operating System: NonStop operating system uses message-passing and implements software fault tolerance, does monitoring, and synchronizes resource usage.

Security: It will be the case that if the application/service is business critical, then security follows as a *must have*. HP Safeguard security software can provide AAA services (*authentication, authorization, audit*) with XYGATE products an optional addon for NonStop systems.

Systems Management: NonStop *management* can be performed by HP's systems insight manager (SIM) and other related HP products and complemented by other products such as Tivoli, Unicenter, BMC Patrol, and open source management environments. A diagram of the *stack* is shown in Figure 8.4.

Database and transactions: HP NonStop SQL is a product architected to capitalize on NonStop's MPP, shared-nothing operation. It can serve as a clustered database and offers a fault-tolerant execution model for transparent takeover (failover). Transaction management is handled by the transaction management facility (HP TMF), apparently featuring full ACID properties. Also on offer is the remote database facility (RDF) to aid in DR for geographically dispersed NonStop systems.

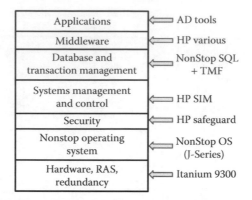

Figure 8.4 HP NonStop integrated stack (2013).

Middleware: NonStop systems support HP's iTP WebServer, SOAP 1.2 protocol, and standard Java Server Pages (JSP), Apache, and other products and environments.

Applications: Modern application development environments (ADEs) and application development tools

Details of these functions and facilities can be found in the reference (http://h20195.www2. hp.com/V2/GetPDF.aspx/4AA4-2988ENW.pdf) and related HP resources on their websites.

Stratus Fault Tolerance

Stratus offers a range of hardware and software products:

ftServer family: The family includes ftServer 2700, ftServer 4700, ftServer 6400.

Operating system: The ftServer family supports Windows Server with Hyper-V virtualization, Red Hat Linux, and VMware vSphere.

RAID: The family supports RAID levels 0, 1, 3, 5, 6, 10, and 50.

RAS: Each system employs fully replicated hardware components that eliminate virtually any SPoF and safeguard data integrity. The server automatically manages its replicated components, executing all processing in lockstep, meaning that a *partner* component can take over from a failed component without loss of *state* knowledge. It also supports hot swappable CPUs, I/O modules and disks, and what are known as customer replaceable units (CRUs).

Architecture: Figure 8.5 shows schematically the Stratus architecture, including the *automated uptime layer*, discussed next.

Automated Uptime Layer

This layer of the architecture employs lockstep techniques to anticipate and prevent some software errors. The ftServer hardware and software combine to handle errors transparently to other software—operating system, middleware, and applications. The Windows drivers are hardened to provide additional availability capability for ft systems.

The management and diagnostic features capture, analyze, and inform Stratus of software problems before they recur, if not corrected *in flight*.

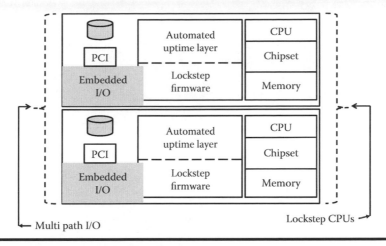

Figure 8.5   Stratus ftServer architecture outline.

ActiveService Architecture

ActiveService is an architecture with capabilities enabling built-in serviceability of ft systems. The systems constantly monitor their own operation and when a fault is detected, the server isolates the condition and automatically opens a call that tells the Stratus support center exactly what action to take. Remote support capabilities enable Stratus service engineers to troubleshoot and resolve problems online (http://www.stratus.com/Solutions/ByITNeed/ FaultTolerance).

Other Clusters

Veritas Clusters (Symantec)

Veritas Cluster Server from Symantec is dubbed an *open* cluster product because it runs on a variety of platforms and supports several database management systems. It is in outline a standard cluster configuration but available across a number of platforms and supports many of the software products native to those platforms, such as replication and other products. Cluster Server provides a solution for detecting risks to application availability and automates the recovery of applications for HA and DR purposes.

Supported Platforms

The Veritas Cluster is essentially *platform and application agnostic* and supported platforms (hardware and operating system) are as follows:

- HP-UX
- IBM AIX Power
- Linux ×86
- Oracle Solaris SPARC
- VMware

Databases, Applications, and Replicators

There is a plethora of software associated with clusters and high availability, including recovery mechanisms. Some of these are listed below.

- Oracle
- DB2
- SQL Server
- Sybase
- Others
- SAP
- BEA
- Siebel
- Exchange
- Oracle applications
- Peoplesoft
- Hitachi TrueCopy
- HP Continuous Access XP/EVA
- EMC SRDF/RecoverPoint/MirrorView
- NetApp SnapMirror
- IBM MetroMirror/Global Mirror/HADR/IBM XIV
- Oracle Data Guard
- Others

Open source clustering is covered in the following URL: http://bonsai.hgc.jp/~mdehoon/software/cluster/software.htm' and URLs generated by the search *cluster software, products*. The latter produces documents on many of the products mentioned above.

Linux Clusters

Overview

Linux is now a stable and accepted operating system and is used in data centers for many applications which might be deemed *critical* but there are some SPoFs in Linux systems and Linux client server configurations—hardware, network components, and applications—so the demand is for the equation *critical = HA* to be solved for Linux.

HA in Linux systems revolves mainly around clustering rather than inbuilt Linux features and there are quite a few contenders in this arena. However, see the URL below for a discussion of HA in Linux storage: *High-availability storage with Linux and DRBD (Distributed Replicated Block Device)*.

DRDB is now included in the Linux kernel according to this article (http://www.ibm.com/developerworks/library/l-drbd/).

There are a series of *Dell* articles on Linux HA, starting with *Architecting Linux High-Availability Clusters—Part 1* referenced[*] in http://www.dell.com/content/topics/global.aspx/power/en/ps4q00_linux?c = us&l = en.

---

[*] I have dismally failed to find any subsequent parts of this *series*! (mid-2013).

Oracle Clusterware

Oracle offers Oracle Clusterware as the underlying clustering solution for Linux systems whenever clustering is required to ensure HA for applications of any kind. A Basic or Premier Oracle Linux Support agreement with Oracle is required but if this is the case, the use of Clusterware is free of charge (http://www.oracle.com/us/faq-clusterware-1728221.pdf).

SUSE Linux Clustering

Geo Clustering for SUSE Linux Enterprise High Availability Extension allows the deployment of physical and virtual Linux clusters between data centers located anywhere in the world. This extends the capabilities of SUSE Linux Enterprise High Availability Extension (for ×86, Power, System z) across unlimited distances (https://www.suse.com/products/highavailability/geo-clustering/).

Red Hat Linux Clustering

The High Availability Add-On enables applications to be highly available by reducing downtime and ensuring that there's no single point of failure in a cluster. It also isolates unresponsive applications and nodes so they can't corrupt critical enterprise data. (Red Hat website)

For reference see http://www.redhat.com/products/enterprise-linux-add-ons/high-availability/.

Linux in the Clouds

Rackspace Knowledge Center website has an article entitled "Architecting High Availability Linux Environments within the Cloud" at the given URL (http://www.rackspace.com/knowledge_center/whitepaper/architecting-high-availability-linux-environments-within-the-cloud).

Linux HPC HA

We have examined some aspects of availability requirements for long-running high performance computing (HPC) jobs, and Linux often plays a part in this environment, for example, HA-OSCAR. See the given reference and references within it for a discussion of this topic (http://www.linuxclustersinstitute.org/conferences/archive/2004/PDF/11-Leangsuksun_C.pdf).

Linux-HA

For open source high availability software for Linux and other platforms see http://www.linux-ha.org/wiki/Main_Page.

Carrier Grade Linux

Carrier Grade Linux (CGL) is a set of specifications which detail standards of availability, scalability, manageability, and service response characteristics which must be met in order for Linux to be considered *carrier grade* (i.e., ready for use within the telecommunications industry = very high availability). The term is particularly applicable as telecom converges technically with data networks and commercial off-the-shelf (COTS) commoditized components such as blade servers.

For reference see http://en.wikipedia.org/wiki/Carrier_Grade_Linux, https://wiki.linuxfoundation .org/en/Carrier_Grade_Linux, and http://www.linuxfoundation.org/sites/main/files/CGL_5.0_ Specification.pdf.

The last reference in the above list contains a detailed list of *availability requirements* for CGL, including single-bit and double-bit ECC specifications.

The referenced URLs in the second don't seem to work properly although the URL itself is accessible.

> *Note:* The above Linux list is not exhaustive, merely a first pass introduction.

VMware Clusters

Clusters in a virtualized environment is a relatively new concept and VMware Clusters are an example of these. It works in the usual way by combining standalone nodes into a single cluster with shared resources and operated with cluster software. With this clustering, it is possible to aggregate ESX Server nodes (virtualized environments with multiple VMs) and manage their resources as if they represented a single host.

Thus, three separate nodes, CPU A with memory a, B with b, and C with c can become a conglomerate cluster of CPUs (A + B + C) with total memory (a + b + c). There are some additional HA facilities which complement and enhance this environment (VMware DRS, VMotion, and Consolidated Backup). See http://www.vmware.com/pdf/vmware_ha_wp.pdf.

> *Note:* Although various vendors' hardware offerings support clustering per se, they are not all the same in features and benefits. They may also behave differently in virtualized and/or cloud environments so do your homework and, if necessary, take advice.

The Web and HA

HA in web applications obviously depends on the HA properties of the underlying hardware and software—applications, middleware, and so on—as well as performance, security, and *liveware* considerations. An article chewing over some parallel considerations to these is interesting:

> *Considerations when implementing high availability for a web application*

For reference see https://www.farbeyondcode.com/Considerations-when-implementing-high-availability-for-a-web-application-5-2861.html.

Service Availability Software

There are a number of vendors of software aimed at increasing availability of services and protecting systems from data loss. One of them is outlined below (Continuity Software). This does not mean that other vendors do not supply similar solutions in this area.

Continuity Software[*]

Continuity Software provides software to mitigate downtime and data-loss risks across enterprise IT systems, including a datacenter's DR, HA, and private cloud environments. The product set comprises of the following:

- *AvailabilityGuard/Enterprise™:* Detect downtime and data loss risks across IT infrastructure, alert the appropriate teams and enable them to collaborate on a solution, correct configuration issues, and other vulnerabilities before they impact business function
- *AvailabilityGuard/DR™:* Detect, alert, and correction function for DR
- *AvailabilityGuard/Cluster™:* Similar functions for clusters
- *AvailabilityGuard/Cloud™:* Ditto for clouds
- *AvailabilityGuard/SAN™:* Ditto for storage area networks

Continuity Software: Services

Continuity Software also offers a DR assurance service, using the AvailabilityGuard software technology set outlined above. Full details of the individual products outlined above and the DR service can be found on the Continuity Software website (http://www.continuitysoftware.com/).

Summary

From the days of *you can choose your cluster: DEC or nothing* to the heady days of choice. This section has outlined what today's IT vendors have to offer, from raw RAS through to RAS enhancements, software RAS, HA environments, clusters, and fault tolerance which are now available in a variety of virtualized and cloud environments. However, with this rich menu comes potential complexity and this could be the undoing of the unwary.

You can empower the system to take some responsibility, for example, via task and operations automation, but ultimately you must be *master and commander* of the environment. The system is probably not familiar with your organization's business and aware of its priorities but you are or should be.

You can only take on this role with knowledge of the business, the system, and the supporting disciplines that are needed to run complex systems and services. If you don't have these, it could run away with you.

> It comes down to a fairly simple choice you have to make: *who is in charge here—me or the system?*

---

[*] Results from Continuity Software.

Chapter 9

High Availability: Transaction Processing and Databases

Note: This section is not a tutorial on OLTP and RDBMS products because such information can be found elsewhere. It is a pointer to, and an overview of any high availability (HA) and, in some cases, disaster recovery (DR) aspects of these two resource managers.

Transaction Processing Systems

Teleprocessing, commonly known as online transaction processing (OLTP) systems, systems have been around since the *stone age* measured on IT timescales. The development phases I saw in IBM might be considered typical of the development of this online version of batch processing in other vendors.

Long, long ago in IBM, there lived several OLTPs that competed for the hand of the princess of processing. *Faster, Bread, Thirst, IMS* (information management system), and *CICS* (customer information control system) were extant in the 1960s and all were doing the online processing jobs very well. However, it became evident to even cash-heavy IBM that these lines of continuing parallel development were divisive and counterproductive. It was decided, sometime in the early 1970s, to rationalize these products, along with several others, to produce what was to be known as the strategic product line (SPL). Even then, some IBM customers persisted in using their home-grown OLTP systems, usually written in assembler (which I used to speak quite well).

What the SPL initiative meant for customers was that if they chose to go the SPL route they wouldn't be left in the lurch by a product being abandoned. Of the several survivors, IMS and CICS were two. Other rationalization came when the multiple data access methods were ironed out with the announcement of VSAM (virtual storage access method) in 1972.

Some TP Systems: OLTP Availability Requirements

The 1970s saw this type of rationalization across vendors and some popular OLTP systems were in use:

- IBM CICS, a spin-off from an OLTP system developed for public utilities, using VSAM, DL/I (data language/one), and eventually DB2 as its database partner.
- IMS/DC, the OLTP part of the IMS. The database partner was IMS DB, initially DL/I, a hierarchical database and eventually the relational DB2.
- DECtp family, including application control management system (ACMS) OLTP which ran on most of its range of servers. It initially used Rdb (a relational product eventually acquired by Oracle) and other database facilities. The DEC products were acquired by Compaq and then by Hewlett Packard, where several still remain.
- Encina (Enterprise Computing in a New Age*), the *great white hope* of open systems computing.
- Tuxedo (transactions for UNIX extended for distributed operations†), a venerable OLTP war horse from the UNIX stable, still used today and the basis for Transaction Processing Council (TPC) benchmarks in many instances.
- Other systems on servers which were available in the 1960s and 1970s, for example, esoteric ones like Pick and multi-user multi-programming system (MUMPS).

A nostalgic journey awaits those of you who wish to pursue these products by searching for them on Wikipedia and elsewhere.

Apart from functionality and performance, the reliance of many key applications on online processing dictated other OLTP requirements—*stability*, *availability*, and *recoverability*. To take an IBM example (again!), it was estimated that some 40% of IMS code was dedicated to logging and availability features. Other products likewise were pursuing the holy grail of availability with similar functions.

TP Systems with Databases

The maturing of these systems and the need for nonpartisan processing across heterogeneous platforms presented its own problems which, in part, the open systems movement sought to address. Again, because this is not a treatise on OLTP, we will concentrate on availability and recoverability aspects here.

A typical OLTP and database system is illustrated in Figure 9.1, a real-life example of which might be CICS/DL/I or CICS/DB2.

Let's take an example. Imagine that for some reason, the Los Angeles emergency service consists of the LA Police Department and the London Fire Brigade and a major incident occurred. The chances that these entities would work together seamlessly are remote, unless they have a common *modus operandi* and commonly understood communications, code words, and so on.

The same problem awaited cross-system OLTP and associated database technologies. To wrap up this preamble, we'll take a short look at the *modus operandi* of OLTP and databases.

---

* Not many people know that.
† Not many people know this either.

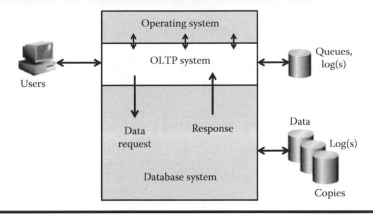

Figure 9.1   Cooperating OLTP and database systems.

The X/Open Distributed Transaction Processing Model: XA and XA+ Concepts*

The X/Open Distributed Transaction Processing (DTP) model comprises three software components:

- An application program (AP) defines transaction boundaries and specifies actions that constitute a transaction.
- Resource managers (RMs, such as databases or file access systems).

A separate component called a transaction manager (TM) assigns identifiers to transactions, monitors their progress, and takes responsibility for transaction completion and for failure recovery.

> The XA standard is an X/Open specification for distributed transaction processing (DTP) across heterogeneous data sources (e.g. Oracle Database and DB2) that was published in 1991. It describes the interface between the transaction coordinator and the data sources that participate in the distributed transaction. Within XA the transaction coordinator is termed the Transaction Manager and the participating data sources are termed the ***Resource Managers***. Transaction Managers and Resource managers that follow this specification are said to be XA compliant.
>
> Some products such as the Oracle database and Oracle WebLogic Server can act as either Transaction Managers or Resource Managers or both within the same XA transaction. Examples of an XA Transaction Manager are: Tuxedo, Oracle WebLogic Server, the Oracle database and IBM WebSphere Application Server. Examples of an XA Resource Manager are: Oracle Database, IBM DB2, SQL Server, IBM MQ-Series and Java Message Service (JMS).
>
> The XA+ specification was meant to be an enhanced specification that would enable distributed transactions to be coordinated across multiple heterogeneous Transaction Managers (e.g. Tuxedo and IBM Encina) as well as dictating how Transaction Managers

---

* Transaction (Xn) API and Transaction API plus (XA+). Even less people know this.

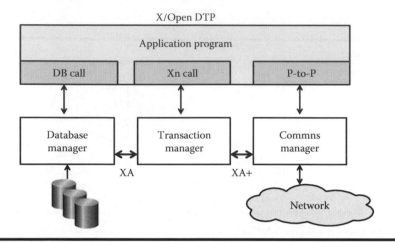

Figure 9.2 X/Open DTP model.

should communicate with multiple RM instances (e.g. Real Application Cluster) (Oracle documentation *XA and Oracle Controlled Distributed Transactions.*)

For reference see http://www.oracle.com/technetwork/products/clustering/overview/distributed-transactions-and-xa-163941.pdf.

A distributed transaction processing (DTP) explanatory diagram is shown in Figure 9.2.

The three *managers* in Figure 9.2 are called *resource managers* in the official documentation. Basically, the model shows an application program making calls to the relational database management systems (RDBMS), the OLTP, and the communications system software. However, the issue is that each *resource manager* may come from a different *stable* (speak a different language) and cannot communicate with each other to generate synergy across the board.

This is where the standards for the calls and the resource manager interfaces comes into play, standards for calls and the XA and XA+ interface specifications. It would be virtually impossible to handle transactions and two-phase commit without them.

Note: Refer to the Oracle document referenced above for a good coverage of this topic.

CICS and RDBMS

The IBM CICS originally supported the DL/I hierarchical database and eventually DB2. Today, CICS transactions can access relational databases by including embedded SQL calls within the body of a CICS application program. Coordinated commitment and the recovery of transactions that include CICS and SQL calls are possible only with relational databases that support the *X/Open XA interface.*

Common RDBMSs supported are DB2, Oracle, Informix, SQL Server, and Sybase (http://publib.boulder.ibm.com/infocenter/txformp/v5r1/index.jsp?topic=%2Fcom.ibm.txseries510.doc%2Ferzhab18.htm).

Relational Database Systems

Some Database History

> ***Note:*** You can pass over this section without losing the thread of this part of the book.

In the 1960s, the repository for data was a simple *file* of one construction or another. They were called *flat files* because that was what they were—no structure until someone added indexing to them. About the mid-1960s, IBM and North American Rockwell cooperated in the development of a *hierarchical* file system, eventually known as IMS DL/I.

About the same time, *network* files appeared with a special interest for manufacturers, for example, chained file management system (CFMS).

- *1960–1970s:* DL/I was useful for bills of material (BoM), for example, whereas CFMS-like files would not only do BoM (*parts breakdown*) but answer *where used* queries for parts or components via many-to-many relationships.
- *1980s:* This saw the emergence of practical RDBMS, probably starting with Oracle in 1979, cleverly building on the System R work of Edgar (Ted) F. Codd of IBM.
- *1990s:* Newer file access methods have emerged, for example, *object-oriented* and *object-relational* (ORDBMS), although object databases were a key plank in the IBM Future Systems (FS) project 40 years ago.
- *2000s:* Other data aggregations of data such as distributed DBs, web-based DBs, semi-structured data and XML, and parallel and multimedia DBs. Next-generation databases include SimpleDB, MongoDB, Apache HBase, and Facebook's Apache Cassandra. These databases handle unstructured data and, as a result, are also ideally suited for handling massive data volumes. See the presentation at http://www.cs.nott.ac.uk/~nza/G51DBS08/lecture18.ppt.

There are at least two other interesting articles on the history of databases, especially DB2 but with references to competition (see http://db2commerce.com/2012/02/02/the-early-history-of-databases-and-db2/; http://en.wikipedia.org/wiki/IBM_DB2).

It is interesting to note that no RDBMS of today actually meets all the rules Ted Codd set forth to define a relational database. The rules can be found in the given reference (http://en.wikipedia.org/wiki/Codd%27s_12_rules).

Early RDBMS

There are several implementations of RDBMS which have come a long way since the pioneering days of Ted Codd and Chris Date, both IBM employees at the time and in their day, as famous as Laurel and Hardy, though not as funny. Oracle and Ingres were early starters in the RDBMS race with others following.

In 1973 when the SystemR project was beginning at IBM, the research team released a series of papers describing the system they were building. Two scientists at Berkeley, Michael Stonebraker and Eugene Wong, became interested in the concept after reading the papers and decided to start a relational database research project of their own. *Ingres* was a developing system that became a commercial proposition in the 1980s, soon to compete with Oracle which had a head start on *newcomers*. Today, Ingres is a commercially supported, open source RDBMS intended to support large commercial and government applications. Ingres has a global community of contributors.

However, Actian Corporation controls the development of Ingres and makes certified binaries available for download, as well as providing worldwide support for the product.

IBM's first commercial product was SQL/DS, released in 1981. IBM announced *DB2* in 1981 but did not deliver until 1983 to demonstrate intent and show it was in the race. In July 1979, *Oracle* (then called relational software) released the *Oracle* database system.

Sybase was formed in 1984 and released a commercial version of its RDBMS in 1987 and went on to pioneer distributed client/server operation instead of just a monolithic central database. Sybase SQL Server was licensed to Microsoft and formed the basis of their own Windows RDBMS *SQL Server* while Sybase still inhabits the UNIX and Linux marketplace.

Informix appeared on the scene to engage the incumbents and was reasonably successful. Informix was acquired by IBM in 2001 and still exists in the IBM RDBMS portfolio alongside DB2.

Other RDBMS also exists. There are dozens of other RDBMS around, of which some are niche products, and a very long list of these can be found on Wikipedia at http://en.wikipedia.org/wiki/List_of_relational_database_management_systems.

Apart from relational features, speed, and other clever tricks, the RDBMS battleground became the software around the database—recovery, logging, journals, snapshots, mirroring, shared database across cluster or geography, and several others. *Availability* is now a frequent buzzword in marketing material from the RDBMS vendors and partners.

That is why we have this chapter—it is an important area in HA environments. We will deal with the vendors, as listed below, in the following discussions which are in no particular order. As with other discussions of vendor products, the minimalist approach is used.

- Microsoft SQL Server
- Oracle 11*g*/12*c*
- Oracle MySQL
- IBM DB2
- IBM Informix 11 and 12
- Ingres
- Sybase
- NoSQL
- NonStop SQL

I will try to emphasis the *availability* aspects over any other *gizmos* which are touted by the vendors, unless these gizmos assist in maintaining or returning to state 1.

SQL Server and HA

Note: This coverage of Microsoft SQL Server and HA concentrates on features and techniques available in and for SQL Server 2012. Information on earlier versions can be found in the references at the end of this discussion and it should be noted that not all HA features from one release are carried forward to the next release. Check the documentation.

Microsoft SQL Server 2014 Community Technology Preview 1

Microsoft SQL Server 2014 brings to market new in-memory capabilities built into the core database, including in-memory OLTP, which complements the existing in-memory data warehousing and BI (business intelligence) capabilities for the most comprehensive in-memory database solution in the market. SQL Server 2014 also provides new cloud capabilities to simplify cloud adoption for SQL databases. At the time of writing, there are limitations[*] on its use and is not considered further in this book. For example, it only runs on ×64 (bit) architecture and is *not* to be used for production purposes.

SQL Server 2014 contains the following *enhancements* for SQL Server *backup* and *restore*:

- SQL Server Backup to URL
- SQL Server Managed Backup to Windows Azure
- Encryption for Backups

For *encryption* in SQL Server 2014, see http://msdn.microsoft.com/en-us/library/dn449489(v = sql.120).aspx.

SQL Server HA Basics

The SQL Server HA Basics are listed as follows:

Windows Server Core: SQL Server 2012 supports deployment in Windows Server Core, a minimal streamlined usage option for Windows Server 2008 (including R2).

Online operations: Online operations support is enhanced in area like re-indexing and adding columns during maintenance operations.

SQL Server on Hyper-V: Instances of SQL Server hosted on the Hyper-V (virtualized) environment has the benefit of *live migration* which enables the migration of virtual machines between hosts with zero downtime.

Clusters: Windows Server failover clustering (WSFC) provides standard clustering features and failover and *hosts* cluster failover at the SQL Server instance level (see later in this section).

These features can be found on the usual Microsoft website and citations therein.

SQL Server AlwaysOn Solutions

This solution set is aimed at providing fault tolerance and DR across several logical and physical layers of infrastructure and application components. These are covered briefly next.

Failover Cluster Instances

This is an enhancement of the SQL Server failover clustering feature which supports multisite clustering across subnets. It thus enables cross-data center failover of SQL Server instances faster and more predictably.

---

[*] See http://technet.microsoft.com/en-gb/evalcenter/dn205290.aspx.

Availability Groups

This SQL Server feature is new to SQL Server 2012 and enhances existing capabilities of database mirroring and helps to ensure the availability of application databases and enable zero data loss through log-based data movement.

Availability groups (AGs) provide manual and automatic failover of a logical group of databases with support for up to four secondary replicas.

Database Mirroring*

Database mirroring maintains two copies of a single database that must reside on different instances of SQL Server database. These server instances typically reside on computers in *different locations* as a DR aid as well as other mirroring purposes. Starting database mirroring on a database initiates a relationship, known as a database mirroring session, between these server instances.

One server instance serves the database to clients (the principal or primary server). The other instance acts as a hot or warm standby server (the mirror or secondary server), depending on the configuration and state of the mirroring session. When a database mirroring session is *synchronized*, database mirroring provides a *hot standby* server that supports rapid failover without a loss of data from committed transactions. When the session is *not synchronized*, the mirror server is typically available as a *warm standby* server (with possible data loss) and recovery obviously takes longer.

Log Shipping

Log shipping consists of three operations:

1. Backing up the transaction log at the primary server instance
2. Copying the transaction log file to the secondary server instance
3. Restoring the log backup on the secondary server instance

The log can be shipped to multiple secondary server instances. In such cases, operations 2 and 3 are duplicated for each secondary server instance.

It is possible to preserve log shipping configurations when upgrading from SQL Servers 2005, 2008, 2008 R2 to SQL Server 2012. Information in the section References URL below describes alternative scenarios and best practices for upgrading a log shipping configuration.

References

These Microsoft references recognize that not every installation will have the latest versions of SQL Server.

1. High Availability with SQL Server 2000 (http://technet.microsoft.com/en-us/library/cc966499.aspx)
2. High Availability with SQL Server 2005, 2008, 2012 (http://msdn.microsoft.com/en-us/library/ms190202(v=sql.110).aspx)
   In the above reference, there is the opportunity to switch (full duplex!) between information on any of these three versions of SQL Server.
3. Upgrading Log shipping to SQL Server 2012 (http://msdn.microsoft.com/en-us/library/cc645954)

---

* *Microsoft Note:* "This feature will be removed in a future version of Microsoft SQL Server. Avoid using this feature in new development work, and plan to modify applications that currently use this feature. We recommend that you use AlwaysOn Availability Groups instead."

Oracle Database and HA*

Introduction

Oracle has branched out over the past 15 years or so from a database supplier to a systems supplier and integrator of its product range which now includes (Sun) hardware and system software, business applications, and middleware, including cloud and virtualization capabilities. Because the underpinning components of a system or service are applications, middleware, hardware, and software, Oracle has developed an HA architecture and HA-aware hardware and software to complete the support chain for these services. Lusser's Law tells us not that the chain is a strong as its weakest link but weaker!

The underpinning elements of hardware and operating systems were alluded to in the last chapter (Chapter 8 under Vendor Products). This section covers the database and related HA features. At the time of writing, the popular choice of Oracle is Oracle 11*g* releases 1 and 2 and Oracle 12*c* was only announced a short while ago. The *g* means grid and the *c* stands for cloud.

Oracle Databases

Oracle 11g (R2.1) HA

Aside from new database functionality, Oracle 11*g* 2.1 lists the following availability features, majoring on reliability, recoverability, timely error detection, and continuous operation:

- *Data guard:* Oracle Data Guard ensures HA, data protection, and DR for enterprise data. Oracle Data Guard provides a comprehensive set of services that create, maintain, manage, and monitor one or more standby databases to enable Oracle databases to survive disasters and data corruption. Oracle Data Guard maintains standby databases as transactionally consistent copies of the primary (production) database.
- *Backup and recovery features:* Backup and recovery of Oracle databases, including RMAN backup and recovery, RMAN data transfer, Oracle Flashback Technology, and user-managed backup and recovery.
- *Oracle Streams:* Oracle Streams enables information sharing. Using Oracle Streams, each unit of shared information is called a *message*, and you can share these messages in a stream. The stream can propagate information within a database or from one database to another, a form of mirroring.
- *Advanced replication:* Advanced replication is a fully integrated feature of the Oracle server: it is not a separate server. Replication uses distributed database technology to share data between multiple sites, but a replicated database and a distributed database are different. Oracle *Golden Gate* offers log-based bidirectional replication.

See references below for overviews and product feature descriptions.

- *Overview:* http://docs.oracle.com/cd/E11882_01/server.112/e17157.pdf
- *Data guard:* http://docs.oracle.com/cd/E11882_01/server.112/e17023.pdf
- *Backup and recovery:* http://docs.oracle.com/cd/E11882_01/backup.112/e10642.pdf

---

* This does not include Oracle Applications.

- *Oracle Streams:* http://docs.oracle.com/cd/E11882_01/server.112/e17069.pdf
- *Advanced replication:* http://docs.oracle.com/cd/E11882_01/server.112/e10706.pdf
- *Oracle Golden Gate:* http://www.oracle.com/us/products/middleware/data-integration/goldengate11g-ds-168062.pdf
- *Reference 11g Release 2 (11.2):* http://docs.oracle.com/cd/E11882_01/index.htm.
- *Reference 11g Release 1 (11.1):* http://docs.oracle.com/cd/B28359_01/index.htm.

Oracle 12c

Oracle 12*c* was *announced* rather like a thinning fog drifting in from the sea—you are not quite sure whether it is there or not. It is finally official so we can cover it here. It has the suffix *c* to announce its cloud credentials including a new *as a service* called Database as a Service or DBaaS.

The literature claims the following:

- Oracle Database 12*c* provides HA features as part of Oracle's Maximum Availability Architecture (MAA).
- Oracle Database 12*c* offers guidance on implementing best practices for HA databases.
- Oracle Database 12*c* enhances Oracle Real Application Clusters (RAC) and Oracle Active Data Guard.
- Oracle Database 12*c* offers new technologies that further enhance Oracle HA offerings.

A starter set of Oracle 12*c* documents are listed in the given URLs (http://www.oracle.com/technetwork/database/availability/maximum-availability-wp-12c-1896116.pdf?ssSourceSiteId=ocomen; http://www.oracle.com/us/products/database/high-availability/overview/index.html). If you want to learn about Oracle technologies, I advise you to join OTN—Oracle Technical Network—where updates and the latest information can be found.

Oracle MAA

Oracle MAA is *Oracle best practices* blueprint based on proven Oracle HA technologies and recommendations. The goal of MAA is to achieve the optimal HA architecture at the lowest cost and complexity.

Oracle High Availability Playing Field

The following are the key capabilities in Oracle Database's 12*c* HA solution set (*):

- MAA Best Practices
- Oracle RACs. See the usual documentation for this.
- Oracle Clusterware is the integrated foundation for Oracle RAC and the High Availability (HA) and resource management framework for all applications on any major platform.
- Data guard—Oracle Data Guard provides the management, monitoring, and automation software infrastructure to create and maintain one or more standby databases to protect Oracle data from failures, disasters, errors, and data corruptions.

- Active data guard enables zero data loss DR across any distance without impacting database performance. It repairs physical corruption without impacting availability.
- Application continuity is an option that masks outages from end users and applications by recovering the in-flight database sessions following recoverable outages.
- Transaction guard[*] is a reliable protocol and tool available with the Oracle Database 12*c* that returns the outcome of the last in-flight transaction after outages that make the database session unavailable. It is used by application continuity to ensure that an in-flight transaction is committed successfully no more than once.
- Golden Gate is a real-time data integration and heterogeneous database replication for continuous availability and zero downtime migration.
- Global data services is an automated workload management solution for replicated databases using replication technologies (such as active data guard, Oracle Golden Gate, etc.).
- Secure backup is a data protection to tape or cloud storage, integrated with recovery manager (RMAN).
- RMAN provides a comprehensive foundation for efficiently backing up and recovering the Oracle database.
- Flashback technologies are data recovery solutions that enable reversing human errors.
- Oracle VM is a virtualization hypervisor.
- Cloud computing (of course, including DBaaS).
- Edition-based redefinition provides an uninterrupted application upgrade.
- Online reorganization is an user access allowed during data reorganization.
- Cross-platform transportable tablespace

(*) This list, along with hyperlinks to the individual components, can be found at the following:

HA Components: http://www.oracle.com/technetwork/database/availability/index.html
Maximum availability architecture: http://www.oracle.com/goto/MAA

> **Note:** Some of the literature for these items flip-flops between headings 12*c* and 11*g* R2 but I assume that key 11*g*R2 functions are carried over to 12*c*.

MySQL

The MySQL development project has made its source code available under the terms of the GNU General Public License, as well as under a variety of proprietary agreements. MySQL, named after co-founder Michael Widenius' daughter, *My*,[†] was owned and sponsored by a single for-profit firm, the Swedish company MySQL AB, now owned by Oracle Corporation. MySQL is popular in web applications and there are several chargeable editions available from Oracle—MySQL *enterprise, standard, cluster, embedded.* See http://www.oracle.com/us/products/mysql/resources/index.html.

---

[*] This does not appear in the list given by Oracle but can be found at http://www.oracle.com/technetwork/database/database-cloud/private/transaction-guard-wp-12c-1966209.pdf.

[†] It is fortunate for the RDBMS community that she wasn't called *Ermintrude, Zipporah, Moonbeam*, or some such *A-lister* name.

MySQL: HA Features

MySQL offers replication modes as follows:

- Asynchronous, the standard type
- Synchronous, the standard type
- Semisynchronous replication, which only returns a *commit* when a secondary (*slave*) server has received the update so that the primary (*master*) server and at least one slave have the update.

It is possible to combine these modes of replication across servers for different purposes, for example, live and testing environments.

MySQL 5.6 (and onward I assume) have replication enhancements and other features to aid the availability cause, *some* of which are listed below:

- Performance
  - Multithreaded slaves
  - Optimized row-based replication
- Failover and recovery
  - Replication failover and administration utilities
  - Crash safe slaves
- Data integrity
  - Replication event checksums
- Development/operations
  - Replication utilities
  - Time-delayed replication

For these, other availability details and cluster/virtualization for MySQL, see http://www.mysql .com/why-mysql/white-papers/mysql-guide-to-high-availability-solutions/ and references herein.

MySQL: HA Services and Support

Oracle offers MySQL training, certification, technical support, and a number of consultancy service offerings. The latter include *HA strategy*, *backup and recovery*, and *HA Jumpstart*. For details of MySQL service offerings, see http://www.mysql.com/services.

A very detailed document on MySQL HA can be found at http://theory.uwinnipeg.ca/mysql/ ha-overview.html.

IBM DB2 Database and HA

IBM DB2 was IBM's original industrial-strength relational offering, following on from the System R project mentioned earlier. Versions of DB2 were subsequently developed to run on IBM platforms other than the mainframe (RS/6000, AS/400) and on non-IBM platforms, such as Hewlett Packard. There was even a version for OS/2.

Today, DB2 is available of platforms IBM z, i (old AS/400), p (Power, AIX), HP-UX, and other UNIX platforms plus the ubiquitous Linux. It should be remembered though that all these versions *do not have identical functionality* so do not assume this.

DB2 for Windows, UNIX, and Linux

The information in this section relates to DB2 10.1, current at the time of writing.

DB2 HA Feature

The DB2 HA feature enables integration between DB2 and cluster managing software. It can operate in two modes:

- Operating system-dependent DB2
  - IBM PowerHA SystemMirror for AIX (formerly known as IBM HACMP)
  - Microsoft Cluster Server for Windows
  - Multi-Computer/ServiceGuard, for Hewlett-Packard
  - Sun Cluster for Solaris

This mode is highly integrated with the operating system.

IBM PowerHA SystemMirror for AIX: http://pic.dhe.ibm.com/infocenter/db2luw/v10r1/index .jsp?topic =%2Fcom.ibm.db2.luw.admin.ha.doc%2Fdoc%2Fc0007500.html
Microsoft Clustering support for Windows: http://pic.dhe.ibm.com/infocenter/db2luw/v10r1/ index.jsp?topic =%2Fcom.ibm.db2.luw.admin.ha.doc%2Fdoc%2Fc0007402.html
Sun Cluster for Solaris: http://pic.dhe.ibm.com/infocenter/db2luw/v10r1/index.jsp?topic =%2Fcom .ibm.db2.luw.admin.ha.doc%2Fdoc%2Fc0007302.html

- Operating system-independent DB2

This mode usually provide more sophisticated features to manage and control the clusters.
DB2 10.1 supports the following operating system-independent cluster managing software:

- Tivoli SA MP
- Veritas Cluster Server

High Availability DR

The *high availability disaster recovery (HADR)* feature of DB2 provides a HA solution for both partial and complete site failures. In this environment, log data are shipped continuously from a primary database to one or more standby (secondary) databases and reapplied to the standby databases. When the primary database fails, applications are redirected to a standby database that automatically takes over the role of the primary database.
DB2 HADR provides the following:

- Fast failover capability
- Negligible impact on performance
- Simplicity of set up and monitoring
- Rolling upgrades with no downtime for running applications
- Transparent failover and failback for applications
- Easy integration with HA clustering software
- Improved DR compared to conventional methods

For more information about HADR, see http://www.redbooks.ibm.com/abstracts/sg247363.html.

DB2 Replication: SQL and Q Replication

Depending on requirements, data replication might be used in the implementation of HA or DR environments. The IBM *InfoSphere Replication Server* provides two approaches for data replication:

- SQL replication because it is based on DB2 tables
- Q replication which is based on a messaging infrastructure instead of staging tables

More information about replication capabilities is from http://www-01.ibm.com/software/data/infosphere/replication-server/features.html?S_CMP = wspace.

See IBM Redbook at http://www.redbooks.ibm.com/abstracts/sg247363.html for a detailed information on HA and DR for Linux, UNIX, and Windows (it comprises *564 pages!... but is well-sectioned and indexed for easy access*).

DB2 for i

This is a 64-bit built-in version of DB2 for the IBM i platform, formerly i5/OS and AS/400. DB2 for i uses the virtualization and large scaling capabilities of the IBM Power System platform, including dynamic logical partitioning, capacity upgrade on demand (CoD), and PowerVM virtualization to cater for changing workloads to provide business continuity in a volatile environment [*a candidate for potential outages!*].

DB2 for i now includes support for solid-state devices (SSDs). See http://www-03.ibm.com/systems/i/software/db2/ and references in it.

DB2 10 for z/OS

DB2's original home was multiple virtual storage (MVS), the version current in 1983 when DB2 was delivered. It has lived on succeeding versions, culminating in z/OS and been made available on other platforms as seen earlier. One major difference between z/OS and other versions is Parallel Sysplex support, which is unique to System z.

DB2 supports database partitioning and some other features related to HA are outlined next. For an overview (381 pages!) of DB2 see http://publib.boulder.ibm.com/epubs/pdf/dsnitm06.pdf.

DB2 pureScale

DB2 pureScale provides a clustered solution that uses multiple hosts to access the same data partition, allowing for increased capacity and continuous availability. It is available on the following platforms:

- z/OS
- Power platforms
- System x Plus with SUSE or Red Hat Linux

The main functions of pureScale are *scalability*, *load balancing*, and *failover clustering*, including common database access across all nodes. The URL for the pureScale website is http://www-01.ibm.com/software/data/db2/linux-unix-windows/purescale/.

An interesting look at pureScale from Triton Consulting can be found in the paper at http://www.triton.co.uk/db2purescale/.

InfoSphere Replication Server for z/OS

InfoSphere Replication Server (now part of IBM InfoSphere Data Replication) distributes, consolidates and synchronizes heterogeneous data for business continuity, workload distribution or business integration scenarios. A summary of features is outlined below.

- Delivers two replication models—message queue-based and SQL-based in one solution, providing asynchronous log-based replication.
- Supports data sharing configurations for DB2 for z/OS in both models; automatically merging the changes captured from the logs.
- Employs queue-based replication, supports high-volume, low-latency data replication with managed conflict detection and resolution.
- Uses SQL-based replication, which maximizes flexibility in managing schedules, transformation, and distribution topologies for populating data warehouses or data marts. [*I am not sure whether people back up these latter databases for DR purposes or reconstruct them from primary data recovered—interesting point.*]
- Maintains data consistency between applications and efficiently manages distribution and consolidation scenarios among multiple locations.
- Supports DB2 for z/OS as both a source and target.

For reference, see http://www-01.ibm.com/software/data/infosphere/replication-server-z/.

DB2 Cross Platform Development

The reference below makes it easier to develop applications using SQL that are portable across the DB2 database family, including DB2 for z/OS Version 10, DB2 for i Version 7.1, and DB2 for Linux, UNIX, and Windows. References to the detailed document for cross-platform development are contained in the document (http://www.ibm.com/developerworks/data/library/techarticle/0206sqlref/0206sqlref.html).

IBM Informix Database and HA

Note: The names of some Informix products within the Informix range have changed their names between versions 11 and 12.

Introduction (Informix 11.70)

Informix is IBM's high volume RDBMS database offering and operates on the following operating systems and environments:

- UNIX
- Linux
- Mac OS X

- Windows operating systems
- Virtual environments
- Cloud environments

As well as RDBMS functions, there are *free developer tools* for Informix applications and several editions, depending on operating system and users' requirements. It can be employed as an embedded RDBMS in applications and, as such, has some of the hardened software characteristics discussed under Software Reliability (Chapter 6).

In addition, applications can be developed in ANSI standard languages such as SQL, SPL, C, C++, .NET, and Java. It also supports the ODBC, JDBC, .NET, ESQL/C, or OLE/DB APIs that are included in IBM Informix Client Software Development Kit (SDK).

There exists an IBM Informix Hypervisor Edition for deploying an image of the Informix database server with IBM PureApplication System or VMware ESX environments. This hypervisor edition is optimized for cloud and virtualization environments and comes with an operating system, otherwise the features on offer are the same.

Availability Features

Fault Tolerance

Availability in pure hardware is normally passive but in software it can take a more active form using intelligent duplication techniques. Informix does this in a number of ways which are explained below.

> *Mirroring:* Informix supports mirroring of data and copies data at the *dbspace*, *blobspace*, or *sbspace* levels. If a failure occurs on the primary data unit (which IBM calls *chunks*), mirroring enables the application to read from and write to the mirror chunk until the primary chunk can be recovered, all without interrupting user access to data. If mirroring is employed for the purposes of operational recovery after failure or DR, all data should be mirrored. If this is not feasible, priority data can be selected at the levels they are mirrored at (*dbspace*). *dbspace* is the basic unit of storage in an Informix RDBMS. *sbspaces* contain only *BLOBS* and *CLOBS* (binary large objects and character large objects).

An alternative to using the RDBMS mirroring is to use the *operating system's* mirroring capability. It is quite feasible to run database server mirroring and operating-system mirroring at the same time because they run independently of each other. In some cases, it might be decided to use both the *database* server mirroring and the mirroring feature provided by your *operating system.* One way of doing this is to let the database server mirror the databases and the operating system the other data.

HA: IBM Informix supports clusters with the usual characteristics and to this end provides cluster management and related software. The Informix MACH 11 cluster and components are outlined next.

Informix MACH 11 Clusters[*]

MACH 11 consists of a group one or more of standby database servers supporting a primary server. To maintain synchronization of data, changes on the primary are replicated on the secondaries via logs from the primary system.

---

[*] See http://www.redbooks.ibm.com/redbooks/pdfs/sg247937.pdf.

MACH 11 clusters can be composed of database server types as follows:

- Shared disk secondary (SDS)
- Remote standby secondary (RSS)
- High availability data replication (HADR)

SDS: This configuration comprises a primary system that owns and manages some data storage that is shared by one or more secondary servers. These secondary servers are kept up to date continuously by accessing log information from the primary server.

RSS: This configuration comprises a primary system and one or more secondary systems that have their own data storage and keep their data current with the primary via the log shipping mechanism used by SDS.

HDR: This environment consists of primary/secondary server pairs with the usual hierarchy of data ownership. The secondary server is updated via the log shipping mechanism which can be synchronous or asynchronous.

These cluster configurations can be mixed and matched in various ways and it is possible for one primary server to be part of more than one cluster, a sort of bigamous arrangement. The configurations can be implemented to provide HA or hardware fault tolerance.

Enterprise replication (ER): This feature allows the replication of data between multiple database systems. It supports full row replication, selective replication, update anywhere, and conflict resolution. ER implements asynchronous data replication, in which network and target database server outages are tolerated via the local server storing transactions until the remote partner server becomes available (similar to message queuing techniques).

The flexible grid: This feature allows the replication of data, data definition language (DDL) statements, and data manipulation language (DML) statements between servers (*everything replication*). These servers can then be used as standalone servers if necessary offering almost limitless scale-out.

Connection manager: This manages client connection to the primary server and redirects them to the secondary if the primary server fails. Multiple instances of the connection manager can be configured on different servers to avoid a single connection manager becoming a SPoF.

Connection Manager

The connection manager (Figure 9.3) is quite clever in routing connection requests.

It is aware of service level agreement (SLA) requirements that are specified to allow knowledge of the type of server needed. The connection manager keeps track of the data quality, latency, workload, server type, and other statistics of relevance. When a connection is requested, the manager directs the connection request to the most suitable choice of destination based on the SLA requirements.

Figure 9.3 demonstrates Informix support for mixed hardware and software environments, in this case Linux, IBM's AIX, and HP-UX.

Double-arrow **1** shows the connection manager features keeping all tables in synchronization and **2** demonstrates keeping a subset of tables in synchronization.

Informix 12.1

Informix 12.1 was announced on March 26, 2013, and was dubbed *evolutionary* rather than revolutionary but as being more robust, simpler and giving better performance than previous versions.

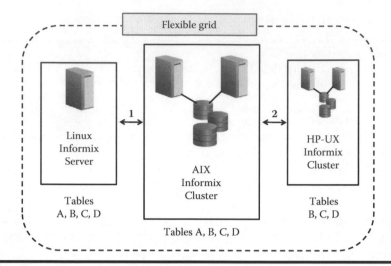

Figure 9.3 Informix connection manager and flexible grid.

The features of interest in the HA arena include the enhancements in the given reference (http://www.iiug.org/library/ids_12/IFMX-1210NewFeaturesWP-2013-03-21.pdf).

Aside: Informix Version 12.1 also has enhanced OLTP, sensor data acquisition, and data analytical features.

Ingres Database and HA

Ingres RDBMS

The Ingres RDBMS has a long history going back over 30 years. From a research project at UC Berkeley and open source project under the Berkeley Software Distribution (BSD) license, it went on to become one of the world's first commercially available RDBMSs and spawned a number of additional projects such as SQL Server, Informix, and Tandem NonStop. The product was brought to market by RTI Inc. (Relational Technology), the company name was changed to Ingres Corporation in the late 1980s. The ASK Group acquired Ingres Corp. in the early 1990s and were subsequently acquired by Computer Associates (CA) in 1994.

On September 22, 2011, Ingres Corporation became Actian Corporation, with a new name and an expanded strategy (see Wikipedia for details and history).

Ingres High Availability Option

This feature is in essence support for clusters running Ingres in failover (Windows, UNIX) and active–active (Linux, Sun) cluster modes. The cluster support includes the following:

- *Clients:* Linux, Windows, UNIX, and MAC
- *Servers:* Web and application servers

- *Shared storage architecture:* Transaction log, database, journal, and checkpoint files for rollback
- WAN or LAN database connectivity
- Ability to add, remove, or replace nodes without impacting any applications running

For further information, see www.actian.com.

Sybase Database and HA

Sybase High Availability Option

(*In later documentation, this is called SAP ASE—Adaptive Server Enterprise*)

In September 2008, Sybase announced its entry into the cluster-database market, releasing Adaptive Server Enterprise Cluster Edition to compete with the likes of Oracle's RAC.

Terminology

ASE with HA option uses the same terms as failover clusters (node, resource groups, ... etc.) but uses following additional specific terms:

Primary database server, secondary database server, and companion server: Primary database server is the first database server registered in the database cluster. The secondary database server is the second database server of the database cluster. Both database servers are known as *companion servers.*

Asymmetric configuration: In asymmetric configuration, the databases of the primary database server can be managed by both primary and secondary database servers. If the secondary database server has its own databases, they cannot failover against the primary host.

Symmetric configuration: In symmetric configuration, both companion database servers can manage all the user databases.

Primary companion databases can failover to the secondary companion server and vice-versa.

Active–passive scenario: In an active–passive scenario, client applications are connected to one database server. The other companion database server is a standby database server. It is only used in case of failover.

Active–Active scenario: In an active–active scenario, client applications run on both companion database servers. Client applications are partitioned between companion database servers.

For example, a finance application may run on the primary database server and a human resource application runs on the secondary database server. In failover cases, configurations must be such that client access and database access can be switched from failing node to surviving companion (server).

Persistence layer: The persistence layer is responsible for data. It features a shared storage capability available to all the physical nodes in the cluster. It is the *glue* that allows the applications of the cluster layer to work.

Use of SAP ASE

SAP ASE is aimed at critical applications that require HA from their data centers. It uses shared-disk clustering, where a number of ASE server instances are grouped into a *cluster* seen as a single system managing the same set of data. This allows application workloads to be balanced among the instances. The software automatically migrates connections if a node fails and runs on most commercial cluster implementations, supporting up to 32 nodes, all accessing a single database if necessary.

The main features of SAP ASE with HA option are as follows:

- Vendor failover cluster solution integration
- Two database servers cluster
- Active/passive, Active/active configurations, depending on the vendor cluster implementation
- Shorter failover delay for large database configurations
- Transparent reconnection (clients and data) after failure

The main reasons for using ASE include the need for HA of applications, workload consolidation, and optimized resource utilization.

SAP ASE with HA option coexists with vendor failover cluster solutions where it uses cluster application programming interfaces (APIs) of vendor solutions to be *cluster aware*. For instance, it is able to *query cluster* to get resource group state or to trigger a failback.

Vendor Availability

ASE with HA option has been generally available since ASE version 12.0 (circa 2000). It is available with ASE 15.7 on following platforms and cluster vendor solutions:

- HP UX—Service guard
- IBM AIX—PowerHA System Mirror
- Sun Solaris—Sun Cluster, Veritas Cluster (VC)
- Red Hat Enterprise Linux (RHEL), VC
- SUSE Enterprise 11/VC
- Windows 2008—Microsoft Cluster Server

Note: SAP ASE with HA option applies only to SAP ASE Enterprise Edition. SAP ASE Cluster Edition is a different product with additional features.

ASE Cluster Requirements

ASE (Adaptive Server (for) Enterprise) is a more recent name for the Sybase High Availability Option and has certain requirements for operation in a cluster environment.

- Shared SAN storage. The SAN must be certified for *raw devices* on SAN.
- The SAN fabric must be multipathing (see Terminology in Appendix 1). All the data devices must be visible on all participating nodes.
- The disk subsystem should support SCSI-3 persistent reservation.

Table 9.1   Sybase Functions Matched to Requirements

Business Requirement	IT Functions
Continuous multisite availability	SAP Sybase ASE
	Transactional replication
	SAP Sybase replication server
Multisite HA: asynchronous	Transactional replication
	SAP Sybase replication server
Site availability	SAP Sybase ASE cluster edition
Server availability	SAP Sybase ASE cluster edition
	SAP Sybase HA option
	Vendor cluster solutions and hardware
Server recovery	Cold standby, hot spare
	Database and log shipping

- Multiple network interface cards (NICs) are also mandatory: you need both public access (from the clients) and high-speed private access (for intranode communications).
- Within a node, the same operating system and architecture are required.

Business Continuity with SAP Sybase

For a good description (with clear diagrams) of this topic and of other aspects of Sybase, see articles by Christian Schmitt at http://scn.sap.com/community/services/blog/authors/chri .schmitt.

Table 9.1 shows the various parts of Sybase used in different HA situations and is taken from Schmitt's excellent coverage referenced above and reproduced here.

The Sybase components can be used in various combinations to suit particular business continuity requirements. In addition, see a demonstration of SAP Sybase on the video at http://video .sybase.com/products/ase/cluster-edition-thawley/SybasePlayerV2.htm.

NoSQL

This is a product of the radical kind I feel—kicking convention and doing its own thing, as they say in California. The quotes below are from Wikipedia.

> Carlo Strozzi used the term *NoSQL* in 1998 to name his lightweight, open-source relational database that did not expose the standard SQL interface. Strozzi suggests that, as the current NoSQL movement "departs from the relational model altogether: it should therefore have been called more appropriately 'NoREL'".

Eric Evans (then a Rackspace employee) reintroduced the term *NoSQL* in early 2009 when Johan Oskarsson of Last.fm wanted to organize an event to discuss open-source distributed databases. The name attempted to label the emergence of a growing number of nonrelational, distributed data stores that often did not attempt to provide atomicity, consistency, isolation and durability guarantees that are key attributes of classic relational database systems.

As far as the subject of this book goes, the *availability* characteristics of NoSQL can also be found in the Wikipedia article, part of it quoted here:

NoSQL has a distributed, fault-tolerant architecture. Several NoSQL systems employ a distributed architecture, with the data held in a redundant manner on several servers. In this way, the system can scale out by adding more servers, and failure of a server can be tolerated. This type of database typically scales horizontally and is used for managing large amounts of data, when the performance and real-time nature is more important than consistency (as in indexing a large number of documents, serving pages on high-traffic web sites, and delivering streaming media).

For reference, see https://en.wikipedia.org/wiki/NoSQL.

Apache Cassandra is a massively scalable *NoSQL* database. Cassandra's technical roots can be found at companies recognized for their ability to effectively manage big data—Google, Amazon, Netflix, and Facebook—with Facebook open sourcing Cassandra to the Apache Foundation in 2009 (http://en.wikipedia.org/wiki/Apache_Cassandra).

NonStopSQL Database

This RDBMS is employed on the HP NonStop fault-tolerant servers of the integrity range. It has the following features:

- *MPP cluster:* Designed as a clustered, massively parallel processor (MPP) architecture built on industry-standard Intel servers (9300 at time of writing).
- *OS integration:* NonStop SQL is tightly integrated with the shared-nothing HP Integrity NonStop platform and operating system.
- *Single database view* across the instances on the cluster nodes.
- *Continuous availability:* The HP NonStop platform provides out-of-the-box database availability, and routine database administration tasks can be done online without bringing down the database.
- *Massive scalability:* As the volume and velocity of data grows, you can add more computing power to the HP NonStop server cluster to get linear performance
- *Application portability:* HP NonStop SQL supports industry standards (ANSI SQL, JDBC, ODBC), as well as Oracle Syntax, to port database applications from other platforms with low risk and cost.
- *Automatic load balancing:* HP NonStop SQL offers query and data virtualization capabilities, enabling an environment that pools and optimizes all resources at the application level.
- *NonStop RDF:* Remote database facility for geographical dispersion and replication of databases.

HP also claim the following features and their related benefits:

- High throughput for instantaneous data replication
- Granular specification of primary and backup databases
- Support for all NonStop TMF (transaction management) configurations
- No lost transactions
- Robust manageability
- Cross-release replication
- Upgrades with no application downtime

For reference, see http://h20195.www2.hp.com/V2/GetDocument.aspx?docname = 4AA33288ENW &cc = us&lc = en.

Summary

The use of databases is often a matter of following the trend and today's trend is relational databases and associated utilities and monitors. Which is the best depends on your requirements and the vendors' offerings. There are, however, people who cling to older databases like IMS DL/I and VSAM plus some other old timers from the 1970s and 1980s.

The future beckons with object databases and other things aimed at standardizing access to data which now lives in a myriad of forms—video, audio, image, character, and so on. *Object abstraction* of data is not new. I remember it as a plank in the Future Systems (FS) plans that IBM was developing in the 1970s and it may have surfaced elsewhere before.

Our theme is availability and whatever mode of storage becomes the norm, it must be chosen on considerations other than just *gee whiz* ones. We as *availabilians* would like to see the data that have the following properties:

- Safety
- Integrity
- Security
- Accessibility
- Compressibility (for replication bandwidth reduction)
- Reproducibility (replication)
- Recoverability

Don't rush to be the first into new database (or any other) technology or you might be first before the company firing squad.

CLOUDS AND VIRTUALIZATION

"There's a long, long trail a'winding into the land of my dreams …"*

This section presents what would never have been presented a decade or so ago in a book on high availability. For that matter, neither would security and nonprocessor peripherals, which I have placed great emphasis on in this book—"… a horse, a horse, my kingdom for a horse" (Shakespeare's Richard III). Here, I have presented an overview of both the topics in this title to set the scene for what availability means in their contexts.

Also, this section is not meant to be a tutorial-style exposition of these topics, merely an introduction for people not familiar with the concepts. I hope it is clearer than some of the texts I consulted when learning about these things myself.

---

* World War I song, lyrics by Stoddard King, music by Zo Elliott.

Chapter 10

High Availability: The Cloud and Virtualization

Introduction[*]

Since I first put toner to paper developing the document on which this book is based, newer concepts have arisen, such as those in the title of this section. *Cloud computing* and the attendant *virtualization* are not immune to component outages, particularly those governed by Murphy's Law, because they are composed of the same *ingredients* as noncloud configurations and managed by *liveware*. In fact, they also have the extra software element of a hypervisor and the possibly added difficulty in monitoring real system components meaningfully in a cloud for availability, performance, and other entities relating to service level agreements (SLAs).

Clouds and virtualization go hand in hand in the provision of services to end users. This partnership is often classed as phase 3 of the development of computing services to end users. The first was the mainframe/mini-dumb terminal model, typified in the 1960s and 1970s by IBM, HP, and DEC machines with nonintelligent screens attached. The second phase, commencing in the 1980s, was the client/server era where intelligent *user stations*, normally PCs, shared functions with the central computer. The main shared functions were as follows:

- Presentation logic
- Application logic
- Database logic

Exactly how these were split (and each could be split down the middle) defined which client/server model they represented. These models ranged from presentation logic on the client and the rest on the central computer (X-windows) through about four models, depending on how you break it down, to everything on the client (workstation computing).

---

[*] For several white papers on these topics, see publication *Virtualization Review* at http://virtualizationreview.com/whitepapers/list/vrt-tech-library-list.aspx.

What Is Cloud Computing?

The definition for cloud computing provided by NIST is as follows:

> Cloud computing is a model for enabling ubiquitous, convenient, on-demand network access to a shared pool of configurable computing resources (e.g., networks, servers, storage, applications, and services) that can be rapidly provisioned and released with minimal management effort or service provider interaction. This cloud model is composed of five essential characteristics, three service models, and four deployment models. (NIST Special Publication 800-145)

Cloud Characteristics

Cloud computing and virtual computing are often confused in terms of their characteristics. Cloud computing comprises the following:

- Centralization of applications, servers, data, and storage resources
- Selective virtualization of IT entities such as servers, storage, applications, desktops, and network components such as switches and routers
- Reliance on the network as the connector between client and provider
- Often used in a *pay as you go* mode, rather like purchasing electricity
- Control and automation shifted to the *provider* for the *client* or *user*, for example, resource management, troubleshooting, change management, and other data center disciplines
- The dynamic creation and modification of virtual resources to meet changing requirements, for example, the addition of a virtual machine or virtual disk. This is often called *elasticity* in a cloud context
- Different manifestations of cloud computing depending on what functions the organization's IT wished to keep and which to offload to a cloud provider

Functions of the Cloud

Cloud computing provides the following facilities:

On-demand self-service: A consumer can unilaterally provision computing capabilities, such as server time and network storage, as needed automatically without requiring human interaction with each service provider.

Broad network access: Capabilities are available over the network and accessed through standard mechanisms that promote use by heterogeneous thin or thick client platforms (e.g., mobile phones, tablets, laptops, and workstations).

Resource pooling: The provider's computing resources are pooled to serve multiple consumers using a multi-tenant model, with different physical and virtual resources dynamically assigned and reassigned according to consumer demand. There is a sense of location independence in that the customer generally has no control or knowledge over the exact location of the provided resources but may be able to specify location at a higher level of abstraction (e.g., country, state, or data center). Examples of resources include storage, processing, memory, and network bandwidth.

Rapid elasticity: Capabilities can be elastically provisioned and released, in some cases automatically, to scale rapidly outward and inward commensurate with demand. To the consumer, the capabilities available for provisioning often appear to be unlimited and can be appropriated in any quantity at any time.

Measured service: Cloud systems automatically control and optimize resource use by leveraging a metering capability at some level of abstraction appropriate to the type of service (e.g., storage, processing, bandwidth, and active user accounts). Resource usage can be monitored, controlled, and reported, providing transparency for both the provider and consumer of the utilized service.

Cloud Service Models

There were four initial service models recognized and on offer in cloud computing:

- Infrastructure as a service (IaaS)
- Platform as a service (PaaS)
- Software as a service (SaaS)
- Information technology as a service (ITaaS)—EMC

For reference, see http://whitepapers.theregister.co.uk/paper/view/3023/esg-it-audit-emc-it-transformation-032013.pdf.

Since then, there have been other *<entity> as a service* entries into the cloud arena such as disaster recovery as a service (DRaaS), high availability as a service (HAaaS)—see reference below, network as a service (NaaS), optimization as a service (OaaS), database as a service (DBaaS), and probably others by now as the *as a service* bug bites. I have seen one recently, LaaS, laboratory as a service—no idea what it offers.

For reference, see http://virtualizationreview.com/Whitepapers/2014/03/VRTVISSOLUTION-5-Reasons-to-Consider/Asset.aspx DRaaS and HAaaS discussion.

We will examine four major "X"aaS contenders here.

1. *IaaS:* This model provides users (or tenants) with shared computing capacity, such as processors, network and storage, which are virtualized, and an operating system (OS). They are not aware of the hypervisor function. All over *facilities* the users install for themselves are not shared.
2. *PaaS:* In this *service*, a layer above IaaS, the user is provided with middleware components, databases, storage, connectivity, caching, monitoring and routing plus reliability features. These may vary with cloud supplier.
3. *SaaS:* Here users share things that are shared in IaaS and PaaS environments plus an application. The application may be shared, but data are isolated for the user's purposes. An application might be installed on multiple machines to provide scalability.
4. *DRaaS:* This service is offered by cloud vendors to clients. An example is the offering by Windstream, a video of which can be seen at http://www.knowledgevaultx.com/kve/the-cloud-many-paths-to-strategic-advantage/.

Figure 10.1 shows where the XaaS (X = I, P, or S) elements fit in the virtualized cloud environment.

For a good source document on the main service models, see http://explainingcomputers.com/cloud.html.

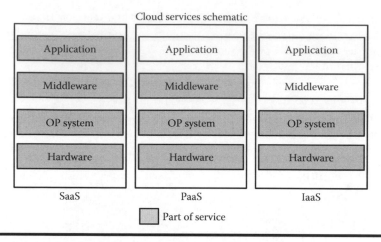

Figure 10.1   Three major cloud delivery models.

Cloud Deployment Models

These models represent the residence and responsibility of the cloud deployment. The most quoted cloud environments are as follows, along with a short description:

■ Community
■ Private
■ Public
■ Hybrid

These cloud environments are discussed in detail as follows:

Community deployment: A community cloud is for the exclusive use of a community, defined as groups of people from different organizations that share a common interest or goal, for example, vertical markets, scientific institutions, or organizations working together on a joint project.

Private deployment: The private cloud is deployed for the exclusive use of the client organization. If the cloud is managed by the client it is known as a *managed private cloud*. If this cloud environment is hosted and operated off the premises, it is called a *hosted private cloud*.

Private clouds offer the client the ability to use existing hardware investments, reduce security fears when sharing infrastructure with others, and eliminate any resource contention between different clients.

Public deployment: In this deployment, the cloud resides on the provider's premises but is *open to the public*. Usage in this scenario is on a *pay as you go* basis and is often termed *utility computing* after the electricity model where you pay for what you use. They have the impression of unlimited capacity that is available on demand.* The user or client need not know or care exactly what machine or where his work is run as long as it fits in with any SLAs he has in force.

Hybrid deployment: In this scenario, two or more distinct cloud infrastructures coexist but share technology that enables the porting of data and applications from one to the other.

---

* This puts me in mind of the old Amdahl CPU *accelerator* on their systems, which a customer could switch on to get temporary extra *horse power* and was charged for it later on a metered basis by Amdahl.

Resource Management in the Cloud

Cloud management means the software and technologies designed for operating and monitoring applications, data and services residing in the cloud. Cloud management tools help ensure a company's cloud computing-based resources are working optimally and properly interacting with users and other services. (Webopedia)

Resource management covers the management of the key resources in a cloud and their measurements (quantification). Major entities, which in the main relate to SLAs, and hence the business, are performance, availability, change, and problem/fault management. Who is responsible for what, when, and why depends on which of the deployment models mentioned above is in operation for a particular client of the cloud provider. Resource management is a key component of meeting SLAs in a cloud environment and this is discussed next.

SLAs and the Cloud*

SLAs for cloud computing are probably more difficult to define because the operating environment is not controlled by the client organization who must define the expectations and the cloud provider will need to map these onto the cloud environment. The SLA(s) will obviously vary depending on which service model (IaaS, PaaS, SaaS) is chosen by the organization.

The document footnote referenced in the title above discusses ten areas of SLAs that a cloud client and a cloud vendor need to consider and agree:

1. Understand roles and responsibilities.
2. Evaluate business level policies.
3. Understand service and deployment model differences.
4. Identify critical performance objectives.
5. Evaluate security and privacy requirements.
6. Identify service management requirements.
7. Prepare for service failure management.
8. Understand the disaster recovery plan.
9. Define an effective management process.
10. Understand the exit process (*in case of nonachievement of SLA criteria, for example*).

Before the client can discuss and agree SLAs with the provider, he must discuss the requirements of the client's own end users, that is, the business users. This implies two *translations*:

1. The translation of the user requirements into an SLA
2. The translation of this SLA into the one or more SLAs by the provider between him and his *providers*, for example, a network *carrier*

The cloud provider will then need an SLA, derived from the client-provider SLA, agreed with the carrier. It might well be the case that there is more than one carrier, hence possibly more than one provider to provider(s) SLAs. It could get complicated unless you *sublet* these *secondary* SLAs to the primary cloud provider [*tertiary SLAs don't bear thinking about*].

---

* See www.cloudstandardscustomercouncil.org/2012_Practical_Guide_to_Cloud_SLAs.pdf.

The subject of SLAs and the cloud may well sway the selection of which cloud provider to use as the choices available are widening.

Cloud Availability* and Security

Cloud Availability

Amil Gupta et al. (*International Journal of Computer Science and Security* 5(4): 2011)[†] outline key areas of cloud computing where issues need to be addressed:

- *System failures* and any ensuing data availability
- *Data errors:* Storage strategy is important, and they suggest configurations of RAIDs 1 and 5 they call *RAID 5+1 Model*.
- *Data migratability:* Can data be moved from one cloud supplier to another? There is a related issue. ...
- *Long-term viability* of the cloud hosting organization
- *Data confidentiality and integrity*
- *Data location:* The client might wish to specify the location of his data for political security, financial security, and security of other reasons.
- *Data security and privacy:* Best of Breed (BoB) encryption methods are required. In addition, the client may wish to specify the location of his data, for example, it must stay in the European Union (EU) or in the USA.
- *Data recovery:* The client needs to specify and understand his RTOs and RPOs and embed them in his SLA(s) with the cloud provider.
- *Regulatory* and user data requirements need to be catered for

There are other papers that, in general, reflect these concerns so we can take them as roughly representative. Is the cloud environment the *nirvana* of HA? Not so according to the next section of this book.

Cloud Outages: A Review

Clouds are not immune to the events which bring down normal IT services but they show different characteristics.

- *To 2012:* The report below, called *Downtime Statistics of Current Cloud Solutions* from an IWGCR (International Working Group on Cloud Computing Resiliency) compilation presents information, gathered from press reports, on cloud outages shows the number of hours of downtime over a number of years from 2008 to 2012. It presents the outages by year, the causes and vendor plus a summary of total hours, availability%, cost/hour, and total outage cost for each vendor. The overall availability for all vendors covered was 99.917%, the best being 99.998%, the worst 99.677%, not bad for volatile environments (http://iwgcr.org/wp-content/uploads/2012/06/IWGCR-Paris.Ranking-002-en.pdf).
- *2013:* There is another *outages* tale told at http://www.computerworld.com/slideshow/detail/108654#.

---

* See references in Appendix 5 under Cloud Computing Availability.
† I have been unable to find the difference between the IJCSS and IJCSIS organizations but both concentrate on IT security issues.

The IWGCR website also has a section on cloud disasters, akin to the disaster section (Never Again) of the Availability Digest referenced in Appendix 5.

Aberdeen: Cloud Storage Outages

A report by Aberdeen Group in April 2013 shows that cloud storage is a lower cost option and gives higher availability than conventional solutions. Some of these costs tie in with their other report on the costs of downtime and the fact that higher availability means lower costs overall. The *downtime reductions* were quoted (as usual for Aberdeen reports) for *Laggards, Industry Average*, and *Best in Class:*

- Best in Class (22.5%)
- Industry Average (15.3%)
- Laggards (7.6%)

The study also showed that recovery times were better for the cloud storage solution too, by 30%, 26%, and 18% for the above classes in order quoted.

Cloud Security

In traditional IT, servers, network, and data were not shared with any other parties, and the network was probably proprietary and fairly safe. Management of the system(s), including backup and recovery, is done with full knowledge of where everything is. In the cloud environments, this is no longer true, particularly in the public cloud which is internet accessible. There are some factors that make security in these environments need careful consideration. The factors are as follows:

- The location of systems and data is often unknown to the user or client.
- Computing resources will be shared with 10s if not 100s of other clients.
- Authentication methods and software will be shared with other clients.
- Disaster recovery and fault tolerance are the responsibility of the cloud provider.
- Intruders are likely to be authenticated users, and you have no demilitarized zone (DMZ).
- You are still getting the financial and other benefits of the cloud but relinquishing control in the process.

A University of Tennessee presentation suggests that most of software security vulnerabilities and issues were carried over into the cloud computing model. In essence, this means that despite its modernity and sophistication, the cloud model has inherited some vulnerability genes from its parents and security is still a key issue in the cloud computing model. The other issues are as ever—availability, performance, and compliance (see http://teaching-ia.appspot.com/files/Cloud_ Computing_Security_Reliability_and_Availability_Issues.pptx).

Another presentation on cloud computing, this time from LogicForce, highlights some areas that any organizations moving to the cloud environment should note the following:

- Security and breaches
- Reliability concerns

- Privacy
- Vendor lock-in
- Loss of control—updates, data location, and other items

For reference, see http://chattanoogataxpractitioners.org/images/PDFs/2012-02-Hampton_Phillip-Cloud_Computing.pdf—"Cloud Computing. New IT Paradigm."

One security breach mentioned in the presentation above is instructive not only in the cloud context, but in the context of MTTR (mean time to repair) and ramp-up time as discussed elsewhere in this book (definition in Appendix 1). The breach is summarized in the presentation as follows:

- June 2011: *Dropbox* accounts accessible without password

  A code update gone awry introduced what the site delicately called an "authentication bug." The error was fixed five minutes after it was discovered, but for a four-hour stretch, the sites defenses were down.

Salutary lesson and other references are provided in this paragraph. This is a perfect example of a fast *fix* (5 minutes) to a logical fault but much longer ramp-up time to normal operation (4 hours or 240 minutes) during which the application is in essence *down*. For other references, see the following URLs for articles on the topic of *Security in the Cloud*. The issues raised, and some solutions, are covered in the first paper listed below, and there is an organization called the "Cloud Security Alliance" also referenced.

- http://www.infoworld.com/d/cloud-computing/download-the-cloud-security-deep-dive-660?source=IFWNLE_nlt_cloud_2014-01-27
- https://cloudsecurityalliance.org/
- https://cloudsecurityalliance.org/research/top-threats/ "The Notorious Nine" paper

There is a mass of useful papers and articles at the site http://www.sans.org/reading-room/whitepapers/logging/?cat = logging.

A Computer Weekly article outlines *five main areas* that need to be understood and acted upon by organizations moving to the cloud (http://www.computerweekly.com/news/2240089111/Top-five-cloud-computing-security-issues).

Finally, in the *Availability Digest*, there is a topical SIEM-related article at the URL (www.availabilitydigest.com).

It pays to keep an eye of the *Availability Digest* as it regularly adds *disaster* tales to its Never Again section. It is also a good source of articles on various aspects of high availability (HA).

Virtualization

What Is Virtualization?

The logical division of a physical machine into multiple *virtual machines*, called VMs or sometimes *guests*.

The concept of virtual systems came mainly from ideas developed in the 1960s and made into a time-sharing software products called CP/CMS (control program/Cambridge monitor system).

CP/CMS became CP-40 and evolved into CP-67, which appeared in 1967. (It also owes something to MIT's Multics*—1969.)

The development of CP-67 culminated in the announcement of VM/370 on August 2, 1972, along with enhancements to the System/370 range of machines. A nuance that amused me at the announcement was that you could run VM/370 under VM/370 *ad infinitum.*

VM/370 was used as a time-sharing system and for program development, and *CMS* came to mean conversational monitor system. It was also the vehicle for running different OSs on a single machine, for example, DOS (disk operating system) and OS, the main OS for large machines and workloads.

Virtual disks attached to users were minidisks into which a real disk had been logically subdivided and given a number. Thus, a user asking for a disk would have a minidisk attached via a command like *attach 291 to <user> as 191.* The user then referred to the virtual disk as 191 when programming or doing other work. Similarly, real tape drives could be attached to a user and *named* 181, 182, and so on to which the user would refer. The *att* command linked a real tape (say 284) to the user as logical tape 181. Both physical tapes and physical disks (and other peripherals) could be detached and used by others when no longer needed. In fact, if this did not happen, the system would grind to a halt with—yes—a *logical* outage.

Within cloud computing, virtual machines go under different names although the base architectures are the same. IBM VMs are called logical partitions (LPARs) and on x86-based machines *virtual machines.*

Full Virtualization

The structure of a virtualized environment as recognized today looks as shown in the Figure 10.2 where *App* stands for application(s), OS for operating system. The *Host OS* is the one that normally controls the hardware platform, which now hosts the VMs. The OSs (guest OSs) on the VMs are unaware that they have been *virtualized* and are completely isolated from the underlying hardware. They *think* they are accessing and controlling the hardware themselves, but their hardware requests are handled for them by the hypervisor. Figure 10.2 shows the structure of two types of hypervisor.

Type 1: This configuration comprises a series of VMs, each containing an OS and application(s) and a hypervisor *OS* to control the allocation of resources—processors, memory, disk, and network interface cards (NICs) across the VMs. This is commonly called a *bare-metal* or *native* hypervisor environment. Examples of bare-metal hypervisors are IBM z/VM for zSeries platforms, IBM PowerVM for Power5, 6, and 7 platforms (what was Risc System/6000), VMW are ESX/ESX1 Server for Windows x86 platforms and Microsoft Hyper-V.

Type 2: This configuration comprises a series of VMs, each containing an OS and application(s) hypervisor *OS* and the *host* or native OS for the hardware platform to control the allocation of resources—processors, memory, disk, and NICs across the VMs. These are commonly called *hosted hypervisors*. Examples of this include VMWare Workstation, VMWare Server, Oracle VM VirtualBox, and Kernel-Based VM (KVM).

---

* The name *Unix* (originally Unics) is itself a pun on *Multics.*

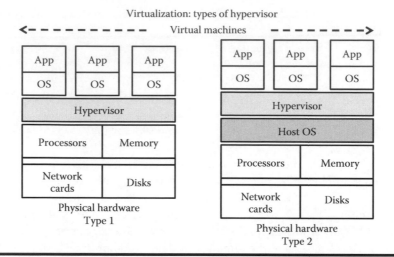

Virtualization: types of hypervisor

Figure 10.2   Two full virtualization environments.

Paravirtualization

Paravirtualization (PV) is similar to full virtualization but has a *thin* hypervisor and necessitates alterations to the guest OSs to function (Figure 10.3).

It therefore has its plusses and minuses as we will see. Paravirtualization is a technique introduced by Xen and is now adopted by other virtualization solution providers. Guests on a paravirtualized system require a modified OS kernel that must be ported to run with Xen. However, because the guest (OS) is aware of the hypervisor, it can run efficiently without any emulation.

Thus, paravirtualization offers better performance and scalability than full virtualization although it has the downside of OS modification and all that entails. However, some flexibility is lost because of this need to modify the OS.

The outline of PV is shown in Figure 10.3. Table 10.1, taken from the reference at the end of this section, shows the efficiency, in terms of the resource *cost* virtualization of the paravirtualization mode against that of full virtualization mode.

Paravirtualization model

Application	Application	Application
Modified OS	Modified OS	Modified OS
Modified driver	Modified driver	Modified driver
Hypervisor (VMM)		

Hardware — CPU, Network HW

Figure 10.3   Paravirtualization schematic.

Table 10.1 Virtualization/Paravirtualization Overheads Compared

Mode	Guest Instances	Virtualization Overhead (%)	System Needs (%)	Total (%)
Full virtualization	5	10 (50 total)	10 (50 total)	100
Paravirtualization	8	2 (16 total)	10 (80 total)	96

Performance and modifications aside, the choice of virtualization type will ultimately depend on the requirements of the system the solution supports. For more detailed aspects, see the reference http://searchservervirtualization.techtarget.com/tip/Paravirtualization-explained.

Security Risks in Virtual Environments

A Symantec/VMware positioning paper "Securing the Promise of Virtualization" outlines for following risks:

- Targeted malware (Neil MacDonald of Gartner claims that all VMs can and will have vulnerabilities, resulting in a breakdown in the isolation "promised" by this layer.)
- *Portable* drive theft (The physical theft of small drives or memory sticks containing important data)
- Data loss due to migration and movement of locations
- Audit scope *creep* due to the existence of data on VM resulting in auditing difficulties
- Missing security updates and patches due to the ease of relocation of VMs
- Reliance on traditional [*security*] barriers that often cannot keep pace with and track the dynamic movement of virtual instances

For reference, see http://www.symantec.com/content/en/us/enterprise/white_papers/b-WP_Securing ThePromiseOfVirtualization_WP_21229614.en-us.pdf.

Vendors and Virtualization

The following sections summarize some of the providers of virtualization platforms, some of which incorporate add-on features to the base hypervisor platform. The function offered by the vendors provided here will evolve so consult the vendor websites for the latest information if planning virtualization *in anger*.

IBM PowerVM

IBM PowerVM is a virtualization platform that runs virtualized AIX, IBM i, and Linux environments on IBM POWER processor-based systems. PowerVM provides customers with the ability to create advanced logical partitions such as micro-partitions (that can be as small as 0.1 core per partition) (http://www-03.ibm.com/systems/power/software/virtualization/).

IBM z/VM

z/VM virtualization technology is designed to allow the capability for running hundreds to thousands of Linux servers on a single mainframe running with other System z operating systems, such as z/OS, or as a large-scale Linux-only enterprise server solution. Certain versions of zVM can host non-Linux workloads such as z/OS, z/VSE (previously DOS), and z/TPF (transaction processing facility). z/VM allows up to four instances of z/VM to be clustered together as members in a single system image, and they can be managed as a single z/VM system and share resources (http://www.vm.ibm.com).

VMware VSphere, ESX, and ESXi

VMware VSphere is a full enterprise virtualization solution that includes server, network, and storage virtualization technologies. VMware ESX and ESXi are server virtualization technologies (http://www.vmware.com).

Microsoft Hyper-V

Microsoft Hyper-V is a virtualization platform from Microsoft that runs on Windows Server 2008/2012. It can in turn run virtualized Linux and Windows environments. The individual virtual environments are called *partitions*. One of the partitions, called the root partition, has to be a Windows partition. Hyper-V can run standalone of on top of Windows 2012. For more information, go to http://www.microsoft.com/windowsserver2008/en/us/hyperv-main.aspx.

HP Integrity Virtual Machines

HP Integrity Virtual Machines is a software virtualization technology within the HP Virtual Server Environment (HP VSE) that enables you to create multiple virtual servers or machines each with its own *guest* OS instance, applications, and users. It supports HP 11i v2 and v3, Windows for Itanium, and Linux for Itanium guests. For more information, go to http://h20338.www2.hp.com/enterprise/us/en/os/hpux11i-partitioning-integrity-vm.html.

Linux KVM

Linux KVM is a virtualization technology that is built into the Linux kernel. This technology enables it to host guest OSs as well as run native applications in that kernel. For more information, go to http://www.linux-kvm.org/page/MainPage.

Solaris Zones

Solaris Zones is an OS virtualization technology that is part of Solaris 10. It has a global zone with a number of zones running within it. Each of these zones has their own node name, virtual network interface, and storage associated with it (http://www.oracle.com/technetwork/systems/containers/index-jsp-140778.html).

Xen

Xen is an open-source type-1(bare-metal) hypervisor, which allows many instances of the same or different OSs to run in parallel on a single machine (or host). Xen is used as the basis for a number of different commercial and open source applications, such as server virtualization, infrastructure as a service (IaaS), desktop virtualization, security applications, embedded and hardware appliances. Xen is frequently used in cloud production environments and is the only type-1 hypervisor that is available as open source (http://wiki.xen.org/wiki/Xen_Overview).

Virtualization and HA

Bill Weinberg,[*] in an article on achieving HA in a virtualized environment, points out some deficiencies in *real* environments, including clustering, and suggests the use of the following things to exploit virtual environments in the quest for HA:

- Elimination of cold (nonvirtual) spares by maintaining snapshots of stable VMs
- Fast failover to warm spares (virtual images)
- Clustering using both virtual and physical (real) machines
- Clustering with virtual clusters spread across physical machines
- Isolation, monitoring, and fast restart of unreliable applications and systems (VM isolation is similar to partition isolation)

He suggests using scripts along with virtualization to implement standard nonvirtual HA scenarios [*do I detect automation here?*]:

- Use local spare VMs for fast failover
- Use spares in VMs on remote systems
- Checkpoint using VM snapshot functionality
- Setting and checking high and low *watermarks* for key resources (key indicators)
- Other technical suggestions involving Linux, management information bases (MIBs), and basic input/output system (BIOS) calls

The article is cited in the footnotes and in addition to the above outlines the ubiquitous *gotchas* and reaches conclusions for IT managers and (availability) architects. He concludes as follows:

> Ultimately, virtualization is just another tool to use to enhance availability and reliability. The heuristics and mechanisms described in this article will not themselves guarantee better uptime and faster fault resolution unless they are integrated into a comprehensive policy regime.

By the final phrase I take Bill's words to mean that virtualization is not a *silver bullet* but a brick or two in the availability wall (http://searchservervirtualization.techtarget.com/tip/Achieving-high-availability-in-a-virtualized-environment).

---

[*] Quotes from Bill Weinberg.

Virtualization Information Sources

An understanding of virtualization is necessary to understand cloud computing, which depends on it. The following are sources of useful information on virtualization and should complement and expand on what has been presented in this book.

1. "Integrating High-availability Tactics into a Virtual Infrastructure" (http://searchserver-virtualization.techtarget.com/ebook/Introduction-to-virtualization-for-administrators/Integrating-high-availability-methods-into-a-virtual-infrastructure)
2. Virtualization website (http://virtualizationreview.com/home.aspx)
3. Virtualization: A Useful Thesis (http://arxiv.org/ftp/arxiv/papers/0910/0910.1719.pdf)
4. Virtualization vendors' comparison (http://virtualization.findthebest.com/)

The first half or more of the document above is a useful introduction to some of the factors affecting availability and a discussion of virtualization, which you may find interesting.

Summary

Virtualization and cloud concepts and their implementation have changed the availability scene in often simplifying the HA task but at the same time often rendering its workings sometimes vague. It is sometimes like a nonmechanic driving a car—you can drive it perfectly but you have no idea what goes on under the metal cover at the front of the vehicle. If it breaks down, you sit at the side of the road and moan.

One fact crosses the border between physical and virtual computing—whatever is under the virtualized/cloud environment is physical—just like the fact that under every substance there are the same electrons, protons, and neutrons—and will obey the same laws and equations and fall over just as often. The trick is to use other VMs as failover vehicles when a primary VM is unwell and there are numerous papers on techniques and products to facilitate this.

> *Note:* This is a warning. Cloud computing is not a silver bullet. Even if it was, you can still shoot yourself in the foot with it.

In embracing virtualization/clouds, perhaps we should keep in mind the physicist Lord Rutherford's thoughts on basic particles and their nature:

1. "I am a great believer in the simplicity of things and as you probably know I am inclined to hang on to broad & simple ideas like grim death until evidence is too strong for my tenacity."
2. "An alleged scientific discovery has no merit unless it can be explained to a barmaid."

I hope any barmaids (and barmen) reading this book are with us so far.

Chapter 11

Disaster Recovery Overview

First, have a definite, clear practical ideal: a goal, an objective. Second, have the necessary means to achieve your ends: wisdom, money, materials, and methods.

Third, adjust all your means to that end.

Aristotle

Aristotle obviously wrote something about disaster recovery (DR), project definition workshops (PDWs), and project initiation documents (PIDs), but the discussions are almost certainly in Greek and I am not aware of any translations. My English version outlined below will need to suffice.

DR Background

A DR Lesson from Space

Location: USS Enterprise, somewhere in space   *Date:* April 1, 2389

Scottie: Houston, we have a problem.

James T. Kirk: What is it Scottie? Klingons, Romulans, hardware, software, spilt coffee. ... Brits run out of tea?

Scottie: I dinnae know Jim. It's an IT problem all right but not as we know it.

JTK: Have you run it though LCARS for an RCA and a CFIA?

Scottie: Nae Jim, it's down as well. That's the wee problem! The other problem is that I dinnae know what RCAs, LCARS and CFIAs are.

JTK: What about the molecular neutron-driven synthesizing backup LCARS on planet Talos IV (to give us flexible, agile, virtualized, easy-to-use cloud-based geo-galactic mirroring with nanosecond failover)?

Scottie: We dinnae have one Jim—Intergalactic Finance said it was too expensive, Talos IV was too far away and you agreed we wouldn't need a DR site anyway—remember?

JTK: Scottie, can you send me a copy of the Intergalactic Early Retirement Option (IERO) document—hardcopy—please? James T Kirk, roger and out.

Disasters Are Rare ... Aren't They?

Note: The information in the next three sections is essentially historical but supports the theses being made here that disasters are *not* rare and when they happen, they are *not* always due to natural causes. Actual numbers may alter over time, hence this rider (Table 11.1).

Another report, outlined next, disputes the idea that disaster situations are caused mainly by natural disasters, except that they may cause other more immediate outages such as major power failures. You must not lose sight of the ultimate cause of the outage and plan accordingly—root cause analysis (RCA).

Key Message: Be Prepared

This Boy Scout motto is apposite in the DR arena because it appears that most installations are unprepared to various degrees according to the Disaster Recovery Preparedness Council (DRPC). The DRPC is an independent research group engaged in IT DR management, research, and benchmarking in order to deliver practical guidance for how organizations can improve business continuity (BC) and DR (www.drbenchmark.org).

Their study[*] covered more than 1000 organizations, from small businesses to large enterprises, to help them to assess their readiness for critical IT systems recovery in virtual environments. It found that 73% of respondents had inadequate overall DR plans. The other drawbacks identified were as follows:

Table 11.1 Organizations Declaring a Disaster in Five Years

Disaster Declarations	Respondents (%)
None	73
One	14
Two	6
Three	3
Five	2
More than five	2
Total with a disaster	27

Source: Building the business case for disaster recovery spending, Forrester Research, Inc., April 2008.

---

[*] Disaster Recovery Preparedness Benchmark Survey.

- General lack of comprehensive DR planning (*it's all in my head boss—don't worry*)
- Lack of DR testing (*it will be alright on the night syndrome*)
- Lack of DR resources—budget and skills (*if you think education and training is costly, try ignorance*)

The report breaks down these drawbacks in terms of levels of inadequacy and suggests some lessons: *Best practices from better prepared organizations* (Section 2) and *What you can do to increase your DR preparedness* (Section 3). The full survey can be seen at http://drbenchmark.org/wp-content/uploads/2014/02/ANNUAL_REPORT-DRPBenchmark_Survey_Results_2014_report.pdf.

*DR Invocation Reasons: Forrester Survey**

As stated previously, the following data are a few years old but the entities involved are probably the same today, even if the actual percentages change.

Forrester: Global Disaster Recovery Preparedness Online Survey
Question: What was the cause(s) or your most significant disaster declaration(s) or major business disruption?, asked of 250 DR decision-makers and influencers.

This survey laid to rest the idea that most DR invocations are due to quirks of nature. It is not so says the survey. Here are the top five reasons given, in order of occurrence and with suggested solutions to avoid or mitigate them:

1. *Power failure (42%)*[†]: Implement a redundant (say, $N + 1$) power supply system [Multiple sources outside the data center might also be a good idea]
2. *IT hardware failure (31%):* Correct and timely maintenance, dedicated trained support
3. *IT network failure (21%):* Replicated, monitored, and well-supported network infrastructure
4. *IT software failure (16%):* Correct and timely maintenance, dedicated trained support
5. *Human error (16%):* Outsourcing to *experts*, remote monitoring, skills

After these come *floods, hurricanes, fire* (and possibly brimstone) plus other causes, including a worrying 4% *don't knows*. I have noticed over many years that in several other, unrelated surveys that the category *other* very often figures highly. Remember that some surveys are what I have called *historical* where *exact numbers* may not still apply but many *causes* will.

End note: Disaster Recovery Journal (DRJ) has teamed with Forrester Research to produce a number of market studies in BC and DR. Each survey contains data for company comparison and benchmarking. The aim is to promote research and publication of best practices and recommendations for the industry. The annual surveys can be accessed via the given URL (https://www.drj.com/resources/forrester-surveys.html). Data within can be used for BC purposes as long as due credit is given to DRJ and Forrester Research. The surveys can be found at the given URL and downloaded (https://www.drj.com/resources/forrester-surveys.html).

- *2012:* The State of Crisis Communication & Risk Management
- *2011:* The State of Business Continuity Preparedness

---

[*] See http://www.drj.com/images/surveys_pdf/forrester/2008Forrester_survey.pdf (contains the results above) and Forrester Research, Inc., State of Enterprise Disaster Recovery Preparedness, Q2 2011.
[†] A similar survey reported in a BCI (Knowledge Base) report puts this top cause down as *disruption from extreme weather (49%)* but my money is on *power* due to weather.

- *2010:* The State of Disaster Recovery Preparedness
- *2009:* Crisis Communication and Risk Management in Business Continuity Preparedness
- *2008:* The State of Business Continuity Preparedness
- *2007:* The State of BC/DR Preparedness

DR Testing: Kaseya Survey

Kaseya: Results of a survey conducted with 6500 IT professionals by Tech Validate for Kaseya. *Question: What is the Current State of Your Disaster Recovery Plan?*

- We have a regularly tested plan for the entire business (16%).
- We have a regularly tested plan for servers and workstations (16%).
- We have a regularly tested plan for just critical servers (24%).
- We have a regularly tested plan for just servers (26%).
- We have no plan in place (18%).

For reference, see www.kaseya.com.

Hence, this chapter. The chapter has three main objectives getting across given as follows:

1. Why DR? Survey above and others like it plus an overview here.
2. What is DR? An *overview*.
3. Where can I get more information and help on DR? Sources given.

Conclusions: Although we don't know the outcome of the disasters or the consequences of indifferent testing in the results of the studies above, one thing is clear—something needs to be done.

Suffice it to say that there will be situations that apply to all countries and industries and those that depend on the *geography* and sometimes the industry. For example, I am not aware of there ever being a tsunami affecting Great Britain or of floods in the Sahara and other deserts. The main thing to recognize is that a disaster is something that renders normal IT operations inoperable for a period, which can harm the business it supports. The decision to invoke DR is a significant one and needs a consistent, logical set of factors to make that decision. If DR is invoked prematurely or a flawed DR process is invoked, then there may be a *double-whammy* DR situation. It will therefore pay to get it right first time, unless you have a DR for a failed or false DR situation (I would call this *nested* DR, a fledgling discipline).

DR: A Point to B Point

We have seen the concept of using the "A" point and "B" point philosophy (PDW) in projects and the same applies here. If your high availability (HA) A point is sufficiently robust to cover DR, the B point, then $A = B$ and you are in good shape. If, however, A is not equal to B, then there is work to be done.

> **Note:** Always remember, if you don't know where you are and don't know your destination, it doesn't matter which way you go. The following sections may be of use in designing the B (recovery) point for your business.

Backup/Restore

Overview

The normal reasons for taking backups and/or archiving is for future use. This might be for short term or DR (backup) or litigation (archiving). In the case of DR, CA at INTEROP 2008 and Softlayer (IBM company) in a service brief suggested the following eminently sensible steps to categorize backup requirements and make it a *horses for courses* method:

- Group data by business value (*that is, by criticality*)
- Identify backup goals plus recovery point objectives (RPOs) and recovery time objectives (RTOs) (*for each group*)
- Identify optimal backup infrastructure solution (*tape, disk, geo-mirrors, etc.*)
- Define a backup strategy based on this infrastructure—data targets, frequency, reporting, logs, and retention plan including transport and locations
- Test it
- Ongoing management, deploying (*appropriate*) combinations of backup, replication, continuous data protection (CDP), and failover (see next sections)

There are a number of ways (modes) of taking copies of or archiving data. Which one is chosen depends on how you plan to recover, to *what point* (RPO) and at *what speed* (RTO) to minimize the business impact of a major failure. Let us look at some ways of taking *copies* of data and associated metadata (indexes, pointers, data definitions, some logs, etc.) plus data/files associated with supporting software such as online transaction processing (OLTP), domain naming service (DNS), and other *middleware.*

Backup Modes

Cold (Offline)

A copy taken when all components (processes) of a system are stopped and the stable data, metadata, and other volatile data backed up without consideration of data changing while being backed up. Copies can be of everything on the system storage or by application or service. It is important for all backup types and modes to know exactly what data—volatile or other—is needed for each service or application.

For DR purposes, non-volatile (fixed) data need to be backed up and stored safely in the event of an invocation of DR when perhaps all primary disks and tapes are lost.

Warm (Online)

A warm online backup is taken where users still have access to the system but with reduced functionality to simplify the backup to preserve consistency between files/data and metafiles being backed up. An example of this reduction might be the suspension of database rights, where data rights may be cached and permanently applied later.

Hot (Online)

An online hot backup is taken with no restrictions on user access but can present difficulties in synchronizing in-flight data and is often ignored.

Backup Types

Full Backup

A full backup backs up all files in a storage area or service irrespective of archive bit settings, last change date, and so on. This means that even dormant data are backed up each time when this kind of backup is run. A study of timesharing users (IBM TSO) once discovered that only 3% of the data involved were altered on any one day. The backups employed were full backups resulting in repeatedly backing up unchanged data. The solution is incremental backups (see below).

Incremental Backup

This backs up files that have been modified since the last full or incremental backup, which saves storage space. One downside of this is that should a restore be necessary, the restore must take place from the most recent full backup and then sequentially from each subsequent incremental backup. Unfortunately, files that have been deleted since the last full backup may also be restored in this operation.

Multilevel Incremental Backup

This type of backup is akin to an incremental backup except, on the nth backup, it backs up the files that have been modified since the last $(n–1)$ level backup. The preceding full backup is considered the level 0 backup version.

Differential Backup

A differential (or delta) backup backs up only the files that have been modified since the last *full backup*. To take an example, if a full backup is taken on Sunday, a differential backup on Monday would backup files modified since Sunday. However, a differential backup taken on Thursday would backup all files modified since Sunday. It thus loses the incremental backup benefit of space saving but usually gains on restoration time.

Synthetic Backup

This is a combination of a full backup with subsequent incremental or differential backups. To combine a full backup with subsequent incremental or differential backups to *masquerade* as a new full backup requires the host to have records of changes and deletions. However, this *new* backup increases the restore speed over that using backup plus incremental/differential.

Progressive Backup

These are scenarios where a single backup is taken and thereafter only incremental backups are taken. This tends to be proprietary because its use requires system knowledge of inactive and deleted files which can be kept for a specified period and then removed.

Data Deduplication

"Data deduplication is the replacement of multiple copies of data—at various levels of granularity—with references to a shared copy in order to save storage space and/or bandwidth" (SNIA Definition).

> Data deduplication looks for redundancy of sequences of bytes across very large comparison windows. Sequences of data (over 8 KB long) are compared to the history of other such sequences. The first uniquely stored version of a sequence is referenced rather than stored again. This process is completely hidden from users and applications so the whole file is readable after it's written. (EMC Glossary)

Data deduplication can operate at the *file*, *block*, or *bit* level (Figure 11.1). In file-level deduplication, if two files are exactly alike, one copy of the file is stored and subsequent iterations receive pointers to the saved file. However, file deduplication is not highly efficient because the change of even a single bit results in a totally different copy of the entire file being stored.

In block deduplication and bit deduplication, the software looks within a file and saves unique iterations of each block.

If a file is updated, only the changed data are saved. This is a far more efficient process than file-level deduplication for the reasons mentioned above.

Block deduplication and *bit* deduplication can achieve compression ratios of about 15:1 but can be larger or smaller according to a TechStorage paper (see Techtarget.com). That site claims source dedupe is less efficient than target dedupe.

Let us discuss *how it works*. Data deduplication is in essence about handling only one copy of an item of data in storing or transmitting it instead of moving multiple copies of identical data.

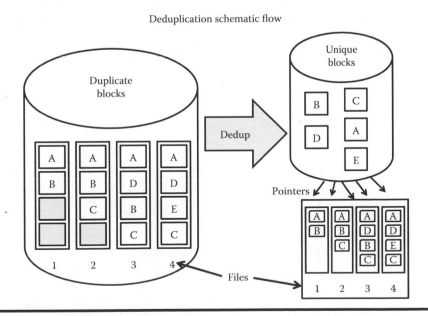

Deduplication schematic flow

Figure 11.1 Data deduplication schematic.

To do this, it is necessary to record just how many data items are identical. When this is done, it is possible to keep one copy and point multiple users to that copy.

The process of deduplication can be employed in a number of ways:

1. *Source based:* Identification of duplicate data segments on the host system before any data are backed up. Some arrays like EMC's and CommVault's offer this capability. This has advantages in reducing bandwidth requirements in sending data to the backup site.
2. *Target based:* Identification of duplicate data segments on the target system. This has the benefit of being able to identify all duplicate data at a site rather than possible multiple sources.
3. *Target copy:* Deduplication on a secondary (copy) backup storage.

Most applications wait for a write transaction to complete before proceeding with further work, and hence, the overall performance decreases considerably. It is a parallel dilemma to using user datagram protocol (UDP) instead of transmission control protocol (TCP) where the latter is diligent in making sure its transmitted blocks have arrived before continuing, with an obvious impact on throughput but in the cause of safety.

Figure 11.2 shows some detail from an EMC paper of 2013 comparing the business data volume (17.3 PB) with the deduplicated volume (5.2 PB) of backup for this data.

Data Replication

"Data replication is continuously maintaining a secondary copy of data—possibly at a remote site—from a primary volume for the purposes of providing high availability and redundancy" (SNIA Definition).

Replication is a mode of *backup* where changes to a primary data source are reflected elsewhere in *real time* for synchronous replication or in a delayed *store and forward* mode for asynchronous replication. It is a common method of *backup* in DR plans and architectures. Which mode is used depends on the distance over which the replication needs to take place.

SYNCH usually operates for distances under 100 km, usually for services where data loss cannot be tolerated, and ASYNC is essentially unlimited.

With synchronous replication, an operation cannot complete at the source system until it has completed on the target system (which you state correctly). However, this introduces a delay on the application, which slows it down and can seriously affect performance. A round-trip signal

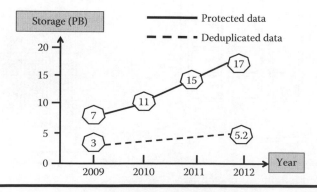

Figure 11.2   Data space savings from deduplication (EMC 2013).

over copper or fiber takes about 20 microseconds per mile. Therefore, if the systems are 100 miles apart, every synchronous operation will add two milliseconds to application processing time. This can seriously slow down an application. Therefore, synchronous replication generally requires that the systems be within a few km of each other, such as in a campus or metropolitan environment.

Asynchronous replication, on the other hand, replicates from a queue of database changes made by the application (or transaction manager). The replication engine reads changes off of the change queue and sends them to the target system for application to the target database. Therefore, the source application is not even aware that replication is going on, and the systems can be separated by great distances – even thousands of miles. The distance penalty is that, as the distance is increased, the number of changes in the replication pipeline increases. It is these changes that will be lost if the replication channel fails.

Replication Agents

With the advent of intelligent storage subsystems or arrays, a lot of function is taken off the host system and performed by the storage array, assuming it has an intelligent array to *converse* with. One sort of replication is the normal *host-based replication* where the system performs the replication in communication with another one. The second way, offloaded from the host, is *array-based replication* where the action may be initiated by the host but the work is done by the arrays involved. Data are replicated array-to-array, possibly over a distance (Figure 11.3).

There are a number of proprietary storage arrays offering replication but nearly all suffer from the *lack of heterogeneous support*, that is, replicating between different types of storage array.

A third way is *network-based replication* but we don't cover that mode here—it can easily be found by a Google search.

Asynchronous Replication

In asynchronous replication (AR), the primary storage array will cache the update transaction data and sends an acknowledgment to its primary host. After a preset time, the primary array sends that update to the array at the remote (secondary) site, that is, there will be a delay in sending.

The remote site acknowledges the transaction to the primary array (and hence to primary host).

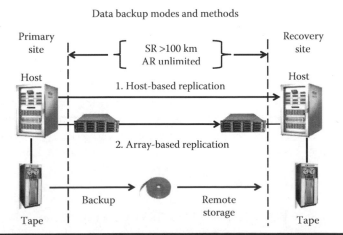

Figure 11.3   Data backup modes and methods with DR in mind.

Synchronous Replication

In the synchronous replication (SR) approach, replication is performed within the source (primary system) update transaction, usually via two-phase commit protocol for consistency.

- The source transaction is not considered complete until the associated update has been successfully replicated at the target system(s).
- The choice of method, AR or SR, depends on various factors, not least the distances involved (see Figure 11.3).
- This scenario has assumed that the replication was handled by the storage array but a similar pattern of *send* and *ack* activity will occur.

For Reference, see http://en.wikipedia.org/wiki/Replication_(computing), where a good source of information on replication and a detailed exposition of the many vendor replication products and techniques can be found.

Heterogeneous Replication

Many organizations use different *brands* of relational database management system (RDBMS), either by choice or by the fact that some applications mandate a particular RDBMS. Either way, there may be a need to implement *RDBMS agnostic* replication in that organization. In its perfect form, this would entail bidirectional replication between all forms and combinations of RDBMS—Oracle, SQL Server, DB2, Sybase, and so on. Heterogeneity can also encompass hardware and operating systems. So, in theory, HW1/OS2/RDBMS3 can replicate to/from HW4/OS5/RDBMS6 in the ideal architecture.

The architecture is illustrated in Figure 11.4 with six popular RDBMS but could contain other RDBMS versions, a huge list of which can be found in Wikipedia.

However, the implementations of this are not quite the same across all HWx, OSx, and RDBMSx versions. In addition, there can be different forms of a particular RDBMS depending on the hosting platform, for example, DB2 on various platforms.

Note: See the appropriate vendor documentation for verification that it fulfils your requirements.

There are other methods of taking copies of data security, recovery and disaster recovery purposes.

Other Types of Backup

Many services may depend on data not stored initially on disk but entered or received on regular basis via some device or other—screens, optical character recognition (OCR), optical mark reader (OMR), handheld devices, telephone, letter, email, and so on. If these business functions are still intact after a DR is declared, there must be a logistics plan for using them at the usual location(s) if IT operations have to be switched elsewhere.

Basically this means the following:

- Main IT equipment disabled for long enough to incur business *damage*—invoke DR
- Main IT plus other related business functions—invoke BC, which as we have seen is related by the well-known equation BC = IT DR ++

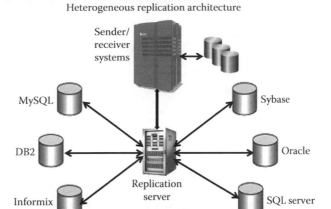

Figure 11.4 Heterogeneous replication schematic.

DR Recovery Time Objective: WAN Optimization

One of the main considerations in locating a DR site is avoiding the *double whammy* of both sites being hit by the same outage cause flood, earthquake, and so on. This is normally solved by having the primary and backup sites being geographically separate, but this brings with it possible issues of backup and replication across large distances.

The basic *equation* is that the slower and less frequent the backup from primary to the DR site, the longer the RTO in a DR situation. This is often tackled by *WAN optimization* and *WAN acceleration* techniques and technology, which are usually combinations of other techniques and specific products.

WAN optimization is achieved by lowering the volume of data and the latency of the network by several techniques, sometimes called *data reduction*, given as follows:

- Data deduplication to reduce the amount of data shipped
- Data compression to reduce the size (not amount) of data transmitted by some ratio x:1, where x might be in double figures
- Latency optimization via transmission protocol *tweaks* such as window size scaling and selective acknowledgments (TCP, UDP, CIFS, NFS, MAPI, HTTP, and HTTPS network protocols). This offers the chance to optimize mixed traffic, for example, production data and backup/replication data streams.
- Data center and local office caching of data with only changes shipped over the network when cached data are requested
- Application acceleration for applications such as RDBMSs

Figures of 30× data transfer speedups are quoted in various places, but I don't think they are the norm—just marketing hype in some cases.

Next is the quality of service (QoS). Networks are now carrying increasing amounts of audio and video data threaten to clog the transmission *pipes*. Important, time-sensitive data need special treatment in such heavy traffic. This can be achieved by rationing bandwidth based on the importance of the data transmitted—less important, less bandwidth allocated. Optimization technology should also monitor traffic and warn network administration of imminent gridlocks as well as identifying current trouble spots.

Vendors of these techniques and products include Cisco, Netex, Riverbed Technology, Silver Peak, Expand Networks, Infineta Systems and F5 Networks (http://en.wikipedia.org/wiki/WAN_optimization).

Gartner Quadrant 2104 report presents the usual quadrant for WAN optimization controllers and the positions of various vendors within it (http://www.riverbed.com/contact/WAN-Optimization-SteelHead.html?CID=70140000000WA0H&LSD=2Q14_Google_AdWords_Steelhead_WAN_MQ).

Backup Product Assessments

Virtualization Review

This report is produced by Info-Tech Research Group Inc. and outlined in Virtualization Review. The report compares fourteen vendors and their backup products. Although each product does basic backup, there are features that differentiate them, such as deduplication:

- *CA Technologies:* CA ARCserve
- *CommVault:* Enterprise Backup/Recovery software
- *Dell AppAssure:* AppAssure, a Dell acquisition
- *Dell Quest vRanger:* vRanger
- *EMC:* Avamar, with deduplication capabilities
- *FalconStor:* FalconStor Continuous Data Protector
- *HP:* Data Protector, integration with HP hardware
- *IBM:* Tivoli Storage Manager
- *Microsoft:* Data Protection Manager
- *NetApp Syncsort:* Software implementation using NetApp hardware
- *PHD Virtual:* Virtual backup solutions (acquired by Unitrends December 2013)
- *Symantec:* Backup Exec and NetBackup
- *Unitrends:* An image-based backup solution with near continuous data protection.
- *Veeam:* Virtual backup, with backup verification, and recovery direct from backups

For reference, see http://virtualizationreview.com/whitepapers/2013/07/symantec-vendor-landscape-virtual-backup-software/asset.aspx?tc = assetpg.

Gartner Quadrant Analysis

Backup products are the subject of a Gartner "Magic Quadrant" report dated June 2013. It analyses and rates vendors who provide features such as traditional backup to tape, backup to conventional disk, backup to the cloud, data reduction (compression and deduplication), snapshot, heterogeneous replication, continuous data protection (CDP), and/or virtual tape library (VTL) support, among other capabilities. The vendors covered are as follows:

- HP
- IBM
- EMC
- Symantec
- CommVault
- NetApp
- Veeam Software

- Actifio
- Dell
- CA Technologies
- Asigra
- EVault
- Acronis
- Syncsort
- FalconStor Software

The report describes the players and outlines their abilities under the heading Strengths and Cautions. This can be useful to an organization *only if it knows its requirements clearly*. The results, which classify the vendors in the usual Gartner Quadrant, showing Niche Players and Visionaries, together with their ability to execute the functions involved, can be found in http://www.actifio. com/2014-gartner-magic-quadrant-enterprise-backup-recovery/.

Backup/Archive: Tape or Disk?

Both obviously have roles to which they are best suited and most installations use a mix of both media for storing *immediate* and *non-immediate* data. Which is used will depend on factors specific to the business in question but considerations common across installations will include the following:

- RTO
- RPO
- Any other time-constraint *demands* of the business impact analysis (BIA)
- Costs and lifetime (*shelf life*) of the media chosen

The obvious route might be *wall to wall* disk if it is cost-effective enough. However, a study by the *University of California* showed the following *activity* profile for disk data:

- 1% of data accessed more than five times.
- 2% accessed less than five times.
- 7% accessed once.
- 90% never accessed.

> *Corollary:* If one can find out if the 90% can be classified and is always the same, it may make sense to commit it to tape. However, if the composition of that 90% varies and sometimes needs rapid access, then tape will not be the answer. By *tape* is often meant LTO (linear tape open), often known as Ultrium. There is much discussion on the relative merits and costs of tape versus disk for backup and recovery purposes, often centered around costs and time to recover.

A paper on LTO lists the following characteristics for tape and disk storage in terms of bit error rate (BER) (Table 11.2):

Bit Rot

A lot of information can be gleaned from the reference http://www.americanscientist.org/issues/ id.3296,y.0,no.,content.true,page.1,css.print/issue.aspx. Some of the causes of bit rot are as follows, with a numeric summary in Table 11.2.

Table 11.2   Published Values for BER

TAPE (Typical LTO Ultrium)	
Midrange Ultrium drive	Hard error rate 1×10^{17} bits
DISK (FC, SAS, SATA)	
Enterprise FC/SAS	1 sector per 1×10^{16} bits
Enterprise SATA	1 sector per 1×10^{15} bits
Desktop SATA	1 sector per 1×10^{14} bits

- *Thermal asperities:* Instances of high heat for a short duration caused by head-disk contact. This is usually the result of heads hitting small *bumps* created by particles embedded in the media surface during the manufacturing process. The heat generated on a single contact may not be sufficient to thermally erase data but may be sufficient after many contacts.
- *Disk head issues:* Disk heads are designed to push particles away, but contaminants can still become lodged between the head and disk; hard particles used in the manufacture of an HDD can cause surface scratches and data erasure any time the disk is rotating.
- *Soft particle corruption:* Other *soft* materials such as stainless steel can come from assembly tooling. Soft particles tend to smear across the surface of the media, rendering the data unreadable.
- *Corrosion:* Although carefully controlled, it can also cause data erasure and may be accelerated by thermal asperity generated heat.

It may be of interest to note that there are various lubricants used in space vehicles that can minimize wear and tear* on moving parts. The surprising fact is that some solid lubricants are more effective than liquid ones in this environment.

It is of personal interest to me to watch if the new substance *graphene* has any applicability to moving parts in IT equipment because much of the work on it is carried out at my *alma mater*, Manchester University.

Tape Costs

Tape is quoted as being 10–15 times lower cost than disk for long-term storage of data and tape life, that is, data preservation is longer than that of disk. Tape today is probably best used for long-term storage, transport, and archiving of data or as the backup medium for applications and services with less rigorous requirements for data protection and RTO.

Remember, that using tape requires replacement disciplines and library functions to be an effective and safe way of storing data. There is a white paper by Sylvatica, dated 2009, which covers "the evolving role of disk and tape in the data center" and can be found at http://www.wellow. co.uk/documents/BestPractices_Whitepaper_July2009.pdf.

A useful set of references can be found in the Nexsan (Imation) link (http://www.nexsan.com/ library/whitepapers.aspx).

There you will find Analyst Reports, Ebooks, Whitepapers, and Solution Briefs. Some are marketing others have very good educational value in data topics.

---

* There is a UK laboratory specializing in this very field and works closely with NASA and other space agencies.

DR Concepts and Considerations

The basic concept of DR is to *get the show back on the road* after it has foundered in some way. If the disaster happened to a circus, they would possibly have to ask themselves *what subset of our acts will be sufficient to keep the customers happy. … and us in business?* A similar quandary can face an IT organization when a disaster strikes IT and their customers (end users) need to be satisfied.

Disasters can take many forms and we needn't dwell on all manifestations of them here—they are spelled out in gory detail in many articles and books. Suffice it to say that a disaster for IT is something of such magnitude that it prevents normal operations and that cannot be solved by normal HA recovery (fix plus ramp-up) actions on the IT system in a reasonable time.

It usually means invoking a duplicate or subset duplicate of the primary systems at the heart of the problem.

Sounds simple, if expensive, but then the following questions arise:

- When do we invoke these emergency systems—what are the criteria for this drastic step?
- Do we duplicate *all our systems* or a *subset* capable of supporting the vital services of the business?
- As a corollary, what business services do we sacrifice if running with the subset option?
- Where do we locate these emergency facilities?
- Who is our sponsor and our leader in all this?
- What do we need to do on a regular basis to ensure the timely functioning of the spare system(s) when disaster strikes—data backups, logs, transaction journaling, etc.?
- Do we have a plan for all this and the skills necessary to handle it?
- We've never bothered with this before, where can we get some help?
- Are we capable of running a PDW to develop this plan or revise an old one?
- Do we have the other skills needed in this area?
- Is the timescale such that we need to buy in skills initially?
- Several other questions will arise as a result of a PDW and from elsewhere
- What have we forgotten? There will be something. Delphi it.

External DR documentation very often takes the shape of *10/8/7 Vital Things in DR*. These can be useful especially if they can be consolidated. However, I am against *prescriptive methods* without knowledge* so I make my case for common sense again.

This is one area of availability management, which can be planned for but not monitored, measured or, in the main, predicted. There are no equations or calculations that I can present that may help in this area. I have quoted earlier examples of disaster situations but others will happen (Probability it will occur: *Murphy's Law*), so forewarned is forearmed.

The DR Scenario

Who Is Involved?

SunGard, the disaster recovery organization have produced a paper entitled "Availability Services—Availability and the Bottom Line" which discusses some business aspects of availability, its impact on business, and responsibilities for it. Surveyed job functions and opinions are very roughly divided into CEO, CIO, CFO, and COO camps of senior personnel.

---

* Remember "A fool with a tool is still a fool."

This section of the document concludes interestingly:

> So whilst there is perhaps no right answer as to who drives adoption of business availability issues—there is perhaps only one answer as to has responsibility and the Nordics perhaps shows the best approach on the face of it. The board needs to pool their vast body of experience and expertise to weave corporate governance, operational efficiencies, strategic (as opposed to point) technology investments and wise economic policies into their journey towards enterprise availability. Give the CIO the control of the ICT estate on a daily basis, but collectively define how to be an available enterprise, and collectively bear the responsibility for it.

For reference, see http://www.sungard.co.uk/Documents/AE_White_Paper.pdf.

No sponsor equates immediately to high risk in any major project.

DR Objectives

We have met the concepts of RTO and RPO before and here they are again (immersion).

Figure 11.5 is a popular way of depicting the recovery requirements of typical services and some of the means of achieving them. The RTO and RPOs recovery times lie somewhere within the large *time* arrow and are denoted—seconds, minutes, hours, days, and so on.

The pointers below the arrow point to typical times that can be achieved using the methods listed below these pointers.

How do we calibrate our system to estimate RTO and RDO? Well, you may have a set of equations to do it but testing your DR methodology is one real way of finding out.

Recovery Factors

Once DR is invoked, it must execute on parameters previously decided and catered for in the plan—what do we recover, to what level/status, where, how and how fast? These requirements will

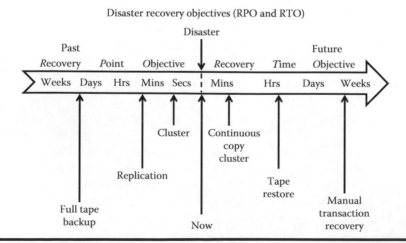

Figure 11.5 DR: Recovery objectives—RPO and RTO.

dictate what steps need to be taken in normal operations to ensure the recovery can take place to satisfy these requirements.

Recovery requirements will emanate from the BIA that categorizes various applications and services by their importance and the essential recovery factors for them. Businesses set great store by BIAs and the documentation from then a valuable *design* aid for IT DR people.

If DR is architected without a solid BIA, then the project is probably doomed. I have seen BIAs involving massive amounts of people time with peer and antagonist reviews to hammer out the real business requirements before a design pen is lifted.

Tiers of DR Availability

In the late 1980s, the SHARE Technical Steering Committee developed a whitepaper that described levels of service for disaster recovery using Tiers 0–6. Since then, a number of businesses using IBM z Series have moved toward an IBM Total Storage solution called the Geographically Dispersed Parallel Sysplex (GDPS), which allows an installation to manage end-to-end application and data availability across multiple geographically separate sites.

This resulted in an additional seventh tier representing the industry's highest level of availability driven by technology improvements:

- *Tier 0:* No off-site data and the prospect of no recovery ever
- *Tier 1:* Data backup but no *hot* recovery site to perform the backup on
- *Tier 2:* Data backup with a hot site for its recovery
- *Tier 3:* Electronic vaulting, with fast communications to and storage at, a remote location
- *Tier 4:* Point-in-time copies for shipping and disk storage of more current data than tape shipping
- *Tier 5:* Transaction integrity to keep primary and secondary (recovery) site data synchronized
- *Tier 6:* Zero and near-Zero data loss that involves some sort of mirroring and essentially split second concurrency
- *Tier 7:* Highly automated, business integrated solution, which is Tier 6 plus auto-recovery upon failure, which eliminates human, and thereby possibly slower, human intervention in the recovery.

If you decided to plot a graph of cost on the vertical axis and tier number horizontal, it would not be surprising to see a roughly positive exponential curve emerge. The type of tiering selected obviously depends on the service and the BIA carried out on it. Refer to https://www.etechservices.com/redbooks/TotalStorageSolutionsforDisasterRecovery.pdf.

DR and Data Tiering[*]

This essentially an aside but a potential area of conflict in the DR scenario. There is interest in the concept of tiering data, that is, storing it on different media (levels) depending on what access data time is needed for the application. Another consideration is cost: slower devices are usually cheaper than faster ones and this often drives the decision to tier. A third factor is the frequency of access of the data.

---

[*] This is sometimes referred to as hierarchical storage, the location in the hierarchy being decided on the data usage patterns.

Table 11.3 Tiered Storage—Media Options

Storage Medium	Relative Access Speed	Access Action
Flash based	Extremely fast	None
Solid state device	Very fast	None
HDD (JBODs)	Fast	Normally none
Tape drives	Relatively slow	Retrieve/mount
Other devices (CDs)	Variable but not fast	Retrieve/access

Automated data tiering is a type of software that moves data files, volumes, or blocks between tiered storage according to company-defined policy. Such data tiering monitors data usage in order to determine where data should be stored. Frequently accessed data will reside, for example, on high performance FiberChannel or solid-state drives, while infrequently accessed data gets moved to lower-cost, high-capacity drives in-house or cloud storage. IBM used to call this hierarchical storage management or HSM.

The issue is that the key consideration relating to DR is *how much data for critical applications is spread across these media and hence, how much of the media do we need to reproduce at the DR site?*

The point being raised here is that a move to data tiering, either in a fixed way by data placement or dynamically using some suitable software, should be accompanied by considerations of the DR implications. Basic storage tier options might look as in Table 11.3.

A Key Factor

The main involvement at the start of DR thinking (yes) and planning are a sponsor and business-aware personnel followed by technical people. This will almost certainly be a virtual team, that is, holding other responsibilities besides DR.

The main person in this project is the *sponsor*, a senior person with a stake in being able to recover the IT business after a catastrophic failure without whom it will not happen. His job is to support the DR plan and implementation and remove any nontechnical hurdles encountered in its planning and execution.

The DR Planning Process

DR: The Steps Involved

In-House DR

The steps suggested for this process vary depending on who you talk to or what literature you read. I have attempted here to distil the experience and wisdom of others in DR in a semiprescriptive manner. As I have said *ad nauseam*, prescriptive lists followed without question are no substitute for common sense and knowledge of your IT and business as one man's meat can be another man's poison.

This conventional wisdom presents the following steps in planning and implementing a DR plan, which assumes that executive management have accepted the requirement for it.

Figure 11.6   The need for a disaster recovery (DR) plan. (Courtesy of Cloudtweaks.)

Get a DR sponsor for the process, preferably an executive who can facilitate the project and give or obtain financial approval. This is important (as in any major project) because his support will almost certainly be needed (Figure 11.6).

> **Aside:** This is where I diverge from *common DR practice* in that I feel a PDW should be the next step to plot the route from Λ (today) to B (the DR environment), produce a PID, and assign roles and responsibilities to the *team*. This is, after all, a project. The A point should include the key business units in the organization, the services they rely on, and their consumption of IT resources. This is of use in the next and subsequent steps in assessing the resource requirements needed in the new (B point) environment. These resources will include people, IT equipment, and costs.

Perform a BIA where the impact on the various business processes of failure(s) of such a magnitude that invocation of DR is mandated. This will assess the *recovery windows* needed for the various interrupted services so as not to have serious effects on the organization's business. This could mean, for example, one service *must be recovered* in 2 hours or less, another in 2 days or less and others that can survive for longer periods without serious business impact. The BIA exercise will involve consideration of RPOs and RTOs for the various business processes (see Figure 9.1).

Another activity related to BIA is the *inventory of resources* required to support each business process or service and vital to its running. This will include files, databases, indexes, logs, middleware files, and so on. It may not include data and files ancillary to the process/service but not vital to the company. Other resource will be data space, CPU, network bandwidth and anything else needed to support the (possibly cut-down) process in the DR environment.

In a situation where the IT resources available or affordable at the DR site are less than those at the primary site, a decision has to be made as to which processes/services will have to be *sacrificed* on the altar of economy.

Further steps in the process involve the following:

1. Define *possible recovery solutions* to meet the RTOs and RPOs. In essence, this means working out how to meet (or better) the recovery targets for the business processes based on their *urgency* as revealed in the BIA:
   a. Tape backup and recovery (full, incremental, differential)
   b. Disk backup and recovery (full, incremental)
   c. Possible use of other media (optical)
   d. Data replication, deduplication, snapshots, log shipping, geographic mirroring (backup methods are outlined at the end of this checklist)

   The information gleaned in step 1 above can help in assessing recovery times for various processes and services. *Speed of recovery* is a prime consideration for high priority business processes.

2. Devise and *document* a DR plan for the above business processes based on their recovery needs as defined in the BIA.

3. Assess the options for the *location of the DR site(s)* based on their *safety*, distance from the primary site, and the logistics of people operating the business in or from the new location. There needs to be the usual hardware, software, and operational considerations (network, server, disk, procedures, etc.) plus the logistics for business use of the new center in a DR situation. This entails a new data center planning exercise (another PDW and PID!), including *costs*.

4. Establish and document DR-related roles and responsibilities:
   a. The criteria and ultimate responsibility for *declaring* a DR cutover
   b. The criteria and responsibility for declaring a return to normal operation (the *all clear*)
   c. Procedures, communications, and logistics for returning to normal operation

5. Establish and staff (probably virtual) a *DR command and control center* (CCC mentioned earlier under War Room) to monitor and direct operations during the DR changeover, preferably not on the site of the disaster! This should be off-site and possibly even mobile with adequate communication facilities. CCCs are regularly used in police, fire, ambulance, and emergency utility situations, such as floods. Some were also set up to deal with crucial situations during the Year 2000 cutover period, although they weren't really needed in the end. A DR CCC *will* be needed in an IT DR situation. A DR CCC is the disaster equivalent of the war room in normal outage situations.

6. Ensure that everyone—apart from the core team(s)- involved/affected by a DR situation is trained to understand what happens and what they need to know and do when *the balloon goes up* and DR is invoked. This will involve considerations of transport, safety, remuneration, communications, and a host of other things, which leads us on to. ...

7. Perform a *walkthrough* of the DR scenario in similar fashion to those carried out with software and availability designs. There are no prescriptions for this—it is, as they say in the movies, *your baby*. Such a DR walkthrough should highlight, in transit, *what if* scenarios, such as the following:
   a. This tape has no label Dave!
   b. This tape has the wrong label.
   c. This tape has nothing on it!
   d. Where are the customer invoice backup tapes?
   e. This tape is so old it's unreadable.
   f. We didn't back up the backup and archive record file—we're doomed!

g. What's the telephone number of our CCC?

h. What do you mean *you didn't know we had one?*

i. All together—shout HELP!

8. *Publish* the DR plan and subsets for non-core persons and seek consensus: internally, perhaps via a Delphi, or externally, using third-party consultants.

9. *Test the DR plan* and revise it in the light of the experience and set a schedule for subsequent tests and revisions. Measure RTO and RDO.

10. Draw a *big* diagram of the process and its flow and put it on every wall in the enterprise.

11. Ensure everyone who might be involved in DR knows the drill.

DR Requirements in Operations

Priority one: Keep the DR site hardware and software and linking network up to date if you want to mimic the primary site *correctly* after the latter's failure and the transfer to the former. You have been warned.

Hardware

The hardware required in the DR center will lie somewhere between complete copy of the primary data center and a minimal subset capable of supporting just the basic business processes critical to the organization, including that needed for backup/restore because this *new* system is *the* business IT system and will eventually transfer back to the recovered primary site.

Network communications will need some consideration because some latent switching and extra networking must be in place already in order to transfer users to the DR center after a failure.

Software

Depending on whether hot, warm, cold, or *bare metal* standby is employed, non-application software will be needed at the DR site, either pre-installed or available for immediate installation (along with the skills needed to achieve this). There will almost certainly be considerations of cost for pre-installed software: *do we have to pay for it if we aren't using it?* Over to IT and finance.

Applications

In-house applications can be ready and waiting to go when DR is declared but proprietary packages may have costs considerations as discussed earlier.

Data

If the business's data are tiered (hierarchical), a decision has to be made as to how much of it is duplicated at the DR site. Data that are historical or only accessed infrequently on an *ad hoc* basis may not need replicating at the recovery site, especially if the data at the primary site are undamaged.

If data at the primary site are destroyed, then it is possible that all tiers need to be replicated. That will all depend on the outcome of a BIA and what priority is assigned to what business functions because this will dictate data requirements.

> ***Summary:*** Enter common sense and knowledge of the business as well as of IT requirements.

DR Cost Considerations

There are obvious cost implications in duplicating some or all the hardware, software, communications, and so on involved in a catastrophic failure scenario can normally be estimated, but there may be other costs, some of them significant, some of them intangible that are listed as follows:

- Outside support and additional internal support
- Customer recompense for consequential loss due to the IT failure
- Loss of potential customers
- Organization reputation
- Share price
- Hosted/cloud support at an external DR site
- Software costs for the backup systems. Some vendors only charge for software in use, others for the licence whether the software is used or not. This can be galling to the finance director if they are never used although it means disasters have been avoided.
- Logistics support—transport, tape shipping, extra premises, overtime payments and physical storage (non-data), etc.
- Accommodation for *displaced* staff if necessary. If your primary and DR sites are geographically separated due to *natureware* considerations, you may need this.

The Backup Site

Details of planning the new site to be the DR site is beyond the scope of this book. However, some points need to be made here. The backup site might be a clone of the primary site or a subset if not all services are to be supported there. If the organization involved is lucky, it may be years before the DR plan needs to be invoked.

However, these glad tidings have a hidden *gotcha*. In a year or more, it is very likely that the primary site will have grown in resource requirements—processor power, storage, network bandwidth, and so on—and this should be reflected in the facilities of the secondary site. The alternative is to accept a degraded service for the duration of the DR operation, that is, until the primary site is nursed back to health. The major consideration here is primary site *capacity planning, with resource needs* reflected in the DR site facilities and in network access.

Although this section is not dealing with BC, it is worth mentioning a few important points here. If the *disaster* involves user accommodation then other things may have to be *backed up*. Examples are copiers, hardcopy documentation, stationery, fax machines, telephones, and other office equipment. In addition, there may be a need for reproducing a subset of any catering, rest rooms, medical rooms, and so on in any *backup* buildings for staff. Another idea from other CCCs is the use of at least two fax machines—one incoming, one outgoing—and satellite phones in case of major telephone failures. The latter were common in Y2K contingency planning. I learned some of this from a UK Water utility believe it or not.

> **Note:** I feel the best way to plan this is by a walkthrough by a team with some of them acting as *devils* advocates' trying to find vulnerabilities in any plan.

Third-Party DR (Outsourcing)

There are alternatives to creating a *DR plan* within an organization, and there are a number of third parties who are active in this area:

- Cloud service providers with DR facilities *in-built*. Some cloud services offer organizations disaster recovery as a service (DRaaS), which backs up the whole environment, not just the data.
- Traditional hosting service providers who provide DR backup facilities for an organization[*]
- DR specialists such as SunGard, IBM, Phoenix, Covenco, EVault, Computer Associates Inc., and others. Some also offer simple data protection and even recovery services.

If this is the route chosen, ensure that the service level agreements (SLAs) are in place for normal operation and DR transfer and operation.

DR and the Cloud

There is a useful article on implementing DR in a cloud environment and another one discussing DR in the context of virtualization.

1. Implementing cloud-based disaster recovery: Six key steps (see http://searchcloudstorage.techtarget.com/feature/Implementing-cloud-based-disaster-recovery-Six-key-steps)
2. Disaster recovery gets a virtualization boost (http://searchitchannel.techtarget.com/news/2240172932/Disaster-recovery-gets-a-virtualization-boost)

HA/DR Options Described

The paper referenced below is specific to SQL Server 2008 R2 and doesn't cover AlwaysOn features, but it is still a useful look at five of the backup/recovery options available for DR. It examines, with case studies:

- Database Mirroring for High Availability and Disaster Recovery
- Geo-Clustering for High Availability and Disaster Recovery
- Failover Clustering for High Availability Combined with SAN-Based Replication for Disaster Recovery
- Peer-to-Peer Replication for High Availability and Disaster Recovery

---

[*] I toured one of these sites in the United Kingdom a few years ago and the utter silence and lack of people activity is quite eerie. There were rows of empty desks and silent keyboards, awaiting the arrival of IT people when a DR situation arises.

See http://sqlblog.com/blogs/kevin_kline/archive/2012/07/26/high-availability-white-papers-and-resources-for-sql-server.aspx.

Disaster Recovery Templates

There are many templates for focusing the mind on what considerations there are in planning and designing for DR but does not preclude the need for knowledge of the organization and its business. Common sense is still in vogue. These are just four templates taken from the Zetta. net Technical Brief "How to Build a Disaster Recovery Plan: Best Practices, Templates and Tools," (http://resources.idgenterprise.com/original/AST-0110849_How_to_Build_a_Disaster_ Recovery_Plan.pdf).

By www.zetta.net.com who specialize in backup, recovery, and archiving:

> http://searchdisasterrecovery.techtarget.com/tip/Top-five-free-disaster-recovery-plan-templates
> *TechTarget*
> http://publib.boulder.ibm.com/iseries/v5r1/ic2924/index.htm?info/rzaj1/rzaj1sampleplan.htm
> *IBM*
> http://www.drp.msu.edu/documentation/stepbystepguide.htm *Michigan State University*
> http://www.tamuct.edu/departments/informationtechnology/extras/ITDisasterRecoveryPlan.
> pdf *Texas A&M University*

There are a number of non-prescriptive articles looking at various aspects of DR and also cloud computing which can be found at http://whitepapershg.tradepub.com/?pt = adv&page = Sungard% 20Availability%20Services.

They are related to Sungard Availability Services and look very useful in giving different perspectives to the subjects of DR and cloud aspects thereof.

> **Note:** On March 31, 2014, Sungard Availability Services was split off from SunGard (www. sungard.com) and became a separate, independent company. If you are looking for information on Sungard Availability Services, you should visit www.sungardas.com.

Summary

DR is important and is becoming more important as businesses rely on IT more and more. Running business of any size today requires robust IT services and running without them well nigh impossible. IT systems will fail and when they do, businesses which rely on them will suffer. When they fail in such a way they can be restored *in situ* and reasonably quickly, business impact is minimized.

If the systems fail catastrophically, they need to be restored as quickly as possible and therein lies the *raison d'être* for quality DR planning and testing and, when necessary, well-managed post-DR implementation.

Don't forget, if your business systems are attacked by a malware entity that prohibits continued business activity, you are probably in uncharted territory and will need to think about it carefully. However, a prerequisite is a good SIEM strategy, which includes recovery as well as detection and analysis.

Of all businesses that close down following a disaster, more than 25% never open their doors again. Insurance Information Institute

Next Steps: You could do worse than re-read this chapter and take heed of some of the references given earlier.

APPENDICES AND HARD SUMS

"For mine own part, it was Greek to me."[*]

(Immersion at the "deep end" of the pool)

This section contains more detail on topics which, if presented in the main body, would possibly impede the reader in his/her understanding of the principles being expounded. It contains some mathematics (hard sums) but an understanding of availability should not be impaired by lack of detailed mathematical *know how*.

This section represents being thrown into the deep end of a swimming pool and being told by the chief information officer (CIO) *Swim*!

---

[*] William Shakespeare, *Julius Caesar*.

Appendix 1

A little knowledge is dangerous.—Proverb

Reliability and Availability: Terminology*

If you haven't read any other parts of this book, read this section and you will be halfway there in availability knowledge.

Advanced persistent threat (APT): An APT is a network attack in which an unauthorized person gains access to a network and stays there undetected for a long period of time. The intention of such an attack is to steal data rather than to cause damage to the network or organization. APT attacks target organizations in sectors with high-value information, such as defense, manufacturing, and the financial industry but others are not immune. The threat may be engineered to mount other attacks at a later date, a sort of an alien *breeding* program.

Application availability: This is when applications can continuously run, even without any information technology (IT) staff on-site. With application availability, businesses will not experience any downtime. Availability (A) is usually expressed as a percentage (%) or a decimal ($0 < A < 1$).

Autonomic computing: This name refers to the self-managing characteristics of distributed computing resources, adapting to unpredictable changes while hiding intrinsic complexity from operators and users. Started by IBM in 2001, this initiative ultimately aims to develop computer systems capable of self-management, to overcome the rapidly growing complexity of computing systems management, and to reduce the barrier that complexity poses to further growth in IT services.

An autonomic system makes decisions on its own, using high-level policies and will constantly check and optimize its status and automatically adapt itself to changing conditions.

Availability (t): It is the probability that a component is able to function at time t. In terms of *state*, then state $(t) = 1$.

Availability types: There are shades of availability between never available and available eternally and some clarifying terminology, generally agreed among IT people, is shown here:

1. *High availability:* This is the ability of a system to provide service to its users during defined service periods, at an acceptable or agreed level. These service periods, as well as

---

* For a detailed Reliability Glossary, see http://www.weibull.com/knowledge/rel_glossary.htm.

a definition of an *acceptable* service level, are either stated in a service level commitment by the service provider, or in a service level agreement (SLA) between end users and the service provider.

2. *Continuous operation:* The ability of a system to provide service to its users at all times, day and night, without scheduled outages to perform system and data maintenance activities.

3. *Continuous availability:* It is the property of a system that provides both *high availability (HA)* and *continuous operation* at the same time. The system must be designed so users experience neither scheduled nor unscheduled outages.

Bare metal recovery: It is the process of rebuilding a computer after a catastrophic failure. The normal bare metal restoration process installs the operating system (OS) from the product disks, install the backup software, and then restore the data. Then, full functionality should be restored by verifying the configuration files, permissions, and so on.

Bathtub curve: It is a plot of the failure rate of a component, whether repairable or not, against time. The failure rate decreases, then stays reasonably constant, before beginning to rise, often rapidly. The shape of this curve roughly resembles a bathtub. Not all items exhibit this behavior but is often used for computer hardware and software.

Business continuity planning (BCP): See https://www.gov.uk/government/uploads/system/uploads/attachment_data/file/137994/Business_Continuity_Managment_Toolkit.pdf.

Belloc, Joseph Hilaire Pierre Rene: He is a French-born naturalized English author (1870–1953), historian, wit, and Catholic scholar. His quotes, like those of Chesterton (q.v.), can add weight to your argument should you need it.

Big data: It is a term applied to data that have characteristics far from those the IT industry has been using over many years. The paper referenced below says *we apply the term big data to any data set that breaks the boundaries and conventional capabilities of IT designed to support day-to-day operations.*

Complexity: It is a long way from simple alphanumeric stuff of the old days.

High transaction volumes: These may be so high that traditional data storage hits queuing bottlenecks in I/O.

IDC definition: Big data technologies describe a new generation of technologies and architectures, designed to economically extract value from very large volumes of a wide variety of data, by enabling high-velocity capture, discovery, and/or analysis. See http://cdn.ttgtmedia.com/deu/Panasas647761.html and http://odbms.org/download/WP-DataStax-BigData.pdf.

Size of data: This may cause bandwidth bottlenecks for records and objects (BLOBS) that are encountered these days.

Variety: All types are now being captured (structured, semi-structured, unstructured).

Velocity: Velocity—how fast the data are coming in.

Volume of content: This may be so high that it exceeds the capacity thresholds of traditional storage and would need hundreds or thousands of disk to satisfy *demand.*

Block diagrams: Availability block diagrams and reliability block diagrams are visual representations of the interactions between contributors to reliability, availability, and maintainability. Each block tends to represent a physical component in the system and its associated reliability/availability (see *RBD*).

Burn-in: It is the initial operation of a component under stress to stabilize its characteristics and to minimize *infant mortality* when in operational use.

Burn out: It is the end-of-life process of a hardware component where failures become more frequent and force the replacement. Software does not suffer *burn out* but obsolescence.

Business continuity (BC): The processes by which an enterprise recovers and restarts its business processes after a major failure in any critical entity supporting the business are called BC. These can be IT facilities, offices, people, transport, and anything else that supports important or critical processes. The object of the BC plan is, in the vernacular, to *get the show on the road again.*

Business continuity management (BCM): The process of managing the process of recovery after a major disruption to business services for whatever reason is called BCM. It may or may not involve IT disruption.

BCM standard (BS25999/ISO 22301): This is a BCM standard published by the British Standards Institution (BSI). It consists of BS 25999-1(2003) and BS 25999-2 (2007).

BS 25999 had been developed by a broad based group of world class experts representing a cross section of industry sectors and government to establish the process, principles, and terminology of BCM. However, the BSI has confirmed that the new International Standard for Business Continuity—ISO 22301 Societal Security Business Continuity Management Systems Requirements—which was officially published in mid-May 2012—will *replace BS 25999* as an ISO standard.

Business impact analysis (BIA): It is an essential component of an organization's business continuance plan—it includes an exploratory component to reveal any vulnerabilities and a planning component to develop strategies for minimizing risk. The result of analysis is a BIA report, which describes the potential risks specific to the organization studied. One of the basic assumptions behind BIA is that every component of the organization is reliant upon the continued functioning of every other component, but that some are more crucial.*

Cascaded failure: A failure which cascades down to cause other failures as a direct result, a sort of *domino* effect is called cascaded failure. Another term used is *collateral* damage.

Command and control center (CCC): It is a term borrowed from the emergency services. It is the hub of control activity by police, fire, and so on in major emergency such as major flooding, terrorist bombs, and earthquakes. In a BCP or disaster recovery (DR) situation, the CCC might be anywhere but certainly not in the data center and probably not in a personnel site as both could be affected by the prevailing emergency. Temporary or even mobile accommodation needs to be available at zero notice time.

Satellite phones may be in order in such cases because in terrorist attacks, particularly in the United Kingdom, where the emergency services may take over the telephone network.

Customer information control system (CICS): It is a TP monitor from IBM that was originally developed to provide transaction processing for public utilities (hence the *customer*) using IBM mainframes. It controls the interaction between applications and users and lets programmers develop screen displays without detailed knowledge of the terminals used—BMS or basic mapping support. It provides terminal routing, password security, transaction logging for error recovery, and activity journals for performance analysis. It has also been made available on nonmainframe platforms including the RS/6000, AS/400, OS/2-based PCs, and a version which ran on HP equipment was produced.

Cluster: It generally refers to multiple servers (nodes) that are linked together in order to handle variable workloads or to provide highly available operation in the event of one or more node failures. Each computer is a multiprocessor system itself. For example, a cluster of four computers, each with 16 CPU cores, would enable 64 unique processing threads to take place simultaneously.

---

* http://searchstorage.techtarget.com/definition/business-impact-analysis.

A cluster of servers provides fault tolerance and/or load balancing. If one server fails, one or more servers are still available. Load balancing software distributes the workload over multiple systems and *locking* software handles the concurrent access to shared data to avoid clashes and the *deadly embrace*, well known to older IT people.

Cluster, HPC: Normally, the most obvious way to apply multiple compute cycles to a complex scientific problem is to use specialized supercomputing hardware—a solution with a very high cost of entry and technical complexity. However, software and hardware advances have made it possible to use existing IT skills and create an HPC environment using commodity servers with high-speed interconnections. These systems can deliver massive computing power at a significantly lower cost of entry and ownership than a supercomputer. This form of HPC is called a commodity HPC cluster. Power is not the only reason for using HPC commodity clustering—availability becomes important as longer jobs are being run, some taking weeks, and failures without a checkpoint mechanism waste a lot of time.

Cluster topologies: Samples of four typical cluster topologies are shown in the next two diagrams. Selection of one or the other depends on user requirements (Figure A1.1).

Clustering hardware comes in three basic flavors, so-called *shared disk, mirrored disk*, and *shared nothing* configurations (http://compnetworking.about.com/od/networkdesign/l/aa041600a. htm).

A *cluster topology* is a specific configuration of two or more pairs of nodes operating under a single cluster administrative framework. All nodes are connected by the cluster interconnect and operate under cluster software control.

You might use a particular topology to run a parallel database application. The different topologies cater for different needs, for example, parallel processing of databases, very HA, or workload scalability.

Topology selection will be based on these requirements for the business application(s) in normal operations and also in failover modes to minimize recovery time and will depend

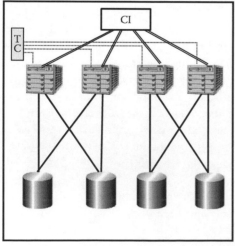
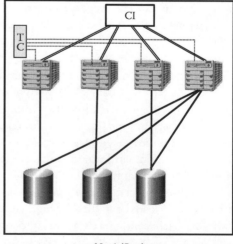

Clustered pairs   *N* + 1 (Star)

Figure A1.1   Cluster topologies 1: Clustered pair and star (*N* + 1). CI, cluster interconnect; TC, communications.

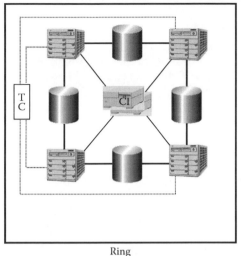
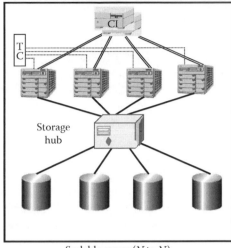

| Ring | Scalable server (*N* to *N*) |

Figure A1.2 Cluster topologies 2: Ring and scalable (*N* + *N*). CI, cluster interconnect; TC, communications.

heavily on the clustering functions provided. Figures A1.1 and A1.2 are typical of Oracle Sun cluster topologies.

A *multisite cluster* is a cluster configuration where the servers are separated geographically and the physical storage is synchronously replicated among the sites. In a geo-dispersed cluster both the public and private network interfaces have to exist in the same network segment, and cluster nodes also must share the same IPsubnet.

Control objectives for information and related technology (COBIT): It is a framework created by ISACA (q.v.) for IT management and IT governance. It is a supporting toolset that allows managers to bridge the gap between control requirements, technical issues, and business risks. ISACA first released COBIT in 1996 and published the current[update] version, COBIT 5, in mid-2012.

COBIT aims *to research, develop, publish, and promote an authoritative, up-to-date, international set of generally accepted* IT control objectives *for day-to-day use by* business managers, *IT professionals, and assurance professionals.* References http://it.safemode.org/ and http://www.qualified-audit-partners.be/?cont = 315&lgn = 1 seem more useful to me than formal sites.

Cold plugging: Computer components are usually described as cold pluggable if the computer system must be powered down to add or remove them. The *recovery* time is that taken to power up and reboot the system and its other components.

Component failure impact analysis (CFIA): It was originally a process defined (but not necessarily invented) by IBM Customer Engineering in the 1980s to improve assessment and quantification of availability. It was a software-based process of analyzing a particular hardware/software configuration to determine the true impact of any individual failed component. Data were supplied by the requestor, usually field personnel.

Cost impact analysis (CIA): This is a very specific part of a BIA where an estimate of financial losses incurred as a result of failure of a certain duration. It is normally expressed in currency/hour for businesses with many transactions per hour with high cumulative value.

Examples are a stock exchange or airline reservation system. A company has to decide on whether to spend more on BC than it would save in losses for the sake of customer loyalty, brand image, and so on.

Criticality: It is a relative measure of the consequences of a *failure* mode and the frequency of its occurrence. In essence, you can choose your own system of rating: A, B, C,… or 1, 2, 3, 4,….

Criticality analysis (CA): It is a procedure by which each potential *failure* mode is ranked according to the combined influence of *severity* and *probability* of occurrence.

Cross site mirroring: It is the process of duplication (mirroring) of data across multiple sites. The sites may be local or remote. Remote sites are often used to avoid total *wipe out* scenarios when all the IT facilities are in an area small enough to be terminally affected by one natural disaster.

Cumulative distribution function (cdf): It is the probability that the variable x takes a value less than or equal to some value x_1, say. In our case of reliability/availability, x takes the form of time t (horizontal axis) and the cdf the probability (vertical axis) of *survival* of the component until a particular time, say t_1. Survival means the component is still available, that is, state = 1. The hazard function is the inverse of the survival function.

Cyber crime: "Cyber crime encompasses any criminal act dealing with computers and networks (called hacking). Additionally, cyber crime also includes traditional crimes conducted through the Internet. For example: hate crimes, telemarketing and Internet fraud, identity theft, and credit card account thefts are considered to be cyber crimes when the illegal activities are committed through the use of a computer and the Internet" (*Webopedia*).

Cyber crime can have an effect on service availability, especially when data are compromised. Distributed denial of service (DDoS), which can flood networks with bogus traffic, will take out a service or services relying on network access and services might be suspended during investigations into other forms of cyber crime.

Cybersecurity: It, also known as IT or computer security, is an information security applied to computers and networks. The field covers all the processes and mechanisms by which computer-based equipment, information, and services are protected from unintended or unauthorized access, change, or destruction. Computer security also includes protection from unplanned events and natural disasters.

Unauthorized access and subsequent use by miscreants can have far-reaching effects on a business—financial, reputational, and company share value. Change, destruction, or locking of data, for example, by external encryption can have similar consequences. Most of these events will constitute and *outage* of physical or logical nature.

Cyclic redundancy check (CRC): It is an error-detecting code commonly used in digital networks and storage devices to detect accidental changes to raw data. Blocks of data entering these systems get a short *check value* based on their contents and on retrieval the calculation is repeated. Corrective action can be taken against presumed data corruption if the check values do not match. CRC, along with LRC, ECC, and parity help to maintain the integrity of data traversing a network. Failure will generate a retransmission of the data, repeated until a threshold is reached.

Data striping (RAID): It is a way of splitting data into sections and storing them across multiple hard disks. Striping is used to increase the efficiency of reading and writing in the disk array. This is because the hard disks work in parallel motion, making the file access faster than using only one hard disk. Native striping is known as RAID 0. Data striping is used in combination with other techniques to deliver other forms of RAID.

Database journaling: Database servers are one major category of server systems, and database software has provided storage redundancy through transaction journaling for many years.

This redundancy defends against simple medium failure or can even be the basis of a remote site DR plan.

A database system, such as SQL Server or Oracle, commits database updates to a transaction journal and to the main database. The transaction journal and the main database storage occupy physically distinct media. Combined with periodic database backups, this protects against any single storage medium failure. Transaction journals also provide some protection against corruption caused by application software failure by storing a history of changes within the database. Corruption introduced by application errors can often be corrected by rolling transactions back to a point in time before the error (see *RPO*).

Transaction journals and backups conveyed to a remote site, together with spare hardware, provide a defense against a complete site failure such as those caused by a natural or man-made disaster.

Database as a service (DBaaS): Some cloud platforms offer options for using a DBaaS, without physically launching a virtual machine instance for the database. In this configuration, application owners do not have to install and maintain the database on their own. Instead, the database service provider takes responsibility for installing and maintaining the database, and application owners pay according to their usage.

For example, Amazon Web Services provides three database services as part of its cloud offering, SimpleDB, a NoSQL key-value store, Amazon Relational Database Service, an SQL-based database service with a MySQL interface, and DynamoDB. Oracle 12*c* offers the facilities to do this.

Cloud databases can offer significant advantages over their traditional counterparts but, at the same time, cloud databases have their share of potential drawbacks, including security and privacy issues as well as the potential loss of or inability to access critical data in the event of a disaster or bankruptcy of the cloud database service provider.

Database hashing: It is the transformation of a string of characters into a usually shorter fixed-length value or key that represents the original string. It is used to index and retrieve items in a database because it is faster to find the item using the shorter hashed key than to find it using the original value. It is also used in many encryption algorithms.

The hashing algorithm is called the *hash function*—probably the term is derived from the idea that the resulting hash value can be thought of as a *mixed up* version of the represented value.

Database replication: Modern RDBMS provide features supporting HA through database replication. This is what we have referred to as a *warm standby* approach, where a copy of the database occupies a physically remote server and transaction journals are transmitted periodically from the active server. It may also be a fully *live* system, where each transaction is applied to multiple copies of the database in real time. The latter system provides the fastest failover recovery time (see *RTO*).

DCIE: See *PUE*.

Data center infrastructure management (DCIM): It extends systems and network management approaches to include the physical and asset-level components. DCIM integrates IT and facility management disciplines to centralize monitoring, management, and intelligent capacity planning of a datacenter's critical systems. The entities which are of interest in DCIM are performance, capacity, assets, configuration, and the *ecosystem* aspects of data centers—power, light, heat, and so on. A central point of control with a wide range of data available is a great asset to availability management, particularly in problem determination.

Deduplication: This is a method of copying data from one place to another but avoiding the transfer of duplicate blocks or records. This reduces the storage needed for copies or even source data and minimizes the bandwidth needed to carry the transferred data across a network. These and other reductions will also reduce costs. Once a deduplicated *file* has been transferred, only changes to the primary need to be transferred subsequently to keep the secondary *file* up to date.

Defect density model: It is a software reliability model alongside software reliability growth model (SRGM, q.v.). It uses parameters such as lines of code (LOC, KLOC), nesting of loops, and I/O to estimate the number of defects in a program, fitting observed fault or defect rates to various mathematical models—Gompertz, Rayleigh, and so on—to predict defect rates in software development.

Defect or failure densities are measured for different types of program and you will find in any book or article about this topic several tables of errors and their classification. The defects are often stated as to which part of the development cycle they occurred in.

Delphi technique: It is a means of obtaining group input from a panel of experts for problem solving. It does not mandate face-to-face contact but for speedy outcomes, this can be done. It involves using two or more rounds of prepared questions to the panel that address a current issue or perhaps an apparently intractable question. Each round is ended by an analysis by a facilitator to check for consensus and the issue resubmitted if none is reached. In essence, the panel is asked to revise their input until they converge toward a feasible solution.

Dependability: This concept represents an amalgam of systematic expositions of the concepts of dependability (Figure A1.3).

It consists of three parts: the *threats* to, the *attributes* of, and the *means* by which dependability is attained, as shown in the figure above, which encompasses our key subjects of reliability and availability.

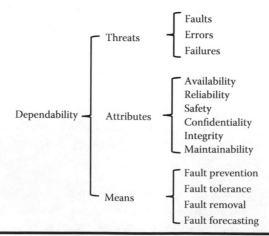

Figure A1.3 The components of dependability. (Data from Avizienis, A. et al., http:// www.google.co.uk/url?sa=t&rct=j&q=&esrc=s&source=web&cd=1&ved=0CCEQFjAA&url= http%3A%2F%2Fwww.researchgate.net%2Fpublication%2F46299378_Dependability_ and_Its_Threats_A_Taxonomy%2Flinks%2F00b4952962001a5330000000&ei=nX4VVN7 zLY_haoDIgrAF&usg=AFQjCNFtYS-muHmfRzUhMmC8K_rwbgaUxw.)

The factors in this diagram represent practically all the aspects of HA and, to a lesser extent, those of DR. *Means* could encompass failure mode and effects analysis (FMEA) and CFIA while *attributes* relates to HA/DR design.

Disaster recovery (DR): This is the process or procedure related to preparing for the continued operation of computing resources after a disaster or failure. This, as we say in Chapter 1, is the IT part of a BCP for an enterprise.

Double bit errors: Errors in the bit patterns of data, usually *detected* in modern hardware by error correction code (ECC), but *not corrected*. Some RAS implementations will issue a retry operation on a double bit error or use a portion of mirrored memory.

Dynamic reconfiguration (DR): It allows administrators to add extra components, including processors and memory, to a system while it is running, without interruption. The OS will recognize these additions and use them. It should also *offline* failing predecessors if that is the reason for the addition of these components. This is normally classes as a RAS feature and is now quite common.

e: Base of natural logarithms $= 2.718281828$, for example, as in $e^{-\lambda t}$, the exponential distribution frequently used in reliability engineering theory. [This might sometimes be written as $\ln(-\lambda t)$ or $\log_e(-\lambda t)$].

Early failure period: That period of life, after final assembly, in which failures occur at an initially high rate because of the presence of defective parts and workmanship. This definition applies to the first part of the bathtub curve (q.v.) for failure rate (infant mortality)

Error correction code (ECC): It is (see Double bit errors) for the detection and correction of single bit errors and the detection of double bit errors and sometimes a retry of the operation. It differs from parity checking in that errors are detected and corrected. It is used in memory, data storage, and communications hardware. It becomes necessary because as data rates increase, so do the numbers of errors. It is implemented via Hamming code (after the person with the surname *Hamming*), which is too complex for me to explain but can be found, as ever, on Wikipedia by searching on *error correction code*.

Enterprise computing in a new age (Encina): It is a UNIX-based TP monitor from Transarc Corporation, Pittsburgh, Pennsylvania, that is layered over OSF's Distributed Computing Environment (DCE). IBM acquired Transarc in 1994 and based its CICS/6000 TP monitor on Encina. Later renamed the IBM Pittsburgh Lab, the company was the first to successfully process one billion transactions in 24 hours, a breakthrough in computing performance. Encina and BEA Tuxedo are the major TP monitors in the UNIX client/server environment.

Encryption: It utilizes mathematical algorithms to transform data so that it can only be read by the intended parties (sender and receiver). In the case of *SSL* (q.v.), the private and public keys provided as part of the server's digital certificate play an important role in securing data sent to and from the web browser.

Error detection: This is self-explanatory but for a detailed exposition see the paper by *Ravishankar K. Iyer* and *Zbigniew Kalbarczyk* of the University of Illinois.* It deals with parity, ECC, CRC, and general error detection and correction. The paper also has a very good, readable coverage of the m-*from*-n theory we have alluded to in this book. *Beware*, however, that some of the URLs referenced in the paper are no longer extant.

Failback (cluster): (See *Failover*.) After a node failure, the applications and resources are normally failed over (transferred) to another node in the cluster. When the failed node rejoins the cluster (after repair, for example), that node now is eligible to be used by applications as

---

* http://courses.engr.illinois.edu/ece542/textbook/hwswerrordetection.pdf.

before. A cluster administrator can set policies on resources and resource groups that allow an application to automatically move back to a node if it becomes available and rejoins the cluster.

Failback (disaster): It is the process over moving services back to the original site or new primary site after a DR invocation and execution. You need a *return ticket* for the DR journey and this should comprise part of the standard DR planning. It is useless to making a journey to somewhere away from home if you have no means of getting back.

Failover (cluster): It is the ability to automatically switch resources over to a redundant or standby server, system, network, or component upon failure of a critical application, server, system, or network. If an individual resource or application fails (but the server does not), server clusters will typically try to re-start the application on the same server: if that fails, it will remove the application's resources and re-starts it on the other server. Failover is a key feature of clustered systems.

Failover (disaster): It is the process of moving vital IT services to another site when the primary site is rendered inoperable and not recoverable in such a period that the business is not affected significantly.

Failure: The event, or inoperable state, in which an item [component], or part of an item, does not, or would not, perform as previously specified. Most of the failure definitions below are from MIL-STD-721. Comments in [*brackets*] are my own to aid and *translate* certain things into IT terms.

> *Failure analysis:* Logical and systematic examination of an equipment or a machine and/or its documentation to detect and analyze the causes, probabilities, and consequences of actual or potential failure.
>
>> [*In our IT terms, the detection and diagnosis of malfunctions in technical systems, in particular, by means of a scheme in which one or more computers monitor the technical* equipment *to signal any malfunction and designate the components responsible for it* (from Business Dictionary: http://www.businessdictionary.com). *It is sometimes called fault analysis*].
>
> *Failure, dependent:* It is the failure that is caused by the failure of and associated item(s). Not independent.
>
> *Failure, independent:* It is the failure that occurs without being caused by the failure of any other item. Not dependent.
>
> *Failure, intermittent:* It is the failure for a limited period of time, followed by the item's recovery of its ability to perform within specified limits without any remedial action.
>
> *Failure mechanism:* It is the physical, chemical, electrical, thermal, or other process which results in failure. In software, failures are not physical but logical.
>
> *Failure mode:* It is the consequence of the mechanism through which the failure occurs, that is, short, open, fracture, and excessive wear (*electrical analogy*).
>
>> [*The manner in which an equipment or* machine failure *can occur. The* typical *failure modes are (1) premature* operation, *as might happen in batch jobs running out of order, (2) failure to* operate *at the prescribed time, again possibly batch jobs run by* cron, *(3) failure to cease operation at the prescribed time, for example overnight batch backup impinging on daytime OLTP, (4) failure during operation, business as usual, and (5) degraded or excessive operational* capability, *performance hit or "overkill" design* (from Business Dictionary: http://www.businessdictionary.com). *The definition does not quite encompass software or malware issues.*]
>
> *Failure, random:* It is the failure whose occurrence is predictable only in probabilistic or statistical sense. This applies to all [*mathematical*] distributions.

Failure, rate: It is the total number of failures within an item population, divided by the total number of life units (q.v.) expended by that population, during a particular measurement interval under stated conditions.

In IT terms, this is the rate of failure per unit time—seconds, hours, days, years—symbol λ. It is evident that this rate is the inverse of the mean time between failures (MTBF), thus:

$$\lambda = \frac{1}{\text{MTBF}}$$

Note: This involves the time between the start of successive failures (MTBF) and not the time between recovery of one failure to the start of the next failure (*mean time to failure* [MTTF]). See Appendix 2 for diagrams and an explanation of these two terms. They can get confused.

Failure mode and effects analysis (FMEA): A procedure by which each potential failure mode in a system is analyzed to determine the results or effects thereof on the system and to classify each potential failure mode according to its severity (see/search MIL-STD-721).

The analysis is known as a *bottom-up* (inductive) approach to finding each potential mode of failure and preventing failures that might occur for every component of a system. It is also used for determining the probable effects on system operation of each failure mode and, in turn, on probable operational success, the results of which can be ranked in order of seriousness.

Failure review board: It is a group of people typically composed of various IT disciplines that determines the status of a failure and who and how it will be addressed. Candidates for the War Room (q.v.).

Failure, transient: See *Transient errors* and *Failure, intermittent*.

Fault tolerance: This is a similar concept to resilience and is outlined in Chapter 4 and demonstrates the principal via RAID technology. It is the ability of an application, computing system, network, or component to continue normal operation even with hardware or software failures. Fault tolerance is normally achieved via component redundancy where the switchover from failing to operating component is transparent and, ideally, instantaneous. If the components involved comprise software as well as hardware, it is important that the former are kept in synchronization. Self-healing could possibly be construed as fault tolerance with or without redundancy. Two concepts are outlined below:

Fault masking: This is a redundancy technique that masks (hides) faults within a set of redundant components. A number of identical components execute the same functions and their outputs *voted* on to remove errors created by a faulty component. This duplicate-voting technique can apply to software as well as hardware. Triple modular redundancy (TMR—Appendix 4 Lesson 9) is a form of fault masking in which modules or components are triplicated and voted. Voting with less than three components would not make sense. In addition, the voting components can be triplicated so that their failures can also be corrected by voting.

Dynamic recovery: This involves automated self-repair of a single component which, in the case of a single computer, requires special hardware and supporting software. See the Rennels paper below and Lesson 9 in Appendix 4. See D. Rennels http://www.cs.ucla.edu/~rennels/article98.pdf.

Forward error correction (FEC): In telecommunication, information theory, and coding theory, FEC is a technique used for controlling errors in data transmission over unreliable or noisy communication channels. The method is for the sender to encode the message in a redundant way by using an ECC. R. Hamming pioneered this field in the 1940s and invented the first ECC in 1950: the Hamming code.

The redundancy allows the receiver to detect a limited number of errors that may occur anywhere in the message and often to correct these errors without retransmission. There are two basic types of FEC codes: block codes and convolution codes.

FEC information is usually added to storage devices to enable recovery of corrupted data, hence its inclusion here.

Geographic mirroring: It is a function that keeps two identical copies of an independent disk pool at two sites to provide HA and DR. The copy owned by the primary node is the *production copy* and the copy owned by a backup node at the other site is the *mirror copy*. User operations and applications access the independent disk pool on the primary node, the node that owns the production copy.

Gotchas: Unexpected happenings and constraints stumbled over in the design, implementation, and operation of hardware systems and associated software. They are related to, and expressed by, Murphy's Law but the math of it is beyond the scope of this book. The damage you will suffer by one or more *gotchas* can be summarized in an equation as

$$\text{Murphy failure intensity (MFI)} = f \text{ (everything in the universe)}$$

Grid computing: The impetus for this type of computing came with the realization that hundred and maybe thousands of desktop and other computers spent a great percentage of their time idle and waiting for work. Attempts were therefore made to try to harness this spare *power* to run applications, particularly scientific ones which could be decomposed, parallelized, and reconstructed. In theory this type of resource sharing could span the globe but would need strict authentication and authorization for it to be commercially acceptable.

Knowledge of parallelism in, and dual executing copies of, software is needed to implement grid computing. "A grid computer is multiple number of same class of computers clustered together. A grid computer is connected through a super fast network and share the devices like disk drives, mass storage, printers and RAM. Grid Computing is a cost efficient solution with respect to Super Computing. The OS has capability of parallelism.

Grid computing combines computers from multiple administrative domains to reach a common goal, to solve a single task, and may then disappear just as quickly" (see Wikipedia). Computing paradigms such as this are often called *cooperative* or *federated* computing.

Gumbel distribution: This is yet another distribution used in reliability studies and is applied to all manner of situations—wind speeds and patterns, floods, and other esoteric things. It is also applied sometimes to software life cycles and failure patterns for prediction and as a possible fit to real software failure data. This is common practice when choosing a distribution for a software model. See the link http://www.weibull.com/hotwire/issue56/relbasics56.htm.

Hard disk drive (HDD): This is the normal drive we are used to. It is an electro-mechanical device unlike the solid-state drive (SSD, q.v.).

Hazard function: This defined the hazard at time t, $h(t)$, as the probability of an event at the interval $[t, t + \delta t]$, when $\delta t \rightarrow 0$. To find an expression for $h(t)$, we should realize that $h(t)$ must be a *conditional probability*: it is conditional on *not* having the event up to time t (or conditional on surviving to time t).

It is expressed as follows (See *Probability Density Function [pdf]*):

$$h(t) = \frac{f(t)}{R(t)} = \frac{f(t)}{[1 - F(t)]}$$

(A1.1)

Reliability: Hazard Function

Heartbeat: It is the communications protocol between members of a cluster that allows one member to detect that the other(s) have failed. There is a *voting* protocol whereby the *successor* to the dead system is elected or, in the case of a two-system cluster, control is passed to the survivor.

High availability (HA): It refers to a system or component that is continuously operational. When a HA solution is implemented, computing systems can continue to perform the tasks they were designed to perform with minimal downtime.

Holistic: (1) It emphasizes the importance of the whole and the interdependence of its parts. (2) It is concerned with wholes rather than analysis or separation into parts.

Hot spare: It is a backup device such as a hard disk or controller that is in a *standby* mode. This means it is online and available should the primary device go offline for any reason or fail. The system software should detect the failure and automatically switch to the hot spare to use as a replacement. Hot spare is commonly used in RAID arrays where additional drives are attached to the controller and left in *standby* mode until a failure occurs.

Hot swapping: It describes the act of replacing components without significant interruption to the system. Components might be disks, memory or, in some cases, CPU cards.

Hoyle: According to... an analogy from card games for stating the rules of *engagement* up front to avoid disputes and, in the 19th century Wild West, getting shot.

Hypervisor: It, also called a virtual machine manager, is a program that allows multiple OSs to share a single hardware host. Each OS appears to have the host's processor, memory, and other resources all to itself. However, the hypervisor is actually controlling the host processor and resources, allocating what is needed to each OS in turn and making sure that the guest OS (called virtual machines) cannot disrupt each other.

Early examples of hypervisors are IBM's VM/370 (Virtual Machine/370) and Amdahl's MDF (multiple domain facility), both Type 1 hypervisors.

Type 1 hypervisor: Also known as a native or bare metal hypervisor, a Type 1 hypervisor runs directly on the host computer's hardware.

Type 2 hypervisor: Also known as a hosted hypervisor, a Type 2 hypervisor runs under an OS environment (OSE).

Hysteresis: It refers to systems that have *memory*, where the effects of the current input (or stimulus) to the system are experienced with a certain lag. Hysteresis phenomena occur in magnetic, ferromagnetic, and ferroelectric materials, as well as in the elastic, electric, and magnetic behavior of materials, in which a lag occurs between the application and the removal of a force or field and its subsequent effect. Electric hysteresis occurs when applying a varying electric field, and elastic hysteresis occurs in response to a varying force.

The term *hysteresis* is sometimes used in other fields, such as economics or biology, where it describes a memory, or lagging effect. In organizations, the IT personnel may understand hysteresis but finance people will not, expecting an immediate return on their investment.

Information dispersal algorithms (IDAs): IDAs provide a methodology for storing information in pieces (dispersed) across multiple servers, possibly at multiple locations, so that redundancy protects the information in the event of a location outage, but unauthorized access at any single location does not provide usable information. Only the originator or a user with a list of the latest pointers with the original dispersal algorithm can properly assemble the complete information. Information dispersal can be implemented using a number of different *information dispersal schemes* (IDS).

Intel cache safe technology: See *Pellston technology.*

Intrusion detection system (IDS): It is a type of security management system for computers and networks. An IDS gathers and analyzes information from various areas within a computer or a network to identify possible security breaches, which include both intrusions (attacks from outside the organization) and misuse (attacks from within the organization). IDS uses *vulnerability assessment* (sometimes referred to as *scanning*), which is a technology developed to assess the security of a computer system or network.

The basic types of IDS are *network-based IDS* and *host-based IDS*. For further information, the reference http://www.intrusion-detection-system-group.co.uk/ is very useful.

ISACA: ISACA (1967) is an international professional association focused on IT governance and was previously known as the *Information Systems Audit and Control Association.* ISACA now goes by its acronym only, to reflect the broad range of IT governance professionals it serves. It is connected with other risk and audit organizations (see Wikipedia).

Take care about too much effort being expended as some 90% of IT people surveyed thought strict compliance to all forms of risk and audit practices was "burdensome."

My suggestion is to review it and tailor it to your own enterprise or business requirements. For reference, see www.isaca.org.

ISO standards: There are a number of ISO and other standards relating to IT. As Hilaire Belloc said of the Commandments *Candidates should not attempt more than 6 of these.* Use these standards by all means but don't *overcook* them, particularly if your organization has its own standards for the areas covered by these ISO/BSI standards. The latter can be overpowering in their attention to detail and can become prescriptive. A number of standards relevant to HA/DR are listed in Table A1.1.

IT infrastructure library (ITIL): It is a mature approach to IT service management (ITSM) and provides a cohesive set of best practice, drawn from the public and private sectors internationally. ITSM derives enormous benefits from a best practice approach. Because ITSM is driven both by technology and the huge range of organizational environments in which it operates, it is in a state of constant evolution.

Table A1.1   Information Technology Standards: ISO and Others

Standard	Area and Outline
ISO 27001	Information security management system standards
ISO 27005	Information security risk management standards
ISO 31000	Risk management: Principles and guidelines
BSI PAS 56:2003	Guide to business continuity
BS 31100	Risk management: Code of practice

Note: BSI, British Standards Institution; ISO, International Standards Organization.

Expert advice and input from ITIL users is both current and practical and combines to generate these IT *best practices* for the discipline (http://www.itil-officialsite.com/).

Just a few lines of code (JAFLOC): It is a lethal remedy that has brought down many a system as in *I can easily fix that with jafloc.* I know because I've seen it happen.

Just a bunch of disks (JBOD): It refers to disks not formatted and accessed in any special way such as RAID, that is, in native mode. Different modes of access are handled by the *access method*, for example, ISAM, VSAM, Relational.

Kilo lines of code (KLOC): It refers to number of LOC expressed in thousands (1000s), a common *unit* in software reliability discourses particularly in the development of reliability models.

Journal files system*: Modern file systems are journaling file systems. By writing information about pending updates to a write-ahead log before committing the updates to disk, journaling enables fast file system recovery after a crash. Although the basic techniques have existed for many years (e.g., IBM's IMS Log Tape Write Ahead, previously WALT, with those words rearranged), journaling has increased in popularity and importance in recent years. Journals can be local or remote for recovery of a remote file system in a failover situation.

Lamda (λ): It is a Greek symbol for "l" (lower case). It is used in reliability theory (and elsewhere) where it represents the inverse of MTBF, that is, $\lambda = 1/\mathrm{MTBF}$ (see *Failure rate*). It is also used to express the wavelength of electromagnetic radiation. λ can be a constant or a function of time $\lambda(t)$ depending on which failure distribution is being employed and the position on the *bathtub* reliability curve.

Life units: It is a measure of use duration applicable to the item (e.g., operating hours/days/months, cycles, distance, rotations, rounds fired, attempts to operate) (MIL-STD-721).

Life units applied to IT component failures are often expressed in life units of thousands or hundreds of thousands of hours, a more practical unit than seconds.

Liveware: It is an expression covering people who interact with IT systems, both passively and actively, and cause changes to the state of a system. The term covers both support personnel and user personnel and, as we have seen, change can have negative as well as positive effects on system state and hence availability. Liveware includes malevolent people too.

Lockstep: It is a technology whereby entities are kept in sync with each other, performing exactly the same operation(s) in parallel. The output of, say, two entities is compared and if one is deemed to be faulty, the other entity takes over.

Lockstep is often applied to CPUs and memory when this kind of work *takeover* is necessary and is a key component in fault tolerant systems such as those marketed by Stratus (ftServer) and HP (Integrity Nonstop). See *Fault tolerance.*

Log shipping: Generic log shipping is a method of maintaining a level of synchronization between a primary systems and a standby system, for example, a DR system. A log is a record of database changes made after a full backup has been taken. In DR, a full copy of a database is installed at the DR site and subsequently updated via change logs to maintain synchronization between primary and DR data. Obviously, there will be some delay in shipping a log and updating the DR database so there will always be a time difference between the states of the primary and DR database.

Log shipping can be implemented for Oracle and SQL Server databases and possibly others. Other *shipping* traffic includes change logs and various activity journals to maintain synchronicity of data and state information of backup and DR systems (secondary) with that of the primary.

---

* See http://research.cs.wisc.edu/adsl/Publications/sba-usenix05.pdf for a detailed discussion of journal file systems.

LOC: It refers to the lines of code in a program, subroutine, or function. It is usually written as *KLOC* (q.v.), equal to 1000 LOC.

Logical volume: It is a simplified view of stored data which is used by coders and other people accessing data. It can mask underlying complexity, such as RAID levels whose handling is left to controller hardware of software.

Logical outage: It is a situation where the components or systems supporting the service are all functioning but the service does not meet the quality of service (QoS) expected by users or necessary for proper functioning of that service. The terms of this QoS are normally contained in an SLA. Examples might be very poor performance, incorrect results, or other limitations on service.

Longitudinal redundancy check (LRC): This is a form of redundancy check that is applied independently to each of a parallel group of bit streams in telecommunications. Data must be divided into transmission blocks, to which the additional check data are added. It is similar in *concept* to CRC. As before, it is employed to ensure correct delivery of data or flag exceptions in data transmissions and invoke a retransmission.

Machine check architecture (MCA): This is a mechanism in which the CPU reports hardware errors to the OSs. This provides a way of detecting and reporting hardware errors, such as system bus errors, ECC errors, parity errors, cache errors, and others. Architectures employed in Windows and IBM environments implement architectures of this nature. Their differences will lie in what a particular architecture is called, what it detects and what the OS does about it.

Maintainability: It is the measure of the ability of an item to be retained in or restored to a specified condition when maintenance is performed by personnel having specified skill levels, using prescribed procedures and resources, at each prescribed level of maintenance and repair (MIL-STD-721—US Military Standard q.v.).

Malware: The word *malware* is short for *malicious software*, often used synonymously with *virus*, but a virus is actually just a specific type of malware. The word *malware* encompasses all harmful software, including all the ones listed below. Most malware these days is produced for profit, and *ransomware* is a good example of this. Ransomware doesn't want to crash a system and delete your files just to cause you trouble. It wants to take something hostage and get a quick payment from you. Some of these examples of malware are limited to personal computers used by individuals but that may not remain the case forever. The perpetrators of these activities may well conclude that extracting money from an organization is easier and more lucrative than attacking an individual.

Note: The era of personal devices being used for business system access is here (BYOD) and therein lies a potential problem.

Virus: It is a type of malware that copies itself by infecting other files, just as viruses in the real world infect biological cells and use those biological cells to reproduce copies of themselves. A virus can do many different things: watch in the background and steal your passwords, display advertisements, or just crash your system. The key thing that makes it a *virus* is how it spreads within a system or across systems if the virus infects a transportable medium, such as an USB stick or even a transaction carrying infected data.

Worm: It is similar to a virus, but it spreads a different way. Rather than infecting files and relying on human activity to move those files around and run them on different systems, a worm spreads over computer networks on its own accord. The worm accesses these system services over the Internet, exploiting any vulnerability, and infecting the computer. The worm then used the new infected computer to continue replicating itself.

Trojan/Trojan Horse: This is a type of malware that disguises itself as a legitimate file. When you download and run the program, the Trojan horse will run in the background, allowing third-parties to access your computer. Trojans can do this for any number of reasons—to monitor activity on your computer, to join your computer to a botnet (q.v.). Trojans may also be used to open the floodgates and download many other types of malware onto a system.

Spyware: It is a type of malicious software that spies on you without your knowledge. It collects a variety of different types of data, depending on the piece of spyware. Different types of malware can function as spyware. There may be malicious spyware included in Trojans that spies on keystrokes to steal financial data, for example.

Keylogger: It is a type of malware that runs in the background, recording every key stroke that a user makes. These keystrokes can include usernames, passwords, credit card numbers, and other sensitive data which can then be uploaded to a malicious server for analysis and criminal use. A virus, worm, or Trojan may function as a keylogger.

Botnet, Bot: A botnet is a large network of computers that are under the botnet creator's control. Each computer functions as a *bot* because it's infected with a specific piece of malware. Once the bot software infects the computer, it will connect to some sort of control server and wait for instructions from the botnet's creator. For example, a botnet may sometimes be used to initiate a DDoS attack (q.v. below).

Rootkit: It is a type of malware designed to burrow deep into a computer, avoiding detection by security programs and users. For example, a rootkit might load before most of Windows, burying itself deep into the system and modifying system functions so that security programs can't detect it. It might hide itself completely, preventing itself from showing up in the Windows task manager. The key thing that makes a type of malware a rootkit is that it's stealthy and focused on hiding itself once it arrives.

Ransomware: It is a fairly new type of malware that tries to extort money from the *owner*. One of the nastiest examples, CryptoLocker, literally encrypts files and demands a payment before they can be accessed again. This is surmountable in a commercial IT environment with adequate HA/DR plans in place but amounts to a DR situation in recovery.

Distributed denial of service (DDoS): This is an attack on a system or systems initiated to *flood* the application(s) with transactions and render them essentially unavailable. It is necessary to distinguish between genuine overloads and a DDoS attack before hitting the panic button. Some product vendors nobly offer the facility to identify DDoS and siphon it off to their own server(s).

For example, Verisign states "When a malicious event is detected, Verisign redirects harmful traffic to a Verisign mitigation site" (http://www.verisigninc.com/en_US/products-and-services/network-intelligence-availability/ddos/mitigation-services/index.xhtml).

Arbor Networks have produced a paper which lists eight key areas that an organization should consider when evaluating DDoS solutions. It is basically aimed at facets of cyberware/malware that can slip through the cracks unless the right defense steps are taken. (http://pages.arbornetworks.com/rs/arbor/images/Arbor_Insight_8_Considerations.pdf?mkt_tok = 3RkMMJWWfF9wsRolsqzJZKXonjHpfsX66%2BsuUaS%2BlMI%2F0ER3fOvrPUfGjI4DS8tjI%2BSLDwEYGJlv6SgFSrjHMatu27gNUxY%3D).

Adware: It often comes along with spyware. It's any type of software that displays advertising on an infected computer. It is seen as more *socially acceptable* than other types of malware but has a nuisance value as well.

One way to tackle these threats is to implement a security operations center (SOC) equipped with products to detect, identify, alert, log, and neutralize threats.

A useful introduction to SOCs, *A Practitioners Guide to Establishing a Security Operation Center*, can be found at http://docs.media.bitpipe.com/io_11x/io_110808/item_723049/WP_Practioners_Guide_to_SOC_July_2013.pdf. Also, see the other security references in Appendix 5 under Security and Malware Sources.

Master/slave: It is a model of communication where one device or process has unidirectional control over one or more other devices. In some systems, a master is elected from a group of eligible devices, with the other devices acting in the role of slaves. The early cluster systems, for example, the DEC VMS Cluster, worked on this basis so that if the master node failed, the cluster failed unless there was a mean of promoting a slave to master.

Mathematical distributions: These are distributions of values for various parameters expressed in terms meaningful to the context. For example, the distribution for *reliability* might plot the probability of failure against time. Distributions can be *continuous* (a smooth curve) or *discrete* (represented as a series of vertical bars).

Two examples of distributions used in reliability theory are Weibull, exponential (continuous), and Poisson (discrete).

Note: Schematics of the two classes of distribution are shown in Lesson 1, found in Appendix 4.

Mean: This is a method of averaging numbers. For a discrete set of numbers, for example, a list of times taken to repair several occurrences of the same fault, the *arithmetic* mean is the sum of the repair times (T) divided by the number of such times, that is:

$$\frac{\sum T_R}{\text{Number of repairs}}$$

The other *mean* value is the *geometric* mean which is the product of the set of numbers to the power of ($1/N$) where N is the number of numbers, that is:

$$\text{Geometric mean } (N \text{ numbers}) = (a1 \times a2 \times a3 \ldots \times aN)^{1/N} = \left(\prod_{1}^{N} a_i \right)^{1/N}$$

Of course, not all faults take the same time to repair (see MTTR), nor is the MTBF the same for each type of fault. Minor hardware faults may take a minute or so to fix or switch a substitute in, a software problem may take minutes, hours, or days. Taking a *mean* of such diverse times can be meaningless. See footnote in the next section and refer to Appendix 4 for the math of this.

Mean residual life (MRL): It is the mean remaining lifetime of a component given that it has reached *age t*. It is defined as

$$\text{MRL}\, r(t) = \frac{\int_t^\infty (u-t)f(u)d}{R(t)}$$

where $f(u)$ is the lifetime probability density function (pdf) (see Appendix 4 for information on pdfs).

Memory mirroring: It is the division of memory on a server into two parts. The first part is mirrored to the second, creating a redundant copy of memory. If a fault occurs within the one section of memory, the memory controller shifts to the *twin* without disruption, and the channels can resynchronize when repairs are completed. Memory mirroring can be compared to RAID1 and replication (q.v.) mirroring for external storage, with a similar downside—memory costs are doubled.

Military handbooks: These are detailed theory and practice documentations produced for and by the US military for use in that sphere of activity and elsewhere that it was applicable. The ones relevant to our study of reliability and availability are shown below—there are others.

MIL-HDBK-217F: US Military Standard for *Reliability Prediction of Electronic Equipment.* It contains some useful reliability information but not all IT-related.

MIL-HDBK-338B: US Military Standard *Electronic Reliability Design Handbook* is what it says on the tin and has useful sections on reliability factors and reliability equations.

MIL-STD-721C: US Military Standard for *definitions* related to reliability and maintainability. It is very useful for the pedant and acronym collector.

Mirroring: It is a technique in which data is written to two duplicate disks simultaneously. Consequently, if one of the disk drives fails, the system can instantly switch to the other disk without any loss of data or service. Disk mirroring is used commonly in on-line database systems where it's critical that the data be accessible at all times and forms part of RAID techniques, along with striping and other techniques.

Mobile security: It is the term normally applied to access security when services are accessed from mobile devices, such as tablets and handheld devices. This can be from anywhere in the world and often from a person's own device. Simple password protection is not thought to be stringent enough to prevent unauthorized access and possible fraud in such environments.

Two-factor authentication is a security process in which the user has to provide two means of identification, one of which is typically a physical token, such as a card, and the other of which is typically something memorized, such as a security code. A common example of two-factor authentication is a bank card: the card itself is the physical item and the personal identification number (PIN) is the data that goes with it. This sort of access needs some modification in the physical aspect for mobile devices.

Monte Carlo methods: Monte Carlo simulation (modeling) is a method for solving engineering problems by sampling methods. The method applies to such things as system reliability and availability modeling by simulating random processes such as life-to-failure (MTTF) and repair times (MTTR).

Mean time between failures (MTBF): The mean time that a system operated without fault before experiencing a fault that causes an outage or downtime. This is the time between the start of one failure and the start of the next after service resumption and is normally used when discussing nonrepairable systems. This can be confused with MTTF. See *MTTF* (below) and Appendix 2 for clarification of this dichotomy.

Mean time to problem determination (MTPD): [*My term but recognized and sometimes named slightly differently by others—but not all*.] The mean (or average) time taken to detect what caused the outage.*

Mean time to failure (MTTF): It is the mean time between resumption of a service and the next outage. This is standard failure interval time for repairable systems (q.v.). This can be confused with MTBF. See Appendix 2 for clarification of this.

Mean time to first failure (MTTFF): This will invoke a machine check for the particular fault for the first time and, presumably, initiate a log. It is of little interest to us. For a nonrepairable item or component, MTTFF is its whole lifetime but a mean time to failure can be obtained from a population of similar devices.

Mean time to repair (MTTR): It is the mean time taken to repair the fault which caused the outage. When using this in the standard availability calculation, remember to add the problem determination time (MTPD) to the *fix/replace* time. If there are any *logistics* times, like traveling to get a part (or just finding it), they should be included, pro-rated, especially when calculating averages.

Look at an example:

Ten repairs took 120 minutes, an average of 12 minutes. However, the 11th failure although taking 12 minutes to fix, lost 60 minutes in *logistics* time so the average fix time is $120 + (12 + 60)/11 = 17.5$ minutes.

Mu (μ): It is the Greek letter lower case "m" used for many scientific things but in reliability engineering it is used as the symbol for *repair rate* or, in software reliability models, cumulative total failures.

Multipathing: In the context of storage, this is related to the ability of a machine (real or virtual) to use multiple routes to and from disk storage for speed and resilience. Older IBM OSs suffered from the deficiency that if I/O started on one path (channel), it had to complete the operation via that same path. Dynamic multipathing was introduced to get round this barrier. Today, some virtual machine implementations allow multipathing based on path optimizing algorithms, choosing a functioning, low latency path for the I/O *on the fly*.

Murphy's Law: If a thing can go wrong it will, one of the many definitions of this law and the rallying point for all availability personnel. Murphy's Law has a sibling called *Sod's Law* which is applied to a situation where a failure has already occurred, hence ... *that's Sod's law* ..., spoken after the event. Murphy's Law is probabilistic and the actual occurrence is a corollary which is Sod's Law (when state = 0). For the history and variations on Murphy's Law, see http://uk.ask.com/wiki/Murphy's_law.

Network monitoring: There are a number of properties of networks for which vendors offer monitors: performance, latency, malware, availability, and others. For example, the availability of a server might be monitored using *pinging* every half minute and recording the state (1 or 0). If the state is 0, then the pinging frequency may be increased until the server returns to operational capacity.

Response times can be monitored by *injecting* transactions into a system and measuring the time between *send message* and *receive reply*.

Network recovery objective (NRO): It indicates the time required to recover or failover network operations. Keep in mind that systems level recovery is not fully complete if customers cannot access the application services via network connections. Hence, the NRO includes the

---

* See Appendix 2 for a discussion of MTBF/MTTR, their derivatives, and their interpretations in this book and in various other sources.

time required to bring online alternate communication links, re-configure routers and, for example, name servers (DNS), and alter client system parameters for alternative TCP/IP addresses.

Comprehensive network failover planning is of equal importance to data recovery in a DR scenario.

Network reduction: This is useful for systems consisting of series and parallel subsystems or components. The method comprises successively reducing the series and parallel structures by equivalent components. Knowledge of the series and parallel reduction formulae is essential for the application of this technique. It is akin to the network reduction technique used in electrical networks where adding to a network involves reducing the existing network to just an electrical input with certain characteristics.

Network interface card (NIC): It is the *gateway* from server to a network. These cards often have intelligence over and above a transport mechanism.

Nonrepairable system: This has been defined as something (component, unit, part) that is discarded on failure. This type of, on the face of it, useless item is mainly discussed in US MIL documents where the terms *mission* and *nonrepairable* are to be found quite often.

NIST: "A non-repairable population is one for which individual items that fail are removed permanently from the population. While the system may be repaired by replacing failed units from either a similar or a different population, the members of the original population dwindle over time until all have eventually failed."

[*My Opinion:* ... *of this topic is that a* "non-repairable item is one used in a fixed time mission, duration T, where repair/replace is not an option." *An example of this is a space exploration flight lasting several years where repair is obviously an impossibility and redundancy not an option because of weight restrictions on the craft. I am assuming that all items in this book are repairable systems (q.v.) and that their statistics, models and equations apply.*]

Online transaction processing (OLTP): It is a class of systems that supports or facilitates high transaction-oriented applications usually over a network. OLTP's primary system features are immediate client feedback and high individual transaction volume. Attributes are input, output, file read/write/update/delete, and the ACID properties.

OLTP is mainly used in industries that rely heavily on the efficient processing of a large number of client transactions, for example, banks, airlines, and retailers.

Paravirtualization (PV): It is an efficient and lightweight form of virtualization introduced by Xen and later adopted by other virtualization solution suppliers. It does not require virtualization extensions from the host CPU and thus enables virtualization on hardware architectures that do not support hardware-assisted virtualization. However, PV guests and control domains require kernel support and drivers that in the past required special kernel builds, but are now part of the Linux kernel as well as other OSs. These live alongside the standard VMs on a system.

Full virtualization can mimic PV by adding modifications to the OS or making the OS completely PV-aware.

Partial outage: It is an outage situation where not all services are affected—just one or perhaps a few. This might be caused by a physical outage of, say, a data disk or the unavailability of data from another system, which has not arrived in time for the necessary processing. That service is thus in limbo for a period, that is, unavailable.

Pellston technology: It is the code name for *Intel Cache Safe Technology.* As cache sizes became larger, the likelihood of cache failures increased. Intel Itanium processors, starting with the Intel Itanium 2 processor, offset this increased likelihood of failures using Intel Cache Safe

Technology. When there is a correctable error in the L3 cache, Cache Safe Technology tests the cache line and corrects the error. If the cache line is found to be defective, it is disabled.

Pi (Π): It is the Greek letter upper case Pi used in math to denote, among other things, the product (multiplication) of factors following it. It is used extensively in availability and reliability theory (see Appendix 4).

Ping utility: The *ping* (*P*acket *I*nter*N*et *G*roper) command is a method for troubleshooting the accessibility of devices. It sends a series of Internet Control Message Protocol (ICMP) Echo messages to an address to determine:

- Whether a remote host is active or inactive. If it isn't, the ping will not be returned within a predetermined time (the *timeout*) and deemed *dead*. The timeout is set by the IT department to take account of delays which are possibly predictable and acceptable.
- The round-trip delay in communicating with the host, the *latency* of the network route (see Lesson 6 in Appendix 4).
- Packet loss in transmission.

The *ping* packet contains 64 bytes—56 data bytes and 8 bytes of ICMP protocol header information. *Ping invento*r was the late Mike Muuss. (See *Traceroute*.)

Post-RAID: It is a series of technologies, partially overlapping, which are being developed in the light of standard RAID's inability to perform with large volumes of data (*big data* q.v.), hence the name. The main topic in post-RAID discussion is erasure codes, a step up from the use of parity and ECC for the reconstruction of data after a failure.

Terms involved in this area include the following:

- Erasure codes—a generic name for failure codes generated to recover data lost due to bit errors which ECC and simple parity cannot handle.
- Reed–Solomon coding
- IDA
- FEC

Power outage: It is the loss of electrical power to components of an IT system or to IT-related accommodation. The *cause* of the outage can be lightning or perhaps component failure. Whatever the cause, the subsequent action is to pin down the *source* of the failure. You cannot do much about lightning (cause) but you can fix the part affected (source) once it has been identified. There may be one cause but many components affected via knock-on effects.

Power redundancy: A power outage in a data center is no respecter of HA or fault-tolerant hardware or software and redundancy applies to power components as much as any other component.

Like other *environment* features, such as air conditioning, fire suppression systems, and smoke detectors, power supplies are potential single points of failure (SPoFs) in a service scenario unless duplicated. A power supply situation with redundancy is illustrated in Figure A1.4. (*Note:* the backup generator in the diagram needs to be driven by fuel or recalcitrant employees on a treadmill!) See *UPS* (uninterruptible power supplies) in this appendix.

Power usage efficiency (PUE): It is determined by dividing the amount of power entering a data center by the power used to run the computer infrastructure within it. It is expressed as a ratio, with overall efficiency improving as the ratio *Power In/IT Power Used* decreases toward 1. It was created by members of the Green Grid, an industry group focused on data center energy efficiency. It is sometimes called power usage effectiveness.

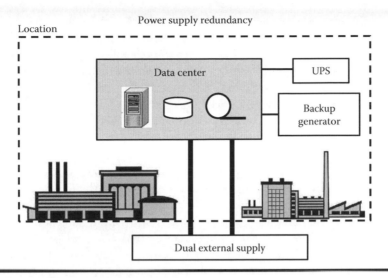

Figure A1.4   Power supply redundancy schematic.

A related metric is *DCIE* = IT equipment power/total facility power × 100%, that is, the inverse of PUE.

Predictions, reliability: Reliability predictions are one of the most common forms of reliability analysis. They predict the failure rate of components and overall system reliability. These predictions are used to evaluate design feasibility, compare design alternatives, identify potential failure areas, trade-off system design factors, and track reliability improvement.

Such predictions are not limited to hardware: for example, the SRGM, which appears in many guises deals with reliability improvements in software development and operation.

Predictive failure analysis (PFA): It allows the server to monitor the status of critical subsystems and to notify the system administrator when components appear to be degrading. In most cases, replacements of failing parts can be performed as part of planned maintenance activity (Figure A1.5).

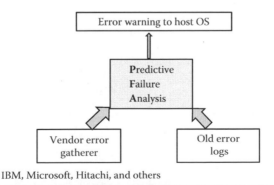

Figure A1.5   Generic predictive failure analysis schematic.

As a result, unscheduled outages can be prevented. A PFA facility usually needs information provided by associated products, usually vendor-specific. For example, IBM PFA relies on remote checks from the *Health Checker for z/OS* to collect data, Microsoft PFA employs *Windows Hardware Error Architecture* (WHEA) while Hitachi uses its *Generalized Error Measurement* feature. Historical error data (logs) are also used in PFA and the general flow of a PFA scenario is shown in Figure A1.5.

The term *predictive failure analysis* was developed by IBM is marked *copyright* by them in some documentation but is freely used by others.

Principle of least privilege (POLP): It is the practice of limiting access to the minimal level that will allow normal functioning. Applied to employees, the POLP translates to giving people the lowest level of user rights that they can have and still do their jobs. The principle is also applied to things other than people, including programs and processes.

The user or system component starts off with no privileges and is only given those considered necessary. This is sometimes difficult since privileges are often assigned to groups of users rather than individuals, depending on the security software used. It may sometimes be necessary to elevate or promote user privileges in certain circumstances, like problem determination or taking emergency action in lieu of another person. If this is deemed necessary in an organization, the security package chosen should possess the granularity of privilege granting to achieve it.

The POLP originated in the US Department of Defense (DoD) in the 1970s and is just one of the tools used in software or system hardening.

Probability: It is the likelihood or chance that something is the case or will happen. Probability theory is used extensively in areas such as statistics, math, science, and philosophy to draw conclusions about the likelihood of potential events and the underlying mechanics of complex systems. We use probability in discussions of reliability and availability (and playing poker[*]).

Probability density function (pdf): This is a way of representing a failure distribution. Probability density is the probability of failure per unit time. When multiplied by the length of a small time interval (δt), the result is the probability of failure in that interval. It is the basic description of the *time to failure* of a component. All other functions related to a components reliability can be derived from the pdf. For example:

$F(t)$—the cumulative distribution function (cdf)

$R(t)$—the survival or reliability function:

$$R(t) = [1 - F(t)]$$

$h(t)$—the hazard rate or hazard function (q.v.):

$$h(t) = \frac{f(t)}{R(t)}$$

$H(t)$—the cumulative hazard function at time t (q.v.):

$$H(t) = \int_0^t h(t)dt$$

---

[*] According to Hoyle of course.

q.v.: *Quod Vide*, Latin for *which see*, used in referring to another part of a document, glossary, or dictionary. Also means other things, such as *quantum vis* (as much as you will) in medicine but that need no concern us.

Quorum (cluster): It is a configuration database or log. It records which nodes are active and which are in standby mode in a cluster environment. It is also used in making decisions if communications in the cluster fail and it becomes two *partitions*.

The partition owning the quorum is allowed to run the application(s) while the other is *removed* from the cluster.

The theory of quorums (or quora) is quite involved and unless you are intimately involved in cluster design and operation, it's perhaps best if you leave it at what is said in this definition.

R: It is the normal character used to represent the reliability of a component—hardware or software, which in the main use the same terminology. This form is often used for the fixed reliability number used in calculation, for example, for parallel components or blocks which is along the bottom of the *bathtub* curve.

R(t): These are the normal characters used to represent the reliability of a component as a time-variable factor. The reliability in this form is expressed in terms of a mathematical function of time $f(t)$

RAID: It is the short form for redundant arrays of independent (or inexpensive in the original definition and original *raison d'être*) disks. It is a category of disk drives that employ two or more drives in combination for fault tolerance and performance. RAID allows the storage of the same data redundantly in a balanced way to improve overall storage performance. There are numerous implementations of RAID, some proprietary but in practice, only about three or four find widespread use. RAID implementations can be effected by hardware (disk controllers and microcode) or software. Both have their plusses and minuses.

RAIN: It (also called channel bonding, redundant array of independent nodes, reliable array of independent nodes, or random array of independent nodes) is a cluster of nodes connected in a network topology with multiple interfaces and redundant storage. RAIN is used to increase fault tolerance and is an implementation of RAID across nodes instead of across disk arrays (http://searchdatacenter.techtarget.com/definition/RAIN).

Ramp-up: It is the process of getting a service (not just the hardware and software) back into operation as per its operating specification. This specification is normally in the form of a SLA. Some systems need time to *stabilize* when starting up again after a failure. It is quite possible for the *ramp-up* time to be greater than the time taken to fix the fault, an example being a NASDAQ failure outlined in the September "Availability Digest." Here is an extract which encapsulates the concept of *ramp-up*:

Nasdaq decided to halt trading at 12:14 PM. Within a **half hour**, Nasdaq had SIP up and running. However, it took another **three hours to test the system** and to evaluate scenarios … to reopen the market for fair and orderly trading … at 3:25 PM.

The time for *ramp-up* after a failure is important in design and in drawing up a SLA and reporting outages. I have no doubts whatsoever that some outage times reported in surveys do not take "ramp up" times into account when calculating the availability of a *service*. This is a mistake.

Rayleigh distribution: It is a special case of the Weibull distribution and has only one parameter. Besides its use in reliability engineering, the Rayleigh distribution is used to analyze noise problems associated with communications systems. It has also been used in some *software* *reliability growth models.* The failure density function and failure rate (hazard function) are shown below. θ or β = Weibull shape parameter, or the characteristic life, defined as where $t = \theta/\beta$, depending on who writes the equation, which is the time at which 63.2% of the units will fail.* The Greek terms used in this and the Weibull distributions vary across authors and papers.

RDBMS: It refers to relational database management system.

RDBMS partitioning: A partition is a division of a logical database or its constituent elements into distinct independent parts. The *splitting* of the database can be done on different criteria: range (of keys), list (name), a hash (partition determination 1, 2, 3, ...), or a composite of these. Database partitioning is normally done for manageability, performance, or availability reasons. For example, sales data for a quarter might be spread across three drives in three partitions—January, February, and March data.

Recovery point objective (RPO): It describes the age of the data you want the ability to restore in the event of a disaster. For example, if your RPO is 6 hours, you want to be able to restore systems back to the state they were in, as of no longer than 6 hours ago. To achieve this, you need to be making backups or other data copies at least every 6 hours. Any data created or modified inside your RPO either will be lost or must be recreated during a recovery. If your RPO is that no data are lost, a synchronous remote copy solution is the only feasible option.

Recovery time objective (RTO): It is the total time needed to recover from a disaster before the business is severely impacted. The RTO is normally decided upon in a BIA. Each major service project should complete a BIA which can be used as the basis for impact analysis of failures affecting that service or business. This time is not a *wish time* but a realistic assessment of how long a service can be down before seriously impacting the business. Some services will specify an RTO of *less than 2 hours*, another *up to 3 days*, and so on, depending on their importance to the enterprise.

Redundancy: It is the use of extra components in a system, usually in parallel, to take over the functionality of a failing component of a similar type. Examples of this are a two-node cluster, dual NICs, and mirrored disk data. Dual NICs usually work via software which monitors them for activity and, when one fails, switches the work to the surviving NIC.

Clusters have software to help the changeover from one system to another when one system fails. In software, *shadow* versions might exist to take over the job of the primary version in the same cluster node if it fails.

Reed–Solomon (RS) codes: These are block-based (not bit or byte) ECCs with uses in a wide range of applications in digital communications and data storage. RS codes are used to correct transmission/storage errors in many systems, including data storage which is our primary interest in them. The basic mechanism is

$$\text{Data input} \rightarrow \text{RS encoder} \rightarrow \text{storage} \rightarrow \text{RS decoder} \rightarrow \text{data retrieval}$$

Reliability R*(t):* This is some measure of the ability of a block or set of blocks to continue to function for long periods. The inverse of reliability is failure rate, thus a highly reliable block or component will have a low failure rate. In an IT system, the main blocks are the hardware and software. Hardware reliability is often statistically derivable, whereas software involves

---

* See http://www.weibull.com/hotwire/issue45/tooltips45.htm (it uses η instead of θ).

human factors (design, coding, and operations) which make failure rates difficult to predict. In the body of this book there are two *bathtub* curves which plot the failure rate of hardware and software over their useful life.

Some elements of reliability theory are covered in Appendix 4, along with other theory elements around the subject of availability. Also, see *Software reliability*. For a general coverage, see the URL (http://infohost.nmt.edu/~olegm/484/Chap3.pdf), titled "Chapter 4—Basic Reliability Math."

Reliability block diagram (RBD): This is a method of modeling how components and subsystems failures combine to cause system failure. We have used them in this book to model the overall reliability of series and parallel blocks which represent components of an IT system or service. These blocks can also be used in a reliability/availability *walkthrough* exercise.

The analysis of systems can be *static*, where all reliability characteristics are known and *time-dependent*, where they vary. Both forms can be handled using an *analytical* method or a *simulation* method.

Reliability growth: Reliability growth is the positive improvement in a reliability parameter over a period of time due to the implementation of corrective actions to system design, operation or maintenance procedures, or the associated manufacturing process. This applies in many areas, particularly software reliability. There are four essential elements involved in achieving reliability growth:
  - Failure mode discovery
  - Feedback of problems identified
  - Failure mode root cause analysis and proposed corrective action
  - Approval and implementation of proposed corrective action.

Fixing a problem by replacing a part with an identical one will not improve reliability but a different solution might have this effect, for example, replacing the part with one of higher reliability or adding an extra one to create a higher level of redundancy.

Repair rate: This is essentially the *antidote* to the failure rate (q.v.) and is normally given the symbol μ. It is very often used in conjunction with the failure rate λ where $(\lambda - \mu)$ figures largely in equations as the net failure rate. This applies to what are known as *repairable* systems.

Equations for reliability of redundant nonrepairable systems obviously do not contain the symbol μ.

Repairable system: This has been defined as an assembly of parts in which parts are replaced when they fail. A system may be comprised of both repairable and nonrepairable parts therefore nonrepairable parts require different statistical models and methods of analysis.

In this book, I have assumed that the items/components/parts are repairable, which they are if you allow *replacement* as variation of a *repair*.

Replication: It is the process of copying and maintaining database objects, such as tables, in multiple databases that make up a distributed database system. Changes applied at one site are captured and stored locally before being forwarded and applied at each of the remote locations.

Replication uses distributed database technology to share data between multiple sites, but a replicated database and a distributed database are not the same. In a distributed database, data is available at many locations, but a particular table resides at only one location. Replication in one form or another is used in maintaining DR sites in anticipation of extended failure of the primary site.

Resilience: It is the ability of an equipment, a machine, or a system to absorb the impact of the failure of one or more components or a significant disturbance in its environment and to still continue to provide an acceptable level of service (*Business Dictionary*). Also, the Latin *resilire*, meaning to *rebound* is essentially the act of springing back to operational readiness after a failure.

This is often applied to IT components in a system, such as CPU and disk. In this context, resilience means the ability of that component to either carry on after a fault or to recover quickly. An apt analogy is a boxer who can take a punch or recover quickly from a knockdown and resume fighting. Resilience in the sense of blocks is an engineering function. However, in the case of a whole system, the resilience is not just a function of the blocks, but involves the whole area of backup, recovery, and problem determination. This is a task for IT personnel.

Risk analysis: See *Risk assessment.*

Risk assessment: The process of identifying, prioritizing, and estimating risks to organizational operations (including mission, functions, image, reputation), organizational assets, individuals, other organizations, and the nation, resulting from the operation of an information system. Part of risk management, it incorporates threat and vulnerability analyses, and considers mitigations provided by security controls planned or in place. It is synonymous with *risk analysis.*

Risk IT: It is an end-to-end, comprehensive view of all risks related to the use of IT and a detailed treatment of risk management, from a senior management perspective to operational issues. Risk IT was published in 2009 by ISACA and is the result of a work group composed of industry experts and some academics.

An important document about Risk IT is the *Practitioner Guide*. It is made up of eight sections:

1. Defining a Risk Universe and Scoping Risk Management
2. Risk Appetite and Risk Tolerance
3. Risk Awareness, Communication and Reporting
4. Expressing and Describing Risk
5. Risk Scenarios
6. Risk Response and Prioritization
7. A Risk Analysis Workflow [*a detailed diagram*]
8. Mitigation of IT Risk Using COBIT and Val IT

For reference, see *The Risk IT Practitioner Guide*, ISACAISBN978-1-60420-116-1 (http://en.wikipedia.org/wiki/Risk_IT).

Risk management: It is the program and supporting processes to manage information security risk to organizational operations (including services, functions, image, reputation), organizational assets, individuals, other organizations, and the nation and includes (1) establishing the context for risk-related activities, (2) assessing risk, (3) responding to risk once determined, and (4) monitoring risk over time.

Roll back: A mode of *database recovery* involving an initial backup, a checkpoint after a period and then resynchronizing the database with roll back/roll forward mechanisms.

It is an *SQL* statement that ends a transaction, undoing any changes made by the transaction. It is the opposite of *commit*, which makes permanent any changes made in the transaction. In the diagram above, reference is made to *dirty pages* which are outlined below.

Dirty page: It is a page in *the cache/buffer pool* that has been updated in memory, where the changes are not yet written (*flushed*) to the data files. It is the opposite of a *clean page*. It is denoted by a *dirty* bit.

Dirty read: It is an operation that retrieves unreliable data, data that were updated by another transaction but not yet *committed*. It is only possible with the *isolation level* known as *read uncommitted* and this kind of operation does not adhere to the *ACID* principle of database design.

This kind of action is important in maintaining data consistency which is an inherent part of availability, particularly in distributed systems.

A *dirty buffer* contains records not yet flushed from cache and thus not on the log data sets. After a system fault, the RDBMS automatically goes into data recovery mode in two ways (Figure A1.6):

- Using *roll forward* (q.v.) to ensure that all database changes prior to the system fault are applied to the database. The work needing to be performed is proportional to the update frequency (volatility) of the database and the time between checkpoints of the database.
- Using *roll back* to ensure all uncommitted changes to the database are undone. The work needing to be performed is proportional to the number and size of uncommitted transaction when the fault occurred.

The time taken to recover, T_{recover}, is

$$T_{\text{recover}} = (\text{roll forward time} + \text{roll back time})$$

Normal checkpointing can periodically identify modified blocks in the buffer cache and bulk write them to the database. The result of this mode of operation is a delay in recovering the database after a system fault. Older versions of Oracle used to make use of *fast-start checkpointing* which always wrote the oldest block first so that every write allows the checkpoint time to be advanced.

Roll forward time is cut by half and roll back time is eliminated. The time to recover is then is the average of the roll forward time:

$$T_{\text{recover}} = (0.5 \text{ roll forward time})$$

Other vendors provide this recovery facility but with either a different name or a different technique (http://www.relationaldbdesign.com/oracle-backup-recovery-features/module4/implement-faststart-parallel-rollback.php).

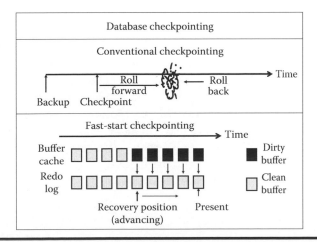

Figure A1.6   Roll back/roll forward database recovery.

Roll forward: In this process, a transaction log is used to *redo,* or *roll forward,* transactions in case of recovery, or an explicit *roll forward* statement. It also stores the before-images of the records that each transaction will change, so it can be used to roll back any transactions that have not committed.

Root cause analysis (RCA): It is a method of problem solving that tries to identify the root causes of faults or problems. This practice tries to solve problems by attempting to identify and correct the root causes of events, as opposed to simply addressing their symptoms. By focusing correction on root causes, problem recurrence can be prevented. RCFA (root cause failure analysis) recognizes that complete prevention of recurrence by one corrective action is not always possible.

For example, an outage may well manifest itself as a power failure but that failure itself may have a deeper, possibly *invisible* cause, such as moisture, external overload, and road works cable severance. Working on the power supply itself might not prevent a repeat occurrence of the outage. Thus, the words *root cause* are significant.

Runbook: It is an electronic or physical document that lists detailed procedures for handling every expected situation that an IT system may experience. Based on changes in system operations, incoming requests and other factors, system administrators determine which procedures to run and when to run them.

Runbook procedures often include complex decision trees that indicate specific steps to follow depending on answers to pre-established questions. It should also be updated with any new procedures or new failure/recovery actions when new types of outages occur. In true HA fashion, there should be redundant identical copies.

> *Aside:* In the DEC accounts of the *golden era,* this type of documentation used to be held in a leather bound *operations procedures* book kept by the main IT systems' console. It also contained, among other things, a record of *system changes* to aid regular maintenance and future problem resolution.

Runbook automation (RBA)[*]*:* It "makes complex procedures easy to repeat while reducing the possibility of human errors. RBA also helps less-skilled IT staffers implement complex activities that span networks, servers, storage, applications, databases and more. IT organizations that take advantage of RBA are able to improve efficiency and service quality while reducing operational costs. Unfortunately, when it comes to flexibility, agility and integration with other tools and processes, especially in today's world of cloud and virtualization—most RBA solutions still fall short."[†] Correctly designed and maintained runbooks are a boon to service availability, especially in volatile operations environments.

Security: It is a condition that results from the establishment and maintenance of protective measures that enable an enterprise to perform its mission or critical functions despite risks posed by threats to its use of information systems. Protective measures may involve a combination of deterrence, avoidance, prevention, detection, recovery, and correction that should form part of the enterprise's risk management approach. *Source:* NIST CNSSI-4009.

---

[*] Not to be confused with IBM's IMS Relative Byte Address (RBA).
[†] http://docs.media.bitpipe.com/io_10x/io_107262/item_602307/WP-Runbook.pdf.

Trusted computer system: It is a system that employs sufficient hardware and software assurance measures to allow its use for processing simultaneously a range of sensitive or classified information. *Source:* NIST CNSSI-4009.

Trusted computing base: It is the totality of protection mechanisms within a computer system, including hardware, firmware, and software, the combination responsible for enforcing a security policy. *Source:* NIST CNSSI-4009.

Trustworthy system: It is the computer hardware, software, and procedures that

1. Are reasonably secure from intrusion and misuse.
2. Provide a reasonable level of availability, reliability, and correct operation.
3. Are reasonably suited to performing their intended functions.
4. Adhere to generally accepted security procedures. *Source:* SP 800-32.

Self-healing: Hardware or software techniques to bypass failures *on the fly* so that processing can continue. This is a developing concept and the enabling technology is not necessarily a *fait accompli* today.

Service (IT): Services as used in this book "refers to the application of business and technical expertise to enable organizations in the creation, management and optimization of or access to information and business processes. The IT services market can be segmented by the type of skills that are employed to deliver the service (design, build, run). There are also different categories of service: business process services, application services and infrastructure services. If these services are outsourced, they are referred to as business process outsourcing (BPO), applications outsourcing (AO) and infrastructure outsourcing" [*Gartner, IT Glossary*].

Sheed, Francis Joseph (1897–1981): An Australian-born lawyer, writer, publisher, and speaker and I used one of his sayings in the Preface to this book and a second in the body of the book. The book of his from which I quoted from was *Theology and Sanity*.

SIEM: It refers to security information and event management systems. It provides security operations information and management functions. The function of a SIEM is to aggregate and manage/analyze event log data for monitoring, reporting, investigation, and auditing purposes. The *functionality* and *scope* of SIEMs (a generic term) varies by vendor.

System components, hardware and software, often generate log data for analysis but manual efforts would be too onerous. SIEMs collect and centrally manage application, system, network, device, security, and user activity from various sources. Also, see *SIM*.

SIEM technology aggregates event data produced by security devices, network infrastructures, systems and applications. The primary data is log data, but SIEM technology can also process other forms of data. Event data is combined with contextual information about users, assets, threats and vulnerabilities. The data is normalized, so that events, data and contextual information from disparate sources can be correlated and analyzed for specific purposes, such as network security event monitoring, user activity monitoring and compliance reporting. The technology provides real-time security monitoring, historical analysis and other support for incident investigation and compliance reporting.

[Gartner]

For reference, see http://whitepapers.theregister.co.uk/paper/view/2584/opinfosec-siemtop-10bestpractices-122210.pdf for SIEM metrics and best practices information.

Sigma (Σ): It is the Greek letter upper case sigma used in math to denote a summation of factors following it. It is used extensively in availability and reliability theory (see Appendix 4).

SIM: It refers to security information management. It is a generic term for activity in the area of systems security, essentially an industry term in related to information security referring to the collection of data (typically log files) into a central repository for trend analysis.

SIM products generally comprise software agents running on the computer systems that are to be monitored, which then send the log information to a centralized server acting as a *security console*. Security alerts are not necessarily given as a *gift* to operations, and it may take some analysis and *digging down* of SIM data accumulated to make knowledgeable decisions on *positive* and *negative* signs of malpractice. This requires security skills in many cases—*a fool with a tool is still a fool*.

For differences and a discussion of SIM and SIEM, see http://en.wikipedia.org/wiki/Security_information_and_event_management and http://en.wikipedia.org/wiki/Security_information_management.

Single bit errors: Errors in the bit patterns of data, usually handled by ECC. Normally, single bit errors are corrected via the parity bit and double bit errors are usually detected and flagged.

Symmetric multiprocessor (SMP): It is a combination of two or more processor systems linked together for either performance (not very good at this) or redundancy/backup.

Sod's Law: See *Murphy's Law*.

Software prototyping: This refers to the activity, 1970s vintage, of creating prototypes of software applications, that is, incomplete versions of the software program being developed. It is an activity that can occur in software development and is comparable to prototyping as known from other fields, such as mechanical engineering or manufacturing (from Wikipedia).

One benefit of prototyping is that the software designer and implementer can get valuable feedback from the users early in the project. The most certain *failure factor* in the development of any user-oriented software is its rejection by users for functional or visual/logistical reasons. This equates to *zero% availability* of the service.

There are, however, advantages to project estimation and management of a prototype approach.

Software reliability: Two definitions for software reliability are as follows: (1) The probability that software will not cause the failure of a system for a specified time under specified conditions. The probability is a function of the inputs to and use of the system, as well as a function of the existence of faults in the software. The inputs to the system determine whether existing faults, if any, are encountered. (2) The ability of a program to perform a required function under stated conditions for a stated period of time.

Definition (2) is similar to that for hardware reliability. One major difference between hardware and software reliability is that the former is a function of time (wear and tear of electrical and mechanical components), whereas software does not *age* and its reliability depends on other factors.

There exists a detailed theory about software reliability, with terms like MTBF, MTTF, and the like but its predictability, in my opinion, is a little more *fluffy* than that of hardware which relies on understood physical properties. Incidentally, the mid-1990s seems to be the heyday of papers on software reliability.

ISO/IEC 9126: Software engineering—Product quality is an international standard for the evaluation of software quality. The fundamental objective of this standard is to address some of the well known human biases that can adversely affect the delivery and perception of a software development project. It has been replaced by ISO/IEC25010:2011 which can be seen at http://www.iso.org/iso/iso_catalogue/catalogue_tc/catalogue_detail.htm?csnumber = 35733.

Software assurance: It is the level of confidence that software is free from vulnerabilities, either intentionally designed into the software or accidentally inserted at any time during its life cycle and that the software functions in the intended manner. *Source:* CNSSI-4009.

Software error: It is a mistake made by a human being(s) resulting in a fault in the software.

Software fault: It is a defect in the software that may cause a failure if executed. Governed by Murphy's Law (probability).

Software failure: It is a dynamic failure with a piece of executing software. Sod's Law (certainty)

Software hardening: It is a process of configuring a programmable unit's (e.g., server) OSs and applications to reduce its security weaknesses.

Software reliability prediction: It is a forecast of the reliability of software at a future stage in its life or at a point in time. Predictions are usually made via software reliability models.

Software system test and evaluation: It is a process that plans, develops, and documents the qualitative/quantitative demonstration of the fulfilment of all baseline functional performance, operational, and interface requirements.

SRGM: It refers to software reliability growth model. it is one of two distinct types of model of software reliability. The first is the defect density model, the second is SGRM. Within these models, there are subcategories often carrying the name(s) of the developer(s) of the submodel.

Solid-state drive (SSD): It (often incorrectly referred to as a *solid-state disk* or *electronic disk*) is a data storage device that uses integrated circuit assemblies as memory to store data persistently. SSD technology uses electronic interfaces compatible with traditional block input/output (I/O) HDDs. SSDs do not employ any moving mechanical components, which distinguishes them from traditional magnetic disks such as HDDs or floppy disks, which are electromechanical devices containing spinning disks and movable read/write heads (Wikipedia).

Secure sockets layer (SSL): It is a protocol developed by Netscape in 1995, which quickly became the preferred method for securing data transmissions across the Internet. SSL is built into every major web server and web browser and makes use of public-private key encryption techniques, allowing sender and receiver to identify each other.

It is a technology that establishes a secure session link between the visitor's web browser and a website so that all communications transmitted through this link are encrypted and are, therefore, secure. An SSL certificate is basically a file or small piece of code. SSL is also used for transmitting secure email, secure files, and other forms of information. It encompasses the security areas of:

Authentication and verification: The SSL certificate has information about the authenticity of certain details regarding the identity of a person, business or website, which it will display to visitors on your website when they click on the browser's padlock symbol or trust mark. The vetting criteria used by certificate authorities to determine if an SSL certificate should be issued is most stringent with an extended validation (EV) SSL certificate: making it the most trusted SSL certificate available.

Data encryption: The SSL certificate also enables encryption, which means that the sensitive information exchanged via the website cannot be intercepted and read by anyone other than the intended recipient.

We have established the importance of security in maintaining HA of services in an organization.

Standby: It is used in various ways but when applied to clusters it means a node on *standby*, ready to take over the workload of a failing node in the cluster. In essence, it is another word for redundancy. The usual modes of cluster *standby* are outlined below but some can be applied to redundant configurations.

Cold standby: The secondary cluster node acts as backup of another identical primary system. It will be installed and configured only when the primary node breaks down for the first time. Subsequently, in the case of a failure in the primary, the secondary node is powered on and the data restored before finally starting the failed component. Data from primary system can be backed up on a storage system and restored on secondary system as and when required. Recovery times here will be measured in hours or even days.

Warm standby: The software component is installed and available on the secondary node. The secondary node is up and running. In the case of a failure on the primary node, these software components are started on the secondary node. This process is usually automated using a cluster manager. Data are regularly mirrored to secondary system using disk based replication or shared disk. Recovery times will be of the order of a few minutes.

Hot standby: Software components are installed and available on both primary and secondary nodes. The software components on the secondary system are up but will not process data or requests. Data are mirrored in near real time and both systems will have identical data. Data replication is typically done through the software's capabilities and usually provides a recovery time of a few seconds.

Active–active (load balanced): In this method, both the primary and secondary systems are active and processing requests in parallel. Data replication happens through software capabilities and would be bidirectional. If the systems involved are remote, extremely fast communication is required to maintain synchronicity. This generally provides a recovery time that is almost instantaneous.

STONITH: To ensure a failed system does not participate in future cluster activity, STONITH (*shoot the offending node in the head*) is sometimes employed as a *fencing* or *mercy killing* mechanism in cluster management.

Storage efficiency (RAID): It is the percentage of the disk space available which can be used for data, the rest being taken by parity and ECC *data*, which is essentially metadata. It may or may not include space for contingency.

Survival probability (t): It is the probability that a component does not fail in the time interval $(0,t)$. Units of t will usually be of the order of magnitude of MTBF/MTTF.

System: "A system is a collection of components, subsystems and/or assemblies arranged to a specific design in order to achieve desired functions with acceptable performance and reliability. The types of components, their quantities, their qualities, and the manner in which they are arranged within the system have a direct effect on the system's reliability.

The relationship between a system and its components is often misunderstood or oversimplified. For example, the following statement is not valid: *All the components in a system have a 90% reliability at a given time, thus the reliability of the system is 90% for that time.* Unfortunately, poor understanding of the relationship between a system and its constituent components can result in statements like this being accepted as factual, when in reality they are false."

For reference, see http://reliawiki.com/index.php/Basics_of_System_Reliability_Analysis.

Time: It is a fundamental property of the universe that ensures everything doesn't happen at once. It is also useful as the horizontal axis, symbol t or T, in many of the graphs in this and other books. It has no substitute and is not a renewable or repairable resource.

TOGAF: It refers to The Open Group Architectural Framework. This is intended to provide a structured approach for organizations seeking to organize and govern their implementation of technology, particularly software technology. In that sense, its objective is to employ an encompassing conceptual framework to try to ensure that software development projects meet business objectives, that they are systematic and that their results are repeatable. TOGAF was created and is maintained by The Open Group, an independent industry association. It builds on an earlier framework known as TAFIM, or Technical Architecture Framework for Information Management, originally devised by the US Defense Department.

An overview and list of publications for TOGAF 9.1 can be found at http://pubs.opengroup.org/architecture/togaf9-doc/arch/.

Transaction processing: See *OLTP.*

Traceroute: This command allows the determination of the path a packet takes in order to get to a destination from a given source by returning the sequence of *network hops* the packet has traversed. The utility normally comes with the host OS (e.g., Linux or Microsoft Windows), as well as with other software (see *ping*). It can be useful in problem determination of networks to discover what route has been taken by failed transmissions.

Traffic shaping: It is the practice of regulating network data transfer to assure a certain level of performance, QoS, or return on investment. It is sometimes known as *packet shaping*. The practice involves delaying the flow of packets that have been designated as less important or less desired than those of prioritized traffic streams. This is a one way of ensuring that services that are critical or have stringent SLAs receive the necessary resources at the expense of other, less important services or applications.

Regulating the flow of packets into a network is known as *bandwidth throttling*. Regulation of the flow of packets out of a network is known as *rate limiting*.

Transient errors: These are sometimes called *soft* errors, occurring mainly in hardware. They include faults caused by random events that affect computer circuits such as power surges, alpha particles, static electricity, cosmic radiation, other sources of random noise, and extraneous electromagnetic radiation. Soft errors are most common in memory modules but can occur on memory and I/O buses. They can, on detection, be corrected by ECC and checksum validation, for example, CRC (q.v.).

Permanent (hard) errors require the component to be replaced to resume operations except in cases where redundancy is employed. It is replaced or repaired to maintain the redundancy and hence availability characteristics.

Triple modular redundancy (TMR): It is a fault-tolerant technique often used for avoiding errors in integrated circuits. The TMR scheme uses three identical logic blocks performing the same task in tandem with corresponding outputs being compared through majority voters (see Lesson 9 in Appendix 4).

Unplanned outage: This is typically caused by a failure causing the loss of a service or application. It is possible to recover from some unplanned outages (such as disk failure, server failure, power failure, program failure, human error, or *Acts of God*) if you have an adequate backup strategy and built-in system redundancy. However, an unplanned outage that causes a complete system loss, such as that caused by a tornado or fire, requires you to have a detailed DR plan in place in order to recover.

*Uninterruptible power supply (UPS):** Not just a bank of batteries, contrary to popular opinion. An UPS differs from an auxiliary or emergency power system or standby generator

---

* See Wikipedia http://en.wikipedia.org/wiki/Uninterruptible_power_supply.

in that it will provide near-instantaneous protection from input power interruptions, by supplying energy stored in *batteries* or a *flywheel*. The batteries can usually only support the system for a matter of minutes until a more permanent power source comes into operation. UPS battery manufacturers sometimes claim lifetimes of 10 years, people who use them often say 5. There is a useful paper on this topic (http://searchdatacenter.techtarget.com/tip/Data-center-power-backup-isnt-just-about-batteries-anymore).

Vulnerability: It is an exposure to attack and possible compromise of a computer system or service. There are some definitions given below but it basically means that someone can *gatecrash* a private party because there are no doormen vetting people trying to enter.

ISO 27005 defines *vulnerability* as

> "A weakness of an asset or group of assets that can be exploited by one or more threats" where an asset is anything that can has value to the organization, its business operations, and their continuity, including information resources that support the organization's mission.

IETF RFC2828 defines *vulnerability* as

> "A flaw or weakness in a system's design, implementation, or operation and management that could be exploited to violate the system's security policy."

The Committee on National Security Systems of United States of America defined *vulnerability* in *CNSS* Instruction No. 4009 dated April 26, 2010, National Information Assurance Glossary:

> "Vulnerability—Weakness in an IS, system security procedures, internal controls, or implementation that could be exploited."

Many NIST publications define *vulnerability* in an IT contest in different ways: FISMApedia provides a list; NIST SP 800-30, give a broader one:

> "A flaw or weakness in system security procedures, design, implementation, or internal controls that could be exercised (accidentally triggered or intentionally exploited) and result in a security breach or a violation of the system's security policy."

There are other definitions but they and those above all say it is *gatecrashing*, in essence [http://en.wikipedia.org/wiki/Vulnerability_(computing)].

WAN acceleration: A wide area network (WAN) accelerator is an appliance that optimizes bandwidth to improve the end user's experience on a WAN. The appliance, which can be a physical hardware component, software program, or an appliance running in a virtualized environment, speeds up the time it takes for information to flow back and forth across the WAN by using compression and data deduplication techniques to reduce the amount of data that needs to be transmitted. Basically, an accelerator works by caching duplicate files or parts of files so they can be referenced instead of having to be sent across the WAN again. It is an adjunct to, and partially overlaps WAN optimization (q.v.).

WAN optimization: It is a collection of techniques for increasing data-transfer efficiencies across WANs. In 2008, the WAN optimization market was estimated to be $1 billion, and it will about $4.4 billion by 2014 according to the Gartner Group (see Chapter 11 for the techniques employed).

Wearout: It is the process that results in an increase of the failure rate or probability of failure with increasing number of *life units* (q.v) [MIL-STD-721].

XA interface: It is the bidirectional interface between a transaction manager (TM) and a resource manager (RM), for our purposes a database. It is not an ordinary application programming interface (API).

It is a system-level interface between distributed transaction processing (DTP) software components. This is an X/Open specification (http://pubs.opengroup.org/onlinepubs/009680699/toc.pdf).

XA+ interface: It is the DTP bidirectional interface between a TM and a communications resource manager (CRM). This is an X/Open specification (http://pubs.opengroup.org/onlinepubs/008057699/toc.pdf).

X/Open company limited: It is a part of The Open Group, an amalgam of the X/Open Company Ltd. and the Open Software Foundation (OSF). Older readers will remember OSF from the *UNIX Wars* of the late 1980s and early 1990s. DEC were early adopters of OSF's UNIX specification (http://www.opengroup.org/).

Zachman architecture: The framework is named after its creator John Zachman, who first developed the concept in the 1980s at IBM. It has been updated several times since its inception in the early 1980s.

The Zachman Framework is an enterprise architecture framework that provides a formal and highly structured way of viewing and defining an enterprise. It consists of a two dimensional classification matrix based on the intersection of six communication questions (What, Where, When, Why, Who, and How) with five levels, successively transforming the most abstract ideas (scope level) into more concrete ideas (at the operations level).

This framework is a schema for organizing architectural artifacts (in other words, design documents, specifications, and models) that takes into account both whom the artifact targets (e.g., business owner and builder) and what particular issue (e.g., data and functionality) is being addressed. The Zachman Framework is not a methodology in that it does not imply any specific method or process for collecting, managing, or using the information that it describes (http://en.wikipedia.org/wiki/Zachman_Framework).

Zulu principle: The idea of obtaining a great knowledge of a narrow subject, an idea developed from a book by Jim Slater on shares. "However, the term 'Zulu Principle,' the idea that it is easy to become an expert in any sufficiently narrow subject area, had been used in the manufacturing industry for at least 10 years before the publication of Slater's book" (Wikipedia).

My own knowledge of the real Zulu people tells me they have Zulu principles of their own. One of them is never to get to the point of a conversation too early—you must talk about anything but that, perhaps the weather or prices (in units of cattle) for a new wife.

Note: *Jabula fundela!* (Happy Learning—there is no Zulu for *reading* that I can find, only the *learning* substitute word). There is no way of reading an unwritten language.

Summary

The definitions and equations in this appendix are meant to provide a quick reference for readers of the book who temporarily forget a concept and need to pick it up again to progress. It is also part of the *immersion process* I believe will give people a more comfortable feeling when thrown in at the deep end of HA and told to swim.

In this appendix and throughout this book, I have tried to clarify some terms that are used loosely in the availability literature, particularly MTTF and MTBF. Some entries support topics in the body of the book, whereas others are standalone entries but with relevance to learning about *availability*.

Note: I truly feel that the way to progress in the availability world is to feel comfortable with the whole topic even if you do not intend to pursue parts of it, for example, software reliability. It would be nice to be able to answer the question from senior management *Can you give the team an overview of reliability and availability* with *Yes* rather than *Sorry, no, I only know about the hardware RAS of the left hand side of the Hokey Cokey 2000 Chip, boss.*

Appendix 2

He who wastes my time, steals my life.

Anon. but variations abound

Availability: MTBF/MTTF/MTTR Discussion

I think the following discussions are necessary because of the numbers of papers which proffer different interpretations of these times.

Most publications present the availability of a system as

$$A = \frac{MTTF}{MTTF+MTTR} \times 100\% = \frac{\text{interval between failures}}{\text{total operating time}} \times 100\% \qquad \text{(A2.1)}$$

Simple Availability Equation

Some authors replace the *MTTF* (mean time to failure) in the equation with MTBF (mean time between failures) but many do not clearly define what they mean by either. This is what I am attempting to do in this appendix.

The first (left hand) definition is simplistic and fails to distinguish between different component failures which have different times between occurrences (MTTF/MTBF) and different repair times (MTTR [mean time to repair]).[*] This means that recording outages needs to include the MTTF and MTTR for each type of error, which may help in tackling the worst *offenders*.

Interpretation of MTTR

The initials MTTR are used in different ways, depending on which document or book you consult. This section will hopefully clarify this without casting doubts upon the validity of any usage of MTTR.

---

[*] I am including diagnosis time (MTPD) in MTTR here.

373

MTTR (mean time to recover): This can mean the total time to eliminate the fault and return the system to normal operation. This will include
 – (Problem determination time) [*what happened, where, etc.*]
 – + (repair/replace time) [time to *fix* the error + any travel/search time]
 – + (time to normalize service) [*service ramp-up time*]

MTTR (mean time to repair): This can mean the total time to repair/replace the fault. In most cases, this should be read as MMTR(ecover) or MMTR(estoration) as above, in the absence of other parameters to specifically denote repair or replace and normalization or restoration as separate items. Otherwise, it may simply mean the repair time, the second item in MTTR above. However, MTTR can hide a multitude of hidden factors that we will discuss in due course.

The objective of achieving maximum availability is to minimize MTTR, which means minimizing the elements within it where possible. In doing so, we increase the MTTF, and availability is directly proportional to this. However, minimizing this recovery requires an understanding of what constitutes a recovery.

Figure A2.1 shows the components of the MTTR* from a *failure* to a *full recovery*.

This sounds pretty straightforward until one realizes that there needs to be some methodology to minimize 1 and tools, methods, and techniques to achieve low elapsed times for 2, 3, and 4.

> ***Note:*** As the astute reader will see, there is more to an outage than just sticking in a new part, which just happens to be handy, into the system. It needs planning and documenting and this is the reason I have adamantly stuck to emphasizing MTP(problem)D (discovery, determination) and spelling out MTTR (recovery).

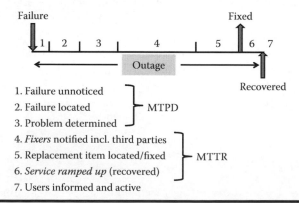

Figure A2.1 Elements of outage diagnosis and recovery times.

---

* See the end of this appendix for one significant variation in these time definitions (Forrester/Zenoss survey in Chapter 2).

Interpretation of MTTF

MTTF is a *reliability* engineering concept where it is calculated from the cumulative probability function for reliability $R(t)$. For a particular component this is a fixed quantity, given by the equation

$$\text{MTTF} = \int_0^t R(t)dt, \quad \text{where } R(t) = [1 - F(t)]$$

See the next section for a discussion of MTTF versus MTBF, vital to understanding or at least playing the reliability game *according to Hoyle*.

Interpretation of MTBF

MTBF can be read as meaning MTTF (as defined above) or, the *measured* time between failures for a component or application/system, depending on how the service level agreement (SLA) is phrased.

MTBF is normally defined as the mean time between the start of a downtime after failure to the start of the next failure. Another definition is the number of failures—the failure rate λ—in an interval divided by the number of units in that interval. In our case, that interval is time.

$$\lambda = \frac{N}{T} = \frac{N}{\sum \text{TBFs}} \quad \frac{1}{\text{MTBF}} \quad \text{since} \quad \frac{\sum \text{TBFs}}{N} = \text{MTBF}$$

(A2.2)

Failure Rate λ and MTBF

The time interval T is made up of the sum of all the times between failures, the TBFs, and the mean time, MTBF, is that sum divided by the number of failures in that interval, N.

Thus, if there are five failures of a component in 10 years, the failure rate is 0.5 per year or per 8,760 hours, then there are $5 \times 100,000/87,600 = 5.7$ failures per 100,000 hours, a common way of stating failures/time.

MTTF and MTBF—The Difference

It is appropriate at this point to further complicate matters by showing the difference between MTTF and MTBF. The MIL-HDBK-338B describes both terms with the same words except that MTTF is applied to *nonrepairable* components and MTBF to *repairable* components. The words *life units* in these definitions refer to the relevant elapsed *unit*—time, cycles, miles, rotations, and so on. For the record, these definitions are as follows (italics are mine used for emphasis):

MTBF: A basic measure of reliability of *repairable items.* The mean number of life units during which all parts of the item perform within their specified limits, during a particular measurement interval under stated conditions [MIL-HDBK-338B].

MTTF: A basic measure of reliability for *nonrepairable items.* The total number of life units of an item population divided by the number of failures within that population, during a particular interval under stated conditions [MIL-HDBK-338B].

MTTF when applied to a nonrepairable unit is a single occurrence of failure because the unit is then totally disabled. The mean value means nothing for a single value. The only time of note after that is the MTTD—mean time to total disintegration. The only way to get a mean time to failure is to take the first failure time across a population of identical nonrepairable units and calculate the mean value. This first failure time is often called MTTFF—mean time to first (and in the case of nonrepairable units, the last) failure.

Another interpretation from other sources is shown in Figure A2.2 where MTTF is the time from end of recovery of failure 1 to the start of failure 2 and MTBF is the time from the start of failure 1 to the start of failure 2. If the *diagnosis* + *recovery* time is short, then

$$\text{When MTBF} \gg \text{MTTR, MTBF} \approx \text{MTTF}(\approx \text{approximately equal to})$$

Even if this relationship is very often true, we still need to define exactly what we mean with these terms for the cases where this approximation is not true. A case in point is software where in testing and repair, they may well be equal to each other or even a case where repair time (MTTR) is greater than the MTTF.

The number of definitions extant can be a bit confusing but as long as you know what you mean and can express what you mean, then it shouldn't matter too much. Figure A2.2 illustrates the parameters MTTR and MTTR for three components of a hypothetical, very basic system. It also shows the situation where each of the elements in the system fails but not all at the same time.

The elements—server, network, and disks—represent a *series* of components comprising a *system*. The diagram after that shows the same configuration with times appended.

The overall availability here will be given by…whose law…?

In the two diagrams above, MTxx is shorthand for the quantities MTBF, MTTF, and MTTR. Txx is shorthand for TTR, TTF, and TBF, single occurrences of the times MTxx for a single failure. xx figures are the mean values of a series of Txx figures.

The mean values (MTxx) are gained from the manipulation of multiple occurrences in the normal manner of calculating a mean.

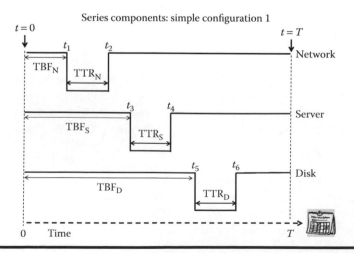

Figure A2.2 Serial device system and availability.

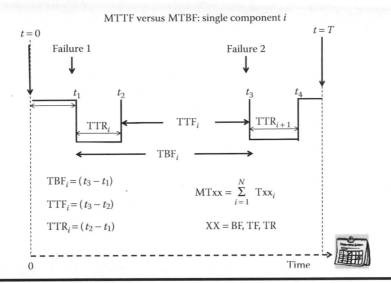

MTTF versus MTBF: single component i

$$TBF_i = (t_3 - t_1)$$

$$TTF_i = (t_3 - t_2)$$

$$TTR_i = (t_2 - t_1)$$

$$MTxx = \sum_{i=1}^{N} Txx_i$$

$$XX = BF, TF, TR$$

Figure A2.3   Schematic showing MTTR, MTTF, and MTBF.

Figure A2.3 shows the following:

- The network failing at time t_1 remaining down until time t_2, MTTR $= (t_2 - t_1)$
- The disks failing at time t_3 remaining down until time t_4, MTTR $= (t_4 - t_3)$
- The server failing at time t_5 remaining down until time t_6, MTTR $= (t_6 - t_5)$

MTTR: Ramp-Up Time

Also note that the time that service is recovered $\neq$ (*not equal to*) the time system is recovered because a *ramp-up time* is often needed after the *system* components are recovered.

This may be short enough to be ignored in some cases, but not in others such as recovery of a data set or file. Figure A2.4 illustrates this idea and remember, ramp-up time can exceed the fix time and therefore needs attention in design, planning, and operations and in devising SLAs. See item 6 in Figure A2.1.

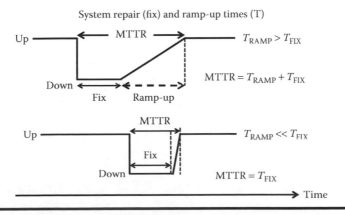

System repair (fix) and ramp-up times (T)

$T_{RAMP} > T_{FIX}$

$MTTR = T_{RAMP} + T_{FIX}$

$T_{RAMP} \ll T_{FIX}$

$MTTR = T_{FIX}$

Figure A2.4   Illustration of ramp-up time in MTTR.

Serial Blocks and Availability—NB

The formula (see Figure A2.3) hides an issue when we consider a system composed of serial devices with different MTBFs and MTTRs.

$$A = \frac{\text{MTTF}}{\text{MTTF} + \text{MTTR}} = \frac{\text{MTTF}}{\text{MTBF}}$$

(A2.3)

Availability in Terms of MTTR, MTTF, and MBTF

Figure A2.5 shows a *system* composed of a network, a server, and some disks attached. The diagram is not to scale but illustrates the situation, probably the real one, where failures in the component parts occur independently and have a different MTBF and MTTR. Note that MTTR here is representing *diagnose + fix + ramp-up* time, essentially *mean time to recover*, which covers both these elements.

Let us put some numbers in for the various values of *t* and *a* value for *T*, our period of observation—see Figure A2.5. Applying the traditional definition of availability (*A*) leads us to three separate availabilities for the network, the disks, and the server. We *cannot* add the MTBFs together because that is meaningless but we can add the outage times together to get the non-availability *N* of the whole system. We can then get the availability *A* from the fact that $A = (1 - N)$.

Look at the previous diagram. In this case,

$$\text{Outage time} = 2 + 3 + 4 = 9 \, \text{units (Easy, even for me)}$$

Operational time? A bit more difficult.

We can use 470 as this or even 550, because in either time interval only one failure (on average) will be experienced by the three components of our simple system.

The units of time used are arbitrary. Call them seconds, hours, or days because it is a ratio we are concerned with, not absolute units. In the terminology of the MIL-documents, this is called a *life unit* (see Terminology in Appendix 1).

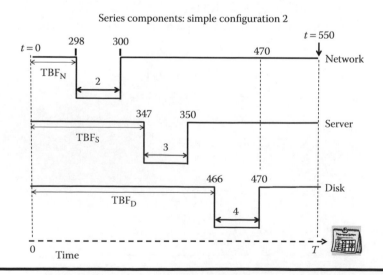

Figure A2.5 Failures in a simple serial system.

> **Remember:** These are *means* and not *precise* figures. Decisions should not be based on their *exactness* as they have a variation about this mean, both from a theoretical viewpoint and in a measurement environment.

Typical MTBF Figures

Manufacturers rarely publish MTBF figures, although they might be available internally. This does not mean they are hiding anything as MTBF numbers can mislead if the recipient is not *au fait* with what we are discussing in this section.

Intel publications list a table of MTBF estimates for a server board and other items which is given in Table A2.1.*

For the published example of a Cisco motherboard, if in Figure A2.6 $\lambda_A = 25°C$, then the MTBF = 335,000 hours, whereas if $\lambda_B = 40°C$, then the MTBF = 165,000 hours—λ_x is the failure rate at temperature *x*.

The MTBFs of the *fan* and *power supplies* for this component are equal to or much greater than the server board. If they were much less, theirs might be the most important figures to consider in assessing reliability. Incidentally, the server board has three cooling fans so the calculation here would be *2 from 3 or 1 from 3 adequate to maintain a working temperature?*

Table A2.1   Real MTBF Numbers for Various Components

Intel Component	MTBF (Hours)
SRCSAS144E RAID controller	449,784
SASMF8I RAID controller	1,031,587
SATA solid-state drive	1,200,000
S1200BTL server board	172,199[a]
Fan	206,885
Power supply	619,607

Note: Also see 2011 Thermal Guidelines for Data Processing Environments ASHRAE TC 9.9 for failure/temperature variation *data* (http://www.eni.com/green-data-center/it_IT/static/pdf/ASHRAE_1.pdf) and (http://www.thegreengrid.org/en/Global/Content/white-papers/WP50-Data Center Efficiency and IT Equipment Reliability at Wider Operating Temperature and Humidity Ranges), which contains a *graph* of failure probability versus temperature.

[a] Varies with ambient air temperature. Temperature is a sensitive factor and changing it by 10°C can cause something like a factor of 2 change in failure rate (see Figure A2.6, a schematic taken from *NASA Technical Memorandum 4322* [TM-4322] relating to electrical junctions).

---

* http://www.intel.com/content/www/us/en/search.html?keyword=mtbf.

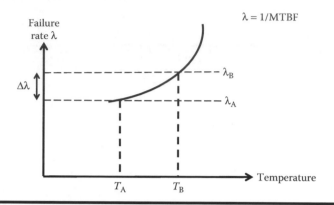

Figure A2.6   Effect of temperature on MTBF.

To give a perspective to these numbers, there are 8,760 hours in a year so in most cases we are talking about MTBFs in terms of several years. For example, the Hitachi 73 GB drive (2005) quoted an MTBF of 1,400,000 power-on hours (160 years).

Heaven knows how long the MTBF would be if it wasn't switched on!

There are a number of other, more detailed tables in this and other documents which, if nothing else, give a feel for the sorts of numbers we are dealing with when talking about MTBF.[*]

Some reliability tools request MTBF figures to perform certain calculations so you need to be aware of the typical numbers involved, otherwise your results may be compromised.

Gathering MTTF/MTBF Figures

Note: One thing that must be remembered is that MTxx (mean) figures are usually for a *component* and not always a *system*. The system will have its own numbers from which to deduce MTxx values. The mean of figures for a system is not the mean of the component means because the mean of A + the mean of B is not always equal to the mean of (A + B).

Outage Records and MTTx Figures

Sometimes an organization (NASA) will collect, record, and analyze large numbers of MTTx figures for prediction purposes. A record of outages might look in skeletal form as follows (and can be as detailed as the organization needs to support its SLAs) (Table A2.2):

Note (1): These classifications should drop out of the RCA if they are not immediately obvious. There may be culprits in these outages other than the obvious *smoking gun*.

Note (2): There must be a baseline for these hours, usually the last failure of this type and time is measured from there. Vertical totals for these MTTF numbers are meaningless

---

[*] In my experience, other vendors are less forthcoming with statistics of this kind.

Table A2.2   Assigning MTxx Times to Different Failures

Failure Type (1)	MTTF (2) (Hours)	MTTR (3) (Hours)	RCA and Notes (4)
Network adapter	13,500	1	Failed-replaced
Firewall *alpha*	21,460	2	Switched to *beta*
Database	n/a	9	Recovered from log
Total		12	

Note: The numbers in the parentheses represents Note (1)–Note (4).

but cumulative totals for individual failure types are not. The numbers in this example are chosen at random and do not represent any manufacturer's figures.

Note (3): The cumulative totals for these should be separate or they may hide a *rogue* failure type. Vertical totals for these MTTR numbers are meaningful as are cumulative totals for individual failure types.

Note (4): RCA should indicate where action to prevent reoccurrence should be taken and what changes to operating procedures are needed to second guess such failures in the future.

Documentation should be available for known or previous errors if the enterprise has a *war room* approach to system failures (see Chapter 10). If these things are not documented, it will be hard to

- Report back to the end users on SLA performance.
- Prevent or anticipate these failures in the future, where possible.
- Learn from the errors and reduce the MTPD (diagnosis) and MTTR (fix) times.
- Show due professionalism.

MTTF and MTTR Interpretation

MTTF versus Lifetime

It is often confusing when an MTTF is quoted as a certain time when the lifetime of that component is many times that MTTF. If a component has an MTTF of 500,000 hours only fails after 57 years (there are 8,760 hours in a year) yet the manufacturer states a lifetime of say 5 years, who is telling the truth?

The answer is that MTTF (and MTTR) are statistical measures derived from a large population so that, for example, in a population of 100 components we should expect a fault every 0.57 years.

This assumes that the failures are independent meaning a failure in one does not cause a failure in another. For a nonrepairable component any "mean" times do not mean anything since the component is rendered inoperable after the first failure. However, the MTTF (or MTTFF mean time to first failure) does have a meaning over a population of identical nonrepairable components. See the end of this appendix for a significant variation in this *time* terminology.

Some MTxx Theory

Repairable systems or components have two basic quantities apart from the *mean* times we have discussed, relating to failures:

- The failure rate λ
- The repair rate μ

(The output of many reliability equations depend on the choice of distribution. For a nonrepairable system or component, there is no μ.)

The effective failure rate, given we are repairing as we go along, is then $(\lambda - \mu)$.

The following equations then hold for the availability of the component in its usual form and then translated into two functions of λ and μ:

$$A(t) = \frac{\mu}{\lambda + \mu} + \frac{\lambda}{\lambda + \mu} e^{-(\lambda + \mu)t}$$

(A2.4)

Instantaneous or Point Availability

$$A_S(t \Rightarrow \infty) = \frac{\mu}{\lambda + \mu}$$

(A2.5)

Steady-State Availability

On the corresponding graphs, the equation for $A(t)$ is an exponentially decreasing curve asymptotic to the steady state line given by Equation A2.5.

In theory, it does not reach this line until infinity but in practice it reaches a number we can use in component reliability calculations long before then (we haven't got the time to wait until infinity).

> **Note:** A detailed reference for this theory can be found in MIL-HDBK-338B and whose contents are outlined in Appendix 5.

MTBF/MTTF Analogy

Imagine the king of Fatland and consider his meals in the daytime. He eats a five-course lunch 12 noon to 2 pm and then a seven-course evening meal starting at 6 pm and ending at 8 pm. What is his MTBM (mean time between meals)? I would say 6 hours (12 noon to 6 pm), whereas his MTT(N)M (mean time to next meal) is 4 hours (2 pm to 6 pm), that is 4 hours from the end of the previous meal. Q.E.D.

Final Word on MTxx

In the reliability/availability literature, much of which I have referred to, there are various definitions and understandings of MTBF, MTTF, MTTFF, and so on. It is possible to have different interpretations of them as long as

- You will preferably draw a diagram similar to those in this Appendix in any discussion/dispute.
- You and everyone else you are addressing agree on the terms.*

---

* This would be equivalent of saying *"According to Hoyle"* before a game of cards.

■ You understand that, however, the terms are used that the availability, expressed as either a decimal or a percentage, is given by the following relationship:

$$\text{Availability} = \frac{\text{time operating}}{\text{time operating} + \text{time down}}$$

As long as we can agree on what *time down* encompasses, we do not have a problem. I believe it should cover problem determination, recover/fix/replace, and ramp-up to normal operations. In this case, you can call the components what you will, with whatever abbreviations you desire, as long as they cover these areas.

In non-numeric terms, the availability of a component/system/service will be a function of the following questions:

■ How often a component fails?
■ How quickly failures can be isolated?
■ How quickly failures can be repaired, replaced, or switched?
■ How long logistics delays, especially time-consuming travel, contribute to downtime?
■ How often preventative measures are taken, for example, in replacements, using a more reliable redundant component?

Forrester/Zenoss MTxx Definitions

The Forrester/Zenoss paper referenced in Chapter 2 uses significantly different terms for the times we have discussed in this book and Appendix as follows:[*]

■ Mean time to resolution (MTTR)
■ Mean time to identify (MTTI) [*Problem determination*]
■ Mean time to know (MTTK) [*Find source of the problem*]
■ Mean time to fix (MTTF)
■ Mean time to verify (MTTV) [*Ramp-up time*]

In the paper, the following *equation* is offered:

$$MTTR = MTTI + MTTK + MTTF + MTTV$$

This does not clash with what we have discussed in this appendix and in various places in this book. In fact, it supports the breakdown we have seen, involving spotting a problem, determining where and what it is, repairing it and ramping up the system to full operating specification. Other papers gloss over the composition of the *resolution* time and this masks the need for tools and action in each component time in this period.

Just one factor is missing in all definitions and erudite discussions of these *times*—MTUD, the mean time to update documentation, forgotten by everyone except us.

Remember, *Those who fail to learn from history are doomed to repeat its mistakes*, and we wouldn't want that, would we?

---

[*] This would be equivalent of saying *'According to Hoyle'* before a game of cards.

Summary

The voluminous literature on the subject of reliability is, in the main, consistent in its treatment of the various concepts involved. An exception, I feel, is that of mean times related to failures of items or components where definitions, and even equations differ from paper to paper. I have set out my stall above which some will agree with and some won't.

From my perspective, it doesn't really matter in the long run as long as the definitions and the resulting equations arrive at the fact that availability is the time an component/system is operating (functioning) according to specification divided by the time it is supposed to be operating (functioning) in that mode.

> *Note:* On the subject of MTTF and MTBF, I have *nailed my colors to the mast* as follows:

- *MTTR*, the mean time to repair, is the average time over multiple repairs of a component/system population to recognize, locate, diagnose, fix, and restore to operational capability any failures that take place in them.
- *MTTF*, the mean time to failure, is the average time between the end of *recovery* of one failure to the *start* of the following failure.
- *MTBF*, the mean time between failures, is the average time from the *start* of one failure to the start of the following one and is composed of the MTTF plus the MTTR.

This is illustrated in Figure A2.7 *for a single component, hence the absence of the* M *for* mean *in the diagram legend. Much of the literature I have consulted agrees with me (or vice versa).*

The *mean* values of these times over N failures are then given by

$$\text{MTTR} = \frac{\sum \text{TTR}_i}{N}, \ \text{MTBF} = \frac{\sum \text{TBF}_i}{N}, \ \text{MTTF} = \frac{\sum \text{TTF}_i}{N} \quad (A2.6)$$

Numeric Summary of MTBF, MTTF, and MTTR

TTR_i, TBF_i, and TTF_i are the individual values of the times *to repair, between failures*, and *to failures*, summed over the values $i = 1$ to N, where N is the number of failures.

Remember, TTR is made up of several elements but going down to the level of calculating mean values for each one is probably counter-productive.

Support for this interpretation of MTTF and MTBF comes from the book *Software Testing and Quality Assurance* (Wiley) jointly produced by NEC and University of Waterloo in its

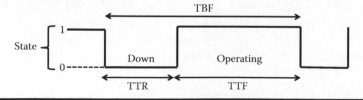

Figure A2.7   Summary and refresher of individual failure times.

Figure 15.1, which relates to these times in the context of software failures. See http://www.soft-waretestinggenius.com/download/staqtpsn.pdf.

And finally... A word from an expert on downtime and broken systems:

When I use a word, it means exactly what I mean it to mean, no more and no less.

Humpty Dumpty (MTTF unknown, MTTR infinite)

Appendix 3

To err is human, to goof twice is a dismissing offence.

Modified proverb

Your HA/DR Route Map and Kitbag

Road to HA/DR

Why are we raising this here and not earlier in the book? Well, I feel that anyone involved in this needs to learn about availability and feel comfortable with the theory, practice, and management disciplines and techniques … then go for it. This is why I've said you should feel your way to a tailored solution to suit your organization. Hopefully, that knowledge and comfort will be aided by this book.

The Stages

There are, as I see it, five main stages in the design of an HA/DR (high availability/disaster recovery) environment where the status of either or both is close to zero on a sliding scale (see Figure A1.5).

Select your team first, then tackle the following, using appropriate management methods and techniques as per Chapter 7:

- Concept and requirements stage
- Design and evaluation stage
- Implementation stage(s)
- Operations stage
- Review and feedback stage

We will look at these former stages as the yardstick for developing both situations of status between 0 and, say, 8 in a little more detail. We will often use flow diagrams in showing these stages. Such diagrams explain things better, show a perspective, and tend to stick in the mind better than dull prose.* If you know it all, please skip to the next major section on total cost of ownership (TCO).

---

* You will by now know my feelings about IT articles which do not have clear diagrams in them, particularly those dealing with networks.

Concept and Design Stages

The flow I envisage for these stages is shown in Figure A3.1, the elements of which are numbered for discussion. The flow includes costs, delta in the case of modification, and risks which come out of any design and implementation.

There is an old saying, normally attributed to the Irish: "Sure if I was going there, I wouldn't be setting off from here!" Unfortunately, in this arena everyone has to start from where they are today and the assessment of that position may not be straightforward.

An *A point* assessment is a review of the HA and DR capabilities of the existing system and this is illustrated graphically in the figure above. How do we do this? To be honest, unless you are fully *au fait* with the subject it may be better to ask a suitable third party to do the assessment for you. Take a look at Figure A3.1 to illustrate the problem semiquantitatively.

1. An example of assessment services on offer can be found at http://2secure.biz/cyber-security-services/disaster-recovery-assessment-drp/. It gives an idea of scope for a DR assessment but does not constitute a recommendation.
2. An article called "If Only I Had Known" at the URL (http://www.disasterrecovery.org/disaster_recovery_knowledge.html) has some salutary observations about DR and attitudes to it.
3. Another article, entitled "Risk Assessment for High Availability," gives a useful insight into areas of concern in HA situations (http://www.rkeytec.com/Pages4/Risk.aspx?track = Customers).

In addition, a suitable search either cross-Internet or at specific vendor sites will yield service offerings on HA assessment. I know there are a couple of such services offered by Oracle and IBM.

The Route in Detail

Use Figure A3.2 as a guide to following the steps outlined here. You may choose to use your own company's methods and techniques or the set outlined in Chapter 7 under Management: The Project—Project Definition Workshop (PDW), FMEA, CFIA, War Room, FRACAS, and the Delphi technique. In addition, there are some *best practices* laid out, especially for change management.

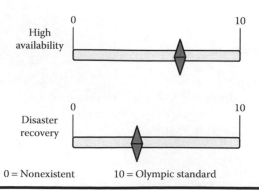

Figure A3.1 Sample assessment of organization's HA/DR status.

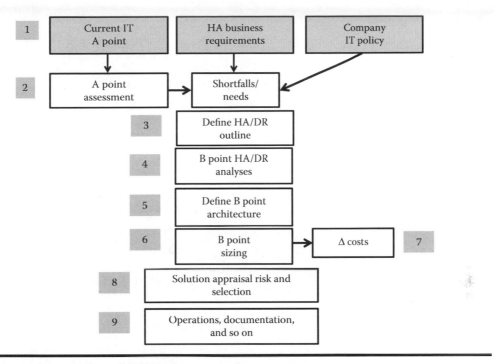

Figure A3.2 DR setup and design stages.

This is the *Kit Bag* in the title to this appendix.

- *Item 1:* This features three boxes representing an assessment of the current IT setup regarding HA and DR (as separate items initially), the business requirements (SLAs) for HA/DR and IT company policy, for example, *Policy 12: z/OS or Linux over my dead body* or similar. It is assumed we have done this or had it done. We now have an A point description (PDW-speak).
- *Item 2:* We have either done or had done an A point (today) assessment and need to fill in the *shortfalls* and other considerations from Item 1 to produce a composite list of what needs remediation and what needs to be added for the HA and DR plans. This is hard work.
- *Item 3:* This step defines in outline the *two plans*—HA and DR, remembering that DR depends very much on the HA setup for its recovery data.
- *Item 4:* This step comprises the detailed work on the components (or blocks) of the two solutions—reliability block diagrams (RBDs), calculations, system *domains*, and so on. This is hard work.
- *Item 5:* The fifth step is a definition of the B point architecture and solid documentation. This should be in a format that will enable people to perform a walkthrough if necessary to check the system and identify unidentified single points of failure (SPoFs) and *gotchas*. The B point is the project *launch pad*.
- *Item 6:* The system(s) configurations should now be in a state that sizing and resources requirements can be estimated.

- *Item 7:* The system(s) configurations should now be in a state that costings can be performed, at least in outline if a vendor is not chosen by now. If existing equipment is being reused, the costings will be a *delta* CaPEX on the existing spend.
- *Item 8:* A solution and risk appraisal will cover a check of the system and the agreement of the end users as to the projected service levels which will be provided—uptime, performance, recovery times ,and anything else agreed in meeting business requirements. [Use the *Delphi technique?*]
- *Item 9:* This takes us into the implementation phase of the project.

Note: The implementation details and effort for the DR site will depend on whether the site is to be *cold, warm,* or *hot.* This decision will also have an impact on the connecting network that will carry the backup/replicated data to and from the primary and secondary (DR) sites.

Implementation Stage

The details of an implementation plan are very specific to a business and its requirements, and no attempt is made here to give chapter and verse on the subject. However, there are some useful sources of information that might aid any implementation plan involving HA and DR. These are sketched out subsequently.

HA Server Implementation—There may be delta implementations to the primary system in areas of redundancy, backup, and so on. There could be either a new system for DR (secondary) or a delta on an existing one deemed inadequate for the DR task designed. Talk to your server vendor but take a look at the IBM Redbook (http://www.redbooks.ibm.com/redbooks/pdfs/sg246769.pdf). It has a lot of generic planning material in its 746 pages that you may find useful.

There is also a Microsoft document that covers the ground in the DR area which could be useful to a DR planner and implementer (http://www.microsoft.com/en-us/download/details.aspx?id = 28373).

HA/DR Network Implementation—For HA/DR network implementation, see the Cisco document at http://www.cisco.com/en/US/docs/solutions/Verticals/EttF/ch6_EttF.html, which is quite detailed. Although it features diagrams with Cisco-labeled products, the underlying ideas are probably applicable to other network devices. It makes sense to implement the network solution to cater for both HA and DR at the same time.

Operations Stage

This stage, like the one above, is IT department-specific and no attempt is made here to teach grandmother to suck eggs. Needless to say, operations and operations procedures will be altered in line with HA/DR requirements that are over and above normal production needs. Just one point to make and that is the procedures can cause more outages than they prevent if not constructed and tested properly.

There will also be a shift in the requirements placed on system monitoring and reporting for both internal IT and the business users (customers, in essence).

Education will almost certainly be required for this new environment and that should become apparent as the specifications are developed (don't forget to budget for it).

Testing is the big bugbear of DR and that is beyond the scope of this book. Unless you are well up in the subject, seek objective advice. Its successful use can save the company pain or, in the worst case, oblivion.

Review/Modification Stage

This stage of any project is the one that gets skipped in the euphoria of completion. In essence, it is a detailed review of the statement *Did we deliver what we said we would and does it fit the users requirements?* and should take place soon after initial implementation or even before.

The *designed* or *delivered* requirements can be summarized under the headings:

■ Functionality delivered and SLA compliance record
■ Overall *performance* of the system—output of various monitoring activities and do they tell us what we need to know—if not, fix it
■ A plan for any enhancements and modifications needed
■ A schedule and agenda for ongoing reviews of the system(s)

Remember: A stitch in time saves nine.

A Short DR Case Study

This is a short rundown of the DR planning and implementation of the DR system at *De Paul Catholic University** in the United States. DePaul was founded in 1898 and is the largest Catholic University in the United States with 23,000 students and 4,000 faculty and staff. It is based in Chicago. The sequence of events leading to their new DR plan was as follows:

■ Previous DR efforts were minimal and were centered around mainframe operations.
■ The plan was updated for Y2000 compliance and they contracted for a hot site but no exercising/testing was done.
■ An IT review was prompted by the move from mainframe to PeopleSoft.
■ The 9/11 disaster prompted further DR scrutiny.
■ The university took steps to update the DR plan:
   – Revision of DR Planning team
   – Production of wallet-sized [DR] cards
   – Verified mission critical business applications
   – Performed a data, hardware, and software inventory
   – Updated processes and procedures
■ The university evaluated three hot site vendors and selected SunGard as a sole vendor based on specific criteria.
■ Obtained executive support and funding, partly based on the downsides of *not* having a workable DR plan.
■ Ran DR tests and reviewed and updated procedures where necessary.

---

* For reference, see http://net.educause.edu/ir/library/powerpoint/CMR0302.pps (*DePaul kindly gave permission to use this material as a case study*).

- Issued final recommendations:
  - Testing is key: IT, evacuation, communications
  - Collaboration with other departments
  - Use business impact analysis (BIA)
  - Analyzed all hot site options [*architecture*]
  - Obtain certification
  - Use consultants/experts
- Network other universities for their experiences.

It is critical to involve stakeholders across your organization so that you can identify what your real priorities are and get sign off from them to verify those priorities. Lastly, without some method of testing you will never know what type of problems or issues you may have and if you truly can recover.

HA and DR: Total Cost of Ownership

TCO Factors

TCO tries to quantify the financial impact of deploying an information technology product over its lifecycle. These technologies include software and hardware, and training. Technology deployment can include the following as part of TCO, remembering that retrofit costing will be a *delta* on *ab initio*[*] costs:

- Computer hardware and programs
  - Network hardware and software [*include monitoring software and its handling by personnel*]
  - Server hardware and Workstation hardware and software [*as above*]
- Costs of extra disks for RAID, taking account of the storage efficiency of the chosen RAID level(s) and including $N + 1$ and contingency storage
  - Installation and integration of hardware and software [*remember internal costs are just as real as buying-in resources*]
  - Purchasing research
- Availability research, design, and planning
  - Warranties and licenses [*vital to have software and hardware cover over the HA operational period*]
  - License tracking—compliance
  - Migration expenses [*this applies especially to retro-fitting*]
  - Risks—susceptibility to vulnerabilities, availability of upgrades, patches and future licensing policies [*this is really contingency costing, part of Business DR*]
- Cost of hardware redundancy, especially RAID, depending on capacity required and RAID level implemented (Figure A3.3)
- Operational expenses
  - Infrastructure (floor space) [*for new or retrofit exercises*]
  - Electricity (for related equipment, cooling, backup power) [*redundancy will add to these costs for retrofit*]
  - Testing costs [*these can be huge*]
  - Downtime, outage, and failure expenses

---

[*] Latin for *from the very beginning* as we have seen.

TCO and ΔTCO for availability projects
Δ = Extra retrofit cost over ordinary design O
AI = Cost of *ab initio* design

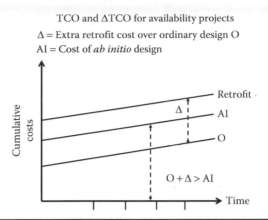

Figure A3.3   TCO scenarios—Schematic of costs.

   – Diminished performance (i.e., users having to wait, diminished money-making ability) [*see Webtorials discussion*]
   – Security (including breaches, loss of reputation, recovery, and prevention) [*plus operations training on any new malware software and SLA reporting*]
■ Development of SLAs
   – Backup and recovery process [*this covers normal BAU and recovery in DR mode but is not incurred until DR is invoked*]
   – Technology training [*remember operations excellence and liveware finger trouble*]
   – Audit (internal and external) [*this could be BAU and not attributable to availability*]
   – Insurance
   – Information technology personnel [*including overtime and travel in the ramp-up period*]
   – Corporate management time [*including training on SLAs and their buy-in for the availability project*]
■ DR/BC costs and any additional insurance for natureware failures
■ Long-term expenses
   – Replacement
■ Maintenance of DR sites (this is additional to the non-DR environment)
   – Future upgrade or scalability expenses and decommissioning

In the case of comparing TCO of existing versus proposed solutions, consideration should put toward the costs required to maintain the existing solution that may not necessarily be required for a proposed solution. Examples include cost of manual processing that is only required to support lack of existing automation and extended support personnel.

Cloud TCO

A crystal ball look by Gartner at the cost elements of cloud computing, dated July 2010, can be viewed in its glory at http://blog.wappwolf.com/wp-content/uploads/2010/11/Gartner-Cloud-lifecycle20101.jpg.

This visual model, a latter-day Nolan curve, shows if nothing else, that TCO is a function of time (t), like reliability $R(t)$, and desired functionality, especially in the XaaS arena.

TCO Summary

Agilent Technologies have proposed a summary model for TCO and this is outlined below:

$$\text{TCO} = C_{\text{acquisition+implementation}} + C_{\text{operations}}$$

$$\text{TCO} = C_{\text{acq}} + C_{\text{pm}} + C_{\text{cm}} + C_{\text{dm}} + C_{\text{tr}} + C_{\text{te}} + C_{\text{rv}} + C_{\text{oth}}$$

where:
- C_{pm} is the cost of preventative maintenance
- C_{cm} is the cost of corrective maintenance
- C_{dm} is the cost of downtime mitigation (*)
- C_{tr} is the cost of technology refresh
- C_{te} is the cost of training and education
- C_{rv} is the resale value or disposal costs
- C_{oth} is other costs
- C_{acq} is of course the cost of acquisition and initial implementation

The (*) in the above list indicates downtime mitigation cost. This cost is stated by Agilent as the cost of mitigating (eliminating) the effects of downtime. This includes a *high availability design* (the subject of this book), ease of maintenance (on-site repair, vendor service, local spares, etc.), and spare capacity in case it is needed.

This model is essentially a design to implement and operate a system but does not include intangible costs/losses incurred by the enterprise when the system does fail, as Mr Murphy predicts it will.

> *Note:* One point here on CSFs (critical success factors) is that conventional wisdom in this area suggests that cost is a *constraint* not a *CSF*.

See Appendix 5 for further references about practical TCO scenarios.

Risk Assessment and Management

A wise man once said to a doubter of the value of his intense devotion to risk possibilities and their elimination or minimization: *you know son, the more risks I find, the luckier I get.*

> Risk is a measure of the extent to which an entity is threatened by a potential circumstance or event, and typically a function of: (i) the adverse impacts that would arise if the circumstance or event occurs: and (ii) the likelihood of occurrence.
>
> Information system-related security risks are those risks that arise from the loss of confidentiality, integrity, or availability of information or information systems and reflect the potential adverse impacts to organizational operations (including mission, functions, image, or reputation), organizational assets, individuals, other organizations, and possibly the Nation.

[NIST 800-30]

You will see by the last phrase of the previous statement that you carry an enormous responsibility on your shoulders—don't let your country down by not factoring *risk* into the HA/DR deliberations.

Who Are the Risk Stakeholders?

There are several categories of people who should be involved in any risk analysis and action plan given as follows:

■ Executives, managers, and, above all, the sponsors, who are the decision makers and removers of nontechnical hurdles
■ Project leader and team who are doing the design, implementation, operations, and subsequent review plans
■ Clients who can indicate their level of risk tolerance and expectations (SLAs)
■ Vendors and other third parties involved who can highlight any risks and considerations associated with their products and services

Risk management is, or should be, a hot topic in today's IT environments.

> ***Note:*** It is not a one-off exercise but an ongoing task throughout the project and afterward.

Where Are the Risks?

There are two broad areas you need to consider as posing risk:

1. The *project* itself. If it fails to deliver a *fit for purpose* system then it's game over.
2. The *deliverables* themselves. There is the possibility that even though they (the system) are designed and implemented well, they can still be at risk of failure due to some outside force or agency. This includes the risks to the security and integrity of the system from outside influences.

> ***Note:*** In all these areas, there needs to be a *risk assessment* and a *risk management* plan of action to handle the identified risks.

How Is Risk Managed?

Apart from ignoring any risk, there are at least four things you can do about them once they are identified and assessed for impact given as follows:

Mitigation: This is a common solution to risk where the flaw, when it occurs, is fixed or sidestepped in some way to reduce the likelihood and impact of it. A good example of mitigation is a software fix (patch).

Transference: This is the act of getting another party to accept risk on *your* behalf. We do this with car and other insurance deals.

Acceptance: This mode simply allows the system to function as planned with a known (identified) risk and take a chance.

Avoidance: This is the practice of removing the vulnerable aspect of the system via an alternative design or perhaps using redundancy.

Availability: Project Risk Management

Most items in the following checklists are phrased in such a way that a *Yes* is good and a *No* requires action. However, to avoid strangling the English language, this way of putting a question has not always been possible.

A subsequent section outlines a means of rating the *No(s)* for importance and developing an action plan to rectify shortfalls recognized.

Obviously, all answers will not be polarized around simple *Yes* and *No* and some *common sense* needs to be applied in rating them and taking action on them.

If you are wise, you will document the output of the assessment, the action plan and follow-up in case of later accusations of lack of due diligence if things go wrong, as Mr Murphy still predicts they will.

> *Note:* The probability of failure is probably inversely proportional to the amount of quality effort put into risk assessment and management.

I have made a sample analysis, based on personal experience, of the first section, User and Business Requirements, of the risk assessment questions with categories of the consequences of *No* answers to the questions posed as follows:

> *Note:* DoA, dead on arrival; NLS, needs life support; PG, possible *gotcha*

You may want to follow suit on the subsequent sections based on knowledge of your own particular circumstances.

User and Business Requirements

There is one reason, and one reason only, for implementing commercial IT solutions and that is business benefit. HA and DR are no exceptions. If it does not assist the end user to provide this benefit, the project may stagnate, lose the confidence of executives, or even die. There will certainly be no emulation in other areas of the business of such a poor solution.

User *expectations* and *requirements* are paramount to success and success yields business benefit.

1. Are there good lines of communication between users and IT (do they get on)? [NLS]
2. Is there a sponsor for the project? [DoA]
3. Is there an agreed business case? [NLS]
4. Are the user requirements understood, defined, and documented as in a PDW or equivalent methodology? [PG]

5. Are there, or will there be, SLAs in place with the users? [NLS]
6. Have the users defined and agreed the business benefits of the project? [PG]
7. Are the users and IT department in agreement on timescales?
8. Are the users aware of any working changes involved in the new system, for example, a new GUI interface, hours of work, new technology, and so on? [PG]
9. Is there a training/induction plan for users, especially new ones? [PG]
10. Have the user departments who will benefit from this project used IT before? [PG]
11. Can the system be implemented without major departmental changes or reorganizations? [DoA]
12. Are you confident that the vendor products and/or services will deliver what these users actually need? [PG]
13. Have you met any of the end users or their management? [PG]

Project Perspective

The project methodology is of prime importance since it is the vehicle to the high availability destination. Research has shown that the cost of correction or backtracking rises rapidly as a project progresses, so 'getting it right first time' is a key objective.

1. Do you and your team know how to run a PDW?
2. Have you run a PDW or had one run?
3. If no, do you have an alternative method?
4. Can you use the Delphi technique if required?
5. Do you have sound project management disciplines?
6. If the project involves third parties, have they worked successfully with you before?
7. If there is a pilot, and are their criteria for measuring its success?
8. Do the people involved in the project work in reasonable proximity to each other for communications and meeting purposes?
9. Has the project timescale been worked out and agreed (as opposed to imposed: *it has to be in and working by June*—signed: I.A.M. Chairman)?

Client/User Perspective

It is important that IT and the end users perceive any incumbent vendor as a partner and not just a *purveyor* of hardware and software products. To achieve this, you must understand what the end user is trying to achieve, his/her expectations and doubts and how well you are placed to help him implement and manage his business solution effectively.

1. Are the vendor personnel likely to be involved in this project aware of it at a sufficient level of detail?
2. If yes, do they have a feasible timescale in which to act?
3. Do you regard yourselves as an end user partner in the project?
4. Does the project use state of the art products? [PG]
5. If yes, does the user have reasonable expectations in the areas of functionality, usability, manageability and performance? [PG]
6. Can you identify the top five end user personnel involved in this project and define their roles?
7. Can the project be resourced using only vendor personnel in your country or region?

8. Are the necessary skills, industry and technical, available in your country/region? [May NLS]
9. Has someone in your chosen vendor(s) worked on projects like this before? [PG]
10. Are the end user's expectations compatible with vendor's?
11. If any vendor business partners are involved, can they answer *Y* to the questions above where applicable?

IT Technical Perspective

The previous sections covered the business and partnership aspects of the proposed solution. There is, however, a technical perspective or *viewpoint* to the solution which is also a critical part of ensuring success.

1. Is the technical solution documented and understood by all involved technically?
2. Is the solution involved *business as usual* and well understood?
3. Does the solution only involve the integration of vendor products?
4. Does the solution only rely on delivered vendor and other technology (as opposed to beta, expected unannounced and vaporware)?
5. Is support for all components of the system adequate and available over most of the country/region?
6. Has this solution, or a similar one, been installed successfully anywhere else?
7. Will all software components be installed and used without modification?
8. Are the performance, reliability, and availability requirements understood?
9. Are the above requirements achievable?
10. Is the proposed or installed hardware configuration adequate to support the solution for the end users?
11. Are the necessary products, prerequisites, and co-requisites on order, including items such as documentation?
12. Are the IT staff trained to handle these types of project?

IT Environment

The new HA (high availability) environment will probably require changes in several areas, particularly in personnel skills, organisation and communications. It may also necessitate changes to development methods and the physical IT environment to avoid expensive 'gotchas' well into the cycle of development.

1. Is the IT department organized to handle any new systems and technologies to be employed, for example, Java, SANs, cloud computing, virtualization, or distributed computing?
2. Are the IT to user lines of communication clear, understood, documented, and agreed?
3. Are any new technologies, with end user implications, familiar to the users of it?
4. Does the IT department know how they will deliver the performance, capacity, availability, and other requirements to meet any SLAs in force?
5. Has the IT department defined and documented the new environment (project perspective of the PDW) after implementation?
6. What are their *green* requirements (power, carbon, etc.), both organization and statutory?
7. Are the business continuity (BC) requirements reflected in the data center environment (sprinklers, halon, etc.)?

Service Management Checklist

The successful running and, when necessary, recovery capability of a systems depend to a great extent on the implementation of service management disciplines. The amount of effort put into each discipline depends on the customer but they are all necessary in one form or another.

The organization should be able to answer *yes* to most of the questions below.

1. Does IT have the architectures/methods/plans/tools/skills for the following disciplines?
    a. Help desk?
    b. Operational procedures?
    c. Performance management?
    d. Capacity planning?
    e. Network management?
    f. Availability management?
    g. Software and configuration management?
    h. Security and audit management?
    i. Change management?
    j. Problem/fault management (as part of availability)?
    k. Print management?
    l. Data management (archive/backup/recovery)?
    m. Business continuity/disaster recovery (BC/DR)?
2. Have you got any third-party offerings in any of these disciplines?
3. If yes, can you handle them effectively?

Technical Checklists

Refer to any available checklists for specific products or configurations for *system assurance* and for any *gotchas*, for example:

1. *Clusters:* Configuration, installation, implementation, operation—*normal* and *failover* (*active/standby*)
2. Other server hardware and software
3. Communications requirements and network changes for HA
4. RDBMS changes and exploitation for HA
5. Operating system changes for HA
6. Related commercial off the shelf (COTs) applications (e.g., SAP) changes or implementation
7. Training requirements defined and in plan
8. Support requirements—internal and external plus vendors and other third parties—coverage 24 × 7
9. Compliance requirements—internal and external regulatory

In IBM, there was a process called *systems assurance* which was an internal but impartial method of examining any technical project or customer bid for *fitness for purpose* or quality. It was based on the principle of not launching a ship which might sink on its first contact with water and was very effective.

The tables and suggestions in this section are illustrative and not mandatory, although the principles should be. These principles should be applied to most projects, large and small, and only differ in the amount of detail in them and effort expended on them.

Availability: Deliverables Risk Management

The *deliverables* comprise the systems and associated resources that deliver the HA environment and the DR environment *and* process. We are talking here about the possible *risks* to the *stable* and *continuing* operation of the systems (including people and processes) which support business activities. The National Institute of Standards and Technology (NIST) documentation, upon which I have drawn heavily, is concerned with success and failure of *missions* such as space flights and warfare activities. Our mission is not as onerous but deserves attention in line with its importance.

The Process

The risk assessment process is shown in Figure A3.4 and described with it.

The Actions:

1. a. Identify and characterize the threat *sources* of concern to the organization, including the nature of the threats and for adversarial threats, capability, intent, and targeting characteristics. Examples are weather, terrorism, and malware.
   b. Identify potential threat *events*, relevance to the organization and the threat sources that could initiate the events. Examples are floods, earthquakes, bombs, poisoning, botnets, and DDoS.
2. Identify vulnerabilities and predisposing conditions that affect the likelihood that threat events of concern result in adverse impacts to the organization, for example, we are 100 ft below sea level and have no flood defenses and we are on the San Andreas fault and the roads to the data center are liable to collapse in an earth tremor.
3. Determine the likelihood that threat events of concern result in adverse impact to the organization, considering
   a. The characteristics of the threat sources that could initiate the events.
   b. The vulnerabilities and predisposing conditions identified.
   c. Organizational susceptibility reflecting safeguards and countermeasures planned or implemented to impede such events. Example is what would happen as a result of the events in 2 occurring?

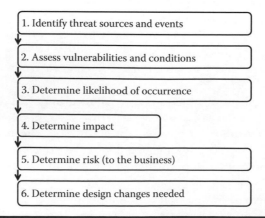

Figure A3.4   HA/DR deliverables risk assessment process.

4. Determine the adverse impact to the organization from threat events of concern considering
   a. The characteristics of the threat sources that could initiate the events.
   b. Organizational susceptibility reflecting safeguards and countermeasures planned or implemented to impede such events.
5. Determine the risk to the organization from threat events of concern considering
   a. The impact that would result from the event.
   b. The likelihood of the event occurring.

Detailed references are found in NIST Guide: http://csrc.nist.gov/publications/nistpubs/800-30/sp800-30.pdf (US Homeland Security); http://www.dhs.gov/xlibrary/assets/nipp_it_baseline_risk_assessment.pdf (Risk Assessment Tables and Plans).

For both types of assessment—*project* and *deliverables*—there needs to be a documented outcome and a documented and resourced plan to remedy deficiencies.

Project Risk Assessment

If there are a few more *No(s)* than *Yes(s)* in an assessment category, mark *medium risk*. If many more, mark *high risk*. All *No(s)* means you are in trouble or will be.

A majority of *Yes(s)* can be flagged *low risk* but still warranting action. Feel free to use your own *assessment* table as long as you have one.

Again, this is only a suggested form—use one that suits your organization.

Table A3.1 contains a rudimentary risk checklist in table format and allows assessments of risk of high, medium, and low. It is a slightly more detailed checklist than our project checklist Table A3.1.

There are some checklists that resemble surrender documents from the World Wars and you can spend more time completing them than fixing real issues.

The URL (http://www.bddk.org.tr/websitesi/turkce/Raporlar/BDDK_Dergi/4214Makale-3.pdf), titled "An Aggregated Information Technology Checklist for Operational Risk Management," covers a lot of ground and I have selected a table from it which will provide risk assessment and management information to whatever level your organization wishes to take it (Table A3.2).

Project Risk Management Plan

Assessing risk is one thing, doing something about it is another. There should be an action plan for the high, then medium, then low-risk elements identified previously (Table A3.3).

Table A3.1   Project Risk Assessment Table

Risk Section	Question	Risk (H, M, L)/Comments
User and Business Requirements	1.	H/Java training sparse
	2.	M/comments
Project Perspective	1.	
	2.	

Table A3.2   Operational Risk: Best Practice

Operational Risks	*Best Practice*
Internal fraud	ISO27001
External fraud	BS7799
Employment practices and safety	CobiT
Clients, products, and business practices	CobiT
Damage to physical assets	ISO27001
Business disruption and system failures	*ITIL*
Execution, delivery, and process management	CobiT

Table A3.3   Identified Risks: Action Plan

Question/Risk	*Action Plan*	*Who*	*By When*
Is the timetable drawn up and verified?/H	Verify timetable with users at the next progress meeting	AB	November 30, 2012
Are current skills adequate for the new environment?/H	Organize product training	DN	December 12, 2012
Changes needed to current problem determination and resolution?/M	Assign and equip the *war room*	Team A	May 5, 2013

Deliverables Risk Management Plan: Specific Risk Areas

Note: The words *quantitative risk* sometimes crop up—they basically mean a value is attached to that risk if it occurs, for example, *if we are offline for 4 hours, the cost to the company will be $124,000.* You may or may not need to employ this factor.

There exist many Internet-based checklists for risk, some specific, some generic. Below are listed three checklists—cloud and cluster—which I think are useful.

Risk in cloud computing: See the documents http://www.coso.org/documents/Cloud%20 Computing%20Thought%20Paper.pdf and http://www.opengroup.org/cloud/cloud/risk. htm on this topic.

Risk in clustering: See the document http://www.continuitysoftware.com/ebooks/top-ten-cluster-high-availability-risks/ on this topic.

Someone said that risk management is a mindset and I can't disagree. The key steps in it are plan, identify, analyze, respond, monitor, and control. If applied all along, it can avoid what people have called *the snowball effect of* one problem compounding others.

The IT Role* in All This

We have seen that the people side of things can impact availability (finger trouble). People can avoid availability issues at the design stage developing skills and experience before, during, and after the HA project. Several of these skills are personal, such as dealing with others. You may not be able to change overnight but I have found in my 35 years in IT that using the items listed below as a checklist can help enormously in *oiling the wheels* of any project. They are also job promotion factors!

- Learn from the past, peers, and, if you are an IT vendor, the competition.
- Try to apply the *So What?* test to things you say and write.
- No ATTAM projects—*All Things To All Men*. They all fail miserably. Set yourself and the *customer* realistic and phased goals—no *Star Trek* stuff on offer.
- Apply FUMP to all designs and their implementations—*F*unctionality, *U*sability, *M*anageability, and *P*erformance. Miss one of these and you are as good as dead in the medium term.
- Strive to be a *trusted advisor* to the client/user on IT architectures of various types (see appendices in this document). If the CIO calls you in for advice, you've made it. If he doesn't, work on the points in this list.
- Develop communications and rapport with the business units in your *customer*, not just with IT people and with developers, implementers, and operations.
- Develop architecture *viewpoints* for different parts of the business—business person, architect, operations, deep *techie*, and *tyre/tire kicker*.
- Sell architecture (and hence IT) as business benefit and not an overhead.
- Be a listener not a brow beater—use the 2:1 rule—you have 2 ears and 1 mouth (unless you are very odd). *Customers* warm to listeners.
- Anticipate needs of business and seek opinions, then, if appropriate, offer advice.
- Isolate technology from architecture: same technology and configuration can display differing viewpoints.
- Be adept at resolving disputes (use Delphi technique where possible).
- Develop and maintain 180° vision of what is going on.
- Mentor/educate others involved: be mentored and taught by them as well.
- Manage risk with and for the *customer* (see section Assessment in Appendix 1).
- If you have time, do a *coffee call* on the *customer*. You'll be surprised what you can dig up in casual conversation.
- Read voraciously and keep learning.

Finally, the golden rules: *Assume Nothing* and the Boy Scout Motto: *Be Prepared*.

Summary

Over the last few years, the concept of what constitutes a data center has evolved from a monolithic cost-center to a dynamic, often distributed environment which is now perceived as giving direct benefit and competitive advantage to a business. In fact, most businesses can no longer

---

* Do you mean ME? Yes.

operate without IT systems, such is their pervasiveness in supporting mission-critical services. E-commerce is an example of the new data center where the speed of change is an order of magnitude greater than in the old data center world.

This does not, however, mean that the traditional data center is obsolete in its entirety because it has a long history of developing disciplines and procedures to ensure correct running and HA of the services it hosted for the business it supports. This document has sought to outline the best current data center practices as they evolve with the commercial and Internet world.

The essence of all this is to detect,* measure, act (manage), and learn from it. The best practices outlined in this document are all about measurement, analysis, assessment, and management. An interesting *maturity* chart, aimed at DCIM (data center infrastructure management), produced by Gartner about Emerson Electric DCIM, shows the stages:

- *Stage 1:* Basic—What do I have?
- *Stage 2:* Reactive—What's happening?
- *Stage 3:* Proactive—What do I need to do?
- *Stage 4:* Optimized—How do I do better?
- *Stage 5:* Autonomic—Do it for me.

I think these classifications are ideal for HA/DR design and their development and I wish I had thought of them first.

These are good stages in which to categorize the phases of HA/DR design and development so as not to attempt to *boil the ocean* on day 1. Think about it. *Finally*

Note: These disciplines *must* be carried over to the new data center or new IT environment if it is to fulfill its role as critical to the business. The daunting world of 7 × 24 × 365, especially for e-commerce, cannot be realized without implementing these (and other) best practices and several e-commerce day 1 failures testify to this. The way these disciplines are implemented may be different, but the base requirement for them remains.

There is a saying, possibly originated by me in the distant past and repeated elsewhere in this book:

"If you can't measure it, you can't manage it. If you can't manage it, you are probably in trouble. If you aren't in trouble now, you will be."

---

* This particularly applies to *malware*, the upcoming *nuisance* and *showstopper*.

Appendix 4

"Mathematics is the supreme judge: from its decisions there is no appeal."

Tobias Dantzig

Availability: Math and Other Topics

In this appendix, we discuss and expand upon some of the math involved in some of the earlier chapters of this book, including the Weibull distribution and its derivative distributions. We will also add some extra details to other aspects of services, which can impact the availability of those services to the end user.

Lesson 1: Multiplication, Summation, and Integration Symbols

The symbol Σ (Greek uppercase *sigma*) denotes a summation of items, and Π (Greek uppercase *pi*) denotes a product or series of multiplications of items. The examples below should make these functions clear:

$$a_1 + a_2 + a_3 + \cdots a_n = \sum_{i=1}^{n} a_i$$

and

$$a_1 \times a_2 \times a_3 \times \cdots \times a_n = \prod_{1}^{n} a_i$$

The summation and integration signs are also used to express the area under discrete and continuous distribution graphs (refer to the next diagram).

Mathematical Distributions

The total area under the discrete graph is the sum of all the elements. The area of the ith element, starting at t_i, is height × width that is $F(i) \times \delta t_i$ for all elements 0 to infinity and $F(i)$ is the value of F at point t_i. We will call this area A_D:

$$A_D = \sum_0^\infty F(i).\delta t_i$$

I have used "." in the above equation to represent a multiplication instead of "×" and will do where confusion with a variable called x might occur, as it does in the integral area below.

As δt_i approaches zero, the discrete graph becomes a continuous curve and the area under this curve, instead of being a discrete summation as seen above, becomes an integration, area A_C, thus:

$$A_C = \int_0^\infty F(x)\,dx$$

Refer to the graphs in Figure A4.1 again to understand these areas.

Sometimes, as we will see later, difficult or unfathomable integrals are often approximated by a summation using a series of discrete *chunks* instead of a continuous curve. We have already seen that areas under curves, for example, the probability density function (pdf), have a meaning when applied to reliability and hence, availability. Cast your eye over these symbols and their meaning again and you will be able to follow the subsequent usage of equations better.

Lesson 2: General Theory of Reliability and Availability

Reliability Distributions

The reliability of any device has a mathematical distribution describing its behavior from which certain values can be obtained. The probability often used in reliability engineering is the *Weibull distribution*. There are many other distributions used in reliability engineering, some of which are applied to software reliability theory. In our discussions here, assume that equivalent mathematical operations would be carried out on these other distributions, many of which are derivations of Weibull.

There are many distributions but in terms of hardware, the Weibull and exponential ones are the main types used for hardware:

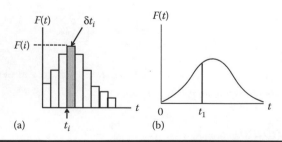

(a)   (b)

Figure A4.1   Areas under (a) discrete (AD) (e.g., Poisson) and (b) continuous (AC) (e.g., Exponential) functions.

- Weibull distribution is used at or below component or part level
- Exponential distribution is used for the life of assemblies of parts or systems of components

The Rayleigh distribution, a subset of Weibull, is often used in discussing software reliability. The Gumbel distribution gets a mention sometimes (see Appendix 1).

pdf Distribution $f(x)$

The Weibull distribution is a general-purpose reliability distribution used to model material strength, times-to-failure of electronic and mechanical components, equipment, or systems.

In its most general case, the three-parameter Weibull pdf* is defined by

$$f(t)=\frac{\beta}{\eta}\frac{(t-\gamma)^{\beta-1}}{\eta}.e^{-(t/\eta)^{\beta}}$$

(A4.1)

A Three Parameter Weibull Probability Density Function

where:
   β = shape parameter
   γ = location parameter
   η = scale parameter

The shape parameter is what gives the Weibull distribution its flexibility and ability to take on other distribution forms. The value of this modeling shape parameter β gives indications of the prevalent failure modes (remember the hardware *bathtub* curve):

- $\beta < 1$ indicates *infant mortality* due to poor production quality or insufficient burn-in.
- $\beta = 1$ indicates random failures that are independent of time, the *exponential* distribution. This is the normal operating phase of life and failures are often due to external events: fire, operator error, deliberate damage, and so on.
- $\beta = 2$, the distribution is the *Rayleigh* form, heading toward the edge of the *bath*.
- β is between 3 and 4, the failure distribution approximates to the *normal* distribution and is effectively *climbing out of the bath.*
- $\beta > 4$ indicates old age and rapid wear out: chip failures, corrosion, fatigue, and so on.

Normally, the equation reduces to a two-parameter Weibull where $\gamma = 0$ and then the pdf looks as follows (Figure A4.2):

$$f(t)=\frac{\beta}{\eta}\left(\frac{t}{\eta}\right)^{\beta-1}.e^{-(t/\eta)^{\beta}}$$

(A4.2)

The Two–Parameter Weibull pdf

---

* For information of *pdf* and *cdf,* see http://www.youtube.com/watch?v=Fvi9A_tEmXQ and http://www.youtube .com/watch?v=-FSTXqZJsFc&feature=related, respectively.

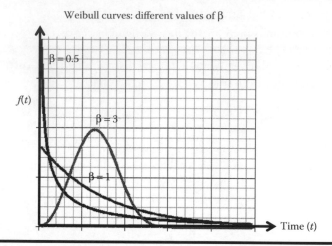

Figure A4.2   Typical Weibull pdfs *f(t)*.

Note that $f(x)$ [not $F(x)$] is the function that can represent entities other than time t in discussing reliability, for example, where x = car reliability, open/closed for stress testing of doors and so on, where t might represent kilometers or number of open/closed and so on. In the IT availability and reliability cases we are interested in, x represents *time* (Figure A4.3).

What does *pdf* mean? The probability that the random variable X takes on a value in the time interval $[a, b]$ is the area under the pdf from a to b, or, in the terms of life data analysis, the Equation A4.2 and Figure A4.2 allow us to calculate the probability of a failure occurring between two different points in time.

However, this sort of information is required infrequently at best. Of greater interest is the probability of a failure occurring before or after a certain time, say a, the equation would return the probability of a failure occurring before time a, *that is, in the period of time 0–a* seconds/hours/days/years.

See YouTube for an excellent video on pdfs at http://www.youtube.com/watch?v=Fvi9A_tEmXQ.

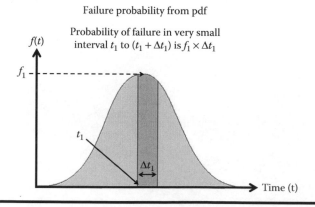

Figure A4.3   Weibull pdf *f(t)*.

cdf introduces the concept of the *cumulative distribution function*. As the name implies, the cdf measures the cumulative probability of a failure occurring before a certain time, say *t*. The equation for the cdf $F(x)$ as a function of the pdf $f(x)$ is

$$F(x) = \int_0^a f(x)\,dx$$

and the cdf is essentially calculating the area under the pdf curve from zero to the point of interest *time* = *a*. We have seen this area calculation at the very beginning of this appendix.

Cumulative Distribution Function $F(x)$

Figure A4.4 shows the cdf distribution curve, $F(x)$.
    The inverse of the $F(x)$ curve represents the availability probability (Figure A4.5).

Note: The lower limit of the integration value varies from distribution to distribution.

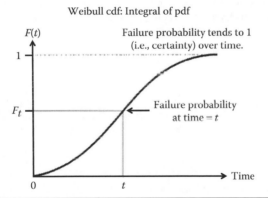

Weibull cdf: Integral of pdf

Figure A4.4   Weibull cdf.

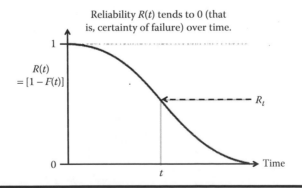

Weibull reliability curve

Figure A4.5   Availability probability from failure probability.

The Weibull distribution has a lower limit of zero. Note that the value of the cdf probability always approaches 1 as time approaches infinity, that is, failure is a certainty.

Lesson 3: Parallel Components (Blocks)

Availability: m-from-n Components[*]

The parallel and series systems we have seen before are special cases of the *m-out-of-n* system, the theory of which is presented here. In the paper referenced here, a *failed* system is denoted ":F" (Failed) and a working one ":G" (Good).

A series system is equivalent to a 1-out-of-*n*:F system and to an *n*-out-of-*n*:G system while a parallel system is equivalent to an *n*-out-of-*n*:F system and to a 1-out-of-*n*:G system. This is stating:

- *Series*: If 1 out of the *n* components fails, the system fails (1-out-of-*n*:F).
- *Series*: If *n* out of *n* components are working (G), the system is working (*n*-out-of *n*:G).
- *Parallel*: If *n* out of *n* components fail, the system fails (*n*-out-of-*n*:F).
- *Parallel*: If 1 out of *n* components is working, the system is working (1-out-of-*n*:G).

Consider a car with a V8 engine. The system is tolerant of failures of up to four cylinders for minimal functioning of the engine and this may be represented by a 4-out-of-8:G system. I am not a car mechanic but I am assuming that three cylinders are not enough for a V8 to move, that is, a (3-out-of-8:F) situation.

m-from-n Examples

There are situations where a function/job is carried out by a number of servers, say *n*, but not all need to be operational for the overall functioning to continue. If the job can carry on with *m* servers ([*n–m*] are down) then this is called an *m-from-n* configuration. Some examples of this configuration are shown below:

1. A 4-engine plane can fly on 1 engine (I hope) so 1-from-4:G.
2. A car needs 4 tyres to work but has a spare in the back so the equation should be 4-from-5:G but 3-from-5:Crash or 3-from-5:Fine.
3. A 4-drive RAID system might be 3-from-4:G and 2-from-4:F.

Note: As we state in the footnote, our notation substitutes *m-out-of-n* for the cited paper's *k-out-of-n* but the end result is the same. We also drop the :F and :G notation for the remainder of this discussion.

m-from-n Theory

We saw in the main text of the book diagrams and formulae for two blocks or components in *series* and in *parallel*. Now we want to look at the cases where not all the components are functioning either because they have failed or they are waiting in *standby mode* to take over the work from a failed *companion* (Figure A4.6).

---

[*] For technical details (in this reference called *k-from-n*), see http://media.wiley.com/product_data/excerpt/1X/04713976/047139761X.pdf.

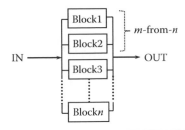

n active blocks in parallel

Figure A4.6 Parallel blocks *m*-from-*n* available.

In theory, with parallel blocks, only 1 needs to be available unless there are special considerations such as performance, where some number of blocks between 1 and *n* is required. This is likely, especially if an service level agreement (SLA) has a performance *rider* alongside the availability requirements.

The general case formula is outlined below and some examples given of its solution for a few cases.

m-*from*-n Redundant Blocks

The general reliability formula of the reliability of a selection of parallel blocks is

$$R_{m\text{-from-}n}(t) = \sum_{i=0}^{n-m}\left[\frac{n!}{(n-i)!\,i!}\right]R_m^{n-i}[1-R_m(t)]^i \tag{A4.3}$$

Reliability of System of m *Blocks from* n

where:
    m is the number of modules/blocks required for the service and being supported
    n is the total number of modules/blocks available

n! *(factorial) means* n × (n–1) × (n–2) × ... × 3 × 2 × 1

Look at the following example:

Example A4.1

$n = 5$, $m = 3$ (thus $[n-m] = 2$) and reliability of each $R = 0.95$. Using the formula we have just seen above:

$$\begin{aligned}R_{3\text{-from-}5}(t) &= \sum_{i=0}^{2}\left[\frac{5!}{(5-i)!\,i!}\right]R_m^{5-i}[1-R_m(t)]^i\\ &= R_m^5(t) + 5R_m^4(t)[1-R_m(t)] + 10R_m^3(t)[1-R_m(t)]^2\\ &= 10(0.95)^3 - 15(0.95)^4 + 6(0.95)^5 = 0.9988\end{aligned}$$

Thus, the probability of 3 blocks out of the 5 being available is 0.9988.

Active and Standby Redundancy

Introduction

Redundant component or parts are used to increase the effective overall reliability and availability of a configuration performing a job. In the general case, a distinction is made between repairable components and nonrepairable ones. Nonrepairable does not mean the component is intrinsically irreparable but that repair is not convenient or possible. Examples might be a computer circuit (inconvenient while operational) and a space satellite (impossible but might be capable of repair if someone could get up to it). In the case of IT studies and calculations, the components are considered nonrepairable, that is, they cannot be maintained *in flight* as some mechanical or electrical installations can be.

Many configurations, including disk arrays and clusters of nodes, are arranged in different ways where there is redundancy but all participants are not necessarily active, that is, working as they would normally. This can be quite deliberate as a backup measure should one or more components fail and need to be substituted. Thus, there are modes like active:active where the spare component is operational (or *energized*) and active:standby where the partner component is inactive.

Energizing in a software scenario might mean starting it up from scratch.

Summary of Redundancy Systems*

The summary of redundancy systems is illustrated in Table A4.1.

Table A4.1 Redundancy: Repairable and Nonrepairable Systems

Nonrepairable Systems	Repairable Systems
Full Redundancy	**Full Redundancy**
Traditional approach	Markovian approach
State analysis approach	Combined unit approach
	Expectation/transition approach
Standby Redundancy	System failure rate approach
Traditional approach	Periodically maintained systems
Perfect switching	Impact of redundancy on maintainability
Imperfect switching	
Efficient Levels of Redundancy	**Standby Redundancy**
	Markovian approach
	Expectation transition model

---

* Report RADC-TR-77-287 by ROME Air Development Center.

Types of Redundancy

In a situation with parallel components, there are two main ways of operating:

1. *Active redundancy* is the condition in which both components are functioning and, in most cases, share the work they normally do (Figure A4.7).
2. *Standby redundancy* is the condition in which one component is functioning while the other is capable of functioning but is not operational.

An example of active redundancy is an aircraft with four engines, all of which are operating. *It is called an active/active configuration of 4 from 4*. If however it was a testing flight and one engine was deliberately disabled but capable of running, it would be called an active/standby configuration of 3 from 4. The idea would be that the plane can fly on those 3 engines but if one fails but 3 are definitely needed, the 4th engine can be brought *online* so to say.

The general statement for this kind of redundancy is *m-from-n*, *3 from 4* in the example above.

Calculations of the reliability of configurations with standby units depends on factors like with or without repair, whether standby (redundancy) is active or passive, and other factors.

For situations where $R_i(t)$ is not the same for each of the i components, the solution to the equations gets a bit more involved but can still be done using the individual reliability values R_1, R_2, ... R_n. In normal IT situations, the parallel components would be the same and for reliability calculations, assumed to be of the same reliability R. The general calculation would consider L sets of n components in parallel. In the case $L = 1$.

The reliability of this $L = 1$, n component system is:

$$R(t) = [1 - (1 - e^{-\lambda t})^n]$$

and the mean time to first failure (MTTFF) is given by:

$$M = \int_0^\infty [1 - (1 - e^{-\lambda t})^n] \, dt$$

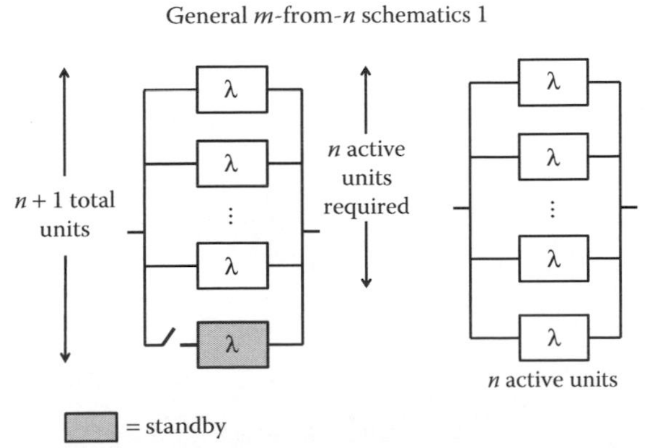

General *m*-from-*n* schematics 1

= standby

Figure A4.7   General schematic of active and standby configurations (1).

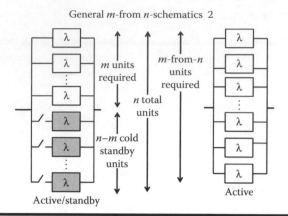

General *m*-from *n*-schematics 2

Figure A4.8   *m* active/(*n*–*m*) standby and *m*-from-*n*: *n* active (2).

The general case of *m active* units with *(n–m)* cold *standby* units in a total of *n* units with *m required* for acceptable functioning of the configuration is shown in Figure A4.8. If one of the *m* units fails, another from the cold units needs to become operational to keep the functioning count at *m* units.

> ***Note:*** As we said above, we might just need 1 out of the *n* parallel blocks to be available for normal functioning. However, there may be situations where more than one *path* needs to be available, for example, for performance or perhaps for reasons of load balancing across the parallel components or units.

Real m-*from*-n Example

Figure A4.9. shows a cluster configuration with duplex RAID controllers supporting a RAID storage array.

To continue operations upon failure of any component, it is necessary to have at least one component from the two working for the cluster nodes and RAID controller. The RAID array requires three disks from four to be operational to continue working.

Redundancy: *m*-from-*n* real-life schematic

1-from-2   Cluster

1-from-2   Duplex controllers

3-from-4   1   2   ⋯   *n*   RAID cluster

RAID disks

Figure A4.9   Simple real *m*-from-*n* configuration examples.

Math of m-*from*-n Configurations

Configurations like the diagram above normally quote reliability functions in terms of λ, the failure rate. The failure rate for configurations is given by the equation in the following tables where *configuration* means *m of n must be working* where *m* and *n* are 1, 2, ... *n* (Table A4.2).

An excellent discussion of these configurations, called *Applied R&M Manual for Defense Systems Part D—Supporting Theory: Chapter 6*, can be found at http://www.sars.org.uk/old-site-archive/BOK/Applied%20R&M%20Manual%20for%20Defense%20Systems%20(GR-77)/p4c06.pdf.

Standby Redundancy

The table above applies to configurations where all units are identical, the standby units are not energized, that is, need action on them to make them active to replace a failed active unit. Energizing a *unit* might mean taking action on a standby cluster node to bring it to the active state but having a switching time = 0 (Table A4.3).

An Example of These Equations

Ravishankar Iyer and Zbigniew Kalbarczyk demonstrate that a simplex (single component system) can have a higher reliability than a triple modular redundancy one (TMR) where two out of the three modules are required for normal operation.[*] Using the equation $\lambda = 1/\text{MTTF}$ format, they

Table A4.2   Reliability Equations: Reliability of Active Redundancy

Configuration	Reliability R(t)
1 of 2	$2e^{-\lambda t} - e^{-2\lambda t}$
1 of 3	$3e^{-\lambda t} - 3e^{-2\lambda t} + e^{-3\lambda t}$
1 of 4	$4e^{-\lambda t} - 6e^{-2\lambda t} + 4e^{-3\lambda t} - e^{-4\lambda t}$
1 of *n*	$\sum_{k=1}^{n} (-1)^{k+1} \, [n!/k!(n-k)!]e^{-k\lambda t}$
2 of 3	$3e^{-2\lambda t} - 2e^{-3\lambda t}$
3 of 4	$4e^{-3\lambda t} - 3e^{-4\lambda t}$
n–1 of *n*	$ne^{-(n-1)\lambda t} - (n-1)e^{-n\lambda t}$
2 of 4	$3e^{-4\lambda t} - 8e^{-3\lambda t} + 6e^{-2\lambda}$
3 of 5	$6e^{-5\lambda t} - 15e^{-4\lambda t} + 10e^{-3\lambda t}$
(*n*–2) of *n*	$n![2(n-2!)]e^{(n-2)\lambda t} + (2n-n^2)e^{-(n-1)\lambda t} + (n-1!)/2(n-3)!e^{-n\lambda t}$
m of *n*	$\sum_{k=m}^{n} n!/[k!(n-k)!](e^{-\lambda t})^k \, (1-e^{-\lambda t})^{(n-k)}$

---

[*] http://courses.engr.illinois.edu/ece542/textbook/hwswerrordetection.pdf.

Table A4.3 Reliability Equations: Reliability of Standby Redundancy

Configuration	Reliability R(t)
1 of 2	$e^{-\lambda t} + \lambda t e^{-\lambda t}$
1 of 3	$e^{-\lambda t} + \lambda t e^{-\lambda t} + 0.5(\lambda t)^2 e^{-\lambda t}$
1 of n	$\displaystyle\sum_{r=0}^{n-1} e^{-\lambda t}(\lambda t)^r/r!$
m of n	$\displaystyle e^{-m\lambda t}\sum_{k=0}^{n-m} m\lambda t^k/k!$

demonstrate that the MTTF of the simplex system is greater than that of the 2-from-3 TMR system, thus:

$$\text{MTTF}_{\text{simplex}}\left(=\frac{1}{\lambda}\right) > \text{MTTF}_{\text{TMR}[2]} = \frac{5}{6\lambda}$$

They go on to say that TMR improves reliability in the short term when all three components or modules are operational but in the longer term can degrade reliability. In the first instance:

$$\text{MTTF}_{\text{TMR}} > \text{MTTR}_{\text{simplex}}$$

After the first TMR failure, the two remaining components provide lower reliability than the simplex system as shown in the first equation (see Lesson 9).

Online Tool for Parallel Components*: Typical Calculation

There are a number of online tools aimed at calculations on the reliability of various configurations of components; some chargeable, some free. Look at: http://reliabilityanalyticstoolkit.appspot.com/ (accessed August 22, 2014) and you will see a tool for calculating various reliability parameters, including the calculation for the reliability of *M* components functioning correctly out of *N*.

Typical Calculation: Active redundancy, with repair, Weibull distribution. The text below accompanies Figure A4.10, reproduced from the referenced website:

> Calculate the effective failure rate of "n" active on-line units with equal failure rates where "m of n" are required for success. Failed units can be repaired. Determine the reliability function, probability density function and hazard function for a wide variety of failure distributions using the Weibull distribution. Calculate the mean time to failure for non-repairable scenarios. Create plots of R(t), f(t) and h(t). Output derived functions to a Microsoft Excel formula format.

A list of components (called units) and their reliability can be modeled with this tool. For example, we might want to model 2 from 3, as shown in the scenario below:

---

* Courtesy of Seymour Morris of Reliability Analytics, www.reliabilityanalytics.com.

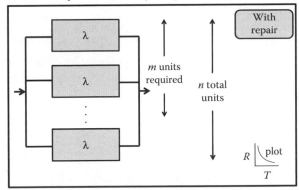

Figure A4.10 Sample *m*-from-*n* computation (reliability analytics).

Unit 1	0.980 (Reliability)
Unit 2	0.990 (Reliability)
Unit 3	0.995 (Reliability)

Other combinations of parameters, probably of little interest to the reader, are as follows:

- Unit name, unit failure rate, $R(t)$, MTBF
- Unit name, Weibull β, Weibull η/$R(t)$, MTBF
- Unit name, symbolic equation (Figure A4.10)

You will be able to do an *m*-from-*n* calculation quite easily to find the availability probability of that configuration. Make some reasonable guesses for the other parameters as they shouldn't affect the final availability number. Using the URL above, try calculating the availability of four (*m*) blocks or components from five (*n*) in parallel.

NB: Realistic IT Redundancy

This area of reliability is quite complicated as it stands but the equations should not be taken too far in complex IT systems. There are some factors native to this theory and some that add complexity when applied to aspects of IT. These can be summarized as follows:

- The reliability of any *switching* device between units is assumed to be zero (perfect).
- The switching time for standby units is assumed to be zero.
- The units are assumed to be identical [same reliability $R(t)$] but in the imperfect switching case the switch and any sensor have a failure distribution.
- Imperfect switching complicates the theory by having different reliabilities for a unit in active and standby modes and a switching time.*
- An exponential failure distribution of units is assumed.

---

* http://www.stat.ncku.edu.tw/faculty_private/jnpan/publication/1998_34_2CIE.pdf.

■ The parallel units inactive/active are identical and fully energized, that is, ready to start work immediately.
■ The standby units are not energized.

> *Note:* This is where the opinions of computer scientists and IT people may possibly part company for a while.

■ Real-life IT has the following characteristics:
  – Some units, like NICs, can be assumed to start as soon as they are invoked in a switch and are normally identical with identical $R(t)$.
  – Switching in intelligent subsystems like disk arrays will not be zero and the standby nodes may be at various *temperatures*.
  – Systems, like cluster nodes, can be unenergized (*cold standby*), partly energized (*warm standby*), or fully energized (*hot standby*), and possibly configurations in between, which makes theory rather difficult to apply.
  – Units that self-repair (like memory mirrors) will take time to switch, but an unknown degree.

The upshot of this is that applying theory at this level in real-life situations can be counterproductive and possibly lead to erroneous conclusions.

> *Note:* The theory was developed mainly for electronic units or components that do not have the variable characteristics outlined for the real IT scenarios above. It certainly will not apply to software scenarios.

Overall Availability Graphs

Figure A4.11 shows the availability of a set of parallel components/blocks for various numbers of them. It should be noted that the availability *payback* may well be exceeded by the costs after utilizing three components/blocks in parallel. The graph represents the overall availability of a number of parallel components or blocks, assuming each has an availability of 98% and is available. It also shows, schematically, the diminishing returns in reliability of extra components in parallel configurations. This can be demonstrated numerically using the online tool described above. The curves illustrate the law of diminishing returns when the number of units in parallel exceeds about four.

The dotted-line graph shows the reliability gained from extra units while the full curve shows the increase in reliability gained by adding units in parallel. Both decrease rapidly as the number of units increases. This graph was recreated from Black's presentation[*] and is based on a book by Allan and Billinton[†] of Manchester University (Figure A4.11).

---

[*] www.slideshare.net/tsaiblake/assuring-reliable-and-secure-it-services.
[†] R. Billinton and R.N. Allan, *Reliability of Engineering Systems* (Plenum Press).

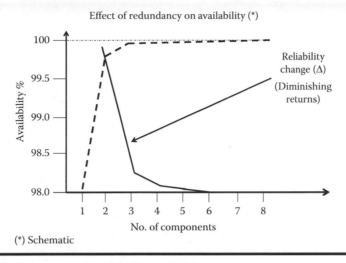

Figure A4.11 **Parallel components/blocks availability.**

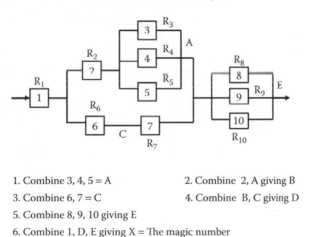

Figure A4.12 **Reliability exercise—Series and parallel components.**

Try This Availability Test

What is the end-to-end reliability of this set of components if all R's = 0.9? If it proves too difficult, make R_i (i = 1 to 10) all equal to one figure, R, and the answer will pop out. (Figure A4.12 provides a reliability exercise pattern.)

Lesson 4: Cluster Speedup Formulae

It should be obvious that putting N systems together in a cluster coupled in some way does not give an aggregate power of $N \times P$ where P is the power (however defined) of one system. We have already seen that IBM only managed a 10% increase in power over a single processor when coupling two 360/65s together, that is, 1.1 P where P is the power of one 360/65.

Why is this important in availability? Well for one reason, the user may be paying for the equipment and if he or she is getting a 10% bonus for 100% extra cost, he or she is not going to be very happy.

Power can be defined in several ways, for example:

- Throughput of batch jobs
- Live transactions per unit time
- Transaction response time
- Commercial benchmark *power*, MIPs, Dhrystone, TPC-C, and VUPs
- Scientific benchmark *power*, MFLOPs, SPEC, Whetstone, LINPACK, and LAPACK
- Other e-mails/h, web frames/s, graphics performance

The end user doesn't understand these but he or she does have expectations of *response* time.

As an aside it may be of interest to note that IBM used to express the power of their multiprocessor systems in terms of throughput of work and might express this as a range such as

$$P_{2\text{proc}} = 1.7 - 1.9 \times P_{1\text{proc}}$$

meaning that two processors, tightly coupled, might give 1.7–1.9 times the throughput of one processor of the same type. Many years ago, the *unit* of power (RPP) was the 370/158-3.

The speedup *laws* we will examine now are basically commercial instruction-processing laws that are amended (1) for more realistic situations (Gunther) and (2) for scientific processing (Gustafson). All other factors—database, memory handling, cache, and so on—are assumed equal.

Amdahl's Law

Amdahl's Law was mentioned in Chapter 4 when discussing the advent of clusters. It is aimed at quantifying the increase in power or throughput of two or more systems in tandem, often called *scalability*. Amdahl's Law is expressed as follows:

$$S(N) = \frac{1}{(1-P)+(P/N)} \tag{A4.4}$$

Amdahl's Speedup Law

where:
   S = speedup factor
   P = fraction of the program that can be parallelized
   N = number of computers/nodes involved
   $(1-P)$ = the part of the program that cannot be parallelized, that is, it remains a serially executing piece of code

As an example, if P is 90%, then $(1-P)$ is 10% or 0.1 in Amdahl's equation, and the execution of code can be speeded up by an asymptotic maximum of a factor of 10, no matter how large the value of N used. For this reason, parallel computing is only useful for either small numbers of processors, or problems with very high values of P, which is sometimes the case with scientific work. In Figure A4.13, no matter how parallel the code elements are, there will always be a portion (shaded) that makes the achievement of a speedup of 10 impossible.

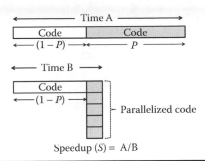

Figure A4.13   Amdahl's law—Parallelization speedup schematic.

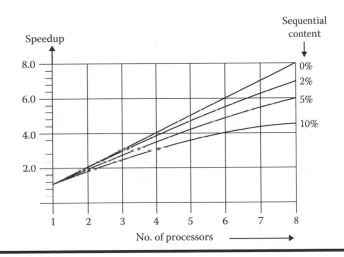

Figure A4.14   Amdahl's law—Speedup curves.

Plotting speedup against number of processors for a variety of parallelizable percentages shows a tailing off of speedup at high N, what is called the law of diminishing returns. Writing parallel code for commercial applications is more difficult than for scientific ones because of the essentially sequential nature of commercial processing.

The plots on the graph in Figure A4.14 show the speedup (S) of programs containing 0%, 2%, 5%, and 10% sequential content with no overheads involved. You can see that the speedup only tails off slightly as the number of processors (N) increases. Obviously the content that can be made parallel is a major factor in speedup.

The scale of Amdahl's Law can be seen in Figure A4.15, which shows the speedup factor extended to very large numbers of processors and higher parallelization factors.

Gunther's Law

Gunther's Law is a modification to Amdahl's Law to take account of overheads when combining processors to produce an increase in speed (speedup).

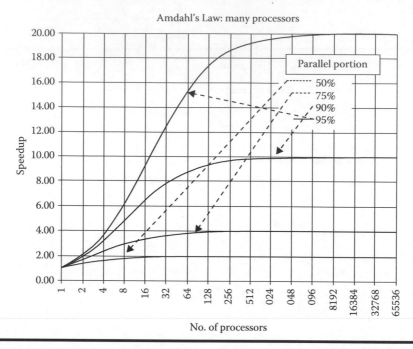

Figure A4.15   Amdahl's law: Many processors—Large *N*, high parallelization %.

The multiprocessor effect is a generic term for the fraction of processing cycles *stolen* by the system (both software and hardware) in order to execute a given workload. Typical sources of multiprocessor overhead include:

1. Operating system (OS) code paths (system calls in UNIX, supervisor calls in MVS, and other OSs)
2. Exchange of shared writable data between processor caches across the system bus
3. Data exchange between processors across the system bus to main memory
4. Lock synchronization of accesses to shared writable data
5. Waiting for an I/O to complete

Even single processors apparently having no work to do have a percentage CPU loading called the *zero utilization effect* where the processor is busy checking queues and other system blocks to see if any work has arrived. When several processors are working in tandem, their interaction also consumes cycles that the program in question might otherwise use.

When these factors are taken into account, Amdahl's Law needs something to recognize this. Figure A4.16 shows the effect of Gunther's Law where the graph illustrates the speedup factor against the number of participating processors.

The multiprocessing (MP) factor causes the *diminishing returns* curve predicted by the Amdahl equation to tail off earlier and flatten off sooner.

The equation now reads

$$C(\alpha, \beta, p) = \frac{p}{\{1 + \alpha[(p-1) + \beta p(p-1)]\}} \tag{A4.5}$$

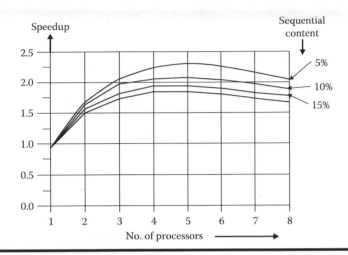

Figure A4.16 Gunther's law—Speedup curves.

where:
  p is as before
  α is a parameter identified with queuing delays
  β is a parameter for additional delays due to pairwise coherency mismatches

In the absence of shared memory, multiple processors (or cores) need to ensure data cache consistency, which generates a performance overhead. The resulting graph is shown above.

When β is 0 (zero), the equation reduces to the Amdahl version of the speedup formula, an analogy of the difference between classical and relativistic physics, which depends on the speed of light.

Gustafson's Law

This law, often known as Gustafson–Barsis' Law, proposes that large data program access to large data sets can be parallelized, that is, computations on it are done in tandem as opposed to in sequence (Figure A4.17). This should result in a speedup of the operation and reduction in elapsed time. It is a modification (some say refutation) of Amdahl's Law which, it is said, pits a limit on the speedup that parallelization can give. Gustafson–Barsis Law does not fully exploit the computing power of an increasing number of processors. Gustafson's Law is illustrated schematically below. The Gustafson–Barsis Law is often written as:

$$S(P) = P - \alpha.(P-1)$$

where:
  S is the speedup factor
  P is the number of processors
  α is the fraction of processing that is not parallelizable

It is easily seen that if all the processing can be parallelized, that is $\alpha = 0$, then the speedup factor is P, the number of processors. This type of speedup is known as *linear* speedup.

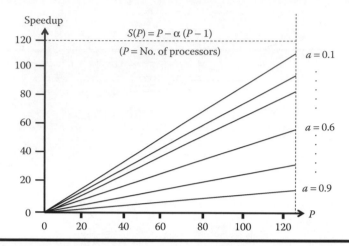

Figure A4.17   Schematic of Gustafson's law—Speedup versus number of processors.

Note: It was in 1988 that Dr. Gustafson wrote the paper "Reevaluating Amdahl's Law" and Dr. Gustafson summarizes this work:

> ...The model is not a contradiction of Amdahl's law as some have stated, but an observation that Amdahl's assumptions don't match the way people use parallel processors. People scale their problems to match the power available, in contrast to Amdahl's assumption that the problem is always the same no matter how capable the computer.

John Gustafson, http://johngustafson.net/glaw.html

Amdahl versus Gunther

Schwartz and Fortune, in their paper titled "Forecasting MySQL Scalability with the Universal Scalability Law" (USL), observe that this USL has a point of maximum throughput after which performance actually degrades, which matches the behavior of real IT systems.

Although this paper discusses scalability in terms of a MySQL environment, much of it is applicable to other software environments too. The authors support their arguments with benchmarks applicable to scalability studies, although some relate to Percona's own version of MySQL, plotting throughput against processor concurrency. They conclude:

> The USL is a model which can help predict a system's scalability. It has all of the necessary and sufficient parameters for predicting the effects of concurrency, contention, and coherency delay. It applies equally well to hardware and software scalability modeling.

For reference, see http://www.percona.com/files/white-papers/forecasting-mysql-scalability.pdf.

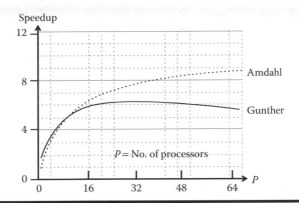

Figure A4.18   Amdahl and Gunther formulae: Speedup results.

It is difficult to compare the Amdahl results with the Gunther results without a graph and the following one does that (Figure A4.18).

For reference, see Gunther at http://arxiv.org/pdf/cs/0210017v1.pdf and http://blogs.msdn.com/b/ddperf/archive/2009/04/29/parallel-scalability-isn-t-child-s-play-part-2-amdahl-s-law-vs-gunther-s-law.aspx#9576239.

You need to remember why we have included this discussion. It is about clusters and the effect on availability of performance shortfalls plus *value for money* for a user-offered clustering as an availability solution.

Performance of a service is also of great importance in SLAs as an *availability as specified* factor in it.

Speedup: Sun-Ni Law

The laws of Amdahl, Gunther, and Gustafson have been tinkered with and discussed since they were proposed. A law that usually accompanies these discussions is the Sun–Ni Law, outlined in the definition below.

> The Sun–Ni law is an approach used in parallel processing that attempts to improve performance. It is also called memory bounded speedup and was proposed by Professors Xian-He Sun and Lionel M. Ni. This law scales up the problem size and tries to find a solution limited only by the amount of memory available. It is a generalization of two other approaches used in parallel computing called Amdahl's law and Gustafson's law.
>
> One of the challenges in parallel computing is to figure out how the performance of the system improves when it is scaled up. As this can be hard to measure, one of the most well-known scalability metrics studied is speedup. Speedup relates the execution of parallel programs running on a certain number of processors and the execution time it takes for the fastest sequential program to solve that problem. One type of speedup approach is to keep the problem size constant, allowing the number of processors that work on the problem to be increased. This is called Amdahl's law and is known as fixed-size speedup.
>
> **(Wisegeek)**

For reference, see http://www.wisegeek.com/what-is-the-sun-ni-law.htm (the above definition) and http://www.dtic.mil/dtic/tr/fulltext/u2/a259227.pdf NASA Contractor Report 189726.

Lesson 5: Some RAID and EC* Math†

RAID configurations can be difficult to handle in terms of resilience, reliability, and storage efficiency but fortunately relatively few RAID levels are in use *in anger*. Much of the material in this lesson is based on existing literature and, in particular, a paper by Andrew (EMC Corporation) and Martin (Polytechnic Institute of New York University) Shooman. The latter has published a book on *Reliability of Computer Systems and Networks*, John Wiley, ISBN 0-471-22460-X (2002). This can now be found online.

> ***Note:*** In the discussion that follows, MTTF is used. As long as the reader understands that it represents the time between failures, we have no confusion with MTBF (see Appendix 2).

RAID Configurations

RAID 0

RAID 0, strictly speaking not a RAID configuration, involves striping of data across several disks with no redundancy. Failure of any one disk in the array can cause irrecoverable data loss. Such a configuration is employed for I/O performance rather than resilience. It doesn't have any!

Figure A4.19 represents a RAID 0 configuration with n disks. If each disk has a capacity of T terabytes, then the nominal total capacity is nT terabytes.

Assuming that λ is the constant failure rate (failures/unit time), the reliability of the system is given by the standard equation:

$$R_S = e^{-n\lambda t} \tag{A4.6}$$

The mean time to failure MTTF is given by the equation:

$$\text{MTTF} = \int_0^\infty e^{-n\lambda t}\, dt = \frac{1}{n\lambda} \tag{A4.7}$$

This number applies over the range 0 to infinity. Theoretical documents take this integral from –(minus) infinity to +(plus) infinity but we take it from 0 to infinity since the curve starts at time = 0. We want to have a target reliability up to time t_1.

Call this target R_g, the reliability goal. This will be represented by the width of the curve $F(t)$ between 0 and t_1:

$$R_g = e^{-n\lambda t_1}$$

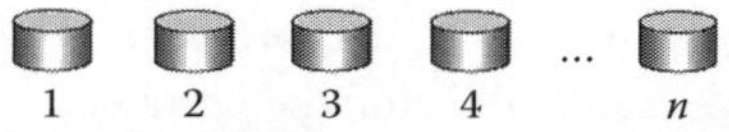

Figure A4.19 RAID 0 schematic—*n* volumes.

---

* Erasure Codes (information dispersal [IDA], forward error correction [FEC], etc.).
† Based on an article by A.M. and M.L. Shooman. "A Comparison of RAID Storage Schemes: Reliability and Efficiency," reproduced with permission.

$$\log_e(R_g) = -n\lambda t_1 \text{ or } \ln R_g = -n\lambda t_1$$

$$t_1 = -\frac{\ln(R_g)}{n\lambda} \qquad (A4.8)$$

Thus, we can conclude from the last equation that

$$t \propto \frac{1}{n}$$

This means that for a desired R goal, the time in which it can be achieved is reduced the larger the number of disks in the configuration. This is what is called the *so-what?* test.

RAID 1

RAID 1, to remind us, is a configuration that mirrors or duplicates *prime* data. If the prime data is another RAID configuration, it becomes one of the *nested* RAID levels we have alluded to previously (Figure A4.20).

In this section, we use the types of equation employed in the RAID 0 discussion above.

The probability of one of a pair of the disks (say, 1 and 1a) is the probability of both being available minus the probability of neither being available, that is:

$$R_{\text{both}} = e^{-\lambda t} + e^{-\lambda t} - e^{-2\lambda t} = 2e^{-\lambda t} - e^{-2\lambda t} \qquad (A4.9)$$

The reliability of the *chain* of mirrored disk (courtesy of Lusser) is:

$$R_{\text{system}} = (2e^{-\lambda t} - e^{-2\lambda t})^n \qquad (A4.10)$$

The MTTF of the system then is

$$\text{MTTF} = \int_0^{\infty} [(2e^{-\lambda t} - e^{-2\lambda t})^n]\,dt \qquad (A4.11)$$

where λ is the constant but independent failure rate (1/MTTF). The integral in Equation A4.11 has no general solution, so an approximation can be used.

This approximation for a quantity x is

$$e^{-x} \cong \left(1 - x + \frac{x^2}{2}\right)$$

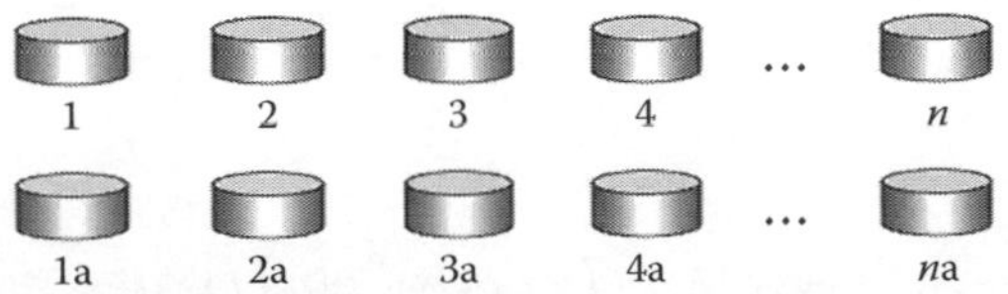

Figure A4.20 RAID 1 reliability schematic.

Using this approximation to get the value of R_g yields the following equation to find the new value of t_1 (see RAID 0 discussion above):

$$R_g = \left\{ 2\left[1 - \lambda t_1 + \frac{(\lambda t_1)^2}{2} \right] - \left[1 - 2\lambda t_1 + \frac{(2\lambda t_1)^2}{2} \right] \right\}^n$$

This reduces to the following equation from which we can obtain t_1:

$$R_g = [1 - (\lambda t_1)^2]^n \tag{A4.12}$$

Expanded Values of R_g

$$t_1 = \frac{[1 - (R_g)^{1/n}]^{1/2}}{\lambda} \tag{A4.13}$$

Time Width for Reliability Goal—RAID 1

RAID 3

RAID 3 is a configuration of striped disks with a parity disk for recovery purposes. The math is quite involved and the reader is referred to the paper by Shooman and Shooman. The value of t_1 that emerges is

$$t_1 = \left[\frac{(1 - R_g)}{n(n+1)\lambda^2} \right]^{0.5} \tag{A4.14}$$

Time Width for Reliability Goal R_g*—RAID 3*

RAID 5

An expression (beyond the scope of this book and my grey matter) for RAID 5 reliability and MTTF was derived by Andrew Shooman and is reproduced below:

$$\text{For } N = 4, \quad R(t) = (4e^{-3\lambda t} - 3e^{-4\lambda t})^{n/3}$$

$$\text{For } N = 8, \quad R(t) = (8e^{-7\lambda t} - 7e^{-8\lambda t})^{n/7} \tag{A4.15}$$

RAID 5 Reliability Approximations

where N is the size of the RAID groups, here using $N = 4$ and $N = 8$, as the often implemented group sizes, and they presented reliability equations for these two values.

From the exponential approximation used in the RAID 1 calculation above, Messrs. Shooman (M. and A.) derive the following value for t_1:

$$t_1 = \frac{\sqrt[2]{[2/N(N-1)]\left[(1 - R_g)^{(N-1)/n} \right]}}{\lambda} \tag{A4.16}$$

Value of t_1 *as a Function of* N *and* R_g

RAID 6

The math for this and the other RAID levels is available in the Shooman (A. and M.) references given below:

Shooman, Andrew M., *RAID Reliability: Mean Time to Data Loss for RAID 1, RAID 5 and RAID 6*. Technical report, EMC Corporation, May 2010 and http://www.xcdsystem.com/rams2012/cdrom/papers/143.pdf (same authors).

The latest RAID paper from these authors is Andrew M. Shooman and Martin L. Shooman. "Reliability and Storage Capacity of Repairable RAID Systems." *Proceedings of the Computer Measurement Group Annual Conference*, November 2013.

Erasure Codes

The math of this is buried in theory developed for telecommunications error detection and recovery and is extended to storage. We have already discussed some of the parameters, but often with different interpretations plus some new terms. I'll list and describe them here although you should be aware of other views on and descriptions of these entities.

AFR: Annual failure rate

MTTF: Mean time to failure, but be careful as to whether the context is a simple disk failure of the failure to be able to access a database across a RAID configuration.

MTTR: Mean time to repair (or restore). Again, the context is important. It may mean repairing a disk or replacing it. It may also mean recovering a RAID configuration via a *restore*.

MTBF: Mean time between failures. This represents the mean of the times between start of failure i to the start of the next one ($i+1$).

MTBDL: Mean time between data loss is the mean value of the time to the *first loss* of some data block in the system. This is roughly the equivalent of MTTFF in normal hardware reliability theory.

MTTDL: Mean time to data loss is the mean time between two consecutive data losses. It can be applied to the mean time before a *given block* is lost due to error. In such cases, it is practical to add a suffix to the quantity, for example. $MTTDL_{OBJ}$ or $MTTDL_{SYS}$ for the loss of a given block or the disk (sub)system, respectively.* This is the data loss entity normally used in loss calculations.

MTTS: Mean time to complete HDD (disk) media scrub

λ: Failure rate of a disk (and related to MTTF as before)

μ: Repair rate of a disk (and related to MTTR as before)

UBER: Unrecoverable bit error rate.

MTTDL Equations[†]

There are different equations for calculating MTTDL for RAID configurations and these are outlined subsequently.

---

[*] An MTTDL calculator can be found at http://www.zetta.net/blog/calculating-mean-time-to-data-loss-and-probability-of-silent-data-corruption/.

[†] Messrs Greenan, Plank, and Wylie disagree with the validity of MTTDL and propose another metric NOMDL. See text above and their paper (c. 2010) at https://www.usenix.org/legacy/event/hotstorage10/tech/full_papers/Greenan.pdf.

General Expression

$$\text{MTTDL} = \frac{\text{MTTF}^{(X+1)}}{\text{No. of data loss combinations} \times \text{MTTR}^X} \tag{A4.17}$$

General MTTDL Formula

where:

X = simultaneous erasure tolerance ($x = 2$ for RAID 6, 1 for RAID 5, for example)

If N is the number of disks, then:

RAID 0

$$\text{MTTDL}_{\text{RAID0}} = \frac{\text{MTTF}^1}{N} = \frac{\text{MTTF}}{N} \tag{A4.18}$$

MTTDL Formula for RAID 0 (Striping)

RAID 5

$$\text{MTTDL}_{\text{RAID5}} = \frac{\text{MTTF}^2}{\text{MTTR} \times N \times (N-1)} \tag{A4.19}$$

MTTDL Formula for RAID 5 / 2-Way Mirror

RAID 6

$$\text{MTTDL}_{\text{RAID6}} = \frac{\text{MTTF}^3}{\text{MTTR}^2 \times N \times (N-1) \times (N-2)} \tag{A4.20}$$

MTTDL Formula for RAID 6 / 3-Way Mirror

NOMDL

Greenan et al. initially proposed a metric magnitude of data loss (MDL), the expected amount of data loss in a system within time t. Subsequently they decided that the metric did not work well across all systems where the number of disks varied. They decided to normalize the MDL to the usable capacity of the target systems, giving the modified metric normalized MDL (NOMDL). Their paper, referenced in the footnote, concludes that while NOMDL is meaningful, understandable, calculable, and comparable, MTTDL is merely calculable!

TTLd

The buck doesn't stop there however. Elerath and Pecht argue that *latent defects* (LDs) should be considered, particularly in large RAID groups. In the scrubbing activity, data on the disks is read and checked against its parity bits even when the data is not being requested by a user. The corrupt data is corrected, media *bad spots* mapped out, and the data moved to *good* locations on the disk.

Enhanced Reliability Modeling of RAID Storage Systems. For reference, see http://www2 .informatik.hu-berlin.de/~wolter/teaching/seminar07/030_enhancedReliabilityModelingOfRaid .pdf.

The significance of undiscovered LDs is apparent when a catastrophic (operational) failure ultimately occurs. The LD, combined with the operational failure, constitutes a double disk failure (DDF), defeating the reliability gains achieved by $(N + 1)$ RAID.

Their argument is that the times that need to be considered are not only operational times to failure (they call these TTop) but also times to LD (TTLd). In addition, we then have times to repair for both scenarios (TTR and TTScrub). I think they are assuming that LDs will occur as per Murphy's Law, which had probably already anticipated this scenario.

Two of the conclusions Elerath and Pecht make are:

- Including estimates for LDs shows DDFs as much as 4000 times greater than the MTTDL-based estimates and has messages for the RAID architect in terms of the best RAID group size and the effects of an increasing failure rate
- Short scrub durations will improve reliability but the extensive scrubbing needed to support high-capacity disks will impact performance to an unacceptable degree

How this impacts the *erasure code* schemes is not clear, but I suppose the old adage applies to whichever scheme you choose: *You pay your money and you make your choice.*

Availability: Replication versus Erasure Coding

In Chapter 4 of this book, the discussion on erasure coding quoted in a paper by Weatherspoon and Kubiatowicz has been provided (https://oceanstore.cs.berkeley.edu/publications/papers/pdf/erasure_iptps.pdf).

Some of the math in there covers the case of fragments of data spread across all the machines in the world with a certain percentage of them down and considers the availability of the data in certain cases. The parameters involved are as follows:

- P_0 is the probability that a block is available.
- n is the total number of fragments (total disks).
- m is the number of fragments needed for reconstruction (coding disks).
- N is the total number of machines in the world.
- M is the number of currently unavailable machines.

P_0 is equal to the number of ways we can arrange unavailable fragments on unreachable servers *times* the number of ways we can arrange available fragments of reachable servers *divided* by the total number of ways we can arrange all the fragments on all the servers. If there are 1 million machines, 10% of which are currently down, storing two replicas provides an availability of 0.99. Erasure Coding of rate $r = 1/2$ with 32 fragments gives an availability of 0.999999998 yet *consumes the same amount of storage and bandwidth, supporting the theory that fragmentation increases availability.*

Lesson 6: Math of Monitoring

In the section on monitoring, we saw the use of *ping* in detecting outages and measuring availability. The use of ping has some benefits in the assessment of the performance of the server and the network leading to it. The discussion which follows is mainly the application of simple queuing theory and is *optional* if you feel your ability at performing *hard sums* is limited.

What follows is really simple queuing theory applied to the ping process.

Ping: Useful Aside

There is a useful spin-off from the timing of a *ping* from our synthetic *user* to server and back. What follows assumes that the traversal time to and from the server is known. Before we tackle this, some elementary performance queuing theory in needed.

For a component of a system performing work, simple queuing theory tells us that the response time T_R is equal to the native service time T_S of the component plus waiting (queuing) time T_W, that is, the total time taken to do its particular job is

$$T_R = T_S + T_W$$

The *component* might be a network line, a server, a disk array, and so on. In fact it could be anything that performs a service as part of a system and takes a finite time to do it. The response times of all the components of a system combine in some way to give the overall response time of the system performing a particular task, for example, processing a transaction. Furthermore, the wait/queue time is given by the equation:

$$T_W = \frac{T_S \times \rho}{(1-\rho)}$$

where ρ is the utilization (or % *busyness*) of that component and so this yields the equation:

$$T_R = T_S + \frac{T_S \times \rho}{(1-\rho)} \tag{A4.21}$$

Service and Response Times' Relationship

For the monitoring situation we are envisaging, imagine the following system comprising a monitor/injector station, a network, and a server. Any disk access and data movement times will be included in the server time for simplicity. We are not avoiding them, simply including them in the server's working time (Figure A4.21).

Let us set up the following parameters for our configuration, using C as the identifier for the server/peripheral combinations or complex (see Figure A4.21):

- $T_S(N)$ is the service time for the network, $T_W(N)$ the wait time for the network, and $\rho(N)$ the network utilization for a simple ping or a transaction (X_N).
- $T_S(S)$ is the service time for the server doing CPU work only, $T_S(C)$ is the service time for the complex as seen from the network, $T_W(C)$ the wait time for the server, and $\rho(S)$ the server utilization as defined by the general Equation A4.21.

The entity $\rho(C)$, the utilization of the Complex, has no real meaning and is irrelevant in the context of our discussion.

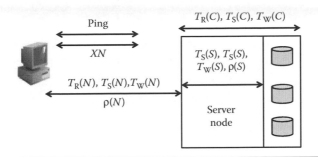

Figure A4.21 Monitoring Scenario and Pinging: Performance information.

Note: It should be noted that the value of ρ at which queuing becomes severe depends on the service time of the server—faster service time equals bigger ρ is tolerated before queuing takes its toll on response times. For slow devices, a utilization of 30% is high, 80% for fast devices is high, but may be tolerable.

Note: It is important here in discussing the *ping* to separate the service time of the CPU from the service time of the server/disk complex, since when dealing with the *ping* situation, there is no disk involvement, only CPU, whereas there is for a normal transaction.

Ping Math

The total network response time for the *ping* transaction is

$$T_R(N) = T_S(N) + T_W(N)$$

Since the wait time $T_W(N)$ for the network transmitting a ping is negligible because of a near-zero value of ρ(N), the service time $T_S(N)$ is the measured response time $T_R(N)$ for the ping *packet* since $T_W(N) = 0$. The ping packet contains 64 bytes—56 data bytes and 8 bytes of protocol header information, so that on a 64 Kb (8 KB) link, the link utilization for a ping would be 0.08%. This will not involve much queuing on an otherwise unloaded *line*. This figure then is essentially the *network latency*.

Since the ping packet is small and the only demands that the receiving server *bat* the packet back to the sender, the equation for the server reads:

$$T_R(S) = T_S(S) + T_W(S) = 0$$

Thus, the total response time for the ping *transaction* alone is

$$T_R(N+S) \cong T_S(N) \text{ since } T_W(N), T_S(S), \text{ and } T_W(S) \text{ are all} \cong 0$$

in the *quiet* period when the *ping* represents the total network and server traffic.

Transaction (*XN*) Math

Since we know the network service time for a 64-byte ping, it is a simple exercise to calculate the network service time, $T_S(N_{xn})$, for the mean transaction traffic of length L bytes:

$$T_S(N_{XN}) = \frac{L}{64} \times T_s(N)$$

where $T_S(N)$ is the service time for our 64-byte *ping* above. Apparently some *pings* are 32 bytes in length but the principle of the calculation is the same.

   Imagine that the ping occurs

1. During the night (or other time) when there are no real users active, time taken T_S—this is the ping time in Ping Math above.
2. During the day alongside real users and transactions, time taken by the *ping* $T_{XN+PING}$

Hopefully, this will give us a handle on the *ambient* network utilization in scenario 2 above. Let's examine the math of this. The equation

$$T_R = T_S + \frac{T_S \times \rho}{(1-\rho)}$$

can be rearranged by judicious math to read a form we will use next:

$$T_R = \frac{T_S}{(1-\rho)}$$

Assuming that the total *ping* response time is approximately the *ping* network service time, then if we use the measured ping response times for the environments of *ping*-only and (*ping* + *XN*), shown in (1) and (2) above, we get the following equation *for the ping response time* as measured in the mixed ping/transaction environment where the utilization of the transmission medium may be significant:

$$\text{Ping response}(\text{ping} + XN) = \frac{T_R(N)(\text{ping alone})}{(1-\rho_N)} \cong \frac{T_S(N)(\text{ping alone})}{(1-\rho_N)} \qquad \text{(A4.22)}$$

Network Utilization via Ping Response Time

We have just measured $T_R(\text{ping} + XN)$ and measured $T_R(\text{ping}) = T_S(\text{ping})$ before, thus the *ambient** network utilization ρ_N can be found using the Equation A4.22 above. It may seem odd that the transaction's details don't appear in Equation A4.22—they do, since they contribute to the utilization ρ that we are calculating and which causes the ping to slow down according to the Equation A4.22.

   As an example, imagine the ping-only response time was 0.120 seconds and the response in the mixed environment was 0.276. Substituting in Equation A4.22 will yield a value for ρ_N of 0.565 or roughly 57% for the network utilization.

---

* I use "ambient" here to mean the utilization at the point in time when the measurements are made. This will almost certainly vary during the day, at weekends, and at other times such as quarter end, year end, and so on.

Ping Sequence Sample

This sample was taken on a DOS system which employs a 32 byte ping packet length (Table A4.4).

> ***Corollary:*** If you want to do network capacity planning, it might be feasible to run two driver systems when in test mode, one injecting pings and the other pseudo transactions— xn1, xn2, … and so on. This should yield the network utilizations, as calculated above, and response times for individual transactions xn_i, where $i = 1, 2, 3, … n$.

> ***A Queuing Story:*** When at Oracle I was teaching a performance course which involved a discussion of elementary queuing theory. During the session, an Italian (who I knew) suggested that queuing theory did not apply in Italy. He was right, since nobody in Italy ever queues—it is just every man or woman for himself or herself.

Lesson 7: Software Reliability/Availability

Overview

Software reliability[*] is a special aspect of reliability engineering. System reliability, by definition, includes all parts of the system, including hardware, software, supporting infrastructure (including critical external interfaces), operators, and procedures. There are significant differences, however, in how software and hardware behave. Most hardware unreliability is the result of a component

Table A4.4   Ping Output and Details

ping oracle.com
Pinging oracle.com [137.254.120.50] with 32 bytes of data:
Reply from 137.254.120.50: bytes = 32 time = 167 ms TTL = 235
Reply from 137.254.120.50: bytes = 32 time = 167 ms TTL = 235
Reply from 137.254.120.50: bytes = 32 time = 167 ms TTL = 235
Reply from 137.254.120.50: bytes = 32 time = 167 ms TTL = 235
Ping statistics for 137.254.120.50:
Packets: Sent = 4, Received = 4, Lost = 0 (0% Loss)
Approximate round trip times in milli-seconds:
Minimum = 167 ms, Maximum = 167 ms, Average = 167 ms

---

[*] Extracted and condensed from Wikipedia and added to http://en.wikipedia.org/wiki/Reliability_engineering #Software_reliability.

or material failure that results in the system not performing its intended function. Repairing or replacing the hardware component restores the system to its original operating state. However, software does not fail in the same sense that hardware fails. Instead, software unreliability is the result of unanticipated results of software logic operations.

Despite this difference in the source of failure between software and hardware, several software reliability models based on statistics have been proposed to quantify what we experience with software: the longer software is run, the higher the probability that it will eventually be used in an untested manner and exhibit a LD that results in a failure according to Messrs. Shooman, Musa, and Denney.

Software reliability depends on the following:

■ Feasible requirements—no ATTAM* applications
■ Good specifications—documented and agreed with users
■ Good design and coding—abiding by established software development (coding) standards, walkthroughs, and peer reviews
■ Good testing and implementation—phased, unit tests, pilot, review, modification
■ First class final documentation across the board for error resolution and change control

According to many sources, software reliability also depends a great deal on the volatility of the specifications—*could we just change this to ...* and *it's just a few lines of code (JAFLOC)*.

Software reliability engineering (SRE) relies heavily on a disciplined software engineering process to anticipate and design against unintended consequences. There is more overlap between software quality engineering and SRE than between hardware quality and reliability.

A good software development plan is a key aspect of the software reliability program. The software development plan describes the design and coding standards, peer reviews, unit tests, configuration management, software metrics, and software models to be used during software development.

A common reliability metric is the number of software faults, usually expressed as faults per thousand lines of code (KLOCs). This metric, along with software execution time, is key to most software reliability models and estimates.

Software Reliability Theory

Although the theory of software reliability uses mathematical distributions and looks at first glance as rigorous as hardware theory, it is not quite so. This is due to certain differences:

■ The large element of human frailty in the design, coding, and testing of software products.
■ Software reliability is not a function of time when fully operational.
■ No errors develop that are not already there, that is, it doesn't react to moisture or corrode like hardware.
■ Software does not *wear out* like hardware.
■ Software is definitely repairable (once you've found out what is wrong) but will need testing .

---

* *All Things To All Men* (or women, but ATTAW doesn't have the same ring to it).

- Software in general is not affected by environmental factors such as overheating, weather, and so on. It is only affected inasmuch as it will fail if the hardware on which it runs fails for some reason.
- Redundancy cannot be implemented as simply as duplicate hardware solutions as there needs to be communication and preservation of *state* information if duplicate modules are used as *backup*.
- N module redundancy ($N > 3$) can be implemented but requires effort to compare the output of each module to detect and correct failures, rather like a cluster forum.
- Hardware systems can be built using standard components and interface standards. This is more difficult in a software environment where reusable code might only exist within a team or, at best, within an organization. There are no standard parts for software, except some standardized logic structures and, in the scientific world, standard subroutines for various calculations.

So, despite the fact that software reliability looks on a par with hardware when looking at the myriad equations and mathematical distributions, it is just this proliferation that makes software reliability a fluid subject. This explains why there are many more models in SRE than there are in the hardware world.

The Failure/Defect Density Models

In this book, we have divided models into the two classes given as follows:

- Time between defects and cumulative defects encountered
- Density of defects or defects per unit time

Note: This saves the initial confusion which troubled me when I came across classes or categories called *prediction* and *estimation*, *black box*, and *white box* and several categories and subcategories. I hope this classification makes life easier for the reader too.

The models have quite esoteric names and a selection of them follows:

- Goel–Okumoto Non-homogeneous Poisson Process model (NHPP)
- Musa Execution Time model
- Musa–Okumoto Logarithmic Model
- Goel Generalized NHPP model
- Shooman Exponential model
- Generalized Poisson model
- IBM Binomial and Poisson model

We will cover only the first three models, with two cases outlined for the Musa models—the *basic execution* model and the *logarithmic* model.

The fault count models are concerned with the number of failures seen or faults detected in given testing intervals or *units*—calendar time, execution time, number of test cases, and so on. When faults are removed from the software, the number of failures experienced per unit of measurement will decrease.

Two ways of measuring and hopefully predicting the reliability of software are as follows:

■ Measure the trend of cumulative failure count $\mu(\tau)$—SRGM model
■ Measure the trend of the number of failures per unit time $\lambda(\tau)$—defect density

where τ is the time in execution of the program. We are interested in the second case of *defect density* or *failure count*. Defects occur in software from the first coding stages through to the end of life (EOL) of a program and it is desirable to be able to make defect predictions about new, developing software based on data from existing, working software.

Common Terms Used in Most Models

$N(t)$, $m(t)$	Total number of failures experienced by time t.
$P[N(t) = n]$	The probability of there being n errors by time t.
$\mu(t)$	Expected number of failures expected by time t, thus $\mu(t) = E[N(t)]$.
$\lambda(t)$	Failure intensity which is the derivative (differentiated) of the mean value function, that is, $\lambda(t) = d\mu/dt$, the number of failures/unit time.
t, τ	Elapsed (calendar) time and CPU time, respectively.
N, N_0	Initial number of faults present in the software prior to testing.
$z(t)$	Per-fault hazard rate, which represents the probability that a fault, that had not been activated so far, will cause a failure instantaneously when activated. This term is usually assumed to be a constant (ϕ) by many of the models.

Goel–Okumoto NHPP Model

This model assumes that failures in a software system occur at random times due to faults. Based on the study of actual failure data across many systems, Goel and Okumoto proposed the following structure to the model (see above for the parameters):

$$\mu(t) = N(1 - e^{-\varphi t}) \text{ and } \lambda(t) = N\varphi e^{-\varphi t} = \varphi[N - \mu(t)]$$

The model assumes the following:

■ The expected number of failures observed by time t follows a Poisson distribution, mean value $\mu(t)$.
■ The number of software failures that occur in interval $(t + \Delta t)$ is proportional to the number of undetected faults, $[N - \mu(t)]$.
■ There is no correlation between the numbers of failures detected in the failure intervals $(0, t_1)$, (t_1, t_2), ... (t_{n-1}, t_n), that is, they are independent.
■ The fault removal process when failures are detected is instantaneous and perfect.
■ The per-fault hazard rate is fixed at a constant given by ϕ [see $z(t)$ above].

Musa Models

John Musa's model has two forms, the *basic* and the *logarithmic* (developed with Okumoto) and often known as the Musa–Okumoto model.

The assumptions in Musa's basic model are as follows:

- Software faults are independent of each other and distributed with a constant rate of encounter (equidistant in time).
- A mixture of instructions and the execution time between failures is large compared with the instruction execution time.
- The sets of input data for each run of the software are selected at random.
- All failures are observed.
- The fault causing the failure is corrected immediately otherwise a recurrence of that failure is *not* counted.

There are different treatments of the Musa models and one is covered here[*] in the subsection Model A and the standard treatment of the two Musa models in Model B and Model C, followed by a schematic graph in subsection Graphical Model D.

Model A—The *owner* of the paper from which this math is quoted is the only identifier I have for the author of the paper referenced in the footnote.

The Rome Reliability Toolkit[†] suggests the following equation for the initial software:

$$\lambda_0 = \frac{rKN_0}{I} \text{ failures per CPU second}$$

where:

r = processor speed in instructions/second
K = fault exposure ratio (a constant as far as we are concerned)
N_0 = total no. of faults in the initial program (at $\tau = 0$)
I = no. of *object* instructions which is determined by LOC × expansion ratio

Object instructions are in essence *machine* instructions. The number of such instructions in say L lines of code will depend on which language the instructions are in. Higher level languages like COBOL will generate lower level instruction in Assembler code so a 5000-statement program in COBOL will generate more machine (or object) instructions than an assembler program of the same size.

This is illustrated in the Table A4.5, taken from the Rome Reliability Toolkit (1993). Because of the age of these figures (1993), it is hard to see how 4GLs would be handled in these models[‡]:

Following this, the procedure develops as follows:

Let us call the ratio $r/I = k$, which is used in the following equations. The failure intensity in Musa's Basic Execution model is given by:

$$\lambda(t) = Kf[N - \mu(t)]$$

---

[*] http://incoming-proxy.ist.edu.gr/stfs_public/cs/msc/ReadingMaterial_MMSE-SEPE_oct2011/Software%20 Quality/Software%20Reliability%20Model%20Study.pdf.

[†] Obtainable from www.quanterion.com.

[‡] Many years ago, in estimating the resource consumption of a COBOL program of size N, IBM used a factor of 3 for the consumption by an Assembler program size N.

Table A4.5 Musa Model: Expansion Ratios

Programming Language	Expansion Ratio
Assembler	1 (base unit)
Macro assembler	1.5
C	2.5
COBOL	3
FORTRAN	3
Ada	4.5

Note: This looks the same as the Goel–Okumoto equation except the factor *Kf* replaces the ϕ of that model.

Model B (Musa's Basic Execution Model)—This uses the assumption that the decrease in failure intensity (rate) is *constant* and states that the failure intensity is a function of the average number of failures experienced at any point in time, that is, the failure probability. This is expressed in the equations that follow. An assumption for this model is:

$$\lambda(\mu) = \lambda_0 \left(1 - \frac{\mu}{v_0} \right)$$

That is, the failure intensity is a function of the average number of failures experienced at any given point in time.

$$\mu(\tau) = \lambda_0 \left(1 - \frac{\mu}{v_0} \right) \text{ and } \lambda(\tau) = \lambda_0 e^{-(\lambda_0 \tau / v_0)} \tag{A4.23}$$

Musa Basic Model Failure Rate/Intensity

where:
$\lambda(\mu)$ = failure intensity
λ_0 = initial failure intensity at the start of execution
μ = average numbers of failures/unit time at a given point in time
v_0 = total number of failures over an infinite time

Model C (Musa–Okumoto Logarithmic Model)—A base assumption for this model is expressed as a decreasing rate with time, that is

$$\mu(t) = \frac{1}{\theta} e^{(\lambda_0 \theta \tau + 1)}$$

Logarithmic Model

$$\mu(\tau) = v_0(1 - e^{\lambda_0\tau/v_0})$$

Basic Model

(A4.24)

Musa – Okumoto Logarithmic Model Failure Rate

θ is a parameter representing a *nonlinear* drop in failure intensity in this model.

Graphical Model D—Graphical representation of these models, showing some of the parameters used in the equations above, can be found in Figure A4.22.

It shows the graphs of failure intensity versus cumulative number of failures and a point somewhere on the horizontal axis is taken as infinite time, denoted by v_0. The curves intersect the vertical axis at the initial failure intensity and, true to the model, decreases over time until at *infinity* it becomes either zero (basic model) or progresses asymptotically to zero.

These figures are $\lambda_0(L)$ for the log curve and $\lambda_0(B)$ for the basic line. The lower the values of these quantities, the higher the reliability of the corresponding software.

The relationship between the failure intensity (rate) and the reliability of the software is given by the expression (similar to its exponential hardware cousin):

$$R(\tau) = e^{-\lambda\tau}$$

A model such as this demonstrates a decreasing failure rate for residual software errors, which is what some models assume.

There are a number of other models in this class which are listed below:

■ Goel generalized NHPP model
■ Shooman exponential model
■ Generalized Poisson model
■ IBM binomial and Poisson model

These can be found in numerous papers and presentations on the Internet.

Times between Failure Models

This is another group of models, each tailored for the situation whose data fits the model:

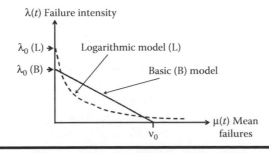

Figure A4.22 Basic and logarithmic models—Failure intensity versus time.

- Jelinski–Moranda model
- Schick and Wolverton model
- Goel and Okumoto imperfect debugging model
- Littlewood–Verrall Bayesian model

Numerous articles and presentations on these can be found by a judicious search on the Internet.

So What?

Michael Lyu has this to say about models and their usefulness. The chapter numbers mentioned below refer to the following book, edited by him (http://www.cse.cuhk.edu.hk/~lyu/book/reliability/):

> For the "*so what*" question, the answer is two-fold. First, if there is no software reliability measurement, there is no evidence of a quantifiable software development process which can be engineered and improved. The application of software reliability models indicate the maturity of an underlying software development process from industry viewpoint. Secondly, even though we cannot guarantee the accuracy of an SRGM for a particular project in advance, we can still use the SRGM prediction results to confirm the readiness (or otherwise) of the software project in terms of its reliability. Chapter 9, for example, takes this point further for industry practice. Besides, whether an SRGM is applicable can also be tested by a trend analysis, which is handled in Chapter 10.

Software vendors are interested in this kind of *crystal-ball* gazing to assess the quality of new outgoing software and resource planning for the maintenance stage of the software's life, that is, between ship and EOL.

Rayleigh Distribution

The Rayleigh pdf and cdf functions are shown below:

$$f(x,\sigma) = \frac{x}{\sigma^2} e^{-(x^2/2\sigma^2)} \text{ and } F(x) = [1 - e^{-(x^2/2\sigma^2)}]$$

(A4.25)

Rayleigh pdf and cdf Functions

An anonymous Internet paper outlines the prediction of software reliability through the various stages of code development and these are listed in Table A4.5 and Figure A4.23.

The plot of the observed defects (failures) are shown for the various stages of development and matched against a Rayleigh curve. Instead if real time on the horizontal axis, the stages of development are shown instead. As we have seen before, this axis can be kilometers before failure, rotations before a spinning component fails, and so on. This diagram shows the defect count at various stages of the development cycle from inception to integration testing of the *suite* and is plotted against the Rayleigh distribution (Table A4.6).

The diagram and the table above illustrate the relative timescales for each phase of the development cycle, the table outlining the meaning of the terms.

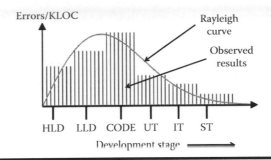

Figure A4.23 Rayleigh distribution for software development.

Table A4.6   Errors in Development Stages and Timescales

Software Stage	Timescale (Relative)
HLD (high-level design)	0.5
LLD (low-level design)	1.5
Coding (implementation)	2.5
UT (unit testing)	3.5
IT (integration testing)	4.5
ST (system testing)	5.5

Some Equations for Model Shapes[*]

This short section is just to illustrate the equations for the curves shown in the diagram above. Most of the models fall into either the *concave* or *S-shaped* camps so don't worry about the names below since they are simply showing the two *types* of the model.

NHPP—The nonhomogeneous Poisson process exponential model is of the *concave* shape, given by the equation below:

$$m(t) = a(1 - e^{-br})$$

$$a(t) = a \text{ and } b(t) = b$$

(A4.26)

Software Reliability Concave Model

where:
$m(t)$ is the expected number of errors detected by time t
$a(t)$ is the error content function, that is, the number of errors in the software including the initial and introduced errors at time t
$b(t)$ is the error detection rate per error at time t

---

[*] http://users.encs.concordia.ca/~dssouli/INSE%206250%20folder/Survey%20papers%2012%20folder/S_Reliability.pptx, a presentation by N. Naseri and J. Vazquez entitled "Software Reliability."

Inflection *S*-Shaped Model—This represents the *S-curve* of the NHPP P–N–Z model (Pham–Nordmann–Zhang), given by the equation below:

$$m(t) = \frac{1}{(1+\beta e^{-bt})} \, [(c+a)(1-e^{-bt})]$$

$$a(t) = c + a(1-e^{-at})$$

$$b(t) = \frac{1}{(1+\beta e^{-bt})} \tag{A4.27}$$

Software Reliability S-Shaped Model

m(*t*) is the expected number of errors detected by time *t*

a(*t*) is the error content function, that is, the number of errors in the software including the initial and introduced errors at time *t*

b(*t*) is the error detection rate per error at time *t*

Lesson 8: Additional RAS Features

The reliability, availability, and serviceability (RAS) features presented in Chapter 2 are more or less common to modern hardware and, in some cases, software as well. There are other features, some bordering on proprietary, which have been added to hardware implementations which are perhaps worth recording here.

Sometimes the same feature goes under a different name depending on which vendor is trying to impress you.

Upmarket RAS Features

RAS is an evolving feature, adding new facilities to increase hardware availability, though it must be remembered that hardware is only part of the availability equation.

> *Note:* These are *extras* which not every vendor has implemented. Where a vendor is identified by a feature, it does not necessarily mean that feature is unique to that vendor—simply that it was found in their literature. Also, presenting this list of RAS *add-ons* does not imply completeness. You need not read every line—just marvel at the new features.

Processor

The following features have been added to their products by various vendors but most of them are now universal in modern CPU hardware.

- Processor fabric bus protection
- Dynamic processor de-allocation
- Dynamic processor sparing
- Using **c**(apacity) **o**(n) **d**(emand) cores (IBM)
- Advanced machine check architecture (MCA)
- Using capacity from spare pool
- Core error recovery

- Bad data containment (for error recovery)
- Alternate processor recovery
- Partition core contained check-stop
- Persistent processor de-allocation
- Mid-plane connection for inter-nodal communication
- Electronically isolated partitioning [*domains*]
- Corrected machine check interrupt (CMCI) for PFA (see below)

I/O Subsystem

The following features have been added to their products by various vendors, some proprietary, but most of them are now universal in modern disk storage.

- GX+ bus persistent de-allocation (IBM)
- Quick Path Interconnect (QPI) Viral Mode—uncorrectable error notification (Intel)
- QPI protocol protection via CRC (Intel)
- QPI self-healing (Intel)
- ECC I/O hub with freeze behavior
- PCI bus enhanced error detection
- PCI bus enhanced error recovery
- PCI–PCI bridge enhanced error handling
- Redundant channel link

Memory Availability

The following features have been added to many main memory subsytems by various vendor. They are often the same feature with a different name.

- ECC in L2 and L3 cache and elsewhere (various I/O paths)
- Failed DIMM identification (for selective replacement)
- Fine-grained memory mirroring
- Memory sparing with CoD at IPL time
- CRC plus retry on memory data bus (CPU to buffer)
- Data bus (memory buffer to DRAM) ECC plus retry
- Dynamic memory channel repair
- L1 parity check plus retry/set delete
- L2 cache line delete
- L3 cache line delete
- Self-healing L2, L3 directory caches (HP)
- L4 cache line sparing (HP)
- Special uncorrectable error handling
- Active memory™ (IBM) mirroring for hypervisor

Fault Detection and Isolation

The following features have been added to their products by various vendors but most of them are now universal in modern hardware.

- Run-time diagnostics
- First failure data capture (FFDC)—data for exception handlers (IBM)

- Platform FFDC diagnostics
- I/O FFDC diagnostics
- OS FFDC
- Storage protection keys
- Error log analysis
- Service processor (SP) support for:
  - Wire tests
  - Component initialization data

Clocks and Service Processor

- Dynamic SP failover at run time/redundant SP
- Clock failover at run time/redundant clock (IBM Sysplex)

Serviceability

- Boot-time progress indicators
- Firmware (embedded software) error codes
- (Relevant) OS error codes
- Inventory collection for maintenance uses
- Environmental and power warnings
- Extended error data collection
- I/O drawer redundant connections
- I/O drawer hot add and concurrent repair
- Hot GX adapter (Infiniband connection) add and repair
- Concurrent add of powered I/O rack
- SP mutual surveillance with the OS hypervisor
- Dynamic firmware update with Hardware Management Console (HMC)
- Service agent *Call Home* application
- Service indicators—guiding light or light path LEDs
- SP support for BIST for logic/arrays, wire tests, and component initialization
- System dump for memory, VM hypervisor, SP
- OS error reporting to HMC for analysis
- RMC secure error transmission subsystem
- Health check scheduled operations with HMC
- Operator panel (real or virtual)
- Concurrent Op panel maintenance
- Redundant HMCs
- Automated server recovery/restart
- Clustering support
- Repair and verify guided maintenance
- Concurrent OS kernel update (OS equivalent of hardware hot-swap)
- Hot-node add
- Cold-node repair
- Concurrent-node repair

For a description of many of these features, see, via searches, appropriate IBM Redbooks and documents on Intel Xeon processor family (RAS features).

Predictive Failure Analysis

PFA is a term for predicting hard errors based on machine checking features and error history logs. This is used by several vendors but may differ in name. See Terminology in Appendix 1 for more details on this. The software equivalent of the hardware models are the various mathematical models which serve essentially as software *PFAs*.

Lesson 9: Triple Modular Redundancy

TMR was one of the first forms of hardware redundancy, introduced by J. (Johann) Von Neumann in 1956. It is an example of trading performance for reliability of a *unit* of components (Figure A4.24).

The basic principle is to ensure a correct result from a component, it would be nice to have it checked in some way. TMR attempts this by asking three components to do the task in hand and then a *voter* component compares the outputs. If all are in agreement, there is no problem and the output is accepted.

However, if there is disagreement, the voter (arbiter) will take a majority decision—in this case 2 from 3. The odd number of components (3) assures there will not be a tie in the voting. There is an assumption that the three components have independent failure patterns so that one can't bring down the others when it fails. It also assumes the voter is 100% reliable. If the voter is not 100% reliable (and nothing is) then the voters themselves are duplicated.

In the single voter case, assume the reliability of each component module is R, then the reliability of the system R_{SYS} can be shown to be

$$R_{SYS} = R^3 + (2 \text{ from } 3) R^2 (1 - R)$$

If we assume for the moment that $R_{SYS} + R$, then $3R^2 - 2R^3 - R = 0$, which is true when solved for $R = 0$, 0.5, and 1, giving no increase in reliability over the simplex counterpart.

The schematic of the simple, single-voter scenario is shown in Figure A.24 and the duplicated voter scenario in Figure A.25 below.

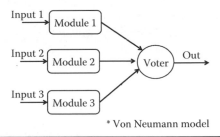

* Von Neumann model

Figure A4.24 TMR (Von Neumann model)—Single voter.

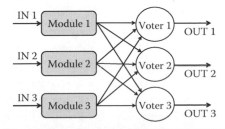

Figure A4.25 TMR with triple voters.

$$R_{SYS} = R^3 + \frac{(3!)}{(2!+1!)} R^2(1-R) = (3R^2 - 2R^3)$$

(A4.28)

Reliability of Single Vote TMR

In real life, it is quite possible for the outputs to feed into a second system like the first and the same procedure followed again and so on until the end of the chain. An example of the use of TMR can be found in some spacecraft where three processors are used where one would suffice for performance requirements.

Lesson 10: Cyber Crime, Security, and Availability

The Issue

Had this book been written 10 or so years ago, this section would be blank. However, the increasing incidence of crimes affecting computing has migrated from being a nuisance, perpetrated by competing *geeks*, for individuals on home PCs to being a major, worldwide and growing issue for business and public organizations. This type of activity is often called *cyber crime* and the software agents which implement it *malware*.

The interconnection between systems made possible by the Internet has its own advantages and disadvantages that were not seen to any degree in the days of proprietary systems.

Some of the new terminology of this scenario include the following:

- *Vulnerability* or how open is your IT to attack from outside
- *Assessment* of the business areas' importance and the impact of their disruption
- *Scanning* for possible *anomalies* in IT behavior, particularly the network
- *Analysis* of the data gathered from the scanning
- *Correlation* of data from different sources to isolate *events* that might signal some kind of external or internal *intrusion* into systems
- *Mitigation* of the effects of the intrusion or *breach*
- *Patching* to solve immediate issues
- *Protection* from future occurrences by tools and techniques
- *SIEM* (see below)
- *Botnets, distributed denial of service (DDoS), virus, phishing, credit card fraud, spoofing, net extortion, identity theft, hardware hijacking, spam, crypto blackmail*, and other types of intrusion, including deliberate theft or destruction of important data for either gain, malice, or sheer fun. Whatever the reasons, the effect is the same.

Note: Even if you don't understand them, it is useful to recognize the names but, more importantly, do something about them. Saying it is too difficult to understand is not really a valid reason for passivity. When teaching children road safety, you don't need to tell them all about the different types and models of cars they might get hit by—you just tell them not to walk in front of anything that moves on the road.

The Solution

The way these threats are tackled is via a methodology and not the *seat of the pants* reactive technique. There are a number of ... *Management* systems in IT—performance, capacity, change, and others. One of the latest is *Security Information Event Management Systems* (SIEM), where the word *event* is significant.

The management of events entails trapping practically everything that goes on in the system—servers, network, and so on—and analyzing it for events that are out of the ordinary and may represent some form of *attack* on the system. The motto might be *if it moves or changes, log it.* It is rather like gathering masses of data about radio signals from space and trying to analyze them for some signs of Extra Terrestrial Intelligence (ETI and the search SETI).

> ***Note:*** Event trapping is fairly easy: the analysis, conclusions, mitigation, and prevention of reoccurrence a little harder. How this is done is down to the organization involved and any tools and techniques employed by them. Enter security analytics, outlined in the next section.

Security Analytics

A paper by Arbor Networks on the product "Pravail Security Analytics" proposes the following reasons and output for a security analytics product[*]:

- Upload packet captures for a comprehensive security and threat check
- Determining if the network is overly targeted
- Employing network forensics and incident management
- Identifying attackers and tracking advanced persistent threats (APTs)
- Identifying indicators and warnings of threats
- Finding zero-day attacks in historical data
- Data exfiltration and what files are being transmitted
- Baselining the network, to determine what is normal and comparing it with other organizations
- Unmask attackers through profiling and monitoring over long periods
- Analyze network data and produce audit and compliance reports
- Review and assess the effectiveness of the security controls

As ever, these controls may need to be tiered to suit the criticality of the services affected by intrusions (www.arbornetworks.com).

Another useful paper, sponsored by HP, "SANS Security Analytics Survey" outlines the needs of and for security analytics and presents survey results on the issues confronting organizations in this area (http://whitepapers.theregister.co.uk/paper/download/delayed/3222/sans-security-analystics-survey-2013-hp.pdf).

Zero Trust Security Model

In many IT areas, the use of standards, models, and policies is recommended and security is no exception. In 2010, Forrester Research proposed a "Zero Trust" Model for security which, in

---

[*] There are other vendors of products which operate in this field of security analytics.

essence, suggest we treat everyone and everything as untrustworthy, including internal personnel. Surveys have shown that internal people can be as *security malicious* as external agents, data spies, and other miscreants.

Basic characteristics of the zero trust model are as follows:

- All resources are securely accessed regardless of location
- Strict least privilege control is mandatory
- All network traffic is inspected and logged

There are a number of security areas listed in the reference below, including wireless and network access control.

For reference, see the IBM sponsored paper at http://www-01.ibm.com/common/ssi/cgi-bin/ssialias?subtype=WH&infotype=SA&appname=SWGE_WG_WG_USEN&htmlfid=WGL03038USEN&attachment=WGL03038USEN.PDF for a description of the need for this model and its implementation.

Security Information Event Management

The term security information (and) event management (SIEM—Gartner 2005) describes the product capabilities of gathering, analyzing, and presenting information from network and security devices: identity and access management applications; vulnerability management and policy compliance tools; OS, database and application logs, and external threat data. Figure A4.26 shows in outline how SIEM activity flows in a loop through the activities involved.

The diagram is generic and specific vendor products will vary in their approach to monitoring, analysis, results presentation, and so on.

Security Management Flow

SIEM usually consolidates log source event data from thousands of device endpoints and applications distributed throughout a network. It performs immediate normalization and correlation activities on raw data to distinguish real threats from false positives.

Typical SIEM capabilities include the following:

- *Data aggregation:* Security events, network events, firewall events, application logs, OS information, and other data.

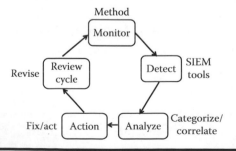

Figure A4.26   Schematic of SIEM.

- *Correlation:* Looking for common attributes and linked events to try to assess if a threat is present. The sophistication of this process depends on the software chosen. Mosaic Security Research listed 85 different SIEM products extant at January 2012.
- *Alerts:* These can be generated and issued, in a variety of ways, after the correlation stage identifies a *positive* threat or potential threat.
- *Data retention:* Event and other data can be kept for long periods to analyze and correlate data over time.
- *Applications logs:* These can collect data on services such as ERP, workflow, database activity, management activity, and other data.

According to the Gartner report referenced below, the leading SIEM product vendors are as follows:

- HP ArcSight
- IBM-Q1 Labs
- McAfee
- Splunk
- LogRhythm

For a Gartner Group SIEM magic quadrant discussion, diagram, and other magic quadrant vendors, see their report and a summary in Appendix 1 of this book (http://www.gartner.com/technology/reprints.do?id=1-1FN1ULD&ct=130514&st=sg).

SIEM Best Practices

These notes are summarized from a paper by Scott Gordon CISSP (2010), via AccelOps, Inc.* It is entitled "Operationalizing Information Security: Put the Top 10 SIEM Best Practices to Work" and encapsulates the main messages in security monitoring, recording, and subsequent or real-time analysis.

An ideal SIEM should provide real-time event data and also search and report on historical incident data. Collecting data is easier than analyzing and correlating it. In a security context, correlation essentially means asking "are these incidents I've just logged symptomatic of something untoward going on in my system or are they just a collection of trivial unrelated events?"

These are the key practices to capture and correlate events:

1. *Requirements:* Establish key monitoring and reporting requirements prior to deployment. This would include objectives, targets, compliance controls, implementation, and workflow [*a kind of RBD*].
2. *Implementation:* Determine the scope of implementation, infrastructure audit targets [*I read this as due diligence*], activation phases, and configuration.
3. *Compliance:* Identify compliance requirements and automate compliance processes and the management of audit data including accessibility, integrity, retention, disposal, and evidence requisites.
4. *Access control:* Monitor and report on key status, violations, and anomalous access to critical resources.

---

* http://www.accelops.com/. A vendor of SIEM products and services.

5. *Perimeter defenses:* Monitor and report on key status, configuration changes, violations/attacks, and anomalous activity associated with perimeter defenses.
6. *Resource integrity:* Monitor and report on key status, configuration changes and patches, backup processes, vulnerabilities [*pentests*], threats, and anomalous activity affecting network and system resources integrity and availability.
7. *Intrusion detection:* Monitor, respond to, and report on key status, notifications, and incidents regarding intrusion detection/prevention network and system threats, attacks, and anomalous activity.
8. *Malware defenses:* Monitor and report on key status, threats, issues, violations, and activity supporting malware controls.
9. *Application defenses:* Monitor and report on key status, configuration changes, issues, violations, and anomalous activity regarding web, database, and other application defenses.
10. *Acceptable use:* Monitor and report on key status, issues, violations, and activity regarding the acceptable use of resources and information.

In short, you need to assess what your vital assets are, how vulnerable they are to threats (internal and external), how you spot them, what to do about them when you do find them, and then document it and do it.

Security: Denial of Service*

A specific threat to availability is a *denial of service* (DoS) attack. A DoS attack is characterized by an explicit attempt by attackers to prevent legitimate users of a service from using it. Examples include the following:

■ Attempts to *flood* a network, thereby preventing legitimate network traffic from being processed
■ Attempts to disrupt connections between two machines, thereby preventing access to a service
■ Attempts to prevent a particular individual from accessing a service
■ Attempts to disrupt service to a specific system or person

The National Institute of Standards and Technology (NIST) document referenced recommends defining the motivations of each threat source and the potential actions of these sources, one of which is outlined below.

> *Tip:* Subscribing to NIST security newsletters will keep you abreast of the wide-ranging security aspects of IT and other systems.

Security: Insider Threats

A recent survey of hundreds of IT staff across the world commissioned by the security firm Cyber-Ark Software showed that 74% of the respondents believed that the insider threat to their

---

* See http://www.cert.org/tech_tips/denial_of_service.html, and for solutions, see http://www.cert.org/advisories/CA-2000-01.html. Also see http://nvlpubs.nist.gov/nistpubs/SpecialPublications/NIST.SP.800-53r4.pdf.

organizations was greater than that posed by external cyber criminals. Examples[*] of dangerous situations in an IT environment can include:

- Administrative users who are not required to periodically change their elevated *super user* credentials. This leads to privileged account passwords that may never expire, becoming known to too many current and former workers.
- Computers and network appliances that share common username and password logins, exposing large portions of the infrastructure should a single account be compromised.
- The storing of administrative passwords on spreadsheets that are placed in well-known or unmonitored locations.
- Failure to adopt a *continuous auditing* approach to security; never enacting the processes to search out new vulnerabilities and mitigate them before they provide the opening for an attack.

Physical machine room security is another issue. People, insiders or outsiders, being able to walk into a machine room unhindered may present a danger to security. Remember that much of the intrusion damage to systems is attributed to *insiders*, that is, people who work for the same company as you.

James Bond has made such intrusions in several movies I have seen—and got away with it. Your company might not.

Security: Mobile Devices (BYOD)

A lot of attention is being lavished on mobile access,[†] bring your own device (BYOD), to corporate systems with the obvious benefits of personnel access from anywhere on a *need to access* basis. Since this kind of access is not in a controlled environment, there is a need to guard this perimeter access to prevent malicious access to company systems and possible ensuing damage. As well as compromising company data, this illegal access may result in an outage—physical or logical.

Figures from Enterprise Management Associates (www.enterprisemanagement.com) suggest that three types of mobile devices would figure in *roaming* access: laptops, tablets, and smartphones. Furthermore, it says that the majority of laptops are supplied (and presumably maintained) by the company but the majority of tablets and smartphones are acquired by the end user. The last two items are therefore possible security exposures if used for personal business.

There is a NIST ITL document NIST Special Publication 800-124 Revision 1, "Guidelines for Managing the Security of Mobile Devices in the Enterprise," which offers guidelines to improve the security of mobile devices (http://csrc.nist.gov/publications/nistbul/itlbul2013_07.pdf plus); "Guide to Malware Incident Prevention and Handling for Desktops and Laptops" (NIST Special Publication) (http://nvlpubs.nist.gov/nistpubs/SpecialPublications/NIST.SP.800-83r1.pdf).

---

[*] Philip Lieberman, CEO of *Lieberman Software*.
[†] By 2015, the world's mobile worker population will reach 1.3 billion, representing 37.2% of the total workforce: *IDC study, Worldwide Mobile Worker Population 2011–2015 Forecast.*

Kaspersky Lab's Global IT Risks survey, which is conducted by research consultancy B2B International, is now in its third year. In the latest survey, there are a number of findings related to security in general and BYOD in particular. Among the many findings and statistics are:

- The average cost of an IT security breach is $50,000 (£32,000) for an SMB and $649,000 (£430,00) for enterprises
- Less than 10% have a BYOD security policy implemented, which is asking for trouble in the future
- Nearly 1/2 have nothing
- Fear of security breaches happening is high in most organizations (in Japan, 93% of organizations feel the threat is very real)

In addition, a warning about BYOD security is issued in the paper "Mobile Security" found at http://resources.idgenterprise.com/original/AST-0106323_marble_cso.pdf, which is sponsored by Marble Security (www.marblesecurity.com).

The same organization provides a white paper "Nine Critical Threats," which exist in the mobile access area (http://go.marblesecurity.com/NineThreatsWPwebsite_Marblelandingpage052013.html).

A Gartner/Sophos paper "Magic Quadrant for Mobile Data Protection" (September 2013) presents a number of vendor offerings, listing strengths and weaknesses, and then placing them in the familiar Gartner Quadrant.

It also "tracks software security utilities that enforce confidentiality policies by encrypting data and then managing access to that encrypted data on the primary and secondary storage systems of end-user devices" (http://www.gartner.com/technology/reprints.do?id=1-1H1RO5G&ct=130710&st=sb).

Security breaches are a real possibility and threaten to disrupt services and hence availability. BYOD appears to be a neglected area of security, which presents a big exposure to business organizations.

BYOD Security Steps

- Develop a mobile device security policy. The policy should define what types of organizational resources can be accessed via mobile devices, what types of mobile devices are permitted, degrees of access, and how provisioning should be handled.
- Develop system threat models for mobile devices and the resources accessed through such devices. Threat modeling helps organizations to identify security requirements and to design effective solutions.
- Consider the merits of each provided security service, determine the needed services, and design and acquire solutions which provide the services. Categories of services to be considered include general policy, data communication and storage, user and device authentication, and applications.
- Implement and test a pilot of the mobile device solution before putting the solution into production. Consider connectivity, protection, authentication, application functionality, solution management, logging, and performance of the mobile device solution.
- Fully secure each organization-issued mobile device before allowing access. This ensures a basic level of trust in the device before it is exposed to threats.
- Develop some form of security for owner-possession devices, maybe even forbidding them.
- Maintain mobile device security on a regular basis. Organizations should periodically assess mobile device policies and procedures to ensure that users are properly following them.

Security: WiFi in the Enterprise

Many people employ WiFi[*] devices for personal use and often wonder what are all the other stations shown on their device when, for example, checking for signal strength. They are other users, you are *connecting* to them and vice versa. These signals fly through the air and are thus accessible to anyone who has a receiving device. According to the paper (http://resources.idgenterprise.com/original/AST-0111237_Documents_PDF_FutureOfWiFi.pdf), WiFi is being increasingly used in enterprises and presents its own security issues.

WiFi is being used for inter-office and intra-office communications as well as between offices and warehouses, factories, and other sites. As with any business communications, there are security issues to be considered, assessed, and catered for.

The initial WiFi security protocol WEP (Wired Equivalent Privacy) had some shortfalls which Wi-Fi Protected Access (WPA) sought to address. Wi-Fi Protected Access II (WPA2) security protocol followed. These security certification programs were developed by the Wi-Fi Alliance to secure wireless computer networks in response to weaknesses in the earlier systems (http://en.wikipedia.org/wiki/Wi-Fi_Protected_Access).

There is also a NIST document dealing with Wireless security "Guidelines for Securing Wireless Local Area Networks (WLANS)," which can be found at http://csrc.nist.gov/publications/nistpubs/800-153/sp800-153.pdf.

Security: The Database

A paper by McAfee entitled "A Practical Guide to Database Security" gives a concise treatment of the topic and makes reference to an organization which had hundreds of thousands of client records compromised resulting in large losses and incurred expenses. The source of the paper is given at the end of this section.

> Why is database security so important? For a company that has suffered a serious data breach, it boils down to monetary damage in its many forms: business disruption, bad publicity, stiff fines for noncompliance, and undermined customer confidence. But most damaging of all is the trouble that it creates when it comes to signing up new customers. A tarnished reputation is a big objection for sales and business development to overcome. That's why data security in general and database security in particular are a crucial part of any company's overall corporate health.

One aspect of databases which other entities do not normally possess is the fact that its main purpose in life is to be accessed and data inserted, deleted, and retrieved. The paper points out that databases are prone to threats that cannot be handled by firewalls and other standard security mechanisms, including perimeter defenses.

It also points out that the *intruders* are not always *young loners* bent on mischief but *organized crime syndicates* who see this area as easier than robbing banks and stagecoaches *a la* Jesse James or Dick Turpin.

A *Ponemon Institute* study found that organization *insiders and third parties* are the most common causes of breaches of data security, although much of it is attributable to negligence.

---

[*] IEEE Standard 802.11. See http://www.webopedia.com/TERM/8/802_11.html for succinct definitions of variations of this standard.

This fact has the hidden implication that *outsiders* might find it easier to breach data security by using an *insider*, with their access privileges as a *tool*. Recent years have shown that the number of reported vulnerabilities has increased and vendors struggle to develop and distribute *patches* in a reasonable time.

This presents a window of opportunity for the ever-vigilant, increasingly clever criminal mind.

The document goes on to discuss methods and organizations which can help to mitigate these exposures:

- Perimeter security
- Native DBMS auditing
- Sarbanes–Oxley Act requiring financial companies to have *effective controls* in place, not necessarily technical or too specific
- Payment Card Industry Data Security Standard (PCI DSS) which is quite specific about protection measures for credit cards
- International data privacy and security regulations, many country-specific
- Initiatives mainly specific to the United States
- State and federal personal data protection laws
- Health Information Portability and Accountability Act (HIPAA)
- Statements on Standards—SAS 70, SSAE 16

The paper then discusses "Five Principles for Protecting the Database" and "Five Practical First Steps" and then outlines monitoring requirements and a McAfee product.

It is a useful document which, in terms of our HA quest, attempts to head off *logical outages* caused by database compromise or corruption (http://virtualizationreview.com/~/media/1F034B6 B076D446F990EA6A144D275F0.pdf).

Distributed DoS

This topic is covered in a Frost and Sullivan white paper entitled "Why Anti-DDoS Products and Services are Critical for Today's Business Environment."

It covers several factors of concern under the following areas (http://enterpriseinnovation.net/ whitepaper/protecting-against-ddos-threats-hacktivist-age):

- Integrity and confidentiality versus availability
- Protecting the business from the DDoS threat

Security: DNS Servers

A paper by Infoblox claims that in 2012, 7.8 million new malware threats emerged and mobile threats increased by 1000%. It states that the second most prominent attack *vector* after HTTP is DNS and unless your business is totally independent of the Internet, you may be affected, and Murphy's Law says you probably will (http://www.infoblox.com/sites/infobloxcom/files/resources/ infoblox-whitepaper-dns-servers-secure-available-network.pdf).

The steps suggested by them for protecting DNS are as follows:

- Hardening appliances, OSs, and applications
- Applying the principles of high availability

- Continually updating critical information on bad domains and security issues from various *credible sources* around the world
- Protecting against DNS cache poisoning, which in essence redirects traffic to the attacker's address
- Taking DNS away from malware and APTs (see Appendix 1)

Cost of Cyber Crime

A Poneman report (2013), sponsored by HP Enterprise Security, on the cost of cyber crime (to the business, not the perpetrators) was based on a representative sample of 234 organizations in six countries. The summary findings in the report are as follows:

> Ponemon Institute's 2013 Cost of Cyber Crime study finds the average company in the U.S. experiences more than 100 successful cyber attacks each year at a cost of $11.6M. That's an increase of 26% from last year. Companies in other regions fared better, but still experienced significant losses. This year's annual study was conducted in the United States, United Kingdom, Germany, Australia, Japan and France and surveyed over 230 organizations. But the study also shows that companies who implement enabling security technologies reduced losses by nearly $4M, and those employing good security governance practices reduced costs by an average of $1.5M.

The paper can be found at http://www.hpenterprisesecurity.com/ponemon-2013-cost-of-cyber-crime-study-reports.

The reference above also has links to the costs involved in cyber crime across the six *individual countries* as well as globally: the United States, the United Kingdom, Germany, France, Australia, and Japan.

Cost of Cyber Crime Prevention versus Risk

Some papers maintain that the costs of protecting against cybercrime exceed the losses incurred because of them and sometimes suggest that maybe it isn't worth it. This has to be one that an organization has to work out for itself but some of the literature on it should help them to do that. Some of them may feel about it like governments think about blackmail—once you give in, the blackmailer comes back for more.

The two UK reports referenced here are quite detailed and specific and should be useful to any organization or company anywhere in the world (https://www.gov.uk/government/uploads/system/uploads/attachment_data/file/60943/the-cost-of-cyber-crime-full-report.pdf; http://www.cam.ac.uk/research/news/how-much-does-cybercrime-cost).

Comprehensive vulnerability detection requires tracking the latest threats as they emerge and evolve in real-time. Qualys *Vulnerability Research Team* claims to perform continuous vulnerability research in this key area.

To check out the top 10 vulnerabilities, new detections for critical vulnerabilities, vulnerabilities with exploits for obsolete software, and much more, visit their page at https://www.qualys.com/research/.

There are other useful security items accessible from this URL:

- Security alerts
- Security advisories

- Obsolete software vulnerabilities
- Top 10 vulnerabilities
- Law of vulnerabilities, defined by Wolfgang Kandek of CTO
- A knowledge base
- Open source projects
- SANs @ Risk section

The literature in this area is vast and evolving but if your organization wants to stay ahead of the *bad guys*, there will have to be a continuing investment in this area. Finally, it is usual to call in experts for tackling this new field of IT management unless you are already well equipped with such people and expertise.

As a UK television advertisement used to say about road safety: "You know it makes sense."

Security Literature

Tripwire is a company offering IT security products, services, and literature (white papers, data-sheets, etc.) and offers a website specializing in security matters. The Resources section of this site offers the following *learning* materials:

- Datasheets
- White papers
- Podcasts
- Solution briefs
- Video walkthroughs
- Videocasts
- Webcasts

The URL (http://www.tripwire.com/it-resources/category/type/white-paper/#resource-type/) points to the white papers resources page, the content of most of them being obvious from the well chosen titles.

Summary

In keeping with the presenter's prayer "Tell them what you are going to tell them, tell them and tell them what you've told them." Here is a summary of the topics in this Appendix:

Lesson 1: Multiplication, Summation, and Integration Symbols—review and reminder
Lesson 2: General Theory of Reliability and Availability
Lesson 3: Parallel Components (Blocks)—simplemath
Lesson 4: Cluster Speedup Formulae—Amdahl, Gustafson, Gunther
Lesson 5: Some RAID and EC Math
Lesson 6: Math of Monitoring—availability
Lesson 7: Software Reliability/Availability—theory and models
Lesson 8: Additional RAS Features—over and above *vanilla* RAS
Lesson 9: Triple Modular Redundancy (TMR)—the *voting* system for redundant components with an example from space
Lesson 10: Cyber Crime, Security, and Availability—the upcoming *outage* cause

The coverage in this Appendix is as far as I understand the topics and I hope that it is of use to people who need an introduction to these topics. As in Chapter 3, I have tried the *immersion* approach to getting my message across with *tasters* in Chapter 2 (Availability: An Overview section) and Chapter 3 (Availability Entities section). These themes are revisited as the book progresses and hopefully made doubly clear in these Appendices.

In this way, I hope that any fear of terms and math has dissolved during the course of this book and you will enjoy studying them. Anyone needing further information is referred to the many references in this book and to Appendix 1 to refresh on various terms and ideas.

Appendix 5

Once I put your book down I couldn't pick it up again.

Mark Twain

Availability: Organizations and References[*]

In preparing this book I have referred to various organizations, numerous papers, and articles. Wherever I have quoted material, it is acknowledged and permission has been obtained where necessary. Some materials I have quoted are from printed output with no visible source. If permission was needed for these materials, I would like to apologize.

Much of the material, even on the same topic, varies enormously in how it approaches the subject, and it is this which has made the job of *translating* advanced material into a common language familiar to nonspecialist IT people somewhat difficult.

For those who want to delve deeper than this book, or read about the same topics from a different perspective, the references in this appendix should help.

Note: My personal recommendation would be an organization to stock a library of relevant books to save the individuals multiple expense in their personal purchases.

Reliability/Availability Organizations

Note: This section is not exhaustive and covers only the organizations I have looked at in some detail. There will be other organizations with similar aims and functions and covers only the organizations I have looked at in some detail. Forgive me if I have excluded your favourite group as I know there are many, many more.

---

[*] I am not suggesting everyone should read all these items, but some may find references to topics which are of interest to them and not found in this book.

Reliability Information Analysis Center

The *Reliability Information Analysis Center* (RIAC), formerly known as the Reliability Analysis Center (RAC), has been serving as a Department of Defense (DoD) Information Analysis Center (IAC) for more than 35 years. As such, the RIAC is a center of excellence and technical focal point for information, data, analysis, training, and technical assistance in the engineering fields of reliability, maintainability, quality, supportability, and interoperability (RMQSI).

Although chartered by the DoD, the RIAC undertakes a variety of other government organization and industrial support projects each year. The team includes Wyle Laboratories, Quanterion Solutions, the University of Maryland Center for Risk and Reliability, the Penn State University Applied Research Laboratory, and the State University of New York Institute of Technology. Resources at their nationwide locations include over 2000 employees of various technical backgrounds and expertise. The RIAC claims to provide total, turnkey solutions to customers, including training, consulting services, and publications and tools for both government and commercial businesses.

You should be aware that nearly all their literature is chargeable. See http://theriac.org/.

Uptime Institute

The Uptime Institute, an independent division of The 451 Group, provides education, publications, consulting, certifications, conferences and seminars, independent research, and thought leadership for the enterprise data center industry and for data center professionals. The Uptime Institute is an unbiased, third-party data center research, education, and consulting organization focused on improving data center performance and efficiency through collaboration and innovation.

The Uptime Institute serves all stakeholders of the data center industry, including enterprise and third-party operation, manufacturers, providers, and engineers. This collaborative approach, completed with the Uptime Institute's capability to recognize trends on a global basis and to interface directly with owners, results in solutions and invocations freed from regional constraints for the benefit of worldwide data center industry.

Founded in 1993, the Institute pioneered the creation and facilitation of end-user knowledge communities to improve reliability and uninterruptible availability—uptime—in data center facilities and Information Technology organizations. In 2009, the Institute was acquired by The 451 Group, a technology-industry analyst company focusing on the business of enterprise IT innovation.

This is taken from their website.
http://uptimeinstitute.com/

The 451 Group, the parent company of 451 Research, the Uptime Institute, and, from January 2013, the Yankee Group, is the research, data, and business advisory group. The Yankee Group is the preeminent research, data, and advisory firm (see http://uptimeinstitute.com/).

IEEE Reliability Society

The Institute of Electrical and Electronics Engineers (IEEE) sponsors an organization devoted to reliability in engineering, the IEEE Reliability Society (IEEE RS). The Reliability Society promotes industry-wide acceptance of a systematic approach to design that will help to ensure reliable products. To that end, they promote reliability not just in engineering, but in maintenance and analysis as well.

The Society encourages collaborative effort and information sharing among its membership, which encompasses organizations and individuals involved in all areas of engineering, including aerospace, transportation systems, medical electronics, computers, and communications (http://en.wikipedia.org/wiki/Business_continuity_planning and http://rs.ieee.org/).

> ***Note:*** Please note that much of IEEE documentation, like that from RIAC, is chargeable, usually about $31.

Storage Networking Industry Association

As a not-for-profit association, the Storage Networking Industry Association (SNIA) enables its 400+ members to develop robust solutions for storing and managing the massive volumes of information generated by today's businesses. For more than a decade, we have been working to bring recognition of storage issues to the IT world, making storage less complicated for the end-user.

As a result, the SNIA has adopted the role of industry catalyst for the development of storage solution specifications and technologies, global standards, and storage education. It has a number of technical communities working on storage-related topics, including data protection and storage security. SNIA publishes "availability" articles and has also published a very detailed and thorough article on RAID, which every RAID-serious person should consult. There is also a "3-Year Strategic Plan for 2012–2015," all of which can be found on their website (www.snia.org).

Availability Digest

I have found the website of Availability Digest invaluable for general topics relating to availability and reliability, and also some spine-chilling service failures under the heading "Never Again."

I would consider it compulsory reading for any availability "nerd" or involved management.

> The digest of current topics on High Availability and Continuous Availability. High Availability *recovers* from the effects of downtime. Continuous Availability *avoids* the effects of downtime. The Digest includes case studies, horror stories, best practices, availability issues, product reviews, recommended reading, and some mathematical nerd stuff.
>
> **Words from the website!**

For reference, see http://www.availabilitydigest.com/ Joining as a member is a GOOD idea.

Service Availability Forum

The Service Availability Forum (SAF or SA Forum) is a consortium that develops, publishes, educates on, and promotes open specifications for carrier-grade and mission-critical systems. SA Forum specifications enable faster development and deployment of commercial off-the-shelf (COTS) ecosystems for highly available platforms.

The SA Forum was formed in December 2001 as a successor to the HA (High Availability) Forum that pioneered the standard-based architecture high availability systems. SA Forum produced a white paper entitled "Providing Open Architecture High Availability Solutions."

The member companies of the SA Forum represent all levels of the IT spectrum:

- Hardware vendors
- Firmware vendors
- Operating system vendors
- Middleware providers
- Application providers
- Network equipment providers
- Integrators
- Academic institutions

The list also includes Oracle, HP, Ericsson, Radisys, and Emerson (www.saforum.org).

On the SA Forum website, you can find a *very useful* white paper, attributed to the "HA Forum," which will be of interest to "high availability" people (see http://www.saforum.org/doc/AdobeViewer. asp?doc_filename=%2FHOA%2Fassn16627%2Fdocuments%2FProviding%20Open%20 Architecture%20High%20Availability%20Solutions.pdf&sfind=&print=1&docid=428821). Even if you don't plan to read the white paper completely, it is well worth a glance.

What Is OpenSAF Then?

OpenSAF stands for Open Service Availability Framework. OpenSAF is an open source community with projects focused on HA middleware.

The goal of OpenSAF projects is to develop HA middleware that is consistent with SA Forum specifications. OpenSAF is freely available to anyone under the LGPLv2.1 (*Lesser General Public License*) and anyone may contribute to the project. The OpenSAF Foundation is a not-for-profit organization established by leading communications and computing companies to facilitate the work of the OpenSAF project and to accelerate the adoption of OpenSAF in commercial products.

The Foundation was inaugurated on January 22, 2008, by leading communications and enterprise computing companies: Emerson Network Power, Ericsson, HP, Nokia Siemens Networks, and Sun Microsystems (now Oracle/Sun). Oracle acquired GoAhead, one of the key implementers of OpenSAF products, in about 2012 (see http://www.opensaf.org/FAQ~184594~14944.htm).

Carnegie Mellon Software Engineering Institute

The Carnegie Mellon Software Engineering Institute (SEI) works closely with defense and government organizations, industry, and academia to continually improve software-intensive systems. Our core purpose is to help organizations such as yours to improve their software engineering capabilities and to develop or acquire the right software, defect free, within budget and on time, every time. To accomplish this, the SEI:

- Performs research to explore promising solutions to software engineering problems
- Identifies and codifies technological and methodological solutions
- Tests and refines the solutions through pilot programs that help industry and government solve their problems
- Widely disseminates proven solutions through training, licensing, and publication of best practices

Since 1984, the SEI has served the USA as a federally funded research and development center based at Carnegie Mellon University.

There are other organizations dedicated to reliability in its many manifestations.

Most of these can be found by web searches on various terms relating to "reliability" (see http://www.sei.cmu.edu/).

ROC Project—Software Resilience

The Recovery-Oriented Computing (ROC) project is a joint research project of Berkeley and Stanford that is investigating novel techniques for building highly dependable Internet services. In a significant divergence from traditional fault-tolerance approaches, ROC emphasizes *recovery* from failures rather than failure-avoidance. This philosophy is motivated by the observation that even the most robust systems still occasionally encounter failures due to human operator error, transient or permanent hardware failure, and software anomalies resulting from "Heisenbugs" (see later under "Software Reliability") or software aging.

See Brown, A., and D. Patterson at http://roc.cs.berkeley.edu/roc_overview.html.

There are numerous articles on software reliability, most of them suggesting methods of development to achieve fault detection, avoidance, in-flight correction, and the like, while acknowledging that even with the best development disciplines, errors are inevitable. Software reliability is by no means "business as usual" as hardware RAS seems to be for most vendors (see http://ubiquity.acm.org/article.cfm?id=1241853).

Business Continuity Today

Business Continuity Today is an online educational publication and resource portal that is sponsored by Vision Solutions, Inc. The aim of *Business Continuity Today* is to help IT professionals and other executives better understand the issues, strategies, and technologies surrounding the resiliency and recovery of IT systems—an indispensible building block of business continuity planning (BCP).

www.businesscontinuitytoday.com

Disaster Recovery Institute

DRI International (originally called the Disaster Recovery Institute International) was founded in 1988 as a nonprofit organization with a mission to make the world prepared. As the global education and certification body in business continuity and disaster recovery planning, DRI International sets the standard for professionalism. There are more than 10,000 active certified professionals worldwide. A DRI credential ensures employers that candidates understand the tenets of business continuity. It is the only certification that requires maintaining a current degree of knowledge through continuing education. DRI International organizes major industry events throughout the world. It offers corporate training programs and partnerships with colleges and universities.

DRI certifies individual professionals from more than 100 countries and conducts training in more than 50 of those nations. DRI advises numerous governments and organizations in creating national and international standards for preparedness as well as working with private sector leaders and professional associations to promote readiness.

www.drii.org/

There is a readable DRI minimanual called *Professional Practices for Business Continuity Practitioners* at https://www.drii.org/docs/professionprac.pdf.

Business Continuity Institute

The Business Continuity Institute (BCI) is a leading institute for business continuity (BC). It was established in 1994, and has now become the leading membership and certifying organization for BC professionals worldwide. Its purpose is to promote the art and science of BC worldwide. The BCI has over 4000 members in more than 85 countries. It offers, among other things, education in BC-related topics. In terms of resources, it offers a "Knowledge Bank" at http://www.thebci.org/index.php/resources/knowledgebank, which covers, in .pdf format, the following subjects in outline:

- Business continuity (20 files)
- IT disaster recovery and resilience (2 files)
- Regulations, standards, and guidelines (14 files)
- Risk management and insurance (8 files)
- Supply chain continuity (6 files)
- Threats and horizon scanning (5 files)

The parent website is www.thebci.com.

Information Availability Institute

The Information Availability Institute provides research and education that helps business professionals of all disciplines to understand and apply information availability technologies. It is sponsored by Vision Solutions (see http://www.visionsolutions.com/IAI/systemoptimization.html).

International Working Group on Cloud Computing Resiliency

The International Working Group on Cloud Computing Resiliency (IWGCR) is a working group with a mission to monitor and analyze cloud computing resiliency. The working group comprises IT executives, academic researchers, and industry representatives. A list of who does what in which area of activity can be found on the website:

www.iwgcr.org

TMMi Foundation

The TMM*i* (Test Maturity Model Integrated) Foundation is an organization dedicated to improving test processes and practice. It is a nonprofit-making organization and the focus of the Foundation's activities is on the development of a common, robust *model* of test process assessment and improvement in IT organizations. The process model is applied very often to software quality and has five levels (five is the highest) of accreditation of maturity of an organization's testing process (www.tmmi.org and http://www.tmmi.org/pdf/TMMi.Framework.pdf):

1. Initial
2. Managed
3. Defined

4. Measured

5. Optimization

Center for Software Reliability

The Center for Software Reliability (CSR) at City University London is an independent research center in the School of Informatics, founded in 1983. As its name suggests, its early research concerned the reliability of software—particularly the problems of measurement, assurance, and prediction of reliability using probabilistic modeling—but this quickly expanded into a much wider systems viewpoint, taking account of different threats to dependability.

CSR now addresses the *dependability* of systems, taking account, for example, of safety and security as well as reliability. The current approach is now aimed at wider systems made up of software, hardware, people, and organizations.

The CSR collaborates widely with academic and industrial organizations in Europe and the United States (see http://www.city.ac.uk/informatics/school-organization/center-for-software-reliability).

CloudTweaks

Established in 2009, CloudTweaks.com claims to be one of the fastest-growing cloud computing resources on the web and to have a growing niche community comprising technology professionals, representatives of government agencies, financial institutions, technology firms, and Fortune 500 organizations.

CloudTweaks.com connects brands to an audience consisting of businesspersons and managers of growing businesses, entrepreneurs, and early adopters. The site also has some very amusing cartoons on the theme of cloud technology (see www.cloudtweaks.com).

In line with my thesis about the importance of security and monitoring for malware of all kinds, I have included "security organizations" as a section. There is a useful Qualys document "4 Key Steps to Automate IT Security Compliance," which is a vendor document and hence is not listed in the next section alongside organizations (see http://www.qualys.com/forms/whitepapers/4_key_steps/).

Security Organizations

Security? I Can't Be Bothered

The following paragraph from a paper entitled "Review of Availability of Advice on Security for Small/Medium Sized Organizations" lists some of the excuses an enterprise gives as to why it shouldn't break into a sweat over security. I believe that this can be applied to all organizations great and small. It is from the UK Information Commissioners Office, an independent authority, with at the URL which is given following the list:

> At the same time, there are a number of blockers and constraints for implementing security, including issues such as the following:
>
> ▪ Insufficient time, desire, and priority to understand or address the need for security.
> ▪ Ignorance of what needs to be done.

- Lack of cash or credit, especially following a recession.
- No expertise or suitable resources available.
- A "just in time," short term focus.
- Perception that security is an unnecessary overhead.
- An aversion to paperwork, policies, and procedures.
- A perception that security is something for techies, not business people.
- A feeling that the enterprise is too small to be affected.
- Operating in an environment that demands and accepts a high tolerance of risks.

Given the statistics and examples in this book of security breaches caused by malware and negligence, ignoring the security aspects of systems is foolish. Malware has now appeared on the IT radar, not only as a business risk but also as a possible availability exposure. Take advice. Don't try to put the fire out yourself before calling the fire brigade (http://search.ico.org.uk/ico/search?q = security).

Cloud Security Alliance

The Cloud Security Alliance (CSA) is a not-for-profit organization with a mission to promote the use of best practices for providing security assurance within cloud computing, and to provide education on the uses of cloud computing to help secure all other forms of computing. The CSA is led by a broad coalition of industry practitioners, corporations, associations, and other key stakeholders.

Mission: "To promote the use of best practices for providing security assurance within Cloud Computing, and provide education on the uses of Cloud Computing to help secure all other forms of computing." The group has a large number of corporate members (over 120) and a small group of affiliate members. Among the former group are Adobe, Cisco, Citrix, Microsoft, Amazon, HP, Hitachi, Ernst & Young, and Google.

The website offers a number of white papers on subjects relating to cloud security, including the pragmatic "Scanning Your Cloud Environment" and "Protecting the Cloud." See www.cloudsecurityalliance.org for more details.

CSO Online

CSO provides news, analysis, and research on a broad range of security and risk management topics. Areas of focus include information security, physical security, BC, identity and access management, loss prevention, and more. *CSO Magazine* and CSOonline.com are published by CXO Media Inc., which is an International Data Group (IDG) company.

CSO publishes a magazine on security issues and solutions. The subscription is *free* for U.S. residents and is *chargeable* for residents of Canada and other countries (see http://www.csoonline.com/about-cso).

dark READING

Dark Reading's Security Monitoring Tech Center is a portal for news, product information, technical data, and best practices related to the monitoring of IT security events and status. Claiming to be aimed at executives and business people as well as security and IT professionals, the Security Monitoring Tech Center is a single community dedicated to the tools and techniques used to analyze security activity and detect potential threats to the business (see http://www.darkreading.com/).

Cyber Security and Information Systems IAC

The Cyber Security and Information Systems IAC (CSIAC) is a DoD IAC sponsored by the Defense Technical Information Center (DTIC). The CSIAC is a consolidation of three predecessor IACs: the Data and Analysis Center for Software (DACS), the Information Assurance Technology IAC (IATAC), and the Modeling & Simulation IAC (MSIAC), with the addition of the knowledge management and information sharing technical area (see www.thecsiac.com(/about)).

Center for International Security and Cooperation

The CISAC which is the Center for International Security and Cooperation should not be confused with the CSIAC (Cyber Security and Information Systems Information Analysis Center). The ambit of CISAC is wider than IT but does include a subsection entitled *Cybersecurity Threats and the Future of the Internet* (see http://cisac.stanford.edu/).

Other Reliability/Security Resources

The following URL contains further information on organizations, conferences, and journals related to reliability and hence availability:
  http://crr.umd.edu/resources
  Symantec website: www.symantec.com Useful articles

> My opinion is that security and malware detection and neutralization are key issues in maintaining high availability and the time to plan for it is not *when* it happens but *before* it happens, because happen it will—Murphy has spoken.

Books, Articles, and Websites

Major Reliability/Availability Information Sources

There is a reference section in Appendix 5, which is quite specific in the areas it covers. However, there are some general sources of information on reliability and availability which you can use to perhaps answer questions not covered directly in this book. The following are the sources of general information I have found useful in researching this book:

- Wikipedia (this will pop up in almost any search you care to make)
- National Institute of Standards and Technology (NIST)
- NASA
- http://www.weibull.com/

- ReliaSoft
- Reliability Analytics, which provides useful information and has free online tools
- MIL Handbooks (see Appendix 2)
- IBM Red Books (search IBM on the word "redbooks, <topic>"), for example, "redbooks, reliability"
- Cisco and Microsoft websites having useful information on many topics related to HA/DR
- Subscription white papers from various bodies, although I must confess I found many of them pure marketing, content-free, or both

Note: If you don't get further than, say, Chapter 1, then the above-listed references will take you a long way toward availability "guru-dom," if you use sensible search terms.

Other Information Sources

Books

- *Reliability Theory and Practice*—Igor Bazovsky (Dover Publications) ISBN 0-486-43867-8 (1961).
  The book that nearly every other book and paper about reliability quotes. It essentially covers RAS without actually naming it thus. I found it useful in understanding certain aspects of reliability which other sources failed to enlighten me on.
- *Weibull*: www.weibull.com/basics
  This site is closely linked to the Reliasoft site given in the following. The URL given here takes you to a page which is the basis of delving into various aspects of reliability in a very readable and understandable form. Try this site for refreshing some of the topics in this book.
- *Blueprints for High Availability*—Marcus, Stern (Wiley) ISBN 0-471-35601-8 (2000)
  This is a good, readable book covering among other things, redundancy, clustering, network aspects, and backup/recovery. It is quite specific in many places while discussing the subject, for example, domain name server (DNS) or RAID.
- United States Army Reliability/Availability Technical Manual (1/2007); see http://www .wbdg.org/ccb/ARMYCOE/COETM/tm_5_698_1.pdf.

This manual gives a good introduction to many facets of availability and reliability and includes some theory. It is worth a perusal and printing for reference.

- *High Availability and Disaster Recovery*—Klaus Schmidt (Springer) ISBN-10 3-540-24460-3 and ISBN-13 978-3-540-24460-8
  This book is from someone who has obviously worked at the "coalface" of IT. It provides some useful, relevant background, a good section on RAID, some detailed availability product considerations, and a detailed disaster recovery (DR) section. It also covers some important "management" aspects. I feel it is not a manager's book.
- *High Availability*—Piedad and Hawkins (Prentice Hall) ISBN 0-13-096288-0 (2001)
  This book mainly covers organizational and checklist aspects of high availability and is somewhat less specific in discussing hardware and software aspects than that of Marcus and Stern. It is probably more useful for a senior IT person in overall control. It does however have a detailed section on service level agreements (SLAs) and SLA Management key HA elements.

■ *High Availability Network Fundamentals*—Chris Oggerino (Cisco Press) ISBN 1-58713-017-3 (2001)

This book is mainly about networks and Cisco products but is useful for its many illustrative worked-out examples and a reasonable coverage of theory. Much of the theory presented is not limited to network components, so don't dismiss it as of no interest if you are a server or disk guru.

■ *Design of Real-Time Computer Systems*—James Martin (Prentice Hall) Library of Congress Catalog Card Number 67-18923 (1967)

This book stands the *test of time* in many areas. Chapter 7 of the book, Reliability and Standby, is very useful and forward looking. Not sure if you can still get a copy except perhaps on eBay.

■ *Websites quoted in context in the body of this document*

Many of these are very useful, though some represent hard work. One problem I found with them is the translation of the coverage of "reliability" into understandable IT terms from pure mathematical treatment, for example, the Weibull distribution, its parameters, and what they mean in terms of reliability and availability.

■ *Vendor websites*, searching on "availability" and other words such as "theory," "practice," "high," "checklists," and so on.

Oracle, IBM, HP, Stratus, Microsoft, Dell, Cisco, and others contain useful general information, and some information specific to their own products. I have found the Cisco, Intel, and IBM websites the most useful for general coverage of many topics. In case of IBM, the Redbook series can be very useful for general learning as opposed to product education.

■ IBM Redbooks (www.redbooks.ibm.com)

Other Sources

■ Wikipedia

This is a fantastic site for information about almost anything and anyone. I base my judgment on its first-class treatment of subjects.

■ Availability Digest (www.availabilitydigest.com)

This is a very useful site for all aspects of availability, including descriptions of "eye-watering" system outages.

■ Security (www.csoonline.com)

This website offers a good selection of articles which can be narrowed down by a judicious search, such as "high availability." I feel that security is somewhat neglected considering the rapid rise in security breaches involving compromising identity, passwords, and, more importantly, vital data. Organizations that neglect this area of availability in the next few years will do so at their peril.

■ ReliaSoft (www.reliasoft.com)

ReliaSoft specializes in software, training, and consulting for reliability engineering and related fields. Wilde Analysis Ltd. in Cheshire, United Kingdom, is the regional distribution partner in the United Kingdom. The latter has given much advice and guidance to me in the preparation of this book.

■ Software Reliability: See http://journal.thedacs.com/enews/enews5-reliability.php and articles referenced therein. See also http://www.softwarereliability.com/.

■ Reliability Analytics (www.reliabilityanalytics.com)

Reliability Analytics (RA) specializes in developing custom analytical models for evaluating system reliability, including system reliability modeling and analysis, reliability prediction, product support, and other custom solutions. RA has been of significant assistance in the preparation of this book.

■ Ops A La Carte: Reliapedia (http://www.opsalacarte.com/Pages/resources/resources_techpapers.htm)

Ops A La Carte is a company that offers a range of reliability services, education, and training. Services offered include software testing, root cause analysis (RCA), failure modes and effects analysis (FMEA), accelerated reliability test methods, and an extensive array of lab services such as HALT, HASS, and ALT.

Their website also contains a "Resources" section of which Reliapedia, a repository of reliability information, is a major part. Access to this section is chargeable and consists of three levels of access, depending on user requirements. This section has been of considerable help in the assessment and verification of material for this book.

Reference Sites for RAID

This is not an exhaustive list, but covers sites which I have found approach the topic in slightly different ways to give a greater understanding by their synergy. They also have unique features, such as calculation tools and animation, which create this synergy.

The website www.ecs.umass.edu/ece/koren/architecture/Raid/raidhome.html comprises the following sections:

■ An Introduction to RAID
■ The Need for RAID
■ Data Striping & Redundancy
■ Different Types of RAID (0, 1, 2, 3, 4, 5, 6, 10) and backup requirements
■ Tool for Storage Efficiency (RAID 1, 2, 3, 4, 5, 6)
  Results: Number of storage disks
     Number of redundant disks
     Storage efficiency (redundant/storage disks) as %
■ Cost & Performance Issues
■ Reliability Issues in RAID
■ Tool for Reliability (RAID 5 and 6)
  Failure Types: Double/triple disk failure
     System crash and disk failure
     Disk failure/double disk failure + bit error
  Results: Reliability of disk array
  MTTDL (Mean Time to Data Loss)
■ Glossary

The "Tools" section allows calculations to be done for *Storage Efficiency* and *Reliability* for the above-specified RAID levels. Input is user generated and includes knowledge of MTTF, MMTR, and related concepts.

The website www.acnc.com/raid covers RAID levels 0, 1, 2, 3, 4, 5, 6, 10, 50, and 0+1. It also has very interesting animation for several of these levels. It is an informative site.

The website http://stoicjoker.com/RAIDMoreInfo.html has very interesting diagrams and useful notes on the following:

- Characteristics and advantages of each RAID level
- Disadvantages of that RAID level
- Recommended applications for that RAID level

The website http://en.wikipedia.org/wiki/Standard_RAID_levels is a useful site offering detailed math in some areas (parity generation) and discussions (but not for all RAIDs covered) of the following:

1. Failure rate
2. Performance
3. Parity handling
4. Recovery issues
5. Latency (RAID 5)
6. Efficiency (redundant/total) (RAID 6)
7. Implementation
8. Nonstandard RAID
9. Non-RAID architectures
10. References

The website http://docs.oracle.com/cd/E19269-01/820-1847-20/appendixf.html covers the topic "Selecting the Best RAID Level" and includes a table of characteristics to compare RAID levels 0, 1, 1E, 5, 5EE, 6, 10, 50, and 60 in the following:

- Redundancy
- Disk drive capacity usage
- Read performance
- Write performance
- Built-in hot sparing
- Minimum disk drives

A "must-see" site for RAID details and fascinating *animation* of several levels of RAID (see http://www.acnc.com/raid)

Other sites with RAID calculation facilities are as follows:

https://www.grijpink.eu/tools/raid/index.php
http://www.synology.com/support/RAID_calculator.php?lang=us
http://www.ibeast.com/content/tools/RaidCalc/RaidCalc.asp
http://www.raid-calculator.com/default.aspx

The SNIA site http://www.snia.org/sites/default/files/SNIADDFv1.2_with_Errata_A_Applied.pdf has very detailed diagrams of various RAID configurations (levels). If you need to delve deeply into RAID configurations, this is the site you need to refer to.

Modeling the Reliability of RAID Sets: This publication by a Dell engineer covers the reliability of various levels of RAID, both normal and nested. The math is very clear and understandable. It's a very good document and covers a lot of ground in its four pages (see http://www.dell.com/downloads/global/power/ps2q08-20080190-Long.pdf).

This is another Dell paper that covers similar ground and is worth a glance: http://www.dell.com/content/topics/global.aspx/power/en/ps1q02_long?c=us&l=en&cs=04

Post-RAID Technology

This section contains references for information on technologies which may complement, and possibly eventually replace, current RAID technology. Their main aim is to eliminate, or at least mollify, the drawbacks in RAID technology in the area of very large data conglomerations. Terms in this arena include Erasure Coding (EC3), BitSpread, Reed-Solomon coding, and others.

In particular, the functions of backup/mirror/recover of RAID technology data can take a very long time which may prevent organizations achieving their RPOs/RTO objectives in recovery situations.

1. This paper looks at current RAID and Amplidata's EC3 implementation, showing graphs of expected failure probabilities for levels of RAID.

    It also covers the newer EC *technology* (the *theory* is older than RAID, however); see http://www.intel.com/content/dam/www/public/us/en/documents/white-papers/big-data-amplidata-storage-paper.pdf.

2. The first URL is a presentation by James Plank entitled "All about Erasure Codes." It is detailed and covers 53 foils. One key advantage of his presentation over papers on the subject is that it is 90% visual and the subject matter is also visual.

    The second URL is a detailed paper on the same topic and represents a useful adjunct to the presentation; see http://web.eecs.utk.edu/~mbeck/classes/cs560/560/notes/Erasure/2004-ICL.pdf and http://static.usenix.org/event/fast09/tech/full_papers/plank/plank_html/.

3. A large, mathematically detailed paper, submitted in part fulfilment of a PhD and entitled "Reliability and Power-Efficiency in Erasure Coded Storage Systems" (see http://citeseerx.ist.psu.edu/viewdoc/download?doi=10.1.1.160.1517&rep=rep1&type=pdf).

4. This readable paper covers RAID, its problems, the possible use of solid state devices (SSDs), and erasure codes/object storage. It also contains an Appendix with short notes on the various RAID levels, standard, and proprietary (see http://www.amplidata.com/pdf/The-RAID-Catastrophe.pdf).

Reference Sites for Software Reliability

Software Fault Tolerance: A Tutorial (66 p.)—NASA/TM-2000-210616; see http://dmi.uib.es/~jproenza/case/torres-pomales00software.pdf.

Software Reliability Growth Model (Weibull site): http://www.weibull.com/hotwire/issue84/relbasics84.htm.

Software Reliability—Nasari, Vazquez (presentation with maths): http://users.encs.concordia.ca/~dssouli/INSE%206250%20folder/Survey%20papers%2012%20folder/S_Reliability.pptx.

Software Reliability—Article by Wohlin et al. Covers main software reliability models and testing: http://www.wohlin.eu/softrel01.pdf.

Software Reliability—Article by Jiantao Pan. Contains *bathtub* curves: http://www.ece.cmu.edu/~koopman/des_s99/sw_reliability/.

Software Reliability Engineering: A Roadmap—Article by Michael R. Lyu: http://www.cse
.cuhk.edu.hk/lyu/_media/conference/lyu-reliability07.pdf?id=home&cache=cache.
Handbook of Software Reliability Engineering—Michael R. Lyu (editor): http://www.cse.cuhk.
edu.hk/~lyu/book/reliability/ McGraw-Hill (1996).

This is simply a selection I have come across and looked at. There are many others around and this
selection does not imply superiority over others.

Security and Malware Sources*

1. *The hacktivist threat to enterprise security*: http://searchsecurity.techtarget.com/magazine-
   Content/The-hacktivist-threat-to-enterprise-security?asrc = EM_ERU_19291242.
2. *Malware trends: The rise of cross-platform malware*: http://searchsecurity.techtarget.com/maga-
   zineContent/Malware-trends-The-rise-of-cross-platform-malware?asrc = EM_ERU_19291243.
3. *Flame malware analysis: How to defend against fraudulent certificates*: http://searchse-
   curity.techtarget.com/tip/Flame-malware-analysis-How-to-defend-against-fraudulent-
   certificates?asrc = EM_ERU_19290802.
4. *Use cybercrime statistics to combat organized cybercrime*: http://searchsecurity.techtarget.com/
   answer/Use-cybercrime-statistics-to-combat-organized-cybercrime?asrc=EM_ERU_19291244.
5. *Picking the best enterprise antivirus product*: http://searchsecurity.techtarget.com/answer/Picking-
   the-best-enterprise-antivirus-product-Does-AV-research-count?asrc = EM_ERU_19291246
6. *Botnet (from Wikipedia)*
   "A botnet is a collection of Internet connected computers whose security defenses have
   been breached and control ceded to a malicious party. Each such compromised device,
   known as a 'bot,' is created when a computer is penetrated by software from a *malware*
   distribution, otherwise known as a malicious software. The controller of a botnet is able
   to direct the activities of these compromised computers through communication channels
   formed by standards-based network protocols such as IRC(Internet Relay Chat) and HTTP
   (Hypertext Transfer Protocol)."
7. *The NIST site* (see above).
8. *IBM Report March 2013: IBM X-Force 2012 Trend and Risk Report*
   This is a very thorough and detailed report on various threats to business and the growth
   in type and volume of "attacks"; see http://public.dhe.ibm.com/common/ssi/ecm/en/
   wgl03027usen/WGL03027USEN.PDF.
9. *CSO List of security-related sources on tools, templates, and policies. Even policies and templates
   can be useful learning vehicles as they expose the breadth of the topic in hand*; see http://www
   .csoonline.com/article/486324/security-tools-templates-policies?source = cso_top5.
   Another useful article about penetration testing can also be found on the CSOONLINE website at:
   http://www.csoonline.com/article/636040/penetration-tests-10-tips-for-a-successful-program
   June 26, 2013: Why Business Is Losing the War against Cybercrime: http://www.csoonline
   .com/article/735511/why-business-is-losing-the-war-against-cybercrime?source   =
   CSONLF_nlt_update_2013-06-27

---

* These are current at the time of writing, but others will appear as time passes and the threat increases. Keep
watching the IT media (*a la* "Close Encounters …").

10. *Data Breaches:* See Verizon report and bear in mind that people who lose their data often lose their business: http://www.verizonenterprise.com/resources/reports/rp_data-breach-investigations-report-2013_en_xg.pdf.
11. A useful glossary outlining newer (and some of the more outlandish) malware items can be found at http://searchsecurity.techtarget.com/definition/Malware-Glossary.

     Within this document are links to related items concerning malware.

System Monitoring[*]

Remember: If you can't measure it, you can't manage it.[†]

There are obviously monitoring tools and related software described on the websites of major vendors like HP, Cisco, IBM, Microsoft, and so on. The following sites are useful alternatives to these, although these major vendors often have connections with third parties.

Integrated Research (www.ir.com): http://www.prognosis.com/infrastructure (infrastructure), http://www.prognosis.com/uc (unified communications).
Managed Methods Inc. JaxView: www.managedmethods.com/content/9.html.
Solarwinds: Watch It!: http://www.solarwinds.com/products/toolsets/standard/watchit.aspx.
Site24x7: Website Monitoring (including availability): http://www.site24x7.com/features.html.
Paessler: Network Availability: http://www.paessler.com/network_availability.
Free Ping Utility: http://www.paessler.com/info/ping_utility.
Kaseya: Website Availability: http://www.kaseya.com/solutions/it-tools.aspx.
Free Ping Utility: http://www.kaseya.com/solutions/it-tools.aspx.
monitor.us: General Free Tools: http://www.monitor.us/website-monitoring.
Uptime/Web Monitoring: http://www.monitor.us/free-monitoring-features/website-uptime-monitoring.
Free Tools List ("for monitoring your site's uptime"): http://sixrevisions.com/tools/12-excellent-free-tools-for-monitoring-your-sites-uptime/.

Cloud Computing Availability

Book: *Reliability and Availability of Cloud Computing* (Eric Bauer, Randee Adams) ISBN: 978-1-1181-7701-3, September 2012, Wiley-IEEE Press.
Stratus White Paper: http://www.stratus.com/~/media/Stratus/Files/Library/WhitePapers/ServerVirtualizationandCloudComputing.pdf.
IBM View of Security and Availability: http://www.redbooks.ibm.com/redpapers/pdfs/redp4614.pdf.
Readable PowerPoint Presentation: http://teaching-ia.appspot.com/files/Cloud_Computing_Security_Reliability_and_Availability_Issues.pptx.
Cloud Computing Availability—paper by Scott Page: http://www.ccbc.ir/files_site/files/r_10_130217100506.pdf.
Cloud Security Alliance Courseware: https://cloudsecurityalliance.org/education/white-papers-and-educational-material/courseware/.

---

[*] For availability, capacity, and intrusion detection.
[†] *One accurate measurement is worth a thousand expert opinions*—Grace Hopper, Rear Admiral US Navy and COBOL pioneer.

Cost of Ownership (TCO) Sites

1. Security Management and Operations (Enterprise Strategy Group 2012): http://docs.media
.bitpipe.com/io_10x/io_109246/item_670363/Esg%20Research%20final%20sponsor%20
report_%20security%20management%20and%20operations.pdf.
2. Improving Availability and Lowering TCO with HP Integrity Servers and Open VMS
(Thomas Pisello): http://h71000.www7.hp.com/openvms/whitepapers/alinean_tco.pdf.
3. Using Availability Analysis to Reduce Total Cost of Ownership: http://www.theriac.org/
DeskReference/PDFs/2010Q2/2010JournalQ2_WEB.pdf.

Green Data Center Environment

1. APC (Schneider) articles and white papers on power and related issues (http://www.apc
.com/prod_docs/results.cfm).
2. Green data center news and articles. Registration required for full benefit (http://www
.greendatacenternews.org/).
3. Searches on words of "green" interest will generate other specific items in this area.
Unfortunately I have found that, in general, "green" means "cost."

Disaster Recovery References

There are numerous articles and e-books on DR, written by people who know more about the
topic than I have outlined in Chapter 11 so at this point I will provide some references.

> **Note:** *It is probably a wise thing to decide your DR priorities via at least a BIA before diving into
> any particular reference to check which one tallies with your needs.*

The Shortcut Guide to Untangling the Differences between High Availability and Disaster Recovery,
sponsored by ARC serve. A very useful and readable e-book from Realtime Publishers
(85 pages); see http://www.realtimepublishers.com/disaster-recovery/.
The Shortcut Guide to Availability, Continuity and Disaster Recovery, sponsored by MARATHON.
It is another readable guide on our subject, see http://nexus.realtimepublishers.com/sgacdr.php/.
IBM Redbook, related to an IBM product (FileNetPp8) but with much useful generic information about DR and backup; see http://www.redbooks.ibm.com/redbooks/pdfs/sg247744.pdf.
IBM Redbook about Tivoli Storage Manager but with masses of generic DR and backup infor-
mation, including a recovery speed table for various configurations; see http://www.redbooks
.ibm.com/redbooks/pdfs/sg246844.pdf.
Other similar papers can be found by searching on "disaster recovery, <vendor name>" and
further qualifying the search if necessary.

Other Reliability Sites*

1. The U.S. government website "Information Technology" covers all aspects of IT, especially
security. It is well worth an hour or two's browse to find out what is relevant to you (see http://
www.nist.gov/information-technology-portal.cfm).

---

* From http://asq.org/links/reliability.html.

2. Barringer & Associates has made Wallodi Weibull's reliability papers available for download. Many of the papers are from Robert Abernathy's book, *The New Weibull Handbook* (www.barringer1.com/wa.htm).

3. The Equipment Reliability Institute is an engineering school that focuses on the reliability and durability of equipment in the aircraft, automobile, telecom systems, and satellite industries. Although the institute charges a fee for its courses and consulting, its website has plenty of free information in the form of newsletters, articles, a message board, and a reliability glossary (www.equipment-reliability.com).

4. The European Safety and Reliability Association (ESRA) is a nonprofit umbrella organization with a membership consisting of national professional societies, industrial organizations, and higher education institutions. ESRA's website has information on becoming a member, conference listings, safety and reliability links, and e-copies of the ESRA newsletter (www.esrahomepage.org).

5. Reliability Center Inc. has a website with features such as forums on various topics, a newsletter and articles, links to other organizations, a definitions page, and a search service (www.reliability.com).

6. This consumer review site for the reliability industry includes news, articles, reviews, question-and-answer pages on many topics, and what is called the Reliability Hall of Fame (www.reliabilityweb.com).

7. The Reliability, Maintainability, and Supportability Partnership (RMSP) is an organization that fosters networking among organizations and people interested in reliability engineering. Its home page features free articles, reliability links, the RMSP quarterly newsletter, events listings, and job opportunity listings (www.rmspartnership.org).

8. The Society for Maintenance and Reliability Professionals (SMRP) is devoted to promoting maintenance and reliability education for people and production and quality processes. On its website, visit the library for abstracts and articles from recent conferences or the popular discussion network for threads on topics such as maintenance training, motor management software, and best practices (www.smrp.org).

9. The Society of Reliability Engineers (SRE) provides visitors information regarding officers, chapters, and directors. In addition, users can read the full text of the organization newsletter, Lambda Notes (www.sre.org).

10. Supported by Reliasoft, this site is a premier source of information, discussion, and tools for reliability engineering. From the home page, click on "Reliability Growth Analysis Online Reference" for principles and theory, "Reliability Glossary" for a complete list of terms, or "Reliability Hotwire" to read the latest e-zine on improving reliability practices (www.weibull.com).

I think there is enough reading and reference material here to last a lifetime and beyond. I trust you will be selective in what you pursue from this massive list, nearly all of which I have consulted (but not necessarily read). I wish you the best of luck.

Appendix 6

"Room service? Send up a larger room."

Henry "Groucho" Marx

Service Management: Where Next?

At the risk of turning the reader to drink, I'll reiterate the whole ethos of this book—the *availability of a service working according to its specification* and not just the correct working of individual components. We have seen, *ad nauseam*, that systems of hardware and software may work smoothly but not according to what the user expects.

We have broken a service into three components: people, processes, and products. Products have been covered in this book and in several others. What we are trying to obtain are processes and competent people who will complement the products and meet end-use expectations as expressed in a *service level agreement*.

You will see figures for availability in survey after survey and wonder whether the fuss about availability in most systems work fine, don't they?. Most systems work fine. First of all, they don't—make sure the ones that don't aren't yours. Second, the surveys are not usually carried out with end users (the IT customers) so we don't really see the *working-to-specification* part of the availability equation.

> *Note:* The objective then is not just high availability hardware and software but *delighted end users*, to coin a phrase. This means unflinching concentration on the *service* and not the nuts and bolts of the systems supporting it. The following sections cover some aspects of giving a first class service to users.

Information Technology Infrastructure Library[*]

The **Information Technology Infrastructure Library** (ITIL) is a set of practices for IT service management (ITSM) that focuses on aligning IT services with the needs of business. In its current form (known as ITILv3 and ITIL 2011 edition), ITIL is

---

[*] http://www.itil-officialsite.com/AboutITIL/WhatisITIL.aspx.

published in a series of five core publications, each of which covers an ITSM lifecycle stage. ITILv3 underpins ISO/IEC20000 (previously BS15000), the International Service Management Standard for ITSM, although differences between the two frameworks do exist.

ITIL describes procedures, tasks, and checklists that are not organization-specific, used by an organization for establishing a minimum level of competency. It allows the organization to establish a baseline from which it can plan, implement, and measure. It is used to demonstrate compliance and to measure improvement.

The names *ITIL* and *IT Infrastructure Library* are registered trademarks of the United Kingdom's Office of Government Commerce (OGC)—now part of the Cabinet Office. Following this move, the ownership is now listed as being with HM Government rather than OGC.

ITIL Availability Management

Availability management targets allowing organizations to sustain the IT service availability to support the business at a justifiable cost. The high-level activities realize availability requirements, compile availability plan, monitor availability, and monitor maintenance obligations.

Availability management addresses the ability of an IT component to perform at an agreed level over a period of time.

- *Reliability:* Ability of an IT component to perform at an agreed level at described conditions.
- *Maintainability:* The ability of an IT component to remain in, or be restored to, an operational state.
- *Serviceability:* The ability for an external supplier to maintain the availability of component or function under a third-party contract.
- *Resilience:* A measure of freedom from operational failure and a method of keeping services reliable. One popular method of resilience is redundancy.
- *Security:* A service may have associated data. Security refers to the confidentiality, integrity, and availability of that data. Availability gives a clear overview of the end-to-end availability of the system.

I have emphasized the need for architectures several times in this book, so I ought to outline what these architectures are. I have seen diagrams of *architectures* that have not been *architected*—they are simply what someone called *wiring diagrams* of the system as they were cobbled together over the years. In other words, they are more of an accident than a design.

Service Architectures

Architecture in an IT context means different things to different people. Some draw a wiring diagram of their current system, however badly put together, and call in an *architecture*. Architecture gurus, in my opinion, make architectures into a scientific cult and often render then incomprehensible. Things should be simple but no simpler, according to Einstein and I agree. What follows is hopefully a pragmatic approach to IT architectures, including High Availability/Disaster Recovery (HA/DR).

Architecture versus String and Sealing Wax

I did some basic work on architectures and on the flow of their development, and the following is a summary of my deliberations and research. It is, against my earlier advice, only a checklist but I feel it will give a different perspective to the development of HA/DR systems. It is advantageous to an organization if the HA/DR can fit within enterprise architectures and standards and not, if possible, bend the rules too much.

System Architectures

The output of an architecture study should ideally be a product-independent architecture which can have one or more implementations. Indeed there may be cases where more than one architecture match the customer requirements and may be amenable to several implementations. In essence, it is a level of abstraction above the hardware, software, and other operational entities.

It is vital that an IT architect understands the difference between an *architecture* and an *implementation*. An architecture is often independent of how it is implemented; for example, a drawing of a house architecture might be *implemented* in brick, stone, wood, or even paper if you live in Japan. Only by assessing the detailed needs of the occupant that it is possible to guide the architecture to the most appropriate implementation. For example, if a person lives at the foot of a volcano, which spews hot volcanic ash out every other week, it would be inadvisable to implement the design in wood (or paper).

One Architecture or Several?

If the business units (BUs) within an enterprise use separate systems, then it is possible to have a different architecture of the same category for each strategic business unit (SBU), for example, two different availability architectures. If they share systems, this is more difficult. Once an architecture has been defined, it can probably be reused in a *diluted form* as an architecture for another system. Sun Microsystems had a Reusable Enterprise Architecture Library (REAL) containing this sort of information. I am not sure if it currently exists.

For example, a backup/recovery architecture can be reduced in availability features and size for a system whose requirements are not as stringent. This would mean reducing the hardware redundancy employed, and possibly the amount of software, to reduce the cost to match the benefit. This is known as *architecture reuse*, a very cost-effective and time-saving way of doing things.

Warnings: The following guidelines might help in designing architecures:

1. It is crucial to designing successful architectures that they avoid solutions to which there is no known problem.
2. A wiring diagram is not an architecture.
3. Neither is a beautiful diagram of what you already have (self-fulfilling prophecy).
4. An architecture should be amenable to different implementations.
5. It should be capable of being explained to a barmaid (Rutherford) (Table A6.1).

Table A6.1 Enterprise Architectures: My View of Categories

Architecture	*Definition*
Information architecture	This architecture defines the business questions that IT is to address, including the major information repositories in the business, the information flow between them, and the access methodology.
Storage architecture	This architecture defines the storage strategy for the business. It is also a subarchitecture to many of the other architectures, such as the availability, application, coexistence, and management architectures.
Application architecture	The application architecture defines the major applications, their interaction, and their delivery. For example, client/server, thin client, web-based, and *n*-tier.
Coexistence architecture	This architecture defines the integration of the major systems supporting the information architecture. It will include the definition of the interfaces between major systems, for example, provision of services for both homogeneous and heterogeneous environments.
Security architecture	This architecture defines the security requirements for the information architecture. This will probably be a requirement for multilevel security. For example, the demands of an Internet installation will typically be more stringent that those of an extranet. BYOD makes this architecture *KEY* to data and application security and hence, to *business continuity*.
Availability architecture	This architecture defines how the availability criteria that are required for each major component of the information architecture will be met. It would include subarchitectures such as backup and recovery strategy, archive strategy, disaster recovery planning. There should be major input from the business, for example, business impact analysis (BIA).
Management architecture	This architecture defines the support strategy for the services that maintain the information architecture, including systems, storage, networks, and applications.
Development architecture	This architecture defines the development environment, test and quality assurance (QA) processes, and deployment strategy. It should include function and load testing of the application(s) and an estimate of software maturity that enables it to be issued.
Production architecture	This architecture defines the production schema for applications and day-to-day operations, such as backup, housekeeping, and so on.
Data architecture	This architecture defines the characteristics of the data that flows through the information architecture. It would typically provide data volumes, storage technologies (RDBMS, text files), availability and security requirements, volatility, and importance.
Web/ e-commerce architecture	This architecture defines the web/e-commerce infrastructure, the delivery targets and mechanisms, and how the security and availability requirements are addressed. This will involve several of the other architectures in this table, for example, availability and security.

(Continued)

Table A6.1 (Continued) Enterprise Architectures: My View of Categories

Architecture	Definition
Enterprise printing architecture	This describes the framework for supporting the printing needs of the organization or SBU. This includes factors such as security, priorities, color, synchronous and asynchronous printing, and so on.
Cloud and virtualization architecture	This is new on the architecture scene pioneered by Zachman, TOGAF, and others, and is outlined here for completeness in handling entities new to HA.

Where is your *network architecture* I hear you cry? Network architecture is not covered in Table A6.1 as a separate item since it really underpins the other architectures and, as such, depends on the physical requirements of the supported architectures. In other words, it cannot be designed in isolation from the other architectures outlined in the table.

Architectures

Availability Architectures: HA Documentation

To my knowledge, there are no formal attempts to define availability architectures along the Zachman or TOGAF lines (see Appendix 1), although several vendors outline ways of using hardware and software to produce availability implementation schematics. Some of these are cited at the end of this section. Availability, like beauty, is in the eye of the beholder and what is important to him or her as an organization.

I feel that a strict, formally rigorous architecture in this area might be a hindrance rather than a help, hence my reference above to what I consider useful vendor schematics. I have seen people shying from tough implementation and operational decisions by hiding behind the *need to develop a formal architecture before proceeding*. Having said that, there are some sources of information on what are loosely described as high availability (HA) architectures, although in reality they are implementations. These are outlined subsequently.

Some architectures are specific to the vendors' products, while others are more generic and could be applied to various situations. The base architecture is a clustered configuration with switched HA disks (SAN, RAID, etc.) and often the implementation of HA features in accompanying software—Oracle, DNS, and so on.

Windows: See http://technet.microsoft.com/en-us/library/cc750543.aspx (HA architecture overview) and http://windowsitpro.com/networking/high-availability-system-architecture (Article 15702 referenced in URL above).

Cisco: See http://www.cisco.com/c/en/us/solutions/collateral/data-center-virtualization/unified-computing/white_paper_c11-553711.pdf (network-oriented white paper).

IBM: See http://public.dhe.ibm.com/software/data/sw-library/services/High_Availability_Architecture.pdf (offering IBM HA architecture services).

Oracle: http://www.oracle.com/technetwork/database/features/availability/maa-090890.html (has further references within this document).

Dell: See http://www.dell.com/downloads/global/power/ps2q05-20040265-rad.pdf (HA for Oracle 10*g* but generic in places).

Amazon Web Services: See http://www.slideshare.net/harishganesan/architecture-blueprints-for-achieving-high-availability-in-aws (architecture blueprints for achieving HA in Amazon Web Services [AWS]).

Other sources: See http://info.servicenow.com/LP = 1935 (advanced HA white paper); http://www.drj.com/articles/online-exclusive/continuous-application-availability-strategy-for-business-resiliency.html (article/white paper); and http://conningtech.files.wordpress.com/2010/09/system-high-availability-architecture.pdf (detailed presentation).

Clouds and Architectures

The commonly accepted three-level approach for planning and implementing cloud computing is

■ Cloud reference *model*
■ Cloud reference *architecture*
■ Cloud reference *implementation*

The last *reference* entity is not well defined but can be intuitively developed based on the model, architecture, and business requirements. Don't forget these because if you get hung up on architectures, you may well throw out the baby with the bath water. The other thing I would say about models and architectures is that in my experience they can get detached from the reality of IT business and become an almost academic subject.

I find a quote from Chairman Mao's *Little Red Book* appropriate in this context::

> When we look at a thing, we must examine its essence and treat its appearance merely as an Usher at the threshold, and once we cross the threshold, we must grasp the essence of the thing: this is the only reliable and scientific method of analysis.

If your eyes glaze at the thought of *third normal forms* and *abstract syntax notation* (ASN-1), take a leaf out of Mao's book and use what you understand about the essence of the topic in the pursuit of IT support for business services. If you struggle to employ abstruse architecture concepts at the expense of providing an HA service, my view is: drop the architecture. As I have already said, it is a good delaying tactic to plead architectural shortfalls as an excuse for not getting on with implementations.

Cloud Life Cycle

Before we examine the reference *model* and the reference *architecture* (RA), it is instructive to look briefly at the Architecture and Interoperability Roadmap produced by AgilePath (Figure A6.1).

Cloud Reference Models

Different *Cloud reference models* can be considered, such as those published by the following:

■ The Open Cloud Consortium.
■ Cloud Services Foundation RA.*

---

* http://blogs.technet.com/b/cloudsolutions/archive/2013/08/15/cloud-services-foundation-reference-architecture-overview.aspx.

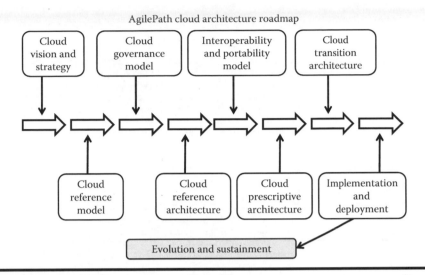

Figure A6.1   AgilePath cloud architecture roadmap.

- NIST Cloud Computing RA.
- The Cloud Security Alliance.
- The Cloud Computing Reference Model (CC-RM) and RA framework from AgilePath.
- The Accenture Cloud Reference Model for Application Architecture with its seven layers. Like the open systems interconnection (OSI) Model for networks, this cloud model is layered to separate concerns and abstract details.

The layered models can be looked at as the cloud equivalent of the OSI and SNA 7-layer models, which are well known. The NIST model involved SaaS, PaaS, and IaaS across the four deployment models. The entities involved (or *actors* in NIST parlance) are as follows:

Cloud consumer: A person or organization that maintains a business relationship with, and uses service from, *Cloud providers.*

Cloud provider: A person, organization, or entity responsible for making a service available to *cloud consumers.*

Cloud auditor: A party that can conduct independent assessment of cloud services, information system operations, performance, and security of the cloud implementation.

Cloud broker: An entity that manages the use, performance, and delivery of cloud services, and negotiates relationships between *cloud providers* and *cloud consumers.*

Cloud carrier: The intermediary that provides connectivity and transport of cloud services from *cloud providers* to *cloud consumers.*

Generic Cloud Reference Model

The general Cloud reference model is given in Figure A6.2 (http://www.architecting-the-enterprise.com/enterprise_architecture/articles/cloud_computing_requires_enterprise_architecture_and_togaf_9_can_show_the_way.php).

Abstraction layer	Functionality
Application	Sets up the application program and architecture, e.g., batch, HPC, portal
Transformation	Transforms application program representation to cloud representation, e.g., data encryption
Control	Prescribes the optimized set of compute resources to meet application requirements, e.g., SLA needs
Instantiation	Provisions and maintains a deployment of virtual appliances with the right SW, data, and configuration
Appliance	Adds the middleware to the virtual machine, e.g., load balancer, web server, database server
Virtual	Manages the set of virtualized logical compute units, e.g., server images, storage volumes, static IP addresses
Physical	Maintains the physical compute equipment, e.g., servers, NAS, SAN, routers

Figure A6.2   General cloud reference model.

Cloud RA

Like the models, there are variations in RA. The IBM RA, presented in the following, is claimed by the IBM to be very close to the NIST architecture and might be taken as representative of general thinking and consensus about cloud computing architecture (Figure A6.3).

IBM's Cloud Computing RA (CCRA) is a blueprint to guide IBM development teams and field practitioners in the design of public and private clouds. IBM created it from the collective

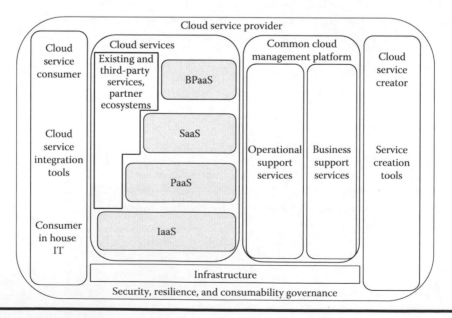

Figure A6.3   IBM cloud RA.

experiences of hundreds of cloud client engagements and information from the implementation of IBM-hosted clouds.

A Reference Architecture (RA) provides a blueprint of a "to-be" model with a well-defined scope, requirements it satisfies, and the architectural decisions it realizes. It includes prescriptive architecture and product recommendations in the form of cloud adoption patterns. By delivering best practices in a standardized, methodical way, an RA ensures globally consistent delivery and high-quality project results.

For reference, see https://www.ibm.com/developerworks/community/wikis/home?lang=en#!/wiki/Wf3cce8ff09b3_49d2_8ee7_4e49c1ef5d22/page/IBM Cloud Computing Reference Architecture 3.0 and http://www.ibm.com/developerworks/rational/library/enterprise-architecture-cloud.

If you want to compare the architectures, visit the article at http://cloudcomputing.sys-con.com/node/1752894, which compares the RA of the Big Three (IBM, HP, and Microsoft):

See Figure A6.3 for IBM Cloud RA, and finally, don't forget to read and absorb the messages in Appendix 7.

Appendix 7

Those who fail to learn from history are doomed to repeat its mistakes.

Final Visual Summary

"Glad the hole isn't at our end Fred."

ROLES & RESPONSIBILITIES,
+ Cooperation

DOCUMENTATION
(Living)

COMMUNICATIONS,
+ Centers of Control
(War Room, SOC, CCC, etc·)

ACCOUNTABILITY
("Carrying the Can")

PLAN & DESIGN,
+ Execute & Review,
+ Prioritize & Delegate

SECURITY
(Let Paranoia Be Your Watchword)

tcritchley07@gmail.com   xperassociates@gmail.com

489

Index

Note: Locators followed by "*f*" and "*t*" denote figures and tables in the text.

A

Aberdeen Group study, 61, 61*f*
Abstract syntax notation (ASN), 484
ACID. *See* Atomicity, consistency, isolation, and durability (ACID)
ACMS. *See* Application control management system (ACMS)
Active modes, 57
Adaptive Server for Enterprise (ASE), 286
Advanced persistent threat (APT), 335, 449
Adware, 352
AGREE (Advisory Group for Reliability of Electronic Equipment), 109
Alerts, 233
Amazon Web Services (AWS), 341, 484
Amdahl's law, 420–421, 421*f*, 422*f*, 425
Analysis, failure, 344
Anarchy, 25
Application availability, 335
Application control management system (ACMS), 268
Application development environments (ADE), 260
Application programming interfaces (API), 27, 170, 286, 370
Applications outsourcing (AO), 365
Architecture reuse, 481
ASN. *See* Abstract syntax notation (ASN)
Assurance, software, 367
Asynchronous transfer mode (ATM), 157
Atomicity, consistency, isolation, and durability (ACID), 186
Authentication bug, 300
Automation
    data center, 22–23
    network change/configuration, 23
    vendors, 23–24
Autonomic computing, 145, 335

Availability (*A*), 111
    7 R's (SNIA), 16–18
    architectures, 69–72
    calculations, 50
        vs. costs, 124
        operational, 41
    and change, 18–19, 18*f*
        monitoring and, 20–22
        operations, 20
        software, 20
    classification
        fault tolerance, 57
        outage analogy, 56–57
        performance and, 64–65, 64*t*
        redundancy, 57
        requirements, sample, 57–59
    concepts, 49–51
        first dip in water, 49
        hardware reliability, 109–110, 109*f*
        parameters, 50–51
        software reliability, 110–111, 111*f*
    definitions, 15
    drivers in flux, 4–6
    equations, 113*f*, 114–117
    factors
        planned and unplanned outages, 125–126, 126*f*
        planned downtime, 126–128, 126*f*, 127*t*
        unplanned downtime, 127*f*, 128–139
    historical scenarios, 8–10
        component repair, 9
        in-flight diagnostics, 10
        other diagnostics, 9
        planar technology, 8
        power-on-self-test, 9
    historical view, 6–8
    IDC and, 53–54
    mathematical issues, 105–107
    Murphy's law of, 4

Availability (*A*) (*Continued*)
 organizations, 461–478
 parallel blocks, 118–119
 probability, 107–108
 quantitative, 16
 redundant blocks, effect, 117–119, 117*f*, 118*f*
 risks to business services, 5*t*
 state variable, 25*f*
 time available/elapsed time, 117
 time factors in outage, 114–116, 115*f*
 tool, 113
 types, 24–28
  binary, 24–25
  continuous availability, 336
  continuous operation, 336
  Duke of York, 25–26
  hierarchy example, 26–27
  hierarchy of failures, 26, 27*f*
  high availability, 335–336
  state parameters, 27–28, 28*f*
Availability groups (AG), 274
Availability, HA design spectrum
 anticipation, 159–160
 application design
  conventional programs, 147
  web applications, 147–148
 application monitoring, 155
 automation, 155–156
 change management, 158
 cleanliness, 159
 configuration
  data, 150
  environment, 150–151
  hardware, 149
  networks, 150
  operating system, 150
 engineering design
  self-healing and other items, 146
  self-healing hardware and software, 145
 eternal vigilance, 161–162
 location, 162
 monitoring, 159
 network design, 165–166
 operations excellence
  data center efficiency, 154
  first class runbook, 153
  performance and capacity, 154
  software level issues, 153–154
  system time, 154
 organization, 160–161
 outside consultancy, 151
 partnerships, 157
 performance/capacity management, 158–159
 proactive monitoring, 151–152
 reactive recovery, 156–157
 retrospective analysis, 154–155

 systems design/modification, 145
 teamwork, 160
 technical support excellence, 152
 vendor support, 151
Availability, math
 active and standby redundancy
  math of *m*-from-*n* configurations, 415
  online tool for parallel components, 416–417
  overall availability graphs, 418–419
  realistic IT redundancy, 417–418
  real *m*-from-*n* example, 414
  reliability of active redundancy, 415*t*–416*t*
  repairable and nonrepairable systems, 412*t*
  types of redundancy, 413–414
 additional RAS features
  clocks and service processor, 446
  fault detection and isolation, 445–446
  I/O subsystem, 445
  memory availability, 445
  predictive failure analysis, 447
  processor, 444–445
  serviceability, 446
  upmarket, 444
 cluster speedup formulae
  Amdahl's Law, 420–421
  Amdahl *vs.* Gunther, 424–425
  Gunther's Law, 421–423
  Gustafson's Law, 423–424
  Sun–Ni Law, 425
 cyber crime, security, and
  BYOD security steps, 454
  cost of cyber crime, 457
  database, 455–456
  denial of service, 452
  distributed DoS, 456
  DNS servers, 456–457
  insider threats, 452–453
  issue, 448
  mobile devices (BYOD), 453–454
  risk *vs.* cost of cyber crime prevention, 457–458
  security analytics, 449
  security information event management, 450
  security literature, 458
  security management flow, 450–451
  SIEM, 451–452
  solution, 449
  WiFi in enterprise, 455
  zero trust security model, 449–450
 math of monitoring
  ping, 432–433, 433*f*
  ping math, 433
  ping sequence sample, 435
  transaction (*XN*), 434
 multiplication, summation, and integration symbols, 405–406

parallel components
    m-from-*n* components, 410
    m-from-*n* examples, 410
    m-from-*n* redundant blocks, 411
    m-from-*n* theory, 410–411
RAID and EC math
    erasure codes, 429
    RAID configurations, 426–429
software reliability/availability
    failure/defect density models, 437–444
    overview, 435–436
    software reliability theory, 436–437
triple modular redundancy, 447–448

B

Backup product assessments
  backup/archive
    bit rot, 319–320
    tape costs, 320
  Gartner quadrant analysis, 318–319
  virtualization review, 318
Backup/restore
  backup modes
    cold (offline), 311
    hot (online), 311
    and methods, 315*f*
    warm (online), 311
  backup types
    differential, 312
    full, 312
    incremental, 312
    multilevel incremental, 312
    progressive, 312
    synthetic, 312
  data deduplication, 313–314, 313*f*
  data replication
    asynchronous, 315
    backup modes and methods, 315*f*
    heterogeneous, 316, 317*f*
    replication agents, 315
    synchronous, 316
  overview, 311
  types of backup, 316
  WAN optimization, 317–318
Bandwidth throttling, 369
Bare metal, 301
  hypervisor, 347
  recovery, 336
Basic input/output system (BIOS), 9, 305
Bathtub curves, 336
  failure modes, 110*t*
  hardware reliability, 109–110, 109*f*
  software reliability, 110–111, 111*f*
BCM standard (BS25999/ISO 22301), 337
Berkeley Software Distribution (BSD), 284

Best of Breed (BoB), 298
BIA. *See* Business impact analysis (BIA)
Big data, 69, 94–95, 336
Bills of material (BoM), 271
Binary availability, 24–25
BIST. *See* Built-in self-test (BIST)
Blacklisting, 71
Block diagrams, 336
BlockSim, 120
Bohrbug software error, 185
Books, articles, and websites
  major reliability/availability information sources,
    469–470
  other information sources, 470–478
Bot, 475
Botnet, bot, 351
Bottom-up (inductive) approach, 345
BPO. *See* Business process outsourcing (BPO)
Bring your own device (BYOD), 453
British Standards Institution (BSI), 337
BSD. *See* Berkeley Software Distribution (BSD)
Built-in self-test (BIST), 9
Burn-in/out, 336
Business continuity (BC), 5, 34, 197, 308, 337,
    398, 466
  plan, 31–32
  relationships of BIA, DR and, 33
Business Continuity Institute (BCI), 466
Business continuity management (BCM), 337
Business continuity plan (BCP), 31–32, 198, 336
Business Continuity Today, 465
Business impact analysis (BIA), 32, 59, 155, 169, 199,
    337, 392
Business/IT recovery requirements, 34*f*
Business process outsourcing (BPO), 365
Business services availability, risks, 5*t*
Business units (BU), 481
BYOD. *See* Bring your own device (BYOD)

C

Cambridge monitor system (CMS), 300
Carrier Grade Linux (CGL), 263
Cascaded failure, 337
Center for Software Reliability (CSR), 467
Central electronic complex (CEC), 191
CFIA. *See* Component failure impact
    analysis (CFIA)
Chained file management system (CFMS), 271
Channel bonding, 359
Chip-kill DRAM, 70
Cisco network configuration, 121–123, 122*f*
Cloud
  availability, 298–299
  characteristics, 294
  deployment models, 296

Cloud (*Continued*)
    functions of, 294–295
    resource management in, 297
    security, 299–300
    service models, 295–296
    SLAs and, 297–298
Cloud computing, 293–294
Cloud Computing RA (CCRA), 486
Cloud Computing Reference Model (CC-RM), 485
Cloud databases, 341
Cloud Security Alliance (CSA), 300, 468
Clusters, 66, 66*f*, 72, 337–339
    architecture, 74–82
        components, 74–77
        configurations of commercial cluster, 74,
            75*f*, 76*f*
        HPC, 77–82
    IBM, 251
    Linux, 262–264
        carrier grade, 263–264
        clouds, 263
        HA, 263
        HPC HA, 263
        Oracle clusterware, 263
        overview, 262
        Red Hat, 263
        SUSE, 263
        VMware clusters, 264
    MACH 11, 282–283
    Oracle HA, 255–256
    production, 67–69
    requirements of ASE, 286–287
    service availability software, 264–265
    speedup formulae, 419–425
        Amdahl's Law, 420–421, 421*f*, 422*f*
        Amdahl *vs.* Gunther, 424–425, 425*f*
        Gunther's Law, 421–423, 423*f*
        Gustafson's Law, 423–424, 424*f*
        Sun–Ni Law, 425
    VC (Symantec), 261–262
        databases, applications, and replicators, 262
        supported platforms, 261
    web and HA, 264
CMS. *See* Cambridge monitor system (CMS)
Cold plugging, 339
Command and control center (CCC), 226, 337
Commercial acceptance of grid computing, 83
Commercial off-the-shelf (COTS), 145, 263, 463
Commodity HPC cluster, 338
Communications resource manager (CRM), 371
Complex systems, 120
    solution methods, 121
    system failure combinations, 120–121
Component failure impact analysis (CFIA), 25–26, 141,
        198, 339
Computer Associates (CA), 284
Computer security, 340

Continuity software, 265
Continuous data protection (CDP), 311
Control objectives for information and related
        technology (COBIT), 339
Control program (CP), 300
Corrected machine check interrupt (CMCI), 445
Cost impact analysis (CIA), 59, 339
Coupling facility (CF), 252
Criticality analysis (CA), 340
Critical success factors (CSF), 212, 394
Cross site mirroring, 340
Cumulative distribution function (cdf), 106,
        107*f*, 340
Customer information control system (CICS), 39,
        267, 337
Customer replaceable units (CRU), 9, 260
Cyber crime, 340, 437
Cybersecurity, 340
Cyber Security and Information Systems IAC
        (CSIAC), 469
Cyclic redundancy checks (CRC), 71, 258, 340

D

Data and Analysis Center for Software (DACS), 469
Database as a service (DBaaS), 295, 341
Database hashing, 341
Database journaling, 340–341
Database replication, 341
Database system, 341
Data Center Automation, 22–23
Data center infrastructure management (DCIM),
        233, 341
Data deduplication, 313–314, 313*f*
Data definition language (DDL), 283
Data encryption, 367
Data manipulation language (DML), 283
Data processing (DP), 19, 40
Data reduction, 317
Data replication, 314–316
Data striping (RAID), 340
DB2
    10 for z/OS
        cross platform development, 281
        DB2 pureScale, 280–281
        InfoSphere Replication Server for, 281
    database and HA of IBM, 278–280
    for i, 280
Deduplication, 342
Defect density, 180
Defense Technical Information Center (DTIC), 469
Degraded mode, 25–26
Delphi technique, 215, 342
Demilitarized zone (DMZ), 299
Denial of service (DoS), 452
Department of Defense (DoD), 462
Dependability, 342

Dependent, failure, 344
Digital Equipment Corporation (DEC), 67–68, 74, 155, 209
Dirty
    buffer, 363
    page, 362
    read, 363
Disaster recovery (DR), 5, 33, 33*f*, 58, 85, 199, 253, 307, 343, 470
    A to B point, 310
    concepts and considerations, 321–324
    Forrester survey, invocation reasons, 309–310
    Kaseya survey, 310
    key message, 308–309
    organizations declaring, 308*t*
    planning process, 324–330
    from space, 307–308
    steps involved, 324–327
Disaster recovery as a service (DRaaS), 295
Disaster Recovery Institute International, 465
Disaster Recovery Preparedness Council (DRPC), 308
Disk operating system (DOS), 301
Distributed Computing Environment (DCE), 343
Distributed denial of service (DDoS), 164, 340, 351
Distributed Replicated Block Device (DRBD), 262
Distributed transaction processing (DTP), 269, 371
DML. *See* Data manipulation language (DML)
Domain/LPAR structure, 73–74, 73*f*
Domain name server (DNS), 134
Domain name service (DNS), 200, 311
Domain reduction, 142
Domains, 73
DOS. *See* Disk operating system (DOS)
Double bit errors, 343
Double disk failure (DDF), 431
Downtime, 34–35, 112
    causes, 129
    other gotchas, 133–135, 134*f*
    planned, 126–128
    unplanned
        availability, 136–137
        data loss causes, 132–133, 132*t*
        disasters, 128–129, 129*t*
        external electromagnetic radiation, 131
        low impact outages, 135–136
        outage reasons, 138–139, 138*f*, 139*f*
        reduction initiatives, 135, 136*t*
        security, 128
Downtime Statistics of Current Cloud Solutions, 298
DRAM. *See* Dynamic RAM (DRAM)
DRBD. *See* Distributed Replicated Block Device (DRBD)
DR concepts and considerations
    objectives, 322
    recovery factors, 322–323, 322*f*
    scenario, 321–322

tiers of DR availability
    data tiering, 323–324
    key factor, 324
DR planning process
    requirements in operations
        applications, 327
        backup site, 328–329
        cloud, 329
        cost considerations, 328
        data, 327–328
        disaster recovery templates, 330
        HA/DR options, 329–330
        hardware, 327
        software, 327
        third-party DR (outsourcing), 329
    steps involved, 324–327
Dual drive failure protection, 90
Duke of York availability, 25–26
Dynamic processor resiliency (DPR), 257
Dynamic RAM (DRAM), 70, 87
Dynamic reconfiguration (DR), 58, 69, 73, 343

E

Early warning system (EWS), 6
Elasticity, 294
Encryption, 343
End of life (EOL), 438
End user experience (EUE), 239
End user monitoring (EUM), 239
Enterprise computing in a new age (Encina), 343
Enterprise replication (ER), 283
Enterprise Resource Planning (ERP), 155
Erasure codes, 97–101, 98*f*
Error correction code (ECC), 58, 70–71, 86–87, 90–91, 96, 101, 145, 257, 343
Error density, 180
Error detection, 343
Error, software, 367
European Safety and Reliability Association (ESRA), 478
Evaluating Data Center and Colocation High-Availability Service Delivery, 135
Extended error correction (EEC), 70
Extra Terrestrial Intelligence (ETI), 449

F

Facilitator, 215
Failback (cluster/disaster), 343
Failover, 57
Failover clusters, 74, 343
Failure, 344–345
Failure intensity, 176
Failure mode and effects analysis (FMEA), 26, 198, 343, 472

Failure mode effects and criticality analysis (FMECA), 26, 198
Failure reporting and corrective action system (FRACAS), 223
    steps for handling failures, 223–225
Failure review board, 226, 345
Failure, software, 367
Fault analysis, 344
Fault management architecture (FMA), 255
Fault, software, 367
Fault tolerance, 345
    dynamic recovery, 345
    fault masking, 345
Fault tree analysis (FTA), 26
Federated computing, 344
Field replaceable units (FRU), 9, 192, 257
File transfer protocol (FTP), 167
First failure data capture (FFDC), 250, 445
Fixed-size speedup, 425
Forward error correction (FEC), 97, 346
Functions of cloud, 294–295

G

Geographically Dispersed Parallel Sysplex (GDPS), 323
Geographic mirroring, 346
Global positioning system (GPS), 129
Goel–Okumoto NHPP model, 438
Gotchas, 346
Graceful degradation, 234
Grid computing, 82–83, 83*f*, 346
    availability, 82–83
    commercial, 83
Gumbel distribution, 346
Gunther's Law, 421–423, 423*f*
Gustafson's law, 423–424, 424*f*, 425

H

HA (high availability). *See* High availability (HA)
Hacking, 340
HA cluster, 74
HA design spectrum, availability
    anticipation, 159–160
    application design
        conventional programs, 147
        web applications, 147–148
    application monitoring, 155
    automation, 155–156
    change management, 158
    cleanliness, 159
    configuration, 149–151
        data, 150
        environment, 150–151
        hardware, 149
        networks, 150
        operating system, 150

engineering design
    self-healing and other items, 146
    self-healing hardware and software, 145
    eternal vigilance, 161–162
    location, 162
    monitoring, 159
    network design, 165–166
    operations excellence, 152–154
        data center efficiency, 154
        first class runbook, 153
        performance and capacity, 154
        software level issues, 153–154
        system time, 154
    organization, 160–161
    outside consultancy, 151
    partnerships, 157
    performance/capacity management, 158–159
    proactive monitoring, 151–152
    reactive recovery, 156–157
    retrospective analysis, 154–155
    systems design/modification, 145
    teamwork, 160
    technical support excellence, 152
    vendor support, 151
Hadoop process, 94
HA/DR (high availability/disaster recovery), 387
    road
        DR case study, 391–392
        stages, 387–391
        total cost of ownership, 392–394
    route map and kitbag, 387
HA management
    component failure impact analysis, 220–223
        other factors, 222
        quantitative, 222
        schematic, 221–222
        walkthrough and risk analysis, 220–221
    Delphi techniques and intensive planning, 215–217
        flowchart, 216*f*
        steps, 216–217
    FMEA process, 217–220
        analogy, 218
        CFIA activity, 219*t*
        risk evaluation methods, 219–220
        steps, 218
    start-up and design phase, 209–215
        management flow, 209–210
        management framework, 210, 211*f*
        multistage PDW, 215
        outline of PDW, 212
        PDW method overview, 212–213, 213*f*
        PID structure and purpose, 213–215
        project definition workshop, 210–211
        project initiation document, 213
Hamming code, 86–87, 90

HA operations
    change/configuration management, 226–228
        control, 226–227, 227*f*
        operation, 227–228
        patch management, 228
    escalation management, 238
    event management, 233
    faults
        actions to neglect, 236
        management, 233–235
    help desk architecture and implementation, 238
    performance management, 229–230, 229*f*
    problem
        determination, 232
        management, 237–238
    resource management, 238–239
    security management, 230–231
    war room, 225–226
Hard disk drives (HDD), 90, 92–93, 96, 346
Hardening, software, 367
Hard errors, 9
Hardware management console (HMC), 190
Hash function, 341
Hazard function, 346–347
Health Information Portability and Accountability Act
        (HIPAA), 456
Heartbeat, 347
Heisenberg's uncertainty principle, 185
Heisenbug software error, 185
Hewlett-Packard (HP) HA
    HP hardware and software
        servers, 256
        services, 256–257
        software, 256
    HP nonstop integrity servers
        nonstop architecture and stack, 258–259
        nonstop stack functions, 259–260
    integrity servers, 257–258
Hierarchical storage, 323
High availability (HA), 198, 347
    assessing cost of, 64
    attitude to, 60–61
    cloud and virtualization, 293–306
    commercial, 77
    cost *vs.* benefit, 60, 60*f*
    design
        errors in cluster, 81
        mistakes, 65
        spectrum. *See* HA design spectrum,
          availability
    development, 65–69, 66*f*
        servers, 65–67
        systems and subsystems, 67–69
    Hewlett-Packard (HP)
        HP hardware and software, 256–257
        HP nonstop integrity servers, 258–260
        integrity servers, 257–258

IBM DB2 database and, 278–280
IBM informix database
    availability features, 282–283
    Informix 11.70, 281–282
    Informix 12.1, 284–285
Ingres database, 284–285
Linux, 263
Linux HPC, 263
management, 209–222. *See* HA
        management
MySQL
    features, 278
    services and support, 278
operations, 225–238. *See* HA operations
Oracle database and, 275–277
    key capabilities, 276–277
    Oracle 11g (R2.1) HA, 275–276
    Oracle 12c, 276
    Oracle MAA, 276
Oracle Sun, 254–255
other clusters, 261
in scientific computing, 80
service availability software, 264–265
SQL server and, 272–274
    AlwaysOn solutions, 273–274
    basics, 273
    Microsoft SQL server 2014 community
        technology, 273
Stratus fault tolerance, 260–261
Sybase database and, 285–288
technologies, 68*f*
transaction processing and databases,
        267–288
vendor products, 249–265
virtualization and, 305
web and, 264
High availability as a service (HAaaS), 295
High availability disaster recovery (HADR),
        279, 283
High performance computing/computation (HPC), 66,
        77–83, 170, 263
    clusters
        applications, 79
        generic, 77–78, 78*f*
        Oscar configuration, 78–79, 79*f*
    Linux HPC HA, 263
HIPAA. *See* Health Information Portability
        and Accountability Act (HIPAA)
Holistic, 347
Hosted hypervisors, 301, 347
Hosted private cloud, 296
Hot spare, 347
Hot swapping, 347
Hoyle, 347
HP Virtual Server Environment (HP VSE), 304
Hypervisor, 347
Hysteresis, 347

I

IAC. *See* Information Analysis Center (IAC)
IBM availability and reliability
  IBM clusters, 251
  IBM hardware, 250–251
  parallel sysplex, 251–254, 252*f*
    future series/system, 253–254
    high availability services, 253
  virtualization, 251
IBM DB2 database and HA
  DB2 for Windows, UNIX, and Linux
    DB2 HA feature, 279
    high availability DR, 279–280
    SQL and Q replication, 280
  for i, 280
IBM informix database
  availability features
    connection manager, 283
    fault tolerance, 282
    informix MACH 11 clusters, 282–283
    Informix 11.70, 281–282
    Informix 12.1, 284–285
IBM mainframe, 45
Identified risks, 402*t*
IEEE Reliability Society (IEEE RS), 462
IMS. *See* Information management system (IMS)
Independence property, 186
Independent, failure, 344
Infant mortality, 51
Inflection *S*-shaped model, 444
In-flight diagnostics, 10
Information Analysis Center (IAC), 462
Information Assurance Technology IAC (IATAC), 469
Information dispersal algorithms (IDA), 348
Information dispersal scheme (IDS), 348
Information management system (IMS), 29–30, 39, 267
Information Systems Audit and Control Association, 348
Information technology as a service (ITaaS), 295
Information Technology Infrastructure Library
    (ITIL), 348
  availability management, 480–481, 483
  defined, 479–480
Infrastructure as a service (IaaS), 295
Ingres database and HA
  Ingres high availability option, 284–285
  Ingres RDBMS, 284
In-house DR, 324–327
Institute of Electrical and Electronics Engineers
    (IEEE), 462
Integrated services digital network (ISDN), 150
Intel cache safe technology, 71
Intelligent storage elements (ISE), 101
Interaction of wares, failure elements, 35–37, 35*t*–36*t*, 36*f*
Intergalactic Early Retirement Option (IERO), 308
Intermittent, failure, 344
Internal data corporation (IDC), 53–54

International Data Group (IDG), 468
International Working Group on Cloud Computing
    Resiliency (IWGCR), 298, 466
Internet Control Message Protocol (ICMP), 356
Internet service provider (ISP), 144
Intrusion detection system (IDS), 348
ISACA, 348
ISO standards, 348
ITIL. *See* Information Technology Infrastructure
    Library (ITIL)
IT service management (ITSM), 348, 479
IT structure
  hardware overview, 40–42
  scenario of web, 41*f*
  schematic, 40
  software layers, 40*f*

J

Java Message Service (JMS), 269
Java Server Pages (JSP), 260
Journal files system, 349
Just a bunch of disks (JBOD), 349
Just a few lines of code (JAFLOC), 349

K

Kernel-Based VM (KVM), 301
Keylogger, 351
Key performance indicators (KPI), 42, 159
Kilo lines of code (KLOC), 349
Knowledge modules (KM), 205, 233
KPIs (key performance indicators), 42, 159

L

Laggards, 153
Lamda (λ), 349
Latent defects (LD), 430
The 4th Law of Thermodynamics, 4
Least squares estimate (LSE), 180
Life unit, 349, 378
Lines of code (LOC), 176
Liveware, 349
Load balancing (LB), 74, 76–77, 76*f*
Local area network (LAN), 141
Lockstep memory, 71
Logical outage, 29, 30*f*, 349
Logical partitions (LPAR), 72–73, 252, 301
Logical volume, 85, 350
Longitudinal redundancy check (LRC), 71, 163, 350
Lusser's Law, 108–109, 117

M

Machine check architecture (MCA), 257, 350
Magnitude of data loss (MDL), 430

Maintainability, 350
Maintenance devices (MD), 9
Malicious software, 475
Malware, 350
    adware, 352
    botnet, bot, 351
    distributed denial of service (DDoS), 351
    keylogger, 351
    ransomware, 350–351
    rootkit, 351
    spyware, 351
    trojan/trojan horse, 351
    virus, 350
    worm, 351
Managed private cloud, 296
Management disciplines, 200–201
Management information bases (MIB), 305
Management of operations phase, 223–225
Massively parallel processors (MPP), 65–66, 71, 257, 288
Master/slave, 352
Mathematical distributions, 352
Mathematical issues, availability
    Lusser's Law, 108–109
    probabilities availability, 107–108
    reliability graphs, guide, 105–107
    system series, 108*f*
Maximum availability architecture (MAA), 255
Maximum likelihood estimates (MLE), 180
Mean, 352
Mean residual life (MRL), 352–353
Mean time between failure (MTBF), 54, 84, 93, 105, 112, 206, 353, 373
    failure rates, 124–125, 125*f*
    figures, typical, 379–380
    gathering MTTF figures, 380
    interpretation of, 375
    and MTTF difference, 375–377
    various components, 379*t*
Mean time for problem determination (MTPD), 114
Mean time to data loss (MTTDL), 472
Mean time to failure (MTTF), 96, 98, 354, 373
    gathering MTBF figures, 380
    interpretation of, 375
    and MTBF difference, 375–377
Mean time to first failure (MTTFF), 354
Mean time to problem determination (MTPD), 354
Mean time to repair (MTTR), 84, 97–98, 112–113, 115, 175, 300, 354
    interpretation of, 373–374
Mean time to total disintegration (MTTD), 376
Mechanism, failure, 344
Memory bounded speedup, 425
Memory mirroring, 353
Mirrored disk, 338
Mirroring, 353
Mobile security, 353
Mode, failure, 344

Modeling & Simulation IAC (MSIAC), 469
Monitoring stack, 240
Monitor layers, 240
Monte Carlo methods, 353
MTBF. *See* Mean time between failure (MTBF)
MTTD. *See* Mean time to total disintegration (MTTD)
MTTDL. *See* Mean time to data loss (MTTDL)
MTTF. *See* Mean time to failure (MTTF)
MTTF and MTTR Interpretation, 381–383
    final word on MTxx, 382–383
    Forrester/Zenoss MTxx definitions, 383
    MTBF/MTTF analogy, 382
    MTTF *vs.* lifetime, 381
    MTxx theory, 381–382
MTTR (mean time to repair), 84, 97–98, 112–113, 115, 175, 300, 354, 374, 377
    interpretation of, 373–374
Mu (μ), 354
Multipathing, 354
Multiple virtual storage (MVS), 39, 280
Multiprocessing (MP) factor, 422
Multisite cluster, 339
Multi-user multi-programming system (MUMPS), 268
Murphy's Law, 354
    of availability, 4
Musa–Okumoto model, 438
Musa's model, 438–441
    expansion ratios, 440*t*
    graphical, 441
    logarithmic, 440–441
    model A, 439
MySQL
    HA features, 278
    HA services and support, 278

N

National Aeronautics and Space Administration (NASA), 8
National Institute of Standards and Technology (NIST), 400, 452, 469
Native hypervisor environment, 301
Nested RAID, 88–89
Network as a service (NaaS), 295
Network change/configuration automation, 23
Network interface cards (NIC), 118, 163, 287, 301, 355
Network monitoring, 354
Network recovery objective (NRO), 354–355
Network reduction, 355
Network reliability/availability, 163–169
    design for availability, 165–166
    file transfer reliability, 167–169
    network DR, 169
    network outages, 164
    network types, 164
    protocols and redundancy, 163
    security, 166–167

NIST. *See* National Institute of Standards and Technology (NIST)
Nonavailability (*N*), 112
    penalty, 60–64
    types, 28–30
Nonhomogeneous Poisson process (NHPP) exponential model, 443
Nonredundant blocks, 108
Nonrepairable system, 355
NonStopSQL database, 288–289
Nonvolatile storage (NVS), 191
Normalized MDL (NOMDL), 430
NoSQL, 287–288

O

Object-oriented and object-relational (ORDBMS), 271
Office of Government Commerce (OGC), 480
Online availability tool, 113
Online transaction processing (OLTP), 29, 39, 150, 267, 311, 355
Open Software Foundation (OSF), 371
Open systems interconnection (OSI), 485
Operating system (OS), 150, 230
Operational pain factors and availability impacts, 21*t*
Operational risk, 402*t*
Optimization as a service (OaaS), 295
Oracle database and HA, 275–277
    key capabilities, 276–277
    Oracle 11g (R2.1) HA, 275–276
    Oracle 12c, 276
    Oracle MAA, 276
Oracle RAC 12c, 255–256
Oracle Sun HA
    Oracle HA clusters, 255–256
    Sun HA
        hardware range, 254–255
        Oracle Sun M5-32, 255
        super cluster, 255
Outage. *See* Logical outage; Physical outage
Outage loss factors, 62
Outage records and MTTx figures, 380–381

P

Packet shaping, 369
Parallel blocks, 123
Paravirtualization (PV), 302, 355
Partial outage, 355
Partitioning, 72
Partitions, 304
Payment Card Industry Data Security Standard (PCI DSS), 456
Pellston technology, 355–356
Pentests, 183
Peripatetic operation, 225
Personal identification number (PIN), 353

Physical outage, 28–29
Pi (∏), 356
PID. *See* Project initiation document (PID)
Ping utility, 356
Planar technology, 8
Platform as a service (PaaS), 295
Post-RAID, 356
Power-on self-test, 9
Power outage, 356
Power usage efficiency (PUE), 356–357
Predictive failure analysis (PFA), 357–358
Preliminary activities of HA
    BC Plan, 199–200
    pre-production, 198–199
Principle of least privilege (POLP), 358
Probability, 358
    availability, 107–108
    failure, 107*f*
Probability density function (pdf), 105, 106*f*, 353, 406
Project definition workshops (PDW), 198, 307, 388
Project initiation document (PID), 211, 213, 307
    notes, 214–215
    purpose, 213–214
    structure, 214
Project risk management plan, 401–402

Q

Quality of service (QoS), 147, 199, 350
Quantitative availability, 16
Quick path interconnect (QPI), 258, 445
Quorum (cluster), 359

R

Radio Corporation of America (RCA), 6
RAID. *See* Redundant arrays of inexpensive disks (RAID)
RAIN, 359
Ramp-up, 29, 31, 116, 166
    backout and, 227
    fix plus, 321
    IT personnel, 393
    in MTTR, 114, 300, 377, 377f, 378
    in MTTV, 383
    in outage, 56
    service ramp-up time, 374
Random access memory (RAM), 70
Random, failure, 344
RAS. *See* Reliability, availability, and serviceability (RAS)
Rate, failure, 345
Rate limiting, 369
Rayleigh distribution, 359, 442–443, 443*f*
RDBMS, 360
    partitioning, 360
REAL. *See* Reusable Enterprise Architecture Library (REAL)

Real application cluster (RAC), 255
Real user monitoring (RUM), 239
Recovery analogy, 56–57, 57*f*
Recovery manager (RMAN), 277
Recovery-Oriented Computing (ROC), 465
Recovery point objectives (RPO), 311, 360
Recovery time objectives (RTO), 33, 311, 360
Red Hat Enterprise Linux (RHEL), 286
Reduced instruction set computing (RISC), 66
Redundancy, 360
Redundant arrays of inexpensive disks (RAID), 83–84,
     85*f*, 86*f*, 88*f*, 144
   architecture, 83–101
     configurations, 86–90, 89*f*, 90*f*
     less relevant, 90–94
     and levels, 84–86
     origins of, 83–84
     post-RAID environment, 94–97
   hybrid, 93
   non-RAID, 96–97
   storage efficiency, 91, 91*t*
   successor qualifications, 97–98
Redundant bit steering (RBS), 70–71
Reed–Solomon (RS) codes, 360
Reference architecture (RA), 484, 487
Relational database management system (RDBMS),
     157, 270
Relational database systems
   database history, 271
   early RDBMS, 271–272
Reliability
   of active redundancy, 415*t*–416*t*
   analytics, 417*f*
   and availability, 335–371
   complex system, 121
   different configurations, 122*f*
   exercise, 419*f*
   graphs, guide
     cdf, 107
     pdf, 105–107
   growth, 361
   hardware, 109–110, 109*f*
   HPC, 80–81
   IBM availability and
     IBM clusters, 251
     IBM hardware, 250–251
     virtualization, 251
     z Series parallel sysplex, 251–254, 252*f*
   information sources, 469–470
   network, 163–169
     design for availability, 165–166
     file transfer reliability, 167–169
     network DR, 169
     network outages, 164
     network types, 164
     protocols and redundancy, 163
     security, 166–167

organizations, 461
properties of software
   ACID properties, 186
   two-phase commit, 186–187
RAID 1, 427*f*
of RAID sets, 474
security resources, 469
software, 110–111, 111*f*, 171, 366
   assessment questions, 188
   current status, 187
   defect count, 180–181
   documentation, 173
   failure/defect density models, 437–444
   fault tolerance (ft), 184–185
   hardening, 182
   installation, 182–183
   model entities, 176–177
   output verification, 170–171
   overview, 435–436
   penetration testing, 183–184
   problem flow, 171–172
   quality, 169–170
   scenario, 175
   shape characterization, 177–178
   software testing model, 173–174
   software testing steps, 172
   SRE models, 175–178
   SRGM, 178–180
   standard IEEE 1633–2008, 181
   theory, 436–437
   time-based *vs.* defect-based, 178
   version control, 183
of standby redundancy, 416*t*
steady-state value of, 50*f*
subsystem, 189–193
   availability, 192–193
   hardware outside server, 190–192
   liveware reliability, 193
theory of availability and
   cdf distribution, 409–410, 409*f*
   pdf distribution $f(x)$, 407–409, 408*f*
   reliability distributions, 406–407
Reliability Analysis Center (RAC), 462
Reliability analytics (RA), 472
Reliability, availability, and serviceability (RAS), 13–14,
     35, 51, 145, 250, 444
   beyond hardware, 14
   features
     fault tolerance, 72
     hot-plug hardware, 69
     input/output, 71
     memory, 70–71
     power/cooling, 71–72
     processors, 69
     storage, 71
Reliability block diagrams (RBD), 27, 51, 120, 120*f*,
     121*f*, 145, 221, 361, 389

Reliability growth, 361
Reliability Information Analysis Center (RIAC), 462
   availability digest, 463
      BCI, 466
      Business Continuity Today, 465
      Carnegie Mellon Software Engineering Institute,
         464–465
      center for software reliability, 467
      CloudTweaks, 467
      Disaster Recovery Institute, 465–466
      IEEE reliability society, 462–463
      Information Availability Institute, 466
      IWGCR, 466
      OpenSAF, 464
      ROC project, 465
      service availability forum, 463–464
      storage networking industry association, 463
      TMM*i* Foundation, 466–467
      uptime institute, 462
Reliability, Maintainability, and Supportability
      Partnership (RMSP), 478
Reliability, maintainability, quality,
      supportability, and interoperability
      (RMQSI), 462
ReliaSoft, 120
Remote database facility (RDF), 259
Remote standby secondary (RSS), 283
Remote terminal emulator (RTE), 240
Repairable system, 361
Repair rate, 361
Replication, 361
Resource management in cloud, 297
Resource manager (RM), 269, 370
RETAIN, 225
Return on investment (ROI), 17, 63
Reusable Enterprise Architecture Library
      (REAL), 481
Review board, failure, 345
Revision control, 183
Risk analysis. *See* Risk assessment
Risk assessment, 362
Risk assessment and management, 394–403
   deliverables risk management,
      400–402, 400*f*
   IT role, 403
   project risk management, 396–399
   risk areas, 402
   risk managed, 395–396
   risk stakeholders, 395
   user and business requirements, 396–397
Risk IT, 362
Risk management, 362
Roll back, 362–363
   dirty page, 362
   dirty read, 363
Roll forward, 364
Root cause analysis (RCA), 154, 225, 232, 308, 364, 472

Rootkit, 351
Root partition, 304
Runbook automation (RBA), 364
Runbooks, 156, 364

S

SAGE (semiautomatic ground environment)
      system, 6–7
SAN. *See* Storage area networks (SAN)
SBU. *See* Strategic business unit (SBU)
Scalability, 420
Scalable memory interconnect (SMI), 258
Scalable processor architecture (SPARC), 254
Secure sockets layer (SSL), 146, 367
   authentication and verification, 367
   data encryption, 367
Security, 364
   trusted computer system, 365
   trusted computing base, 365
   trustworthy system, 365
Security information event management system (SIEM),
      231, 449
Security operations center (SOC), 352
Security organizations
   center for international security and
      cooperation, 469
   CSA, 468
   CSIAC, 469
   CSO online, 468–469
   other reliability/security resources, 469
Self-healing storage, 100
Semiautomatic ground environment (SAGE)
      system, 6–7
Series blocks, 123
Server domain architecture, 72–74
Service
   processor, 73
   vs. systems, 49, 49*f*
Service availability forum (SAF), 463
Service availability software, 264–265
Service Domain Concept, 141–143
Service level agreement (SLA), 42–43, 55, 116, 143, 198,
      283, 293, 375, 411, 470
   availability and QoS, 201
   cloud, 297–298
   dawn of realism, 42
   defined, 43
   elements of, 201–203, 202*f*
   importance of, 43
   IT
      benefits of potential, 204
      service delivery, 204–205
   potential business benefits of, 203–204
   reneging on, 207–209
   reporting of availability, 206–207,
      206*f*, 208*t*

specifics, 202–203
structure and samples, 205–206
types, 203
Service life cycle, 43–44
Service management
architectures
AgilePath cloud architecture roadmap, 485f
cloud reference model, 486f
clouds, 484
HA documentation, 483–484
IBM cloud RA, 486f
availability management of ITIL, 480–483
architecture *vs.* string and sealing wax, 481
enterprise architectures, 482t–483t
service architectures, 480, 481
elements, 45–49
availability management in, 48f
hierarchy, 47
operations support, 46
scope of, 45–49
service, 48–49, 48f
systems management, 47
user support, 46
ITIL, 479–480
Service monitors
availability measurement, 239–240
availability monitors, 242–244
benchmarks, 243–244
EUE tools, 243
related monitors, 244
disaster recovery, 244–245
observer of system behavior, 241f
synthetic user of system, 242f
system resource monitors, 241–242
viewpoint approach to documentation, 245
Shared disk, 338
Shared disk secondary (SDS), 283
Shared file system (SFS), 77
SIEM, 365
Sigma (Σ), 365
Simple network management protocol (SNMP), 91
SIM (systems insight manager), 259, 366
Single bit errors, 366
Single large expensive drive (SLED), 84
Single point of failure (SPoF), 57, 74, 77–78, 84, 87, 108, 164, 252, 356, 389
SLA. *See* Service level agreement (SLA)
SNMP. *See* Simple network management protocol (SNMP)
Snowball effect, 402
Society for Maintenance and Reliability Professionals (SMRP), 478
Society of Reliability Engineers (SRE), 478
Soft errors, 9, 369
Software
errors, 185
failure costs, 62–63, 63f

prototyping, 366
universe, 188–189
Software as a service (SaaS), 295
Software Engineering Institute (SEI), 464
Software reliability, 171
assessment questions, 188
current status, 187
failure/defect density models, 437–444
models, 175–185
defect count, 180–181
entities, 176–177
fault tolerance (ft), 184–185
hardening, 182
installation, 182–183
penetration testing, 183–184
shape characterization, 177–178
software scenario, 175
SRE, 175–176
standard IEEE 1633–2008, 181
time-based *vs.* defect-based, 178
version control, 183
output verification, 170–171
overview, 435–436
problem flow, 171–172
software
documentation, 173
quality, 169–170
testing model, 173–174
testing steps, 172
SRGM, 178–180
theory, 436–437
Software reliability engineering (SRE), 50, 62, 175, 436
Software reliability growth model (SRGM), 178, 342, 367
Software reliability prediction, 367
Solid-state drives (SSD), 67, 92–94, 280, 367
Solid-state storage (SSS), 92
Speed of recovery, 326
Spyware, 351
SQL server and HA, 272–274
AlwaysOn solutions, 273–274
availability groups, 274
database mirroring, 274
failover cluster instances, 273
log shipping, 274
basics, 273
Microsoft SQL server 2014 community technology, 273
Standard Performance Evaluation Corporation (SPEC), 243
Standby, 367–368
active–active (load balanced), 368
cold, 368
hot, 368
warm, 368
Standby modes, 57

Steady-state reliability, 50, 50*f*
STONITH (shoot the offending node in the head), 368
Storage area networks (SAN), 9, 75, 222
Storage efficiency (RAID), 368
Storage Networking Industry Association (SNIA), 463
Strategic business unit (SBU), 481
Strategic product line (SPL), 267
Stratus fault tolerance
    ActiveService architecture, 261
    automated uptime layer, 260–261
Stripe of mirrors, 89
Subsystem reliability, 189–193
    availability, 192–193
    hardware outside server
        disk subsystem RAS, 190–191
        disk subsystem reliability, 190
        tape reliability/RAS, 191–192
    liveware reliability, 193
Subsystems, 141
Sun–Ni Law, 425
Survival probability (t), 368
Switchover. *See* Failover
Sybase database and HA
    ASE cluster requirements, 286–287
    business continuity with SAP sybase, 287
    terminology, 285
    use of SAP ASE, 286
    vendor availability, 286
Symmetric multiprocessors (SMP), 65–66, 68, 257, 366
Synthetic transactions, 241
System, 50
    assurance, 399
    availability classes, 55*t*
    failure, 131
    management, 43
System controller (SC), 69, 74
System network architecture (SNA), 163
Systems insight manager (SIM), 259
Systems managed storage (SMS), 254
System under test (SUT), 183

T

Target reliability, 187
TCP. *See* Transmission control protocol (TCP)
Tiered storage, 324*t*
Time, 368
Times between failure models, 441–442
TMM*i* (Test Maturity Model Integrated), 466
TOGAF, 369
Total cost of ownership (TCO), 42, 64, 149, 387
    cloud, 393
    factors, 392–393
    schematic of costs, 393

TP systems
    with databases
        CICS and RDBMS, 270
        X/open distributed transaction processing model, 269–270
    OLTP availability requirements, 268
Traffic shaping, 369
Transaction manager (TM), 269, 370
Transaction processing. *See* Online transaction processing (OLTP)
Transaction Processing Council (TPC), 243, 268
Transient errors, 9, 369
Transient, failure, 345
Transmission control protocol (TCP), 314
Triple modular redundancy (TMR), 257, 345, 369
Trojan/trojan horse, 351
Trouble ticketing, 237
True outage, 29
Trusted computer system, 365
Trusted computing base, 365
Trustworthy system, 365
Turbo-Delphi technique, 215
Two-phase commit (2PC), 186

U

Ultrium, 319
Uninterruptible power supply (UPS), 144, 369–370
Universal Scalability Law (USL), 424
Unplanned outage, 369
User acceptance tests (UAT), 172
User datagram protocol (UDP), 314
User service, concept, 45
Utility computing, 296

V

Vendors and virtualization
    HA, 305
    HP integrity virtual machines, 304
    IBM PowerVM, 303
    IBM z/VM, 304
    information sources, 306
    Linux KVM, 304
    Microsoft hyper-V, 304
    Solaris zones, 304
    VMware VSphere, ESX, and ESXi, 304
    Xen, 305
Veritas Cluster (VC), 286
Virtualization
    full, 301–302, 302*f*
    paravirtualization, 302–303
    security risks in virtual environments, 303
    vendors and. *See* Vendors and virtualization
Virtual machines, 347
Virtual private network (VPN), 163
Virtual recovery, 156

Virtual storage access method (VSAM), 267
Virtual telecommunications access method (VTAM), 39
Virus, 350
Visual availability, 17*f*
VSAM (virtual storage access method), 267
Vulnerability, 370

W

Wagon master, 218
WAN. *See* Wide area network (WAN)
Warm standby approach, 341
Wearout, 370
Web and HA, 264
Weibull distribution, 109, 113*f*, 406
Wide area network (WAN), 141
    acceleration, 370
    optimization, 317–318, 370

Wi-Fi Protected Access (WPA), 455
Windows Hardware Error Architecture
        (WHEA), 358
Windows Server failover clustering (WSFC), 273
Wired Equivalent Privacy (WEP), 453
Wiring diagrams, 480

X

XA+ interface, 371
XA interface, 370–371
X/Open company limited, 371

Z

Zachman architecture, 371
Zero utilization effect, 422
Zulu principle, 371

Printed and bound by CPI Group (UK) Ltd, Croydon, CR0 4YY

25/10/2024

01779408-0002